Using Russian

Using Russian is a guide to Russian usage for those who have already
acquired the basics of the language and wish to extend their
knowledge. Unlike conventional grammars, it gives special attention to
those areas of vocabulary and grammar which cause most difficulty to
English speakers, and focuses on questions of style and register which
are all too often ignored. Clear, readable and easy to consult, it will
prove invaluable to students seeking to improve their fluency and
confidence in Russian.

   This second edition has been substantially revised and expanded to
incorporate fresh material and up-to-date information. Many of the
original sections have been rewritten, the passages illustrating register
are all fresh and one brand new chapter has been added, providing a
clear picture of Russian usage in the twenty-first century.

DEREK OFFORD is Professor of Russian Intellectual History at the
University of Bristol, where he has served as Chairman of the School
of Modern Languages and Head of Department. His previous
publications include *Portraits of Early Russian Liberals* (1985), *The
Russian Revolutionary Movement in the 1880s* (1986) and *Modern
Russian: An Advanced Grammar Course* (1993), as well as numerous
articles and chapters on classical Russian literature and thought.

NATALIA GOGOLITSYNA is Language Assistant at the University of
Bristol. She has taught Russian as a second language at St Petersburg
Pedagogical University, and has been a visiting academic at the
University of Essex. Her previous publications include *Problems of
Translation: Russian Words and Concepts with No Exact Equivalents in
English* (1995) and various articles on culture-specific words and
concepts.

Companion titles

Using Russian

A guide to contemporary usage

Second edition, revised and augmented

DEREK OFFORD
University of Bristol

NATALIA GOGOLITSYNA
University of Bristol

CAMBRIDGE
UNIVERSITY PRESS

CAMBRIDGE UNIVERSITY PRESS
Cambridge, New York, Melbourne, Madrid, Cape Town, Singapore, São Paulo,
Delhi, Dubai, Tokyo, Mexico City

Cambridge University Press
The Edinburgh Building, Cambridge CB2 8RU, UK

www.cambridge.org
Information on this title: www.cambridge.org/9780521547611

First edition published November 1996. Reprinted 1998 (twice), 2000, 2003, 2004
Second edition published 2005
4th printing 2010

Printed in the United Kingdom at the University Press, Cambridge

A catalogue record for this publication is available from the British Library

ISBN 978-0-521-54761-1 Paperback

Contents

Preface to the first edition

This book, like the volumes already published in the series on contemporary usage in French, German and Spanish, is aimed at the advanced learner who has studied the basic grammar of the language and is now striving for a more comprehensive and sophisticated knowledge. To this end the book includes much material on register, vocabulary, verbal etiquette and word-formation, as well as material on the subjects of morphology, prepositions and syntax with which the post-A-level student should already have some familiarity. The book is not conceived as a comprehensive grammar, although the main grammatical topics that trouble the English-speaking student are quite fully covered in the later chapters. The approach adopted is not prescriptive. That is to say an attempt is made to show the range of linguistic phenomena that might be encountered in modern Russian and to define the limits within which they are used rather than to lay down rules for usage.

While offering, it is hoped, a multi-faceted view of the modern language, two purposes are kept in mind throughout the book.

Firstly, it is intended to demonstrate that Russian, like any other modern language with which the student may be familiar, is not a stable, uniform abstraction that is applied inflexibly in all situations. As a living language spoken by millions of individuals of different ages from different backgrounds and in different situations, Russian exists in many varieties. Words, forms and constructions which are appropriate in one context may be quite out of place in another. Even apparently hard-and-fast grammatical rules may be relaxed, to the frustration of the foreign student who has laboriously mastered them. Chapter 1 therefore aims to make the student aware of the existence of variety in the Russian language, and this variety is borne in mind and examples of it indicated in all the chapters that follow.

Secondly, the book attempts to address problems that the English-speaking student of Russian may find especially taxing. Russian operates, of course, according to quite different grammatical principles from those to which the English-speaker is accustomed. (One thinks in particular of its system of declension of nouns, pronouns, adjectives, numerals and participles and of the aspectual distinction that runs through the Russian verbal system.) Moreover, in the field of vocabulary correspondences between Russian and English words are often limited or inexact and similarities can be misleading. Again, in certain situations Russians simply do not express themselves in the same way as English-speakers in a similar situation, or at least a direct translation of what an English-speaker would say in that situation would seem to a Russian to some degree unnatural. Much attention is therefore devoted in this book to problems of non-equivalence in the two languages in vocabulary, phraseology and verbal etiquette as well as grammar.

Beyond these purposes it is also hoped that the book, through its broad approach, will increase the student's general awareness of the structure and resources of the Russian language, and that his or her understanding and appreciation of the immense vitality and depth of experience of the Russian people may thus in some small way be enhanced.

Preface to the second edition

This new edition of *Using Russian: a Guide to Contemporary Usage* represents an extensively revised and augmented version of the first edition, which was published in 1996. Whereas the first edition consisted of ten chapters the current edition has twelve and is some ninety pages longer than the first. Our thanks are due to Cambridge University Press for allowing this enlargement.

Some material in the first edition that is now out-of-date or that is for some other reason of less interest than it was in 1996 (for example, neologisms associated with the period of *glásnost'* and *perestróika*) has been excised or reduced. On the other hand, much fresh material has been incorporated, especially in the first five chapters and the last chapter. The main changes that have been made are as follows.

Chapter 1 is based on sections 1–5 inclusive of the first chapter of the first edition but the material has been substantially rewritten and considerably expanded. Section 1.1, on the distribution of the Russian language, has been revised in the light of information in the most recent Russian census (2002). Section 1.2, on varieties of language, has been slightly expanded to include material on the distinction drawn, for example by David Crystal, between written and spoken language. Section 1.3, on registers in contemporary Russian, contains some fresh examples of usage and a new section (1.3.6) on the language of the internet (a subject to which this new edition as a whole pays much attention). Section 1.4, which is also new, briefly illustrates differences in register as reflected in vocabulary by taking about two dozen common words and identifying some of their equivalents in low and high registers. A further new section (1.6), on current debate about standard Russian, deals with concerns about the lowering of the standard that have arisen as a result of the perceived linguistic permissiveness that has accompanied the political, economic and social transformation of Russia over the last ten years.

The seven passages that were used to illustrate register in the first edition (located at 1.6 in that edition) have all been excised as now somewhat stale and have been replaced by thirteen fresh passages. Colloquial speech, the neutral register, the scientific/academic style, the official/business style, the style of journalism and political debate, and the language of imaginative literature are all illustrated in the new edition by two passages each. There is also a passage that illustrates and explicitly discusses the style of email. This latter passage, taken together with one of the passages exemplifying colloquial language on the basis of conversation in an internet chatroom, gives insight into the new register of Netspeak. The thirteen passages illustrating register, and the translations of and commentaries on them, now take up the whole of

Chapter 2, from which it is hoped a broad view of the range of register available in contemporary Russian will emerge.

Additions have also been made to the two chapters (Chapters 3 and 4 of the new edition) that deal with problems of meaning and translation (one on Russian words and one on English words). In Chapter 3, for example, a few new entries have been inserted in each of the sections on homonyms (3.1), paronyms (3.4) and *faux amis* (3.5) and a new section (3.7) has been included on Russian words that are difficult to render in English because of their cultural specificity. In 4.1 some new entries have been added and some further possible translations have been provided in entries that were already included in this section in the first edition.

In the chapter on vocabulary and idiom (now Chapter 5) the first section, on neologisms, has been rewritten in order to take account of the recent expansion of Russian lexis by means of the adoption of loanwords, the extension of the use of colloquial words and the elevation of demotic words to the level of everyday colloquial speech. This section now includes sub-sections on slang (5.1.4) and on the new vocabulary associated with computing (5.1.5). The last three sections of Chapter 5 (5.7–5.9) have also been slightly expanded and contain more extensive literal translation of, and fuller comment on, the idioms, proverbs and similes that they present than the equivalent sections in the first edition.

In what is now Chapter 6, section 6.8, on the language of public notices, and section 6.10, on acronyms and alphabetisms, have been slightly expanded to reflect contemporary practice. We have also appended a short section on the popular Russian conversational genre of the joke, or 'anecdote', to the end of this chapter (6.13).

The last four chapters of the first edition (Chapters 8–11 inclusive in this second edition) have required much less substantial revision than the earlier chapters, because they concern morphology and syntax, which have been relatively little affected by innovation over the eight years that have elapsed since the publication of the first edition. No significant cuts have been made to these chapters, because we feel that it remains useful for advanced learners to have at hand a fairly exhaustive compendium of information on grammar alongside the material on those aspects of language (register and vocabulary) that are subject to greater and more rapid change.

Finally, a new chapter has been included on stress (Chapter 12), on the grounds that it is important for the advanced learner to master Russian stress patterns, which are complex, and that study of them has been relatively neglected in English-language books on Russian. In keeping with the spirit of the series this new chapter devotes some attention to variation in usage.

All the material from the first edition which remains substantially unchanged in this second edition has been reviewed. Mistakes and flaws identified in the first edition have been corrected and further minor alterations have been made with respect to both content and presentation.

Our revision of the first edition has been informed by recent literature on debate about the standard in English and on the impact of the internet on the English language as well as by new work on the Russian language. We have also been able to make use of online resources on the Russian language that were not available when the first edition was being prepared. The new sources that we have consulted are included in the revised list of sources that appears on pp. xix–xxi.

Cross-referencing and the two indexes (a list of the Russian words and affixes to which the book refers and an index of topics covered) have of course been revised to take account of all the changes made.

DO, NG
Bristol, July 2004

Acknowledgements

Every effort has been made to secure necessary permissions to reproduce copyright material in this work, though in some cases it has proved impossible to trace or contact copyright holders. If any omissions are brought to our notice, we will be happy to include appropriate acknowledgements on reprinting, and in any subsequent edition.

We thank Penguin Books for permission to reproduce the English translation of an extract from Pushkin's poem that is given in section 2.11.

We also warmly thank the following: Tat'iana Dimoglo, for material on neologisms and orthography and for general linguistic advice; Elena Gogolitsyna, for material and advice on contemporary slang and computing terminology; Yurii Gogolitsyn for his invaluable technical assistance; John Steeds, FRS, for his help with translation of the passage on physics reproduced at 2.5; Helen Barton of Cambridge University Press for her guidance and for her prompt and patient responses to all our queries; Kay McKechnie for her careful reading of the typescript and the many improvements that she introduced at the copy-editing stage; and Alison Powell of Cambridge University Press for overseeing production of the book. For any mistakes, misapprehensions and imperfections of presentation that might remain in spite of the best efforts of all who have helped us in various ways we ourselves accept sole responsibility.

DO, NG,
Bristol, August 2004

Sources

Reference works

Avanesov, R. I., ed., *Орфоэпический словарь русского языка*, Русский язык, Moscow, 1985

Borras, F. M., and R. F. Christian, *Russian Syntax*, 2nd edn, Clarendon Press, Oxford, 1979

Chernyshev, V. I., et al., eds., *Словарь современного русского литературного языка*, Академия наук СССР, 17 vols., Moscow, 1950–65

Comrie, Bernard, Gerald Stone and Maria Polinsky, *The Russian Language in the Twentieth Century*, 2nd edn, revised and expanded, of *The Russian Language since the Revolution*, by Bernard Comrie and Gerald Stone, Clarendon Press, Oxford, 1996

Evgen'eva, A. P., *Словарь синонимов русского языка*, Наука, 2 vols., Leningrad, 1970–1

Forbes' Russian Grammar, 3rd edn, revised and enlarged by J. C. Dumbreck, Oxford University Press, 1964

Galperin, I. R., ed., *New English–Russian Dictionary*, 2 vols., Soviet Encyclopaedia Publishing House, Moscow, 1972

The Oxford Russian Dictionary (Russian–English, English–Russian), revised and updated by Colin Howlett, Oxford University Press, Oxford and New York, 1993

Ozhegov, S. I., *Словарь русского языка*, 20th edn, Русский язык, Moscow, 1988

Pulkina, I. M., *A Short Russian Reference Grammar*, translated from the Russian by V. Korotky, 7th edn, Русский язык, Moscow, 1984

Ryazanova-Clarke, Larissa, and Terence Wade, *The Russian Language Today*, Routledge, London and New York, 1999

Unbegaun, B. O., *Russian Grammar*, Oxford University Press, 1957

Vinogradov, V. V., et al., *Грамматика русского языка*, Академия наук СССР, 2 vols. in 3 books, Moscow, 1960

Vlasto, A. P., *A Linguistic History of Russia to the End of the Eighteenth Century*, Clarendon Press, Oxford, 1988

Wade, Terence, *A Comprehensive Russian Grammar*, 2nd edn, revised and expanded, ed. Michael J. de Holman, Blackwell, Oxford, and Malden, Mass., 2000

Wade, Terence, and Nijole White, *Using Russian Synonyms*, Cambridge University Press, 2003

Ward, Dennis, *The Russian Language Today: System and Anomaly*, Hutchinson University Library, London, 1965

Wheeler, Marcus, *The Oxford Russian–English Dictionary*, 2nd edn, Clarendon Press, Oxford, 1990

We have also made use, especially in Chapters 9–11, of material from Derek Offord, *Modern Russian: an Advanced Grammar Course*, Bristol Classical Press and Duckworth, London, 1993.

Specific references

Many sections in this book (indicated by the references in brackets after the titles below) draw on the works on particular areas of vocabulary or grammar in the following list or relate to areas more fully dealt with in those works.

Akulenko, V. V., ed., *Англо-русский и русско-английский словарь 'ложных друзей переводчика'*, Советская энциклопедия, Moscow, 1969 (3.5)

Avanesov, R. I., and V. G. Orlova, eds., *Русская диалектология*, 2nd edn, Наука, Moscow, 1965 (1.5)

Bex, Tony, and Richard J. Watts, *Standard English: the Widening Debate*, Routledge, London and New York, 1999 (1.6)

Bivon, R., *Element Order*, Cambridge University Press, 1971 (11.14)

Bratus, B. V., *The Formation and Expressive Use of Diminutives*, Cambridge University Press, 1969 (8.8)

Cooper, Brian, 'Problems with the in-laws: the terminology of Russian family relationships', *Journal of Russian Studies*, no. 52 (1987), pp. 37–45 (6.7)

Crystal, David, *Language and the Internet*, Cambridge University Press, 2001 (1.3.6)

Davison, R. M., *The Use of the Genitive in Negative Constructions*, Cambridge University Press, 1967 (11.1.6)

Flegon, A., *За пределами русских словарей*, Flegon Press, London, 1973 (5.6)

Fomina, M. I., *Современный русский язык: лексикология*, 3rd edn, Высшая школа, Moscow, 1990 (3.1.1–3.4)

Foote, I. M., *Verbs of Motion*, Cambridge University Press, 1967 (11.7)

Formanovskaia, N. I., *Употребление русского речевого этикета*, Русский язык, Moscow, 1982 (7.1–7.2, 7.4–7.16)

Forsyth, James, *A Grammar of Aspect: Usage and Meaning in the Russian Verb*, Cambridge University Press, 1970 (11.5)

Gogolitsyna, N., 'BYT: a Russian word study', *Rusistika*, no. 17 (March 1998), pp. 3–6 (3.7)

Gogolitsyna, N., 'New developments in Russian vocabulary', *Rusistika*, no. 12 (December 1995), pp. 32–3 (5.1)

Gogolitsyna, N., 'The Russian Intelligentsia', *Rusistika*, no. 25 (spring 2002), pp. 14–22 (3.7)

Gogolitsyna, N., 'Svoboda and Volya: Russian words and concepts', *Rusistika*, no. 19 (March 1999), pp. 22–5 (3.7)

Harrison, W., *The Expression of the Passive Voice*, Cambridge University Press, 1967 (11.8, 11.11.4)

Ivanova, Tat'iana, '"Лингвоэкология" или Ильич как бренд', *Литературная газета*, no. 16 (April 2003) (1.6)

Khlebtsova, Ol'ga, 'Как бы русский язык', *Литературная газета*, no. 11 (March 2003) (1.6)

Klimenko, A., *Эффективный самоучитель работы на ПК. Основной курс*, Diasoft, Moscow, St Petersburg and Kiev, 2003 (5.1.5)

Kuz'min, S. S., and N. L. Shchadrin, *Русско–английский словарь пословиц и поговорок*, Русский язык, Moscow, 1989 (5.7–5.8)

Maksimov, V. I., et al., *Словарь перестройки*, Златоуст, St Petersburg, 1992 (5.1)

Mustajoki, Arto, *Падеж дополнения в русских отрицательных предложениях*, Slavica Helsingiensa, 2, Helsinki, 1985 (11.1.6)

Norbury, J. K. W., *Word Formation in the Noun and Adjective*, Cambridge University Press, 1967 (Chapter 8)

Palazhchenko, P., *Мой несистематический словарь. Русско-английский. Англо-русский. (Из записной книжки переводчика)*, 3rd edn, Р. Валент, Moscow, 2003 (Chapters 3–5)

Pereiaslov, Nikolai, 'Литература и клавиатура', *Литературная газета*, no. 21 (May–June 2003) (1.3.6)

Rassudova, O. P., *Употребление видов глагола*, Moscow University Press, 1971 (11.5)

Room, Adrian, 'Russian personal names since the Revolution', *Journal of Russian Studies*, nos. 45 (1983), pp. 19–24 and 46 (1983), pp. 13–18 (7.3)

Rozental', D. E., *Практическая стилистика русского языка*, 4th edn, Высшая школа, Moscow, 1977 (esp 1.3)

Rozental', D. E., and M. A. Telenkova, *Словарь-справочник лингвистических терминов*, 3rd edn, Просвещение, Moscow, 1985 (Glossary)

Shanskii, N. M., and E. A. Bystrova, *700 фразеологических оборотов русского языка*, Русский язык, Moscow, 1975 (5.7)

Suslova, A. P., and A. V. Superanskaia, *О русских именах*, 3rd revised edn, Лениздат, Leningrad, 1991 (7.3)

Valgina, N. S., *Синтаксис современного русского языка*, 3rd edn, Высшая школа, Moscow, 1991 (esp 11.14–11.15)

Vasiléva, A. N., *Particles in Colloquial Russian*, translated by V. Korotky and K. Villiers, Progress Publishers, Moscow, 1972 (5.4)

Vsevolodova, M. V., 'Употребление кратких и полных прилагательных', *Русский язык за рубежом*, 1971, no. 3, pp. 65–8 and 1972, no. 1, pp. 59–64 (11.3)

Wade, Terence, *Prepositions in Modern Russian*, University of Durham, 1983 (Chapter 10)

Zemskaia, E. A., and D. N. Shmelev, eds., *Городское просторечие: Проблемы изучения*, Наука, Moscow, 1984 (1.3.2)

In addition we have made use of some of the many online resources to which students of the Russian language may now turn, e.g. <www.gazeta.ru>, <www.smi.ru>, <www.nns.ru>, <www.gramma.ru> and various sites that have been set up under the auspices of the Government of the Russian Federation's Council for the Russian Language (Совет по русскому языку при Правительстве Российской Федерации), e.g. <www.slovari.gramota.ru>, <www.spravka.gramota.ru>, <www.learning-russian.gramota.ru>, <www.navigator.gramota.ru>.

Note on transcription, stress marks and transliteration

Where it has been necessary to indicate precisely how a Russian word is pronounced (e.g. in the sections on regional variation in 1.5) a standard system of phonetic transcription has been used, according to which the Cyrillic consonants have the following values:

б	в	г	д	ж	з	й	к	л	м	н	п	р	с	т	ф	х	ц	ч	ш	щ
b	*v*	*g*	*d*	*ž*	*z*	*j*	*k*	*l*	*m*	*n*	*p*	*r*	*s*	*t*	*f*	*x*	*c*	*č'*	*š*	*šš'*

The symbol ′ placed after a letter indicates that the preceding consonant is soft, e.g. *l'es* (лес). Since most consonants, when they precede the vowels represented by the Russian letters **e, ё, и, ю** and **я**, are soft, these letters will in effect be transcribed, within this phonetic system, as *'e, 'o, 'i, 'u, 'a* respectively, e.g. *i'ul'a* (июля). The symbol ′ may also indicate the presence of a soft sign in the Russian word, e.g. *noč'* (ночь).

Stress is indicated in this book by the use of an acute accent over the stressed vowel, e.g. хлéба. In words which may be stressed in different places by different speakers an acute accent is placed over both the vowels that may bear the stress, e.g. кóмпáс. The secondary stress (see Glossary) that may occur in some words, especially compound nouns or adjectives, is marked by a grave accent.

The system of transliteration used to render Russian names (e.g. *Petia*, i.e. Пéтя), place names and other Russian words in Roman script is that used in *The Slavonic and East European Review*. In this book stress has been marked in these transliterated forms (e.g. *Púshkin, perestróika*), as well as in Cyrillic forms (Пýшкин, перестрóйка) unless the Cyrillic form, with stress indicated, is adjacent to the transliterated form.

Glossary of linguistic terms

Besides providing explanation of terms used in this book, the following glossary should aid understanding of the linguistic concepts required for advanced study of Russian. It will in any case be found that many educated Russians have a high degree of awareness of the grammar of their language and that in talking about it they will use some of the terms defined here. Numbers in brackets refer to the section(s) in this book that deal(s) with the phenomenon in question.

accusative case (вини́тельный паде́ж): the case in which the direct object of a transitive verb is expressed, e.g. Óльга чита́ет **кни́гу**, *Ol'ga is reading **a book*** (9.1.2, 10.1.2, 10.3.1, 11.1.2).

acronym (звукова́я аббревиату́ра): word made up of the initial letters of other words, e.g. *laser (light amplification by the stimulated emission of radiation)* (6.10).

active voice (действи́тельный зало́г): construction in which the subject of the verb itself performs the action, e.g. *The boy **stroked** the cat*; cf. **passive voice**.

adjective (и́мя прилага́тельное): word that qualifies a noun, e.g. *a **red** pen*.

adverb (наре́чие): word modifying the meaning of a verb, adjective or adverb, e.g. *Peter walks **slowly, quite** big, **very** quickly* (9.4, 11.14(c)).

adversative conjunction (противи́тельный сою́з): conjunction expressing contrast, e.g. *but*.

affix (а́ффикс): an element added to a root or stem to modify its meaning or use, e.g. ***un**willing, wonder**ful***. **Prefixes, infixes** and **suffixes** (q.v.) are all types of affix.

affricate (аффрика́та): consonant sound beginning as a **plosive** (q.v.) and passing into the corresponding **fricative** (q.v.), e.g. the initial and final sounds in ***church***, i.e. *t* + *š*. Standard Russian has two affricates, *c* (ц) and *č* (ч).

akan'e (а́канье): loss of distinction between the phonemes *a* and *o* in the pretonic syllable of a word (i.e. the syllable preceding the stress), e.g. *Maskvá* (Москва́; see 1.5.1). А́канье is a feature of pronunciation of Muscovite Russian, other C dialects and the S regional dialect.

alphabetism (бу́квенная аббревиату́ра): word consisting of initial capital letters of other words, e.g. **ОО́Н** (Организа́ция Объединённых На́ций, *United Nations Organisation*) (6.10).

animacy (одушевлённость): grammatical category embracing nouns that denote living things; in Russian, inflection of the accusative singular of most masculine nouns and of the accusative plural of nouns of all genders is determined by whether they are classified as animate or inanimate (see 11.1.3).

attributive adjective (атрибути́вное прилага́тельное): a descriptive adjective which qualifies a noun or noun-equivalent directly, e.g. *the new* car (9.3.1); cf. **predicative adjective**.

biaspectual verb (двувидово́й глаго́л): verb in which one form may function as either imperfective or perfective, e.g. **веле́ть, ра́нить**.

buffer vowel (бе́глое о): vowel added for the sake of euphony in certain situations to some Russian prepositions and prefixes which end in a consonant, e.g. в**о** внима́ние, перед**о** мно́й, сожг**у́**.

calque (ка́лька): a loan translation, i.e. a compound word or phrase that is a literal translation of a foreign expression, e.g. Eng *motorway* from Ger *Autobahn*; влия́ние, *influence*.

cardinal numeral (коли́чественное числи́тельное): numeral expressing *how many*, e.g. *five* (9.5, 11.4); cf. **ordinal numeral**.

case (паде́ж): morphological variant of a noun, pronoun, adjective, numeral or participle which expresses the relation of that word to other words in the clause.

clause (предложе́ние): word group containing a subject and predicate, e.g. *I shall do it* [main/principal clause] *as soon as I can* [subordinate clause]. (An overt subject, however, is not always present, e.g. in the imperative *Do it!*) See also **main clause, subordinate clause**.

cognates (однокоренны́е/однокорневы́е слова́): words that are etymologically related or derived from the same root, e.g. Eng *mother*, Fr *mère*, Ger *Mutter*, Russ мать, Sp *madre*; or, within Russian, стари́к, ста́рость, стару́ха, ста́рый, устаре́лый, etc.

colloquial (разгово́рный): informal or familiar style, expression or form widely used in everyday speech (1.3.1).

complement (дополне́ние): word or group of words that completes the meaning of an utterance, esp a noun or noun phrase that directly defines the subject, e.g. *She is a teacher* (11.1.10); see also **object**.

conditional mood (усло́вное наклоне́ние): verbal form expressing condition or hypothesis, e.g. *if it rains; if it were to rain* (11.9).

conjugation (спряже́ние): system of verb inflections expressing tense, mood, voice, person and number.

conjunction (сою́з): word used to connect words, groups of words or sentences, indicating the relationship of the connected elements, e.g. *dogs and cats* (coordinating conjunction); *I had supper after they had gone* (subordinating temporal conjunction); *I like curry although it's hot* (subordinating concessive conjunction); *She drank some water because she was thirsty* (subordinating causal conjunction) (11.12.1–11.12.3).

consonant (согла́сный): any speech sound other than a vowel, i.e. sound produced by some obstruction of the airstream (see also **affricate, fricative, plosive**); also any letter representing such a sound.

coordinating conjunction (сочини́тельный сою́з): a conjunction connecting two words, groups of words or sentences and indicating that both are independent and have the same function and importance, e.g. **and** (11.12.1).

dative case (да́тельный падёж): the case used to denote the indirect object of a verb, e.g. *I gave it **to my father***; Она́ посла́ла **мне** письмо́, *She sent the letter **to me*** (see 9.1.2, 9.1.8, 10.1.4, 10.3.3, 11.1.7–11.1.8).

declension (склоне́ние): system of inflections of noun, pronoun, adjective, numeral or participle expressing gender, case and number.

defective verb (недоста́точный глаго́л): verb which for some reason lacks some personal form or forms, e.g. **победи́ть** which has no first-person-singular form.

denominal preposition (отымённый предло́г): preposition derived from a noun, e.g. **по отноше́нию к**, *with regard to* (10.2).

devoicing (девокализа́ция, оглуше́ние): transformation of a **voiced consonant** into a **voiceless consonant** (q.v.), e.g. pronunciation of final *b* of раб as ***p***.

dialect (диале́кт): a variety of language distinguished from others by features of its sound system, vocabulary, morphology and syntax. Dialects may be geographic (i.e. spoken by people of the same territory) or social (i.e. spoken by people of the same class, social or occupational group). In Russian the term **наре́чие** designates a regional dialect spoken over a very wide area, whilst the term **го́вор** designates a local dialect confined to a much smaller area (1.5).

direct object (прямо́е дополне́ние): the thing on which the action denoted by a transitive verb is directed, e.g. *I broke a **window**; She bought a **newspaper*** (11.1.2–11.1.3, 11.1.6).

disjunctive conjunction (раздели́тельный сою́з): conjunction which unites clauses or sentences but separates meanings, e.g. ***or***.

dual number (дво́йственное число́): a grammatical form indicating duality; the form is obsolete in Russian but remnants of it survive, e.g. in plurals such as **глаза́** and **у́ши** and in the use of genitive singular forms of nouns after the numerals *2, 3* and *4*.

ellipsis (э́ллипсис): omission of a word or words whose meaning will be understood by the listener or reader, e.g. *after all [**that has been said**]*; Вы меня́ [**спра́шиваете**]? [**Are**] *you* [**asking**] *me?* (11.13).

ending (оконча́ние): in Russian, inflectional suffix added to a word to indicate its case, number, tense, mood, etc. in a particular context.

faux ami (ло́жный друг): a word in a foreign language that does not mean what a foreigner, on the basis of her or his own language, might expect it to mean, e.g. Russian **трансля́ция** does not mean *translation* (3.5).

fricative (фрикати́вный): consonant sound produced by the breath being forced through a narrow opening, e.g. Eng *f, v, s, z* and *th* in both *th*at and *th*ink.

genitive case (роди́тельный падёж): the case expressing possession, e.g. кни́га **бра́та**, *(my) brother's book* (9.1.2, 9.1.4, 9.1.7, 10.1.3, 10.3.2, 11.1.4–11.1.6).

gerund (дееприча́стие): in Russian, verb form invariable in gender, case and number which may be derived from verbs of either aspect and which defines the relationship in time of one action to another action denoted by the main verb of the sentence, e.g. Она́ гуля́ла, **напева́я** мело́дию, *She strolled,* ***humming*** *a tune* (imperfective gerund denoting simultaneous action); **Прове́рив** рабо́ту, он закры́л тетра́дь, ***Having checked*** *his work, he closed the exercise-book* (perfective gerund denoting prior action) (9.7.1–9.7.2, 11.11.1).

government (управле́ние): way in which a word controls the form of another word, e.g. the verb горди́ться governs an object in the instrumental case; the preposition о́коло governs a noun or noun-equivalent in the genitive case.

grammar (грамма́тика): rules of morphology and syntax of a language.

hard sign (твёрдый знак): the letter **ъ**, as in e.g. разъе́хаться, the function of which is explained at 8.2.2.

homoform (омофо́рма): a word identical with another word only when it is in one of the several morphological forms that it may adopt, e.g. **лечу́** (3.2).

homograph (омо́граф): a word written in the same way as another word but pronounced in a different way and having different meaning, e.g. **пото́м**, i.e. по́том and пото́м (3.3).

homonym (омо́ним): a word having the same sound as another word and written in the same way, but having a different meaning and possibly a different origin, e.g. ***bank*** (side of river and financial institution) (3.1.1–3.1.2).

homophone (омофо́н): a word which sounds the same as another word but is written differently, e.g. ***bare/bear, right/write*** (3.2).

iakan'e (я́канье): pronunciation of *'e* as *'a* after a soft consonant in the pretonic syllable. In **strong** (си́льное) я́канье, pretonic *'a* replaces *'e* irrespective of the quality of the vowel in the stressed syllable, e.g. *n'aslá* (несла́), *s'alóm* (село́м), *n'asú* (несу́), *t'ap'ér'* (тепе́рь). In **moderate** (уме́ренное) я́канье, pretonic *'a* replaces *'e* only before hard consonants, e.g. *n'aslá* (несла́), *s'alóm* (село́м), *n'asú* (несу́), but *t'ep'ér'* (тепе́рь) where *p* is soft.

idiom (идио́ма): expression peculiar to a language, group of words with a single meaning which cannot readily be derived from the meanings of the individual component words, e.g. Eng ***to spill the beans***, Russ **Ви́лами на/по воде́ пи́сано**, *It's still up in the air* (5.7).

ikan'e (и́канье): pronunciation of the vowels *'e* and *'a* in the pretonic syllable after a soft consonant as *'i*, e.g. *d'it'éj* (дете́й), *n'islá* (несла́), *t'ip'ér'* (тепе́рь), *vz'ilá* (взяла́), *r'idý* (ряды́), *t'inú* (тяну́).

imperative mood (повели́тельное наклоне́ние): verbal mood expressing command, invitation, suggestion, entreaty, request, etc., e.g. ***come in, sit down*** (6.8, 9.6.11, 11.5.6).

imperfective aspect (несоверше́нный вид): describes an action without reference to its extent and thus presents it as incomplete, e.g. Она **пе́ла**, *She **was singing/used to sing*** (11.5); cf. **perfective aspect**.

indicative mood (изъяви́тельное наклоне́ние): mood which affirms or denies that the action or state denoted by the verb in question is an actual fact, e.g. *I **read**, she **went**, they **were sitting**, the sun **was not shining***.

indirect object (ко́свенное дополне́ние): a noun, pronoun or phrase denoting an object indirectly affected by an action, e.g. *He gave the book* [direct object] ***to his sister*** [indirect object]. See also **dative case**.

indirect speech (also called **reported speech**; ко́свенная речь): discourse in which the substance of sb's words or thoughts is related without being quoted verbatim, e.g. *He told me **that he would do it**, She said **she was twenty*** (11.6).

infinitive (инфинити́в): verb form expressing the idea of an action without reference to person or number, e.g. ***to speak**, **говори́ть***.

infix (и́нфикс): element inserted in the middle of a word to modify its meaning or use, e.g. запи́**сыва**ть (8.6); English, unlike Russian, has no infixes.

inflection (also **flexion**; оконча́ние): the grammatical ending that expresses relations of case, tense, number, gender, etc. in nouns, pronouns, adjectives, numerals, verbs and participles, e.g. бра́**та**, себе́, но́**вого**, трё**х**, чита́**ю**, сидя́**щая**.

instrumental case (твори́тельный паде́ж): the case denoting the agent **by** which or the instrument **with** which sth is done, e.g. подпи́санный **им** догово́р, *the treaty signed **by him***, писа́ть **карандашо́м**, *to write **with a pencil*** (9.1.2, 9.1.8, 10.1.5, 10.3.4, 11.1.9–11.1.10).

interjection (междоме́тие): an exclamatory word, invariable in form, which is thrown into an utterance to express emotion, e.g. ***oh!, ox!*** (5.5).

intransitive verb (непереxо́дный глаго́л): a verb that does not require a direct object, e.g. *The sun **rises**, A crowd **gathered*** (4.4, 11.8).

isogloss (изогло́сса): a line separating one region from another which differs from it in a feature of dialect. The isogloss may indicate e.g. the limits of distribution of a certain word or the boundary beyond which one phenomenon (e.g. о́канье) is replaced by another (а́канье).

lexical (лекси́ческий): relating to vocabulary (as opposed to grammar).

locative case (ме́стный паде́ж): the case which indicates location of an object; used after the prepositions в and на (9.1.2, 9.1.5, 10.1.6, 10.3.5, 11.1.11); see also **prepositional case**.

long form (of adjective; по́лная фо́рма): full form that must be used when a Russian adjective is attributive, e.g. **ру́сский, но́вая, бе́лое, си́льные**, etc. (9.3.1); cf. **short form**, which may be used when the adjective is predicative.

main clause (гла́вное предложе́ние): a clause which can stand independently, e.g. *I went home* [main clause] *after I had spoken to you* [**subordinate clause**, q.v.].

mobile vowel (бе́глый гла́сный): one of the vowels **o**, **ё** or **e** when (a) they precede the final consonant of a masculine noun in its nominative singular form but disappear once an inflection is added, e.g. у́гол (угла́, etc.; see 9.1.3), or (b) are inserted in certain types of feminine or neuter noun which in the genitive plural have a **zero ending** (q.v.), e.g. доска́ (досо́к), полоте́нце (полоте́нец; see 9.1.7).

modal particle (мода́льная части́ца): a short indeclinable word which emphasises, intensifies or in some other way expresses the speaker's emotion or attitude, e.g. **ведь**, **же** (5.4).

modal verb (мода́льный глаго́л): verb (e.g. Eng *can*, *could*, *may*; Russ **мочь**) expressing possibility, permissibility, obligation, etc., and followed by another verb which it modifies (4.3).

monosyllable (односло́жное сло́во): word comprising one syllable, e.g. *cat*, *word*.

mood (наклоне́ние): form of the verb that indicates how the speaker views an action or state, i.e. whether it is seen as matter-of-fact, desirable, contingent on sth else, etc. See also **conditional**, **imperative**, **indicative**, **subjunctive**.

morphology (морфоло́гия): study of the forms of words. **Inflectional morphology** (see **inflection**) relates to the declension of nouns, pronouns, adjectives, numerals and participles and conjugation of verbs (see Chapter 9). **Lexical** (q.v.) **morphology** relates to **word-formation** (q.v.; see Chapter 8).

neologism (неологи́зм): a new word or phrase (e.g. **грант**, **теневи́к**), or the use of an old word in a new sense (e.g. **боеви́к**) (5.1).

nominative case (имени́тельный паде́ж): the case in which the subject is expressed, e.g. **О́льга** чита́ет кни́гу, *Ol′ga is reading a book* (9.1.2, 10.1.1, 11.1.1).

number (числ0́): the grammatical property of a word which indicates whether it is singular, dual (q.v.) or plural. The difference between *car/cars*, *mouse/mice*, *I am/we are* is in each instance a difference of number.

numeral (числи́тельное): a word denoting number, e.g. *two*, *five*; see also **cardinal numeral** and **ordinal numeral**.

object (дополне́ние): see **direct object** and **indirect object**.

oblique case (ко́свенный паде́ж): any case other than the nominative (and in other Slavonic languages, vocative), i.e. in Russian accusative, genitive, dative, instrumental, prepositional. In this book the term is used to embrace the last four of these cases, but not generally the accusative.

okan′e (о́канье): the phoneme *o* preserves its value in the pretonic syllable, e.g. *sová* (сова́); cf. **akan′e** above. In **full** (по́лное) о́канье *o* retains its value even in the syllable before the pretonic syllable, e.g. *molodój* (молодо́й). In **incomplete** (непо́лное) о́канье, *o* in the syllable preceding the pretonic syllable is reduced to ə, e.g. *məlokó* (молокó) (1.5).

Old Church Slavonic (церко̀внославя́нский язы́к): the South Slav language that was used by the early Slav missionaries, in the ninth and tenth centuries, for the transmission of Christian teaching to other Slav peoples; the basis of the language used in Russia for liturgical purposes and most literary forms before westernisation in the eighteenth century.

ordinal numeral (поря́дковое числи́тельное): numeral indicating place in order or sequence, e.g. *second, fifth*.

orthography (орфогра́фия): correct or accepted use of the written characters of a language.

paradigm (паради́гма): table setting out the system of inflection of a word.

paronym (паро́ним): a word which may be confused with another to which it is close in sound, written form and possibly meaning, and which may be of similar origin, e.g. *principal/principle*. In this book the term is used in a broad sense to include all easily confused words, even those of quite different origin, e.g. **бре́мя, вре́мя** (3.4).

participle (прича́стие): a verb form that combines both the qualities of a verb (e.g. transitiveness or intransitiveness, active or passive meaning, tense and aspect, but not person) and the qualities of a noun (e.g. gender, case and number). Russian has present and past active participles and present and past passive participles (9.7.3–9.7.6, 11.11.2–11.11.4).

passive voice (страда́тельный зало́г): the form of a verb which indicates that the subject suffered the action, i.e. was not itself the agent, e.g. *I was hit by a stone, They were taught French by their mother*.

perfective aspect (соверше́нный вид): describes an action restricted in its extent and thus presents it as complete; perfectives relate to the beginning of an action (e.g. **зазвене́ть**, *to start to ring*), the limited duration of an action (e.g. **посиде́ть**, *to sit for a while*), or the completion of an action (e.g. **вы́пить**, *to drink up*) (11.5); cf. **imperfective aspect**.

periphrasis (перифра́за): complicated, round-about expression, use of more words than is strictly speaking necessary, e.g. *in this day and age*.

person (лицо́): form of the verb which represents: (a) the person/persons or thing/things speaking (i.e. 1st pers, e.g. *I/we read*); (b) the person/persons or thing/things spoken to (i.e. 2nd pers, e.g. *you read*); or (c) the person/persons or thing/things spoken about (i.e. 3rd pers, e.g. *he/she reads, they read*).

phrase (фра́за): group of words lacking a finite verb but felt to express a single idea or to constitute a discrete element in a sentence.

plosive (взрывно́й): consonant sound produced by momentary stoppage of the air passage at some point, e.g. Russ *b* and *p* (labial plosives), *d* and *t* (dental plosives), *g* and *k* (velar plosives); also sometimes called an 'occlusive'(смы́чный) or a 'stop'.

predicate (сказу́емое): word or group of words which says sth about the subject, e.g. *I am **studying languages**; Cats **catch mice***. A verb is generally the chief part of the predicate.

predicative adjective (предикати́вное прилага́тельное): adjective that forms part of the predicate, i.e. which is separated from the noun it qualifies by some part of the verb *to be* or, in Russian, by part of the verb *to be* that is understood, e.g. *The book was **interesting**,* Кни́га была́ **интере́сна**.

prefix (приста́вка): element added to the beginning of a word to modify its meaning, e.g. ***pre**determine,* **при**ходи́ть (8.3–8.5).

preposition (предло́г): word that defines the relation of a noun or pronoun to some other word, e.g. *The book is **on** the table; I went **across** the road; A plane flew **over** the houses* (Chapter 10).

prepositional case (предло́жный паде́ж): case used after certain prepositions when they have certain meanings (9.1.2, 9.1.5, 9.1.8, 10.1.6, 10.3.5, 11.1.11); see also **locative case**.

present perfect continuous: the tense which in English indicates that an action begun in the past is still continuing, e.g. *I **have been living** here for three years*. In Russian this tense must be rendered by an imperfective verb in the present tense (11.6).

pretonic syllable (предуда́рный слог): the syllable before the stress, e.g. Москва́.

pronoun (местоиме́ние): word used instead of a noun, e.g. ***he, she*** (9.2, 11.2).

prosthetic (also **prothetic**; протети́ческий): sound inserted at the beginning of a word for ease of pronunciation, e.g. the sound *n* in на **н**его́ (9.2).

proverb (посло́вица): short familiar sentence expressing a supposed truth or moral lesson, e.g. ***Every cloud has a silver lining*** (5.8).

register (стиль): a variety of language determined by such factors as medium, subject-matter, purpose and situation (1.2–1.4, 1.6).

relative pronoun (относи́тельное местоиме́ние): a word which introduces a subordinate clause describing a preceding noun or pronoun (the antecedent), e.g. Eng ***who, which***, Russ **кото́рый**, e.g. *The man **who** sells newspapers; The table **which** I bought yesterday* (11.2.1).

reported speech: see **indirect speech**.

root (ко́рень): the base of a word which bears its fundamental meaning, e.g. стол in **сто́л**ик, **сто́л**овая, на**сто́л**ьный, etc.

secondary stress (второстепе́нное ударе́ние): in long words, especially compound words, a syllable other than the main stressed syllable which may also need to be pronounced with additional force. Secondary stress is marked in this book by a grave accent, e.g. церко̀внославя́нский.

semantic (семанти́ческий): relating to meaning.

sentence (предложе́ние): minimum complete utterance, e.g. ***I told him; Come back!***

short form (of adjective; кра́ткая фо́рма): the truncated masculine, feminine, neuter and plural forms, e.g. **нов, нова́, но́во, но́вы**, which in modern Russian are indeclinable and which may only be used predicatively (9.3.2, 11.3); see also **predicative adjective**.

simile (сравне́ние): rhetorical likening of a thing to sth else, e.g. *drunk as a lord, like a bolt from the blue* (5.9).

Slavonicism (славяни́зм): a form of **Old Church Slavonic** (q.v.) origin. Many Slavonicisms exist in Russian alongside East Slav forms. They are characterised by (a) certain phonetic features, notably (with the Slavonicism first in each pair): **прах/по́рох, мла́дший/молодо́й, среда́/середи́на, расте́ние/рост, ладья́/ло́дка, граждани́н/горожа́нин, ночь/всено́щная, еди́ный/оди́н, юро́дивый/уро́д**); (b) certain prefixes, e.g. **избра́ть** (cf. **вы́брать**), **низверга́ть, чрезме́рный** (cf. **че́рез**), **предви́деть** (cf. **пе́ред**), **преступле́ние** (cf. **переступа́ть**); (c) certain suffixes, e.g. **пе́рвенец, сочу́вствие, жизнь, моли́тва, святы́ня, творе́ние, горя́щий** (cf. **горя́чий**), **богате́йший, широча́йший**. Slavonicisms tend to have a more bookish flavour than related Russian forms of East Slav origin and tend to occur in more elevated varieties of language.

soft sign (мя́гкий знак): the letter **ь**, the function of which is to indicate that the preceding consonant is soft. The soft sign is normally transliterated by the symbol ′ or by an apostrophe.

stress (ударе́ние): in all Russian words of more than one syllable, as in such English words, one syllable is pronounced with more force than the other(s). This stress is marked in this book, as in most textbooks, by an acute accent, but it is not normally indicated in Russian publications. Russian stress patterns (Chapter 12) are numerous and complex.

stump–compound (аббревиату́ра): word compounded of segments of other words, e.g. **тера́кт** (террористи́ческий акт, *terrorist act*).

subject (подлежа́щее): the agent performing the action expressed by the verb in an active sentence, or the person on whom or the thing on which the action of a passive sentence is performed, e.g. *The priest delivered a sermon; We saw the queen; The man was struck by lightning.*

subjunctive mood (сослага́тельное наклоне́ние): the verbal mood which indicates that the action or state denoted by the verb in question is regarded as hypothetical or subject to another action or state, e.g. *I wish he were right; I demand that it be done* (11.10).

subordinate clause (прида́точное предложе́ние): clause which cannot function as a sentence in its own right but is dependent on another clause which can, e.g. *I think* [main clause] *that she is nice* [subordinate clause]; *I like the house* [main clause] *which you have bought* [subordinate clause]; *I went to bed* [main clause] *because it was late* [subordinate clause].

subordinating conjunction (подчини́тельный сою́з): conjunction introducing a subordinate clause, e.g. *although, after, because* (11.12.2–11.12.3).

substantivised adjective (субстантиви́рованное прилага́тельное): word which has adjectival form but is used as a noun, e.g. **моро́женое**, *ice-cream*; **столо́вая**, *dining-room*.

suffix (су́ффикс): element added to the end of a root or stem to modify its use or meaning, e.g. *writer, happiness* (8.7–8.11).

syntax (си́нтаксис): grammatical structure in a sentence, or study of that structure.

tense (вре́мя): verbal form indicating whether the action or state denoted by the verb is viewed as past, present or future.

transitive verb (перехо́дный глаго́л): verb that requires a direct object, e.g. *I **bought** a car* (4.4, 11.8).

tsokan'e (цо́канье): loss of distinction between the affricates (q.v.) *c* and *č'*. In **hard** (твёрдое) цо́канье the standard soft hushing affricate *č'* is replaced by a hard hissing affricate *c*, e.g. *cúdo* (чу́до). In **soft** (мя́гкое) цо́канье *č'* is replaced by a soft hissing *c'*, e.g. *c'údo*.

velar (задненёбный): consonant sound produced by raising the back of the top of the tongue against the soft palate (нёбо); in Russian the sounds *g, k, x*.

vocative case (зва́тельный паде́ж): case used in direct personal address; now defunct in Russian, except in relics such as **Бо́же** and **го́споди** and in certain colloquial forms in the spoken language (see 7.3.1). (The vocative survives in other Slavonic languages, e.g. Czech, Polish, Serbo-Croat.)

voiced consonant (зво́нкий согла́сный): consonant produced with the vocal cords vibrating, e.g. Russian *b, v, g, d, ž, z*; see also **voiceless consonant**.

voiceless consonant (глухо́й согла́сный): consonant produced without vibration of the vocal cords, e.g. Russian *p, f, k, t, š, s, x, c, č', šš'*.

vowel (гла́сный): sound produced by passage of air through mouth without obstruction of the airstream, e.g. *a, e, i, o, u*.

word-formation (словообразова́ние): formation of new words by combining roots and affixes or by other means; also the study of the structure of words and the laws of their formation in a language (Chapter 8).

zero ending (нулево́е оконча́ние): ending of a Russian noun in an oblique case in which no inflection is present e.g. солда́т, *soldier* (which is genitive plural as well as nominative singular); жён (gen pl; nom sg жена́, *wife*); мест (gen pl; nom sg ме́сто, *place*).

List of abbreviations

acc	accusative	math	mathematical
act	active	med	medical
adj	adjective	mil	military
adv	adverb	mus	musical
agric	agricultural	N	North
biol	biological	n	neuter
C	Central	NE	North-East
col	column	nom	nominative
collect	collective	non-refl	non-reflexive
conj	conjunction	NW	North-West
D	demotic	obs	obsolete
dat	dative	OCS	Old Church Slavonic
dimin	diminutive	offic	official
E	East	part	participle
econ	economic	pass	passive
Eng	English	pej	pejorative
esp	especially	pers	person
f	feminine	pf	perfective
fig	figurative	phil	philosophical
fin	financial	pl	plural
Fr	French	poet	poetic
fut	future	pol	political
gen	genitive	prep	prepositional
geog	geographical	pres	present
geol	geological	R	register
Ger	German	refl	reflexive
gram	grammatical	rhet	rhetorical
imp	imperative	Russ	Russian
impers	impersonal	sb	somebody
impf	imperfective	SE	South-East
incl	including	sg	singular
indecl	indeclinable	Sp	Spanish
infin	infinitive	sth	something
instr	instrumental	subst	substantivised
iron	ironical	SW	South-West
lit	literally	tech	technical
loc	locative	theat	theatrical
m	masculine	vulg	vulgar

The Russian particle -нибýдь is frequently abbreviated to -н.

1 Varieties of language and register

1.1 The Russian language and its distribution

The Russian language belongs to the East Slav group of languages, itself part of the Slavonic branch of the Indo-European family. The relationship of Russian to the other modern European languages is illustrated by Figure 1 (which includes only languages still used by substantial numbers of speakers).

It is difficult to give accurate up-to-date figures for the number of people for whom Russian is their native or first language, or at least their first language for some purpose or purposes (e.g. professional or social). This difficulty arises for several reasons. Firstly, we are dealing with several different categories of user, including the following: ethnic Russians who are citizens of the Russian Federation; ethnic Russians who are citizens of other former republics of the Soviet Union; members of other ethnic groups who are citizens of the Russian Federation; and members of other ethnic groups who are citizens of other former republics of the Soviet Union but who continue to use Russian at work or at home, perhaps because their community or family is mainly Russian-speaking. It is not always easy to define whether Russian is the first or second language of at least the latter two groups. Secondly, there has been much migration between the regions and states of the former Soviet Union since the collapse of the Union in 1991, with the result that numbers and proportions of ethnic Russians or other speakers of Russian in each former republic may have changed significantly over the last thirteen years. Thirdly, considerable numbers of both ethnic Russians and members of non-Russian ethnic groups who grew up in Russia or the Soviet Union using Russian as their first language have in the same period emigrated from the Russian Federation to countries outside the former Soviet Union. The number of Jews in the Russian Federation, for example, fell from roughly 540,000 in 1989 to 230,000 in 2002 and the number of Russian Germans has declined over the same period from 840,000 to 600,000. It is difficult to determine how many émigrés continue to use Russian as their first language, or for how long they do so, after their emigration.

The most easily quantifiable group of Russian-speakers, of course, is the citizenry of the Russian Federation, of which Russian is the official language. According to the census of the Russian Federation carried out in 2002, the population of the Federation was a little over 145 million,[1] of whom some 116 million (i.e. almost 80 per cent) describe themselves as ethnically Russian.

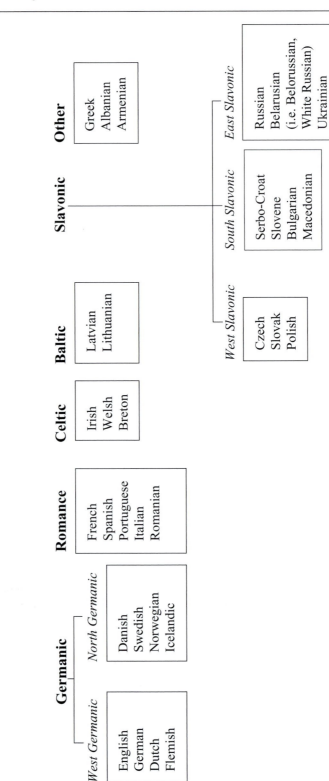

Fig. 1.   The Indo-European languages

Among the remaining 20 per cent, or approximately 29 million, of the population of the Russian Federation (many of whom will also consider Russian their first language) 160 nationalities were represented, according to the 2002 census. The largest of these non-Russian groups, in descending order, were Tatars (of whom there were over five million), Ukrainians (almost three million, although their number in the Russian Federation has been decreasing), Bashkirs and Chuvashes (over a million each), and Chechens and Armenians (also over a million each, and their numbers in the Russian Federation have been increasing). Figure 2 shows the composition of the population of the Russian Federation by ethnic group, as revealed by the 2002 census.

Of the non-Russian citizens of the Federation the Ukrainians and Belorussians (whose numbers in the Russian Federation have also been decreasing) are ethnically close to the Russians. Their languages (i.e. Ukrainian and Belorussian respectively) are closely related to Russian, which Ukrainians and Belorussians are likely also to speak with native or near-native facility. However, many of the non-Russian citizens of the Russian Federation (e.g. Estonians, Kazakhs, Latvians) belong to quite different ethnic groups from the Russians, including non-European groups. They may therefore speak a language that is only distantly related to Russian (e.g. Latvian, which is also Indo-European) or that belongs to a different linguistic group (e.g. Estonian, which is a Finno-Ugric language, or Kazakh, which is a Turkic language).[2] These non-Russian citizens of the Federation have varying degrees of command of Russian. A substantial number of them consider Russian their first language.

It needs to be borne in mind, incidentally, that different Russian terms are used to denote the different types of 'Russian' who have been identified in the preceding paragraphs. The substantivised adjective ру́сский (f ру́сская) denotes a person who is ethnically Russian. Used as an adjective, this word also denotes the Russian language (ру́сский язы́к). The noun россия́нин (f россия́нка), on the other hand, conveys the broader concept of a person who is a citizen of the Russian Federation but who is not necessarily ethnically Russian. The adjective росси́йский has a correspondingly broader sense than the adjective ру́сский, as, for example, in the name of the country itself (Росси́йская Федера́ция), which denotes a political rather than an ethnic, linguistic or cultural entity.

The numbers of ethnic Russian and non-Russian speakers of Russian outside the Russian Federation are more difficult to quantify. Some idea of their number can be gauged from the fact that at the time of the 1989 census (the last census carried out in the Soviet era) there were 25 million ethnic Russians living in other republics of the Soviet Union (see 6.11.1 for a list of these republics), the majority of them in Ukraine. Moreover, since Russian was used as a second language throughout the non-Russian areas of the Union, whose total

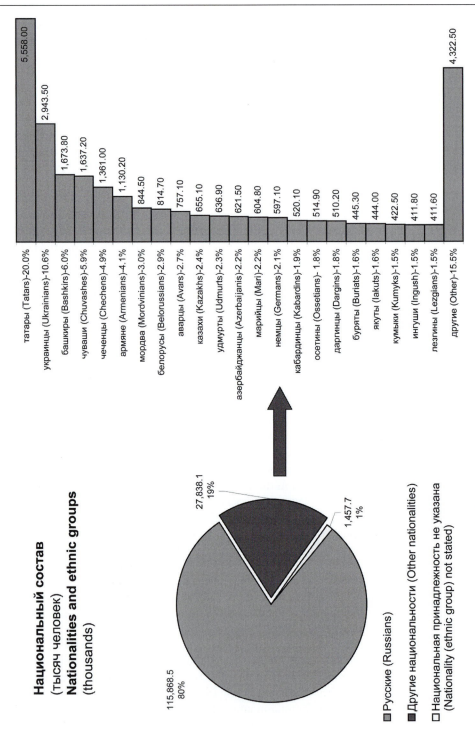

Fig. 2.   Population of the Russian Federation by ethnic group, according to the 2002 census

population in 1989 was 287 million, one may assume that the language
was used as a first or second language by at least a further 50 million
Soviet citizens. However, the status of the Russian language is now
diminishing in the former Soviet republics in proportion as the
languages of the ethnic groups that are dominant in the new states (e.g.
Kazakhs in Kazakhstan) are promoted, particularly within the
educational system. Admittedly Russian remains a lingua franca for
commercial and diplomatic transactions in the former Soviet republics,
especially among the older generation of speakers who were educated
in Soviet times, when Russian was the dominant language throughout
the Union. On the other hand, the rise of English as the language of
global communication, and therefore the first foreign language to be
taught in schools, may further weaken the status of Russian outside the
Russian Federation. One may predict that in twenty or thirty years
Russian will be less widely spoken in the former Soviet republics than
it is today, especially in those countries with a relatively small residual
ethnic Russian population (e.g. Lithuania). It is also possible that many
people who do speak Russian in those countries will use it less than
they do today and that they will have a poorer command of it than
non-Russians who speak Russian there now.

Russian is of course also spoken, with varying degrees of fluency,
accuracy and proximity to the Russian now spoken in Russia itself, by
many émigrés or their descendants in countries outside the former
Soviet Union. Russians, or members of other ethnic groups who were
formerly Soviet citizens, have left the Soviet Union – or not returned
to it – at four main periods in the last ninety years or so: in the years
immediately or soon after the Bolshevik revolution of 1917; after the
Second World War (1939–45), following their displacement; in the
Brézhnev period (especially in the 1970s, after the granting of
permission to Jews to leave the country); and from the mid-1980s,
following the further relaxation of emigration controls. The principal
destinations of these emigrants, at one time or another, have been
France, Germany, Britain, the US and Israel. Many members of the
Russian diaspora are permanently settled abroad but some – mainly
more recent émigrés – are only temporarily resident outside Russia,
perhaps because they are working or studying abroad.

Russian is also spoken by millions of people as a foreign language,
especially people from Africa, Asia, Latin America and Eastern Europe
who received all or most of their higher education in the Soviet
Union. Moreover, Russian has been widely taught outside Russia
since the Second World War, particularly when the Soviet Union was
at its most powerful from the 1960s to the1980s. Organisations such as
the International Association of Teachers of the Russian Language and
Literature (Междунаро́дная ассоциа́ция преподава́телей ру́сского
языка́ or МАПРЯ́Л) were set up in the Soviet period to support such
activity. However, the number of foreigners learning Russian
(estimated at some 20 million in 1979) has diminished in the

post-Soviet period, following the demise of Russian hegemony in the Eastern bloc countries (East Germany, Poland, Czechoslovakia, Hungary, Romania and Bulgaria) and the weakening of Russian influence in various states in other parts of the world (e.g. Cuba, Angola, Ethiopia, North Yemen and Vietnam).

It should be added, finally, that Russian is one of the official and working languages of the United Nations and UNESCO.

Although Russian is thus widely distributed, and although it is also the language in which one of the world's great bodies of imaginative literature has been created over the last two and a half centuries, it is with the varieties of Russian that are spoken by ethnic Russians in Russia today that this book is primarily concerned.

1.2 Varieties of language

The student learning a foreign language in a systematic way will generally study a form of it, or the single form of it, which educated native speakers consider normative, e.g. 'BBC English', Parisian French, Tuscan Italian, Mandarin or Cantonese. In the case of Russian this normative form is what Russians refer to as the 'literary language' (литерату́рный язы́к). However, the term 'literary language' suggests to an English-speaker exclusively the written language, and the expression 'standard Russian' is therefore preferred in this book. Standard Russian embraces the spoken language of educated people as well as the written language, and its spoken form is based on educated Muscovite speech.

Study of the normative form of a language should inculcate a standard pronunciation and vocabulary and 'correct' grammatical rules. It is essential that the foreign student absorb such a norm both in order that he or she should be able to communicate with educated speakers of the language in a way acceptable to the largest possible number of them, and in order to establish criteria in his or her own mind for judging correctness and error in the language.

However, there comes a point in one's study of a foreign language when it also becomes necessary to recognise that the concept of norms is to some extent theoretical and abstract. This is so because a living language is constantly evolving and because innumerable varieties of it exist both within what is regarded as the norm and beyond the limits of that norm.

For one thing, what people consider correct changes with the passage of time. For example, authoritative Russian dictionaries indicate end stress throughout the future tense in the verbs помести́ть and посели́ть (помести́шь, etc., посели́шь, etc.), but many educated speakers now consider поме́стишь, etc. and посе́лишь, etc. normal and correct. As far as the historical evolution of Russian is concerned, the student needs to be aware that while the Russian of Пу́шкин, Турге́нев and Толсто́й is easily comprehensible to Russians today, it differs in some respects morphologically and especially lexically from the contemporary language. Moreover, Russian is undergoing rapid change at the present time. This change is due to some extent to the global technological and managerial revolution of the late twentieth century, with its large new vocabulary, but also to the quite sudden breakdown of the communist order in Russia and the political, economic, social and cultural innovations and dislocations which that breakdown has entailed. The concerns that these linguistic changes have generated among educated Russians are dealt with in section 1.6 below.

More importantly from the point of view of this book, the language spoken in Russia today, while having a common core, has numerous varieties, as do modern English, French, German, Spanish and so on. For native users of a language do not all use their language in the same way. The language they use may vary depending on such factors as where they come from, which social group they belong to, whether they are speaking or writing, and how formal the context is in which they are communicating. In other words varieties of language are, in the terminology of the Romanian linguist Coseriu, diatopic (that is to say, characteristic of a particular place, as are regional dialects), diastratic (characteristic of a certain stratum, as are social dialects), diamesic (determined by medium, e.g. whether the example of language is written or spoken), or diaphasic (determined by degree of formality).

The last two types of variation are particularly important for us here, since no individual speaker of a language, whatever region or class he or she emanates from and irrespective of whether he or she writes and speaks what is considered the standard form of the language, uses the language in the same way in all situations. People make linguistic choices, which are determined by the situation in which they find themselves, selecting certain lexical, morphological and syntactic forms from among the options available in their language. They may even vary their pronunciation (and in Russian, their stress) according to the context. It is important for advanced learners of a language to be aware of this variety in the language's use, both in order that they may be sensitive to the nuances of what they hear and read and in order that they themselves may use language that is appropriate in a given situation and has the desired impact. After all, a sophisticated expression used in the wrong context may sound laughably pompous, while a coarse turn of phrase addressed to the wrong company may cause offence.

Bearing in mind what has been said about variety, one needs when studying language to reflect on the following factors. Who is using the language in a given instance, and with what intent? What form of communication is being used? What is its subject-matter? And what is the context? In other words, one should consider the user, purpose, medium, field and situation.

Factors relating to the speaker himself or herself which help to determine the type of language he or she uses are the speaker's age, sex, place of origin (see 1.5), level of education and social position or status. These factors may impinge on language directly, by affecting a person's accent, way of addressing others, range of vocabulary and command of grammar, and indirectly, by shaping and delimiting a person's knowledge and experience.

The purpose of communication in a given instance also has a bearing on the form of language used. One may be using language merely to impart information, as is the case for example in a scholarly article or lecture, a textbook or a weather forecast; or to persuade, as is the case in an editorial article, a lawyer's speech in court or a political broadcast; or merely for social intercourse, as is the case in a conversation with friends. Language used for the first purpose is likely to be logical, coherent, matter-of-fact, relatively sophisticated syntactically and shorn of emotional expressiveness. Language used for the last purpose, on the other hand, is likely to be less rational and less complex syntactically, and may deploy a range of emotional and expressive resources.

The medium used for communication also significantly affects the language used. Perhaps the most important distinction to be made under this heading is the distinction between spoken and written forms of language. The distinction has been defined by David Crystal in the following way. Speech is time-bound and transient. The speaker has particular addressees in mind. Because of the probable lack of forethought and the speed of delivery the constructions used are relatively simple and loose. There is a higher incidence of coordinating conjunctions than subordinating conjunctions. Spoken language may incorporate slang, nonsense words and obscenity. Utterances may be repeated or rephrased and comments interpolated. It is prone to error, but there is an opportunity for the speaker to reformulate what has been said. Such factors as loudness, intonation, tempo, rhythm and pause play an important role. In the event of face-to-face communication extra-linguistic aids to communication might be used, such as expression, gesture and posture. Speech is suited to social intercourse, the expression of personal feelings, opinions and attitudes. Writing, on the other hand, is space-bound and permanent. The writer is separated from the person addressed, that is to say the reader. The written language tends to be carefully organised and its syntax relatively intricate. There is a higher incidence of subordination in it than there is in speech. Documents may be edited and corrected before they are disseminated and format and graphic conventions may strengthen their impact. Writing is suited to the recording of facts and the exposition of ideas. It should be noted, though, that there is no simple correlation between speech and informality, on the one hand, and writing and formality on the other. While the written language tends to be more formal than the spoken language it is not necessarily so. For example, the written language in the form of a letter to a partner, friend or relation is likely to be less formal than such examples of the spoken language as an academic lecture, a radio or television interview, or a political speech.

As for field, language is affected by subject-matter in an obvious way, inasmuch as fields of activity and branches of knowledge have their special terminology, for example, political, philosophical, scientific, medical, musical, literary, sporting, professional and so forth. However, the effect of field on language may go further than terminology. Groups have distinctive ways of expressing themselves: doctors, for example, are likely to describe patients' symptoms in language altogether different from that used by patients themselves.

Finally, regarding situation, one's mode of expression may be affected by the nature of the relationship that exists between the user and the person or people with whom he or she is communicating. Language is likely to vary according to such factors as whether one is speaking, for example, to one's elders (with any one of a range of nuances from respect, deference, sympathy or affection to condescension or intolerance), to children (lovingly, reproachfully, sternly), to a superior or junior at work, or to an intimate or a stranger.

1.3   Registers

The varieties of language that result from the interaction of the factors described in 1.2 represent stylistic levels which, in common with authors of other books in this series, we shall term registers.[3] Although the number of registers that may be identified is quite large, for the purposes of this book a scale will be used on which three main registers are marked (low, neutral and high). These registers will be referred to throughout the book as R1, R2 and R3, respectively. Beyond the first of these registers lie demotic speech (1.3.2) and vulgar language (5.6) and within R3 lie various functional styles (функциона́льные сти́ли) which will be classified here as scientific or academic style, official, legal or business style, and the styles of journalism and political debate (1.3.4).

These registers, which are examined in more detail below, broadly speaking reflect a spectrum ranging from informality, in the case of R1, to formality, in the case of R3. Insofar as this spectrum reveals a view of language as low (сни́женный), neutral (нейтра́льный) or high (высо́кий), it may be traced back in Russia to the work of the poet, scientist and student of language Lomonósov, who in his *Предисло́вие о по́льзе книг церко́вных в росси́йском языке́* (*Preface on the Use of Church Books in the Russian Language*, 1758) famously defined three linguistic styles (ни́зкий, посре́дственный, высо́кий) and laid down the genres in which it seemed appropriate to use each of them. To a considerable extent this spectrum of register runs parallel to that which ranges from the colloquial form of spoken Russian at one end to a bookish form of the written language at the other (although, as has already been noted in the previous section, certain spoken media may be more formal than certain written media).

It is important to appreciate that the boundaries between linguistic registers are constantly shifting. In particular it should be noted with

regard to modern, post-Soviet Russian that what only recently might
have been considered improper at a higher level than R1 may now be
considered quite acceptable, or at least might be widely used, in R2.
Similarly, what was recently felt to be sub-standard may now be
widespread in R1. This lowering of boundaries and the broadening of
what was previously considered the standard, and also reactions to
these changes, are examined in more detail in 1.6 below.

Passages exemplifying the various registers described in this section
are provided, with translation and commentary, in Chapter 2.

1.3.1   The colloquial register (R1)

The principal function of this register is social intercourse. Its medium
is dialogue or conversation and its field is one's personal relationships
and practical everyday dealings with others. It is therefore distinguished
by relative spontaneity, simplicity and the absence of forethought or
technical or official tone. Non-lexical features, such as intonation,
pauses, stress, rhythm and tempo, play an important part in it. Meaning
is reinforced by non-linguistic resources such as facial expression and
gesture. The function, medium and field of the register account for
many of the factors which it tends to exhibit in the areas of
pronunciation, vocabulary and phraseology, word-formation,
morphology and syntax.

pronunciation • Articulation is often careless and indistinct, and vowels may be reduced
or consonants lost as a result of lazy or rapid delivery, e.g. *grú* (говорю́),
zdrássti (здра́вствуй), *u t'á* (у тебя́), *tóka* (то́лько), *vaššé* (вообще́),
p'iis'át (пятьдеся́т). Local accent is marked (e.g. with а́канье and
associated phenomena or о́канье, treatment of *g* as occlusive or
fricative; see 1.5). Stress may differ from the accepted norm (e.g.
до́говор, при́говор, позво́нишь, разви́лось, разви́лись instead
of догово́р, пригово́р, позвони́шь, развило́сь, развили́сь,
respectively).

vocabulary • This tends to be basic and concrete since the register is concerned with
the practicalities of life. All parts of speech are represented in numerous
colloquial forms, i.e. nouns (e.g. зади́ра, *bully*; карто́шка, *potato*;
толкотня́, *crush, scrum*); adjectives (e.g. долговя́зый, *lanky*; дото́шный,
meticulous; мудрёный, *odd*; работя́щий, *hard-working*; расхля́банный,
lax); verbs (e.g. арта́читься, *to dig one's heels in* (fig); дры́хнуть and
вздремну́ть (pf), *to have a nap*; вопи́ть, *to wail, howl*; впихну́ть (pf), *to
cram in*; гро́хнуть(ся) (pf), *to bang, crash*; ехи́дничать, *to gossip
maliciously*; куроле́сить, *to play tricks*; ме́шкать, *to linger, loiter*;
огоро́шить (pf), *to take aback*; перебо́рщивать, *to overdo* (lit *to make too
much borshch*); помере́ть (pf), *to die*; прихворну́ть (pf), *to be unwell*;
секре́тничать, *to be secretive*; тарато́рить, *to jabber, natter*; тормоши́ть,
to pull about, pester); adverbs (e.g. ба́ста, *enough*; вконе́ц, *completely*;
втихомо́лку, *on the quiet*; давне́нько, *for quite some time now*;
исподтишка́, *on the sly*; ми́гом, *in a flash*; многова́то, *a bit too*

much/many; нагишо́м, *stark naked*; недосу́г, *haven't/hasn't got time (to do sth)*; помале́ньку, *gradually, gently, tolerably*; потихо́ньку, *slowly, softly, on the sly*; хороше́нько, *well and truly*; часте́нько, *quite often*; чу́точку, *a tiny bit*); and pronouns (э́такий, *what a/such a*). Some colloquial words are derived from the same root as non-colloquial words (e.g. карто́шка, cf. карто́фель; помере́ть, cf. умере́ть).

- The speaker has frequent recourse to various types of filler words (e.g. зна́чит, ти́па, ка́к бы, в смы́сле), hesitation markers (e.g. гм), comment clauses (e.g. предста́вь себе́; see 5.3 on all of these), and attempts to engage an interlocutor, real or imagined (e.g. зна́ешь, понима́ете, ви́дите). The language's means of expressing emotion, notably modal particles (e.g. ведь, же; see 5.4) and interjections (e.g. ах, тсс; 5.5), may be exploited. Informal modes of address predominate (7.2–7.3). People conversing in the colloquial register are more likely to address each other as ты than as вы and to call each other by their first names, indeed by diminutive forms of them (7.3.1), than by the combined first name and patronymic.

phraseology

- Idioms (5.7) and expressive turns of phrase are used, giving a variety of tones, for example ironic, scornful, jocular. Phraseology may be structurally distinctive, e.g. бе́з году неде́ля, *only a few days*; гляде́ть в о́ба, *to be on one's guard*; ждать не дожда́ться, *to be on tenterhooks*; из ко́жи вон лезть, *to do one's utmost*; танцева́ть от пе́чки, *to start again from the beginning*; э́то ежу́ я́сно, *any fool could see it* (lit *it's clear to a hedgehog*).

word-formation

- Bookish suffixes, especially those of Old Church Slavonic origin, are relatively scarce, but many other noun suffixes (see 8.7) abound and indeed occur mainly in this register, e.g. -а́к (проста́к, *simple-minded fellow*); -я́к (добря́к, *good-natured bloke*); -а́ка (зева́ка, *idler*); -я́ка (гуля́ка, *playboy*); -а́н (старика́н, *old chap*); -я́н (грубия́н, *boor*); -а́ч (борода́ч, *bloke with a beard*); -а́ш (алка́ш, *alcoholic*; торга́ш, *small trader, mercenary person*); -ёжка (зубрёжка, *cramming*, i.e. study); -ень (ба́ловень, *spoilt brat*); -ла (вороти́ла, *bigwig*); -лка (раздева́лка, *cloakroom*); -ня́ (возня́, *row, racket*); -отня́ (беготня́, *running about, bustle*); -тя́й (лентя́й, *lazy person*); -у́н (болту́н, *chatterbox*); -у́ха (толсту́ха, *fat woman*); -ы́ш (малы́ш, *kid*); -я́га (бедня́га, *poor devil*). Diminutive and pejorative suffixes (8.8) indicate a speaker's attitudes, e.g. -о́к (сыно́к, *dear son*); -и́шка (лгуни́шка, *wretched liar*); -и́шко (городи́шко, *little town* or *ghastly town*); -и́ща (бороди́ща, *hideous beard*). The adjectival suffix -у́щий (большу́щий, *whacking great*), the adjectival prefix пре- (преглу́пый, *really stupid*), and the verbal suffix -ничать (бродя́жничать, *to be a tramp*) are also characteristic of the colloquial register.

morphology

- In some masculine nouns certain forms may be preferred to standard forms in some cases, e.g. prep sg in -у́ (в отпуску́ instead of в о́тпуске, *on leave*; 9.1.5); nom pl in -а́ (сектора́ instead of се́кторы, *sectors*; 9.1.6); gen pl in zero ending (грамм, помидо́р instead of гра́ммов, *of grammes*, помидо́ров, *of tomatoes*; 9.1.7). Diminutive forms of first names may be used in a truncated vocative form, e.g. Тань, *Tania* (7.3.1). The suffix -ей may be preferred in short comparatives (e.g. быстре́й instead of быстре́е, *quicker*) and the prefix по- is commonly attached to such comparatives (e.g. полу́чше, *a bit better*, 9.3.3). The infinitive forms вида́ть, слыха́ть may be preferred to ви́деть, *to see*, слы́шать, *to hear* (3.4). There is a tendency to simplification, which entails weakening of certain grammatical rules, e.g. a speaker may fail to decline all components of a numeral in an oblique case (11.4.3, note 2) or both parts of a compound word (e.g. полго́дом ра́ньше, *half a year earlier*, instead of полуго́дом). Forms may be used which strictly speaking are grammatically incorrect, e.g. Ты умне́е на́шего instead of Ты умне́е нас, *You're brighter than us*, and even к пе́рвому ма́рту instead of к пе́рвому ма́рта, *by 1 March*. Nouns may be used in a case that is incorrect after the preposition that governs them. Thus the dative case is commonly used after по in expressions of time such as по истече́нию, *on expiry*, in which the preposition means *upon, after*, and should strictly speaking govern the prepositional case (по истече́нии; R3).

syntax

- The nature of the colloquial register makes for sentences consisting of only one word (e.g. да, *yes*; нет, *no*; вон, *get away*; марш, *forward*; ка́к же, *of course* (iron); пожа́луйста, *please*), incomplete sentences, and simple sentences. In complex sentences coordinating conjunctions are much more frequent than subordinating conjunctions. Syntax may be disjointed, with repetitions (e.g. да, да, да, *yes, yes, yes*), weak links, breaks in sentences and interpolations of various sorts (e.g. providing comment, clarification or correction). Questions and exclamations abound. Rules dictating the government of words may be relaxed, e.g. a preposition might govern an infinitive (насчёт поговори́ть, *about having a chat*) or might be combined with a word other than a noun, pronoun or adjective (Отло́жим разгово́р на по́сле обе́да, *Let's put off our conversation until after dinner*). Speakers frequently resort to ellipsis e.g. Я к вам, *I'm [coming] to [see] you*; 11.13) and other distinctive constructions, which may involve various types of complex predicate, e.g. Стоя́ла пе́ла, *[She] was standing singing*; Он возьми́ да и закричи́, *He went and shouted*; она́ то́лько и де́лает, что, *she does nothing but*; Знай себе́ идёт, *He's walking along quite unconcerned* (11.13). Predicates in such constructions may contain particles, e.g. Написа́ть-то напишу́, но она́ не отве́тит, *Well, I'll write, but she won't reply* (5.4) or they may consist of interjections, e.g. стук, *banged* (5.5).

It is worth adding, finally, that the low style is notable for what it lacks as well as for what it contains. It eschews the complex subordinate clauses, gerunds, active participles and passive constructions involving reflexive verbs that are characteristic of the high style as well as much sophisticated or specialised vocabulary and many set phrases and formulae.

1.3.2 Demotic speech (D)

Beneath the normal colloquial register, which may be used by all social groups in informal situations, there are other linguistic strata whose elements, unlike much in R1, may still sound more or less unacceptable and discordant in R2. These strata include what will here be termed 'demotic' (просторе́чие, which is sometimes also translated as 'popular speech'), as well as youth slang (молодёжный сленг; see 5.1.4), thieves' cant (блатно́й язы́к), prison slang (тюре́мный жарго́н) and vulgar language (5.6).

Demotic is the spontaneous, informal speech of the uneducated (or, if it is used by the educated, then it is used for special effect). It lies outside the bounds of what is considered the literary standard (though, as has been said, that standard is constantly shifting and continually admits elements which were recently considered unacceptable). Unlike the various registers embraced by the standard language, demotic speech observes no norms. It is distinguished to some extent, as illustrated by the following examples of features of mainly Muscovite просторе́чие, by stress and morphological and syntactic peculiarities, but above all by a layer of racy vocabulary.

stress

- Some nouns are stressed on a different syllable from that which bears the stress in the standard language, e.g. доку́мент (докуме́нт, *document*); кило́метр (киломе́тр, *kilometre*); мага́зин (магази́н, *shop*); мо́лодежь (молодёжь, *youth*); по́ртфель (портфе́ль (m), *briefcase*); шо́фер (шофёр, *driver*).

- Stress variation also affects some verb forms, e.g. зво́нишь, etc. (standard звони́шь, *you ring*); гна́ла (гнала́, *chased*); отда́ла (отдала́, *gave back*), and the short forms of past passive participles, e.g. приве́дено (приведено́, *brought*); приве́зено (привезено́, *brought (by transport)*); прине́сено (принесено́, *brought (by hand)*).

vocabulary

- Use of words considered unacceptable in standard usage, e.g. nouns such as балбе́с, *coarse, idle person*; башка́, *head, nut*; забулды́га, *debauched person*; образи́на, *ugly mug*; пу́зо, *belly, gut*; хапу́га, *thief, scrounger*; adjectives such as му́торный, *disagreeable and dreary*; нахра́пистый, *high-handed*; verbs such as барахли́ть, *to stutter* (of engine, machine, heart); бреха́ть (брешу́, бре́шешь), *to bark, talk nonsense, tell lies*; дре́йфить/сдре́йфить, *to be a coward*; лимо́нить/слимо́нить, *to nick*; нали́зываться/нализа́ться, *to get pissed*; обалдева́ть/обалде́ть, *to become stupefied*; околпа́чивать/околпа́чить, *to fool, dupe*; оття́гиваться/оттяну́ться, *to have a good time, to have fun*; рехну́ться (pf), *to go off one's head*; спере́ть (pf; сопру́, сопрёшь), *to nick*; укоко́шить (pf), *to kill, knock off*; улепётывать/улепетну́ть, *to rush off*; ха́пать/ха́пнуть, *to pinch, scrounge*; and adverbs such as да́веча, *recently*; отродя́сь, *never in one's life*.

word-formation

- Use of the verbal suffix -ану́ть (see also 8.11), e.g. звездану́ть (pf), *to bash*; садану́ть (pf), *to hit hard, bash*.

morphology

- The nominative plural form in -á for masculine nouns is more widespread than in the standard language (e.g. шоферá, *drivers*) (9.1.6).

- Types of declension may be confused, e.g. use of -ов as a genitive plural flexion for nouns other than masculine nouns, as in местóв (see also 1.5.3).

- The form скóлько врéмя?, *how much time/what is the time?* in which the noun is not declined (instead of standard скóлько врéмени?).

- Verbal conjugations may also be confused (e.g. махáю instead of машý, from махáть, *I wave*), or other non-standard forms may be found (e.g. жгётся instead of жжётся, *it burns*).

- Use of certain non-standard imperative forms, e.g. едь instead of ешь, *eat*, and éхай instead of поезжáй, *go (by transport)*.

- Non-reflexive forms may be substituted for reflexive forms, especially in gerunds and active participles, e.g. сидéл задýмавши instead of сидéл задýмавшись, *sat thinking*, and загорéвший дом instead of загорéвшийся дом, *the house which has caught fire*.

- Use of past passive participial forms in -тый where in the standard language the ending -нный would be used, e.g. порвáтый (пóрванный, *torn*).

syntax

- Loose and broad use of prepositions, e.g. чéрез in the sense of *because of* (из-за), e.g. Чéрез негó опоздáл(а), *I was late because of him*. Non-standard use of prepositions after verbs, e.g. (standard forms in brackets) беспокóиться про когó-н (о ком-н), *to worry about sb*, and рáдоваться о чём-н (рáдоваться чемý-н), *to be glad at sth*.

1.3.3   The neutral register (R2)

This is the norm of an educated speaker, the standard form of the language that is used for polite but not especially formal communication. It might be used in broadcasting, among colleagues at work, by educated people who do not know each other very well, by teachers to their pupils. It is the register that the foreign student as a rule first learns and which is most suitable for his or her first official or social contacts with native speakers. It is 'correct' without being fussy or pedantic. This register is perhaps best defined in negative terms, as lacking the distinctive colloquial features of R1 and the bookish features of R3, though it may to some extent contain elements of both without altogether taking on a colloquial or bookish colouring. Both forms of address, ты and вы, are possible in R2, depending on the degree of intimacy between the people speaking. First names and patronymics are likely to be used between acquaintances. On the other hand, secondary diminutive forms of first names (e.g. Ната́шенька, Та́нечка; see 7.3.1) might seem overfamiliar.

1.3.4 The higher register (R3)

This register is most commonly the vehicle for ideas which have been thought out in advance and are expressed in uninterrupted monologue. The exposition of such ideas may follow established patterns. Language in the higher register is therefore relatively well organised and formal and may have recourse to set phrases and formulaic expressions. It eschews elements that can be identified as colloquial (1.3.1), including regional variation (1.5). Vocabulary may be sophisticated, specialised or terminological. Syntax may be complex. Constructions containing reflexive verbs used in a passive sense (11.8), gerunds (11.11.1) and active participles (11.11.2) are used freely. Nouns in the same case, especially the genitive, may be 'threaded' together (so-called нани́зывание падеже́й), e.g. представи́тель Министе́рства вну́тренних дел Герма́нии, (lit) *a representative of the Ministry of the Interior of Germany*. Nouns may be preceded by adjectival phrases containing nouns, e.g. пе́рвое в ми́ре коммунисти́ческое госуда́рство, *the first communist state in the world*.

Within this register the following functional styles may be identified.

(a) Academic/scientific style (нау́чный стиль)

The purpose of this functional style is to report information. The style may be appropriate in any medium from a monograph, learned article or textbook to a lecture or seminar. It may also be used in many fields, indeed in any academic discipline from the natural sciences (e.g. physics, chemistry and biology), through the social sciences (e.g. politics, sociology and economics) to the humanities (e.g. philosophy, philology and the study of literature). (It should be noted that the Russian word нау́ка, like the German word *Wissenschaft*, has a broader range than the English *science*, embracing all academic work, not merely the natural and social sciences.) The language of the academic style is characterised by logical and orderly development (hence the copious use of transition words (5.2)). It is carefully formulated with explanation of the relationships between things (hence the use of numerous subordinating conjunctions (11.12.2)). Choice of words is precise. Much vocabulary is terminological and words are used in their literal meanings. Verbs which would occur in R1/R2 might be replaced by phrases consisting of verb + verbal noun (e.g. происхо́дит рост instead of растёт, *grows*; име́ет ме́сто повыше́ние температу́ры instead of повыша́ется температу́ра, *the temperature rises*). Various means are used to express a copula for which English would use some form of the verb *to be*, e.g. состои́т из, заключа́ется в, представля́ет собо́й, all meaning *is* (4.2). This style is shorn of artistry and lacks the expressive devices of the colloquial language described in 1.3.1.

(b) *Official/business style (официа́льно-делово́й стиль)*

Like the academic style, this functional style has as its purpose communication in the sense of reporting. It may be found in treaties, legislation, regulations, codes of practice, forms, certificates, official correspondence and even public notices. Its field spans diplomacy, law, administration and commerce and even some of the standard methods of address in letters (7.17). Whereas in other styles clichés may be a defect, here they are more or less *de rigueur*. The language of this style is therefore characterised by numerous formulae, e.g.: в отве́т на Ваш запро́с, *in reply to your enquiry* (7.17); свиде́тельствовать кому́-либо уваже́ние, *to pay one's respects to sb*; в рабо́чем поря́дке, *in due course*; в обы́чном режи́ме, *when things are normal* (a Putinism, it seems). Material is arranged according to some generally accepted form. Terminology abounds. So also do the following phenomena: set phrases (e.g. вступи́ть в си́лу, *to come into effect*; исполня́ть обя́занности, *to fulfil obligations*; подлежи́т подтвержде́нию, *is subject to confirmation*); abbreviations (6.9); verbal nouns (see e.g. 8.7.1); prepositional phrases based on a noun (e.g. в де́ле, *in the matter of*; в соотве́тствии с, *in conformity with*; с це́лью, *with the object of*); complex conjunctions (ввиду́ того́, что, *in view of the fact that*; в связи́ с тем, что, *in connection with the fact that*; всле́дствие того́, что, *owing to the fact that*; see 11.12.3); and formulaic links (на слу́чай, е́сли, *in the event that*; с тем усло́вием, что, *on condition that*). Word order tends to be straightforward. The official/business style is impersonal and eschews the expressive resources of the colloquial register. It is also relatively stable and resistant to change.

(c) *The styles of journalism and political debate (публицисти́ческий стиль)*

This functional style, or set of styles, differs from the academic/scientific and the official/business styles in that it may be designed to persuade as well as to record or inform. Its medium may be serious journalistic reporting in written form (in which case its purpose may be primarily informative) or journalistic comment, a polemical article, a political speech, propaganda, a pamphlet, or even a slogan (in which case its primary purpose is to persuade, to influence opinion). The style is characterised by socio-political vocabulary. It easily absorbs neologisms (5.1). It resorts to certain stereotypes and clichés (дать зелёную у́лицу, *to give the green light*) and periphrasis (e.g. вы́разить наде́жду, *to express the hope*; ока́зывать по́мощь, *to render assistance*; пита́ть не́нависть, *to harbour hatred*; принима́ть реше́ние, *to take a decision*; производи́ть осмо́тр, *to carry out an inspection*). Introductory constructions indicate the source of information (e.g. как сообща́ет наш корреспонде́нт, *as our correspondent reports*; по да́нным, *according to information*). Unlike the academic and official styles, the styles of journalism and political debate make use of such graphic, emotive and expressive resources of the language as rhetorical devices, repetition, parallelism and exclamation. They are mainly bookish but elements of colloquial language are used to lend them vitality.

1.3.5 Styles of belles-lettres (стили худо́жественной литерату́ры)

Account must also be taken of the language used by the creative artist, although this language stands apart from the scale of register that stretches from the colloquial informality of R1 to the mainly bookish formality of R3. Unlike the varieties of language dealt with in 1.3.1 to 1.3.4 inclusive, the language of the work of imaginative literature has an aesthetic function as well as a communicative one. It may be contrasted in particular with the academic style of R3, which expounds ideas in conceptual terms and literally, for the language of the work of art expresses ideas with the help of images and uses words in non-literal ways. The medium of the language of belles-lettres may be a poem, a play, a short story, a novel, or even a song. As for register, the language of belles-lettres may, according to the author's purpose and subject-matter, embrace all the registers and styles examined in 1.3.1 to 1.3.4, even the demotic and – nowadays – the vulgar. Unlike the impersonal, objective styles of R3 (academic/scientific and official/ business), it may be personal and subjective. It makes use of the resources that the language possesses for expressing emotion and attitude (e.g. modal particles, interjections, diminutive and pejorative suffixes, the syntax of R1). It may deploy dialect words, jargon, professional or common parlance or archaisms to lend a particular colouring. Tone may be varied, from the elevated to the ironic or parodic.

1.3.6 Language of the internet (язы́к интерне́та)

Finally, mention must be made of the language used on the internet in all its forms, e.g. the world-wide web (Мирова́я паути́на), email (электро́нная по́чта) and chatrooms (ча́ты; sg чат). Netspeak, as the language of the internet may be called in English, contains features of both written and spoken language as they were defined in 1.2 above, following Crystal. Since the world-wide web may be used for informative purposes and as a reference source it contains much material couched in the formal written registers. (Some Russian websites (са́йты; sg сайт) that are of particular use for students of Russian are indicated in the section on Sources.) The language of the chatroom, on the other hand, is highly informal. It does resemble a written medium, inasmuch as it may be edited before dissemination and a record of it remains after it has been disseminated, but at the same time it comes close to (without quite attaining) the immediacy of speech. The language of email comes midway between these extremes, since email is a medium that resembles written correspondence but is generally less formal and is (or is perceived as) more transient. There are grounds, then, for seeing Netspeak as a third medium which, in its totality, embodies features of both writing and speech and which is capable of spawning further new varieties of language.

While use of personal computers is now widespread in Russia among young people, especially in the cities, it may be that Russian users of the internet are still less broadly representative of the Russian population as a whole than are British internet users of the British population as a whole. Nevertheless the introduction of information technology into Russia has had a significant impact on the Russian language, at least in the fields of lexis and phraseology. A large new vocabulary has developed, most of it of English origin. This vocabulary, on such matters as hardware and software, word-processing, and use of the world-wide web and email, is dealt with at 5.1.5, under the general heading of neologisms. At the same time Russian, like English, has developed a distinctive informal register for use in forms of two-way electronic communication. In email this register is characterised by lightly edited or unedited composition, simple syntax and casual forms of greeting and farewell (see 2.13 below). In chatrooms it is characterised by the tendency to spell words as they are pronounced, recourse to slang, adoption of screen names (ники; sg ник) by participants, unconventional punctuation, and use of symbols (smileys (смайлики; sg смайлик) or emoticons) to indicate moods and reactions (see 2.2 below).

There is of course debate as to the extent to which the new linguistic usage promoted by the internet should be welcomed or resisted. To linguistic purists of the sort whose views are described in 1.6 below, the internet may be the bearer of bad linguistic habits. On the other hand, it has been argued, by Nikolai Pereiáslov in a recent article (see Sources), that the internet is capable of transmitting good works of literature alongside the vulgar or pornographic material that is associated with it in the minds of many people. Russians would be unwise, according to this view, to spurn the 'literary continent' that is developing on the internet, lest 'internet literature' (интернéт-литератýра) drift away to an abroad which they will have to discover at a later date, just as in Soviet times they had to discover other, earlier forms of Russian émigré literature.

1.4   Illustration of register in vocabulary

The following table briefly illustrates the levels of language that have been discussed, as they are manifested in Russian lexis, by showing some of the colloquial and high equivalents (R1 and R3 respectively) of the basic neutral words (R2) that are given in the middle column. The table is arranged in accordance with the alphabetical order of the neutral Russian words.

R1	R2		R3
гляде́лки (pl)	глаза́	*eyes*	о́чи (sg о́ко; poet)
башка́	голова́	*head*	глава́
де́вка	де́вушка	*girl*	деви́ца
ба́бки (pl), капу́ста	де́ньги (pl)	*money*	сре́дства (pl)
куме́кать (impf)	ду́мать (impf)	*to think*	мы́слить (impf)
харчи́ (pl)	еда́	*food*	пи́ща
ку́шать (impf), жрать (impf; D)	есть (impf)	*to eat*	вкуша́ть (impf)
ба́ба	жена́	*wife*	супру́га
ба́ба	же́нщина	*woman*	да́ма
мо́рда, ро́жа (D)	лицо́	*face*	лик
ма́ма, мама́ша (D)	мать (f)	*mother*	роди́тельница
колёса (pl; sg колесо́), та́чка (slang)	маши́на	*car*	автомоби́ль (m)
у́йма	мно́го	*much/a lot*	мно́жество
па́рень (m)	молодо́й челове́к	*young man*	ю́ноша
мужи́к	муж	*husband*	супру́г
нагоня́й	наказа́ние	*punishment*	ка́ра
напа́сть (f)	несча́стье	*misfortune*	бе́дствие
одёжа	оде́жда	*clothes*	пла́тье
па́па, папа́ша, ба́тя (D)	оте́ц	*father*	роди́тель (m; *parent* in R2)
подмо́га	по́мощь (f)	*help*	соде́йствие
ла́па (*paw* in R2)	рука́	*hand*	длань (f)
каю́к	смерть (f)	*death*	кончи́на
дры́хнуть (impf)	спать	*to sleep*	почива́ть (impf)
старика́н	стари́к	*old man*	ста́рец
отда́ть концы́*	умира́ть/ умере́ть	*to die*	сконча́ться (pf)

* The verbs **околева́ть/околе́ть** and **подыха́ть/подо́хнуть**, which also mean *to die* and in R2 are used only of animals, may in R1 be used of humans, in which case they have a pejorative tone.

1.5   Regional variation in Russian

Account must be taken, when considering variety in a language, of the existence of geographic as well as social dialects. The higher and neutral registers of a language (R3 and R2) are subject to little, if any, regional variation, but the colloquial form (R1) does vary from one region to another, both when used by relatively uneducated speakers and even when used by educated speakers in informal situations. Regional features often reflect archaic usage that has died out in the standard language and infringe that language's grammatical norms, which the foreign learner is expected to observe.

Considering the enormous size of the territory of the Russian Federation (which stretches over 8,000 kilometres from the border with Belarus in the west to the Bering Strait in the east and some 3,000 kilometres from the Kola Peninsula in the north to the Caucasus in the south and covers in all an area of some 10.5 million square kilometres) the Russian language is surprisingly uniform. The Russian spoken on the Pacific coast in Vladivostók, for example, is easily comprehensible to the Muscovite. This relative uniformity (compared to the greater phonological differences in a much smaller country such as Switzerland) results from the frequent migrations of populations and the lack of major geographical barriers within the country. It has been reinforced in post-revolutionary Russia by such processes as urbanisation and the spread of literacy. Nevertheless, there is regional variation in Russian, in pronunciation, vocabulary, morphology and syntax.

The foreign student is not advised to use regional linguistic features, which do not belong in the standard language or higher registers and which may in any case seem out-of-place unless all the distinctive features of a particular dialect are deployed consistently and comprehensively. The following sections are therefore intended only to give a superficial impression of the extent of regional variation in Russian and to draw attention to a few of the salient regional features. A number of the linguistic terms used in this section are explained in the Glossary.

1.5.1   Standard pronunciation

The regional features listed in 1.5.3 below are deviations from the standard, to which reference is made, unless otherwise indicated, elsewhere in this book. The lexical, morphological and syntactic features of standard Russian are examined in the following chapters, but since standard pronunciation is not dealt with elsewhere it is as well to list here a few of the phonological features of Muscovite speech on which, owing to the status of Moscow as the capital city, standard pronunciation is based.

- **а́канье**: *a* and *o* are both pronounced as *a* when they occur in the syllable before the stress or in the initial syllable of a word, e.g. *travá* (травá), *savá* (совá), *ablaká* (облакá). In other unstressed positions both vowels may be reduced to ə (like the reduced vowel at the beginning of English *about*), e.g. *məlakó* (молокó).

- **и́канье**: after soft consonants *é* and *á* are both pronounced as *'i* when they occur in the syllable before the stress, e.g. *n'islá* (несла́), *vz'ilá* (взяла́), *č'isý* (часы́). This phenomenon is characteristic of many C dialects as well as the standard language.

- In the standard language, as in the N regional dialect and many C dialects (see 1.5.2), the voiced velar *g* is an **occlusive** sound (like Eng *g*). Voiceless *g* becomes *k*, e.g. *nok* (ног), *snék* (снег).

- There are four labiodental fricatives, i.e. hard voiced *v* and soft voiced *v'* and hard unvoiced *f* and soft unvoiced *f'*. At the end of a word or before a voiceless consonant *v* and *v'* are devoiced, e.g. *drof* (дров), *láfka* (ла́вка), *gotóf'fe* (гото́вьте).

- There are two distinct affricates, the hard hissing affricate *c*, as in *cygán* (цыга́н), and the soft hushing affricate *č'* as in *č'aj* (чай). (This distinction is also observed in most S and C dialects.)

1.5.2   Classification of Russian dialects

Dialects are defined not by a single phenomenon but by a set of phenomena, on the basis of a so-called bundle of isoglosses. However, the isoglosses defining the territorial limits of the use of one phenomenon do not necessarily coincide neatly with isoglosses relating to another phenomenon. Identification and classification of Russian dialects is therefore a complex matter that will not be addressed here, except insofar as it is possible to make a broad distinction between the following regional forms of Russian that may be heard in European Russia.

(a)   The N regional dialects (**се́верное наре́чие**), i.e. the Russian spoken north of a line running a little to the north of Nóvgorod, Tver' and Nízhnii Nóvgorod (but excluding St Petersburg). This regional dialect embraces such groups of local dialects as the Ládoga-Tíkhvin group, the Vólogda group and the Kostromá group. The N regional dialect is characterised especially by о́канье and use of occlusive *g*.

(b)   The S regional dialect (**ю́жное наре́чие**), i.e. the Russian spoken from the borders of Belarus and Ukraine in the west and south and up to a line passing through Kolómna, to the north of Kalúga and Riazán'. This regional dialect embraces a SW group of dialects around Smolénsk (influenced by Belorussian features), an Upper Dnepr group, an Upper Desná group around Briansk, the Kursk and Orió́l group, and a group including the Russian of Riazán', Tambóv and Vorónezh. The S regional dialect is characterised especially by а́канье and use of fricative γ.

(c)   The C dialects (**среднеру́сские го́воры**), i.e. the Russian spoken in the lateral strip of territory running from the border with Belarus in the west. This group of dialects embraces the Nóvgorod group and the Pskov group in the west, the group around Moscow, and the group around Vladímir to the east. These transitional dialects exhibit varying mixtures of N and S regional features such as оканье and аканье, occlusive *g* and fricative γ.

1.5.3   Regional features

This section lists some of the principal regional deviations from the standard form of the language which the foreign student will normally learn and indicates in which broad regions these variations from the norm might be encountered. It should be borne in mind that although these deviations may be found in the language of belles-lettres they will generally be altogether absent from the styles classified in 1.3.4 as R3a, R3b and R3c and may occur only infrequently in R2. The degree to which they will occur in R1 will depend on such factors as the speaker's background, education, age and experience, the circumstances in which he or she is speaking and the identity of the person being addressed. In general one may expect such features to occur more markedly in the speech of the poorly educated rural or provincial dweller. It is also important to emphasise that regional features are not so strong as to make any dialect incomprehensible to the speakers of another dialect or to speakers of the standard language.

Note: letters in brackets in this section (e.g. N, S, C, NE, SW) indicate the region(s) in which the features in question may be encountered. However, they do not imply that the feature is exclusive to that area or universal in it, even among the sort of speakers whose speech may exhibit dialect features.

pronunciation (cf. 1.5.1)

- яканье, e.g. *t'ap'ér'* (теперь), *n'as'í* (неси), *s'aló* (село), *n'asú* (несу) (i.e. strong яканье; SE); or before hard consonants only, e.g. *s'aló* (село), *n'asú* (несу) (i.e. moderate яканье; SW).

- оканье, e.g. *sová* (совá) (N regional and some C dialects).

- Fricative γ, e.g. *naγá* (ногá). Correspondingly, devoiced γ becomes *x*, e.g. *nox* (ног), *sn'ex* (снег) (S regional dialect). In some SW regions bordering on Belarus and Ukraine *g* becomes *h*.

- Labiodental *v* and *v'*, when they occur at the end of a word or syllable, are pronounced as bilabial *w*, e.g. *drow* (дров), *láwka* (лáвка) (most S and many W and NE dialects).

- Initial *v* may become *u*, e.g. *um'éste* (вмéсте), *u górod* (в гóрод), and some homophones may result, e.g. внёс, унёс (both pronounced *un'ós*) (some S dialects).

- цоканье, e.g. *caj* (чай), *cýsto* (чи́сто), *cúdo* (чу́до), i.e. hard цоканье (NW and also many C and SE dialects); or *c'aj*, *c'isto*, *c'udo*, i.e. soft цоканье (NE dialects).

- Assimilation producing the long consonant *m* from the combination *bm*, e.g. *ommán* (обмáн) (some N dialects).

- Simplification of the group *st* to *s* in final position, e.g. *mos* (мост) (some N and a few S dialects).

- Occurrence in some words of the combination *mn* instead of standard *vn*, especially *damnó* (давнó) and *ramnó* (равнó) (some N and S dialects).

stress
- Tendency to more innovatory stress in the S dialects, e.g. movement of stress from prefix to stem in the past tense of certain verbs (óтдал → отдáл, *gave back*); shift of stress from preposition to noun in certain phrases (нá берег → на бéрег, *on to the bank*). The NE dialects are more conservative in stress. In the field of stress S practice has affected the evolution of the standard language more than N practice.

vocabulary
- A dialect may have a word different from the standard word to denote a certain phenomenon or action, e.g. (standard forms in brackets):

  бирюк (волк, *wolf*); some S dialects
  бурáк (свёкла, *beetroot*); some S dialects
  вéдро (хорóшая погóда, *fine weather*)
  дóбре (хорошó, *well*); some S dialects
  дюже (óчень, *very much, awfully*); also R1
  кóчет (петýх, *cock(erel)*); some S dialects
  мурáшка (муравéй, *ant*); some SW dialects
  назём/позём (навóз, *manure*); some N dialects
  орáть (пахáть, *to plough*); some N and WC dialects

  Regional words may be used in particular to denote age-old features of rural life such as paths, fences, outhouses, animal sheds, vegetables, parts of a plough or certain implements and utensils.

- A word which in the standard language or in some regions has one meaning may in certain other regions have another meaning or an additional meaning, e.g. жúто (*corn*) may mean *rye* in SW dialects and *barley* in NW dialects; пахáть (*to plough*) may in N dialects also mean *to sweep*; погóда (*weather* in the standard language) may mean *bad weather* in some N dialects and *good weather* in some S dialects.

- Special words may be used in particular dialects to denote phenomena, especially flora, fauna, topography, climate, clothing or architecture, which are peculiar to the region in question, e.g. лáхта, a bay or inlet in NW Russia; рёлка, raised ground in swampy district, islet in river in Siberia; обéдник, a type of sea wind; понёва, a homespun skirt in S Russia; хáта, a peasant hut in S Russia.

morphology
- Treatment of many nouns in -o that in the standard language are neuter, especially nouns with stress on the stem (e.g. дéло, сéно, стáдо), as feminine, e.g. плохáя дéла (плохóе дéло, *a bad business*) (some S and C dialects). This phenomenon is a logical consequence of áканье, since the unstressed final *o* is heard as *a*.

- Declension of the nouns мать, *mother*, and дочь, *daughter*, that differs from the standard declension, e.g. nom sg мáти, acc sg мáтерь (some

N dialects). In some W dialects the nouns ма́тка and до́чка replace
мать and дочь respectively.

- Use of the flexion -e for the genitive singular of nouns in -a after
  prepositions, e.g. без родне́ (без родни́, *without relations*); от жене́ (от
  жены́, *from [one's] wife*); у сестре́ (у сестры́, *at [one's] sister's*).

- Occurrence of fewer nouns than in the standard language with
  nominative plural form in -а́, e.g. гла́зы (глаза́, *eyes*); до́мы (дома́,
  houses); лу́ги (луга́, *meadows*) (some N, W and SW dialects); or,
  conversely, of more nouns with this nominative plural form than in the
  standard language, e.g. деревня́ (дере́вни, *villages*); лошадя́ (ло́шади,
  horses).

- Extension of the genitive plural ending -ов to neuter and even
  feminine nouns, e.g. дело́в (дел), место́в (мест), ба́бов (баб), я́годов
  (я́год) (many S dialects).

- Various deviations from standard flexions in dative, instrumental and
  prepositional plural forms, such as: coincidence of dative and
  instrumental plural forms, e.g. с рука́м (с рука́ми, *with hands*), с нам
  (с на́ми, *with us*) (many N dialects); use of dative and prepositional
  forms of the type гостём, гостёх; лошадём, лошадёх (some S
  dialects); use of instrumental plural endings such as -а́мы,–а́ма, e.g.
  рука́мы, рука́ма (рука́ми, *hands*).

- Use of accusative/genitive pronominal forms мене́, тебе́, себе́
  (S dialects).

- Use of soft *t'* in third-person-singular forms, e.g. *idót'* (идёт) (some S
  and C dialects).

- Various paradigms of мочь, e.g. могу́, мо́гешь, etc.; могу́, могёшь,
  etc.; мо́жу, мо́жешь, etc. (some S dialects).

- Use of first-person-singular forms of second-conjugation verbs
  without epenthetic л or consonant change, e.g. любю́ (люблю́), ходю́
  (хожу́) (some S and SW dialects).

syntax

- Use of certain compound prepositions of the type по-над, по-под,
  which are not found in the standard language (used with instrumental
  to indicate the site of action), e.g. по-под горо́й, *under the hillside*;
  по-над ре́чкой, *over the river* (some N and S dialects).

- Use of certain prepositions with a case different from the case they
  govern in the standard language, e.g. во́зле, ми́мо, по́дле + acc (cf.
  genitive in the standard language), e.g. во́зле реку́ (во́зле реки́, *near the
  river*) (some N dialects).

- Use of c + gen in sense of *out of* (cf. из in the standard language), e.g.
  вы́йти с ко́мнаты, *to go out of the room*; прие́хать с Москвы́, *to come
  from Moscow*.

- Use of nominative rather than distinctive accusative (or accusative/
  genitive) form of a noun which is the direct object of a transitive verb,

e.g. принести́ вода́ (принести́ во́ду, *to bring water*); кача́ть ребёнок (кача́ть ребёнка, *to rock a baby*) (some N dialects).

- Use of за + acc after short comparative adjectives (cf. genitive in the standard language), e.g. Он ста́рше за Са́шу (Он ста́рше Са́ши, *He's older than Sasha*) (some S dialects).

- Use of a pluperfect tense consisting of the past tense of быть + the past tense of the verb denoting the action in question, e.g. А в сентябре́ снег был вы́сыпал, а октя́брь был тёплый, *Snow had fallen in September, but October was warm* (some N dialects).

- Predicative use of perfective gerunds, e.g. Де́рево упа́вши, *A tree is down*; Ка́ша пригоре́вши, *The porridge is burnt* (some NW dialects; note, however, that the form вы́пивши, *drunk*, is used in this way in the standard language).

- Various impersonal constructions involving the use of a short form of a past passive participle, e.g. Свои́ми рука́ми напи́лено, *I sawed it up with my own hands* (lit *with my own hands it has been sawn*); Мно́го бы́ло рабо́тано, *A lot of work has been done*; Си́жено бы́ло у меня́, *I've been sitting around / People have been sitting around at my place*; or use of a past passive participle that does not agree with the noun to which it relates, e.g. Оди́н солда́т похоро́нено здесь, *One soldier is buried here*; Молоко́ проли́т, *Some milk has been spilt*.

- Less differentiation than in the standard language of subordinating conjunctions (which in any case occur less in R1 than in R2 and especially R3; see 11.12.2); correspondingly broader use of certain conjunctions, especially: что in causal sense, e.g. Он хохо́чет над на́ми, что глу́пы дак, *He's laughing at us for being so stupid*; and как in (a) conditional sense (= е́сли, *if*), e.g. Как ти́хо – пое́ду, а ве́тер – дак ни за что, *If it's calm I'll go, but if it's windy I certainly shan't*; (b) causal sense (= потому́ что, *because*), e.g. Ведь я́-то не напишу́, как я негра́мотна, *I shan't write myself, because I can't write*; (c) temporal sense (= когда́, *when*), e.g. Как жа́рко бы́ло, дак ко́шки в траву́ ложи́лись, *When it was hot the cats would lie down in the grass*.

- Use of the emphatic post-positive particle –то (see 5.4 on use of this particle in the standard language). In some dialects (esp N and E) the article changes according to the gender and number of the noun, i.e. сто́л-от, кры́ша-та, окно́-то, столы́-те. In some C dialects the forms –ту and –ти or –ты may be used for the sake of harmony with the ending of the noun to which the particle is attached e.g. на берегу́-ту, без со́ли-ти.

1.6   Current debate about standard Russian

We return at this point to the notion of a linguistic standard that was broached in section 1.2 above. By linguistic standard we mean a canonical form of a language which grammarians and lexicographers have sought to codify and which certain works of literature are felt to exemplify. In some countries it is the function of some institution (e.g. the Académie française in France) to preserve this standard. (In Russia this function is fulfilled by the V. V. Vinográdov Russian Language Institute of the Russian Academy of Sciences, the Linguistics Institute of the Russian Academy of Sciences, the A. S. Púshkin Russian Language Institute, and other institutions.) It will be clear from what was said in 1.2 that the standard is not only the uniform language that educated speakers are believed actually to use but also an exemplary language that it is felt speakers of the language in general ought to aspire to use. In other words, the term 'standard' when applied to a language has both a descriptive and a prescriptive sense.

This book is primarily descriptive. We aim to acquaint students with contemporary Russian usage (its registers and functional styles, lexis, morphology, syntax and stress) as we find it rather than to exhort students to adhere exclusively to usage that a purist might consider as conforming to an educated standard. We therefore have no hesitation in pointing out non-standard features of contemporary Russian. This leaning towards descriptivism rather than prescriptivism, which is in the spirit of the series to which this book belongs, is intended to help the foreign student to become aware of the full stylistic and expressive range that is available to the Russian native speaker. Evidence of such awareness may raise the foreign learner's authority in the eyes of native speakers.

At the same time it is essential that a foreigner learning a language should know what native speakers consider to be standard (the norm at which they will probably feel foreigners should aim) and what they consider sub-standard (and may therefore expect the foreign learner to eschew). In particular, the foreign learner should understand that the freedom that he or she enjoys to use the resources of the language being acquired, especially its sub-standard forms, is on the whole more limited than that enjoyed by native speakers. This statement is true as a matter of fact, inasmuch as there will no doubt be lacunae in knowledge of vocabulary, idiom and grammar that inhibit the foreign user of a language. It also holds good with respect to etiquette. For the relatively limited nature of the foreigner's understanding of the cultural contexts in which the foreign language is used is likely to be felt at some level by native speakers to impose a duty on the foreigner to observe a certain humility and linguistic restraint. The disapproval of native speakers may easily be aroused by deployment of sub-standard forms by the foreign learner in an inappropriate context.

Debates about what the standard form of a language is or should be and about the desirability and feasibility of preserving, purifying or reforming the language are commonplace among peoples whose languages are widely used for political, commercial, administrative, literary and other purposes as well as for everyday social intercourse. With respect to the English language, for example, there has in recent years been much discussion about such questions as the following. Is standard spoken English the same thing as standard written English? (It is widely thought by socio-linguists not to be.) Is there such a thing as standard spoken English at all? Is it right to attempt to impose a standard spoken form of English, including received pronunciation, through the educational system? What are the social implications of such a policy? What political assumptions lie behind the positions taken up on such issues? Such debates are often fuelled by concern that what is thought to be a standard form of language is being polluted by the increasing toleration of non-standard pronunciation (e.g. the pronunciation that characterises what is known as estuary English), or by the influx into a language of lexis that is perceived by educated users as coarse or vulgar, or by the establishment of grammatical phenomena that are considered by such users to be incorrect.

A debate about the state of the Russian standard began in the late 1980s and has quickened in the 1990s and the early years of the twenty-first century. This debate needs to be seen against the background of the political, economic, social and cultural changes (преобразова́ния) that have affected the Russian language in the post-Soviet period. For example, Russians now have much closer contact with the West, as a result of increased opportunities for travel abroad, the influx of a larger number of foreigners into Russia than in the Soviet period, and easier access to Western culture, particularly material and popular culture, through the media and the internet. The one-party state of Soviet times has given way to a state with democratic institutions in which political parties of various complexions compete with one another. A free-market economy is developing. Mass media, including new and independent television stations and newspapers, have proliferated. Women have asserted themselves to a greater extent than before. The Soviet cultural legacy is receding.

The effect of these changes on the Russian language, especially in the areas of lexis and style, may be viewed in different ways. On the one hand they may be seen positively as having enriched Russian with numerous neologisms expressing new concepts or presenting old concepts in a new light (see 5.1 below). They have also helped to release the language from the ideological straitjacket of the Soviet era. It is perhaps indicative of a recognition of the positive effect, or at least the naturalness and legitimacy, of linguistic change that Russian linguists have in recent years become more interested than they were in Soviet times in usage in non-standard registers.

On the other hand the post-Soviet Russian language is widely perceived, particularly by educated speakers brought up in the Soviet period, as having undergone 'barbarisation' (варвариза́ция). It has come to be seen as a vehicle for mass culture. It has received numerous loanwords (заимствования) of international currency. (Resistance to what linguistic conservatives perceive as inundation with foreign words was exemplified as early as 1995 by Solzhenítsyn's *Ру́сский слова́рь языково́го расшире́ния* (*A Russian Dictionary of Linguistic Expansion*).)

Numerous slang words (жаргони́змы) have come into common use, many of them associated with youth culture (and often disseminated through rock music) and others originating in the underworld. The complaint is heard that whereas once people were encouraged to write or speak in a way that was comprehensible to the masses (что́бы бы́ло поня́тно ма́ссам) now the demand is that they write or speak in a way that is entertaining to the masses (что́бы бы́ло заня́тно ма́ссам). Thus the linguistic standard has been broadened and the average level of speech in public contexts lowered. The point is not that mistakes were not made before, of course, for languages are always used loosely by many speakers. Rather it is that lax usage in Russian is now widely disseminated in the mass media (СМИ, i.e. сре́дства ма́ссовой информа́ции), television serials (телесериа́лы), talk shows (ток-шо́у), films, advertising (рекла́ма), contemporary fiction and the public speech of officials and politicians (whose parliamentary debates are broadcast).

We should add to these complaints the fact that there often occurs what might be described as a sort of linguistic inflation. Certain words lose their original worth, because a meaning comes to be attached to them that is more trivial than their original meaning or simply because they are overused. The process applies even to vulgar language (see 5.6) when it becomes habitual. The lexical currency is thus devalued.

In response to the perceived debasement of the standard Russian language, or литерату́рный язы́к, commentators now routinely discuss the 'ecology' of the language (лингвоэколо́гия), expressing concern about the phenomena that have come to be tolerated in public discourse and lamenting the alleged impoverishment of the language. For example, the authors of two recent articles in the paper *Литерату́рная газе́та* (Ivanóva and Khlebtsóva; see Sources) complain about departures from the standard in the areas of pronunciation, enunciation, stress, morphology, syntax, lexis and style that they have observed in the media, even in broadcasts that are not live and in which editors might therefore have been expected to ensure a higher linguistic standard. They criticise correspondents and presenters for halting and stumbling delivery, for speaking inaudibly and with unclear diction, for speaking too quickly and omitting syllables from words, and for pronouncing words in a colloquial or demotic way. They disapprove of the appearance on central television and radio channels of presenters who have a regional accent. (This practice has long since been accepted in British broadcasting; in some respects Russian purists are reacting to the shock of what to them is novel.) They point to examples of non-standard stress, e.g. взя́та, вклю́чат, газопро́вод, новоро́жденный, обле́гчить instead of взята́, *taken*, включа́т, *they will include*, газопрово́д, *gas pipeline*, новорождённый, *new-born*, облегчи́ть, *to facilitate*, respectively.

In the field of grammar, one area of particular concern to such purists is the incorrect or innovative combination of nouns and prepositions, e.g. на прави́тельстве, в Украи́не, instead of в правительстве, *in the government*, на Украйне, *in (the) Ukraine* (see note 1 on на in 10.1.6(c)). Another is the widespread incorrect declension of numerals, e.g. о двухсóт, instead of о двухстáх, *about 200*; к двухтысячепéрвому году instead of к две тысячи пéрвому году, *by 2001*; and двух тысяча трéтий год, instead of две тысячи трéтий год, *2003*. Khlebtsóva points to the use of double subjects (a colloquial phenomenon sometimes known in English as 'heads'), e.g. сегóдняшняя тéма, онá касáется интерéсной проблéмы, *today's subject, it concerns an interesting problem*. More pedantically, perhaps, Ivanóva notes that certain nouns are inflected that should not be, such as the names of settlements (посёлки) and large Cossack villages (станúцы). Conversely, other proper nouns, such as the names of cities and villages, are not inflected when they are in apposition, although strictly speaking they should be, e.g. в гóроде Новосибúрск and в гóроде Бáсра, instead of в гóроде Новосибúрске, *in the city of Novosibirsk*, and в гóроде Бáсре, *in the city of Basra*, respectively.

As far as lexis is concerned, Ivanóva and Khlebtsóva lament the inundation of the language of the media with foreign, especially English, vocabulary (see 5.1.2 below), slang (5.1.4) and professional jargon, especially computing terminology (5.1.5). Furthermore they bemoan the allegedly limited vocabulary of people who work in the media and their consequent underemployment of synonyms and their failure to distinguish between registers. They also complain of the assignation of new meanings to words. For example, the verb ощущáть, *to feel*, Khlebtsóva believes, now does service for дýмать, полагáть, понимáть and считáть (*to think, suppose, understand* and *consider*, respectively), as in the question she has heard put to someone on television: Как вы ощущáете, бýдет ли Амéрика ратифицúровать договóры о разоружéнии? (*How do you feel/What do you think, will America ratify the disarmament treaties?*). (In this modish use ощущáть may be an anglicism.) Similarly the verb озвýчивать/озвýчить has gained currency as a synonym for выражáть/вýразить мнéние, произносúть/произнестú and сказáть (*to express an opinion, utter* and *say*, respectively). At the same time the volume of words that belong to a relatively high stratum of Russian lexis, Ivanóva believes, has diminished.

On the stylistic level Ivanóva criticises pleonasm (e.g. бывший экс-премьéр, *the former ex-premier*, and мировáя глобализáция, *world globalisation*) and presenters' continuing recourse to official clichés (e.g. в настоящий момéнт, *at the present moment*; предпринять мéры, *to undertake measures* (an embellishment of the official phrase принять мéры, *to take measures*). Both authors deplore the ubiquitous use of the vague fillers как бы and тúпа, *sort of/like*, e.g. тúпа сдáли в арéнду, *they sort of rented it out*; как бы реформúруем систéму образовáния, *we're like reforming the education system*; как бы рок-грýппа, *'like, a rock group'*. Indeed it has become possible to talk of какбыйзм as a phenomenon emblematic of the debasement of which defenders of the standard complain.

Those who deploy the language in advertising are held by Khlebtsóva to be particularly culpable, on the grounds that they promote the use of absurd epithets (сáмая огнеопáсная комéдия, *the most inflammable comedy*; супердышащие подгýзники, *superbreathable nappies*), inflated exclamations (Попрóбуй удовóльствие на вкус!, *Try the taste of pleasure!*), and youth slang (Оттянѝсь со вкýсом! or Оторвѝсь по пóлной! *Have a good time! Have fun!*). It is a further source of concern to such commentators that words that were formerly taboo, i.e. words denoting sexual organs or describing bodily functions, have become commonplace in the language of light broadcasting and journalism and popular entertainment. They also complain that an anglicised, or rather americanised, less respectful, more aggressive manner of addressing the listener, viewer or reader is often adopted. This alien manner may extend to use of a rising intonation at the end of an utterance in place of the falling intonation that is characteristic of statements (as opposed to questions) in Russian.

The purists recommend various means of combating the poor linguistic usage of which they complain. (These means might seem to Westerners more or less impracticable and unlikely to produce the results that the purists desire; in fact the purists, like all conservatives in times of rapid change, run the risk of appearing jaundiced and outmoded.) They argue, for example, that Olympiads and other competitions should be organised and given publicity, and that prizes should be awarded for success in them, in order that kudos might be attached to those who demonstrate command of the language. In addition Ivanóva proposes the following measures: that the linguistic competence of people applying for jobs in which they will use the language in a professional capacity be tested; that advertising be scrutinised with a view to eliminating orthographic and logical errors and the use of an aggressive tone; that the language of sections of the media be permanently monitored and that linguists be invited regularly to analyse and comment on the results of this monitoring; that the use of vulgar language, slang, demotic vocabulary or low borrowings from other languages be somehow prohibited in public discourse; and even that editors be fined for poor linguistic usage in the media that they manage.

It is important, finally, to emphasise that although the Russian language has recently changed in significant ways that are examined in this book under such headings as the language of the internet (1.3.6) and neologisms (5.1) it has not undergone fundamental grammatical or for that matter lexical change as a result of the political, economic, social and cultural transformation of Russia in the post-Soviet period. The most important change to which we draw attention here is of a socio-linguistic nature. It is that registers that were once seen as relatively formal, such as the registers of political discourse, broadcasting and journalism on current affairs, have been invaded by the habits and phenomena of colloquial and demotic speech. It is primarily to this redefinition of the boundaries within which varieties of language are used that those concerned with the 'ecology' of the language seem to be objecting, although of course they also fear that unless the norms they advocate are disseminated they will in time be altogether forgotten.

Notes

1. The population has decreased slightly, by almost two million, since 1989, when the last Soviet census was carried out. Nevertheless the Russian Federation is the seventh most populous country in the world, after China, India, the US, Indonesia, Brazil and Pakistan. The census also reveals that: almost three-quarters of the population live in towns (although the process of urbanisation has ceased); women are in the majority; the average age of the population is increasing; the literacy rate (which in any case was very high in Soviet times) has increased; and the birth rate is declining.
2. Many other languages besides Russian and the minority languages already mentioned above are spoken by the numerous ethnic minorities in Russia itself, especially various Finno-Ugric languages (e.g. Karelian, Komi, Mari, Mordvin, Udmurt), Caucasian languages (Abkhaz, Georgian, Ingush, Lezgi), Turkic languages (Iakut, Kirgiz, Turkmen), languages of the Mongolian group (Buriat, Kalmyk), and Tadzhik (a language of the Iranian branch of the Indo-European family).
3. It should be noted that some linguists use the term 'style' to designate 'a variety of language viewed from the point of view of *formality*' and the term 'register' to designate 'a variety of language determined by topic, subject matter or activity, such as the register of mathematics, the register of medicine, or the register of pigeon fancying' (Trudgill in Bex and Watts).

2 Passages illustrating register

All the passages presented below have been edited. Three dots (многото́чие; see 11.15 below) may indicate either a pause in the original text or our own omission of a passage from it.

2.1 R1: from a TV show

The following passage is an excerpt from a popular TV show in which people are confronted, in the presence of a studio audience, by members of their family, partners, friends or enemies about problems in their lives. The context of this excerpt is that a young man (Anton) takes a young woman whom he wants to marry to meet his parents in a provincial town outside Moscow. However, he has to leave her on her own with his parents because he is called back to Moscow by his employer. When he returns a week later he finds that his parents and his girl-friend (Marina) are not talking to one another. When Anton and Marina get back to Moscow Marina tells Anton she is breaking off their relationship. Anton tells the presenter that he has tried to find out from his mother (Ella Georgievna) what has gone wrong.

Анто́н: Я спра́шиваю у ма́мы. Ма́ма чего́-то непоня́тное мне отвеча́ет, ника́к то́лком не мо́жет сказа́ть.

Веду́щий: А дава́йте спро́сим действи́тельно у ма́мы. Ва́ша ма́ма – Э́лла Гео́ргиевна. (Вхо́дит Э́лла Гео́ргиевна) Здра́вствуйте,

5   приса́живайтесь, пожа́луйста. (Анто́ну) Спроси́ у ма́мы.

Анто́н: Ма́ма, вот объясни́ мне наконе́ц, что произошло́.

Э́лла Гео́ргиевна: Да, я слы́шала . . . всё. Зна́ешь что, вот и хорошо́, что она́ уе́хала. Хорошо́, что она́ уе́хала. Я пря́мо уже́ е́ле вы́держиваю всё э́то. Тебе́ така́я жена́ не нужна́ соверше́нно.

10   Веду́щий и Анто́н (вме́сте): Почему́?

Э́лла Гео́ргиевна: Почему́, он спра́шивает почему́? Да потому́, что она́ соверше́нно ничего́ не уме́ет де́лать. Э́то кака́я-то ха́мка. Она́ побыла́ у нас не́сколько дней, и бо́льше мне вообще́ ничего́ не на́до от неё, ни её.

15   Анто́н: Тебе́ любу́ю де́вушку приведи́, тебе́ люба́я не понра́вится.

Э́лла Гео́ргиевна: Вот когда́ бу́дет люба́я, вот когда́ бу́дет друга́я, тогда́ и поговори́м, а вот с э́той . . .

Веду́щий: А с э́той-то что? То, что она́ ничего́ не уме́ет де́лать, э́то же придёт . . .

20   Э́лла Гео́ргиевна: Да она́ вообще́ кака́я-то . . . (сигна́л заглуша́ет сло́во: засра́нка?). А со мной вообще́ сплошна́я гру́бость.

Веду́щий: Что зна́чит . . . ? В прямо́м смы́сле сло́ва?

Э́лла Гео́ргиевна: Да, в прямо́м смы́сле.

Веду́щий: Так э́то на́до лечи́ть.

25 Элла Георгиевна: Ну, вот и лечи́те её. Вот пусть . . . и лечи́те её.

Анто́н: Она́ мне нра́вится, я люблю́ её. Мне́ всё равно́, что ты говори́шь.

Элла Георгиевна: Как э́то всё равно́? Мне всегда́ видне́е, как ты не понима́ешь, что я еди́нственный челове́к, кото́рый хо́чет тебе́
30 добра́. Пока́ ещё.

Анто́н: Она́ всего́ неде́лю побыла́, как ты могла́ что́-то узна́ть?

Элла Георгиевна: Она́ всего́ неде́лю побыла́, и мне хвати́ло вот так (де́лает жест руко́й над голово́й). Е́ле дождала́сь, е́ле дождала́сь.

35 Веду́щий: Чудеса́ . . . И мы е́ле дожда́ли́сь. (Вхо́дит Мари́на) Здра́вствуйте, Мари́ночка. Вы наве́рно дожи́ли до сто́льких лет и не зна́ли, что Вы . . .

Мари́на: Спаси́бо.

Веду́щий: А почему́ так ма́ма говори́т? Попро́буйте нам объясни́ть.
40 Ну, что ж тако́е-то?

Мари́на: Я не хоте́ла сюда́ приходи́ть. Меня́ сюда́ про́сто притащи́ли. (Анто́ну) Так что я хоте́ла тебе́ сказа́ть, что у тебя́ ма́ма про́сто ненорма́льная же́нщина. Ви́димо, по каки́м-то дре́вним тради́циям ма́ма реши́ла прове́рить меня́ на де́вственность. То́
45 есть жена́ её сы́на должна́ быть неви́нной . . .

Веду́щий: Де́вочкой . . .

Мари́на: Да, про́сто, понима́ешь, как бы меня́ это о́чень унижа́ет . . . Понима́ешь, я всегда́ берегла́ себя́ для тебя́, вот, а тут вдруг про́сто . . .

50 Анто́н: Я не понима́ю.

Элла Георгиевна: Анто́н, я еди́нственное, что попроси́ла: 'Мари́на, у меня́ тут есть о́чень хоро́ший знако́мый врач, дава́й потихо́нечку, там э́то, зайдём к нему́, всё бу́дет прекра́сно, же́нщина, посмо́трит тебя́, и я бу́ду знать, что ты
55 действи́тельно . . .'

Мари́на: Ну, для чего́ э́то ну́жно, для чего́? Ведь ваш сын мне доверя́ет.

Элла Георгиевна: Ну вот, когда́ у тебя́ бу́дет твой сын, и ты бу́дешь тогда́ по́лностью доверя́ть . . . про́сто так, слова́м.

60 Анто́н: Заче́м . . .

Мари́на: Да, я ду́маю, что как бы мы в свое́й жи́зни с ним са́ми разберёмся.

Анто́н (ма́тери): Заче́м ты э́то де́лаешь? Заче́м ты в мою́ жизнь вме́шиваешься?

65 Элла Георгиевна: Я то́же ко́е-что уви́дела . . . (Мари́не) И ты зна́ешь, что я хочу́ тебе́ сказа́ть . . . Е́сли ты така́я че́стная, чего́ ты бои́шься тогда́, взять пойти́ и прове́риться? Чего́ ты бои́шься?

Мари́на: Я не бою́сь, про́сто хочу́ вам сказа́ть, что ну́жно доверя́ть немно́го.

70 Элла Георгиевна: Я тебе́ соверше́нно не доверя́ю.

From the television programme 'О́кна' compèred by Dmitrii Nagiev, broadcast on NTV in February 2004

Anton: I ask mum. Mum gives me some answer I don't understand, she just won't give me a straight answer.

Presenter: Well let's ask mum herself. Your mum – Ella Georgievna. [Ella Georgievna appears.] Hello, take a seat please. [To Anton] Ask your mum.

Anton: Mum, will you explain to me now what happened.

Ella Georgievna: Yes, I've heard . . . everything. You know what, it's a good thing that she's gone. It's a good thing that she's gone. I've hardly been able to bear all this. You really don't need a woman like that.

Presenter and Anton [together]: Why's that?

Ella Georgievna: Why, he asks why. Well because she can't do a thing. She's a cow. She was with us for several days and I just don't want anything else to do with her, I don't want her.

Anton: Any girl I brought home you wouldn't like.

Ella Georgievna: When there's another one, when there's another we'll talk about it, but as for this one . . .

Presenter: Well what about this one? The fact that she can't do a thing, it might change . . .

Ella Georgievna: Well she's just a . . . [a bleep muffles the word: possibly 'shit']. And she was just totally rude to me.

Presenter: What do you mean, a . . . ? In the literal sense of the word?

Ella Georgievna: Yes, in the literal sense of the word.

Presenter: Then she needs to be treated for it.

Ella Georgievna: Well, treat her for it then. Let her . . . get treated for it.

Anton: I like her, I love her. I don't care what you say.

Ella Georgievna: What do you mean you don't care? I know better than you, you don't understand that I'm the only person who wishes you well. For the time being.

Anton: She was with you for just a week, how could you find anything out?

Ella Georgievna: She was with us for just a week, and that was enough for me [makes a gesture over her head]. I could hardly wait, I could hardly wait.

Presenter: Amazing . . . And we can hardly wait either. [Marina appears.] Hello Marina. You've obviously lived all these years without knowing you were a . . .

Marina: Thank you.

Presenter: And why's mum saying that? Try and explain it to us. So what's it all about then?

Marina: I didn't want to come here. I've just been dragged here. [To Anton] Anyway, I wanted to tell you that your mum's just not a normal woman. Obviously your mum decided to go along with some ancient tradition and check up on my virginity. That's to say her son's wife had to be an innocent . . .

Presenter: Little girl . . .

Marina: Yes, so you see, like, how much that degrades me . . . Do you understand, I was saving myself all the time for you, that's what, and then all of a sudden I get this . . .

Anton: I don't understand.

Ella Georgievna: Anton, the only thing I asked of her was: 'Marina, I've got a very good friend here who's a doctor, let's pop round there on the quiet, well, let's go and see the doctor, it'll be all right, it's a woman and she'll have a look at you and I'll know that you really are . . .'

Marina: What's that necessary for, what for? After all, your son trusts me.

Ella Georgievna: Well, when you have a son of your own you'll completely trust . . . just words.

Anton: Why . . .

Marina: Yes, I think that we'll, like, sort out our own lives for ourselves.

Anton [to his mother]: Why are you doing this? Why are you interfering in my life?

Ella Georgievna: I've seen a thing or two myself . . . [To Marina] And you know what I want to say to you . . . If you're such a good girl, then what have you got to be afraid of, why don't you just go and get checked? What are you afraid of?

Marina: I'm not afraid of anything, I just want to tell you that you've got to trust people a bit.

Ella Georgievna: I don't trust you at all.

The television programme from which the excerpt is taken follows the format of Western talk shows such as ITV's *Trisha* and is therefore symptomatic of the influx of Western popular culture into Russia.

Linguistically the excerpt illustrates the colloquial register that people use for discussion, or argument, about highly personal matters. Utterances are frequently incomplete or incoherent and people may repeat themselves, e.g. хорошо́, что она́ уе́хала (8), Почему́, он спра́шивает почему́ (11). The colloquial features of the passage include the following.

modes of address • Use of the familiar second-person-singular personal pronoun ты (26, 28, 31), second-person-singular verb forms, e.g. Зна́ешь (7, 65), понима́ешь (47), де́лаешь (63), вме́шиваешься (64), and second-person-singular imperative forms, e.g. объясни́ (6). The familiar forms of address are not confined to people who know each other well (i.e. Ella Georgievna and her son, Anton, and Anton and his girl-friend, Marina). Ella Georgievna also addresses Marina in this way (and in this case the familiar form has a tone of condescension or contempt). The presenter too at one point uses the familiar second-person-singular imperative form Спроси́ when addressing Anton (5), thus entering into the intimate spirit of the exchanges.

vocabulary • Words such as сплошна́я (21), the derogatory ха́мка (12).

• Diminutive or familiar forms: потихо́нечку (53) and Мари́ночка (36), a diminutive form of Мари́на (used by the presenter).

• Repeated use by all three participants of the word вот, which occurs in the expression вот так (32–3), or which may serve as a filler (6, 7, 17, 25, 48, 58). In one utterance by Ella Georgievna this word occurs three times (16–17). Other fillers are used too: вообще́ (which is a favourite of Ella Georgievna's: 13, 20, 21), and про́сто (41, 49) and как бы (47, 61), both of which are characteristic of Marina's speech.

• Use of modal particles, e.g. the post-positive particle -то (18), ж(е) (19, 40) and ну (40, 56, 58).

syntax • Turns of phrase such as Ну, что ж тако́е-то (40), а тут вдруг про́сто (48-9), там это (53), and про́сто так (59).

- Use of a clause with the second-person-singular imperative form in a conditional or concessive sense: любую девушку приведи (15), *if you [one] were to bring any girl* or *whatever girl you [one] might bring.*

- Use of the verb взять to suggest sudden action (67).

2.2 R1: based on a conversation in a Russian internet chatroom

	A:	Здравствуйте, добрые мои знакомые. С новым Годом!
	B to A:	А незнакомые?
	C to D:	так вот если не секрет, кроме того, что вы обитаете на небесах, где ваша земельная дислокация!!
5	E to F:	это я уже видела, ну и как ты думаешь удовлетворить?
	F to E:	я не знаю твоих запросов:)))
	G to F:	главное отличие компьютера от мозов заключается в том, что им пользуются
	H to I:	И что дальше?
10	I to H:	такси проезжает мимо, торможу его, а он мне типа до города стольник, а мине деенех так жалка и ваще такая красивая, а он – стольник, грю 30 тока и улыбаюсь во все 32 зуба
	A:	И незнакомые, хотя таких практически нет, здрасти
	C to E:	браво!! а что вы ещё видели! а лучше скажите что вы показивали!!!
15	I to A:	здрасти
	D to C:	ну во-первых, на ты:) а во-вторых, моя замечательная, как ты заметил, дислакация, в г. К.
	A to I:	С праздником, радость моя!
	F to G:	смелая мысль, на личном опыте основана?
20	E to C:	вы о чём?
	A to B:	ты Наташа?
	C to E:	ну с кем ты там говоришь о том, что ты видела!!
	B to A:	Да...А вы...?
	B to A again:	Пардон...ты
25	H to I:	Не томи душу! Рассказывай!
	E to C:	ни скем я одна
	I to H:	привёз он меня и телефончик оставляет, грит, назад поедите, вызывайте и лыбится
	A to B:	спасибо, конечно
30	G to F:	ты смеёшься над правдой
	C to D:	ну вот наконецто убираем границы будм только на ты!! а о г. К. ничего не слыхал!!
	F to G:	нет, правду я люблю:))
	C to E:	а сейчас расплачусь, такая милая, нежная маленькая и одна!! могу я скрасить твоё одиночество!
35		
	D to C:	очень зря...наш город присвоил себе статус города невест...в И. они перевелись, а у нас наоборот:))
	I to H:	да ничего такого, просто кода я уже утро стояла на остановке и мёрзла опять же, а маршрутки ещё не ходили, опять этот парень подкатывает
40		
	H to I:	И всё?!?!
	E to C:	я не одна я с охраной
	G to B:	винзип плохой попался, хотел такси вызвать, прислали девушку

45

50

B to A:	Есть ещё вариа́нт, о кото́ром спра́шивают: побе́да))))
C to D:	ва́у, ва́у!! скро́мно! и вопро́с в спи́ну! – ты за́мужем!?
A to B:	сейча́с не на́до, лу́чше со мной пообща́йся
C to E:	ах, вон оно́ как!!! да мы вро́де бы и с охра́ной мо́жем договори́ться, и наконе́ц уедини́ться!!!
I to H:	мда . . . ка́к-то нескла́дно рассказа́ла
D to C:	Сде́лаешь предложе́ние, е́сли нет?:)
E to C:	со мной бу́дет трудне́е договори́ться
C to D:	ну сего́дня пра́здник, почему́ бы и нет, но я ду́маю нам сто́ило бы немно́го бо́лее узна́ть друг дру́га!!
H to I:	– Норма́льно! Дава́й вы́пьем за взаимопонима́ние!

A:	*Hello, my good friends. Happy New Year.*
B to A:	*And what about strangers?*
C to D:	*and so if it isn't a secret, apart from the fact that you live on another planet, where's your base on Earth!!*
E to F:	*i've seen that already, so how do you intend to satisfy me?*
F to E:	*i don't know your needs :)))*
G to F:	*the main difference between a computer and brans [brains] is that people use it*
H to I:	*And what else?*
I to H:	*a taxi goes past, i wave him down, and he says to me like it'll cost you a hundred to get to town but i'm so meeean with money and anyway i'm so gorgeous and he's asking for a hundred so i say thirty and that's it and I give him a great big smile . . .*
A:	*And strangers as well, although there aren't many of them [i.e. A claims to know almost everybody].*
C to E:	*bravo!! and what else have you seen! or better still tell us what you've showen [shown]!!!!*
I to A:	*hi*
D to C:	*well firstly let's be on familiar terms:)) [that is to say, on terms which in Russian make possible the use of the informal personal pronoun* ты *as the means of address] and secondly, my lovely, as you've noticed, my base is in K. [D names a provincial Russian town here].*
A to I:	*Happy holiday, my lovely!*
F to G:	*it's a bold idea, is it based on personal experience?:)*
E to C:	*what are you on about?*
A to B:	*are you Natasha?*
C to E:	*so who are you talking to there about what you've seen!!*
B to A:	*Yes . . . And are you . . . ? [B uses A's screen name here.]*
B to A again:	*i beg your pardon . . . [B is apologising for having used the formal pronoun* вы *instead of the informal* ты *now that she is getting to know A.]*
H to I:	*Don't keep me on tenterhooks! Tell all!*
E to C:	*i'm not withanyone [sic] i'm alone*
I to H:	*he gave me a lift and he hands me his telephone number and says when you go back you call me and he gives me a leer*
A to B:	*thanks, of course*
G to F:	*you're laughing at the truth*
C to D:	*well at last we're breaking down the barriers then and we'll be on familiar terms all the time!! [i.e. they will address each other using the pronoun* ты*] and i haven't heard a thing about K.!! [the town that D has named]*
F to G:	*no, i love the truth:))*
	[At this point A asks B about the implications of her screen name.]

C to E:	*i'm going to burst into tears, such a sweet delicate little thing and all on her own!! i'm the one who can relieve your loneliness!*
	[B now replies to A's enquiry about her screen name.]
D to C:	*it's a great shame you haven't ... we've got the reputation of a town full of girls who want to get married ... they've run out of them in I. [D names a neighbouring Russian town], but it's quite the opposite here:))*
I to H:	*nothing special, it's just that wen i was standing freezing at the bus stop this morning all over again, and no minibuses were running, this guy drives up again*
H to I:	*And that's all there is to it?!?!*
E to C:	*i'm not alone i've got a minder*
G to B:	*i've got a dud zip file, i wanted to call a taxi, they sent a girl*
B to A:	*There's another scenario that people ask about: conquest))))*
C to D:	*wow, wow!! how modest of you! and the big question! – are you married!?*
A to B:	*not yet, it would be better for you to get to know me*
C to E:	*oh, so that's how it is!!! well we could sort of come to an agreement with the minder, and then get to be on our own!!!!*
I to H:	*hm ... i didn't put it too well*
D to C:	*If not, will you propose?:)*
E to C:	*you'll find i'm more difficult to come to an agreement with [i.e. more difficult than the minder]*
C to D:	*well today's a holiday, so why not, but i think it would be worth our while to get to know each other a bit better!!*
H to I:	*OK! Let's drink to mutual understanding!*

Of the participants in this conversation A, C, F, G and H are male and B, D, E and I are female (as is clear from grammatical forms used in the Russian, as well as from the content of the conversation).

The passage reflects the chaotic reality of the internet chatroom where numerous concurrent conversations go on in public, most of them quite independently of one another but within view of the other participants, and some of them not easily intelligible to outsiders who do not know what has been said before.

From the linguistic point of view the passage illustrates the extreme informality of speech in this medium. The participants, even those who are apparently communicating with one another for the first time, express themselves with a greater freedom (exemplified by frequent sexual innuendo) than would be usual among strangers if they were suddenly brought physically together in a social situation.

The normal conventions of written language, which tends towards a standard and is subject to editing, correction and revision, are not observed in this cybertext. Consequently usage is extremely lax. For instance, letters are omitted (thus мозо́в for мозго́в (7), будм for бу́дем (31), кода́ for когда́ (38)). Words are misspelt, owing to careless keying of characters or possibly to ignorance of correct usage, e.g. пока́зивали (14) for пока́зывали, пое́дите (27) for пое́дете, расказа́ла (49) for рассказа́ла. Words are incorrectly joined together (скем (26) for с кем). Punctuation is often omitted, e.g. full stops at the end of sentences, the comma or full stop required after ни с кем (26), and the hyphen required in наконе́ц-то (31). Incorrect punctuation marks may be used, e.g. exclamation marks instead of a question mark

(4, 14). Participants frequently insert emoticons into the text (6, 16, 33, 37, 44), that is to say they use a new form of punctuation that has developed in the language of the internet. Rules relating to the use of capitals are also broken. Thus a lower-case form is generally used for the first letter of the first word of a sentence.

We try in our translation to preserve the flavour of the original cybertext by imitating the typing errors and lax usage of the participants in the chatroom, omitting or misusing certain marks of punctuation, and using lower-case letters instead of capitals where the participants themselves have done so.

Participants' spelling of words in this text, besides containing mistakes, sometimes also reflects pronunciation in rapid speech, e.g. ващé for вообщé (11), грю for говорю́ (12), тóка for тóлько (12), здрáсти for здрáвствуйте (15), грит for говори́т (27). Participant D's spelling of the word дислокáция as дислакáция (17) reflects the phenomenon of ákan'e (see 1.5 above) in the second syllable. Participant I spells some words in the affected, drawn-out way in which she claims to have pronounced them in the conversation that she reports, e.g. минé (11; i.e. мне), деéнех (11; i.e. дéнег).

Besides intermittently reflecting colloquial pronunciation, the passage also illustrates many other colloquial speech habits, e.g. use of:

- the informal pronoun ты (5, 16, 21, etc.), the related possessive forms твои́х (6) and твоё (35), and second-person-singular verb forms, especially imperatives, e.g. Сдéлаешь (50); Не томи́ (25); Расскáзывай (25); пообщáйся (46); давáй (54). Three of the participants actually discuss or allude to such informal usage (16, 24, 31);

- the very familiar form of address рáдость моя́ (18);

- simple syntax. Many sentences are constructed around an understood verb *to be*, e.g. éсли не секрéт (3); где вáша земéльная дислокáция (3-4); на ли́чном óпыте оснóвана? (19); ты Натáша (21); я не однá (42); я с охрáной (42); ты зáмужем!? (45); сегóдня прáздник (52). Subordination, where it occurs, is of a simple kind: see e.g. the clauses introduced by éсли (3, 50), хотя́ (13), что (3, 7), как (16), когдá (38) and котóрый (44). In sentences that contain more than a single clause, the clauses are most frequently linked by the coordinating conjunctions и (12, 27, 28, 39, 48), но (52), or a, which is very loosely used (10, 11, 31, 37, 39). Often ideas are linked by no conjunction at all, so that sentences may take on a rambling quality;

- verbs in the present tense, in order to give a sense of immediacy to reported events, e.g. такси́ проезжáет ми́мо (10); опя́ть э́тот пáрень подкáтывает (39–40);

- ellipsis (see 11.13 below), e.g. он мне (10, i.e. *he [says] to me*); он – стóльник (11–12, i.e. *he [says/asks for] a hundred-rouble note*); вы о чём? (20, i.e. *you [are talking] about what?*);

- slovenly expressions, e.g. типа (10), вро́де бы (47), both meaning *like* or *sort of* (see the comments in 1.5 above about какбыи́зм);

- colloquial words or expressions and colloquial variants of words, e.g. улыба́ться во все 32 зу́ба (12), lit *to smile with all thirty-two teeth*; томи́ть ду́шу (25), lit *to torment the soul*, i.e. *to keep sb in suspense*; телефо́нчик (27), *telephone number*; лы́бится (28), *smiles*, i.e. улыба́ется; слыха́л (32), instead of слы́шал; зря (36), *to no purpose, for nothing*; маршру́тка (39), a diminutive equivalent of маршру́тное такси́, *a fixed-route taxi*; подка́тывает (40), *to roll up* (trans), in the sense of *to drive up* (intrans); нескла́дно (49), *awkwardly, not well*. The expression вопро́с в спи́ну (45), used by C, may be a conscious or unconscious muddling of two established expressions, вопро́с в лоб, *a blunt question*, and нож в спи́ну, *a stab in the back*;

- modish usage, slang or jargon, e.g. дислока́ция, *stationing of troops*, in the sense of *place where one lives* (4); the verb тормози́ть, *to brake*, in the sense of *to wave down a vehicle* (10); сто́льник, *hundred-rouble note* (11); охра́на (42), *guard* in the sense of *minder*; винзи́п, *zip file* (43), a term from the language of computing;

- particles, e.g. ну or ну и (5, 16, 22, 31, 52); же (39); -то (31); a as a means of introducing a question (2, 23);

- interjections, e.g. бра́во! (14), ва́у, ва́у! (45), ax (47), and phrases of an interjectional nature, e.g. вон оно́ как! (47);

- fillers, e.g. мда (49) and вот (31).

Occasionally a turn of phrase occurs that is associated with a higher register, but such turns of phrase are used only for some clear stylistic reason. For example, participant C deploys the high-flown expression обита́ть на небеса́х (3), lit *to dwell in the heavens*, for jocular effect, and later on he employs the phrase скра́сить одино́чество (34), *to relieve loneliness*, euphemistically as a means of making a sexual advance. Again, G uses the bookish copula заключа́ется в том, что (7; see 4.2 below) because he is delivering himself of what he thinks is a rather clever aphorism.

On greetings of the sort С но́вым Го́дом! (1) and С пра́здником! (18), which are stylistically neutral, see 7.8 below.

2.3   R2: magazine interview with a popular actor

– В одно́м из интервью́ ты сказа́л, что 'уме́ешь дово́льствоваться ма́лым'. Э́то фо́рмула пра́вильного отноше́ния к жи́зни?

– Э́то моя́ защи́тная реа́кция. Чем ме́ньше име́ешь, тем ме́ньше теря́ешь.

5   – Зна́чит, э́то боя́знь потеря́ть?

– Да я не сто́лько бою́сь, ско́лько не люблю́ разочаро́вываться. Не люблю́ создава́ть себе́ пробле́мы.

– Говорят, от нахлынувшей известности ты испытываешь скорее неловкость, чем удовольствие.

10   – Знаешь, мне всё-таки проще, чем другим. Я никогда не стремился к славе, поэтому не испытываю никакого душевного подъёма или головокружения. Некоторые даже не верят, что популярность может тяготить. Мне говорят – да ты что, ты же актёр, ты должен был этого хотеть. А я чувствую себя неудобно. Поэтому хожу, глядя в

15   пол. Мне сложно быть всегда на виду. Особенно в имидже своего парня, который выпивает, матерится и одновременно защищает людей, закон. Хотя мой Ларин – совсем не положительный герой. Он обычный питерский разгильдяй, но со своими убеждениями и позицией.

20   – А ты сам насколько близок и насколько далёк от этого образа?
– Далёк, поскольку у меня другая профессия. А близок во всём остальном. Я ничего не играю в сериале ... Вот ездить, отдыхать, плавать – это по мне. Есть же такие области, где нужно просто ездить по миру ...

25   – Дмитрий Крылов так делает передачу про разные страны.
– Я ему завидую белой завистью. И я бы с удовольствием сделал семейную передачу о том, как мы путешествуем. Общался бы с людьми: 'Ну, как у вас тут, почём сигареты?' Жизненная была бы передача ... Но это только мечта. С другой стороны, у неё

30   есть шансы сбыться! Мечтал же я когда-то ничего не делать и получать деньги – и в конце концов я этого добился. Бог услышал мои молитвы и послал мне наш милицейский сериал. Не прилагаю никаких усилий, чтобы как-то выигрышно себя подать. Всё получается само собой.

35   – Но в начале-то, наверное, пришлось постараться, заслужить авторитет ...
– В начале мы относились к этому как к обыкновенной халтуре. Был 1994 год. Помню, отсняли первых восемь серий. Но на РТР, где тогда всё только начиналось, это оказалось никому не нужно.

40   Мы про сериал благополучно забыли. Через полтора года его вдруг решили показать, уже на ТНТ. Он вышел без всякой рекламы. И на следующий день мы проснулись знаменитыми.

From the Russian edition of *Cosmopolitan*, December 2002

Q: *In one interview you said that 'you're able to be contented with very little'. Is that a formula for the right attitude to life?*
A: *It's my defence reflex. The less you have the less you lose.*
Q: *So you're afraid of losing things?*
A: *Well it's not so much that I'm afraid as that I don't like being disillusioned. I don't like making problems for myself.*
Q: *People say that fame has brought you more embarrassment than pleasure.*
A: *You know, actually I've found it easier than others do. I never strove for fame and so I don't feel at all uplifted or dizzy as a result of it. Some people just don't believe that popularity can be a burden. People say to me 'What do you mean, you're an actor, aren't you, you must have wanted this.' And I feel uncomfortable. So now I go round staring at the ground. I find it hard to be on show all the time. Especially in the image of the guy I play, who's always drinking and swearing*

*and at the same time defending people and the law. Although my Larin's far
from a positive hero. He's your normal Petersburg layabout, but he's got things
he believes in and views of his own.*

Q: *And how close are you to this character, and how far away from him?*

A: *A long way away in that I've got a different job. But close in all other respects.
I'm not acting in the series . . . Travelling, relaxing, swimming, that's what I like
doing. In fact there are walks of life where all one has to do is travel round the
world . . .*

Q: *That's how Dmitrii Krylov makes programmes about various countries.*

A: *I'm green with envy. I'd happily make a family film about us travelling. I'd mix
with people and ask them how they're doing and how much cigarettes cost. It'd be
a down-to-earth film . . . But it's just a dream. On the other hand it could come
true. After all, there was a time when I dreamt of doing nothing and making
money and I ended up managing that. God heard my prayers and sent me our
police series. I don't make any effort to put myself forward. Things just happen.*

Q: *But I expect you had to try hard to start with, to gain authority . . .*

A: *To start with we approached it as hack-work. It was 1994. They shot the first
eight episodes, I recall. But at RTR, where things were only just beginning,
nobody wanted it as it turned out. We happily forgot about the series. A year
and a half later they suddenly decided to show it, on TNT by this time. It was
broadcast without being advertised beforehand. And the next day we woke up
famous.*

Although this extract is an example of the written language it is at the
lower end of R2 and tends towards R1, since it is based on an
interview. We may assume that it has been somewhat edited and
therefore tidied up for the purposes of publication in written form,
but the conversational origin of the piece is still very much in
evidence.

The familiar form of address (ты) is used by the interviewer. Syntax
is simple, with little subordination. Sentences tend to be short (over 80
per cent are of ten words or less). There is frequent recourse to это as a
subject, e.g. Это фо́рмула пра́вильного отноше́ния к жи́зни? (2), Это
моя́ защи́тная реа́кция (3), это боя́знь потеря́ть? (5), это по мне́ (23)
and это то́лько мечта́ (29). The colloquial interrogative adverb почём,
how much, is preferred to the stylistically neutral ско́лько (28) and the
colloquial preposition про, *about*, is preferred to the neutral preposition
о (40). Some of the vocabulary has a colloquial flavour, e.g.
матери́ться, *to eff and blind* (16), разгильдя́й, *layabout* (18), халту́ра,
hack-work (37). There are expressive particles, such as postpositive -то
(35), же (13, 23) and ну (28), and colloquial turns of phrase (especially
when the actor is quoting his own imagined words), e.g. да ты что́ (4),
это по мне́ (23) and как у вас тут? (28). The interviewer also uses the
colloquial particle а to introduce a question (20, and on several other
occasions in the interview from which this passage is taken).

At the same time the vigour and spontaneity of speech have perhaps
been lost to some extent in the transformation of the interview into
the rather bland form required by the genre of the magazine feature.
What is printed, while linguistically simple, is grammatically correct,
fluent and coherent.

2.4   R2: question-and-answer session with President Putin

Кала́шников В., Тюме́нская о́бласть: Влади́мир Влади́мирович, Вам за четы́ре го́да не успе́ть сде́лать всё то, что Вы наме́тили.

Пу́тин В.В.: Вы помо́жете – мы сде́лаем.

Кала́шников В.: Необходи́мо увели́чить срок до семи́ лет. Спаси́бо.

5   Пу́тин В.В.: Я уже́ отвеча́л на э́ти вопро́сы и ещё раз хочу́ подтверди́ть свою́ пози́цию. Коне́чно, э́то стремле́ние к определённой стаби́льности, но така́я стаби́льность мо́жет перерасти́ и в засто́й. Всегда́ мо́жно найти́ аргуме́нты, ссыла́ясь на кото́рые мо́жно беспреде́льно увели́чивать срок пребыва́ния

10   у вла́сти того́ или друго́го нача́льника, того́ и́ли ино́го руководи́теля. Коне́чно, мо́жет быть, и пять лет бы́ло бы ничего́, ка́к-то ци́фра бо́лее окру́глая. Ду́маю, что семь – э́то совсе́м многова́то.

      Е́сли сего́дня исполня́ть те обя́занности, кото́рые до́лжен

15   исполня́ть глава́ госуда́рства росси́йского, то, име́я в виду́ огро́мное коли́чество накопи́вшихся пробле́м, рабо́тать ну́жно с по́лной отда́чей сил. Е́сли семь лет с по́лной отда́чей вот так рабо́тать, с ума́ мо́жно сойти́, понима́ете?

      Е́сть и друга́я составля́ющая э́той пробле́мы. Вы зна́ете, я

20   сам ду́мал то́же над э́тим, и получа́ется, что мы хоти́м дости́чь стаби́льности путём подры́ва Основно́го зако́на госуда́рства – Конститу́ции. Как то́лько начнём пра́вить Конститу́цию – э́то уже́ путь к како́й-то нестаби́льной ситуа́ции. Вот сто́ит то́лько нача́ть, пото́м не останови́ться бу́дет. Поэ́тому лу́чше не тро́гать

25   Основно́й зако́н госуда́рства и рабо́тать в тех ра́мках, кото́рые те лю́ди, кото́рые рабо́тали над э́тим зако́ном, заложи́ли. Четы́ре го́да небольшо́й, но и нема́ленький срок. Два ра́за по четы́ре го́да если челове́к отрабо́тал норма́льно, лю́ди э́то всё равно́ пойму́т и оце́нят. Э́то бу́дет во́семь лет. И пото́м зада́ча

30   любо́го руководи́теля – тем бо́лее тако́го ра́нга – заключа́ется в том, что́бы предложи́ть о́бществу челове́ка, кото́рого он счита́ет досто́йным рабо́тать на э́том ме́сте да́льше. Е́сли лю́ди соглася́тся, зна́чит, подде́ржат. И э́то бу́дет продолже́ние того́, что де́лается сейча́с. Но в э́том слу́чае, да́же если э́то

35   челове́к досто́йный, о́пытный, всё равно́ э́то друго́й челове́к, с ним прихо́дят све́жие лю́ди, све́жие иде́и, све́жие подхо́ды к реше́нию тех пробле́м, кото́рые стоя́т пе́ред страно́й. Э́то всегда́ в плюс.

Published on the website www.Putin2004.ru

V. Kalashnikov, Tiumen' Province: Vladimir Vladimirovich, you won't be able to do everything you've planned in the space of four years [i.e. in the presidential term of office].

V. V. Putin: We'll get it done with your help.

V. Kalashnikov: The term needs to be increased to seven years. Thank you.

V. V. Putin: I've already answered these questions and I'd like to reaffirm my position. Of course, it's a desire for a certain stability, but such stability might also turn into stagnation. One can always find arguments by reference to which one can infinitely increase the time that this or that boss or this or that leader stays in power. Of course, maybe five years would be all right, a more rounded figure as it were. I think seven is rather a lot.

If today one is to carry out the duties which the head of the Russian state must carry out then bearing in mind the huge number of problems that have accumulated one has to work at full steam. If one was to work like that at full steam for seven years one could go mad, do you understand?

There's another component to the problem as well. You know I thought about this myself too and it's that we want to achieve stability by undermining the Fundamental Law of State, the Constitution. The moment we start to amend the Constitution, that's already the road to an unstable situation. You only have to start and you won't be able to stop. Therefore it's better not to touch the Fundamental Law of State and to work within the framework that the people who worked on that law have laid down. Four years is not a big term but it's not a small one either. Twice four years if a person has worked all right, people will be able to understand and value that. That'll be eight years. And then the task of any leader, especially of that rank, is to offer society a person whom he considers worthy of carrying on work in that position. If people agree then they'll support [him]. And that'll be a continuation of what is happening now. But in that event, even if this is a worthy, experienced person nevertheless it's a different person and with him come fresh people, fresh ideas, [and] fresh approaches to solving the problems facing the country. That's always a plus.

This is an answer to one of many questions put to President Putin by people from various parts of Russia at a face-to-face meeting held in Moscow University on 12 February 2004 during the presidential election campaign. In terms of register President Putin's answer is fairly neutral. As an example of the spoken rather than the written language it exhibits many conversational features, especially with regard to syntax, e.g.

- reliance on constructions with a verb 'to be' (stated or understood), and often with э́то: э́то стремле́ние к определённой стаби́льности (6–7); пять лет бы́ло бы ничего́ (11–12); э́то совсе́м многова́то (12–13); э́то уже́ путь к како́й-то нестаби́льной ситуа́ции (22–3); Четы́ре го́да небольшо́й, но и нема́ленький срок (27); Э́то бу́дет во́семь лет (29); э́то бу́дет продолже́ние (33); э́то друго́й челове́к (35); Э́то всегда́ в плюс (37–8);

- sentences built around an impersonal form + infinitive: мо́жно найти́ (8); рабо́тать ну́жно (16); с ума́ мо́жно сойти́ (18); лу́чше не тро́гать (24);

- the colloquial construction Вот сто́ит то́лько нача́ть (23–4);

- the colloquial form многова́то (13) and the expression всё равно́ (35);

- engagement with the listener: понима́ете? (18), Вы зна́ете (19).

At the same time the importance of the President's office and the serious political subject-matter tend to raise the language above the very informal, colloquial levels illustrated in the passages at 2.1 and 2.2, as indicated by the following features:

- the copula заключа́ется в том, что́бы (30–1);
- past active participial form накопи́вшихся (16);
- imperfective gerunds: ссыла́ясь (8), име́я в виду́ (15);
- the use of the formal mode of address, Вы (2, 3, etc.).

There are also a few examples of the terminology and phrasing of the professional politician, some of them perhaps characteristic of President Putin in particular, e.g. подтверди́ть свою́ пози́цию (6); с по́лной отда́чей сил (17); составля́ющая (19) as a noun meaning *component*; путь к (23) рабо́тать в тех ра́мках, кото́рые те лю́ди, кото́рые рабо́тали над э́тим зако́ном, заложи́ли (25–6); Э́то всегда́ в плюс (37–8).

2.5   R3a: academic style (modern historiography)

Такова́ 'официа́льная анке́та' Победоно́сцева. Его́ 'послужно́й спи́сок', 'мунди́р'. А что 'под мунди́ром'? Какова́ биогра́фия души́ 'вели́кого реакционе́ра'? Каки́е челове́ческие чу́вства дви́гали его́ посту́пками? Зада́ть э́ти вопро́сы ле́гче, чем на них

5   отве́тить. Победоно́сцев был челове́ком сло́жной, во мно́гом зага́дочной вну́тренней жи́зни, кото́рую он тща́тельно скрыва́л от посторо́нних взо́ров. Характе́рно, что он в отли́чие от большинства́ госуда́рственных де́ятелей, уше́дших на поко́й, не озабо́тился написа́нием мемуа́ров (представля́вших бы уж то́чно не ме́ньший

10   интере́с, чем мемуа́ры Ви́тте). Ре́дко-ре́дко распа́хивается его́ душа́ в пи́сьмах к са́мым инти́мным корреспонде́нтам, да ещё в не́которых за́писях несистемати́ческого, разро́зненного дневника́...А вокру́г челове́ка, не рыда́ющего в чужи́е жиле́тки, в Росси́и неизбе́жно возника́ет атмосфе́ра таи́нственности, спле́тен, до́мыслов...

15   Дово́льно распространённым явля́ется мне́ние о Победоно́сцеве как о безду́шном сухаре́-бюрокра́те, зану́дном ста́рце со скрипу́чим го́лосом. Изве́стно, что Алексе́я Каре́нина в 'А́нне Каре́ниной' Толсто́й спи́сывал с Константи́на Петро́вича. Протоиере́й Гео́ргий Флоро́вский вообще́ называ́ет о́бер-прокуро́ра 'ледяны́м челове́ком'.

20   Когда́ смо́тришь на по́здние фотогра́фии 'вели́кого инквизи́тора ру́сской обще́ственности', действи́тельно ка́жется, что на э́том сухо́м, суро́во-аскети́ческом, лишённом традицио́нной ру́сской доброду́шной окру́глости лице́ в при́нципе не мо́жет игра́ть улы́бка, что бескро́вные, безжи́зненные гу́бы э́того получино́вника,

25   полумона́ха спосо́бны произноси́ть слова́ исключи́тельно прика́зов или моли́тв. Но свиде́тельства мно́жества люде́й, обща́вшихся с о́бер-прокуро́ром, рису́ют его́ совсе́м ина́че. В.В.Ро́занов, вспомина́я встре́чу с шестѝдесятивосьмиле́тним Победоно́сцевым в о́бществе, где преоблада́ли молоды́е лю́ди, изумля́ется: '...э́тот стари́к

30   каза́лся моло́же нас всех, по кра́йней ме́ре живе́е, оживлённее в движе́нии, ре́чи, лёгкой, изя́щной шутли́вости, бесспо́рном уме́, свети́вшемся в его́ глаза́х...'. Францу́зский посла́нник в Росси́и Мори́с Палеоло́г та́кже запо́мнил 'соверше́нную простоту́ и вели́кое обая́ние мане́р и ре́чи' 'ру́сского Торквема́ды'. Оконча́тельно

35   же разруша́ют привы́чный о́браз Победоно́сцева его́ пи́сьма и дневники́. В них ощуща́ешь живу́ю, стра́стную, уме́ющую глубоко́ и

то́нко чу́вствовать ду́шу. И скоре́е мо́жно упрекну́ть Константи́на Петро́вича в изли́шней эмоциона́льности и впечатли́тельности, не́жели в холо́дности.

From a chapter by S. V. Sergéev in *Вели́кие госуда́рственные де́ятели России*, ed. A. F. Kiseliốv (Moscow: Гуманита́рный изда́тельский центр ВЛА́ДОС, 1996)

Such is Pobedonostsev's 'curriculum vitae'. His 'service record', his 'uniform'. But what lies beneath the uniform? What is the biography of the soul of the 'great reactionary'? What human feelings governed his actions? It is easier to pose these questions than to answer them. Pobedonostsev was a man whose inner life was complex and in many respects enigmatic and who carefully concealed that life from the gaze of others. It is typical of him that unlike the majority of statesmen when they went into retirement he did not trouble to write any memoirs (which would certainly have been of no less interest than those of Witte). Just occasionally his soul bursts open in letters to the correspondents with whom he is most intimate and in a few of the entries in his unsystematic diary, of which there are various bits, as well . . . But in Russia a man who does not cry on other people's shoulders is inevitably enveloped in an atmosphere of mystery, gossip and conjecture . . .

There is a quite widespread view of Pobedonostsev as a soulless, dry-as-dust bureaucrat, a tedious monastic elder with a croaky voice. It is well known that it was on Konstantin Petrovich that Tolstoi modelled Aleksei Karenin in 'Anna Karenina'. Archpriest Georgii Florovskii always calls the Chief Procurator 'an ice man'. When you look at the photographs of the 'grand inquisitor of Russian public opinion' [that were] taken towards the end of his life it does indeed seem that it was as a matter of principle out of the question that a smile should play on this sternly ascetic face, which lacked the usual Russian genial rotundity, and that the bloodless, lifeless lips of this man who was half official, half monk were capable of enunciating nothing but the words of commands or prayers. And yet the testimony of many people who met the Chief Procurator paints quite a different picture of him. V. V. Rozanov, recalling an encounter with the sixty-eight-year-old Pobedonostsev at a social gathering at which young people predominated, was astonished to find that 'this old man seemed younger than any of us, or at least more vivacious, more animated by virtue of his movements, speech, gentle, graceful humour and the indisputable intellect that shone in his eyes . . .' The French minister in Russia, Maurice Paléologue, also remembered 'the utter simplicity' of the 'Russian Torquemada' and 'the great charm of his manners and speech'. The usual image of Pobedonostsev is utterly destroyed by his letters and diaries, in which you sense a vivacious, passionate soul that has a capacity for profound and delicate feeling. In fact you could sooner reproach Konstantin Petrovich for an excess of emotion and impressionability than for coldness.

This is an extract from a piece of historical scholarship on the late nineteenth-century conservative statesman Pobedonóstsev who in the 1880s occupied the position of Chief Procurator of the Holy Synod and acted as mentor to the emperor, Alexander III.

The passage is characterised by grammatical correctness, linguistic precision, and the smooth flow of the argument. The author displays his erudition by his wide range of reference and occasional quotation. He strives to achieve literary effect by such means as use of rhetorical questions (А что 'под мунди́ром'? etc.), marks of omission (o; see

11.15) and the rhetorical device of anaphora (как о безду́шном сухаре́-бюрокра́те, зану́дном ста́рце (16) and the two clauses beginning with что in the same sentence (21–6)).

At the same time the passage is not without more informal features (e.g. the rather colloquial word зану́дном (16) and the dearth of specialised vocabulary). It is as if the author is attempting to show that post-Soviet scholarship, like post-Soviet political and cultural life in general, is becoming lighter and more widely accessible.

Syntactic features which do place the passage in a relatively formal register include use of the following:

- a gerund: вспомина́я (27);

- present active participles: рыда́ющего (13), уме́ющую (36);

- past active participles: уше́дших (8), представля́вших (9), обща́вшихся (26), свети́вшемся (32, in a quotation);

- complex adjectival phrases preceding nouns: сло́жной, во мно́гом зага́дочной вну́тренней жи́зни, (5–6) and на э́том сухо́м, суро́во-аскети́ческом, лишённом традицио́нной ру́сской доброду́шной окру́глости лице́ (21–3);

- the verb явля́ться (15);

- the somewhat archaic conjunction не́жели, *than* (39), which has a rather literary flavour, instead of the usual modern form чем.

2.6   R3a: academic style (scientific writing)

Синхротро́нное излуче́ние – электромагни́тное излуче́ние у̀льтрарелятиви́стских электро́нов и́ли позитро́нов, ускоря́емых в цикли́ческих ускори́телях – в после́днее вре́мя ста́ло важне́йшим инструме́нтом иссле́дования сво́йств вещества́. Во всём ми́ре

5 создаю́тся це́нтры по испо́льзованию синхротро́нного излуче́ния, стро́ятся дорогосто́ящие исто́чники. В 1999 году́ в Москве́, в Росси́йском нау́чном це́нтре 'Курча́товский институ́т' на́чал функциони́ровать исто́чник синхротро́нного излуче́ния – накопи́тель электро́нов на 2,5 ГэВ (и э́то дополни́тельно к

10 шести́ уже́ де́йствующим в Росси́и исто́чникам – синхротро́нам и накопи́телям в Москве́, Новосиби́рске и То́мске) . . .

В настоя́щее вре́мя синхротро́нное излуче́ние (СИ) испо́льзуется практи́чески во всех областя́х совреме́нной нау́ки, где изуча́ется взаимоде́йствие электромагни́тного излуче́ния с вещество́м. Высо́кая

15 я́ркость исто́чников СИ позволя́ет проводи́ть спектроскопи́ческие иссле́дования с экстрема́льно высо́ким спектра́льным разреше́нием при бо́лее коро́тких экспози́циях. Испо́льзование поляризацио́нных сво́йств СИ даёт возмо́жность иссле́довать простра́нственную анизотропи́ю объе́ктов. Иссле́дование поглоще́ния и

20 флюоресце́нции га́зов и паро́в несёт информа́цию о строе́нии вну́тренних оболо́чек а́томов. Иссле́дование молекуля́рных спе́ктров с по́мощью СИ позволя́ет получи́ть информа́цию о

25

процессах фотоионизáции и фотодиссоциáции в молекулáрных систéмах. Успéшно применяется СИ в биолóгии, в чáстности, для рентгéноструктýрного исслéдования бйополимéров, для рентгéновской микроскопйи, для спектрофотометрúческих измерéний с временнýм разрешéнием.

30

Наряду́ с многочúсленными применéниями СИ в наýчных исслéдованиях, есть ряд рабóт, имéющих вáжное прикладнóе значéние, в чáстности, по рентгéновской микролитогрáфии. СИ тáкже испóльзуется для исслéдования радиациóнного воздéйствия на материáлы и прибóры в услóвиях вáкуума, чтò óчень вáжно для космúческого материаловéдения. Рентгéновское монохроматизúрованное СИ применяется в рентгенодиагнóстике,

35

чтò позволяет существéнно снúзить радиациóнную нагру́зку на человéка при рентгéновском обслéдовании. Возмóжно применéние СИ в радиациóнной технолóгии и радиациóнно-химúческих процéссах. В послéднее врéмя наблюдáется бýрное развúтие рабóт по применéнию СИ и в наýке, и в тéхнике, создаются нóвые

40

истóчники СИ трéтьего и четвёртого поколéний.

From an article published by Moscow University in 2001

Synchrotron radiation (the electro-magnetic radiation of ultra-relativistic electrons or positrons which are speeded up in cyclical accelerators) has recently become a crucial tool for the investigation of the properties of matter. All over the world centres for the use of synchrotron radiation are being set up and costly sources are being constructed. A synchrotron radiation source started functioning in the Kurchatov Institute in Moscow in 1999. This is a 2.5 gigavolt electron storage facility. (It is in addition to six sources already operating in Russia, synchrotrons and storage facilities in Moscow, Novosibirsk and Tomsk)...

Synchrotron radiation is now used in virtually all fields of modern science where the interaction of electromagnetic radiation and matter is studied. The high brightness of sources of SR enables one to carry out spectroscopic investigations with an extremely high spectral resolution with shorter exposures than previously. Use of the polarisation properties of SR makes it possible to investigate the spatial anisotropy of objects. Investigation of the absorption and fluorescence of gases and vapours produces information about the structure of the inner shells of atoms. Investigation of molecular spectra with the aid of SR enables one to obtain information about the processes of photoionisation and photodissociation in molecular systems. SR is being successfully applied in biology, in particular for X-ray fine-structure investigation of biopolymers, for X-ray microscopy, and for spectro-photometric measurements with time resolution.

Alongside the numerous applications of SR in scientific research there is a whole body of work that is of great practical importance, in particular in the field of X-ray microlithography. SR is also used for research into the effect of radiation on materials and instruments under vacuum conditions, which is very important for our knowledge of materials in space. Monochromatic SR [generated from] X-rays is used in radiological diagnostics, which makes it possible substantially to reduce the amount of radiation to which a person is exposed when undergoing X-ray investigation. It may be possible to use SR in radiation technology and radiation-chemical processes. Recent years have seen work connected with the application of SR in science and technology move forward rapidly and new third- and fourth-generation sources of SR are being developed.

This passage is distinguished by precision and by the careful, logical development of ideas. Words are used unambiguously and in an impersonal way. There is no emotional content and such linguistic features as modal particles, interjections and diminutives are therefore altogether lacking. Features characteristic of the formal scientific register include the following.

vocabulary

- Specialised vocabulary, much of which is of Western origin. This vocabulary is either in the form of calques (e.g. ускори́тель (3), разреше́ние (16)), or in the form of loanwords: синхротро́нный (1), электромагни́тный (1), электро́н (2), позитро́н (2), цикли́ческий (3), спектроскопи́ческий (15), экстрема́льно (16), спектра́льный (16), поляризацио́нный (17), анизотропи́я (19), флюоресце́нция (20), молекуля́рный (21), фотоиониза́ция (23), фотодиссоциа́ция (23), информа́ция (22), биополиме́р (25), рентге́новский (26), микролитогра́фия (30), ва́куум (32), etc.

- Abundance of verbal nouns, especially with the suffix -ние: излуче́ние (1), иссле́дование (4), испо́льзование (5), разреше́ние (16), поглоще́ние (19), строе́ние (20), измере́ние (27), примене́ние (28), значе́ние (30), возде́йствие (32), обсле́дование (36).

- Abbreviations: ГэВ (9), СИ (12, etc.).

phrasing

- Set phrases and formulaic phrasing: в после́днее вре́мя (3, 38); в настоя́щее вре́мя (12); позволя́ет проводи́ть (15); даёт возмо́жность (18); несёт информа́цию (20); позволя́ет получи́ть (22); в ча́стности (30); име́ющих ва́жное прикладно́е значе́ние (29–30).

grammatical forms

- Participles of various sorts, viz: present active, де́йствующим (10), име́ющих (29); present passive, ускоря́емых (2).

syntax

- Frequent use of reflexive imperfectives in a passive sense, giving an objective, impersonal air to the passage, e.g. создаю́тся (5, 39), стро́ятся (6), испо́льзуется (12, 31), изуча́ется (13), применя́ется (24, 34), наблюда́ется (38).

- Verbal nouns combined with при: при бо́лее коро́тких экспози́циях (17), при рентге́новском обсле́довании (36).

- Combination of по with nouns in the sense of *in the field of, in connection with*: по испо́льзованию (5), по рентге́новской микролитогра́фии (30), по примене́нию (39).

- Complex adjectival phrase preceding noun: к шести́ уже́ де́йствующим в Росси́и исто́чникам (9–10).

- Parenthetical explanation to support assertions: элѐктромагни́тное излуче́ние . . . в цикли́ческих ускори́телях (1–3).

- Use of что̀ to refer to all the matter in the preceding clause (32, 35).

2.7   R3b: official/business style (legal)

1. Рекла́ма должна́ быть распознава́ема без специа́льных зна́ний или без примене́ния техни́ческих сре́дств и́менно как рекла́ма непосре́дственно в моме́нт ее представле́ния незави́симо от фо́рмы и́ли от испо́льзуемого сре́дства распростране́ния.

5   Испо́льзование в ра̀дио-, тѐле-, вѝдео-, а̀удио- и кѝнопроду́кции, а та́кже в печа́тной проду́кции нерекла́много хара́ктера целенапра́вленного обраще́ния внима́ния потреби́телей рекла́мы на конкре́тную ма́рку (моде́ль, арти́кул) това́ра ли́бо на изготови́теля, исполни́теля, продавца́ для формирова́ния и поддержа́ния интере́са

10   к ним без надлежа́щего предвари́тельного сообще́ния об э́том (в ча́стности, путём поме́тки 'на права́х рекла́мы') не допуска́ется.

Если ра̀дио-, тѐле-, вѝдео-, а̀удио- и кѝнопроду́кция, а та́кже печа́тная проду́кция распространя́ются частя́ми (се́риями), сообще́ния о рекла́ме та́кже должны́ повторя́ться соотве́тственно

15   коли́честву часте́й (се́рий).

Организа́циям сре́дств ма́ссовой информа́ции запреща́ется взима́ть пла́ту за размеще́ние рекла́мы под ви́дом информацио́нного, редакцио́нного и́ли а́вторского материа́ла.

2. Рекла́ма на террито́рии Росси́йской Федера́ции распространя́ется

20   на ру́сском языке́ и по усмотре́нию рекламода́телей дополни́тельно на госуда́рственных языка́х респу́блик и родны́х языка́х наро́дов Росси́йской Федера́ции. Да́нное положе́ние не распространя́ется на радиовеща́ние, телевизио́нное веща́ние и печа́тные изда́ния, осуществля́емые исключи́тельно на госуда́рственных языка́х

25   респу́блик, родны́х языка́х наро́дов Росси́йской Федера́ции и иностра́нных языка́х, а та́кже на зарегистри́рованные това́рные зна́ки (зна́ки обслу́живания).

3. Рекла́ма това́ров, рекла́ма о само́м рекламода́теле, е́сли осуществля́емая им де́ятельность тре́бует специа́льного разреше́ния

30   (лице́нзии), но тако́е разреше́ние (лице́нзия) не полу́чено, а та́кже рекла́ма това́ров, запрещённых к произво́дству и реализа́ции в соотве́тствии с законода́тельством Росси́йской Федера́ции, не допуска́ется.

Если де́ятельность рекламода́теля подлежи́т лицензи́рованию,

35   в рекла́ме должны́ быть ука́заны но́мер лице́нзии, а та́кже наименова́ние о́ргана, вы́давшего э́ту лице́нзию.

4. Рекла́ма това́ров, подлежа́щих обяза́тельной сертифика́ции, должна́ сопровожда́ться поме́ткой 'подлежи́т обяза́тельной сертифика́ции'.

40   5. Испо́льзование в рекла́ме объе́ктов исключи́тельных прав (интеллектуа́льной со́бственности) допуска́ется в поря́дке, предусмо́тренном законода́тельством Росси́йской Федера́ции.

6. Рекла́ма не должна́ побужда́ть гра́ждан к наси́лию, агре́ссии, возбужда́ть па́нику, а та́кже побужда́ть к опа́сным де́йствиям,

45   спосо́бным нанести́ вред здоро́вью физи́ческих лиц и́ли угрожа́ющим
     их безопа́сности.

From a law on advertising

*1. An advertisement must be recognisable as such at the moment when it is
displayed, without any specialist knowledge or resort to technical resources, [and]
irrespective of its form or the means of dissemination being used.*

*It is not permitted in a radio, television, video, audio, or cinematographic output,
or in a printed work which is not of an advertising nature, to purposely draw
the attention of the consumer of the advertisement to a specific brand (model,
article) of a product or to a manufacturer, performer, or seller for the purpose of
creating and maintaining interest in them without proper preliminary notification
to this effect (in particular by means of the sign 'this has been authorised as an
advertisement').*

*If a radio, television, video, audio, or cinematographic output or a printed work
is disseminated in parts (series) the notification that it is an advertisement must
also be repeated as many times as there are parts (series).*

*Mass media organisations are prohibited from making a charge for carrying an
advertisement under the guise of news, editorial or authorial material.*

*2. Within the territory of the Russian Federation advertisements shall be in
Russian and, at the discretion of the advertisers, additionally in the state languages of the republics and the native languages of the peoples of the Russian
Federation. This provision shall not extend to radio broadcasting, television
broadcasting and printed works that are exclusively in the state languages of
the republics, the native languages of the peoples of the Russian Federation, or
foreign languages, or to registered trade marks (service marks).*

*3. It is not permitted to advertise products or to advertise the advertiser himself if
the activity in which he is engaged requires special permission (a licence) and that
permission (the licence) has not been obtained, or to advertise products which it
is prohibited to produce or sell under the laws of the Russian Federation.*

*If the activity of the advertiser is subject to licensing the number of the licence and
the name of the body which issued the licence must be shown in the advertisement.*

*4. The advertisement of products which are liable to compulsory certification must
be accompanied by the sign 'liable to compulsory certification'.*

*5. The use in an advertisement of things to which there are exclusive rights
(intellectual property) is permitted in accordance with the provisions laid down
by the laws of the Russian Federation.*

*6. An advertisement must not provoke citizens to violence or aggression or cause
panic or incite dangerous actions which might damage the health of physical
persons or threaten their safety.*

This text is drawn from a recent law passed by the Russian parliament
on advertising. It is the first of two texts presented here to illustrate the
formal, written register that is used in official, legal and business
documents. It exemplifies language used in a dry, unemotional way for
the purpose of setting out laws, regulations, codes of practice, duties,

obligations and rights, or for recording binding treaties, agreements, understandings, contracts and so forth. The great precision for which authors of texts written in this register must strive (exemplified in this document by the frequent recourse to parenthetical definitions (8, 11, 13, 15, 27, 30, 41) necessitates grammatical accuracy. At the same time the requirement that ideas be expressed in such a way that misunderstandings or differences of interpretation cannot arise tends to produce inelegant sentences which are intended to be read rather than heard and whose sense may not be clear until the reader reaches the end of them (see the second sentence in clause 1 and the first sentence in clause 3).

Authors of this sort of document generally follow a well-established pattern (e.g., in this text, the division of the statute into 'articles' and the sub-division of articles into clauses). They observe certain conventions and utilise certain formulae. They eschew those resources of the language which convey emotional nuance (e.g. modal particles, interjections and diminutives) and which are deployed in social intercourse (or even in the high register that is used for persuasive purposes (see 2.10 below)). They also eschew the non-literal use of language and the rhetorical or stylistic devices (e.g. metaphor, simile) which may characterise texts produced by imaginative writers who are striving for aesthetic impact (devices which may also be encountered in the academic register (see 2.5 above)).

Leaving aside linguistic features that are notable by their absence, we may say that the principal positive feature characteristic of the high register in general that is found in this text is the free use of participles of all descriptions, especially present and past active participles and present passive participles, all of which are sparingly used in lower registers, e.g.

- present active participles: подлежа́щих (37), угрожа́ющим (45);

- past active participle: вы́давшего (36);

- present passive participles: распознава́ема (1), испо́льзуемого (4), осуществля́емые (24);

- past passive participles (which, however, do not belong so exclusively in the high register): полу́чено (30), запрещённых (31), ука́заны (35).

Features of high register evident in this text that are particularly associated with those sub-divisions of high register which have informative rather than persuasive purpose (i.e. the sub-divisions classified here as R3a and R3b) include the following.

word-formation • Predilection for verbal nouns, especially with the suffix -ние: примене́ние (2), представле́ние (3), распростране́ние (4), испо́льзование (5), обраще́ние (6), формирова́ние (9), поддержа́ние (9), сообще́ние (10), размеще́ние (17), реализа́ция (31), лицензи́рование (34).

syntax

- Use of reflexive imperfectives in a passive sense, giving the text an impersonal flavour: не допуска́ется (11), распространя́ются (13; see also 19, 22), повторя́ться (14), запреща́ется (16), сопровожда́ться (38).

- 'Threading' of nouns in the genitive case: нерекла́много хара́ктера целенапра́вленного обраще́ния внима́ния потреби́телей рекла́мы (7), in which there are no fewer than five nouns in succession in the genitive case. The sequence is made even more cumbersome than a sequence of this length normally would be by the fact that the first noun in the genitive (хара́ктера) relates to the noun проду́кция but the last four nouns (обраще́ния, внима́ния, потреби́телей, рекла́мы) relate to the noun испо́льзование with which the sentence begins.

- Use of the prepositional phrase в соотве́тствии с (32), which also has a very formal flavour.

There are various other formal words or turns of phrase in the text that are characteristic of the official sub-division of the high register, e.g. незави́симо от (3), надлежа́щий (10), соотве́тственно (14), по усмотре́нию (20), дополни́тельно (20), подлежи́т . . . сертифика́ции (37), в поря́дке, предусмо́тренном . . . (41–2).

2.8   R3b: official/business style (commercial)

ДОГОВО́Р № ПК-1290

ку́пли–прода́жи векселе́й

Санкт-Петербу́рг   '5' ноября́ 2004 г.

1. ПРЕДМЕ́Т ДОГОВО́РА

5   **1.1. ПРОДАВЕ́Ц** продаёт векселя́, ука́занные в п. 1.2. настоя́щего догово́ра, явля́ющиеся его́ со́бственностью, не находя́щиеся в зало́ге и не состоя́щие под аре́стом, а **БАНК** приобрета́ет их в со́бственность и обязу́ется оплати́ть их сто́имость.
1.2. Объе́ктом ку́пли–прода́жи явля́ются просты́е векселя́ . . .

2. ЦЕНА́ ДОГОВО́РА

10   **2.1. БАНК** приобрета́ет векселя́, ука́занные в п. 1.2. по цене́ – 25 007 000,00 (Два́дцать пять миллио́нов семь ты́сяч рубле́й).
2.2. Су́мма к перечисле́нию на расчётный счёт **ПРОДАВЦА́** – 25 007 000,00 (Два́дцать пять миллио́нов семь ты́сяч рубле́й).

3. ОБЯ́ЗАННОСТИ СТОРО́Н

15   **3.1. ПРОДАВЕ́Ц** обя́зан переда́ть векселя́, ука́занные в п. 1.2., **БА́НКУ** в тече́ние одного́ ба́нковского дня с моме́нта подписа́ния настоя́щего догово́ра с бла́нковым индоссаме́нтом.
3.2. БАНК обя́зан в тече́ние одного́ ба́нковского дня́ от да́ты 20   заключе́ния настоя́щего Догово́ра перечи́слить **ПРОДАВЦУ́** су́мму,

указанную в п. 2.2. настоящего Договора, но не ра́нее исполне́ния **ПРОДАВЦО́М** обяза́тельств, предусмо́тренных п. 3.1.

3.3. ПРОДАВЕ́Ц гаранти́рует, что он име́ет все полномо́чия, необходи́мые для переда́чи **БА́НКУ** пра́ва со́бственности на векселя́,
25 не обременённые никаки́м зало́гом и́ли други́ми права́ми тре́тьих лиц, и что векселя́ передаю́тся **ПРОДАВЦО́М БА́НКУ** вме́сте со все́ми права́ми, кото́рыми они́ наделены́.

3.4. В слу́чае несоблюде́ния **БА́НКОМ** сро́ка перечисле́ния де́нежных сре́дств, предусмо́тренного п. 3.2. настоя́щего Договора,
30 **ПРОДАВЕ́Ц** выпла́чивает **БА́НКУ** пе́ню в разме́ре 0,3 (Три деся́тых) проце́нта от цены́ заде́ржанных векселе́й за ка́ждый день просро́чки.

4. СРОК ДЕ́ЙСТВИЯ ДОГОВО́РА

4.1. Догово́р вступа́ет в си́лу с моме́нта его́ подписа́ния Сторона́ми и де́йствует до по́лного исполне́ния Сторона́ми свои́х обяза́тельств,
35 предусмо́тренных настоя́щим Догово́ром.

4.2. Де́йствие настоя́щего Договора мо́жет быть прекращено́ по взаи́мному согла́сию Сторо́н.

5. ФОРС-МАЖО́Р

5.1. Ни одна́ из сторо́н не несёт отве́тственности в слу́чае
40 невыполне́ния, несвоевре́менного и́ли ненадлежа́щего выполне́ния е́ю како́го-либо обяза́тельства по настоя́щему договору, е́сли ука́занное невыполне́ние, несвоевре́менное и́ли ненадлежа́щее выполне́ние обусло́влены исключи́тельно наступле́нием и/и́ли де́йствием обстоя́тельств непреодоли́мой си́лы (форс-мажо́рных
45 обстоя́тельств).

5.2. Затро́нутая форс-мажо́рными обстоя́тельствами сторона́ без промедле́ния, но не поздне́е чем че́рез 3 (три) ба́нковских дня по́сле наступле́ния форс-мажо́рных обстоя́тельств в пи́сьменной фо́рме информи́рует другу́ю сто́рону об э́тих обстоя́тельствах и
50 об их после́дствиях и принима́ет все возмо́жные ме́ры с це́лью максима́льно ограни́чить отрица́тельные после́дствия, вы́званные ука́занными форс-мажо́рными обстоя́тельствами.

6. ОСО́БЫЕ УСЛО́ВИЯ

6.1. Все измене́ния и дополне́ния к настоя́щему Догово́ру возмо́жны
55 при усло́вии взаи́много согла́сия Сторо́н и должны́ оформля́ться Приложе́ниями к настоя́щему Догово́ру.

6.2. Догово́р соста́влен в двух экземпля́рах, име́ющих ра́вную юриди́ческую си́лу.

6.3. Все спо́ры, вытека́ющие из примене́ния и толкова́ния
60 настоя́щего Догово́ра, подлежа́т рассмотре́нию в Арбитра́жном суде́ Санкт-Петербу́рга и Ленингра́дской о́бласти.

AGREEMENT No. PK 1290
Purchase and Sale of Bills of Exchange
St Petersburg 5 November 2004

1. The subject of the agreement

1.1 *The **VENDOR** shall sell the Bills of Exchange specified in clause 1.2 of this Agreement, the said Bills being his own property which has not been mortgaged or sequestered, whereas the **BANK** shall assume ownership of them and shall undertake to pay their cost.*
1.2 *The following Bills of Exchange are the object of this sale and purchase . . .*

2. The value of the agreement

2.1 *The **BANK** shall acquire the Bills of Exchange specified in clause 1.2 to the value of 25,007,000.00 (twenty-five million seven thousand roubles).*
2.2 *The sum to be transferred to the account of the **VENDOR** is 25,007,000.00 (twenty-five million seven thousand roubles).*

3. Obligations of the parties [to the agreement]

3.1 *The **VENDOR** shall surrender the Bills of Exchange specified in clause 1.2 to the **BANK** with a Form of Endorsement within one banking day of the signing of this Agreement.*
3.2 *The **BANK** shall transfer to the **VENDOR** the sum specified in clause 2.2 of this Agreement within one banking day of the date on which this Agreement was made but not prior to the fulfilment by the **VENDOR** of the obligations stipulated in clause 3.1.*
3.3 *The **VENDOR** guarantees that he has full authority to transfer rights of ownership of the Bills of Exchange to the **BANK** [and that this authority] is unencumbered by any mortgage or other rights possessed by third parties and that the Bills of Exchange are being transferred to the **BANK** by the **VENDOR** together with any rights associated with them.*
3.4 *In the event that the **BANK** fails to transfer funds by the deadline stipulated in clause 3.2 of this Agreement the **BANK** shall pay the **VENDOR** a fine amounting to 0.3 (three tenths) of one per cent of the sum that is overdue for each day that it is overdue.*

4. Operative period of this agreement

4.1 *The Agreement shall come into force from the moment it is signed by the Parties and shall remain in force until the Parties have fully discharged the obligations stipulated in this Agreement.*
4.2 *This Agreement may be terminated by mutual consent of the [two] Parties.*

5. Force majeure

5.1 *Neither Party is responsible in the event that it fails to fulfil any obligation imposed [upon it] by this Agreement, or fails to fulfil any obligation on time or in the proper way, if the failure to fulfil the obligation or the failure to fulfil it on time or in the proper way is due exclusively to the onset and/or operation of circumstances outside its control (force majeure).*
5.2 *The Party affected by force majeure shall inform the other Party of these circumstances and their consequences in writing without delay and no later than 3 (three) banking days after the onset of the circumstances [in question] and shall take all possible steps to limit as far as possible the adverse consequences of the specified circumstances outside its control.*

6. Special conditions

6.1 *Changes and additions may be made to this Agreement on condition that both Parties consent to them and they must be formally recorded in Addenda to this Agreement.*
6.2 *The Agreement is made in two copies, which have equal legal force.*
6.3 *All disputes arising out of the application and interpretation of this Agreement shall be dealt with by the Court of Arbitration of St Petersburg and Leningrad Province.*

This text, being drawn from a contractual document about sale and purchase, exemplifies language used for the sole purpose of providing an unambiguous record of a binding agreement between two parties. Like the legislative text presented in 2.7 above, it is therefore devoid of linguistic features that convey emotional nuance. It also resembles the legislative text, and the academic and scientific texts at 2.5 and 2.6 respectively, by virtue of its grammatical accuracy, syntactic complexity and great precision. At the same time it has certain distinctive features that are characteristic of legal usage, besides specialised terminology, e.g.:

- numbered clauses;

- repeated cross-referencing;

- use of capital letters and bold type to highlight headings and key terms;

- use (albeit sparing) of initial capital letters (as in English legalese) in nouns denoting certain documents or persons, e.g. Догово́р, Сторона́;

- the use of conventional abbreviations, e.g. п. for пункт, *point* (translated in this context as *clause*);

- rendering of monetary sums both with numerals and in full written form in brackets. (Note the absence of commas where English-speakers would expect them, to indicate units of thousands or millions, and the use of the comma instead of the full stop to indicate a decimal point (12, 14). See 6.3 for further examples.)

We have tried to adhere in our translation of this text to usage in the equivalent English register. Note in particular that in English the modal verb *shall* is used (e.g. in this passage *shall sell, shall assume, shall come*) in order to express contractual obligation that is conveyed in Russian by a verb in the present tense (продаёт, приобрета́ет, вступа́ет) or, in some instances, by some part of the verb обяза́ть, *to bind, oblige* (обязу́ется, обя́зан).
Other points of note, including features indicative of high register:

vocabulary
- specialised financial or legal terminology, much of it of Western origin, e.g. ве́ксель (2, etc.), расчётный счёт (13), ба́нковский день (17), бла́нковый индоссаме́нт (18);

- other official parlance: предусмо́тренный (22, 29), ненадлежа́щий (40, 42), оформля́ться (54);

- abundance of verbal nouns, especially with the suffix -ние: перечисле́ние (13), подписа́ние (17, 33), заключе́ние (20), исполне́ние (21, 34), выполне́ние (40, 42), наступле́ние (43, 47), промедле́ние (46), измене́ние (53), дополне́ние (53), примене́ние (58), толкова́ние (58), рассмотре́ние (59). Some of these verbal nouns are negated forms, e.g. несоблюде́ние (28), невыполне́ние (39, 42);

phraseology

- formulaic phrases, especially certain combinations of verb + noun, e.g. приобрета́ть в со́бственность (7), име́ть все полномо́чия (23), вступа́ть в си́лу (33), по взаи́мному согла́сию (35–6), нести́ отве́тственность (39), в пи́сьменной фо́рме (47–8), принима́ть все возмо́жные ме́ры (49), име́ть ра́вную юриди́ческую си́лу (56–7), подлежа́ть рассмотре́нию (59);

- formal prepositional phrases, e.g. в слу́чае несоблюде́ния (28), с це́лью (49), при усло́вии (54);

grammatical forms

- present active participles, which lend the text a very formal flavour, e.g. явля́ющиеся (6), находя́щиеся (6), состоя́щие (7), име́ющих (56), вытека́ющие (58);

- numerous past passive participles: ука́занные (5, 11, 16), предусмо́тренных (22), обременённые (25), наделены́ (27), прекращено́ (36), обусло́влены (43), затро́нутая (45), вы́званные (50), соста́влен (56);

syntax

- use of reflexive imperfectives in a passive sense, e.g. обязу́ется (8), передаю́тся (26), должны́ оформля́ться (54);

- complex adjectival phrase preceding noun: затро́нутая форс-мажо́рными обстоя́тельствами сторона́ (45);

- use of явля́ться as copula (9).

2.9   R3c: political journalism (reporting)

В МОСКВЕ́ ОТКРЫВА́ЕТСЯ СА́ММИТ РОССИ́Я-ЕС
На нём реши́тся вопро́с вхожде́ния в ВТО

Президе́нт Росси́и Влади́мир Пу́тин сего́дня в Кремле́ бу́дет обсужда́ть с руково́дством Евросою́за отноше́ния Москвы́ и
5   Брюссе́ля. Традицио́нный са́ммит Росси́я-ЕС, проводя́щийся два́жды в год, на э́тот раз 'бу́дет нерядовы́м'. Это – пе́рвая встре́ча на вы́сшем у́ровне по́сле расшире́ния Евросою́за.

У главы́ росси́йского госуда́рства не плани́руется отде́льных двусторо́нних встреч с уча́стниками са́ммита. На перегово́ры
10   в Москву́ при́были два представи́теля Ирла́ндии – страны́, председа́тельствующей ны́не в ЕС, а та́кже глава́ Еврокоми́ссии.

В ра́мках са́ммита Росси́я-ЕС, открыва́ющегося сего́дня в Москве́, ожида́ется подписа́ние двусторо́ннего соглаше́ния по вступле́нию РФ во Всеми́рную торго́вую организа́цию (ВТО).

15 Как сообщи́ли в Минэкономразви́тия, 'э́то соглаше́ние ста́нет
фи́нишем шестиле́тнего марафо́на перегово́ров Росси́и и Евросою́за
о присоедине́нии к э́той влия́тельной междунаро́дной организа́ции'.
Накану́не глава́ Минэкономразви́тия (МЭРТ) Ге́рман Греф сообщи́л
журнали́стам, что 'большинство́ пози́ций, обсужда́емых сторона́ми,
20 уже́ согласо́ваны'.

В хо́де предыду́щего ра́унда двусторо́нних перегово́ров в Пари́же
на мину́вшей неде́ле Греф и комисса́р Евросою́за по торго́вле
дости́гли, по слова́м еврокомисса́ра, 'суще́ственного прогре́сса по
таки́м ва́жным пробле́мам, как до́ступ европе́йских компа́ний на
25 ры́нок това́ров РФ, а та́кже по вну́тренним росси́йским це́нам
на эне́ргию'. В свою́ о́чередь, Греф подтверди́л, что 'Евросою́з
понима́ет на́ши пози́ции и идёт на компроми́сс'. До́лгое вре́мя
вну́тренние росси́йские це́ны на эне́ргию остава́лись гла́вным
внешнеторго́вым противоре́чием ме́жду двумя́ сторона́ми. Евросою́з
30 тре́бовал от Росси́и их суще́ственного повыше́ния, аргументи́руя
это тем, что 'дешёвая эне́ргия, испо́льзующаяся в промы́шленности,
создаёт преиму́щество для росси́йских това́ров на европе́йском
ры́нке'.

Вступле́ние РФ в ВТО уже́ официа́льно поддержа́ли поря́дка
35 десяти́ стран. Ожида́ется, что Евросою́з к ним присоедини́тся
уже́ сего́дня. На сего́дняшний день чле́нами э́той влия́тельной
организа́ции явля́ются 147 стран, передаёт **ИТАР-ТАСС**.

Izvestiia, Friday 21 May 2004

RUSSIA–EU SUMMIT OPENS IN MOSCOW
The question of entry to the WTO will be decided at it

*The Russian President, Vladimir Putin, will discuss relations between Moscow
and Brussels with leaders of the EU in the Kremlin today. This time the
traditional twice-yearly Russia–EU summit 'will be out of the ordinary'. This
is the first top-level meeting since enlargement of the European Union.*

*There are no plans for separate bilateral talks between the head of the Russian
state and the participants at the summit. Two representatives of Ireland, the
country holding the EU presidency, have come to Moscow for the talks together
with the head of the European Commission.*

*It is expected that a bilateral agreement on the entry of the Russian Federation
into the World Trade Organisation (WTO) will be signed within the framework
of the Russia–EU summit which opens in Moscow today. The Ministry of
Economic Development has said in a statement that 'this agreement will be the
finish of a six-year marathon of talks between Russia and the European Union
on joining this influential international organisation'. On the eve of the summit
the head of the Ministry of Economic Development (MED), German Gref,
told journalists that 'most of the matters being discussed by the [two] sides [had]
already been resolved'.*

*During the previous round of bilateral talks in Paris last week [Mr] Gref and
the European Union Commissioner for Trade 'made substantive progress', in the
words of the Eurocommissioner, 'on important questions such as internal Russian
energy prices as well as access to the Russian market for European companies'. Mr
Gref in turn confirmed that 'the European Commission understands our position
and is making compromises'. For a long time internal Russian energy prices had
been the main point on which the two sides differed when it came to foreign trade.*

The European Commission was demanding that Russia substantially increase these prices on the grounds that 'cheap energy for industry [was] creating an advantage for Russian goods in the European marketplace'.

Russia's entry into the WTO has already been officially supported by some ten countries. It is expected that the European Union will join it as early as today. As of today 147 countries are members of this influential organisation, ITAR-TASS reports.

This is the first of two passages that illustrate the register of political journalism. Unlike the following text (2.10), this report of a political summit is intended to inform rather than to persuade. It is therefore written in a dry, impersonal register very close to that of R3a and R3b, but with an admixture of distinctive political terminology and idiom. Features of R3 in general, or the political variety of it in particular, include the following.

grammatical forms
- Present active participles: проводя́щийся (5), председа́тельствующей (11), открыва́ющегося (12), испо́льзующаяся (31).
- Present passive participles: обсужда́емых (19).
- Imperfective gerund: аргументи́руя (30).
- Reflexive verbs used in a passive sense: открыва́ется (1), реши́тся (2), плани́руется (8), ожида́ется (13, 35).

vocabulary
- The slightly inflated adjective мину́вший in the phrase на мину́вшей неде́ле (22), instead of the neutral про́шлой.

phraseology
- Official turns of phrase (sometimes in quotations of politicians' words): в ра́мках са́ммита (12), соглаше́ние по вступле́нию (13–14), идёт на компроми́сс (27), создаёт преиму́щество для (32).

syntax
- Use of явля́ться as copula (37).
- Occasional complex sentence structure, e.g. как до́ступ европе́йских компа́ний на ры́нок това́ров РФ, а та́кже по вну́тренним росси́йским це́нам на эне́ргию (25–6); Евросою́з тре́бовал от Росси́и их суще́ственного повыше́ния, аргументи́руя э́то тем, что ... (29–31). On the whole, though, syntax is uncomplicated, as befits a text with informative purpose for the general reader.

abbreviation
- ЕС (1, etc.), РФ (14, 25, 34), ВТО (2, 14, 34), МЭРТ (18), ИТА́Р-ТАСС (37).

stump-compounds
- Евросою́з (4, etc.), Еврокоми́ссия (11), Минэкономразви́тия (15, 18), еврокомисса́р (23).

political terminology
- са́ммит (1, etc.), встре́ча на вы́сшем у́ровне (6–7), двусторо́нние встре́чи (9), двусторо́ннее соглаше́ние (13), в хо́де предыду́щего ра́унда двусторо́нних перегово́ров (21).

modish phrases
- э́то соглаше́ние ста́нет фи́нишем ... марафо́на (15–16), суще́ственный прогре́сс (23).

2.10   R3c: political journalism (comment)

The following passage is from a political commentary prompted by the first trial of an American soldier charged with abusing Iraqi detainees.

АРА́БСКАЯ ТЮРЕ́МНАЯ СКА́ЗКА ДЛЯ БУ́ША

И вот тут, со́бственно, для америка́нцев и конкре́тно кома́нды Бу́ша начина́ется большо́е ми́нное по́ле. Америка́нцы пыта́ются вести́ в Ира́ке так называ́емую 'цивилизо́ванную войну́', переходя́щую в 'цивилизо́ванную оккупа́цию' и обра́тно. Составно́й ча́стью

5   тако́й поли́тики в своё вре́мя, в ча́стности, ста́ло то, что на оккупи́рованной террито́рии ме́стному населе́нию без како́й бы то ни́ бы́ло прове́рки на благонадёжность оста́вили на рука́х ору́жие. Я́вно, су́дя по всему́, не отла́жена цензу́ра в ме́стных

10 СМИ. При э́том все пре́жние структу́ры ти́па бы́вшей пра́вящей па́ртии Баа́с и́ли ира́кской а́рмии бы́ли скоропости́жно распу́щены. Лю́ди, привы́кшие подчиня́ться дикта́торской во́ле и 'ходи́ть стро́ем под ружьём', оста́лись не у дел. Никто́ да́же не пыта́лся зада́ться вопро́сом – а вдруг с ни́ми, на цини́чный восто́чный мане́р, мо́жно

15 бы́ло бы договори́ться, сде́лав, опя́ть же рассужда́я цини́чно, послу́шными марионе́тками. Нет, ста́вка в ира́кской войне́ была́ сде́лана дово́льно идеалисти́ческая. И, похо́же, в и́скреннем расчёте на то́, что, возлюби́в америка́нцев за счастли́вое избавле́ние от ва́рвара-дикта́тора, ира́кский наро́д с воодушевле́нием при́мется

20 стро́ить институ́ты гражда́нского о́бщества и демокра́тии. Одна́ко ж почему́-то не случи́лось. Вме́сто благода́рности партиза́нская война́ с кра́йне неприя́тным ислами́стским отте́нком.

В   конте́ксте   восто́чного   мировоззре́ния   и   полити́ческой филосо́фии скоре́е всего́ и коммента́рии, и чи́сто обыва́тельское

25 восприя́тие подо́бных проце́ссов бу́дут совсе́м ины́ми, чем ожида́ют лю́ди с àнглосаксо́нским правосозна́нием. В э́том уви́дят проявле́ние посты́дной сла́бости америка́нцев, уви́дят сти́мул к тому́, что́бы ещё акти́внее боро́ться с даю́щими слаби́ну оккупа́нтами, прибега́я в том числе́ к са́мым ва́рварским ме́тодам – похище́нию люде́й, ка́зням в

30 онла́йне, гро́мким и крова́вым тера́ктам про́тив ми́рных жи́телей в са́мых ра́зных стра́нах и пр. В Вашингто́не, похо́же, забы́ли, как са́ми неда́вно осужда́ли Садда́ма Хусе́йна за то, что он трави́л га́зом восста́вших ку́рдов, а восста́вших ши́итов ира́кская а́рмия вообще́ вы́резала це́лыми селе́ниями с же́нщинами и детьми́. Верне́е,

35 в Вашингто́не забы́ли о том, что америка́нцы пришли́ в страну́, кото́рая до неда́внего вре́мени контроли́ровалась и управля́лась, прито́м контроли́ровалась абсолю́тно, то́лько таки́ми ме́тодами, а други́х ме́тодов она́ вообще́ не зна́ет. Тепе́рь ей предлага́ется оцени́ть все пре́лести 'справедли́вого суда́'. Не оце́нят! С то́чки

40 же зре́ния 'вну́треннего потребле́ния' эффе́кт, коне́чно, мо́жет оказа́ться бо́лее благоприя́тным. Э́то, безусло́вно, ста́нет да́нью америка́нской политкорре́ктности, демократи́ческим тради́циям и про́чно укорени́вшемуся в населе́нии уваже́нию к со́бственной а́рмии, в кото́рой ви́дят институ́т, несу́щий са́мые благоро́дные

45 ми́ссии по всему́ ми́ру. Одна́ко и в Аме́рике найду́тся те, кто все равно́ бу́дет ворча́ть: мол, капра́л Си́витц отду́вается за Ра́мсфелда

и про́чее вашингто́нское нача́льство. Не говоря́ уже́ о том, что сам он мо́жет стать своего́ ро́да 'америка́нским Буда́новым', вы́звав далеко́ не однозна́чную реа́кцию на его́ осужде́ние 'на потре́бу'
50 Ира́ку.

Izvestiia, Friday 21 May 2004

Bush's Arabian prison tale
And this is really where a great minefield begins for the Americans and specifically for Bush's team. The Americans are trying in Iraq to wage a so-called 'civilised war' that turns into a 'civilised occupation' and back again. In particular it was at one time an integral part of this policy to leave weapons in the hands of the local populace of the occupied territory without any checks as to the reliability of the populace. To all appearances the local mass media have not been censored. At the same time all previous structures like the former ruling Baath Party or the Iraqi army have been prematurely dismantled. People who had become accustomed to submitting to the will of a dictator and 'marching under arms' found themselves with no role. Nobody even tried to ask themselves: supposing we could come to an understanding with them, in the cynical oriental manner, and make them obedient puppets, if one again puts it cynically. No, the gamble that was taken in the Iraq war was quite idealistic. And it looks as if it was taken in the sincere belief that the Iraqi people, having come to love the Americans for rescuing them from a barbaric dictator, would enthusiastically set about building the institutions of civil society and democracy. And yet for some reason that hasn't happened. Instead of gratitude there is a guerrilla war with an extremely unpleasant Islamicist complexion.

In the context of the oriental outlook and political philosophy the perception of such trials both by commentators and among ordinary people will most probably be quite different from what people with an Anglo-Saxon legal consciousness expect. They will see in this a sign of shameful American weakness, they will see an encouragement to people to fight more actively against occupiers who have given [the Iraqis] a bit of rope and to resort among other things to the most barbaric methods – kidnapping people, online executions, well-publicised acts of terrorism against peaceful inhabitants in various countries, and so forth. It looks as if they have forgotten in Washington how they themselves were recently condemning Saddam Hussein for gassing Kurdish insurgents and how the Iraqi army in general would slaughter whole villages of Shiite insurgents including women and children. More likely still they have forgotten in Washington that the Americans have come to a country which until recently had been controlled and governed, and controlled absolutely, only by methods of this sort and which knows no other methods. Now it is being suggested to it [Iraq] that it should prize all the delights 'of a fair trial'. They won't prize them!

From the point of view of 'domestic consumption' the effect [of the trial] may of course be more favourable. It will undoubtedly be a sop to American political correctness, democratic traditions and the deep-rooted respect specifically for the army, which people see as an institution that carries out the most noble missions all over the world. However, even in America there are those who will be grumbling: Corporal Sivits, they'll say, is carrying the can for Rumsfeld and other Washington chiefs. Not to mention the fact that he himself might become a sort of 'American Budanov' [a Russian officer accused of shooting a Chechen girl], provoking a reaction to his condemnation 'to satisfy the Iraqis' that will not be straightforward by any means.

Like the previous passage, this text contains various features of high register, including the use of active participles and in particular the prolific use of gerunds. However, its purpose is not merely to inform but also to put a point of view and to this end the author deploys a sprinkling of colloquial expressions, often with a hint of irony. The passage is also notable for the care that the author takes to sustain his argument, especially by means of frequent use of transitional words (see 5.2), and for his maintenance of a sense of contact with the reader by means of various conversational devices. Features of R3 in general and of the political variety of it in particular include the following.

grammatical forms

- Present active participles: переходя́щую (4), даю́щими (28), несу́щий (44).

- Past active participles: привы́кшие (12), восста́вших (33), укорени́вшемуся (43).

- Imperfective gerunds: су́дя (9; in a set expression), рассужда́я (15), прибега́я (28).

- Perfective gerunds: сде́лав (15), возлюби́в (18), вы́звав (48).

syntax

- Use of стать as copula: Составно́й ча́стью тако́й поли́тики . . . ста́ло то, что (5–6).

- Occasional complex sentence structure, especially involving use of some variant of the phrase то́, что, viz. на то́, что (18), за то́, что (32), о то́м, что (35, 47), к тому́, что́бы (27).

phraseology

- Modish expressions: конкре́тно (2), начина́ется большо́е ми́нное по́ле (3), в том числе́ in the sense of *among other things* (38–9).

- Colloquial expressions, used with a hint of incredulity or mockery: а вдруг (14), отдува́ется за (46).

- Phrases that appear to be quotations, or that are placed in quotation marks to highlight them, perhaps with ironic intent: 'цивилизо́ванную войну́', (4), 'цивилизо́ванную оккупа́цию' (5), 'ходи́ть стро́ем под ружьём' (12–13), 'справедли́вого суда́' (39), 'вну́треннего потребле́ния' (40), 'америка́нским Буда́новым' (48), 'на потре́бу' (49).

- Transitional words and phrases which maintain the flow of an argument: При э́том (10), Одна́ко (20, 45), В конте́ксте (23), В э́том (26), Верне́е (34), С то́чки же зре́ния (39–40), Не говоря́ уже́ (47).

- Devices suggestive of engagement with the reader: И вот тут (2), Нет (16), похо́же (17, 31), the exclamation Не оце́нят! (39), коне́чно (40), безусло́вно (41) and the particle мол indicating reported speech (46).

2.11   Classical poetry

It should not be forgotten, even in a book on contemporary usage, that a magnificent literature has been created in Russian over the last two hundred and fifty years and that this literature has greatly enriched the Russian language and continues to inform the consciousness of educated Russians. It is generally agreed among Russians that the outstanding representative of their literature is the poet Alexander Púshkin (1799–1837), who helped to fashion the modern literary language and exercised a seminal influence on many of the great classical and twentieth-century writers. Púshkin's poetry is not well-known to western readers, partly because of the near impossibility of translating it successfully. However, it continues to have a vitality and resonance for educated Russians that it is hard to understand in societies where poetry is generally of narrower appeal. It is therefore by no means a purely academic exercise for the contemporary foreign student of the modern language to emulate educated Russians by learning passages of Púshkin by heart.

We therefore offer here the opening lines of Púshkin's narrative poem 'Мѐдный всáдник' ('The Bronze Horseman'), written in 1833. (The reference is to the statue of Peter the Great (ruled 1696–1725) erected on the bank of the River Nevá in St Petersburg by the eighteenth-century French sculptor Falconet at the behest of Catherine the Great (ruled 1762–96).) Púshkin begins his poem by imagining Peter contemplating the foundation of his northern capital in the marshy wasteland near the mouth of the Nevá. He then paints a sparkling picture of St Petersburg, the city that by Púshkin's lifetime had sprung up there. The extract ends with Púshkin comparing St Petersburg, the 'window' that Peter had cut into Europe, to the older, more conservative and inward-looking capital Moscow, which was associated with traditional Russian institutions such as autocracy and the Orthodox Church.

> На берегý пустьíнных волн
> Стоя́л *Он*, дум вели́ких полн,
> И вдаль гляде́л. Пред ним широ́ко
> Рекá неслáся; бéдный чёлн
> 5 По ней стреми́лся одино́ко.
> По мши́стым, то́пким берегáм
> Черне́ли и́збы здесь и там,
> Прию́т убо́гого чухо́нца;
> И лес, неве́домый лучáм
> 10 В тумáне спря́танного со́лнца
> Круго́м шуме́л.
>
> И ду́мал Он:
> Отсе́ль грози́ть мы бу́дем шве́ду.
> Здесь бу́дет го́род заложён
> 15 На зло́ надме́нному сосе́ду.
> Приро́дой здесь нам суждено́
> В Евро́пу проруби́ть окно́,
> Ного́ю твёрдой стать при мо́ре.
> Сюдá по но́вым им волнáм
> 20 Все флáги в го́сти бу́дут к нам
> И запиру́ем на просто́ре.

Прошло́ сто лет, и ю́ный град,
Полно́щных стран краса́ и ди́во,
Из тьмы́ лесо́в, из то́пи блат
25 Вознёсся пы́шно, горделиво;
Где пре́жде фи́нский рыболо́в,
Печа́льный па́сынок приро́ды,
Оди́н у ни́зких берего́в
Броса́л в неве́домые во́ды
30 Свой ве́тхий не́вод, ны́не там
По оживлённым берега́м
Грома́ды стро́йные тесня́тся
Дворцо́в и ба́шен; корабли́
Толпо́й со всех концо́в земли́
35 К бога́тым при́станям стремя́тся;
В грани́т оде́лася Нева́;
Мосты́ пови́сли над вода́ми;
Темнозелёными сада́ми
Её покры́лись острова́,
40 И пе́ред мла́дшею столи́цей
Поме́ркла ста́рая Москва́,
Как пе́ред но́вою цари́цей
Порфироно́сная вдова́.

On a deserted wave-swept shore, He stood, filled with lofty thoughts, and gazed into the distance. Before him the river sped on its wide course; a humble, lonely skiff moved fast on its surface. On the mossy and swampy banks black huts were dotted here and there – the homes of miserable Finns; and the forest, impenetrable to the rays of the sun shrouded in mist, murmured all around.

And thus He thought: 'From here we shall threaten the Swede; here a city shall be founded, to spite our arrogant neighbour. Here we are destined by Nature to cut a window into Europe; and to gain a firm foothold by the sea. Here, over waters new to them, ships of every flag will come to visit us, and, unconstrained, we shall make merry.'

A hundred years passed, and the young city, the ornament and marvel of the northern climes, rose, resplendent and stately, from the dark forests and the swamps. Where once the Finnish fisherman, Nature's wretched stepson, alone on the low-lying banks, cast his ancient net into unknown waters, now along the banks astir with life tall and graceful palaces and towers cluster; ships from all the ends of the earth hasten in throngs to the rich quays; the Neva has clothed herself in granite; bridges hang above the waters; her islands have become covered with dark-green gardens; and old Moscow has paled before the younger capital, like a dowager clad in purple before a new empress.

Prose translation from *The Penguin Book of Russian Verse*, introduced and
edited by Dimítri Obolénsky

It is impossible in a brief description of Pushkin's language and style to capture the beauty of this passage. Pushkin's verse derives dignity, coherence and harmony from its diction, rhyme (*aababccdcdefefgghcch*, etc.), and rhythm. (The metre is iambic tetrameter with an additional (ninth) syllable in lines with feminine rhyme (i.e. rhyme in which the stress is on the penultimate syllable).) Linguistic features that distinguish this passage from the modern spoken language include:

- Slavonicisms, which give the passage a lofty tone, as befits the subject of national destiny that Púshkin is addressing: Пред (3), град (21), блат (23), Полно́щных (22);

- other examples of poetic diction: the elevated verb вознести́сь (24) and the now obsolete adverb Отсе́ль (12);

- feminine instrumental singular forms, in both nouns and adjectives, in -ою: Ного́ю (17), мла́дшею (39), но́вою (41). These forms are more common in poetry and literary registers than in prose and ordinary speech;

- the forms несла́ся (4) and оде́лася (35), in which the reflexive particle retains its full form in spite of the preceding vowel. These forms too are poetic.

Stylistic features that enhance the dignity of Púshkin's verse, or lend it elegance or charm, or help the poet to develop his themes, include:

- inversions, some of which convey the gravity of the subject-matter: дум вели́ких полн (2): Ного́ю твёрдой (17), Полно́щных стран краса́ и ди́во (22), Грома́ды стро́йные (31);

- symmetry: Из тьмы́ лесо́в, из то́пи блат (23); the sustained contrast between the deserted wasteland that Peter has surveyed (Где пре́жде . . . (25)) and the magnificent city that has subsequently been built there (ны́не там . . . (29)); the comparison of Moscow to a widow, which is achieved by two pairs of lines (39–40 and 41–2) that are perfectly balanced: И пе́ред мла́дшею столи́цей/Поме́ркла ста́рая Москва́,/Как пе́ред но́вою цари́цей/Порфироно́сная вдова́;

- the quasi-deification of Peter the Great, the awesome presence akin to the God of Genesis who is denoted by the pronoun Он (spelt with a capital letter; 2, 11). In both lines the pronoun derives additional weight from its position after the verb;

- personification of the River Nevá, which is clothed in granite (35), and of Moscow (40–2);

- an alliterative quality that enhances the musicality of the verse: Печа́льный па́сынок приро́ды (26); Свой ве́тхий не́вод, ны́не там (29); пе́ред мла́дшею столи́цей/Поме́ркла ста́рая Москва (39–42).

2.12 Literary prose

The passage offered here as an illustration of modern literary prose is from 'Níka', a short story by Víktor Pelévin. In clear, precise, simple prose Pelévin's narrator describes his relationship with Níka (a diminutive form of the female name Veroníka). Níka is a rather simple creature who is never seen with a book and likes eating, sleeping and gazing out of the window. The narrator, who seems to be an artistic intellectual and would like to confide in and share his views with a partner, is disconcerted by Níka's air of indifference and independence, but is attracted by her grace, charm and natural spirituality. As the relationship culminates in betrayal the reader's normal expectations are subverted when it turns out that Níka is not a woman but a cat.

Не то́ чтобы Ни́ка была́ равноду́шна к удо́бствам – она́ с патологи́ческим постоя́нством ока́зывалась в том са́мом кре́сле, куда́ мне хоте́лось сесть, – но предме́ты существова́ли для неё, то́лько пока́ она́ и́ми по́льзовалась, а пото́м исчеза́ли. Наве́рное,

5 поэ́тому у неё не́ было практи́чески ничего́ своего́; я иногда́ ду́мал, что и́менно тако́й тип и пыта́лись вы́вести коммуни́сты дре́вности, не име́я поня́тия, как бу́дет вы́глядеть результа́т их уси́лий. С чужи́ми чу́вствами она́ не счита́лась, но не и́з-за скве́рного скла́да хара́ктера, а оттого́, что ча́сто не дога́дывалась о существова́нии

10 э́тих чувств. Когда́ она́ случа́йно разби́ла стари́нную са́харницу кузнецо́вского фарфо́ра, стоя́вшую на шкафу́, и я че́рез час по́сле э́того неожи́данно для себя́ дал ей пощёчину, Ни́ка про́сто не поняла́, за что её уда́рили, – она́ вы́скочила вон и, когда́ я пришёл извиня́ться, мо́лча отверну́лась к стене́. Для Ни́ки са́харница была́ про́сто

15 усечённым ко́нусом из блестя́щего материа́ла, наби́тым бума́жками; для меня́ – чем-то вро́де копи́лки, где храни́лись со́бранные за всю жизнь доказа́тельства реа́льности бытия́: страни́чка из давно́ не существу́ющей записно́й кни́жки с телефо́ном, по кото́рому я так и не позвони́л; биле́т в кино́ с неото́рванным контро́лем; ма́ленькая

20 фотогра́фия и не́сколько незапо́лненных апте́чных реце́птов. Мне бы́ло сты́дно пе́ред Ни́кой, а извиня́ться бы́ло глу́по; я не знал, что де́лать, и оттого́ говори́л витиева́то и пу́тано:
    – Ни́ка, не серди́сь. Хлам име́ет над челове́ком стра́нную власть. Вы́кинуть каки́е-нибудь тре́снувшие очки́ означа́ет призна́ть, что

25 це́лый мир, уви́денный сквозь них, навсегда́ оста́лся за спино́й, и́ли, наоборо́т и то же са́мое, оказа́лся впереди́, в ца́рстве надвига́ющегося небытия́... Ни́ка, е́сли б ты меня́ понима́ла... Обло́мки про́шлого стано́вятся подо́бием якоре́й, привя́зывающих ду́шу к уже́ не существу́ющему, из чего́ ви́дно, что нет и того́, что обы́чно понима́ют

30 под душо́й, потому́ что...
    Я и́з-под ладо́ни гля́нул на неё и уви́дел, как она́ зева́ет. Бог зна́ет, о чём она́ ду́мала, но мои́ слова́ не проника́ли в её ма́ленькую краси́вую го́лову – с таки́м же успе́хом я мог бы говори́ть с дива́ном, на кото́ром она́ сиде́ла.

Víktor Pelévin, 'Níka', *Generation 'П': Расска́зы* (Moscow:
Vagrius, 2001)

It's not that Nika was indifferent to comfort – with pathological permanency she turned up in the very chair I wanted to sit in – but things existed for her only while she was using them, and then disappeared. That's probably why she had practically nothing of her own; I sometimes thought that this was exactly the type that the communists of old had tried to breed, having no idea what the outcome of their efforts would look like. She did not take account of the feelings of others, and not because her character was bad but because she often did not suspect that they existed. When she accidentally broke an antique sugar-bowl made of Kuznetsov china which used to stand on the dresser, and an hour later I slapped her face without knowing I was going to do it, Nika simply did not understand what she was being hit for – she just rushed out and when I came to say I was sorry, she silently turned her face to the wall. To Nika the sugar-bowl was just a truncated cone made of shiny material and filled with pieces of paper; to me it was a sort of money-box, where the proofs of the reality of being that I had gathered throughout my life were stored: a little page from a note-book that had long ago ceased to exist with a telephone number that I did not ring; a cinema ticket with a stub that had not been torn off; a little photograph and several blank prescriptions. I was ashamed of myself but felt it was stupid to apologise; I did not know what to do and so I spoke in a rhetorical and muddled way:

'Don't be angry, Nika. Old things have strange power over you. To throw away a pair of cracked spectacles is to admit that the whole world that you have viewed through them is left in the past forever, or vice versa, it's ahead of you, in the realm of impending non-being, which is the same thing . . . Nika, if only you could understand me . . . Fragments of the past take on the likeness of moorings that tie us to things that no longer exist, from which you can see that what people usually understand as the soul doesn't exist either, because . . .'

I looked at her from under the palm of my hand and saw her yawn. God knows what she was thinking about, but my words did not penetrate her beautiful little head – I might have had the same effect if I had been speaking to the sofa on which she was sitting.

This is an example of the modern written language in its most highly crafted form. The passage has an elegant, polished quality. It is the antithesis of the spontaneous, broken utterances of colloquial speech and the informal variety of the language of the internet, as exemplified in 2.1 and 2.2 above. The purpose of the user differs too from that of the authors of other texts presented in this section: it is not to inform, as in the formal registers illustrated in 2.5–8 inclusive, but to produce an aesthetic impact on readers.

The passage contains a number of features characteristic of higher registers, especially a gerund and participles of various sorts, viz.:

- imperfective gerund: имёя (7);

- present active participles: существу́ющей (18; see also 29), привя́зывающих (28);

- past active participles: стоя́вшую (11), тре́снувшие (24);

- past passive participle: уви́денный (25); this is not a commonly used form and is less likely to be encountered in R1 and R2 than many participles of this type;

- adjectival phrases before nouns: со́бранные за всю жизнь доказа́тельства реа́льности бытия́ (16–17); из давно́ не существу́ющей записно́й кни́жки (17–18);

- complex syntax with much subordination: то́лько пока́... (4); я иногда́ ду́мал, что... (5–6); не име́я поня́тия, как... (7); Когда́ она́ случа́йно разби́ла... (10); когда́ я пришёл извиня́ться... (13); с телефо́ном, по кото́рому я так и не позвони́л... (18–19); на кото́ром она́ сиде́ла... (34); and the avowedly rhetorical из чего́ ви́дно, что нет и того́, что обы́чно понима́ют под душо́й, потому́ что... (29–30).

On the other hand there are none of the impersonal reflexive verbs used in a passive sense that are common in R3a and R3b. Nor are there any examples of 'threading of cases' or any of the prepositional phrases, formulae and conventions that characterise R3b in particular.

It should be emphasised that although there are no colloquial features in this passage their absence is not a necessary attribute of literary prose, which may of course encompass colloquial and even demotic forms, especially within the direct speech of characters. It is not a prevalence of formal or informal features that distinguishes this register but its aesthetic purpose. In the passage given here this purpose is evident not only in the careful construction of sentences, as illustrated by the use of active participles (which have an especially literary flavour) and by the examples of complex syntax given above, but also in:

- occasional alliterative patterns: с патологи́ческим постоя́нством (1–2), и́з-за скве́рного скла́да (8), стари́нную са́харницу кузнецо́вского фарфо́ра, стоя́вшую на шкафу́ (10–11);

- syntactic balance and symmetry: Не то́ чтобы Ни́ка была́ равноду́шна к удо́бствам... но предме́ты существова́ли для неё (1–3); не и́з-за скве́рного скла́да хара́ктера, а оттого́, что... (8–9); витиева́то и пу́тано (22).

- implicit intertextual reference, to Nabókov, whose sense of the reality of things that have not happened informs details such as the page from the narrator's diary with a telephone number that has never been called and the cinema ticket that has not been used. (Elsewhere in the story there is also explicit and implicit reference to the early twentieth-century writer Búnin, whose presence is felt in the story's subtle eroticism.)

2.13 Language of the internet

А́втор :
Да́та :

Чё вы тут за фуфло́ разво́дите?

5 В интерне́те язык люде́й есте́ственным о́бразом кра́йне си́льно меня́ется, и Ва́ши нездоро́вые иде́и о чистоте́ языка́ не в си́лах э́тому помеша́ть:)

На мой взгляд, гораздо поучительней было бы проанализировать эти искажения под влиянием жизни в интернете и выявить причины таких изменений.

10 Я не имею в виду словечки типа 'онлайн' или 'виртуальный', я про то, что подавляющее большинство меняет свой стиль правописания в пользу 'как слышу так и пишу'... особенно в чатах это сильно распространено, где приходится очень много печатать...

По-моему очень даже замечательно заменять к примеру 'тс, тьс'
15 на 'ц'... например 'общаться-общаца', 'знакомиться-знакомица' Точки в конце предложений ставятся крайне редко, обычно стараются сказать всю мысль одним предложением, и в конце бухнуть смайлик, прямо как я щас:) Кстати 'сейчас-щас' это тоже нечто:)

20 Ну а о целой культуре, с центром на сайте www... я вообще молчу, так как Вы к такому просто не готовы наверняка:)) А будущее то именно там:)

Ну в общем таких вещей очень много, и вряд ли стоит так сразу отмахиваться от подобного подхода к языку в интернете, а вот
25 осветить их ох как стоило бы:) И с деревенщиной из глубинки России тоже никакой связи это не имеет:)

P.S. бывают в инете конечно же и дети, у которых сложное предложение, состоящее из трёх простых, и ни одной запятой:) Это конечно же не то, о чём я говорил. Я как раз имею в виду подобные
30 изменения в языке без искажения смысла и понимаемости.

From:...
Date:...

What a load of crap you're talking.

People's language naturally changes a great deal on the internet, and your unhealthy ideas about linguistic purity can't stop it changing:)

I think it would be much more instructive to analyse the changes that have taken place under the influence of the internet and to bring out the reasons for them. I don't mean words like 'online' or 'virtual', what I'm saying is that the vast majority of people change their spelling and write it like they hear it... that's what people do in chatrooms in particular, where they have to type a lot... For instance I think it's really cool to replace 'тс, тьс' with 'ц'... for example 'общаться-общаца' ['to socialise with'], 'знакомиться-знакомица' [to meet] Full stops are very rarely put at the end of sentences, people usually try to say their whole thought in a single sentence, and bung in a smiley at the end, just like me now [щас]:) Incidentally сейчас-щас [i.e. how the word for 'now' is spelt], that's another thing:)

And as for the whole culture centred on site www...com [a pornographic website], I'm not going to say anything about it because I'm sure you're just not ready for it:)) But that's where the future's at:)

Well there are lots of things like that and one really shouldn't dismiss that sort of approach to language on the internet out of hand, when it would be really worthwhile to bring them out into the open:) And this hasn't got anything to do with being like a yokel out of the depths of Russia either:)

P.S. there are of course also kids on the net for whom a complex sentence is three simple ones without a single comma:) That's not what I've been talking about of course. What I've got in mind is changes in language without distorting the sense and comprehensibility [of it].

This text is a message sent as an email to an officially funded Russian website devoted to maintenance of linguistic standards. The author (who is a male, as the masculine form of the verb in the second sentence of the *post scriptum* indicates) is addressing the subject of linguistic usage on the internet. At the same time he self-consciously uses his message to illustrate distinctive features of the email register. Layout, punctuation, vocabulary, syntax and style, and to a lesser extent orthography, all impart to the message a characteristically informal tone which, given the nature of the site to which the message is addressed, is challenging and slightly subversive.

layout
- As an email, the text is preceded by an indication of the subject, author and date. It closes, as a letter also might, with a *post scriptum*.

- The author strives to accommodate each idea within a single sentence, as he says people try to do when communicating on the internet (16–17). This habit may lend sentences a rather rambling nature (see especially the fourth and sixth sentences; compare the participants in the chatroom conversation at 2.2 above). Moreover, a sentence may itself constitute a separate paragraph. This is the case with the first five sentences of the message, and in the next three paragraphs too the material which follows the opening sentence is not much more than an appended afterthought.

punctuation
- The author relies mainly on commas or многото́чие (three dots) to indicate pauses in his train of thought, avoiding the use of colons and semi-colons.

- More often than not he omits the full stop, thus adhering to what he says is normal practice on the internet (16).

- In lieu of full stops he very frequently uses the expressive device of the emoticon, or smiley (6, 18, 19, 21, 22, 25, 26, 28), another habit characteristic of informal language on the internet to which he draws attention (17–18).

vocabulary
- Internet terminology: интерне́т (4), онла́йн (10), виртуа́льный (10), чат (12), сма́йлик (18), сайт (20) and the abbreviated form ине́те (27).

- Colloquial forms: По-мо́ему (14), к приме́ру (14), бу́хнуть (18), наверняка́ (21), отма́хиваться (24).

- Diminutive forms: слове́чки (10), глуби́нка (25).

- Particles (see 5.4): ну (20, 23); а (20); post-positive -то (but not preceded in the text by the standard hyphen; 21); же (27, 29).

- The demotic form чё (i.e. что) and the slang word фуфло́ in the opening question (3).

- The interjection: ox (25).

syntax

- Syntax is simple. Only one simple subordinating conjunction, так как (21), is used in the message. Links between ideas are established, if they are explicitly established at all, by use of the coordinating conjunctions и (e.g. 5, 17) and а (24).

- The dominant syntactic technique is use of a simple copula, stated or understood, e.g. Ва́ши нездоро́вые иде́и . . . не в си́лах (5); поучи́тельней бы́ло бы проанализи́ровать (7); это си́льно распространено́, (12–13); э́то то́же не́что (18–19); бу́дущее то и́менно там (21–2); Э́то . . . не то́ . . . (28–9).

- Ellipsis (see 11.13): я про то́, in which some verb such as говори́ть is understood (10–11; it should be noted that the preposition про is colloquial as well).

- Other colloquial expressions, e.g. пря́мо как я щас (18), как раз (29), and the colloquial transition word кста́ти (18).

style

- The author follows the casual practices of ordinary speech. For instance, he makes no attempt to avoid repetition, resorting more than once to the same or similar words or expressions: кра́йне (4, 16); (не) име́ю в виду́(10, 29); к приме́ру (14), наприме́р (15); вообще́ (20), в о́бщем (23); сто́ит (23), сто́ило бы (25); коне́чно же (27, 29).

- He seems also wilfully to cultivate an unpolished style. The phrases Ну а о це́лой культу́ре (20) and освети́ть их ох как сто́ило бы (25) seem particularly inelegant on account of the ugly succession of vowel sounds (*u, a, o*) in the first and the grotesque combination of *ikh* and *okh* in the second.

orthography

- The author refers to the practice of spelling words in a way that reflects actual pronunciation as a fact of linguistic life on the internet (11–13). He also commends this practice himself (14–15) and demonstrates it by his spelling of сейча́с as щас (18–19). All the same, the author's innovations in spelling are actually very limited. In general his orthography is careful and correct (cf. the careless and casual orthography of the passage from a chatroom in 2.2 above).

- Nor is the use of capitals in this message unconventional. After all, each new sentence begins with a capital letter (except the first sentence of the *post scriptum*, which in any case the author may deem to have begun with the abbreviation 'P.S.'). Capitals are even used for the first letter of possessive and personal pronouns (Ва́ши, Вы) denoting the addressee(s) of the message, as is conventional in formal correspondence (5, 21; see 7.17).

absence of
formal features

- Features of the higher formal registers are not altogether absent. There is, for instance, a present active participle, состоя́щее (28), and a reflexive verb used in passive sense, ста́вятся (16). However, there is a notable dearth of such features, there being no examples of gerunds, present passive participles, threading of cases, subordinating conjunctions or complex prepositional phrases.

3 Problems of meaning: Russian words

This chapter lists some of the Russian words that give difficulty to the English-speaking student. The difficulty may arise for any one of several reasons. For example, the Russian word may have a wide range of meaning. It may be easily confused with some other Russian word or words. It may be deceptively similar to some English word. It may occur in a plural form whereas its English equivalent occurs in a singular form or vice versa. Or it may denote some phenomenon or concept that is unfamiliar to an English-speaker.

3.1 Homonyms

Homonyms arise in several ways. Firstly, as a result of phonological change a word may come to coincide in sound and form with another word of different origin (as is the case with the pair лук). Secondly, identical forms may develop as a result of the processes of word-formation, by the addition of distinct suffixes to a root (e.g. ударник). Thirdly, it very often happens that an existing word takes on quite a new meaning (e.g. свет).

We also include here a few words (e.g. нога) which strictly speaking are not homonyms but which have a range of meaning that is unexpected to English-speakers.

Many of the examples given here are full homonyms (i.e. they have identical pronunciation and paradigms, e.g. ключ in its different meanings), while others are partial homonyms (i.e. they do not share all the forms which each word possesses, e.g. мир, which does not have plural forms in its sense of *peace*).

3.1.1 Examples of homonyms

блок	*bloc* (esp pol)
	pulley
брак	*matrimony*
	defective goods, rejects
вид	*air, appearance*
	shape, form, state
	view (e.g. from room)
	species
	aspect (gram term)

вре́мя	*time* *tense* (gram term)
вяза́ть	*to tie* *to knit*
гла́дить/погла́дить	*to stroke* (e.g. animal) *to iron* (clothes; pf also вы́гладить)
гнать	*to chase, drive, pursue* *to distil*
го́лос	*voice* *vote*
го́лубь (m)	*pigeon* *dove*
го́рло	*throat* *neck of bottle* (though as a rule the dimin form го́рлышко is used in this sense, except in the phrase пить из горла́ (D), *to drink straight from the bottle*)
горн	*furnace, forge* *bugle*
губа́	*lip* *bay, inlet* (in northern Russia) *tree fungus*
дере́вня	*country* (i.e. not town) *village*
долг	*duty* *debt*
жать	(жму, жмёшь) *to press, squeeze* (жну, жнёшь) *to reap*
же́ртва	*victim* *sacrifice*
Земля́ **земля́**	*Earth* *land, soil*
икра́	*caviar* *calf* (part of leg)
исто́рия	*history* *story* *affair*
ка́рта	*map* *playing card*

клуб	*club* (society)
	puff, cloud (e.g. of dust)
ключ	*key* (to door); also fig, *clue*
	spring, source (of water)
ко́жа	*skin*
	leather
коло́да	*block* (of wood)
	pack of cards
коса́	*plait*
	scythe
	spit (of land)
кося́к	*door-post*
	shoal (of fish)
	herd (of mares with one stallion)
кула́к	*fist*
	strike force (mil)
	wealthy peasant
курс	*course* (programme of study; path along which sth moves)
	year (of course in educational institution)
	rate of exchange (fin)
ла́ска	*caress, kindness*
	weasel (gen pl ла́сок)
лёгкий	*light*
	easy
леса́ (pl; gen лесо́в)	*forests*
	scaffolding
ле́стница	*staircase*
	ladder
лопа́тка	*shovel*
	shoulder-blade
лук	*onion*
	bow (for shooting arrows)
масси́ровать	*to mass* (mil)
	to massage
мате́рия	*matter* (as opposed to spirit; phil)
	cloth
маши́на	*machine*
	car

мир	*peace* *world* *peasant commune* (in pre–revolutionary Russia)
момéнт	*moment* *factor*
наýка	*science* *learning*
наýчный	*scientific* *academic*
начáло	*beginning* *premiss* (i.e. *postulate*)
нéбо	*sky* *heaven*
ногá	*leg* *foot*
носúть	*to carry* *to wear* (clothes)
óпыт	*experience* *experiment*
пар	*steam* *fallow*
пéтля	*loop* *stitch* *buttonhole* *noose*
плитá	*slab* (e.g. paving–stone) *stove* (for cooking)
пол	*floor* *sex*
пóле поля́ (pl)	*field* *margin* (of page) *brim* (of hat)
полúтика	*policy* *politics*
пóлка	*shelf* *weeding*
пóлька	*Polish woman* *polka* (dance)

поро́ть	*to thrash* (pf вы́пороть)
	to unstitch (pf распоро́ть)
предме́т	*subject* (e.g. of study)
	object (thing, topic)
програ́мма	*programme*
	channel (on TV)
	schedule; учéбная програ́мма, *curriculum*
рома́н	*novel*
	romance
рука́	*arm*
	hand
рысь (f)	*trot*
	lynx
свет	*light*
	world
	society (i.e. the fashionable world)
све́тлый	*bright, radiant*
	light (of colours)
ско́рость (f)	*speed*
	gear (of engine)
сло́во	*word*
	speech, e.g. свобо́да сло́ва, *freedom of speech*; предоста́вить кому́-н сло́во, *to call on sb to speak*
сове́т	*advice*
	soviet (i.e. council)
среда́	*Wednesday* (acc sg сре́ду)
	milieu, environment (acc sg среду́)
стол	*table*
	bureau, office (e.g. па́спортный стол, *passport bureau*)
	board, cuisine (e.g. шве́дский стол, *Smörgåsbord*, lit *Swedish table*)
тень (f)	*shadow*
	shade
тита́н	*titanium* (chemical element)
	Titan (in Greek mythology)
	boiler (old-fashioned bathroom water heater)
трава́	*grass*
	herb
туши́ть	*to extinguish, put out* (pf потуши́ть)
	to braise, stew

тяжёлый	*heavy*
	difficult
уда́рник	*member of strike force* (mil); *shock-worker*
	firing-pin (of gun)
	drummer (in pop group; R1)
учёный	*scientist*
	scholar, learned person
ша́шка	*draught* (in boardgame); игра́ть в ша́шки, *to play draughts*
	sabre
язы́к	*tongue*
	language

3.1.2 Homonyms with different plural forms

In a number of nouns the different meanings that the noun may have are distinguished by use of different nominative plural forms (and, if the noun denotes an inanimate object, this form is identical with the accusative plural form).

- In many such instances one plural form has the usual ending for masculine nouns in -**ы** or -**и** and the other has the stressed ending -**а́** or -**я́** (see 9.1.6), e.g.

nom pl in -ы/-и		**nom pl in -а́/-я́**	
бо́ровы	*hogs, fat men*	**борова́**	*flues*
ко́рпусы	*torsos, hulls*	**корпуса́**	*corps, blocks* (buildings)
ла́гери	*(political) camps*	**лагеря́**	*holiday/prison camps*
мехи́ (pl only)	*bellows*	**меха́**	*furs*
о́бразы	*images*	**образа́**	*icons*
о́рдены	*monastic orders*	**ордена́**	*medals*
по́ясы	*geographical belts*	**пояса́**	*belts* (clothing)
про́воды	*send-off* (no sg)	**провода́**	*(electrical) leads*
про́пуски	*omissions*	**пропуска́**	*passes, permits*
со́боли	*sables* (animals)	**соболя́**	*sables* (furs)
счёты	*abacus* (no sg)	**счета́**	*bills, accounts*
то́ки	*(electric) currents*	**тока́**	*threshing-floors; also birds' mating-places*
то́ны	*tones* (sound)	**тона́**	*tones* (colour)
то́рмозы	*impediments*	**тормоза́**	*brakes* (of vehicle)
хле́бы	*loaves*	**хлеба́**	*crops*
цветы́	*flowers*	**цвета́***	*colours*

*The sg form is цвето́к in the meaning *flower* but цвет in the meaning *colour*.

• Some partial homonyms have other variant plural forms, e.g.

		nom/acc pl	**gen pl**
коле́но	*knee*	коле́ни	коле́ней
	joint (in pipe)	коле́нья	коле́ньев
	bend (in river)	коле́на	коле́н
	generation (obs)	коле́на	коле́н
ко́рень (m)	*root*	ко́рни	корне́й
	roots (used for culinary or medicinal purposes)	коре́нья	коре́ньев
лист	*leaf*	ли́стья	ли́стьев
	sheet of paper	листы́	листо́в
по́вод	*ground, cause (for)*	по́воды	по́водов (к)
	rein	пово́дья	пово́дьев
су́дно	*vessel, craft*	суда́	судо́в
	chamberpot	су́дна	су́ден

3.2 Homophones and homoforms

Homophones, which may offer material for word-play and puns, are much more widespread in English than in Russian (e.g. *bare, bear; right, write*). However, even in Russian they may occur as a result, for example, of а́канье (see e.g. компа́ния), or и́канье (see e.g. леса́), or the devoicing of final voiced consonants (see e.g. гриб), or even the coincidence of a word and a phrase (e.g. немо́й, *dumb* and не мой, *not my*). In a given context it is most unlikely that any confusion as to the meaning of a word which sounds the same as another will arise.

Homoforms (see e.g. вожу́) arise quite frequently as a result of the morphological complexity of Russian.

A very small number of Russian examples is given here to illustrate both these phenomena.

вожу́	*I take on foot* (from води́ть)
	I take by transport (from вози́ть)
гриб	*mushroom*
грипп	*influenza*
груздь (m)	*milk-agaric* (type of mushroom)
грусть (f)	*sadness, melancholy*
дне	prep sg of день, *day*
	prep sg of of дно, *bottom*

дог	*Great Dane*
док	*dock*
есть	(infin) *to eat* (3rd pers sg and pl) *there is/are* (3rd pers sg) *is* (see 4.2)
кампа́ния	*campaign*
компа́ния	*company* (in various senses)
леса́	nom/acc pl of лес, *forest*; also *scaffolding*
лиса́	*fox*
лечу́	*I fly* (from лете́ть) *I cure* (from лечи́ть)
луг	*meadow*
лук	*onion, bow* (see 3.1.1)
печь	f noun, *stove* infin, *to bake*
пила́	*saw* (tool) f past tense of пить, *to drink*
плод	*fruit*
плот	*raft*
поро́г	*threshold*
поро́к	*vice* (fault, sin)
походи́ть	(impf) *to resemble* (pf) *to walk around for a bit*
пруд	*pond*
прут	*twig*
род	*kin, sort, kind, genus, gender*
рот	*mouth*
ста́ли	gen/dat/prep sg of сталь (f), *steel* pl past-tense form of стать, *to become*
стих	*line of verse* m past-tense form of сти́хнуть, *to abate, die down, subside*
столб	*post, pole, column, pillar*
столп	*pillar* (fig, e.g. столп о́бщества, *a pillar of society*)

сходи́ть	(impf) *to come down* (pf) *to go (there and back)*
три	*three* 2nd pers imp of тере́ть, *to rub*
труд **трут**	*labour* *tinder*
туш **тушь** (f)	*flourish* (mus) *Indian ink*
ша́гом	instr sg of шаг, *step, pace* adv, *at walking pace*

3.3 Homographs

Russian has many pairs of homographs, a large number of which result from morphological coincidence (see e.g. адреса, воды, below). Only a very small sample is given here to illustrate the phenomenon.

а́дреса **адреса́**	gen sg of а́дрес, *address* nom pl of а́дрес
а́тлас **атла́с**	*atlas* *satin*
воды́ **во́ды**	gen sg of вода́, *water* nom/acc pl of вода́
за́мок **замо́к**	*castle* *lock*
и́рис **ири́с**	*iris* (flower) *toffee*
мо́ря **моря́**	gen sg of мо́ре, *sea* nom/acc pl of мо́ре
му́ка **мука́**	*torment* *flour*
но́шу **ношу́**	acc sg of но́ша, *burden* 1st pers sg of носи́ть, *to carry*
о́рган **орга́н**	*organ* (biol, pol) *organ* (mus)

пи́сать (vulg)	*to piss* (пи́саю, пи́саешь, etc.)
писа́ть	*to write* (пишу́, пи́шешь, etc.)
пла́чу	1st pers sg of пла́кать, *to cry*
плачу́	1st pers sg of плати́ть, *to pay*
по́ра	*pore*
пора́	*it is time (to)*
по́сле	preposition meaning *after*
после́	prep sg of посо́л, *ambassador, envoy*
по́том	instr sg of пот, *sweat*
пото́м	adv, *then*
сбе́гать	pf, *to run (there and back)*
сбега́ть	impf, *to run down*
се́ло	n past tense of сесть, *to sit down*
село́	*village*
сло́ва	gen sg of сло́во, *word*
слова́	nom pl of сло́во
со́рок	*forty*
соро́к	gen pl of соро́ка, *magpie*
у́же	short comp form of у́зкий, *narrower*
уже́	*already*

3.4 Paronyms

There are in Russian, as in English, many words which may easily be confused with other words that are similar in sound and written form. The problem is compounded when, as is often the case, the two words have related or similar meaning.

This section provides a small sample of such words, including a few whose difference is mainly one of register rather than meaning. In many cases the difference between two forms consists in the fact that one is a Slavonicism and the other a Russian form (e.g. граждани́н, горожа́нин; see Glossary). In others the difference is merely one of gender (e.g. жар, жара́). Some of the less common meanings a Russian word may have are omitted. Not included are verbal clusters derived from the same root by the addition of various prefixes (on which see 8.3).

банк	*bank*	**ба́нка**	*jar, can*
бли́зкий	*near, close*	**бли́жний**	*neighbouring*; Бли́жний восто́к, *Middle East*
бре́мя	*burden*	**вре́мя**	*time, tense*
вида́ть (R1)	*to see*	**ви́деть**	*to see*

Note: вида́ть is used mainly in the infinitive or the past tense and tends to have a frequentative sense.

во́дный	*relating to water*, e.g. во́дное по́ло, *water polo*	**водяно́й**	*aquatic, living in water*, e.g. водяна́я пти́ца, *water bird*; *operated by water*, e.g. водяна́я ме́льница, *water-mill*
во́рон	*raven*	**воро́на**	*crow*
воскресе́нье	*Sunday*	**воскресе́ние**	*resurrection*
высо́кий	*high, tall*	**высо́тный**	*high-rise*, e.g. of building
гла́вный	*main, principal*	**головно́й**	*relating to the head*, e.g. головна́я боль, *headache*

Note: in R1 the form головно́й may also be encountered in the sense *main*, e.g. in the phrase головно́е предприя́тие, *head office*.

горожа́нин	*town-dweller*	**граждани́н**	*citizen*
горя́чий	*hot*	**горя́щий**	*burning*
дальнови́дный	*far-sighted* (prescient)	**дальнозо́ркий**	*long-sighted*
дипломати́ческий	*relating to diplomacy*	**дипломати́чный**	*tactful, shrewd*
драмати́ческий	*relating to drama*	**драмати́чный**	*dramatic, sensational*
дух	*spirit*	**духи́** (pl; gen духо́в)	*scent, perfume*
душ	*shower*	**душа́**	*soul*
жа́лоба	*complaint*	**жа́лованье**	*salary*
жар	*heat* (heat of day, fervour, ardour)	**жара́**	*hot weather*
жесто́кий	*cruel*	**жёсткий**	*hard, tough*
замеча́тельный	*remarkable, splendid*	**значи́тельный**	*significant, considerable*
за́навес	*curtain* (large, e.g. in theatre)	**занаве́ска**	*curtain* (e.g. in house)

здоро́вый	*healthy*	**здра́вый**	*sensible;* здра́вый смысл, *common sense*
земе́льный	*relating to land*	**земляно́й**	*made of earth, earthen*
знамена́тельный	*important, momentous*	**знамени́тый**	*famous, renowned*
изме́на	*betrayal, treachery*	**измене́ние**	*change* (see 4.1)
импе́рский	*imperial*	**импера́торский**	*relating to an emperor*
карье́р	*career* (gallop), e.g. во весь карье́р, *at full speed*	**карье́ра**	*career* (progress in job, etc.)
коро́ткий	*short* (physical)	**кра́ткий**	*brief* (abstract)

ледови́тый	in phrase Се́верный Ледови́тый океа́н, *the Arctic Ocean*
ледо́вый	*taking place on / amid ice,* e.g. Ледо́вое побо́ище, *the Battle on the Ice* (1242); ледо́вые пла́вания, *Arctic voyages*
ледяно́й	*consisting of ice,* e.g. ледяна́я ко́рка, *an ice layer; covered in ice,* e.g. ледяна́я верши́на, *an icy peak; very cold* (also fig), e.g. ледяно́й взгляд, *an icy look*

мане́р (R1)	*manner* (way), e.g. на ру́сский мане́р, *in the Russian manner*	**мане́ра**	*manner* (style); **мане́ры** (pl), *manners*
матема́тик	*mathematician*	**матема́тика**	*mathematics*
материалисти́ческий	*materialist* (relating to matter)	**материалисти́чный**	*materialistic* (coveting goods)
мел	*chalk*	**мель** (f)	*shoal, bank, shallows*
мех	*fur*	**мох**	*moss*

ми́рный	*peaceful*
мирово́й	*relating to the world,* e.g. мирова́я война́, *world war*
всеми́рный	*world-wide*

мол	*pier* also *he says, they say* (particle; see 5.4)	**моль** (f)	*(clothes-)moth*

молодо́й	*young*
мла́дший	*younger, junior*
молодёжный	*relating to the young*
моложа́вый	*young-looking*

му́ха	*fly*		
му́шка	dimin of му́ха; also *beauty-spot*; also *foresight* (on gun), as in взять на му́шку, *to take aim*		
мо́шка	*midge*		
надева́ть/наде́ть	*to put on* (clothing)	**одева́ть/оде́ть**	*to dress* (trans), e.g. оде́ть ребёнка, *to dress a child*
не́бо	*sky, heaven*	**нёбо**	*palate*
неве́жественный	*ignorant*	**неве́жливый**	*rude, impolite*
оби́дный	*offensive*	**оби́дчивый**	*touchy, easily offended*
опа́сливый	*cautious, wary*	**опа́сный**	*dangerous*
осно́ва	*base, basis, foundation*	**основа́ние**	*founding; ground, reason;* also *foot* (of mountain, column)
остава́ться/оста́ться	*to remain, stay behind*		
оставля́ть/оста́вить	*to leave behind*		
остана́вливать(ся)/ останови́ть(ся)	*to stop; transitive form also means to stay,* e.g. в гости́нице, *in a hotel*		
отстава́ть/отста́ть	*to lag behind*		
оста́нки (pl; gen оста́нков)	*remains* (of dead person)	**оста́тки** (pl; gen оста́тков)	*remnants, leftovers*
оте́чество	*fatherland*	**о́тчество**	*patronymic*
паде́ж	*case* (gram)	**падёж**	*cattle plague*
пар	*steam, fallow*	**па́ра**	*pair, couple*
передава́ть/переда́ть	*to pass, transfer*	**предава́ть/преда́ть**	*to betray*
пла́мя	*flame (see 9.1.10)*	**пле́мя**	*tribe (see 9.1.10)*
поднима́ть	*to lift*	**подыма́ть (R1)**	*to lift* (esp with difficulty)
поли́тик	*politician, policy maker*	**поли́тика**	*politics*
полити́ческий	*relating to politics*	**полити́чный**	*careful, tactful*
поня́тливый	*quick to understand*	**поня́тный**	*understandable, intelligible*
посту́пок	*act, deed*	**просту́пок**	*misbehaviour*
пра́здничный	*festive*	**пра́здный**	*idle, vain*

практи́ческий	*practical, i.e. relating to practice, e.g. of help, work*	**практи́чный**	*practical, i.e. having experience, expertise*
прах	*ashes, remains; dust (rhet)*	**по́рох**	*powder*
проводи́ть/провести́	*to conduct, carry out, trick*	**производи́ть/ произвести́**	*to produce, promote; but in the expression* произвести́ о́пыт, *to conduct an experiment*
прохла́дный	*cool*	**холо́дный**	*cold*
проч́сть (pf; R1)	*to read*	**прочита́ть** (pf; R2)	*to read*
ра́вный	*equal*	**ро́вный**	*flat, level, even, exact*
развито́й	*developed, i.e. mature, advanced*	**разви́тый**	*developed (i.e. past pass part of* разви́ть)
рот	*mouth*	**ро́та**	*company* (mil)
свиста́ть (impf; R1)	*to whistle*	**свисте́ть** (impf; R2)	*to whistle*
середи́на	*middle*	**среда́**	*Wednesday milieu, environment* (see 3.1.1)
слу́шать/послу́шать **слы́шать/услы́шать** **слыха́ть** (R1)	*to listen (to)* *to hear* *to hear*		

Note: слыха́ть is used mainly in the infinitive or the past tense and tends to have a frequentative sense.

сосе́дний	*neighbouring*	**сосе́дский**	*belonging to one's neighbour*
состоя́ть (impf)	*to consist (in some contexts to be; see 4.2)*	**состоя́ться** (pf)	*to take place*
сто́ить	*to cost, be worth*	**стоя́ть**	*to stand*
сторона́	*side*	**страна́**	*country* (nation)
теку́чий	*fluid, unstable*	**теку́щий**	*current, present*
те́хник	*technician*	**те́хника**	*technique, technology*
уда́чливый	*lucky*	**уда́чный**	*successful, felicitous*
фи́зик	*physicist*	**фи́зика**	*physics*

хорони́ть (impf)	*to inter*	храни́ть (impf)	*to keep, preserve*
экономи́ческий	*relating to economics*	экономи́чный	*economical*
эле́ктрик	*electrician*	электри́чка	*suburban electric train*

3.5 *Faux amis* (*ло́жные друзья́*)

There are in Russian many words of foreign origin which bring to mind an English word but in fact have or may have quite a different meaning from the English cognate. This section lists a few of these, together with the usual Russian equivalents of the English word with which confusion has arisen.

авантю́ра	*shady enterprise*	**adventure**	приключе́ние
агита́ция	*(political) agitation*	**agitation**	волне́ние (anxiety) т632вога (alarm)
адеква́тный	*identical, appropriate, good*	**adequate**	доста́точный
акаде́мик	*member of the Academy of Sciences*	**academic**	университе́тский преподава́тель (university teacher) учёный (scholar)
академи́ческий	*academic (relating to an academy or to academia)*	**academic**	учёный (scholarly) теорети́ческий (of no practical significance) абстра́ктный (abstract)
аккомпани́ровать (impf) + dat	*to accompany (musically only)*	**to accompany**	провожа́ть/проводи́ть (go with) сопровожда́ть (go with)
аккура́тный	*punctual, neat, tidy, conscientious*	**accurate**	то́чный (precise) ме́ткий (of shooting)
актуа́льный	*topical, pressing*	**actual**	действи́тельный (real) настоя́щий (genuine) существу́ющий (existing)
а́кция	*share (i.e. equity), also political or diplomatic action*	**action** (i.e. an act)	де́йствие, посту́пок
анги́на	*tonsillitis*	**angina**	грудна́я жа́ба
арти́кль (m)	*article (gram term)*	**article**	in other senses: see 4.1
арти́ст	*(performing) artist*	**artist**	in other sense: see 4.1
ассисте́нт	*junior teacher (in higher educational institution)*	**assistant**	помо́щник замести́тель (m; deputy)

ата́ка	*attack* (mil)	**attack**	in other senses: see 4.1
аудие́нция	*audience* (with important person)	**audience**	зри́тели (pl; gen зри́телей; spectators)
афе́ра	*shady transaction*	**affair**	де́ло (matter) рома́н (love affair)
бала́нс	*balance* (econ, fin)	**balance**	равнове́сие (equilibrium)
бассе́йн	*swimming pool, river-basin*	**basin**	таз (washbasin) ми́ска (bowl)
бискви́т	*sponge-cake*	**biscuit**	пече́нье (sweet) суха́рь (m; rusk)
бланк	*form* (to be filled in)	**blank**	про́пуск (omission) пробе́л (in memory) холосто́й заря́д (bullet)
гениа́льный	*of genius*	**genial**	весёлый (jolly) добро́душный (good-natured) доброжела́тельный (benevolent) прия́тный (pleasant) симпати́чный (likeable, nice)
го́спиталь (m)	*(military) hospital*	**hospital**	больни́ца
гума́нный	*humane*	**human**	челове́ческий
дека́да	*ten-day period*	**decade**	десятиле́тие
инструкти́вный	*instructional*	**instructive**	поучи́тельный (edifying) поле́зный (useful)
ка́мера	*chamber, cell, video camera* (R1)	**camera**	фотоаппара́т
капита́л	*capital* (fin)	**capital**	столи́ца (city)
капита́льный	*main, fundamental,* e.g. капита́льный ремо́нт, *major repair*	**capital**	прописна́я бу́ква (letter) Note: сме́ртная казнь, *capital punishment*
карто́н	*cardboard*	**carton**	коро́бка
кекс	*fruit-cake*	**cake**	торт
компози́тор	*composer*	**compositor**	набо́рщик
консервато́рия	*conservatoire*	**conservatory**	оранжере́я, вера́нда
контро́ль (m)	*supervision*	**control**	руково́дство (management) власть (f; power) влия́ние (influence)
конфу́з	*embarrassment*	**confusion**	беспоря́док (disorder) пу́таница (muddle)

			неразбери́ха (R1; muddle)
			толкотня́ (R1; pushing)
корре́ктный	*polite, proper*	**correct**	пра́вильный
кросс	*cross-country race*	**cross**	крест
луна́тик	*sleep-walker*	**lunatic**	сумасше́дший
			умалишённый
магази́н	*shop*	**magazine**	журна́л
майо́р	*major*	**mayor**	мэр
манифеста́ция	*demonstration*	**manifestation**	проявле́ние
момента́льный	*instantaneous*	**momentous**	знамена́тельный
мотори́ст	*mechanic*	**motorist**	автомобили́ст
моцио́н	*exercise* (physical)	**motion**	движе́ние
объекти́в	*lens* (of camera)	**objective**	цель (f)
патети́ческий	*having passion, pathos*	**pathetic**	тро́гательный (touching)
			печа́льный (sad)
			жа́лкий (pitiable)
перспекти́ва (see also проспе́кт)	*perspective* (in art), also *outlook, prospect*	**perspective**	перспекти́ва (in art only)
			то́чка зре́ния (point of view)
поэ́ма	*narrative poem*	**poem** (short)	стихотворе́ние
прете́нзия	*claim, complaint, charge,* as well as *pretension*	**pretension**	прете́нзия (claim)
			притяза́ние (claim)
			претенцио́зность (f; pretentiousness)
принципиа́льный	*of principle, principled,* e.g. принципиа́льный челове́к, *person of integrity*	**principal**	гла́вный (main)
			веду́щий (leading)
про́ба	*test, model* (i.e. *prototype*), *sample*	**probe**	зонд (med, geol)
			иссле́дование (exploration)
проспе́кт	*avenue;* also *prospectus, summary*	**prospect**	перспекти́ва
репети́ция	*rehearsal*	**repetition**	повторе́ние
ре́плика	*rejoinder, cue* (theat)	**replica**	то́чная ко́пия
реце́пт	*prescription* (med), *recipe*	**receipt**	получе́ние (receiving)
			распи́ска, квита́нция (written acknowledgement)
симпати́чный	*nice* (of person)	**sympathetic**	сочу́вствующий (compassionate)
			отзы́вчивый (responsive)
			одобря́ющий (approving)

сквер	small public garden in town	**square**	пло́щадь (f; place) квадра́т (shape)
стаж	length of service, probation	**stage**	сце́на (theat) эта́п (of process)
стул	chair; also stool (med)	**stool**	табуре́тка
схе́ма	diagram, outline, plan, (electrical) circuit; схемати́ческий may mean oversimplified, e.g. схемати́ческий подхо́д, simplistic approach; микросхе́ма, microchip	**scheme**	план (plan) програ́мма (plan) прое́кт (plan) за́мысел (plot) махина́ция (intrigue) в поря́дке веще́й, in the scheme of things подбо́р цвето́в, colour scheme, lit choice of colours
те́зис	argument, point, e.g. основны́е те́зисы, main points, as well as thesis	**thesis**	диссерта́ция (dissertation) те́зис (only in sense of contention, proposition)
темпера́ментный	spirited	**temperamental**	капри́зный (capricious) с но́ровом (obstinate, awkward)
трансля́ция	transmission, relay	**translation**	перево́д
фа́брика	factory	**fabric**	ткань (f)
фамилья́рный	overfamiliar, offhand	**familiar**	знако́мый (known) изве́стный (well-known) привы́чный (customary)
фра́кция	faction	**fraction**	части́ца (small part) дробь (f; math)
характери́стика	reference (testimonial)	**characteristic**	характе́рная черта́
эксперти́за	(expert) examination, analysis, study, test, e.g. эксперти́за на СПИД, AIDS test	**expertise**	зна́ние (knowledge) компете́нтность (f; competence) о́пыт (experience)
электора́т	may correspond to Eng electorate, i.e. all voters, or may have narrower meaning, i.e. group of like-minded voters, constituency, e.g. коммунисти́ческий электора́т, communist voters	**electorate**	избира́тели (pl; electors)

3.6 Problems of number

3.6.1 Nouns with plural form only

Many nouns exist which in English have a singular form but in Russian have only a plural form, at least when they have certain meanings. The word for *a clock*, for example, is **часы** (gen **часо́в**). Such nouns may belong to any of the declension types. In the lists below genitive forms (which cannot be deduced from the nominative forms) are given in brackets.

воро́та (воро́т)	*gate*
вы́боры (вы́боров)	*election*
гра́бли (гра́блей)	*rake*
де́ньги (де́нег)	*money*
джу́нгли (джу́нглей)	*jungle*
дрова́ (дров)	*firewood*
духи́ (духо́в)	*scent, perfume*
носи́лки (носи́лок)	*stretcher*
обо́и (обо́ев)	*wallpaper*
пери́ла (пери́л)	*handrail*
по́хороны (похоро́н)	*funeral*
про́воды (про́водов)	*send-off*, i.e. farewell gathering
са́ни (сане́й)	*sledge*
сли́вки (сли́вок)	*cream*
су́мерки (су́мерек)	*twilight*
су́тки (су́ток)	*day* (24-hour period)
схо́дни (схо́дней)	*gangway, gangplank*
счёты (счётов)	*abacus*
черни́ла (черни́л)	*ink*
ша́хматы (ша́хмат)	*chess*
щи (щей)	*cabbage soup*
я́сли (я́слей; in R1 also ясле́й)	*crèche*

Many Russian nouns which are generally used only in a plural form do correspond to English nouns which also have a plural form, e.g.

брю́ки (брюк)	*trousers*
весы́ (весо́в)	*scales*
за́морозки (за́морозков)	*light frosts*
кавы́чки (кавы́чек)	*quotation marks*
кани́кулы (кани́кул)	*holidays*
коньки́ (конько́в)	*skates*

ку́дри (кудре́й)	*curls*
лохмо́тья (лохмо́тьев)	*rags*
лю́ди (люде́й)	*people*
но́жницы (но́жниц)	*scissors*
очки́ (очко́в)	*spectacles*
перегово́ры (перегово́ров)	*talks, negotiations*
стихи́ (стихо́в)	*verses*
хло́поты (хлопо́т)	*efforts, trouble*
хло́пья (хло́пьев)	*snowflakes, cornflakes*

3.6.2   Nouns with singular form only

Some Russian nouns denoting fruits or vegetables give particular difficulty to the English-speaking student because they are used collectively and, in R2–3 at least, have only a singular form, e.g.

брусни́ка	*red whortleberries, cowberries*
ви́шня	*cherries*
горо́х	*peas*
ежеви́ка	*blackberries*
земляни́ка	*(wild) strawberries*
капу́ста	*cabbage*
карто́фель (m)	*potatoes*
клубни́ка	*(cultivated) strawberries*
клю́ква	*cranberries*
крыжо́вник	*gooseberries*
лук	*onions*
мали́на	*raspberries*
морко́вь (f)	*carrots*
кра́сная сморо́дина	*redcurrants*
чёрная сморо́дина	*blackcurrants*

If it is necessary to refer to one particular unit of the thing in question then one may in some instances use a related word with the suffix -ина (e.g. горо́шина, карто́фелина), or one may insert the word шту́ка, which refers to an individual unit, e.g. пять штук, five of the thing to which reference is being made.

Note 1   In R1 plural forms of some of these nouns may be encountered, e.g. пять ви́шен, *five cherries*; де́сять ежеви́к, *ten blackberries*.

2   There are also of course many nouns denoting fruit and vegetables that do have plural forms, e.g. апельси́н, *orange*; огуре́ц, *cucumber*; помидо́р, *tomato*; я́блоко, *apple* (nom/acc pl апельси́ны, огурцы́, помидо́ры, я́блоки respectively).

3.7   Russian words difficult to render in English

This section deals with a number of common Russian words that are not easy to translate into English because they do not obviously have direct English equivalents. Many of these words without equivalents (безэквивалéнтые словá) are culture-specific. That is to say they denote phenomena, values, preoccupations or a way of viewing the world that are unfamiliar to English-speakers. Their meaning and nuances may in some cases be fully understood only by reference to certain historic or cultural factors that cannot be properly explored here. In addition to such words that are clearly culture-specific we include a few others whose meaning cannot be conveyed by a single English word, so that they have to be rendered in English by a phrase or descriptive paraphrase. We offer various possible translations of the words given, for use in different contexts. In some instances we also provide a brief gloss.

азáртный	*adventurous, animated, passionate*; describes sb who gets carried away with sth (see also увлекáться below) or is prepared to stake a lot on sth, e.g. азáртный человéк = gambler (fig); also азáртные и́гры: *games of chance, gambling*
бездорóжье	absence of roads; bad condition of roads; season when roads are impassable
белорýчка	lit *person with white hands*, i.e. sb who shirks rough or dirty work; *softie*
бýдни	lit *weekdays, working days*; fig humdrum life, colourless existence, the everyday; antonym of прáздники (see below in this section)
быт	*way of life; everyday life, daily routine, habitual pattern of life; drudgery*. The word (which is derived from the verb быть) evokes the material world and a static conservative form of existence.
вóля	*freedom, liberty, free will*. The word implies lack of constraint, natural freedom, even a state close to anarchy.
выступáть/ вы́ступить	to make some public statement or appearance, e.g. вы́ступить в парлáменте, *to speak in Parliament*; вы́ступить в печáти, *to write in the press*; вы́ступить защи́тником, *to appear for the defence* (in court); вы́ступить по рáдио, *to be interviewed on/give a talk on radio*; вы́ступить по телеви́дению, *to appear on television*; вы́ступить с доклáдом, *to give a paper*; вы́ступить с рéчью, *to make a speech*.
ги́бель (f)	*destruction, ruin, wreck, downfall, death* (esp tragic, violent death in war or as a result of an accident)

	English lacks a general noun from the verb *to perish* (погиба́ть/поги́бнуть).
дежу́рная, дежу́рный	person on duty, e.g. at the entrance to a block of flats or to a hotel corridor; the word suggests sb who keeps watch
де́ятель (m)	lit sb who does sth, but usually only meaningful in combination with some adjective, e.g. госуда́рственный де́ятель, *statesman*; литерату́рный де́ятель, *writer, journalist, man of letters*; обще́ственный де́ятель, *public figure*; педагоги́ческий де́ятель, *educator*; полити́ческий де́ятель, *politician*
душе́вный	*sincere, cordial, heartfelt, having soul* (душа́)
закономе́рный	*natural*, in the sense of *bound to happen*; in conformity with some law (i.e. a natural order of things, not necessarily or even primarily a juridical order); *normal* or *regular* in one of these senses; cf. зако́нный, *legitimate*, i.e. in accordance with the criminal or civil law
засто́й	*stagnation* (fig), i.e. political, economic, intellectual stagnation. The word evokes the climate of the Bréznev period of the 1970s as Russians perceived it at the time of *perestróika* in the 1980s.
земля́к/земля́чка	*fellow countryman, fellow-townsman, fellow-villager*; a person from the same district
злой	*evil, bad, wicked, malicious, vicious, unkind, ill-natured, angry*. There is no adjective in English that conveys the full range of meaning of злой, which may be best defined as the antonym of до́брый.
интеллиге́нция	*intelligentsia, professional class(es)*. The word denotes a group of intellectuals who are politically engaged but at the same time are excluded from power and who feel a sense of moral responsibility for the state of their society.
командиро́вка	*business trip, mission, posting*
крупа́	*groats*; a general word for grain from which *kasha* can be made
кру́пный	*big, large, large-scale, outstanding, important; major, well-known*. The adjective implies that all the elements of a thing are large, e.g. кру́пный рис, *long-grain rice*; antonym of ме́лкий (see below in this section).

лицо́	*face; person,* e.g. гражда́нское лицо́, *civilian;* де́йствующее лицо́, *character* (in play); должностно́е лицо́, *an official;* духо́вное лицо́, *clergyman;* подставно́е лицо́, *dummy, man of straw.* Note also: физи́ческое лицо́, *physical person* (leg); юриди́ческое лицо́, *juridical person* (leg).
ли́чность (f)	*personality, individual*
любова́ться/ полюбова́ться	to enjoy looking at sth. The verb may sometimes be translated by Eng *to admire* but it implies feasting one's eyes on sth, including natural beauty.
ме́лкий	*small, fine* (of rain, sand); also *petty, shallow.* The adjective implies that sth is small in all its parts, small-proportioned; antonym of кру́пный (see above in this section).
мещани́н (person) **меща́нство** (the phenomenon) **меща́нский** (adj)	*petty bourgeois person; petty bourgeois behaviour/ attitudes.* The words are used in a figurative sense to evoke sb who is *narrow-minded, philistine,* or such behaviour; in Soviet parlance they were used as pejorative terms to describe a selfish mindset.
мировоззре́ние	view of the world, set of beliefs. The word implies something more systematic and coherent than English *outlook;* cf. German *Weltanschauung.*
ненагля́дный	sth which one cannot take one's eyes off. The word denotes the quality of an object, admiration of which one might express with the verb любова́ться (see above in this section).
новостро́йка	newly erected building, building work in a new town or district. The word brings to mind the rapid urban development of the post-war Soviet period.
обыва́тель (m)	*inhabitant, citizen, the average man, the man in the street;* fig *philistine* in pre-revolutionary days. In Soviet times the word was used as a synonym of мещани́н, i.e. a narrow-minded person without social interests; it may now be reverting to its pre-revolutionary role.
однолю́б	sb who has had only one love in her or his life or who can love only one person at a time
опохмели́ться (pf)	to have a drink to cure a hangover, to have a drink the morning after
отхо́дчивый	describes sb who loses her/his temper with sb else but does not subsequently harbour resentment towards the person who angered her/him

очередно́й	*next in turn, periodic, recurrent, regular, routine, usual.* The word is derived from о́чередь (f), *queue*.
по́двиг	heroic deed, feat, act of heroism, sth done for the general good
по́шлый (adj) **по́шлость** (f)	*morally low, tasteless, rude, common, banal, vulgar;* an object or act that can be described in this way. No single English word has the same field of meaning although *tacky*, a recent borrowing from American English, does convey the same notion of lack of good taste.
пра́здник	*holiday* in sense of *festival, national holiday, festive occasion, occasion for celebration, red-letter day;* antonym of бу́дни (see above in this section)
про́воды (pl; gen про́водов)	*send-off*, occasion or process of seeing off sb who is leaving
просто́р	*space, spaciousness, expanse, scope, freedom, elbow-room.* The word evokes the wide open spaces and seeming infinity of the Russian landscape.
раздо́лье	synonymous with просто́р
разма́х	*scope, range, sweep, scale, span, amplitude.* When applied to character the word may suggest an expansiveness and generosity that is admired.
разру́ха	*ruin, collapse, devastation* (esp after war, revolution or some other cataclysmic event)
рове́сник/ рове́сница	person of the same age
родно́й	*one's own* (by blood relationship), *native*, e.g. родно́й язы́к, *native language*; родны́е, as substantivised noun = *relations, relatives, kith and kin*; antonym of чужо́й (see below in this section). The word has strong positive connotations.
саморо́док (adj **саморо́дный**)	a person who possesses natural gifts but lacks a systematic, thorough education; (of metals) *nugget*, piece of mined metal in chemically pure form
све́рстник/ све́рстница	synonyms of рове́сник/рове́сница, respectively
свой	*one's own, my/your/his/her/our/their own;* close in meaning to родно́й (and therefore also having positive connotations) and an antonym of чужо́й. Note: свой челове́к = person who is not related but whom one trusts. See 11.2.6 on use of свой.

сгла́зить (pf)	*to put the evil eye (on)*
сплошно́й	*unbroken, continuous, all-round, complete, entire, total,* e.g. сплошно́й забо́р, *unbroken fence*; сплошно́е удово́льствие, *complete satisfaction*; сплошна́я гра́мотность, *one-hundred-percent literacy*
срок	*period of time, term, deadline*
стро́йный	*well-proportioned, elegant, shapely, well-balanced, harmonious, orderly, well put together.* The word evokes sth that is aesthetically pleasing, pleasant to the eye.
увлека́ться/ увле́чься + instr	*to be carried away (by), to become keen (on), to be mad (about), to fall for, to become enamoured (of).* The word suggests great enthusiasm.
успева́ть/успе́ть	*to have time (to do sth), to manage (in time), to succeed (in doing sth in time)*
хам/ха́мка ха́мство ха́мский (all pej)	*lout, boor, cow; loutishness, boorishness; loutish, boorish.* Хам denotes a person who behaves in a crude, disgusting way and has no respect for herself/himself or others. (The word is derived from the name of the biblical character Ham, who in Genesis 9 saw his father Noah naked and told his brothers.)
чужо́й	*sb else's, other people's, not mine/ours; foreign, alien, strange.* The word is an antonym of родно́й and свой and therefore has negative connotations.

4 Problems of translation from English into Russian

4.1 English words difficult to render in Russian

This section lists in alphabetical order some of the more common English words which give difficulty for students learning Russian and defines some of the Russian equivalents they may have. The list is intended to encourage the student to think about the precise meaning of the English word in a given context and to consider which of the various possible Russian renderings is appropriate in that context. The lists of Russian equivalents for the English words are not intended to include all possible translations of the English word, merely to draw attention to the ways in which Russian deals with the main fields of meaning which the English word may have. In each entry the Russian word/words which render the meaning of the English word that seems most common or fundamental is/are given first.

Rendering of English prepositions is dealt with separately in 10.4.

English has many phrasal verbs (e.g. *to hold back, hold on, hold up*) in which the precise meaning of the verb is clarified by the following preposition. Translation of phrasal verbs is not considered here except in a very small number of cases. It should be noted that in many cases the function of the English preposition is fulfilled in Russian by a verbal prefix (see 8.3), as well as by a following preposition.

ACCIDENT	несча́стный слу́чай	emphasising effect on victim
	ава́рия	involving machinery, transport, etc., e.g. на электроста́нции, *at a power station*
	круше́ние	*crash*, e.g. круше́ние по́езда, *train crash*; кораблекруше́ние, *shipwreck*
	катастро́фа	*disaster*; also fig
	случа́йность (f)	*chance, contingency*
ADVERTISEMENT	рекла́ма	with a view to selling
	объявле́ние	*announcement* (e.g. of job vacancy)
	ано́нс	short notice about coming event
AGAIN	опя́ть	*once more as before*
	сно́ва	= опя́ть (slightly more bookish)
	за́ново	*anew, afresh*
	ещё раз	*one more time*

AGE	**во́зраст**	stage in one's life
	век	lit *century*; also *age*, e.g. ка́менный век, *the Stone Age*
	пери́од	*period*
	эпо́ха	*epoch*
AGREE	**соглаша́ться/согласи́ться с +** instr	*to concur with*
	соглаша́ться/согласи́ться на + acc	*to consent to*
	сходи́ться/сойти́сь	*to tally* (of figures), *to come to an agreement about*, e.g. сойти́сь в цене́, *to agree a price*
	согласо́вывать/согласова́ть что́-н с ке́м-н (trans)	*to agree sth with sb*
	согласова́ться (impf) с + instr	*gram term*
	договори́ться (pf)	*to come to an arrangement*
APPEARANCE	**появле́ние**	*emergence, coming into view*
	нару́жность (f)	*outward appearance, exterior*
	выступле́ние	*public appearance* (e.g. on stage, television), *speech*
	вид	*air, look, aspect*
APPLICATION	**заявле́ние**	esp for abstract object, e.g. заявле́ние о приёме на рабо́ту, *a job application*
	зая́вка	esp for concrete object, e.g. зая́вка на материа́лы, *an application for materials*
	про́сьба	*request*, e.g. про́сьба о по́мощи, *an application for help*
	наложе́ние	placing on, e.g. наложе́ние повя́зки на ра́ну, e.g. *application of a bandage to a wound*
	примене́ние	putting to use, e.g. примене́ние си́лы, но́вой тео́рии, *application of force, of a new theory*
	испо́льзование	*utilisation*
	прилежа́ние	*diligence*
ARGUMENT	**спор**	*controversy, debate, dispute* (legal)
	ссо́ра	*quarrel*

	раздо́р	*discord, dissension*
	до́вод	*evidence*
	те́зис	*thesis* (see also 3.5)
	аргумента́ция	*argumentation*
ARTICLE	**изде́лие**	*manufactured article*
	това́р	*commodity*
	статья́	in newspaper, journal, treaty, contract
	пункт	in treaty, contract
	арти́кул	= пункт
	арти́кль (m)	gram term; also now *commodity*
ARTIST	**худо́жник**	*creative artist* (e.g. writer, painter, composer)
	арти́ст	*performing artist, artiste*
ASK	**спра́шивать/спроси́ть**	*to enquire*
	проси́ть/попроси́ть	*to request*
	задава́ть/зада́ть вопро́с	*to pose a question*
	справля́ться/спра́виться	*to make enquiries*
	приглаша́ть/пригласи́ть	*to invite*
ATTACK	**нападе́ние**	*assault* (in most senses)
	наступле́ние	*offensive* (mil)
	набе́г	*raid*
	ата́ка	*military attack*
	припа́док	*fit* (med)
	при́ступ	*fit, pang, bout*, e.g. при́ступ гри́ппа, ка́шля, *an attack of flu, coughing*
	инфа́ркт	*heart attack*
BAD	**плохо́й**	general word
	дурно́й	*nasty*, e.g. дурна́я привы́чка, *bad habit*; дурно́й сон, *bad dream*
	парши́вый (R1)	lit *mangy; nasty, lousy*, e.g. парши́вая пого́да, *bad weather*
	злой	*wicked*
	вре́дный	*harmful, detrimental, injurious*
	тяжёлый	*severe*, e.g. тяжёлая боле́знь, *bad illness*; тяжёлое ране́ние, *bad injury*

	гнило́й	*rotten*, e.g. of fruit
	ки́слый	*sour*, e.g. of milk
	ту́хлый	*putrefied*, e.g. of egg
	испо́рченный	*spoiled, off* (of food)
	неподходя́щий	*unsuitable*, e.g. неподходя́щий приме́р, *bad example*
	неблагоприя́тный	*unfavourable*
BALL(S)	шар	spherical object, *billiard ball*
	ша́рик	dimin of шар
	клубо́к	e.g. of wool
	мяч	for games, sport
	мя́чик	dimin of мяч
	ядро́	*cannonball*
	вздор	*nonsense, rubbish*
	чепуха́	= вздор
	я́йца (pl; R1 vulg)	*testicles*
BIG	большо́й	*large*
	кру́пный	*major, large-scale* (see 3.7)
	вели́к/а́/о́/и́	*too big* (see 11.3)
BLUE	си́ний	*dark blue*
	голубо́й	*light blue*
	лазу́рный (poet)	*sky-blue, azure*
	порнофи́льм	*blue film*
	как гром среди́ я́сного не́ба	*like a bolt from the blue*
BODY	те́ло	of human or animal; also solid object, e.g. star
	ту́ловище	*torso*
	труп	*corpse*
	ку́зов	of carriage, car, etc.
	организа́ция	*organisation*
BOX	я́щик	*chest, container*; почто́вый я́щик, *post-box*
	коро́бка	smaller container than я́щик; коро́бка скоросте́й, *gear-box*
	коро́бочка	dimin of коро́бка
	шкату́лка	*casket, trinket box*

	сунду́к	*trunk*
	бу́дка	*booth, kiosk*
	ло́жа	at theatre

Note: А ла́рчик про́сто открыва́лся, *The box just opened*, meaning *The explanation was quite simple* (a quotation from a fable by Krylov).

BRANCH	ветвь (f)	*bough*
	о́трасль (f)	*section, subdivision*, e.g. о́трасль промы́шленности, *branch of industry*
	филиа́л	*subsidiary section of organisation*, e.g. ло́ндонский филиа́л ба́нка, *the London branch of a bank*
BREAK	лома́ть/слома́ть	*to fracture*, e.g. слома́ть но́гу, *to break a leg*; *to cause not to work*, e.g. слома́ть механи́зм, *to break a mechanism*
	разбива́ть/разби́ть	*to smash* (into many pieces), e.g. разби́ть посу́ду, *to break crockery*
	наруша́ть/нару́шить	*to infringe*, e.g. нару́шить зако́н, пра́вило, *to break a law, a rule*
	прерыва́ть/прерва́ть	*to break off, interrupt, sever*, e.g. прерва́ть дипломати́ческие отноше́ния, *to break off diplomatic relations*
	превыша́ть/превы́сить	*to break* (i.e. *exceed*), e.g. превы́сить дозво́ленную ско́рость, *to break a speed limit*
BRIGHT	я́ркий	*vivid*
	све́тлый	*light-coloured, radiant*
	у́мный	*clever*
BROWN	кори́чневый	*cinnamon-coloured*
	ка́рий	*of eyes*
	бу́рый	*reddish brown*, e.g. бу́рый медве́дь, *brown bear*
	шате́н/шате́нка (nouns)	*brown-haired man/woman*
	загоре́лый	*sunburned*
	сму́глый	*of complexion, swarthy*
	шокола́дного цве́та	*chocolate-coloured*
	бе́жевый	*beige*

BRUSH	**щётка**	for cleaning, brushing hair
	кисть (f)	for painting, e.g. маля́рная кисть, *paintbrush*
	ки́сточка	dimin of кисть, e.g. ки́сточка для бритья́, *shaving brush*
	метла́	*broom*
BURN	**горе́ть/сгоре́ть** (intrans)	e.g. дом гори́т, *the house is on fire*
	жечь (trans)	e.g. жечь му́сор, *to burn rubbish*
	сжига́ть/сжечь (trans)	*to burn up, cremate*
	зажига́ть/зажёчь	*to set light to*
	поджига́ть/поджёчь	*to set on fire* (with criminal intent)
	пыла́ть (intrans)	*to blaze, flame, glow*; also fig, e.g. пыла́ть стра́стью, *to burn with passion*
CALL	**звать/позва́ть**	*to call, summon*; impf only also means *to name*, e.g. Как вас зову́т? *What is your name?* (lit *What do they call you?*) Меня́ зову́т А́нна, *My name is Anna.*
	вызыва́ть/вы́звать	*to call out*, e.g. вы́звать врача́, *to call the doctor*
	называ́ть/назва́ть	*to name*
	подзыва́ть/подозва́ть	*to beckon*
	призыва́ть/призва́ть	*to appeal to*
	созыва́ть/созва́ть	*to call together, convoke*
	звони́ть/позвони́ть + dat	*to ring, telephone*
	заходи́ть/зайти́ к + dat	*to call on, visit*
	загля́дывать/загляну́ть к + dat	*to look in on*
CAREFUL	**осторо́жный**	proceeding with caution
	тща́тельный	*thorough, painstaking*
	внима́тельный	*attentive, considerate*
CASE	**слу́чай**	*instance*
	де́ло	*legal case*
	до́воды (pl; gen до́водов)	set of arguments
	обоснова́ние	*basis, grounds*, e.g. обоснова́ние са́нкций, *the case for sanctions*
	ана́лиз конкре́тной ситуа́ции	*a case study*
	больно́й	*(medical) patient*

= container (see also *box*)	**паде́ж**	gram term
	чемода́н	*suitcase*
	футля́р	for spectacles, musical instrument
	витри́на	*glass case*
CATCH	**лови́ть/пойма́ть**	*to seize, ensnare,* e.g. пойма́ть ры́бу, *to catch a fish*
	хвата́ть/хвати́ть ог **схвати́ть**	*to grab, snatch, seize*
	схва́тывать/схвати́ть	*to grasp;* also fig, e.g. схвати́ть смысл, просту́ду (R1), *to catch the sense, a cold*
	застига́ть/засти́гнуть	*to take unawares*
	застава́ть/заста́ть	*to find,* e.g. Я заста́л его́ до́ма, *I caught him at home.*
	заража́ться/зарази́ться + instr	*to be infected with,* e.g. Она́ зарази́лась анги́ной, *She caught tonsillitis.*
	ула́вливать/улови́ть	*to detect, perceive,* e.g. улови́ть звук, нюа́нс, *to catch a sound, nuance*
	зацепля́ться/зацепи́ться	*to get caught up on,* e.g. Рука́в мое́й руба́шки зацепи́лся за иглу́, *The sleeve of my shirt got caught on a thorn.*
	простужа́ться/простуди́ться	*to catch a cold*
CHALLENGE (noun)	**вы́зов**	may translate *challenge* but is not so widely used as this English word; originally means *calling out,* e.g. to duel
	сти́мул	sth that drives one to act
	зада́ча	*(difficult) task*
	пробле́ма	*problem;* has wide range of meaning; close to зада́ча
CHANGE (verb)	**меня́ть**	basic verb
	изменя́ть/измени́ть (trans)	*to change, alter*
	изменя́ться/измени́ться (intrans)	*to change, alter*
	меня́ть or **обме́нивать/ обменя́ть** (also **обмени́ть** in R1)	*to (ex)change* (money), e.g. Дава́йте обменя́ем валю́ту на рубли́, *Let's change our currency into roubles; to change sth for sth else,* e.g. обменя́ть пла́тье, *to change a dress* (e.g. because it is the wrong size)

переменя́ть/перемени́ть	*to shift* (from one position to another), e.g. перемени́ть пози́цию, тон, *to change one's position, tone*
переменя́ться/перемени́ться	intrans of переменя́ть/перемени́ть
разме́нивать/разменя́ть	to change a coin or note into smaller denominations
сменя́ть/смени́ть	*to replace*, e.g. смени́ть бельё, карау́л, ши́ну, *to change linen, a sentry, a tyre*
преобразо́вывать/ преобразова́ть (R3)	*to transform, reform, reorganise*
превраща́ть/преврати́ть (trans)	*to turn* (sth into sth else), e.g. преврати́ть во́ду в лёд, *to turn water into ice*
превраща́ться/преврати́ться	intrans of превраща́ть/преврати́ть
видоизменя́ть/видоизмени́ть (trans; R3)	*to alter, modify*
переса́живаться/пересе́сть	*to change transport*, e.g. Здесь на́до пересе́сть на другу́ю ли́нию, *We must change to another line here.*
переодева́ться/переоде́ться	*to change one's clothes*
переходи́ть/перейти́ на + acc	*to go over* (to sth different), e.g. Она́ перешла́ на другу́ю рабо́ту, *She changed her job.*
переду́мывать/переду́мать (pf)	*to change one's mind* (and think better of it)
разду́мывать/разду́мать (pf)	*to change one's mind* (and decide not to do sth)
оду́мываться/оду́маться (pf)	*to change one's mind* (think again, perhaps in response to warning)

CHANGE (noun)	измене́ние	*alteration*
	обме́н	*exchange*, e.g. of information, opinions, money into different currency
	переме́на	*shift* (from one thing to another)
	разме́н	when note or coin is broken down into money in smaller denomination
	сда́ча	money handed back after purchase, e.g. сда́ча с фу́нта, *change out of a pound*

	ме́лочь (f)	coins of small denominations
	сме́на	*replacement*, e.g. сме́на белья́, карау́ла, *change of linen, guard*
	преобразова́ние	*transformation, reorganisation*
	превраще́ние	*conversion* (into sth else)
	видоизмене́ние	*modification*
	переса́дка	from one vehicle or form of transport to another
CHARACTER	хара́ктер	*nature, personality*
	о́браз	in work of literature
	де́йствующее лицо́	in play
	тип	*type*
	нрав	*disposition*
	осо́ба (f)	*person, individual*
CLEVER	у́мный	*intelligent*
	тала́нтливый	*talented*
	спосо́бный	*capable, able*
	дарови́тый	*gifted*
	одарённый	= дарови́тый
	ло́вкий	*adroit, dexterous*
	иску́сный	*skilful*
	уме́лый	*able, astute*
CLOUD	о́блако	white cloud
	ту́ча	*rain-cloud, storm-cloud*
	клубы́ (pl; gen клубо́в)	клубы́ ды́ма, пы́ли, *cloud of smoke, dust*
COACH	авто́бус	*bus*
	ваго́н	part of train
	каре́та	*horse-drawn carriage*
COAT	пальто́ (indecl)	*overcoat*
	шу́ба	*fur coat*
	дублёнка (R1)	*sheepskin coat*
	ку́ртка	short outdoor jacket
	ветро́вка (R1)	*anorak*
	аля́ска (R1)	*winter coat with fur lining*
	плащ	*raincoat, waterproof cape*

	дождеви́к (R1)	*plastic raincoat*
	шине́ль (f)	*(military) greatcoat*
	шерсть (f)	animal's fur
	слой	*layer* (of paint)
	герб	*coat of arms*
COMPETITION	ко́нкурс	organised contest, e.g. ко́нкурс красоты́, *beauty contest*; also competition to get in somewhere
	состяза́ние	*contest, match*, e.g. состяза́ние по бо́ксу, пла́ванию, фехтова́нию, *boxing, swimming, fencing competition*; also unorganised competition
	соревнова́ние	sporting event
	сопе́рничество	*rivalry*
	конкуре́нция	*(economic) competition*
COPY	ко́пия	*reproduction*
	экземпля́р	*specimen, example*, e.g. У меня́ два экземпля́ра э́той кни́ги, *I have two copies of this book*
	ксе́рокс	*(photo)copy*
COUNTRY	страна́	*state*
	ро́дина	*native land*
	оте́чество	*fatherland*
	ме́стность (f)	*terrain*
	за́ город (motion), за́ городом (location)	outside the city or town
CUT (verb)	ре́зать	basic verb
	нареза́ть/наре́зать	*to cut into pieces, carve, slice*
	отреза́ть/отре́зать	*to cut off*
	среза́ть/сре́зать	*to cut off*; also fig, e.g. сре́зать у́гол, *to cut a corner*
	уреза́ть or уре́зывать/уре́зать (R3, offic)	*to reduce by cutting*, e.g. Прави́тельство уре́зало расхо́ды на обще́ственные ну́жды, *The government has cut public expenditure.*
	сокраща́ть/сократи́ть	*to cut down, curtail*, e.g. сократи́ть расхо́ды, *to cut expenditure*
	прекраща́ть/прекрати́ть	*to cut short, stop*, e.g. Прекрати́ли пода́чу га́за, *They have cut off the gas supply.*

	кро́ить/скро́ить	to cut out (a pattern)
CUT (noun)	сокраще́ние	cutting down, curtailment, cut (fin)
	ски́дка	reduction, discount
	сниже́ние	reduction, e.g. in price
	прекраще́ние	cutting off, cessation
DEVELOPMENT(S)	разви́тие	growth, unfolding, evolution
	разви́тие собы́тий	development of events
	разрабо́тка	working out/up, elaboration
	проявле́ние	photographic
	нала́живание	arrangement, e.g. нала́живание конта́ктов, development of contacts
DIE	умира́ть/умере́ть	to pass away (of natural causes, disease, starvation)
	погиба́ть/поги́бнуть	to perish, be killed (in accident, war, natural disaster)
	сконча́ться (pf; R3)	to pass away
	ложи́ться/лечь костьми́ (R3, rhet)	to lay down one's life (in battle)
DIFFERENCE	ра́зница	extent of disparity
	разли́чие	distinction (individual point of difference)
	разногла́сие	intellectual disagreement
	размо́лвка	tiff
	расхожде́ние	divergence; расхожде́ние во мне́ниях, difference of opinion
DIFFERENT	ра́зный	various, diverse
	разли́чный	divergent
	отли́чный от + gen	different from
	не похо́жий на + acc	dissimilar to
	несхо́дный с + instr	dissimilar to
	отлича́ться от (impf only)	to be different from, e.g. Чем отлича́ется Москва́ от Са̀нкт-Петербу́рга? In what way is Moscow different from St Petersburg?
	друго́й	not the same as before, e.g. По́сле войны́ он был други́м челове́ком, He was a different person after the war.

	иной	= другой
	по-ра́зному	*in different ways*
DREAM	сон	what one sees in one's sleep
	сновиде́ние (R3)	= сон
	мечта́	*daydream, ambition*
	мечта́ние	*reverie*
	(ночно́й) кошма́р	*bad dream, nightmare*
EDGE	кра́й	*brim, brink*
	кро́мка (not common)	in various senses, esp physical, e.g. кро́мка крыла́, мате́рии, *edge of a wing, material*
	остриё	*cutting edge*, e.g. остриё ножа́, *edge of a knife*
	поля́ (pl; gen поле́й)	*margin* (of paper)
	опу́шка	of forest
	грань (f)	*facet*; also *brink* (fig), e.g. на гра́ни войны́, *on the brink of war*
	переве́с	*superiority, advantage*
EDUCATION	образова́ние	general instruction
	обуче́ние	*tuition*, e.g. совме́стное обуче́ние лиц обо́его по́ла, *co-education*
	воспита́ние	*upbringing*
	просвеще́ние	*enlightenment*
ENCOURAGE	поощря́ть/поощри́ть	*to give incentive to*
	ободря́ть/ободри́ть	*to cheer up, hearten*
	сове́товать/посове́товать	*to advise*
	стимули́ровать (impf and pf)	*to stimulate*, e.g. стимули́ровать рост, *to encourage growth*
	спосо́бствовать (+ dat)	*to contribute to, promote*
	подде́рживать/поддержа́ть	*to support*
END	коне́ц	general word
	оконча́ние	*ending, conclusion*; also gram term
	ко́нчик	*tip, point*, e.g. ко́нчик языка́, *end of one's tongue*
	кончи́на (R3; rhet)	*demise*
	кра́й	*edge, limit*, e.g. на краю́ све́та, *at the world's end*

	цель (f)	*aim, goal*
ENJOY	люби́ть	*to like* (sth/doing sth), e.g. Она́ лю́бит му́зыку, игра́ть в те́ннис, *She enjoys music, playing tennis.*
	нра́виться/понра́виться (impers)	*to like*, e.g. Мне понра́вилась пье́са, *I enjoyed the play.*
	наслажда́ться/наслади́ться + instr	*to take delight in*, e.g. наслади́ться приро́дой, *to enjoy nature*
	хорошо́ проводи́ть/провести́ (вре́мя)	*to spend (time) pleasantly*, e.g. Вы хорошо́ провели́ о́тпуск? *Did you enjoy your holiday?*
	весели́ться/повесели́ться	*to enjoy oneself, have a good time*
	по́льзоваться (impf; + instr)	*to have*, e.g. по́льзоваться дове́рием, репута́цией, уваже́нием, *to enjoy trust, a reputation, respect*
	облада́ть + instr	*to possess*, e.g. облада́ть права́ми, хоро́шим здоро́вьем, *to enjoy rights, good health*
EVIDENCE	свиде́тельство	*indication, testimony*
	доказа́тельство	*proof*; пи́сьменные доказа́тельства, *written evidence*
	ули́ка	*piece of (legal) evidence*; неоспори́мая ули́ка, *indisputable evidence*
	при́знак	*sign, indication*
	да́нные (pl; subst adj)	*data*
	основа́ния (pl; gen основа́ний) (ду́мать)	*grounds (for thinking)*
	показа́ние	*(legal) deposition*
EXAMINE	рассма́тривать/рассмотре́ть	*to consider*, e.g. рассмотре́ть вопро́с, *to examine a question*
	осма́тривать/осмотре́ть	*to inspect, look over*, e.g. осмотре́ть бага́ж, больно́го, *to examine baggage, a patient*
	обсле́довать (impf and pf)	*to inspect*, e.g. обсле́довать больно́го, *to examine a patient*
	проверя́ть/прове́рить	*to check, mark (student's work)*
	экзаменова́ть/проэкзаменова́ть + acc	*to conduct an examination of*
	опра́шивать/опроси́ть	*to cross-examine*, e.g. опроси́ть свиде́теля, *to examine a witness*

EXERCISE	упражне́ние	exertion of body or mind, task
	заря́дка	physical activity, *drill*
	трениро́вка	*training*
	моцио́н	*exertion* (of the body for good health), e.g. де́лать моцио́н, *to take exercise*
	уче́ния (pl; gen уче́ний)	*military exercise*
	манёвры (pl; gen манёвров)	*military manoeuvres*
EXPERIENCE	о́пыт	what one has learnt
	пережива́ния (pl; gen пережива́ний)	what one has lived through
	слу́чай	*incident*, e.g. неприя́тный слу́чай, *unpleasant experience*
FACE	лицо́	front part of head; also *exterior*
	ли́чико	dimin of лицо́, e.g. ли́чико ребёнка, *a child's face*
	выраже́ние	*expression*
	ро́жа (R1)	*mug*
	цифербла́т	*dial* (of clock, watch, gauge)
FALL	па́дать/(у)па́сть	basic verb
	выпада́ть/вы́пасть	of rain, snow, in the phrases вы́пал снег, *it snowed*; вы́пали оса́дки (e.g. in weather report), *it rained*
	опада́ть/опа́сть	of leaves
	распада́ться/распа́сться	*to fall to pieces, disintegrate*
	попада́ть/попа́сть кому́-н в ру́ки	*to fall into sb's hands*
	стиха́ть/сти́хнуть	of wind
	снижа́ться/сни́зиться	*to get lower*, e.g. у́ровень, цена́ снижа́ется, *the standard, price is falling*
	влюбля́ться/влюби́ться в + acc	*to fall in love with*
	замолча́ть (pf)	*to fall silent*
FAT	то́лстый	*thick, stout, corpulent*
	по́лный	*portly* (polite)
	жи́рный	*plump* (of people), *greasy, rich, fatty* (of food)

	ту́чный	corpulent, obese
FEAR	боя́знь (f)	dread, e.g. боя́знь темноты́, fear of darkness
	страх	terror
	испу́г	fright
	опасе́ние	apprehension, misgiving
FEEL	чу́вствовать/почу́вствовать	to be aware of
	чу́вствовать себя́ (intrans)	e.g. Как ты чу́вствуешь себя́? How do you feel?
	ощуща́ть/ощути́ть	to sense
	щу́пать/пощу́пать	to explore by touch, e.g. щу́пать кому́-н пульс, to feel sb's pulse
	тро́гать/потро́гать	to run one's hand over
	пробира́ться/пробра́ться о́щупью	to feel one's way
	испы́тывать/испыта́ть	to experience
	пережива́ть/пережи́ть	to endure, suffer, go through
FIGHT	дра́ться/подра́ться с + instr	to scrap, brawl
	сража́ться/срази́ться с + instr	to do battle with, e.g. of armies
	боро́ться	to wrestle, struggle (also fig)
	воева́ть (impf)	to wage war
FIND	находи́ть/найти́	to find (as result of search)
	застава́ть/заста́ть	to come across, encounter, e.g. заста́ть кого́-н до́ма, to find sb at home
	счита́ть/счесть	to consider, e.g. Они́ счита́ют ру́сский язы́к тру́дным, They find Russian difficult.
	встреча́ть/встре́тить	to encounter
	открыва́ть/откры́ть	to discover
	обнару́живать/обнару́жить	to bring to light, e.g. Меха́ник обнару́жил непола́дку в мото́ре, The mechanic found a fault in the engine.
	признава́ть/призна́ть	legal term, e.g. Призна́ли его́ вино́вным, They found him guilty.
FIRE	ого́нь (m)	general word
	пожа́р	conflagration, e.g. лесно́й пожа́р, forest fire

	костёр	*bonfire*
	ками́н	*open fire, fireplace*
	пыл	*ardour*
(AT) FIRST	снача́ла	*at the beginning*
	сперва́ (R1)	= снача́ла
	пре́жде всего́	*first of all, first and foremost*
	впервы́е	*for the first time*
	во-пе́рвых	*in the first place*
	на пе́рвых пора́х	*in the first instance*
	с пе́рвого взгля́да	*at first sight*
FOLLOW	идти́/пойти́ за + instr	*to go after*
	сле́довать/после́довать за + instr	*to go after*
	сле́довать/после́довать + dat	*to emulate*
	следи́ть за + instr	*to watch, track, keep up with*, e.g. ЦРУ следи́т за ни́ми, *The CIA is following them*; следи́ть за полити́ческими собы́тиями, *to follow political developments*
	соблюда́ть/соблюсти́	*to observe*, e.g. соблюсти́ дие́ту, пра́вила, *to follow a diet, rules*
	понима́ть/поня́ть	*to understand*
FOOD	пи́ща	general word
	еда́	what is eaten; еда́ и питьё, *food and drink*
	(пищевы́е) проду́кты	*food products*
	продово́льствие (sg)	*foodstuffs, provisions*
	прови́зия (sg only)	*provisions, victuals*
	консе́рвы (pl; gen консе́рвов)	*canned food*
	ку́хня	*cuisine*
	блю́до	*a dish*
	пита́ние	*nourishment, feeding*
	корм	*animal fodder*
FOREIGN	иностра́нный	general word; Министе́рство иностра́нных дел, *Ministry of Foreign Affairs*
	зарубе́жный	= иностра́нный; зарубе́жная пре́сса, *the foreign press*

	внéшний	*external*; внéшняя полúтика, торгóвля, *foreign policy, trade*
	чужóй	*alien*
FREE	свобóдный	*at liberty, unconstrained*
	непринуждённый	*relaxed, at ease*
	бесплáтный	*free of charge*, e.g. бесплáтное образовáние, *free education*
FREEDOM	свобóда	*freedom* in most senses, e.g. свобóда лúчности, печáти, слóва, собрáний, *freedom of the individual, press, speech, assembly*
	вóля	*free will*; Земля́ и вóля, *Land and Liberty*; Нарóдная вóля, *The People's Will* (nineteenth-century Russian revolutionary parties)
FREEZE	морóзит	*it is freezing, i.e. there is a frost*
	мёрзнуть/замёрзнуть (intrans)	e.g. Óзеро замёрзло, *The lake has frozen.*
	заморáживать/заморóзить (trans)	e.g. заморóженное мя́со, *frozen meat*; also fig, e.g. Правúтельство заморáживает цéны, *The government is freezing prices.*
	покры́ться льдом	*to be covered with ice, as of river, road*
	зя́бнуть/озя́бнуть (intrans)	*to suffer from/feel the cold*
	леденéть/оледенéть (intrans)	*to turn to ice, become numb with cold*
FRIEND	друг	general word
	подрýга	*female friend*
	дружóк	dimin of друг
	прия́тель(ница)	not so close as друг/подрýга
	товáрищ	*comrade, pal*
	знакóмый/знакóмая (subst adj)	*acquaintance*
	сторóнник	*supporter*
	доброжелáтель (m)	*well-wisher*
FRUSTRATION	отчáяние	*despair*
	чýвство безысхóдности	*feeling that there is no way out*
	чýвство бессúлия	*sense of impotence*
	досáда	*annoyance*

	раздраже́ние	*irritation*
	фрустра́ция	esp psychological
	фрустри́рованность (f)	state of being frustrated
FUNNY	смешно́й	*laughable*
	заба́вный	*amusing*
	стра́нный	*strange*
	непоня́тный	*incomprehensible*
	подозри́тельный	*suspicious*
GIRL	де́вочка	*little girl*
	де́вушка	*girl (after puberty)*; also as term of address to (young) woman (see 7.4)
	де́вка (R1, D)	affectionate term; also in folklore, e.g. кра́сна [sic] де́вка, *fair maid*; also pej, i.e. *slut*
	деви́ца	*maiden, virgin*
	продавщи́ца	female shop assistant
GLASS	стекло́	*glass* (as material), *window-pane, windscreen* (of vehicle)
	стака́н	*tumbler*
	рю́мка	*small glass* (for drink)
	рю́мочка	dimin of рю́мка, e.g. *vodka glass*
	фуже́р	*tall glass*, for water, juice (at formal dinner)
	бока́л	*wine glass, goblet, chalice*
	очки́ (pl; gen очко́в)	*spectacles*
GOAL	цель (f)	*aim, purpose*
	воро́та (pl; gen воро́т)	(sport) goalposts and net
	гол	what is scored in sport
GOOD	хоро́ший	general word; хоро́ш собо́й, *good-looking*
	до́брый	in various senses, *kind*
	поле́зный	*useful*
	вы́годный	*profitable*, e.g. вы́годная сде́лка, *a good deal* (i.e. business arrangement)
	уда́чный	*successful*, e.g. уда́чный визи́т, день, перево́д, *a good visit, day, translation*; уда́чная поку́пка, *a good buy*

	интере́сный	interesting
	весёлый	cheerful, e.g. весёлое настрое́ние, good mood
	прия́тный	pleasant, agreeable
	спосо́бный	able, capable
	послу́шный	obedient
	гора́зд (short forms only)	skilful, clever, e.g. Он на всё гора́зд, He's good at everything.
GOVERNMENT	прави́тельство	ruling body
	правле́ние	system of government
	управле́ние + instr	act of governing; also gram term
GREET	здоро́ваться/поздоро́ваться с + instr	to say hello to
	приве́тствовать	to welcome (also fig, e.g. приве́тствовать предложе́ние, to welcome a proposal)
	встреча́ть/встре́тить	to meet, receive
	принима́ть/приня́ть	to receive
GROW	расти́/вы́расти (intrans)	to get bigger
	возраста́ть/возрасти́ (intrans)	to get bigger, increase
	нараста́ть/нарасти́ (intrans)	to accumulate
	подраста́ть/подрасти́ (intrans)	to get a little bigger
	выра́щивать/вы́растить (trans)	to cultivate, e.g. вы́растить о́вощи, to grow vegetables
	увели́чиваться/увели́читься (intrans)	to increase, e.g. Проце́нт сме́ртности увели́чивается, The mortality rate is growing.
	отпуска́ть/отпусти́ть	to let grow, e.g. отпусти́ть во́лосы, бо́роду, to grow one's hair, beard
GUN	ружьё	rifle
	обре́з	sawn-off shot-gun
	пистоле́т	pistol
	револьве́р	revolver
	пулемёт	machine-gun
	пу́шка	cannon

HARD	**твёрдый**	*firm, solid,* e.g. твёрдый грунт, *hard ground;* твёрдый знак, *hard sign*
	тру́дный	*difficult*
	тяжёлый	fig, e.g. тяжёлая рабо́та, *hard work;* тяжёлые усло́вия, *hard conditions;* тяжёлые времена́, *hard times*
	си́льный	*forceful,* e.g. си́льный уда́р, *a hard blow*
	суро́вый	*severe,* e.g. суро́вая зима́, *a hard winter*
	стро́гий	*strict*
	чёрствый	*stale,* e.g. чёрствый хлеб, *hard bread*
(adverb)	**приле́жно** or **мно́го**	*diligently, with application,* e.g. приле́жно/мно́го рабо́тать, *to work hard*
	усе́рдно	= приле́жно
HARVEST	**урожа́й**	*crop, yield*
	жа́тва	*reaping*
	убо́рка	*gathering in,* e.g. убо́рка пшени́цы, карто́шки, *wheat harvest, potato harvest*
	сбор	*gathering,* e.g. сбор фру́ктов, овоще́й, *fruit harvest, vegetable harvest*
HAT	**шля́па**	*hat with brim*
	ша́пка	*fur hat;* вя́заная ша́пка, *knitted hat*
	ке́пка	*peaked cap*
	фура́жка	*peaked cap,* esp mil
	цили́ндр	*top hat*
HAVE	**у** (with noun or pronoun in gen + **есть**)	*to have* (esp concrete objects, e.g. у нас есть чёрная маши́на, *We have a black car.*)
	име́ть	*to have* (with abstract object, e.g. име́ть пра́во, возмо́жность, *to have a right, an opportunity*)
	облада́ть + instr	*to possess* (esp qualities, e.g. облада́ть тала́нтом, хладнокро́вием, *to have talent, presence of mind*)

HEAD	голова́	part of the body
	глава́	fig, e.g. глава́ делега́ции, администра́ции, *head of delegation, administration*
	нача́льник	*chief, superior, boss*
	руководи́тель (m)	*leader, manager*
HEAVY	тяжёлый	general word
	си́льный	e.g. си́льный дождь, на́сморк, уда́р, *heavy rain, a heavy cold, blow;* си́льное движе́ние, *heavy traffic*
	проливно́й	in slightly bookish phrase проливно́й дождь, *heavy rain*
	интенси́вный	in slightly bookish phrase интенси́вное движе́ние, *heavy traffic*
HERE	тут	*here;* also *at this point* (not necessarily spatial)
	здесь	*here*
	сюда́	*to here*
	вот	*here is*
HOLE	дыра́	general word
	ды́рка, ды́рочка	dimins of дыра́: *small hole,* e.g. in clothing
	щель (f)	*tear, slit, crack*
	отве́рстие	*opening, aperture*
	я́ма	*pit, hole* (in road); возду́шная я́ма, *air pocket*
	лу́нка	in sport, e.g. on golf course; in ice (for fishing)
HOLIDAY	о́тпуск	time off work
	пра́здник	*festival,* e.g. Christmas, Easter
	кани́кулы (pl; gen кани́кул)	*school holidays, university vacations*
	свобо́дный день	*free day, day off*
	выходно́й день	day when shop, institution is not working. Note: Я сего́дня выходно́й, *It's my day off;* выходны́е (i.e. pl form) may mean *weekend.*
	о́тдых	*rest, recreation, leisure*

HOT	жа́ркий	e.g. жа́ркая пого́да, *hot weather*
	горя́чий	*hot* (to the touch), e.g. горя́чая вода́, *hot water*, горя́чий суп, *hot soup*
	о́стрый	*spicy, piquant*, e.g. о́стрый со́ус, *a hot sauce*
IDEA	иде́я	general word
	мысль (f)	*thought*
	ду́ма (R3)	*a thought*
	ду́мка	dimin of ду́ма
	поня́тие	*concept, understanding*
	представле́ние	*notion*; Представле́ния не име́ю, *I've no idea.*
	план	*plan*
	за́мысел	*scheme, project*
	наме́рение	*intention*
INFORM	информи́ровать/ проинформи́ровать + acc	*to notify*
	сообща́ть/сообщи́ть + dat	*to report to*
	извеща́ть/извести́ть + acc (R3b)	*to notify*
	осведомля́ть/осве́домить + acc (R3b, negative overtone)	*to notify*
	ста́вить/поста́вить кого́-н в изве́стность (R3b)	*to notify*
	доноси́ть/донести́ на + acc	*to denounce, inform against*
INTEREST	интере́с	*attention, pursuit*
	заинтересо́ванность (f)	*concern, stake (in)*, e.g. заинтересо́ванность в результа́те, *an interest in the outcome*
	проце́нты (pl; gen проце́нтов)	premium paid for use of money
	до́ля	*financial share*
INTRODUCE	представля́ть/предста́вить	*to present, introduce* (a person), e.g. Она́ предста́вила мне Ивано́ва, *She introduced Ivanov to me.*
	вводи́ть/ввести́	*to bring in*, e.g. ввести́ но́вый зако́н, *to introduce a new law*

	вноси́ть/внести́	*to incorporate*, e.g. внести́ попра́вку в докуме́нт, *to introduce a correction in a document*
INVOLVE	вовлека́ть/вовле́чь в + acc	*to draw in*, e.g. Он был вовлечён в манифеста́цию, *He got involved in the demonstration.*
	впу́тываться/впу́таться в + acc	*to be drawn in* (= passive of вовлека́ть/вовле́чь)
	уча́ствовать (impf only) в + prep	*to be involved in*, i.e. *take part in*
	вме́шиваться/вмеша́ться в + acc	*to get involved in*, i.e. *interfere/meddle in*
JOB	рабо́та	*work, employment*
	до́лжность (f)	position held
	обя́занность (f)	*duty, responsibility*
	ме́сто	post
	пост	*post*, e.g. высо́кий пост, *good job*
	поруче́ние	*mission, assignment*
	зада́ча	*task*
LAST	после́дний	last in series, e.g. после́днее и́мя в спи́ске, *the last name in a list*
	про́шлый	most recently past, e.g. на про́шлой неде́ле, *last week*
LAW	зако́н	*rule, statute*; also scientific formula
	пра́во	the subject or its study
	правопоря́док	*law and order*
	пра́вило	*rule, regulation*
	профе́ссия юри́ста	*the legal profession*
	юриди́ческий	in expressions such as юриди́ческая шко́ла, *law school*; юриди́ческий факульте́т, *law faculty*
LEADER	ли́дер	*(political) leader*
	руководи́тель (m)	*director, manager*
	вождь (m; R3, rhet)	*chief*
	передова́я статья́	*leading article (in newspaper)*
LEARN	учи́ться/научи́ться + dat of subject learned	*to learn, study*, e.g. учи́ться матема́тике, *to learn mathematics*

	учи́ть/вы́учить + acc	*to learn, memorise*
	изуча́ть/изучи́ть + acc	*to study*, e.g. изуча́ть матема́тику, *to learn mathematics*; pf изучи́ть implies mastery
	занима́ться/заня́ться + instr	*to study*, e.g. занима́ться ру́сским языко́м, *to learn Russian*
	узнава́ть/узна́ть	*to find out*
LEAVE	**выходи́ть/вы́йти**	*to go out*
	выезжа́ть/вы́ехать	*to go out* (by transport)
	уходи́ть/уйти́	*to go away*
	уезжа́ть/уе́хать	*to go away* (by transport)
	улета́ть/улете́ть	*to go away by plane, fly off*
	отправля́ться/отпра́виться	*to set off*
	отходи́ть/отойти́	*to depart* (of transport), e.g. По́езд отхо́дит в по́лдень, *The train leaves at midday.*
	вылета́ть/вы́лететь	*to depart* (of plane)
	удаля́ться/удали́ться	*to withdraw*
	оставля́ть/оста́вить	*to leave behind*; also *to bequeath*
	покида́ть/поки́нуть	*to abandon, forsake*
	броса́ть/бро́сить	*to abandon, forsake*, e.g. бро́сить жену́, *to leave one's wife*
	забыва́ть/забы́ть	to forget to take, e.g. Я забы́л зо́нтик в авто́бусе, *I left my umbrella on the bus.*
LIGHT	**свет**	general word
	освеще́ние	*lighting, illumination*
	просве́т	*shaft of light, patch of light*
	ого́нь (m)	on plane, ship; огни́ (pl; gen огне́й), *lights* (in buildings)
	ла́мпа	*lamp*
	фа́ра	*headlight* (on vehicle)
	светофо́р	*traffic light*
	проже́ктор	*searchlight*
	ра́мпа	*spotlight* (in theatre)
LINE	**ли́ния**	in various senses
	ряд	*row, series*
	верёвка	*cord, rope*

	леса́ (pl лёсы, gen лёс; dimin ле́ска)	*fishing-line*
	строка́	*on page*
LONG	**дли́нный**	*spatial*, e.g. дли́нная у́лица, *a long street*
	до́лгий	*temporal*, e.g. до́лгое вре́мя, *a long time*
(A) LONG TIME	**до́лго**	*a long time*
	задо́лго до + gen	*long before*, e.g. задо́лго до конца́, *long before the end*
	надо́лго	*for a long time*, e.g. Он уе́хал надо́лго, *He went away for a long time.*
	давно́	*long ago*; also *for a long time*, in the sense of *long since*, e.g. Я давно́ изуча́ю ру́сский язы́к, *I have been studying Russian for a long time.*
LOOK	**смотре́ть/посмотре́ть на** + acc	*to look at, watch*
	гляде́ть/погляде́ть на + acc	*to look/peer/gaze at*
	вы́глядеть (impf)	*to have a certain appearance*, e.g. Он вы́глядит хорошо́, *He looks well.*
	похо́же на дождь	*it looks like rain*
	взгля́дывать/взгляну́ть на + acc	*to glance at*
	Слу́шай(те)!	*Look!* i.e. *Listen!*
	уха́живать за + instr	*to look after (care for)*
	присма́тривать/присмотре́ть за + instr	*to look after (keep an eye on)*
LOSE	**теря́ть/потеря́ть**	*in various senses*
	утра́чивать/утра́тить (R3)	e.g. утра́тить иллю́зии, *to lose one's illusions*
	лиша́ться/лиши́ться + gen	*to be deprived of*, e.g. лиша́ться води́тельских прав, *to lose one's driving licence*
	прои́грывать/проигра́ть	*game, bet, etc.*
	заблужда́ться/заблуди́ться	*to lose one's way, get lost*

	отставать/отстать	of timepiece, e.g. Мои часы́ отстаю́т на де́сять мину́т в день, *My watch loses ten minutes a day.*
MAKE	де́лать/сде́лать	in various senses
	производи́ть/произвести́	*to produce*
	изготовля́ть/изгото́вить	*to manufacture*
	выраба́тывать/вы́работать	*to manufacture, produce, work out, draw up*
	выде́лывать/вы́делать	*to manufacture, process*
	гото́вить/пригото́вить	*to cook, prepare*
	вари́ть/свари́ть	*to cook* (by boiling)
	заставля́ть/заста́вить + infin	*to compel* (sb to do sth)
	зараба́тывать/зарабо́тать	*to earn*
	вы́йти (pf)	in construction Из неё вы́йдет хоро́шая учи́тельница, *She will make a good teacher.*
MANAGE	руководи́ть (impf only) + instr	*to direct, be in charge of*
	управля́ть (impf only) + instr	*to direct, be in charge of*
	заве́довать (impf only) + instr	*to direct, be in charge of*
	справля́ться/спра́виться с + instr	*to cope with*
	уме́ть/суме́ть + infin	*to know how (to do sth)*
	умудря́ться/умудри́ться + infin	*to contrive (to do sth)*
	удава́ться/уда́ться (3rd pers only; impers)	*to succeed*, e.g. Мне/ему́/ей удало́сь зако́нчить свою́ диссерта́цию, *I/he/she managed to finish my/his/her dissertation.*
	успева́ть/успе́ть на + acc, к + dat	*to be in time (for)*, e.g. Он успе́л к по́езду, *He managed to catch the train.*
	обходи́ться/обойти́сь	*to get by*, e.g. Мы обойдёмся, *We'll manage.*
MARRIAGE	сва́дьба	*wedding*
	жени́тьба	*process of getting married (from point of view of man)*
	заму́жество	*married state (for woman)*
	брак	*matrimony*
	супру́жество (R3)	*wedlock*

	союз	(fig) union, alliance
MARRY	жени́ться (impf and pf) на + prep	to get married (of man to woman)
	выходи́ть/вы́йти за́муж за + acc	to get married (of woman to man; lit to go out behind a husband)
	жени́ться/пожени́ться	to get married (of couple)
	венча́ться/обвенча́ться	to get married (of couple in church)
	венча́ть/обвенча́ть (trans)	to marry (i.e. what the officiating priest does)
MEAN	име́ть в виду́	to have in mind
	подразумева́ть	to imply, i.e. convey a meaning
	хоте́ть сказа́ть	to intend to say
	зна́чить	to signify, have significance
	означа́ть	to signify, stand for, e.g. Что означа́ют бу́квы США? What do the letters USA mean?
	намерева́ться	to intend to
	наме́рен/наме́рена/наме́рены (m/f/pl forms used as predicate) + infin	intend(s) (to do sth)
MEET	встреча́ть/встре́тить + acc	to meet (by chance), go to meet, e.g. Мы встре́тили их в аэропорту́, We met them at the airport.
	встреча́ться/встре́титься с + instr	to meet with (by arrangement); also to encounter, e.g. встре́титься с затрудне́ниями, to meet difficulties
	знако́миться/познако́миться с + instr	to make the acquaintance of, e.g. Он познако́мился с ней в Ри́ме, He met her in Rome.
MEETING	встре́ча	encounter
	свида́ние	appointment, rendezvous
	собра́ние	gathering (formal, e.g. party meeting)
	заседа́ние	formal session (people sitting and discussing)
	совеща́ние	(high-level) conference (people consulted, decisions made)
	ми́тинг	political rally

MISS	тосковáть по + dat	*to long for, yearn for*, e.g. тосковáть по рóдине, *to miss one's country*
	скучáть по + dat	similar to тосковáть but not so strong
	опáздывать/опоздáть на + acc	*to be late for*, e.g. опоздáть на пóезд, *to miss a train*
	не попадáть/попáсть в + acc	*to fail to hit*, e.g. Пýля не попáла в цель, *The bullet missed the target.*
	пропускáть/пропустúть	*to fail to attend*, e.g. пропустúть заня́тия, *to miss classes*
	проходúть/пройтú мúмо + gen	*to go past*, e.g. Онá прошлá мúмо поворóта, *She missed the turning.*
MOVE	двúгать/двúнуть (trans)	to change the position of sth, set in motion
	двúгать/двúнуть + instr	to move part of one's body, e.g. двúнуть пáльцем, *to move one's finger*
	подвигáть/подвúнуть (trans)	to move sth a bit
	отодвигáть/отодвúнуть (trans)	*to move aside*
	отодвигáться/отодвúнуться (intrans)	*to move aside*
	передвигáть/передвúнуть	*to shift* (from one place to another), e.g. передвúнуть стрéлки часóв назáд, *to move the clock back*
	сдвигáть/сдвúнуть (trans)	*to shift, budge* (from some point), e.g. сдвúнуть кровáть с её мéста, *to move the bed from its place*
	сдвигáться/сдвúнуться (intrans)	*to shift, budge* (from some point)
	шевелúться/шевельнýться	*to stir*
	переезжáть/переéхать	to move to new accommodation, e.g. переéхать на нóвую квартúру, *to move to a new flat*
	перебирáться/перебрáться	= переезжáть/переéхать in the sense above
	переходúть/перейтú	*to go across, transfer*, e.g. перейтú на нóвую рабóту, *to move to a new job*
	трóгать/трóнуть	*to touch, affect* (emotionally), e.g. Егó любéзность трóнула меня́ до слёз, *His kindness moved me to tears.*
	идтú	*to go, proceed*

	идти́ + instr	to move piece in board game, e.g. Он идёт пе́шкой, *He is moving a pawn.*
	развива́ться/разви́ться (intrans)	*to develop* (of events, action), e.g. Собы́тия бы́стро развива́ются, *Events are moving quickly.*
MUCH	мно́го	*a lot*
	намно́го	*by a large margin*
	гора́здо	with short comp adj, e.g. гора́здо лу́чше, *much better*
	сли́шком (мно́го)	*too much*
	о́чень	with verbs, *very much*, e.g. Э́та пье́са мне о́чень нра́вится, *I like this play very much.*
NAME	и́мя (n)	in various senses, incl *given name*
	о́тчество	*patronymic*
	фами́лия	*surname*
	кли́чка	*nickname*, name of pet
	про́звище	*nickname, sobriquet*
	назва́ние	*designation, appellation*
	репута́ция	*reputation*
NEED	нужда́	*need, necessity, want*
	необходи́мость (f)	*necessity, inevitability*
	потре́бность (f)	*requirement*
	нищета́	*poverty, indigence*
NICE	прия́тный	*pleasant, agreeable*
	симпати́чный	*likeable* (of person)
	до́брый	*kind, good*
	любе́зный	*kind, courteous*
	ми́лый	*sweet, lovable*
	обая́тельный	*charming* (of person)
	преле́стный	*delightful, charming* (of thing)
	ую́тный	*comfortable, cosy*
	вку́сный	of food, *tasty*
NIGHT	ночь (f)	general word

	ве́чер	*evening*, time of day up until bedtime, e.g. сего́дня ве́чером, *tonight*
NOTE	запи́ска	written message or memorandum
	заме́тка	a mark, e.g. заме́тки на поля́х, *notes in the margin*
	поме́тка	sth jotted down
	замеча́ние	*observation, remark*
	примеча́ние	additional observation, *footnote*
	но́та	musical note
	банкно́та (банкно́т also possible)	*bank-note*
NOW	сейча́с	*at the present moment; just now* (in the past); *presently, soon* (in the future)
	тепе́рь	*now, nowadays, today* (esp in contrast to the past)
	ны́не (R3, obs)	*nowadays*
	то . . . то	*now . . . now*, e.g. то дождь, то снег, *now rain, now snow*
NUMBER	число́	in various senses; also *date*
	но́мер	of bus, journal, etc.; also *hotel room*
	телефо́н	*telephone number*
	ци́фра	*figure, numeral*
	коли́чество	*quantity*
OLD	ста́рый	in various senses
	пожило́й	*middle-aged* (showing signs of ageing)
	пре́жний	*previous*
	бы́вший	*former, ex-*, e.g. бы́вший президе́нт, *the ex-President*
	стари́нный	*ancient*, e.g. стари́нный го́род, *an old city*
	дре́вний	*ancient* (even older than стари́нный), e.g. дре́вняя исто́рия, *ancient history*
	ве́тхий	*dilapidated*; also in phrase Ве́тхий заве́т, *the Old Testament*

	устаре́лый	obsolete, out-of-date
ORDER	зака́зывать/заказа́ть	to book, reserve, e.g. заказа́ть стол в рестора́не, to reserve a table in a restaurant
	прика́зывать/приказа́ть + dat + infin or что́бы	to order (sb to do sth)
	веле́ть (impf and pf; R3) + dat + infin or что́бы	to order (sb to do sth), e.g. Я веле́л ему́ вы́йти, I ordered him to leave.
PART	часть (f)	portion, component
	до́ля	share
	уча́стие	participation, e.g. принима́ть/приня́ть уча́стие в чём-н, to take part in sth
	роль (f)	role, e.g. in play; игра́ть роль, to play a part (also fig); исполня́ть/испо́лнить роль, to take a part (in play)
	па́ртия	musical part
	край	of country, region
PAY	плати́ть/заплати́ть кому́-н за что́-н	to pay sb for sth
	опла́чивать/оплати́ть что́-н	to pay for sth, e.g. оплати́ть расхо́ды, счёт, to pay the expenses, the bill

Note: Russians themselves may say оплати́ть за что́-н, but this usage is considered incorrect.

	отпла́чивать/отплати́ть кому́-н	to repay sb, pay sb back
	выпла́чивать/вы́платить	to pay out, e.g. вы́платить зарпла́ты, to pay wages
	упла́чивать/уплати́ть что́-н	to pay sth (which is due), e.g. уплати́ть взнос, нало́г, to pay a subscription, tax
	распла́чиваться/расплати́ться с + instr	to settle accounts with
	поплати́ться (pf) жи́знью за что́-н	to pay with one's life for sth
	свиде́тельствовать/засвиде́тельствовать своё почте́ние (R3b)	to pay one's respects

	обраща́ть/обрати́ть внима́ние на + асс	to pay attention to
	навеща́ть/навести́ть кого́-н	to pay a visit to sb
PAY(MENT)	платёж	in various senses; платёж в рассро́чку, *payment in instalments*; платёж нали́чными, *cash payment*
	пла́та	for amenities, services, e.g. пла́та за газ, обуче́ние, *payment for gas, tuition*
	опла́та	of costs, e.g. опла́та кварти́ры, пита́ния, прое́зда, *payment for a flat, food, travel*
	упла́та	of sum due, e.g. упла́та по́шлины, *payment of duty*
	зарпла́та	*wages, salary*
	полу́чка (R1)	= зарпла́та
	жа́лованье	*salary*
	взнос	*subscription*
PEOPLE	лю́ди	individuals, persons
	наро́д	*a people (ethnic group)*
POUR	лить (trans and intrans)	basic verb
	налива́ть/нали́ть (trans)	e.g. нали́ть напи́ток, *to pour a drink*
	разлива́ть/разли́ть	*to pour out (to several people)*
	сы́пать (impf; trans)	basic verb, of solids, e.g. сы́пать рис, *to pour rice*
	сы́паться (impf; intrans)	of solids, e.g. Песо́к сы́плется из мешка́, *Sand is pouring from the sack.*
	вали́ть (impf)	fig, e.g. Дым вали́л из до́ма, *Smoke was pouring from the house.*
	хлы́нуть (pf; intrans)	*to gush (of blood, water); also fig,* e.g. На у́лицу хлы́нула толпа́, *A crowd poured into the street.*
POWER	власть (f)	*authority*
	си́ла	*strength, force;* лошади́ная си́ла, *horse power*
	эне́ргия	*energy,* e.g. я́дерная эне́ргия, *nuclear power*
	мощь (f)	*might*

	мо́щность (f)	esp tech, e.g. мо́щность дви́гателя, *the power of an engine*
	держа́ва	an influential state; сверхдержа́ва, *a superpower*
	спосо́бность (f)	*ability, capacity*
	сте́пень (f)	math term
PRESENT (adj)	настоя́щий	now existing; настоя́щее вре́мя, *the present time* or *the present tense*
	совреме́нный	*modern, contemporary*
	ны́нешний	*today's*, e.g. ны́нешнее прави́тельство, *the present government*
	прису́тствующий	in attendance, in the place in question
PREVENT	меша́ть/помеша́ть + dat + infin	*to hinder, impede, stop* (sb from doing sth)
	предотвраща́ть/предотврати́ть	*to avert, stave off, forestall*
	препя́тствовать/воспрепя́тствовать + dat	*to obstruct, impede*
PUT	класть/положи́ть	into lying position
	ста́вить/поста́вить	into standing position
	сажа́ть/посади́ть	into sitting position. Note also: посади́ть кого́-н в тюрьму́, *to put sb in prison*
	укла́дывать/уложи́ть	*to lay*, e.g. уложи́ть ребёнка в посте́ль, *to put a child to bed*
	вставля́ть/вста́вить	*to insert*, e.g., вста́вить ключ в замо́к, *to put a key in a lock*
	ве́шать/пове́сить	*to hang*, e.g. пове́сить бельё на верёвку, *to put washing on a line*
	помеща́ть/помести́ть	*to place, accommodate*, e.g. помести́ть госте́й в свобо́дную ко́мнату, *to put guests in a spare room*; помести́ть де́ньги в сберка́ссу, *to put money in a savings bank*
	дева́ть/деть (in past tense дева́ть = деть)	*to do with*, e.g. Куда́ ты дева́л/дел кни́гу? *Where have you put the book?*
	засо́вывать/засу́нуть	*to shove in*, e.g. засу́нуть ру́ку в карма́н, *to put one's hand in one's pocket*

	высо́вывать/вы́сунуть	to stick out, e.g. вы́сунуть язы́к, to put one's tongue out
	задава́ть/зада́ть	in the phrase зада́ть вопро́с, to put a question
	выдвига́ть/вы́двинуть	to put forward, e.g. вы́двинуть тео́рию, to put forward a theory
	надева́ть/наде́ть	to put on, e.g. наде́ть шля́пу, to put on a hat
	откла́дывать/отложи́ть	to put off, defer
	убира́ть/убра́ть	to put away, clear up
QUEEN	короле́ва	monarch
	да́ма	playing card
	ферзь (m)	chess piece
	ма́тка	of insect, e.g. bee, ant
	гомосексуали́ст	homosexual
	голубо́й (subst adj; R1)	gay
QUIET	ти́хий	not loud, tranquil, calm
	бесшу́мный	noiseless, e.g. бесшу́мная маши́на, a quiet car
	споко́йный	tranquil, calm, peaceful
	молчали́вый	taciturn
REACH	доходи́ть/дойти́ до + gen	to get as far as (on foot)
	доезжа́ть/дое́хать до + gen	to get as far as (by transport)
	добира́ться/добра́ться до + gen	= доходи́ть/дойти́ and доезжа́ть/дое́хать, but implies some difficulty
	доноси́ться/донести́сь до + gen	to carry (of e.g. news, sounds, smells), e.g. До неё донёсся слух, A rumour reached her.
	дотя́гиваться/дотяну́ться до + gen	by touching, e.g. Я могу́ дотяну́ться до потолка́, I can reach the ceiling.
	достава́ть/доста́ть до + gen	to stretch as far as (of things and people)
	достига́ть/дости́гнуть + gen	to attain, e.g. дости́гнуть це́ли, to reach a goal
REALISE	понима́ть/поня́ть	to understand
	осознава́ть/осозна́ть	to acknowledge, e.g. осозна́ть оши́бку, to realise one's mistake

	отдава́ть/отда́ть себе́ отчёт в чём-н (R3)	*to be/become aware of sth (esp a difficulty)*
	осуществля́ть/осуществи́ть	*to bring into being, accomplish*
	реализова́ть (impf and pf)	*to convert into money; also to implement*, e.g. реализова́ть план, *to realise a plan*
REMEMBER	по́мнить (impf)	basic verb
	вспомина́ть/вспо́мнить	*to recall, recollect*
	запомина́ть/запо́мнить	*to memorise*
	помина́ть	in phrase Не помина́й(те) меня́ ли́хом, *Remember me kindly.*
	Note also the phrase **переда́й(те) приве́т** + dat, *remember (me) to*, i.e. *give my regards to.*	
RESPONSIBILITY	отве́тственность (f) обя́занность (f)	*answerability, obligation*, e.g. обя́занности мини́стра, *the minister's responsibilities*
RICH	бога́тый	*in various senses*
	зажи́точный	*well-to-do, prosperous*
	обеспе́ченный	*well provided-for*
	роско́шный	*luxurious, sumptuous*
	изоби́лующий + instr	*abounding in*, e.g. райо́н изоби́лующий приро́дными ресу́рсами, *a region rich in natural resources*
	ту́чный	*fertile*, e.g. ту́чная по́чва, *rich soil*
	жи́рный	*fatty (of food)*
	пря́ный	*spicy (of food)*
	сла́дкий	*sweet (of food)*
RISE	восходи́ть/взойти́	*to mount, ascend*, e.g. Со́лнце восхо́дит в шесть часо́в, *The sun rises at six o'clock.*
	встава́ть/встать	*to get up*
	поднима́ться/подня́ться	*to go up*
	повыша́ться/повы́ситься	*to get higher*, e.g. Це́ны повыша́ются, *Prices are rising.*
	увели́чиваться/увели́читься	*to increase*
	возраста́ть/возрасти́	*to grow*

	возвыша́ться/возвы́ситься над + instr	*to tower over*
	продвига́ться/продви́нуться	*to be promoted, gain advancement*
	восстава́ть/восста́ть на + acc	*to rebel against*
	воскреса́ть/воскре́снуть	*to be resurrected*, e.g. Христо́с воскре́с из мёртвых, *Christ rose from the dead.*
ROOM	ко́мната	*general word*
	но́мер	*hotel room*
	аудито́рия	*auditorium, classroom*
	зал	*hall, assembly room*; зал ожида́ния, *waiting-room*
	ме́сто	*space*
RUBBISH	му́сор	*refuse*
	сор	*litter, dust*
	дрянь (f)	*trash*
	ру́хлядь (f)	*junk (old and broken things)*
	хлам	*junk (things no longer needed)*
	ерунда́	*nonsense*
	чепуха́	= ерунда́
	вздор (more bookish)	*nonsense*
	нести́ ахине́ю (R1)	*to talk rubbish*
SAVE	спаса́ть/спасти́	*to rescue*
	бере́чь (impf)	*to put by, preserve*, e.g. бере́чь свои́ си́лы, *to save one's strength*
	сберега́ть/сбере́чь	*to put money by*
	оставля́ть/оста́вить	*to put aside (for future use)*, e.g. оста́вить буты́лку молока́ на за́втра, *to save a bottle of milk for tomorrow*
	избавля́ть/изба́вить кого́-н от чего́-н	*to spare sb sth*, e.g. Э́то изба́вило меня́ от мно́гих хлопо́т, *This saved me a lot of trouble.*
	эконо́мить/сэконо́мить (на + ргер)	*to use sparingly, economise (on)*, e.g. эконо́мить вре́мя, труд, *to save time, labour*
	выга́дывать/вы́гадать	*to gain*, e.g. вы́гадать вре́мя, *to save time*

SCENE	**сцéна**	in various senses
	зрéлище	*spectacle*
	явлéние	part of drama
	декорáция	*set, décor*
	скандáл	*scandalous event, row*
	пейзáж	*landscape*
	мéсто	*place*, e.g. мéсто преступлéния, *the scene of the crime*
SERIOUS	**серьёзный**	in various senses
	тяжёлый	*grave*, e.g. тяжёлая болéзнь, *a serious illness*
	óстрый	*acute*, e.g. óстрая проблéма, *a serious problem*
SERVICE	**слýжба**	in various senses
	услýга	*assistance, good turn*, e.g. окáзывать/оказáть комý-н услýгу, *to do sb a service*; also *facility*, e.g. коммунáльные услýги, *public services*
	служéние (R3)	act, process of serving, e.g. служéние мýзе, *serving one's muse*
	обслýживание	*attention*, e.g. in shop, restaurant; also *servicing, maintenance*, e.g. обслýживание машúны, *of a car*
	самообслýживание	*self-service*
	сéрвис	*attention* (from waiter, etc.)
	сервúз	set of crockery
	обрáд	*rite, ceremony*
	подáча	at tennis, etc.
SHAKE	**трястú** (impf; trans)	basic verb
	трястúсь (impf; intrans)	basic verb
	потрясáть/потрястú (trans)	*to rock, stagger* (fig), e.g. Онá былá потрясенá этим собы́тием, *She was shaken by this event.*
	встря́хивать/встряхнýть	*to shake up, rouse*; встряхнýть кóсти, *to shake dice*
	встря́хиваться/встряхнýться	*to shake oneself*
	вытря́хивать/вы́тряхнуть	*to shake out*, e.g. вы́тряхнуть скáтерть, *to shake out the table-cloth*

	стря́хивать/стряхну́ть	*to shake off*
	дрожа́ть (impf; intrans)	*to tremble, shiver*, e.g. Она́ дрожи́т от хо́лода, *She is shaking with cold.*
	подрыва́ть/подорва́ть	*to undermine*, e.g. подорва́ть чью-н ве́ру, *to shake sb's faith*
	грози́ть/погрози́ть + instr	*to make a threatening gesture with*, e.g. грози́ть кому́-н кулако́м, па́льцем, *to shake one's fist, finger at sb*
	кача́ть/покача́ть голово́й	*to shake one's head*
	пожима́ть/пожа́ть кому́-н ру́ку	*to shake hands with sb*
SHINE	**блесте́ть** (impf)	*to glitter, sparkle*, e.g. Его́ глаза́ блесте́ли ра́достью, *His eyes shone with joy.*
	блесну́ть (pf)	*to sparkle, glint*
	блиста́ть (impf)	*to shine* (esp fig), e.g. блиста́ть на сце́не, *to shine on the stage*
	сверка́ть (impf)	*to sparkle, glitter, gleam*
	сверкну́ть (pf)	*to flash*
	сия́ть	*to beam*, e.g. Со́лнце сия́ет, *The sun is shining* (viewer's subjective impression).
	свети́ть	of source of light, e.g. Ла́мпа све́тит я́рко, *The lamp is shining brightly* (objective statement).
	свети́ться	*to gleam, glint*, esp when giving light is not seen as the primary function of the subject, e.g. Её глаза́ свети́лись, *Her eyes were shining.*
	горе́ть (impf)	*to be on* (of light)
	мерца́ть (impf)	*to twinkle, flicker*, e.g. Звезда́ мерца́ет, *The star is shining.*
SHOE	**ту́фля**	*outdoor shoe*
	та́почка	*slipper, flipflop*
	босоно́жка	*sandal*
	башма́к	*clog*
	боти́нок (pl боти́нки, боти́нок)	*ankle-high boot*
	сапо́г (pl сапоги́, сапо́г)	*high boot*
	ва́ленок (pl ва́ленки, ва́ленок)	*felt boots*

	кроссо́вки (pl; gen кроссо́вок)	*trainers*
	о́бувь (f)	*footwear*
SHOOT	стреля́ть (impf)	basic verb
	застре́ливать/застрели́ть	*to shoot dead*
	обстре́ливать/обстреля́ть	*to bombard*
	расстре́ливать/расстреля́ть	*to execute by shooting*
	подстре́ливать/подстрели́ть	*to wound by shooting*
	мча́ться (impf)	*to tear along*
	проноси́ться/пронести́сь ми́мо + gen	*to rush past*
	бить по воро́там	*to shoot at goal*
	снима́ть/снять фильм	*to shoot a film*
SHOP	магази́н	general word
	ла́вка	*small shop, store*
	универма́г	*department store*
	гастроно́м	*food shop*
SHOW	пока́зывать/показа́ть	general word
	проявля́ть/прояви́ть	*to manifest, e.g.* прояви́ть интере́с к му́зыке, *to show an interest in music*
SIDE	сторона́	in various senses
	бок	of body or physical object
	склон	*slope, e.g.* склон холма́, горы́, *side of a hill, mountain*
	бе́рег	*bank, shore, e.g.* бе́рег реки́, о́зера, *side of a river, lake*
	край	*edge, e.g.* сиде́ть на краю́ крова́ти, *to sit on the side of the bed*
	обо́чина	of road
	борт	of ship
	кома́нда	*team*
	нару́жность (f)	*outside, exterior*
SIGHT	зре́ние	*vision*
	вид	*aspect, view*
	взгля́д	*glance, opinion, e.g.* на пе́рвый взгляд, *at first sight*
	зре́лище	*spectacle*

	достопримеча́тельность (f)	touristic attraction
	прице́л	aiming device

Note: also the phrase **знать** кого́-н **в лицо́**, *to know sb by sight*.

SIT	**сиде́ть**	*to be seated*
	сади́ться/сесть	*to sit down*
	приса́живаться/присе́сть	*to take a seat*
	проси́живать/просиде́ть	*to sit* (for a defined time)
	заседа́ть (intrans)	*to be in session*, e.g. Парла́мент заседа́ет, *Parliament is sitting.*
	быть чле́ном	*to be a member of*, i.e. *to sit on* (a committee)
	держа́ть экза́мен	*to sit an exam*
	сдава́ть экза́мен	= держа́ть экза́мен
SKIN	**ко́жа**	*in various senses*
	шку́ра	*hide, pelt* (of animal)
	ко́жица	*thin skin*, e.g. ко́жица виногра́да, колбасы́, помидо́ра, *grape skin, sausage skin, tomato skin*
	кожура́	*peel* (of fruit, e.g. apple)
	ко́рка	*thick skin, rind* (e.g. of an orange, cheese)
	шелуха́	crackly dry skin (e.g. of onion)
	пе́нка	on milk, etc.
SMALL	**ма́ленький**	*in various senses*
	небольшо́й	= ма́ленький
	ма́л (short form predominates)	*little, too small*, e.g. Э́та ша́пка мне мала́, *This hat is too small for me.*
	немногочи́сленный	*not numerous*, e.g. немногочи́сленная гру́ппа, *a small group*
	ме́лкий	*petty, unimportant, trivial*, of small calibre, status or denomination, etc., e.g. ме́лкий шрифт, *small print*; ме́лкая со́шка, *small fry*; ме́лкие де́ньги, *small change*
	ме́лочный	*small-minded*
	незначи́тельный	*insignificant*, e.g. игра́ть незначи́тельную роль, *to play a small part*

	второстепе́нный	*second-rate*
	плохо́й	*bad, poor,* e.g. плохо́й аппети́т, урожа́й, *a small appetite, harvest*
	скро́мный	*modest,* e.g. скро́мный дохо́д, *a small income*
SMELL (verb)	па́хнуть (intrans; impers) + instr	*to have the odour (of),* e.g. Здесь па́хнет га́рью, табако́м, *It smells of burning, tobacco here.*
	попа́хивать (intrans; impers; R1) + instr	*to smell slightly of*
	ду́рно па́хнуть (intrans)	*to emit a bad smell*
	воня́ть (impf; intrans) + instr	*to stink, reek (of),* e.g. В ку́хне воня́ет ры́бой, *It smells of fish in the kitchen.*
	чу́ять/почу́ять (trans)	of animals, to perceive by smelling, e.g. Волк почу́ял за́йца, *The wolf smelt a hare.*
	чу́вствовать/почу́вствовать	of humans, to perceive by smelling
	слы́шать/услы́шать (за́пах)	= чу́вствовать
	ню́хать/поню́хать	*to sniff*
	проню́хивать/проню́хать	*to smell out, get wind of* (also fig)
	обоня́ть (impf)	to have a sense of smell
SMELL (noun)	за́пах	*odour*
	обоня́ние	*sense of smell*
	арома́т	*aroma*
	благоуха́ние	*fragrance*
	вонь (f)	*stink, stench*
SOUND	звук	general word
	шум	*noise,* e.g. шум ве́тра, дождя́, мо́ря, *the sound of the wind, rain, sea*
	визг	*scream, squeal, yelp, screech*
	го́мон	*hubbub* (not harmonious)
	гро́хот	*crash, din, thunder*
	гул	*rumble, hum,* e.g. гул движе́ния, *the sound of traffic*
	жужжа́ние	*buzz, drone, humming,* e.g. жужжа́ние пчёл, *the sound of bees*
	журча́ние	*babbling,* e.g. журча́ние воды́, *the sound of water*

	звон	*chinking, clinking*, e.g. звон монéт, стакáнов, *the sound of coins, glasses*
	звонóк	*ring* (sound of bell)
	лéпет	*babble*, e.g. лéпет младéнца, *the sound of a baby*
	раскáт	*roll, peal*, e.g. раскáт грóма, *the sound of thunder*
	свист	*whistling, warbling, hissing*
	скрип	*squeak, scraping*
	стук	*knock, thump, thud, tap*
	тóпот	*treading, tramping*; кóнский тóпот, *the sound of hoofs*
	треск	*crackle*, e.g. треск кострá, *the sound of a bonfire*
	удáр	*clap* (e.g. of thunder)
	шéлест	*rustle* (e.g. of papers, rushes)
	шóрох	*rustle* (soft, indistinct, perhaps of animal)
SPEND	трáтить/истрáтить	*to pay out*, e.g. истрáтить дéньги, *to spend money*
	расхóдовать/израсхóдовать (R3b)	*to expend*, e.g. израсхóдовать дéньги, *to spend money*
	проводи́ть/провести́	*to pass*, e.g. провести́ врéмя, *to spend time*
STAND	стоя́ть	*to be standing*
	простáивать/простоя́ть	*to stand* (for a specified time); *to stand idle*, e.g. Станки́ простáивают, *The machines stand idle.*
	стáвить/постáвить	to put into standing position
	станови́ться/стать	to move into certain positions, e.g. стать на цы́почки, *to stand on tiptoe*
	вставáть/встать	*to get up*
	выноси́ть/вы́нести	*to endure*
	терпéть/потерпéть	*to endure*
	выдéрживать/вы́держать	*to withstand, stand up to*, e.g. Её кни́га не вы́держит кри́тики, *Her book will not stand up to criticism.*
	оставáться/остáться в си́ле	*to remain in force*, e.g. Решéние остаётся в си́ле, *The decision stands.*

	обстоя́ть (impf)	in expression Как обстои́т де́ло, *How do things stand?*
STATE	состоя́ние	*condition*
	положе́ние	*position, state of affairs*
	настрое́ние	*mood, state of mind*
	госуда́рство	body politic
STATION	ста́нция	general word, e.g. радиоста́нция, *radio station*; электроста́нция, *power station*; also small railway station, underground station
	вокза́л	*railway terminus, mainline station*
	уча́сток	in phrases избира́тельный уча́сток, *polling station*, and полице́йский уча́сток, *police station*
	запра́вочный пункт/ запра́вочная ста́нция	*filling station*
STEP	шаг	*pace*
	ступе́нь (f)	on flight of stairs
	ступе́нька	= ступе́нь; also *step* on ladder
	ле́стница	*ladder, staircase*
	стремя́нка	*step-ladder*
	подно́жка	*footboard* (of vehicle)
	крыльцо́	steps into building, *porch*
	по́ступь (f)	*tread*, e.g. тяжёлая по́ступь, *heavy step*
	похо́дка	*gait, way of walking*
	ме́ра	*measure*, e.g. принима́ть/приня́ть ме́ры, *to take steps*
	па (n, indecl)	*dance step*
	стопа́	in phrase идти́ по чьи́-н стопа́м, *to follow in sb's footsteps*

Note the expression **идти́ в но́гу с** + instr, *to be in step with*.

STOP (verb)	остана́вливать/останови́ть (trans)	*to bring to a halt*
	остана́вливаться/останови́ться (intrans)	*to come to a halt*
	приостана́вливать/ приостанови́ть (trans)	*to suspend*, e.g. приостанови́ть платежи́, *to stop payments*

	прекраща́ть/прекрати́ть (trans)	to arrest progress, e.g. прекрати́ть я́дерные испыта́ния, *to stop nuclear tests*
	прекраща́ться/прекрати́ться (intrans)	*to come to an end*
	перестава́ть/переста́ть + impf infin	*to cease* (doing sth), e.g. Он переста́л писа́ть, *He stopped writing.*
	броса́ть/бро́сить + impf infin	*to give up* (doing sth), e.g. Она́ бро́сила кури́ть, *She has stopped smoking.*
	меша́ть/помеша́ть + dat + infin	*to prevent sb from doing sth*, e.g. Ра́дио меша́ет мне рабо́тать, *The radio is stopping me working.*
	прерыва́ть/прерва́ть	*to interrupt*, i.e. stop (sb) talking
	заде́рживать/задержа́ть	*to detain*, e.g. Он был заде́ржан полице́йским, *He was stopped by a policeman.*
	уде́рживать/удержа́ть от + gen of verbal noun	*to restrain* (sb from doing sth)
	затыка́ть/заткну́ть	*to plug, seal*
STORM	**бу́ря**	*rainstorm, tempest*
	гроза́	*thunderstorm*
	мете́ль (f)	*snowstorm*
	вьюга	*blizzard* (snow swirling)
	пурга́	= вьюга
	бура́н	*snowstorm* (in steppes)
	урага́н	*hurricane*
	шквал	*squall* (at sea); also *barrage* (mil and fig)
	шторм	*gale* (at sea)
	вихрь (m)	*whirlwind*; also fig, e.g. революцио́нный вихрь, *the revolutionary storm*
	град	*hail*; also fig, e.g. град пуль, оскорбле́ний, *a hail of bullets, insults*
	штурм	military assault
STORY	**расска́з**	*tale*
	по́весть (f)	*novella*
	ска́зка	*fairy tale*
	исто́рия	series of events

	анекдо́т	*anecdote, joke*
	фа́була	*plot* (literary term)
	вы́думка	*fabrication, invention*
	небыли́ца	*cock-and-bull story*
	статья́	in newspaper
STRING	верёвка	*cord, rope*
	бечёвка	*twine*
	ни́тка	*thread,* e.g. ни́тка же́мчуга, *a string of pearls*
	струна́	of musical instrument
	ряд	*row, series*
	верени́ца	line of people, animals or vehicles
	цепь (f)	*chain*
STRONG	си́льный	in various senses
	кре́пкий	*sturdy, robust,* e.g. кре́пкий чай, *strong tea*; кре́пкое вино́, *strong wine*
	про́чный	*stout, durable,* e.g. про́чный фунда́мент, *a strong foundation*
	твёрдый	*firm,* e.g. твёрдая ве́ра, *strong faith*
	убеди́тельный	*convincing,* e.g. убеди́тельный до́вод, *a strong argument*
TEACH	учи́ть/научи́ть кого́-н + dat of subject taught or + infin	to give instruction, e.g. Я учу́ его́ испа́нскому языку́, *I am teaching him Spanish*; Она́ научи́ла меня́ игра́ть на скри́пке, *She taught me to play the violin.*
	обуча́ть/обучи́ть	= учи́ть/научи́ть
	проу́чивать/проучи́ть кого́-н (R1)	*to give sb a good lesson*
	преподава́ть (impf)	to give instruction in higher educational institution
TEACHER	учи́тель(ница)	*schoolteacher*
	преподава́тель(ница)	in higher education
	воспита́тель(ница)	sb responsible for general upbringing, including moral upbringing
	наста́вник	*mentor*

THEN	тогда́	*at that time*; also *in that case* in conditional sentences (see 11.9)
	пото́м	*afterwards, next*
	зате́м	*afterwards, next*
THICK	то́лстый	*fat*, e.g. то́лстый ломо́ть, *a thick slice*
	густо́й	*dense*, e.g. густо́й тума́н, *a thick fog*; густо́й суп, *thick soup*
	тупо́й (R1)	*dull-witted*
THIN	то́нкий	*not fat or thick*, e.g. то́нкий ломо́ть, *a thin slice*
	худо́й	*slender*, e.g. худо́е лицо́, *a thin face*
	худоща́вый	*lean*
	исхуда́лый	*emaciated*
	исхуда́вший	= исхуда́лый
	жи́дкий	*of liquid*, e.g. жи́дкий суп, *thin soup*
	ре́дкий	*sparse*, e.g. ре́дкие во́лосы, *thin hair*
	неубеди́тельный	*unconvincing*, e.g. неубеди́тельный до́вод, *a thin argument*
THINK	ду́мать/поду́мать	basic verb
	выду́мывать/вы́думать	*to think up, invent, fabricate*
	обду́мывать/обду́мать	*to think over, ponder*, e.g. Он обду́мал план, *He thought over the plan.*
	приду́мывать/приду́мать	*to think up, devise*, e.g. Они́ приду́мали отгово́рку, *They thought up an excuse.*
	проду́мывать/проду́мать	= обду́мывать/обду́мать
	мы́слить	*to engage in thinking*, e.g. Она́ мы́слит я́сно, *She thinks clearly.*
	счита́ть/счесть + acc + instr	*to consider*, e.g. Я счита́ю сестру́ спосо́бной же́нщиной, *I think my sister is a capable woman*
	мне/тебе́/нам ка́жется	*I/you/we think*
	мне/тебе́/нам ду́мается	= мне/тебе́/нам ка́жется
	быть хоро́шего/высо́кого/ дурно́го мне́ния о ко́м-н	*to think well/highly/badly of sb*
TIME	вре́мя	*in various senses*; also *tense*

раз	*occasion*
эпо́ха	*epoch*
пери́од	*period*
век	*age, century*
срок	*fixed period, term*
моме́нт	*moment,* e.g. в подходя́щий моме́нт, *at the right time*
сезо́н	*season*
слу́чай	*instance,* e.g. в девяти́ слу́чаях из десяти́, *nine times out of ten*
час	*hour, time of day,* e.g. Кото́рый час? *What time is it?* В кото́ром часу́? *At what time?*
такт	*mus term,* e.g. отбива́ть/отби́ть такт, *to keep time*
пора́ + infin	*it is time* (to do sth)
досу́г	*spare time, leisure,* e.g. на досу́ге, *in one's spare time*
в два счёта (R1)	*in no time, in a jiffy*

Note also **во́-время**, *on time*; **впервы́е**, *for the first time*; **заблаговре́менно** (R3), *in good time*.

TOP	верх	in various senses
	верши́на	*summit,* e.g. верши́на горы́, *the top of a mountain*
	верху́шка	*apex,* e.g. верху́шка де́рева, *the top of a tree*
	маку́шка	*top of the head*
	пове́рхность (f)	*surface*
	колпачо́к	of a pen
	кры́шка	*lid,* e.g. кры́шка коро́бки, *the top of a box*
	нача́ло	*beginning,* e.g. нача́ло страни́цы, *the top of the page*
	пе́рвое ме́сто	*first place, pre-eminence*
	во весь го́лос	*at the top of one's voice*
	на седьмо́м не́бе	*on top of the world* (lit *in seventh heaven*)
	наверху́	*on top*
	све́рху	*from the top*

TOUCH	**тро́гать/тро́нуть**	basic verb, e.g. тро́нуть что́-н рука́ми, *to touch sth with one's hands*; also fig, e.g. Её слова́ глубоко́ тро́нули меня́, *Her words touched me deeply.*
	дотра́гиваться/дотро́нуться до + gen	*to make contact with*, e.g. Не дотро́нься до горя́чего утюга́, *Don't touch the hot iron.*
	затра́гивать/затро́нуть	*to affect, touch on*, e.g. затро́нуть те́му, *to touch on a theme*
	каса́ться/косну́ться + gen	*to make contact with*, e.g. косну́ться мяча́, *to touch the ball*; *to touch on*, e.g. косну́ться сло́жного вопро́са, *to touch on a difficult question*
	прикаса́ться/прикосну́ться к + dat	*to touch lightly, brush against*
	достава́ть/доста́ть до + gen	*to reach*, e.g. доста́ть до дна, *to touch the bottom*
	дотя́гиваться/дотяну́ться до + gen	*to stretch as far as*, e.g. Он дотяну́лся до потолка́, *He touched the ceiling.*
	равня́ться/сравня́ться с + instr	*to compare in quality with*, e.g. В матема́тике никто́ не мо́жет сравня́ться с ней, *No one can touch her in mathematics.*
	стрельну́ть (R1)	*to cadge*, e.g. Он стрельну́л у меня́ пятёрку, *He touched me for a fiver.*
	не есть	*not to touch food*
	не пить	*not to touch alcohol*

Note the expression **задева́ть/заде́ть** кого́-н **за живо́е**, *to touch sb to the quick.*

TRY (verb)	**пыта́ться/попыта́ться**	*to attempt*
	про́бовать/попро́бовать	= пыта́ться in R1/2; also *to sample, taste* (food)
	стара́ться/постара́ться	*to attempt* (more effort than пыта́ться)
	стреми́ться (impf) + infin	*to strive* (to do sth)
	ме́рить/поме́рить	*to try on* (shoes, clothing)
TURN (verb)	**повора́чивать/поверну́ть** (trans)	basic verb, e.g. поверну́ть ключ, руль, го́лову, *to turn a key, steering wheel, one's head*
	повора́чиваться/поверну́ться (intrans)	basic verb

вывора́чивать/вы́вернуть	to turn (inside) out, e.g. вы́вернуть карма́н, to turn out one's pocket
завора́чивать/заверну́ть	to turn (a corner), e.g. заверну́ть за́ угол, to turn a corner; also to tighten or to shut off by turning, e.g. заверну́ть га́йку, кран, to tighten a nut, turn off a tap
обора́чиваться/оберну́ться	to turn one's head; to turn out, e.g. Собы́тия оберну́лись ина́че, Events turned out differently.
перевора́чивать/переверну́ть	to turn over, invert, e.g. переверну́ть страни́цу, to turn a page
подвора́чиваться/подверну́ться	to turn up, appear, crop up
развора́чиваться/разверну́ться (intrans)	to swing round, do a U-turn
свора́чивать/сверну́ть	to turn off (in a new direction), e.g. сверну́ть с доро́ги, to turn off the road
крути́ть/покрути́ть	to twist, wind, e.g. покрути́ть ру́чку, to turn a handle
верте́ть (impf; trans) + acc or instr	to rotate, twirl, e.g. Он ве́ртит зо́нтиком, He is twirling his umbrella.
верте́ться (intrans)	to rotate, revolve
враща́ть (trans)	to rotate, revolve
враща́ться (intrans)	to rotate, revolve, e.g. Колесо́ ме́дленно враща́ется, The wheel is slowly turning.
кружи́ться/закружи́ться	to whirl, spin round
направля́ть/напра́вить что́-н **на** + acc	to direct sth at/towards, e.g. напра́вить своё внима́ние на очередну́ю зада́чу, to turn one's attention to the next task
превраща́ть/преврати́ть что́-н **в** + acc	to change sth into (sth)
превраща́ться/преврати́ться в + acc (intrans)	to change into (sth)
станови́ться/стать + instr	to turn into, become, e.g. Он стал пья́ницей, He has turned into a drunkard.
обраща́ться/обрати́ться к кому́-н	to address oneself to sb
переходи́ть/перейти́ к + dat	to switch over to, e.g. Она́ перешла́ к друго́му вопро́су, She turned to another question.

	включа́ть/включи́ть	*to turn on* (switch, tap)
	выключа́ть/вы́ключить	*to turn off* (switch, tap)
	гаси́ть/погаси́ть	*to turn out, extinguish*, e.g. погаси́ть свет, *to turn out the light*
	выгоня́ть/вы́гнать	*to turn out, drive out*, e.g. Оте́ц вы́гнал сы́на и́з дому, *The father turned his son out of the house.*
	прогоня́ть/прогна́ть	*to turn away, banish*
	восстава́ть/восста́ть про́тив + gen	*to turn against*, e.g. Толпа́ восста́ла про́тив мили́ции, *The crowd turned against the police.*
	ока́зываться/оказа́ться + instr	*to turn out/prove to be*, e.g. Она́ оказа́лась прекра́сным адвока́том, *She turned out to be an excellent lawyer.*
	закрыва́ть/закры́ть глаза́ на + acc	*to turn a blind eye to*
	бледне́ть/побледне́ть	*to turn pale*
	красне́ть/покрасне́ть	*to turn red, blush*
USE (verb)	употребля́ть/употреби́ть + acc	in various senses
	по́льзоваться/воспо́льзоваться + instr	*to make use of*, e.g. воспо́льзоваться услу́гами, *to make use of services*
	испо́льзовать (impf and pf) + acc	*to utilise*
	применя́ть/примени́ть	*to apply*, e.g. примени́ть я́дерную эне́ргию, *to use nuclear energy*
	эксплуати́ровать	*to exploit*
	прибега́ть/прибе́гнуть к + dat	*to resort to*
VIEW	вид	what can be seen, e.g. вид на о́зеро, *view of the lake*; вид с пти́чьего полёта, *bird's-eye view*
	взгляд	opinion, e.g. на мой взгляд, *in my view*
	мне́ние	opinion
	убежде́ние	conviction
	то́чка зре́ния	point of view
VILLAGE	село́	community with a church
	дере́вня	smaller community than село́; also means *country(side)*
	посёлок	settlement

VISIT (verb)	посеща́ть/посети́ть	*to call on, go to*, esp places
	навеща́ть/навести́ть	*to call on*, esp people
	наноси́ть/нанести́ визи́т (R3b)	*to pay a visit*
	быть у кого́-н **в гостя́х**	*to be a guest at sb's place*
	идти́/пойти́ **в го́сти** к + dat	*to go to* (as a guest)
	гости́ть/погости́ть **у** + gen	*to stay with* (as a guest)
	заходи́ть/зайти́ к + dat	*to call on*
	быва́ть/побыва́ть **в** + prep	*to spend some time in* (town, country)
	осма́тривать/осмотре́ть	*to inspect*, e.g. осмотре́ть достопримеча́тельности, *to visit the sights*
	сове́товаться/посове́товаться **с** + instr	*to consult* (e.g. doctor)
WAY	путь (m)	*road, path*, esp in abstract sense, e.g. на обра́тном пути́, *on the way back*; на полпути́, *halfway*
	доро́га	*road*
	направле́ние	*direction*
	спо́соб	*means, method*
	сре́дство	*means, method*
	о́браз	*manner, fashion*, e.g. таки́м о́бразом, *in this way*
	вход	*way in*
	вы́ход	*way out*
	перехо́д	*way across*
	расстоя́ние	*distance, way off*

Note: *way* is often not directly translated in adverbial phrases, e.g. по-дру́жески, *in a friendly way*.

WIN	выи́грывать/вы́играть	*to be the victor*, also trans, e.g. вы́играть приз, *to win a prize*
	побежда́ть/победи́ть	*to triumph, prevail*, e.g. Она́ победи́ла в бе́ге, *She won the race.*
	завоёвывать/завоева́ть (trans)	*to gain, secure*, e.g. завоева́ть золоту́ю меда́ль, *to win a gold medal*
	одержа́ть (pf) побе́ду (R3)	*to triumph*
WINDOW	окно́	*general word*; *also free period* for teacher
	око́шко	*dimin of* окно́; e.g. of ticket-office

	фо́рточка	small window within window which can be opened for ventilation
	витри́на	*shop window*
	витра́ж	*stained-glass window*
WORK	рабо́та	in various senses
	труд	*labour*
	слу́жба	official/professional service
	ме́сто	position at work
	заня́тия (pl; gen заня́тий)	*studies, classes* (at school, university)
	зада́ча	*task*
	де́ятельность (f)	*activity*
	произведе́ние	creation produced by artist
	сочине́ние	= произведе́ние; собра́ние сочине́ний Пу́шкина, *collection of Pushkin's works*
	тво́рчество	corpus of works by writer, *œuvre*
WORKER	рабо́тник	sb who does work
	слу́жащий	*white-collar worker*
	рабо́чий	*manual worker*
	трудя́щийся	= рабо́чий, but more respectful
	пролета́рий	*proletarian*
	тру́женик (R3, rhet)	*toiler*
	работя́га (m and f; R1 slightly pej)	*hard worker*
WORLD	мир	in most senses, esp abstract, including e.g. spheres of existence or activity, civilisations
	во всём ми́ре	*all over the world*
	живо́тный мир	*the animal world*
	расти́тельный мир	*the vegetable world*
	нау́чный мир	*the scientific world*
	дре́вний мир	*the ancient world*
	свет	narrower use, tends to be more concrete, e.g. Ста́рый свет, *the Old World*; Но́вый свет, *the New World*; путеше́ствие вокру́г све́та, *journey round the world*
	земно́й шар	*the Earth, globe*
	вселе́нная	*universe*

	общество	*society*
	круги́ (pl; gen круго́в)	*circles*
	жизнь (f)	*life*
WRONG	**не тот/та/то**	not the right thing
	не тогда́	not at the right time
	не там	not in the right place
	не туда́	not to the right place
	не по а́дресу	*to the wrong address*
	непра́вый	of person, e.g. Он непра́в, *He is wrong.*
	непра́вильный	*incorrect*, e.g. непра́вильное реше́ние, *wrong decision*
	оши́бочный	*mistaken, erroneous*
	ошиба́ться/ошиби́ться	*to be mistaken*
	фальши́вый	*false*, e.g. фальши́вая но́та, *wrong note*
	неподходя́щий	*unsuitable*
	не на́до* + impf infin	*it is wrong to/one should not*
	не ну́жно*	= не на́до
	не сле́дует*	= не на́до
	не рабо́тает	*is not functioning*
	поша́ливает (R1)	*plays up from time to time*, e.g. of mechanism

* Stylistically these synonymous forms may be arranged in the following
   ascending order of formality: не на́до, не ну́жно, не сле́дует.

4.2   Translation of the verb *to be*

Translation of the verb *to be* into Russian gives rise to much difficulty, for
it is rendered by some form of its most obvious equivalent, быть, in only
a small proportion of instances. The following list gives some indication
of the numerous verbs to which Russian resorts in contexts in which
an English-speaker might comfortably use some part of the verb *to be*.

- **быть**, which is omitted altogether in the present tense (the omission
  sometimes being indicated by a dash; see 11.15) may be used when the
  complement offers a simple definition of the subject, e.g.

  Вес ребёнка – о́коло четырёх килогра́ммов.
  The child's weight is about four kilogrammes.
  Это **была́** коро́ткая война́.
  It was a short war.

Note: on use of case in the complement of быть see 11.1.10.

- **быва́ть** = *to be* in habitual or frequentative meaning, e.g.

  Её муж рабо́тает в Москве́, но **быва́ет** до́ма на все пра́здники.
  Her husband works in Moscow but is home for all holidays.
  Его́ иностра́нные друзья́ ча́сто у него́ **быва́ли**.
  His foreign friends often came to see him.

- **явля́ться/яви́ться** may be used when the complement defines the subject, e.g.

  Основны́ми исто́чниками облуче́ния персона́ла на я́дерных
  реа́кторах **явля́ются** проду́кты корро́зии металли́ческих
  пове́рхностей труб.
  *The products of corrosion of the metallic surfaces of the pipes are the
  fundamental sources of the irradiation of personnel at nuclear reactors.*
  Состоя́вшиеся в Дама́ске перегово́ры **яви́лись** очередно́й попы́ткой
  найти́ 'ара́бское реше́ние' конфли́кта в Зали́ве.
  *The talks which took place in Damascus were the latest attempt to find an
  'Arab solution' to the Gulf conflict.*

Note 1   As is clear from the flavour of the above examples, явля́ться/яви́ться belongs
mainly in R3.

2   The complement of явля́ться/яви́ться must be in the instrumental case. The
complement is the noun that denotes the broader of the two concepts, whilst
the subject, which is in the nominative case, denotes the more specific
concept, the precise thing on which the speaker or writer wishes to
concentrate.

3   It follows from what is said in note 2 that such relatively vague words as
исто́чник, *source*; **перспекти́ва**, *prospect*; **попы́тка**, *attempt*; **причи́на**, *cause*;
пробле́ма, *problem*; **результа́т**, *result*; **сле́дствие**, *consequence*; **часть**, *part*, will
usually be found in the instrumental case when явля́ться/яви́ться is used.

4   In practice the subject (i.e. the noun in the nominative) often follows
явля́ться/яви́ться (see the first example above) because the phrase at the end
of the sentence carries special weight and it is on this phrase that the speaker
or writer wishes to concentrate (see 11.14 on word order). However, the
choice as to which noun should be put in which case does not actually hinge
on word order.

- **представля́ть собо́й** (impf) is much less common than
  явля́ться/яви́ться but fulfils the same function of bookish substitute
  for быть, e.g.

  Э́ти материа́лы **представля́ют собо́й** обы́чные при́меси леги́рующих
  элеме́нтов ста́ли.
  These materials are the usual admixtures in the alloying elements of steel.

Note: the complement of представля́ть собо́й is in the accusative case.

- **стать** (pf) is now frequently used as an apparent synonym for
  явля́ться/яви́ться, e.g.

  Причи́ной катастро́фы **ста́ли** техни́ческие непола́дки.
  Technical malfunctions were the cause of the disaster.

Закры́тие ба́зы **ста́ло** одно́й из составны́х часте́й програ́ммы по
сокраще́нию ассигнова́ний на оборо́ну.
*The closure of the base was one of the components of a programme of defence
cuts.*

Note: all the points made in notes 1–4 on явля́ться/яви́ться will apply also to стать
when it has this function.

- **заключа́ться в** + prep is frequently used in R2/R3 in the sense *to
consist in*, e.g.

Одна́ из гла́вных причи́н недово́льства лицеи́стов **заключа́ется в**
том, что они́ обеспоко́ены свои́м бу́дущим.
*One of the main causes of the lycée pupils' discontent is that they are worried
about their future.*

- **состоя́ть в** + prep = заключа́ться in this sense, e.g.

Преиму́щество хлорфтороуглеро́дов пе́ред други́ми вещества́ми
состои́т в том, что они́ нетокси́чны.
The advantage of CFCs over other substances is that they are not toxic.

- **составля́ть/соста́вить** = *to constitute, to amount to*; this verb is followed
by the accusative case and is particularly common in statistical contexts,
e.g.

В э́том райо́не армя́не **составля́ют** меньшинство́.
Armenians are a minority in this region.
Температу́ра реа́ктора к моме́нту ги́бели подло́дки **составля́ла**
се́мьдесят гра́дусов.
*The temperature of the reactor at the moment the submarine was destroyed was
70 degrees.*

Note: this verb is particularly common in the phrases **составля́ть/соста́вить часть**, *to
be a part (of)* and **составля́ть/соста́вить исключе́ние**, *to be an exception.*

- **находи́ться** (impf) may be used when *to be* defines the position or
location of people, places or things, and also when state or condition is
being described, e.g.

Президе́нт находи́лся в Крыму́ на о́тдыхе.
The President was on holiday in the Crimea.
Черно́быль **нахо́дится** бли́зко от грани́цы с Белару́сью.
Chernobyl is close to the border with Belarus.
Аэропо́рт **нахо́дится** под контро́лем повста́нцев.
The airport is under the control of the rebels.
Обору́дование **нахо́дится** в отли́чном состоя́нии.
The equipment is in excellent condition.

- **располо́жен** (f **располо́жена**, n **располо́жено**, pl **располо́жены**) may
also be used when location is being described, e.g.

Кипр **располо́жен** киломе́трах в шести́десяти к ю́гу от Ту́рции.
Cyprus is about 60 kilometres south of Turkey.

- **стоя́ть, лежа́ть, сиде́ть** = *to stand, to lie, to be sitting*, respectively, e.g.

  Он **стои́т** в фойе́.
  He's in the foyer.
  Письмо́ **лежи́т** на столе́.
  The letter is on the desk.
  Они́ **сидя́т** в за́ле ожида́ния.
  They're in the waiting room.

- **сто́ить** = *to be worth, to cost*, e.g.

  Ско́лько **сто́ит** цветно́й телеви́зор?
  How much is a colour television set?

- **прису́тствовать** = *to be present*, e.g.

  Она́ **прису́тствовала** на заседа́нии.
  She was at the meeting.

- **рабо́тать** = *to work (as)*, e.g.

  Он **рабо́тает** по́варом.
  He's a cook.

- **служи́ть**, *to serve*, is more or less synonymous with рабо́тать but slightly more formal, e.g.

  Он **слу́жит** в а́рмии.
  He's in the army.

- **приходи́ться** = *to fall* (of dates), *to stand* in a certain relationship to, e.g.

  Правосла́вное Рождество́ **прихо́дится** на седьмо́е января́.
  The Orthodox Christmas is on 7 January.
  Он мне **прихо́дится** пра́дедом.
  He is my great-grandfather.

- **есть** is the copula when the subject and complement are the same, e.g.

  Я начина́ю узнава́ть, кто **есть** кто.
  I am beginning to find out who is who.
  Оши́бка **есть** оши́бка.
  A mistake is a mistake.

Note: есть also occurs in R3, in the scientific/academic or official/business styles, in definitions, e.g. Квадра́т **есть** прямоуго́льник, у кото́рого все сто́роны равны́, *A square is a rectangle all of whose sides are equal.*

- **существова́ть**, *to exist*, may translate *there is/there are*, e.g.

  Я ве́рю, что **существу́ет** Бог.
  I believe there is a God.
  В таки́х ситуа́циях **существу́ет** риск возникнове́ния войны́.
  There is a risk of war breaking out in such situations.

- **иметься** may also translate *there is/there are* in the sense of *to be available*, e.g.

  В го́роде **име́ется** музе́й.
  There is a museum in the town.
  Име́ются интере́сные да́нные об э́том.
  There is interesting information about this.

- **состоя́ться** (pf) may translate *there was/will be* in the sense of *to take place*, e.g.

  В де́сять часо́в **состои́тся** пресс-конфере́нция.
  There will be a press conference at ten o'clock.

Note: the verb *to be* may be used in English purely for emphasis, e.g. *It **was** only then that he realised what had happened.* When it has this purely emphatic function *to be* is not rendered in Russian by any verbal equivalent or substitute. The emphasis is conveyed instead by word order, by the manner of the speaker's delivery, or by use of some adverb such as и́менно, *namely, precisely,* or то́лько, *only,* or by some particle such as же or и (see 5.4 below). Thus the above sentence might be translated: Он то́лько тогда́ по́нял, что случи́лось.

4.3 Translation of English modal auxiliary verbs

Modal verbs express the mood or attitude of the speaker towards an action. The English modals give rise to much difficulty for the English-speaking student trying to render their meaning in a foreign language, as they do for the foreign student of English, because each modal is used in various ways and is more or less interchangeable with one or more other modals in some meanings (e.g. *can/could, can/may, may/might*). Moreover, the differences of meaning between certain modals (e.g. *must, should, ought, may, might*) may be so subtle that English-speakers themselves will not agree on the verbs' precise nuances.

Not all the possible translations of each English modal are given in this section, but most of their important functions are covered.

CAN	(a)	expressing ability or possibility: **мо́жно, мочь**, or (in the sense *to know how* to do sth) **уме́ть**, e.g.

This can be done at once.	**Э́то мо́жно** сде́лать сра́зу.
I can't lift this box.	Не **могу́** подня́ть э́тот я́щик.
He can swim.	Он **уме́ет** пла́вать.

	(b)	expressing request or permission (*can* is synonymous in this sense with *may* except in very formal English): **мо́жно, мочь**, e.g.

Can/May I come in?	**Мо́жно** войти́?
Can I go to the park, mum?	Мам, **мо́жно** пойду́ в парк? (R1)
You can/may smoke.	Вы **мо́жете** кури́ть.

(c)   expressing right, entitlement: **мочь, име́ть пра́во**, e.g.

We can vote at eighteen.	**Мы име́ем пра́во** голосова́ть в восемна́дцать лет.

(d)   with verbs of perception, when *can* bears little meaning: auxiliary omitted, e.g.

I can see a dog.	**Я ви́жу** соба́ку.
Can you hear?	**Слы́шно?**

(e)   expressing doubt: **неуже́ли**, e.g.

Can this be right?	**Неуже́ли** э́то пра́вда?

(f)   in negative (*cannot*), synonymous with *may not, must not*, expressing prohibition: **нельзя́** + impf infin; **не** + 3rd pers pl verb; also **не разреша́ется, воспреща́ется** (R3; formal, e.g. in notices):

You can't go in.	**Нельзя́** входи́ть.
You can't smoke here.	Здесь **не ку́рят.**
	Здесь кури́ть **не разреша́ется.** (R3)
You can't run up and down the escalators.	Бе́гать по эскала́торам **воспреща́ется.**

(g)   *cannot help*: **не мочь не** + infin, e.g.

I can't help laughing.	**Я не могу́ не смея́ться.**

COULD   (a)   past tense of *can*, i.e. = *was/were able to*: use past-tense forms of the translations given under *can* above;

(b)   polite request: **не мо́жете ли вы; не могли́ бы вы; пожа́луйста**, e.g.

Could you help me?	**Не мо́жете ли вы** помо́чь мне?
	Не могли́ бы вы помо́чь мне?
Could you pass the salt?	Переда́йте, **пожа́луйста,** соль.

(c)   *could have* (also *might have*), expressing unfulfilled possibility in past: **мог/могла́/могло́/могли́ бы**, e.g.

She could/might have done it [but did not].	Она́ **могла́ бы** э́то сде́лать.

(d)   *could have* (also *may have, might have*), expressing uncertainty as to whether action took place: **мо́жет быть**, e.g.

She could/might have done it [and may have done].	**Мо́жет быть** она́ и сде́лала э́то.

(e)   expressing emotion, wish: various translations, e.g.

She could have wept for joy.	Она́ **гото́ва была́** запла́кать от ра́дости.
I could have killed him.	**Мне хоте́лось** уби́ть его́.

MAY	(a)	expressing request or permission: see *can* (b);

(b) expressing possibility: **мочь, мо́жет быть, мо́жет** (= мо́жет быть in R1), **пожа́луй** (*perhaps*), **возмо́жно**, e.g.

He may lose his way.	**Он мо́жет** заблуди́ться.
They may have gone home.	Они́, **мо́жет (быть)**, пошли́ домо́й.
She may be right.	Она́, **пожа́луй**, права́.
It may be snowing there.	**Возмо́жно**, там идёт снег.

(c) after verbs of hoping and fearing and in concessive clauses (see 11.10) *may* is not directly translated, a future or subjunctive form of the Russian verb being used instead, e.g.

I hope he may recover.	Наде́юсь, что он **вы́здоровеет**.
I fear he may die.	Я бою́сь, **как бы** он не у́мер.
I shall find you wherever you may be.	Я найду́ вас, **где бы** вы **ни́ были**.

(d) expressing wish in certain phrases:

May the best man win.	**Да победи́т сильне́йший!**
May he rest in peace.	**Мир пра́ху его́!**

(e) *may not*, expressing prohibition: see *can* (f).

MIGHT	(a)	expressing possibility: synonymous with *may* (b) (though *might* is perhaps more colloquial);

(b) *might have* in the sense *could have, may have*: see *could* (c) and (d);

(c) after verbs of hoping and fearing and in concessive clauses: synonymous with *may* (c);

(d) expressing formal polite request in interrogative sentences: various formulae, e.g.

Might I suggest that . . .	**Позво́льте мне** предложи́ть, что́бы . . .
Might I discuss this matter with you tomorrow?	**Мо́жет быть**, вы за́втра разреши́те мне обсуди́ть э́то де́ло с ва́ми?

(e) *might have*, expressing reproach: **мог/могла́/могло́/могли́ бы**, e.g.

You might have told me that.	Вы **могли́ бы** мне сказа́ть э́то.

MUST	(a)	expressing obligation, necessity: **до́лжен/должна́/должны́, на́до, ну́жно, сле́дует** (see also note on 'wrong' in 4.1), e.g.

She must work.	Она́ **должна́** рабо́тать.
We must get up early.	Мы **должны́** встать ра́но.
You must come at once.	Тебе́ **на́до** прийти́ сра́зу же.
(We) must hurry.	**Ну́жно** торопи́ться.
One must observe the rules.	**Сле́дует** соблюда́ть пра́вила.

(b)   expressing certainty: **должно́ быть**, surrounded in the written
language by commas, e.g.

She must have gone.	Она́, **должно́ быть**, ушла́.
He must know this.	Он, **должно́ быть**, зна́ет э́то.

(c)   *must not*, expressing prohibition: see *can* (f).

OUGHT

(a)   expressing advisability, recommendation, obligation (more or less
synonymous with *should*): **сле́довало бы**, **до́лжен/должна́/должны́**,
e.g.

He ought to drink less.	Ему́ **сле́довало бы** поме́ньше пить.
She ought [is obliged] to be at work today.	Она́ **должна́** быть на рабо́те сего́дня.

(b)   *ought not*, expressing inadvisability, prohibition: **не сле́довало бы**,
e.g.

You ought not to laugh at him.	(Вам) **не сле́довало бы** смея́ться над ним.

(c)   *ought to have*, expressing reproach, regret at omission: **сле́довало бы**,
до́лжен был/должна́ была́/должны́ бы́ли бы, e.g.

She ought to have passed her examination.	Она́ **должна́ была́ бы** сдать экза́мен.
You ought to have helped us.	Вам **сле́довало бы** помо́чь нам.

(d)   expressing probability (less certain than *must* (b) but more certain than
may (b) and *might* (a)): **наве́рно(е)**, **вероя́тно**, e.g.

They ought to win.	Они́ **наве́рное** вы́играют.
She ought to be [probably is] home by now.	Она́ **вероя́тно** уже́ до́ма.

SHALL

(a)   expressing first person singular and first person plural of future tense:
future tense, e.g.

I shall write to him.	**Я напишу́** ему́.

(b)   expressing promise or threat (synonymous with *will*): perfective future,
e.g.

You shall receive the money tomorrow.	**Полу́чишь** де́ньги за́втра.
You shall pay for this.	Ты за э́то **запла́тишь**.

(c)   in questions asking whether sth is desirable or obligatory: impersonal
construction with dative subject (or with no subject stated) and
infinitive, e.g.

Shall I call in tomorrow?	**Мне зайти́** за́втра?
Shall I bring you some more vodka?	**Принести́** вам ещё во́дки?

	(d)	in R3b, in legal and diplomatic parlance, expressing obligation (synonymous with *will*): present tense, e.g.

The Russian side shall meet all these costs.	Российская сторона **берёт** на себя все эти расхо́ды.

SHOULD	(a)	synonymous in ordinary English speech with *would* (a), (b) and (c);
	(b)	expressing advisability, recommendation, obligation: more or less synonymous with *ought* (a);
	(c)	*should have*, expressing reproach or regret at omission: more or less synonymous with *ought* (c);
	(d)	expressing probability: more or less synonymous with *ought* (d);
	(e)	expressing modest assertion: various formulae, e.g.

I should think that . . .	**Мне ка́жется**, что . . .
I should say that . . .	**Я бы сказа́л(а)**, что . . .

	(f)	expressing surprise, indignation: various formulae, e.g.

Why should you suspect me?	**С како́й** э́то ста́ти вы меня́ подозрева́ете?
How should I know?	**Отку́да** мне знать?
You should see him!	**Посмотре́ли бы** вы на него́!

	(g)	as a subjunctive form in certain subordinate clauses: **что́бы** + past tense, e.g.

Everybody demanded that he should be punished.	Все потре́бовали, **что́бы** он **был** нака́зан.
I proposed that they should return the money.	Я предложи́л(а), **что́бы** они́ **возврати́ли** де́ньги.

WILL	(a)	as auxiliary forming second and third person singular and plural of future tense (and in ordinary English speech also first person singular and plural forms): future tense, e.g.

She will arrive tomorrow.	Она́ **прие́дет** за́втра.

	(b)	expressing probability, e.g. *She'll be home by now*: more or less synonymous with *ought* (d).
	(c)	expressing habitual action: imperfective verb, e.g.

He'll sit for hours in front of the television.	Он **сиди́т** це́лыми часа́ми пе́ред телеви́зором.

	Note:	*Boys will be boys*, **Ма́льчики остаю́тся ма́льчиками**.
	(d)	expressing polite invitation, exhortation or proposal in the form of a question: see *would* (d);
	(e)	*will not*, expressing refusal or disinclination: various renderings, e.g.

I will not do it.	Э́того я **не сде́лаю**.
	Я **не наме́рен(а)** э́того де́лать.
	Я **не хочу́** э́того де́лать.

WOULD

(a) as second and third person singular and plural auxiliary (and in ordinary speech also first person singular and plural), expressing conditional mood: past-tense form + **бы**, e.g.

| *They would go out if it stopped* | Они́ **вы́шли бы**, е́сли бы |
| *raining.* | прекрати́лся дождь. |

(b) as second and third person singular and plural auxiliary (and in ordinary speech also first person singular and plural) indicating future in indirect speech (see 11.6(a)): perfective future, e.g.

| *I told you I would come.* | Я тебе́ сказа́л, что **приду́**. |
| *He said he would ring me.* | Он сказа́л, что **позвони́т** мне. |

(c) with *like*, expressing wish: **хоте́л/хоте́ла/хоте́ли бы**, **хоте́лось бы**, e.g.

They would like to leave.	Они́ **хоте́ли бы** уйти́.
I would like to thank you	**Мне хоте́лось бы** тепло́
warmly.	поблагодари́ть вас.

(d) expressing polite invitation, exhortation or proposal in the form of a question (more or less synonymous with *will*): various formulae or a modified imperative, e.g.

Would you close the window,	**Вам не тру́дно** закры́ть окно́? or
please?	**Вас не затрудни́т** закры́ть окно́?
Would you wait a moment?	**Подожди́те** мину́точку,
	пожа́луйста.

(e) expressing frequent action in the past: imperfective past, possibly with a suitable adverb or adverbial phrase, e.g.

They would often pick mushrooms	Они́, **быва́ло, собира́ли** грибы́
in the wood.	в лесу́.
As a rule she would read in the	Она́, **как пра́вило, чита́ла** по
evenings.	вечера́м.

4.4 Transitive and intransitive verbs

A particular problem that confronts the English-speaking student of Russian is the morphological or lexical distinction which Russian makes more widely and clearly than English between transitive and intransitive verbs. Many English verbs which may function as either transitive or intransitive forms (e.g. *to improve, to hang*) must be rendered in different ways in Russian depending on whether or not they have a direct object. The student needs to be aware of two types of distinction.

- The distinction between transitive and intransitive usage may be made by the use of non-reflexive and reflexive forms respectively, e.g. Э́та ме́ра улу́чшит ситуа́цию, *This measure will improve* [trans] *the situation* and Ситуа́ция улу́чшится, *The situation will improve* [intrans]. This type of distinction applies to a very large number of common verbs (see 11.8).

- Other English verbs must be rendered in Russian by different verbs depending on whether they are used transitively or intransitively, e.g. Она́ **ве́шает** карти́ну на сте́ну, *She is hanging* [trans] *a picture on the wall*, but Карти́на **виси́т** на стене́, *A picture is hanging* [intrans] *on the wall*.

Common English verbs which must be rendered in Russian by distinct transitive or intransitive forms include the following:

	trans	intrans
to boil	**кипяти́ть/вскипяти́ть**	**кипе́ть/вскипе́ть**
to burn	**жечь/сжечь**	**горе́ть/сгоре́ть**
to drown	**топи́ть/утопи́ть**	**тону́ть/утону́ть**
to grow	**выра́щивать/вы́растить**	**расти́/вы́расти**
to hang	**ве́шать/пове́сить**	**висе́ть**
to hurt	**причиня́ть/причини́ть боль**	**боле́ть**
to rot	**гнои́ть/сгнои́ть**	**гнить/сгнить**
to sink	**топи́ть/потопи́ть** or **затопля́ть/затопи́ть**	**тону́ть/потону́ть** (R1) **тону́ть/затону́ть**
to sit (down)	**сажа́ть/посади́ть**	**сади́ться/сесть**
to smell	**чу́вствовать за́пах** or **ню́хать/поню́хать**	**па́хнуть**
to stand	**ста́вить/поста́вить**	**стоя́ть**

Note: in some cases the Russian transitive and intransitive verbs contain the same root, but in others they are derived from quite distinct roots (e.g. **жечь/сжечь** and **горе́ть/сгоре́ть**).

4.5 Translation of English forms ending in *-ing*

This English form has many functions, and Russian renders these functions in various ways.

(a) English progressive tenses: an imperfective verb, e.g.

I am going home. — Я **иду́** домо́й.
She was writing a letter. — Она́ **писа́ла** письмо́.
They'll be watching TV tonight. — Они́ **бу́дут смотре́ть** телеви́зор сего́дня ве́чером.

(b) attendant action: a separate clause, which in R3 might contain a gerund (see 9.7.1–9.7.2, 11.11.1), e.g.

He broke his leg while playing football.　**Пока́ он игра́л/Игра́я** в футбо́л, он слома́л себе́ но́гу.

(c) action prior to that denoted by the main verb: a subordinate clause, which in R3 may contain a perfective gerund, e.g.

I telephoned him on finding out about this.　**Узна́в** об э́том, я позвони́л(а) ему́.

After discussing the matter they came to a decision.　**Обсуди́в** де́ло, они́ пришли́ к реше́нию.

(d) in an English phrase describing a noun (equivalent to a relative clause): either a relative clause with **кото́рый** or, in R3, an active participle (see 9.7.3–9.7.4, 11.11.2), e.g.

a factory producing lorries　заво́д, **кото́рый произво́дит/ производя́щий** грузовики́

for a firm specialising in trade with Russia　для фи́рмы, **кото́рая специализи́руется/ специализи́рующейся** в торго́вле с Росси́ей

(e) English verbal noun describing some action or process, result or place of action, material, inner state or abstract concept: a Russian verbal noun (possibly with the suffix **-ние**, see 8.7.1), e.g.

reading	**чте́ние**
teaching	**обуче́ние**
building	**зда́ние**
lodging	**жили́ще**
lining	**подкла́дка**
feeling	**чу́вство**
hearing	**слух**

(f) English gerund, denoting some activity: verbal noun or infinitive, e.g.

His favourite subject is drawing.　Его́ люби́мый предме́т – **рисова́ние**.

I like playing chess.　Я люблю́ **игра́ть** в ша́хматы.

(g) after verbs of perception: subordinate clause introduced by **как**, e.g.

I heard you singing.　Я слы́шал(а), **как** ты **пе́ла**.

We saw him getting on a bus.　Мы **ви́дели, как** он **сади́лся** в авто́бус.

(h) after the verb *to keep*: **всё** + imperfective verb or **не переstaváть** + imperfective infinitive, e.g.

She kept (on) repeating the same words.

Она́ **всё повторя́ла** те же слова́/Она́ **не переставала повторя́ть** те же слова́.

(i)   after *from* used with verbs such as *prevent, stop*: Russian infinitive, e.g.

You are preventing/stopping me from working.
Ты меша́ешь мне **рабо́тать**.

(j)   often a construction containing **то** in the case appropriate in the context followed by **что́бы** + infinitive may be used, e.g.

We all have an interest in taking the best decisions.
Все мы заинтересо́ваны **в том, что́бы** приня́ть наилу́чшие реше́ния.

4.6   Translation of *too, also, as well*

The distinction between **та́кже** and **то́же** gives rise to problems for English-speakers. Та́кже may be used in most circumstances, but то́же is more restricted in its use. The following distinction can be made:

• **то́же** may be used when an additional subject is performing an action, e.g.

Ты идёшь в кино́? Я **то́же** пойду́.
Are you going to the cinema? I'll come too.
Я люблю́ му́зыку. Жена́ **то́же** лю́бит му́зыку.
I like music. My wife likes music too.

• **та́кже** (often in the phrase **а та́кже**) is used when a single subject is performing an additional action or performing an action that affects an additional object, e.g.

Я сего́дня был(а́) на вы́ставке, **а та́кже** порабо́тал(а).
I went to an exhibition today and did a bit of work too.
Я интересу́юсь литерату́рой, **а та́кже** теа́тром.
I'm interested in literature and also in the theatre.

It should be noted that **и** is very often used in the sense of *also, too, as well*, e.g.

Экономи́ческий кри́зис приведёт к безрабо́тице. Возни́кнут **и** социа́льные пробле́мы.
The economic crisis will lead to unemployment. Social problems will also arise.
Над Антаркти́кой обнару́жена огро́мная дыра́. Наблюда́ется уменьше́ние озо́нового сло́я **и** над мно́гими гу́сто населёнными райо́нами плане́ты.
A huge hole has been discovered over Antarctica. A reduction in the ozone layer is being observed over many densely populated regions of the planet as well.

Note: in clauses with a negative verb и may have the meaning *either*, e.g.
Премье́р-мини́стр не объясни́л, почему́ инфля́ция подняла́сь до тако́го у́ровня. В его́ ре́чи не нашли́ ме́ста **и** други́е о́стрые пробле́мы, *The prime minister did not explain why inflation had risen to such a [high] level. Other serious problems found no place either in his speech.*

5 Vocabulary and idiom

5.1 Neologisms

The radical changes in Russian life since the mid-1980s, the sudden greatly increased exposure to Western influence, and the introduction of large numbers of new institutions, habits and concepts have led to the flooding of the Russian language with neologisms. These neologisms relate to almost every area of life, but are especially numerous in such fields as politics, economics, social problems, law and order, science and technology, education, culture, sport and fashion.

Many of the neologisms are loanwords from other languages, nowadays mainly from English. Neologisms of this type may require slight phonetic adaptation, especially when the English word contains the letter *c* followed by *e* or *i*, e.g. **геноци́д**, *genocide*. The majority of them are absorbed into Russian without morphological adaptation, if they are nouns (e.g. **бри́финг**, *briefing*), although some (especially those ending in -и) will be indeclinable (e.g. **пабли́сити** (n) *publicity*). However, the adjectives and verbs among loanwords, and also many borrowed nouns, require the addition of Russian affixes to the foreign root (e.g. **вертика́льный**, *top-down* (of management); **митингова́ть**, *to take part in meetings* (R1, pej); **са̀мофинанси́рование**, *self-financing*).

Many other neologisms are derived from existing Russian resources by various means, including composition of acronyms (e.g. **бомж**, *vagrant*), affixation (e.g. **теневи́к**, person who operates in the shadow economy) and polysemanticisation (e.g. **отмыва́ть/отмы́ть**, *to launder* (money)), perhaps on the basis of some foreign model (e.g. **я́стреб**, *hawk*, used in a figurative sense).

The following section very briefly indicates the main waves of Russian lexical borrowing. In 5.1.2 and 5.1.3 we provide a small number of examples of very recent loanwords from English and of neologisms derived wholly or partly from existing Russian words or roots. These words belong in R2, and may therefore be used in most contexts, unless otherwise indicated. In 5.1.4 we deal with slang of various sorts. Section 5.1.5 looks at the large body of new terminology that relates to computing.

5.1.1 Western loanwords in Russian

A large number of words have entered Russian from non-Slavonic peoples and languages at various times in its history, for instance: from the Varangians who established the Riurikid dynasty in the ninth century (e.g. **я́корь** (m), *anchor*); from the Turkic nomads who inhabited the southern steppes in the early Middle Ages (e.g. **ло́шадь** (f), *horse*); from Greek around the time of the conversion of Russia to Christianity in the tenth century (e.g. **а́нгел**, *angel*; **ева́нгелие**, *the Gospels*); from the Tatars who ruled over Russia from the thirteenth to the fifteenth centuries (e.g. **де́ньги** (pl), *money*; **тамо́жня**, *customs*; **ярлы́к**, *label*); from German, from the time of Peter the Great at the beginning of the eighteenth century (e.g. **банк**, *bank*; **университе́т**, *university*; **флю́гер**, *weather-vane*); from French, from the middle of the eighteenth century on (e.g. **жиле́т**, *waistcoat*; **орке́стр**, *orchestra*; **пье́са**, *play*).

In the twentieth century a huge number of words of foreign, especially English, origin entered Russian, e.g. **автостра́да**, *motorway*; **грейпфру́т**, *grapefruit*; **джаз**, *jazz*; **кокте́йль** (m), *cocktail*; **комба́йн**, *combine (harvester)*; **та́нкер**, *tanker*; **тра́улер**, *trawler*; **тролле́йбус**, *trolleybus* (all borrowed in the 1930s); **аквала́нг**, *aqualung*; **бадминто́н**, *badminton*; **бики́ни** (n, indecl), *bikini*; **хо́бби** (n, indecl), *hobby* (all in the post-Stalinist period when Zhdanovism abated and attitudes towards things Western relaxed).

The influx of borrowings from English has been particularly rapid since the introduction *of glásnost'* by Gorbachóv in the mid-1980s and the subsequent break-up of the Soviet Union.[1] These neologisms had meanings which existing Russian words did not convey, or at least did not convey with the necessary flavour, e.g. **бестсе́ллер**, *bestseller*; **ва́учер**, *voucher*; **глобализа́ция**, *globalisation*; **диа́спора**, *diaspora*; **до́нор**, *donor*; **импи́чмент**, *impeachment* (which in application to Russian political life only became possible with the establishment of a bicameral parliament); **иннова́ция**, *innovation*; **инфраструкту́ра**, *infrastructure*; **клип**, *clip* (i.e. short TV item); **консе́нсус**, *consensus*; **консо́рциум**, *consortium*; **корру́пция**, *corruption* (in political and financial sense); **ло́бби** (n, indecl) *lobby* (i.e. pressure group), **лобби́рование**, *lobbying*, and **лобби́ст**, *lobbyist*; **марафо́н**, *marathon* (in fig sense); **мафио́зи** (m, indecl), *member of the mafia*, and **ма́фия**, *mafia*; **менталите́т**, *mentality*; **наркобизнес** *(illegal) drugs business*; **наркома́ния**, *drug addiction*; **но́у-ха́у** (pl, indecl), *know-how*; **порнобизнес**, *pornography business*; **приорите́т**, *priority*, and **приорите́тный**, *having priority*; **ре́йтинг**, *rating*; **респонде́нт**, *respondent*, e.g. to questionnaire; **рок-му́зыка**, *rock music*; **рэ́кет**, *racket* (i.e. crime), and **рэкети́р**, *racketeer*; **спо́нсор**, *sponsor* (also *sugar-daddy*, i.e. man who keeps a mistress); **тинэ́йджер**, *teenager*; **три́ллер**, *thriller*; **фа́кс**, *fax*; **хари́зма**, *charisma*, and **харизмати́ческий**, *charismatic*; **хо́спис**, *hospice*; **ча́ртерный рейс**, *charter flight*.

A particularly large number of the loanwords of the late twentieth century had to do with the new economic conditions in which centralised planning and state ownership were giving way to private ownership and a free market, e.g. **бро́кер**, *broker*; **гиперинфля́ция**, *hyperinflation*; **дивиде́нд**, *dividend*; **ди́лер**, *dealer* (on stock exchange); **инве́стор**, *investor*; **индекса́ция**, *indexation*; **оффшо́рный**, *offshore*; **приватиза́ция**, *privatisation*, and **приватизи́ровать** (impf and pf), *to privatise*; **хо́лдинг-компа́ния**, *holding company*. Other foreign words relating to economic matters that had already been borrowed in pre-revolutionary and early Soviet times achieved a new currency in the post-communist period, e.g. **а́кция**, *share, equity*; **аре́нда**, *leasing*; **би́знес** (tone now neutral), *business* (i.e. economic activity); **би́ржа**, *stock exchange*.

5.1.2 Recent loanwords from English

Although loanwords from English are of course particularly easy for English-speaking learners of Russian to grasp and deploy, they do need to be studied carefully. For one thing a loanword may be used in a much narrower sense than its equivalent in the language from which it is borrowed. Thus **и́мидж** means *image* only in the sense of character as perceived by the public; **крайм**, *crime*, and **суици́д**, *suicide*, denote not an individual action but only an organised social phenomenon; and **секс**, *sex*, has the relatively restricted meaning of sexual activity. Moreover, once accommodated by a language a loanword takes on a life of its own. It may acquire new meaning and even become a false friend (as have many of the *faux amis* in 3.5). English-speakers should also be aware that stress in a Russian loanword may fall on a syllable different from the one on which they would expect to find it, as in **марке́тинг**, *marketing*, **монито́ринг**, *monitoring*, and **пена́льти**, *penalty* (sporting term).

It is also sensible to use very recent loanwords from English with some caution, since their position in the language may still be insecure and some of them will in due course be discarded. Furthermore such words may be perceived in different ways by different native speakers. While in some circles use of western loanwords may give the speech of the user an attractively cosmopolitan air, in others the alien tinge that they lend to speech may be unwelcome. It should also be remembered that many neologisms may be incomprehensible to large numbers of Russians, particularly to older people, who find it hard to keep abreast of the changes that are taking place, and to the poorly educated, who are unfamiliar with the Western languages and societies from which the new words and concepts are drawn.

There follows a short list of some English words and phrases that have been recently borrowed or that have recently acquired new meaning:

ба́ксы (pl; gen **ба́ксов**)	*bucks* (i.e. *dollars*)
бебиси́ттер	*babysitter*
бренд	*brand* (in its commercial sense)
грант	*grant*
дефо́лт	collapse of the rouble in August 1998
имиджме́йкер	*image-maker*
импи́чмент	*impeachment*
индика́тор	*indicator* (e.g. political, sociological)

ка́стинг	*casting* (*for film, TV*)
ки́ллер	*hitman*
клони́ровать(ся)	*to clone/be cloned*
ме́неджер	*manager* (but not the top person; the Russian term is not so prestigious as *manager*)
ме́сседж	(*political*) *message*
ньюсме́йкер	*newsmaker*
олига́рхи	*oligarchs* (i.e. men who have accumulated enormous wealth as a result of privatisation of Soviet state resources)
пиа́р	*PR*
пиа́рить	*to promote, plug*
пиа́рщик	*PR man/woman, spin-doctor*
саспе́нс	*suspense* (of novels and films)
се́конд-хе́нд	*second-hand*
ток-шо́у	*talk show*
хе́длайн	*headline*
хэ́ппенинг	*a happening* (i.e. event)
эксклюзи́вное интервью́	*exclusive interview*

5.1.3   Neologisms derived from existing Russian words

The following list contains a small number of neologisms (phrases as well as words) derived from the resources of Russian rather than foreign languages, although some of them contain elements that were originally borrowed (e.g. **нефтедо́ллары**). The list includes existing words that have recently taken on new meaning in certain circles (e.g. **вменя́емый**), words formed through composition (e.g. **банкома́т**) and phraseological calques (**раска́чивание ло́дки**).

Many neologisms of this sort, particularly those that are used in an ironic or jocular way, may be classified as slang, to which the next section is devoted.

The polysemanticisation that some of the words in this section illustrate can of course enrich a language. However, when it results in the creation of clichés or vogue expressions with little substance, as is the case with some of the words and phrases given below, then equally polysemanticisation may lead to a certain linguistic impoverishment, the sort of inflation to which reference was made in 1.6.

банкома́т	*cashpoint*
боеви́к	*combatant, fighter*, now used e.g. of militant fundamentalists, e.g. чече́нские боевики́, *Chechen fighters*

бюдже́тник	*sb who is on the state payroll*
включа́ть/включи́ть счётчик	*to start the clock ticking* (lit *to switch on the meter*)
вменя́емый	*reasonable* (originally a legal term meaning *responsible, of sound mind*)
Вор до́лжен сиде́ть в тюрьме́.	*A thief should be in prison* (said about the *oligarchs* (see 5.1.2 above); a quotation from a popular film).
Восто́к – де́ло то́нкое.	lit *The East is a delicate matter* (said as counsel of caution when dealing with Eastern nations which function in a way unfamiliar to Europeans; also a quotation from a popular film).
во́тум дове́рия/недове́рия	*vote of confidence/no confidence*
гражда́нское неповинове́ние	*civil disobedience*
гуманита́рная по́мощь	*humanitarian aid*
дава́ть/дать зелёный свет	*to give the green light*
забива́ть/заби́ть гол в свои́ воро́та	*to score an own goal*
За держа́ву оби́дно.	*I feel for my country* (i.e. because it is suffering or being humiliated; another quotation from a popular film).
зашка́ливать/зашка́лить (его́ зашка́лило)	*to send off the scale* (he went through the ceiling/went ballistic)
зна́ковое собы́тие	*meaningful event*, i.e. sign of the times
конверти́руемая валю́та	*convertible currency*
ма́лый би́знес	*small business*
многопарти́йная систе́ма	*multi-party system*
нало́г на доба́вленную сто́имость (НДС)	*Value Added Tax (VAT)*
нетрудовы́е дохо́ды	*illegal earnings*
нефтедо́ллары	*petro-dollars*, i.e. foreign currency earned by export of Russian oil
оборотни в погонах	lit *werewolves with epaulettes* (i.e. police who are themselves engaged in criminal activity)
о́бщество с ограни́ченной отве́тственностью	*limited liability company*

однозна́чный/однозна́чно	lit *simple, monosemantic*; used to describe (over-)simplified or black-and-white approach to complex issues
озву́чивать/озву́чить	*to publicise, give voice to*
ору́жие ма́ссового уничтоже́ния	*weapons of mass destruction*
отмыва́ние де́нег	*money-laundering*
охо́та за ве́дьмами	*witch hunt*
порну́ха	*porn*
постсове́тское простра́нство	*post-Soviet space*
раска́чивание ло́дки	*rocking the boat*
режи́м	in the sense of *mode*, e.g. в обы́чном режи́ме, *in normal mode*
рокиро́вка ка́дров	*reshuffle* (lit *castling* [chess term] *of personnel*)
ры́ночная эконо́мика	*market economy*
сиде́ть на игле́	*to be addicted* (lit *to sit on the needle*)
сиде́ть на нефтяно́й игле́	*to be dependent on oil* (said of the contemporary Russian economy)
слови́к	member of security forces, which are known collectively as силова́я структу́ра
теа́тр одного́ актёра	*one-man band* (lit *one-actor theatre*)
теневáя эконо́мика	*shadow economy*
теневи́к	person operating in the shadow economy
тру́бка	*mobile* (telephone)
у́зник со́вести	*prisoner of conscience*
уте́чка мозго́в	*brain drain*
челно́к	originally *shuttle*; now also sb who goes abroad to buy goods cheaply and resells them in Russia for profit
челове́ческий фа́ктор	*the human factor*
черну́ха	the negative side of life or its depiction
четвёртая власть	*the fourth estate*, i.e. the media

It has also been pointed out, for example by Ryazanova-Clarke and Wade (see Sources), that with the re-emergence of the Church as an officially acceptable institution in Russia in the post-Soviet era new life has been given to words and expressions with a religious colouring, including some Slavonicisms embedded in biblical expressions, e.g. всу́е, *in vain*; глас вопию́щего в пусты́не, *a voice in the wilderness*; земля́ обетова́нная, *the promised land*; зени́ца о́ка, *the apple of one's eye*; златой теле́ц, *the golden calf*; и и́же с ни́ми, *and others of that ilk*; ищи́те и обря́щете, *seek and ye shall find*; о́ко за о́ко, зуб за зуб, *an eye for an eye, a tooth for a tooth*; при́тча во язы́цех, *the talk of the town*. These expressions may have a range of functions. They might for example be used for rhetorical purposes (especially in the language of nationalistic politicians and commentators), or as a means available to people of more Westernist outlook of disparaging nationalistic forces, or simply as a jocular device in everyday speech. They may accordingly be classified as nowadays belonging either to R3 or R1 depending on their context.

5.1.4   Slang

Slang is a stratum of lexis that defies the standard and is unorthodox and more or less subversive. It is associated particularly with youth and marginal groups. The words which abound in youth slang (молодёжный сленг) relate especially to parents, sex, drink, drugs, fighting and the police, for instance: (to denote parents) ро́дичи (lit *relatives* in R1), шнурки́ (lit *shoe-laces*); and (in the meaning *to have sex*) попа́риться, попи́литься, потелефо́нить, поуда́читься (all pf). Further varieties of slang are associated with business (делово́й сленг, о́фисный жарго́н), the criminal underworld (воровско́е арго́ (indecl), блатно́й язы́к, or фе́ня) and the world of computer-users (see 5.1.5 below). Some slang is derived from foreign words, e.g. гри́ны, '*greens*' (i.e. *dollars*; gen гри́нов); дри́нкать, *to drink*; кредитну́ться, *to get a loan*; о́лды, *oldies* (i.e. *parents*).

There follows a short list of examples of slang of one sort or another that have been in vogue at some time over the past ten years or so. However, foreign learners should use such words with caution, both because slang is by definition non-standard and because it tends to become dated more quickly than other areas of lexis (indeed some of the expressions listed here that are now modish may well seem stale by the time this book is published).

ба́бки (pl; gen ба́бок)	*money*
брат	*member of criminal fraternity*
братва́	*criminal fraternity*
глюк	*hallucination*; у него́ глю́ки, *He's hallucinating / seeing things.*
дедовщи́на	*bullying of new recruits by older soldiers* (деды́, i.e. *grand-dads*)
де́мбель (m)	*demobilisation*
демократиза́тор	*(policeman's) truncheon*

деревя́нные	*roubles (i.e. wooden things)*
забива́ть/заби́ть	*to arrange, book, secure*, e.g. заби́ть сто́лик, *to get a table* (in bar, restaurant)
Заби́то.	*It's settled.*
зака́зчик	*sb who puts out a contract, i.e. hires a hitman*
зака́зывать/заказа́ть кого́-н	*to put out a contract on sb (i.e. to arrange to have sb killed)*
заморо́чиваться	*to get into/caught up in a mess*
заморо́чки (sg заморо́чка; gen pl заморо́чек)	*snags, hitches*
зелёные	*greens (i.e. dollars; = гри́ны)*; also *people concerned with protection of the environment as a political issue*
кайф	*kicks*
ки́ска	*very attractive girl*
клёвый (adv **клёво**) (now dated)	*brill, knockout, fantastic*
коси́ть/закоси́ть (от слу́жбы)	*to dodge (military service)*
крёстный оте́ц	*godfather*, i.e. leader of criminal clan
круто́й (adv **кру́то**)	*cool, wicked*
кры́ша	*protection* (i.e. criminal racket)
крышева́ть	*to give protection*
лом	*unwillingness to do sth because one is too lazy*, e.g. мне э́то в лом, *I can't be bothered.*
лох	*sucker, dolt*
лохотро́н	*scam*
мент	*policeman*
моби́ла	*mobile (telephone)*; slang variant of моби́льник (R1), which is also a recent neologism
надри́нкаться (pf)	*to get pissed*
нае́зд	*pressure, threat*
наезжа́ть/нае́хать на кого́-н	*to threaten/put pressure on sb*
нал (= нали́чные (де́ньги))	*cash*
обло́м	*flop, failure, fiasco*
обломи́ться (pf)	*to make a wrong decision, cock sth up*
отморо́зок	*freak; person without any principles*

отрыва́ться/оторва́ться	*to have a good time, to have fun*
оття́гиваться/оттяну́ться	= отрыва́ться/оторва́ться
паркова́ть/запаркова́ть **ба́бки**	*to invest in something secure* (lit *to park one's money*)
прика́лываться (impf; R1)	*to joke (make cutting remarks)*
прико́л (R1)	*(barbed) joke*
проко́л	*foul-up, cock-up, gaffe*
разбо́рка	*showdown, infighting, sorting-out*
расколо́ть	lit *to chop, split*; in new slang *to make sb talk*, e.g. Меня́ не раско́лешь, *You won't get anything out of me.*
раскру́тка (adj **раскру́ченный**)	*hype (hyped)*, e.g. раскру́ченная певи́ца, *hyped singer*
слеза́ть/слезть с иглы́	*to come off drugs* (lit *to come off the needle*)
смоли́ть (impf)	*to smoke a lot* (including hashish)
срыва́ться/сорва́ться	*to come off the wagon* (i.e. *to start drinking again*)
стёб	*buffoonery, mockery, self-mockery*, perhaps with implication that the fun touches a raw nerve
страши́лка	*horror film*
то́рмоз	*bore, slow tedious person* (lit *brake*)
тусова́ться	*to hang about together*
тусо́вка	*get-together, do*
устра́ивать/устро́ить бу́чу (now dated)	*to have a fight* (= дра́ться/подра́ться)
фиг	*indicates rude gesture*; equivalent to *damn* in some phrases, e.g. Мне всё по́ фиг, *I couldn't give a damn.*

Note: пофиги́зм, *couldn't-care-less attitude*. See also 5.5 on interjections indicating annoyance.

халя́ва	*freebie*; на халя́ву, *for free*
ча́йник	*layman, non-specialist*, not an expert (lit *tea-pot*)
шту́ка	*a thousand* (in roubles or foreign currency)
штукату́рка	*heavily made-up woman* (lit *plastering*)

5.1.5 Computing terminology

One area of vocabulary which has greatly expanded in recent years is the field of terminology relating to computing and the internet.

Neologisms in this field include both loanwords (almost entirely from English) and existing Russian words that have taken on new meaning.

basic components and functions of the PC (основны́е компоне́нты и фу́нкции ПК)	персона́льный компью́тер	*personal computer*
	рабо́чий стол	*desktop*
	монито́р/диспле́й	*monitor*
	экра́н	*screen*
	клавиату́ра	*keyboard*
	кла́виша	*key*
	мышь (f), мы́шка	*mouse*
	жёсткий диск	*hard disk*
	ги́бкий диск	*soft disk, floppy*
	ла́зерный компа́кт-диск	*CD*
	ла́зерный прои́грыватель	*CD player*
	диск DVD	*DVD*
	при́нтер	*printer*
	звукова́я пла́та	*sound card*
	ска́нер	*scanner*
	моде́м	*modem*
	устро́йство	*device*
	хране́ние информа́ции	*information storage*
	многозада́чность (f)	*multitasking*
	па́мять (f)	*memory*
using the computer (испо́льзование компью́тера)	по́льзователь (m)	*user*
	операцио́нная систе́ма	*operating system*
	паро́ль (m)	*password*
	програ́мма	*program*
	устано́вка	*installation*
	пане́ль (f) инструме́нтов	*toolbar*
	портфе́ль (m)	*briefcase*
	меню́ (n, indecl)	*menu*
	щёлкать/щёлкнуть (на кно́пке)	*to click (on a button)*
	(двойно́й) щелчо́к	*(double) click*
	формати́рование	*formatting*
	редакти́рование	*editing*
	копи́рование	*copying*
	перемеще́ние	*moving*

переименова́ние	*renaming*
выреза́ние	*cutting*
скле́ивание	*pasting*
выделе́ние	*highlighting*
вста́вка	*insertion, pasting*
удале́ние	*deletion*
заме́на	*replacing*
сохраня́ть/сохрани́ть	*to save*
докуме́нт	*document*
файл	*file*
па́пка	*folder*
табли́ца	*table*
столбе́ц	*column*
яче́йка	*cell*
те́ма	*subject*
окно́	*window*
значо́к	*icon*
шрифт	*font*
жи́рный шрифт	*bold*
курси́в	*italics*
си́мвол	*symbol*
правописа́ние	*spelling*
по умолча́нию	*default*
корзи́на	*recycle bin* (normally *waste bin*)
ви́рус	*virus*
защи́та от ви́русов	*virus protection*
антиви́русная програ́мма	*antivirus program*

commands and control buttons (кома́нды и кно́пки управле́ния)	Пуск	*Start*
	Откры́ть	*Open*
	Пра́вка	*Edit*
	Вид	*View*
	Найти́	*Find*
	Наза́д	*Back*
	Вперёд	*Forward*
	Созда́ть	*Create*
	Вы́резать	*Cut*
	Вста́вить	*Insert*
	Удали́ть	*Delete*

Копи́ровать	*Copy*
Сохрани́ть (как)	*Save (as)*
Отме́на	*Cancel*
Восстанови́ть	*Restore*
Сверну́ть	*Minimise* (lit *Roll up*)
Разверну́ть	*Maximise* (lit *Unroll*)
Печа́ть (f)	*Print*
Приостанови́ть	*Pause*
Вы́ход	*Exit*
Закры́ть	*Close*
И́збранное	*Favourites* (lit *Selected*)
Обзо́р	*Browse* (lit *Survey*)
Пара́метры (pl; sg пара́метр)	*Options*
Спра́вка	*Help*
Ярлы́к	*Shortcut* (lit *Label*)
Настро́йка	*Settings*
Се́рвис	*Tools*
Очи́стить корзи́ну	*Empty recycle bin*
Вы́ключить компью́тер	*Shut down computer*
Перезагрузи́ть	*Restart*

the internet (интерне́т, инэ́т)	Мирова́я паути́на	*World Wide Web*
	поставщи́к услу́г интерне́та	*internet service provider*
	подключе́ние к се́ти	*connecting to the net*
	онла́йн (adj онла́йновый)	*online*
	навига́ция	*navigating, surfing*
	бра́узер	*browser*
	информацио́нный порта́л	*information gateway*
	сайт	*site*
	закла́дка	*bookmark*
	дома́шняя страни́чка	*home page*
	ник	*screen name*
	По́иск	*Search*
	Перехо́д	*Go*
	Да́лее	*Next*
	Домо́й	*Home*
	Загру́зка	*Download*
	загружа́ть/загрузи́ть	*to download*
	ви́део-конфере́нция	*video-conference*

	завершéние сеáнса	*log off*
email (электрóнная пóчта (R2); емéля, мейл, мы́ло all R1))	электрóнный áдрес	*email address*
	сообщéние	*message*
	От	*From*
	Комý	*To* (lit *To whom*)
	Предмéт	*Subject*
	вложéние	*attachment*
	Создáть сообщéние	*Compile/New message*
	Отпрáвить	*Send*
	Отвéтить	*Reply*
	Пересла́ть	*Forward*
	отправи́тель (m)	*sender*
	получа́тель (m)	*recipient*
	почтóвый я́щик	*mailbox*
	входя́щие	*inbox*
	предыду́щее	*previous*
	слéдующее	*next*
	адреса́т	*addressee*
	áдресная кни́га	*address book*
	спи́сок рассы́лки	*mailing list*
	нежелáтельная пóчта	*junk mail*
	спам	*spam*
	соба́чка (R1)	*@*
slang (жаргони́змы; all R1)	апдáтиться/проапдáтиться	*to update*
	броди́лка	*browser* (= брáузер)
	звуковýха	*sound card*
	ЗЫ	*PS* (because these Cyrillic letters are produced by the keys that produce *p* and *s* on an English keyboard, and users do not think it worth switching to Roman just to key in these two letters (which in Russian correspondence are always written in Roman))
	имхó	*in my (humble) opinion* (the Russian form is made up of the initial letters of the four English words in this phrase)
	клáва	*keyboard* (= клавиату́ра); топта́ть кла́ву, *to type*

клик	*click* (= щелчо́к)
по ле́вому/пра́вому кли́ку	*mouse left/right click*
комп, компа́шка	*computer*
кры́са	*mouse* (lit *rat*)
месса́га	*message*
мы́лить/намы́лить	*to send by email*
про́га	*program*
скача́ть	*download*
трабл	*trouble, problem*
ха́кер	*hacker*
ю́зать	*to use*
ю́зер	*user*

5.2   Transition words

The words or phrases in the following list are frequently used to link points and give coherence to an argument. Many of them (e.g. **во-пе́рвых**, etc.) are by their nature more likely to feature in the written language and the more formal speech of R3 than in the colloquial language of R1, and may therefore be contrasted with some of the fillers given in the following section.

без (вся́кого) сомне́ния	*without (any) doubt*
в конце́ концо́в	*in the end, after all*
в са́мом де́ле	*indeed (confirms preceding idea)*
на са́мом де́ле	*in fact (contradicts preceding idea)*
во вся́ком слу́чае	*in any case*
во-пе́рвых	*firstly*
во-вторы́х	*secondly*
в-тре́тьих	*thirdly*
ведь	*you see, you know*
вкра́тце (R3)	*briefly, succinctly*
и́бо (R3)	*for, i.e. because (cf. Fr car)*
ита́к	*thus, so*
к моему́/на́шему прискорбию (R3)	*to my/our regret*
к тому́ же	*besides*
коро́че говоря́	*in short*
кро́ме того́	*moreover*
наконе́ц	*lastly*

наоборо́т	*on the contrary*
наприме́р	*for example*
несомне́нно	*undoubtedly*
одна́ко	*however*
одни́м сло́вом	*in a word, in short*
поэ́тому	*consequently*
пре́жде всего́	*first of all, above all*
с одно́й стороны́ . . . с друго́й стороны́	*on the one hand . . . on the other hand*
само́ собо́й разуме́ется	*it goes without saying*
сверх того́	*moreover*
сле́довательно	*consequently*
сле́дует отме́тить (R3)	*it must be noted*
таки́м о́бразом	*in this way*
тем не ме́нее	*nevertheless*
то́ есть	*that is (to say)*

5.3 Fillers

Alongside transitional expressions of the sort exemplified in 5.2, which give coherence to a line of thought, languages have a stock of words or phrases that may be inserted in an utterance for various other purposes. Such interpolations might represent a speaker's comment on the reliability of information (e.g. **ка́жется**), indicate the source or status of the information (e.g. **по-мо́ему**), describe the way an idea is expressed (**ины́ми слова́ми**), make some sort of appeal by a speaker to his or her interlocutor (**понима́ешь**), or express a speaker's attitude to what is said (**на беду́**). Often interpolations mean very little, serving mainly to fill out an utterance, perhaps in order to give the speaker time to marshal further thoughts. (Interpolations of this latter sort are known in Russian as **слова́-парази́ты**.) Unlike the transition words given in 5.2 most of the fillers given in this section belong primarily to the more informal spoken register (R1).

In the expressions in the following list which address an interlocutor (e.g. **вообрази́(те) (себе́)**) both the second-person-singular and the second-person-plural forms are given.

ви́дишь/ви́дите ли	*do you see*
ви́дно	*evidently, obviously*
вообрази́(те) (себе́)	*fancy, just imagine*
вот	*so there we are*
гм	*er . . .*
говоря́т	*they say*

гру́бо выража́ясь	*roughly speaking*
действи́тельно	*really*
допу́стим	*let's suppose, say*
други́ми слова́ми	*in other words*
зна́ешь/зна́ете	*you know*
знать	*evidently, it seems*
зна́чит	*so, then*
извини́(те)	*excuse (me for saying so)*
ины́ми слова́ми	= други́ми слова́ми
к сожале́нию	*unfortunately*
к сча́стью	*fortunately*
как бы	*sort of, like*
коне́чно	*of course*
кста́ти (сказа́ть)	*by the way*
ме́жду на́ми	*between ourselves*
ме́жду про́чим	*incidentally*
на беду́	*unfortunately*
не пове́ришь/пове́рите	*you won't believe it*
ну	*well*
по всей вероя́тности	*in all probability*
по кра́йней ме́ре	*at least*
по пра́вде сказа́ть	*to tell the truth*
позво́ль(те)	*allow (me to say it)*
поми́луй(те)	*pardon (me) (as expression of objection)*
понима́ешь/понима́ете	*(do) you understand*
по́просту говоря́	*to put it simply*
предста́вь(те) себе́	*imagine*
прости́(те)	*forgive (me for saying it)*
пря́мо ска́жем	*let's be frank*
са́мое гла́вное	*the main thing*
скажи́(те) на ми́лость	*you don't say* (iron)
слу́шай(те)	*listen*
согласи́шься/согласи́тесь	*you'll agree*
так	*so*
так сказа́ть	*so to speak*
ти́па	*sort of, like*
чего́ до́брого	*who knows* (anticipating sth unpleasant)
что называ́ется	*as they say*

5.4   Modal particles

Modal particles are not often encountered in the relatively objective varieties of the formal written language (esp R3a/R3b) but in the spoken language, and in particular in colloquial conversation, where subjective utterances abound, they are extremely important. However, they are not easy for the English-speaking student to master, since English often achieves the nuances that particles convey by means of tone of voice or intonation rather than by lexical means. Moreover, the precise meaning or function of the Russian particles is elusive, partly because they are in most cases polysemantic and also because they interact with word order, phrasal stress and intonation to produce complex and variable nuances.

This section lists a number of the less elusive functions of the most important modal particles. At the end of the section a list is given of other particles which have a lexical or morphological function rather than a modal one.

а

(a) placed at the end of an utterance, exhorts the hearer to give an answer or agree to sth, e.g.

Моро́женое дать, **а**?	*Want an ice-cream?*
Всё в поря́дке, **а**?	*Is everything all right then?*
Ты гото́в(а)? Пое́дем, **а**?	*Are you ready? Shall we go then?*

(b) occurs in vocative expressions (see 7.3.1) when a diminutive name is repeated, in which case the particle is placed between the two words in the vocative, e.g.

Тань, а Тань! Как ты ду́маешь, мне на ве́чер пойти́?	*Tania, what do you think, should I go to the party?*
Мам, а мам! Ты помо́жешь мне?	*Mum! Will you help me?*

(c) placed at the beginning of an utterance, gives a spontaneous link with what has been said or assumed, e.g.

– Отку́да э́то у тебя́ тако́й краси́вый шарф?	*'Where did you get such a lovely scarf?'*
– **А** муж подари́л.	*'My husband gave it to me as a present.'*
– Ми́тю мо́жно?	*'Can I speak to Mitia?'*
– **А** он на рабо́те.	*'He's at work.'*
– **А** когда́ бу́дет?	*'When will he get home?'*
– В шесть. **А** кто его́ спра́шивает?	*'At six. Who's that asking for him?'*

ведь

(a) expresses mild assertion of sth which the speaker considers obvious; sometimes this assertion constitutes an objection to another point of view, e.g.

Ведь ина́че и быть не мо́жет.	*For it just couldn't be otherwise.*

Пора́ у́жинать. Мы **ведь** с утра́ ничего́ не е́ли.	*It's time to have supper. After all, we haven't eaten since this morning.*
– То́ля, наде́нь ша́пку.	*'Tolia, put your hat on.'*
– Не хочу́.	*'I don't want to.'*
– **Ведь** де́сять гра́дусов ни́же нуля́.	*'But it's minus 10.'*
– Не бу́ду чита́ть э́ти кни́ги.	*'I'm not going to read these books.'*
– **Ведь** прова́лишься на экза́мене.	*'Then you'll fail your exam.'*

(b)   expresses gentle reproach or warning, e.g.

Ну, хва́тит! Я **ведь** сказа́л(а), что не на́до шуме́ть.	*That's enough. I told you not to make a noise.*
Ты **ведь** совсе́м не обраща́ешь внима́ния на мои́ слова́.	*You just don't pay any attention to what I say.*

(c)   expresses surprise at an unexpected discovery, e.g.

– Где моя́ ша́пка?	*'Where's my hat?'*
– Я её на ве́шалку пове́сил.	*'I hung it on the peg.'*
– А **ведь** её там нет.	*'But it isn't there.'*
Я **ведь** не по́нял(а), что она́ уже́ аспира́нтка.	*I hadn't realised that she was already a postgraduate.*

(d)   in questions, encourages sb to give the answer the speaker wants to hear; in this sense fulfils the same role as the English tail question, as in the following examples:

Ты **ведь** побу́дешь у нас?	*You will come and stay with us for a bit, won't you?*
Ведь не опозда́ете?	*You won't be late, will you?*

вот

(a)   expresses demonstrative meaning, which may be rendered in English by *this* or *here*, e.g.

Они́ живу́т **вот** в э́том до́ме.	*They live in this house here.*
Попро́буй **вот** э́тот сала́т. Он о́чень вку́сный.	*Try this salad here. It's very nice.*

(b)   with interrogative pronouns and adverbs, lends emphasis of the sort rendered in English by the verb *to be*, e.g.

Вот где он упа́л.	*This is where he fell over.*
Вот почему́ я посове́товал(а) тебе́ не выходи́ть.	*That's why I advised you not to go out.*
Вот что я име́ю в виду́.	*This is what I have in mind.*

(c)   with the future tense, may express promise, resolution, warning or threat, e.g.

Я бро́шу пить. **Вот** уви́дишь.	*I'll give up drinking. You'll see.*

Здесь ско́льзко. **Вот** упадёшь сейча́с!	*It's slippery. You'll fall.*
Ты разби́л(а) окно́. **Вот** расскажу́ роди́телям о твои́х проде́лках.	*You've broken the window. I'll tell your parents about your pranks.*

(d) in exclamations, may express such sentiments as surprise or indignation, in which case the particle itself is stressed, e.g.

– Президе́нт у́мер.	*'The president has died.'*
– **Во́т** как?	*'Really?'*
Во́т как ты тепе́рь живёшь!	*So that's the way you live now, is it?*
Во́т что ты де́лаешь по вечера́м! Пья́нствуешь.	*So that's what you do in the evenings. You get drunk.*

(e) in exclamations, may also intensify the speaker's emotional response to sth, e.g.

Вот хорошо́, что нас не забы́ли!	*It's so nice that you haven't forgotten us.*

да

(a) expresses objection or remonstration in a very familiar tone, e.g.

Да я бы на твоём ме́сте э́того не сде́лал(а).	*I wouldn't have done that if I'd been in your place.*

(b) expresses agreement or concession (see also ну (d), уж (b)), e.g.

– Мо́жно, я сейча́с вы́йду?	*'Can I leave now?'*
– **Да** выходи́, мне всё равно́.	*'Go ahead, it's all the same to me.'*
– Я, пожа́луй, спрошу́ О́лю.	*'I might ask Olia.'*
– **Да** спроси́. То́лько вряд ли она́ тебе́ ска́жет.	*'Go ahead and ask her. But I don't suppose she'll tell you.'*

(c) expresses insistent suggestion, friendly advice or reassurance, e.g.

Да не шуми́те. Я рабо́таю.	*Don't make a racket. I'm working.*
Да не беспоко́йся, па́па сейча́с подойдёт.	*Don't worry, daddy'll come back in a minute.*

(d) in a vague answer, carries a casual, indifferent tone, e.g.

– Куда́ она́ уе́хала?	*'Where's she gone off to?'*
– **Да** не зна́ю. Говоря́т в Сиби́рь.	*'Oh, I don't know. Siberia I think.'*

(e) with an indefinite pronoun containing the particle -**нибудь**, expresses certainty against a background of vagueness, e.g.

Что́-**нибудь да** ку́пим.	*We're sure to buy something or other.*
Кого́-**нибудь да** заста́нешь до́ма.	*You're bound to find someone in.*

(f) In exclamatory questions, expresses amazement, e.g.

Да ра́зве ты не зна́л(а), что он жена́т?	*Surely you knew he was married?*

	Да заблуди́ться среди́ бе́ла дня!	*What! Get lost in broad daylight?*
	Не мо́жет быть.	*That's not possible.*

ещё (a) expresses a feeling on the speaker's part that sth is unreasonable or does not correspond to reality, e.g.

А **ещё** меха́ник!	*And you call yourself a mechanic!*
А **ещё** говори́шь, что неспосо́бен/неспосо́бна к му́зыке.	*And you still say you've no aptitude for music!*

(b) expresses emphatic affirmation or denial, e.g.

Ещё бы!	*I'll say!*
– Ну, нае́лся?	*'Have you had enough to eat?'*
– **Ещё как** нае́лся!	*'I'll say.'*

же (a) categoric emphasis on what the speaker considers a compelling point or an indisputable fact, e.g.

Ра́зве ты идёшь на рабо́ту? У тебя́ **же** температу́ра.	*Surely you're not going to work? You've got a temperature after all.*
Я не уме́ю игра́ть в ша́хматы. Вы **же** са́ми зна́ете, что не уме́ю.	*I can't play chess. You yourself know very well that I can't.*

(b) with imperatives, expresses insistence on the part of the speaker together with impatience or irritation, feigned at least, that the order has to be given or repeated, e.g.

Алёша! **Иди́ же** скоре́е сюда́.	*Aliosha, come here at once.*

(c) in questions, may indicate that the speaker cannot envisage or accept any answer other than the one he or she invites, e.g.

Вы **же** не солжёте?	*You surely wouldn't tell a lie, would you?*
Ты **же** не бу́дешь утвержда́ть, что не зна́ешь?	*You're surely not going to say you don't know, are you?*

(d) in questions framed with an interrogative pronoun or adverb, may express incredulity or perplexity on the speaker's part, in which case it may correspond to the English suffix *-ever*, e.g.

Где же ты был(а́)?	*Wherever have you been?*
Почему́ же вы возража́ете на э́то?	*Why on earth do you object to this?*
Что же ему́ подари́ть на Рождество́?	*Whatever can we give him for Christmas?*

(e) may also be used in questions in which the speaker asks for precise information, e.g.

Вы говори́те, что кто́-то поги́б. **Кто же** поги́б?	*You say that somebody was killed. Who exactly was killed?*

Вы то́же живёте в це́нтре го́рода? На **како́й же** у́лице?	*So you live in the centre as well? Which street do you live in?*

Note 1   же may be shortened to **ж**.

     2   же is generally placed immediately after the word or phrase which it highlights.

и   (a)   expresses emphasis, in which case it has the same function as и́менно (see note at end of 4.2), e.g.

Она́ была́ на конфере́нции. Мы там **и** познако́мились.	*She was at the conference. That's where we met.*
Мы подошли́ к кафе́. 'Вот тут **и** пообе́даем', сказа́ла она́.	*We approached a café. 'This is where we're going to eat,' she said.*

    (b)   may correspond to **да́же**, *even*, e.g.

Ка́жется, на́ша кома́нда вы́играла, а я **и** не слы́шал(а) об э́том.	*Apparently our side won, and I didn't even hear about it.*

    (c)   may correspond to **хотя́**, *although*, e.g.

И тепло́ на у́лице, а я не хочу́ выходи́ть.	*I don't want to go out, although it's warm outside.*

    (d)   may increase uncertainty, e.g.

– Мо́жет быть, вы чита́ли э́ту кни́гу?	*'You may have read this book.'*
– Мо́жет быть, **и** чита́л(а).	*'I may have done.'*

    (e)   with an interjection, may intensify an exclamation, e.g.

Ох, и обо́рвыш ты!	*God, you're scruffy!*
Он уме́ет игра́ть на скри́пке. **Ох и** игра́ет!	*He can play the violin. Oh, and how he plays!*

-ка   (a)   attached to imperative forms, produces gentle informal exhortation or friendly advice, e.g.

Ле́ночка, **вы́йди-ка** сюда́ на мину́тку.	*Lenochka, come out here for a moment would you.*
Посмотри́те-ка, как она́ похороше́ла.	*Just look how pretty she's become.*
Поди́те-ка вы отдыха́ть. Вы нарабо́тались.	*Go and have a rest. You've worn yourself out with work.*

    (b)   attached to an imperative used in a conditional sense (see 11.9, note 3), expresses a challenge to sb to do sth perceived as difficult, e.g.

Поговори́те-ка с э́тим па́рнем – уви́дите, како́й он тру́дный.	*You try speaking to this lad and you'll see how difficult he is.*

| **Посто́й-ка** на моро́зе без перча́ток! | *You just try standing out in the frost without gloves on.* |

(c)   attached to the first-person-singular form of a perfective verb, indicates irresolution in the speaker, e.g.

| А **пойду́-ка** я на рабо́ту пешко́м. | *I think I might walk to work.* |
| **Куплю́-ка** до́чке но́вую ю́бку. | *Perhaps I'll buy my daughter a new skirt.* |

ли

(a)   with a perfective infinitive, expresses vague intention or hesitancy on the part of the speaker, e.g.

В теа́тр что **ли** сходи́ть?	*Shall we go to the theatre? I don't know.*
Предупреди́ть **ли** мне их?	*Should I perhaps warn them?*
Не купи́ть **ли** конфе́т?	*Shouldn't we buy some sweets?*

(b)   combined with **не**, expresses a very polite request or suggestion (which may be ironical), e.g.

Не ска́жете ли вы мне, как пройти́ на Кра́сную пло́щадь?	*Could you possibly tell me the way to Red Square?*
Не мо́жешь ли ты помолча́ть?	*You couldn't possibly be quiet for a bit, could you?*
Не потру́дитесь ли вы вы́йти? (iron)	*Would you be so kind as to leave?*

ну

(a)   exhorts sb to say or do sth, e.g.

Ну, как дела́?	*Well, how are things?*
Ну, говори́, где ты побыва́л(а).	*Come on, tell us where you've been.*
Ну, пойдёмте.	*Well, let's be going.*

(b)   reinforces the expression of attitudes such as objection, bewilderment, annoyance, frustration, e.g.

| **Ну** что мне с тобо́й де́лать? Совсе́м не слу́шаешься. | *What on earth am I to do with you? You just don't do what I say.* |
| **Ну** ско́лько раз тебе́ говори́ть, что на́до снять ту́фли? | *However many times have I got to tell you to take your shoes off?* |

(c)   introduces expressive exclamations, e.g.

Ну, кака́я уда́ча!	*Well, what a stroke of luck!*
Ну, коне́чно!	*But of course!*
Ну, у́жас!	*But that's terrible!*

(d)   expresses qualified permission or acceptance (see also да (b)), e.g.

– Я уста́л(а).	*'I'm tired.'*
– **Ну**, передохнём.	*'Let's take a breather then.'*
– Мо́жно, я посмотрю́ на ваш мотоци́кл?	*'Can I have a look at your motor-bike?'*
– **Ну**, посмотри́те.	*'All right.'*

(e) in D, precedes a verb in the infinitive to stress the intensity of an action, e.g.

Начался́ спор, а он **ну́ крича́ть!**   *An argument broke out, and did he shout!*

(f) in D, with the accusative form of a personal pronoun, expresses strong disapproval, e.g.

А ну́ тебя́!   *Get lost!*

– Принима́й лека́рство.   'Take the medicine.'
– **Ну́ его́!**   'To hell with it!'

(g) also acts as a filler when the speaker is trying to collect her or his thoughts, e.g.

Не зна́ю. **Ну** ... Что сказа́ть?   *I don't know. Well ... What can I*
Попыта́юсь узна́ть.   *say? I'll try to find out.*

так   (a) introduces a suggestion in response to a setback, in which case так often corresponds to English *then*, e.g.

– Здесь нет мы́ла.   'There's no soap here.'
– **Так** принеси́!   'Then bring some.'

Его́ не бу́дет? **Так** мы обойдёмся   *He won't be there? Then we'll get*
без него́.   *by without him.*

(b) with the same word used twice (так being placed between the word or words used twice), indicates concession on the part of the speaker, or acceptance of a suggestion, or that some property is fully manifested, e.g.

– Дава́йте встре́тимся в кино́.   'Let's meet in the cinema. Is that
Согла́сны?   OK?'
– **В кино́ так в кино́.**   'The cinema it is then.'

– Как пое́дем домо́й? Дава́й на   'How shall we get home? Shall we get
такси́?   a taxi?'
– **На такси́ так на такси́.**   'All right then, we'll get a taxi.'

В Сиби́ри зимо́й уж **хо́лодно так**   *God, it's cold in Siberia in winter.*
хо́лодно.

(c) expresses approximation with time, distance, quantity, etc., e.g.

– Когда́ прие́дешь?   'When will you get here?'
– Часо́в **так** в шесть.   'About six o'clock.'

– Далеко́ до це́нтра?   'Is it far to the centre?'
– **Так** киломе́тра два.   'About two kilometres or so.'

– Ско́лько ве́сит ры́ба?   'How much does the fish weigh?'
– Килогра́мм **так** пять.   'About five kilos.'

–то

(a) stresses sth, e.g.

В то́м-то и де́ло. | *That's just it.*
Зо́нтик-то не забу́дь. Идёт | *Don't forget your umbrella. It's*
дождь. | *raining.*

(b) in stressing part of an utterance, may reinforce a contrast, e.g.

Сте́ны-то уже́ постро́ены, но | *The walls are built but there isn't a*
кры́ши ещё нет. | *roof yet.*
Я-то вы́полнил(а) своё обеща́ние, | *I've fulfilled my promise, but you're*
а вы ме́длите. | *procrastinating.*

(c) in constructions in which a word is repeated and in which –то stands after the word when it is first used, expresses concession, e.g.

Писа́ть-то пишу́, а она́ не чита́ет | *She doesn't read my letters, although*
мои́ пи́сьма. | *I make a point of writing to her.*
Занима́ться-то занима́лся/ | *I failed the exam, although I*
занима́лась, а на экза́мене | *worked really hard.*
провали́лся/провали́лась. |

(d) in certain phrases expressing strong negation, has a euphemistic nuance, e.g.

Кни́га **не осо́бенно-то** интере́сна. | *The book's pretty dull.*
Мне **не о́чень-то** хоте́лось | *I really didn't want to talk to her.*
говори́ть с ней. |
Не та́к-то про́сто бы́ло его́ | *It wasn't all that easy to calm him*
успоко́ить. | *down.*

(e) in exclamations with a tone of admiration or wonder, e.g.

Она́ краса́вица. **Каки́е глаза́-то!** | *She's beautiful. What wonderful*
| *eyes!*
Наро́ду-то на ры́нке! Что там | *What a lot of people at the market!*
продаю́т? | *What are they selling there?*

(f) lends intimacy or informality to an utterance, e.g.

В теа́тр-то ходи́л(а) вчера́? | *Did you go to the theatre yesterday*
| *then?*
'Как тебя́ **звать-то**?' – спроси́л | *'What should we call you then?'*
врач ребёнка. | *the doctor asked the child.*

Note: used as a particle –то is always attached to the word that it is intended to emphasise; it cannot stand on its own and never bears the stress.

уж

(a) intensifies some word denoting affirmation, negation or degree, e.g.

– Ты уста́л(а)? | *'Are you tired?'*
– **Да уж**. Е́ле иду́. | *'I certainly am. I can hardly move.'*

Он **уж совсе́м** переста́л заходи́ть | *He's completely given up calling on*
к нам. | *us.*

(b)   expresses acceptance or concession, perhaps reluctant, e.g.

– Дай мне свой зо́нтик на́ день.	*'Will you lend me your umbrella for the day?'*
– Бери́ **уж**, то́лько не забу́дь его́ в по́езде.	*'All right, but don't leave it on the train.'*
– Дым тебе́ меша́ет? Мо́жет, попроси́ть, чтоб не кури́ли?	*'Is the smoke bothering you? Shall we ask them to stop smoking?'*
– **Уж** пусть они́ ку́рят.	*'Oh, let them smoke.'*

(c)   with an imperative, lends the order a blunt but good-natured tone, an air of camaraderie, e.g.

| **Молчи́ уж** об э́том. Тебе́ не́чем горди́ться. | *You'd better keep quiet about that. You've got nothing to be proud of.* |
| **Иди́ уж.** | *Get a move on.* |

| хоть (бы)
хотя́ (бы) | (a) | may mean *if only* or *at least*, or may have the same meaning as **да́же**, *even*, or **да́же е́сли**, *even if*, especially in set phrases, e.g. |

Приезжа́й **хоть** на оди́н день.	*Do come, if only just for a day.*
Ах, **хоть бы** одно́ письмо́ от неё!	*Oh, if only there were just one letter from her!*
Хоть убе́й, не скажу́.	*I couldn't tell you to save my life. (lit Even if you kill me I won't tell you)*

(b)   introduces an example which readily springs to the speaker's mind; in this use it may be translated by *for example, to take only*, e.g.

| Лю́ди лени́вы. Взять **хоть** тебя́. | *People are lazy. Take you for example.* |

| что | (a) | may introduce a question, perhaps with a tone of surprise, disapproval or indignation, e.g. |

| **Что**, боли́т желу́док? | *So you've got stomach-ache, have you?* |
| **Что**, он говори́т, что не зна́ет меня́? | *What! He says he doesn't know me?* |

(b)   combines with a personal pronoun in the nominative to form elliptical exclamations in which some verb such as говори́ть is understood, e.g.

– Мо́жет быть, ску́шаешь ещё что́-нибудь?	*'Would you like to have something else to eat?'*
– **Что ты!** я сыт(а́).	*'What are you saying? I'm full.'*
– Я тебе́ заплачу́ за пи́во.	*'I'll pay you for the beer.'*
– **Что ты!** Не на́до!	*'For goodness sake! It's not necessary.'*

Miscellaneous particles	–то –нибу́дь –ли́бо }	form indefinite pronouns (see 11.2.5)
	де́скать	indicates reported speech, e.g. Он, де́скать, не слы́шал, *He said he hadn't heard.*
	мол	contraction of мо́лвил; = де́скать
	–с (obs)	(= су́дарь or суда́рыня) form of address to a social superior, e.g. serf to lord; also used ironically; widely encountered in classical literature
	–ся (–сь)	forms reflexive verbs (11.8)
	я́кобы	*allegedly, ostensibly, supposedly,* e.g. я́кобы невозмо́жная зада́ча, *a supposedly impossible task* (but the speaker does not believe it to be so)

5.5 Interjections

Interjections by their nature belong to the colloquial speech of R1. The following list gives some common interjections with translations that attempt to capture their flavour rather than the literal meaning of the words.

admiration	ах!	*wow!*
	балдёж! (slang)	*great!*
	блеск!	*brill!*
	блестя́ще!	*brilliant!*
	замеча́тельно!	*wonderful!*
	здо́рово!	*great!*
	изуми́тельно!	*super!*
	отпа́д!	*great!*
	су́пер!	*super!*
	улёт!	*magic!*
	чуде́сно!	*marvellous!*
agreement	договори́лись	*OK, agreed*
	замётано	*OK, agreed*
	есть (mil)	*yes, sir/ay, ay, sir*
	идёт	*all right*
	ла́дно	*OK, fine*
	хорошо́	*good*
annoyance	к чёрту его́!	*to hell with him/it!*

	пошёл к чёрту!/пошёл на́ фиг!	*go to hell!*
	пошёл на́ хер! (vulg)	*go to hell!*
	блин! (D)	*bother/damn/sod it!*
	Ну, блин, ты даёшь! (slightly vulg)	*What the hell are you doing?*
	тьфу, надое́л/а/о/и	*oh damn, I'm fed up with it/you*
	наплева́ть на + acc	*to hell with, damn*
	прова́ливай!	*clear off, get lost!*
	убира́йся!	*clear off, get lost!*
	чёрта с два!	*like hell!*
	чёрт возьми́!/чёрт побери́!	*to hell with it!*
	хрен с + instr (vulg)	*to hell with*

Note: see also 5.6 on vulgar language.

disbelief, surprise	ах!	*oh!*
	Бо́же мой!	*my God!*
	го́споди!	*good heavens, good gracious!*
	вот ещё!	*whatever next!*
	во́т как!/во́т что!	*really?*
	вот так та́к! (R2)	*well, I never!*
	ё моё (R1)	*well, I never!*
	ни фига́ себе́! (D)	*well, I never!*
	ну и ну!	*well, well!*
fright, pain	ай!	*oh! ouch*
	ах!	*ah! oh!*
	ой!	*ouch!*
	ох!	*ah! oh!*
objection	ни в ко́ем слу́чае!	*no way!*
	ни за что на све́те!	*not for anything!*
	ничего́ подо́бного!	*nothing of the sort!*
warning	внима́ние!	*attention!*
	осторо́жно!	*careful!*
	смотри́(те)!	*look out!*
miscellaneous	Бог (его́) зна́ет!	*God knows!*
	брысь!	*shoo! (to cat)*
	будь здоро́в/здоро́ва/бу́дьте здоро́вы!	*God bless! (when sb sneezes)*

вот-вот!	*that's it!* (expressing approval)
вот так!	= вот-вот
вот тебе!	*take that!* (accompanying blow)
вот тебе и + nom	*so much for*
вот тебе на!	*well, how do you like that!*
давай	*come on* (encouragement)
давай давай	*go on/pull the other leg* (when sb is told sth implausible)
ещё бы!	*I'll say!* (expressing confirmation)
лёгок/легка на помине	*talk of the devil* (on appearance of sb one has been talking about)
на	*here you are/here, take it*, e.g. Ná кни́гу, *Here, take the book.*
так тебе/вам и надо	*it serves you right*
поделом тебе/вам! (R3, obs)	*it serves you right*
ра́ди Бо́га	*for God's sake*
тсс!	*shh! hush!*
фу!	*ugh!* (expressing revulsion)
чего доброго!	*who knows!* (anticipating sth unpleasant)
чтоб не сглазить!	*touch wood!*

| **interjectional predicate** | Some interjectional forms, most of them derived from verbs, may serve as a predicate in R1, e.g. |

Айда́ в го́род.	*They set off and were in town in no time.*
Я **бах/бац/хлоп** его́ по спине́.	*I banged/slapped him on the back.*
Он – **прыг** на кры́шу.	*He leapt on to the roof.*
Он – **стук** в стекло́.	*He knocked on the window.*
Они́ – **шмыг** в тень.	*They nipped into the shadow.*

5.6   Vulgar language

This section must be prefaced by a triple warning. Firstly, the foreign student should be aware that no matter how good one's command of another people's language one may strike a discordant note or even give offence to a native speaker if one falls into very familiar registers in general and the vulgar register in particular. Secondly, it cannot be overemphasised that a vulgar word may have a greater impact in the Russian context than does its English lexical equivalent (even though the same anatomical features and sentiments are involved), since the English word occurs in a society that uses such vocabulary, for better or for worse, with relative freedom. Thirdly, it should be understood that whereas in Britain vulgar language may nowadays be used as freely by women as by men, in Russia the use of such language by a woman is likely to shock both men and women more than the use of that language by a man. The foreign student of Russian should therefore avoid using vulgar language if he, or especially she, wishes to win acceptance in any sort of 'polite' Russian society.

On the other hand, with the sudden influx into Russia of things Western, including pornography, vulgar language is a reality of Russian life that foreign students are much more likely to encounter now than they would have been in Soviet times. It has also found its way on a large scale into serious literature, including works published in Russia as well as those published abroad by émigrés. The introduction of vulgar language into works of art may be traced to the brief thaw under Khrushchóv. Vulgar words occur, for example, in Solzhenítsyn's *Оди́н день Ива́на Дени́совича* (*A Day in the Life of Ivan Denisovich*). In the age of *glásnost'* and the post-Soviet era such language has come to be widely used with great freedom in the works of writers such as Aleshkóvskii, Venedíkt Eroféev, Limónov, Nárbikova, Petrushévskaia, Evgénii Popóv and Zínik, some of whom, it should be noted, are women, and many of whom are writers of literary note. The foreign student may therefore usefully acquire a passive knowledge of this area of language.

The word meaning *foul language*, **мат**, is derived from мать, *mother*, expressions of abuse towards one's mother being the most offensive sort of obscenity. Further expressions of the same origin include **ма́терный язы́к** and **матерщи́на** (which also mean *foul language*) and the verbs **матери́ться**, *to use foul language*, and **матюка́ться**, *to eff and blind*.

A small selection of the very numerous obscenities available to the Russian-speaker is given below.

блева́ть (блюю́, блюёшь)	*to puke*
еба́ть (ебу́, ебёшь; past tense ёб, ебли́)	*to fuck*; also *to curse, discipline severely*
отъеби́сь от меня́	*fuck off*
ёбля	*fucking* (noun)
взъёбка	*a bollocking*
ёбаный	*fucking* (adj)
еба́ться с чем-н	*to fuck about with sth*
заёба (m and f)	*pain-in-the-arse*
ёб твою́ мать	*fucking* (as epithet; lit *fuck your mother*)
тра́хать/тра́хнуть (less vulg than еба́ть)	*to screw, bonk*

пи́сать (пи́саю, пи́саешь)/**попи́сать**	*to piss*
ссать (ссу, ссышь)/**посса́ть**	*to piss*
отлива́ть/отли́ть	*to have a piss, take a leak*
жо́па (dimin **жо́пка)**	*arse*
жополи́з	*arse-licker*
бздеть (бзжу, бздишь)	*to fart (silently), foul the air, bullshit; to shit oneself, i.e. to be afraid*
бздун	*fart (weak person), coward*
перде́ть (перди́т)/**пёрнуть**	*to fart*
пердёж	*farting*
перду́н	*farter, old fart*
срать (сру, срёшь)/**насра́ть**	*to shit*
ему́ насра́ть	*he doesn't give a shit*
засра́нец	*arse-hole, shit (i.e. person)*
обсира́ть/обосра́ть кого́-н	*to shit all over sb (fig)*
дерьмо́	*crap, dung (also person)*
говно́	*shit*
говню́к	*shit (bag) (i.e. person)*
пизда́	*cunt*
пи́здить/спи́здить	*to swipe, nick, steal*
хуй (dimin **хуёк)**	*prick (also person)*
ни хуя́	*fuck all*
пошёл на́ хуй	*fuck off*
хер	= хуй
ни хера́	= ни хуя́
хуйня́	*shit (nonsense, rubbish)*
херня́	= хуйня́
хуёвый	*lousy, fucking awful*
херо́вый	= хуёвый
муда́к	*arsehole (person)*
мудня́	*bollocks (nonsense)*
дрочи́ла (m and f)	*wanker*
дрочи́ть	*to masturbate*
сво́лочь (f)	*swine, bastard*
блядь (f)	*whore; also used as exclamation: sod it!*
ку́рва	*tart*

5.7 Idioms

An idiom is an expression peculiar to a particular language. It may have a rough equivalent in another language, but its meaning may not be readily apparent to a foreigner or even logically explicable.

Russian is particularly rich in its stock of idiomatic expressions, which are a source of pride to native speakers. These expressions lend colour and vitality to a speaker's language and appropriate use of them enhances the speaker's authority.

The idioms given in this section are widely used in modern Russian. While many of them are colloquial, they may well be deployed in the literary language and in R3c as well as in everyday speech in order to impart vitality, vividness and even an air of authentic national distinctiveness. On the other hand they are unlikely to be encountered in the formal objective registers of R3a and R3b.

The idioms are arranged in alphabetical order according to the letter with which the key word, usually a noun, begins. Where only one member of an aspectual pair of verbs appears either that member predominates or only that member may be used in the idiom in question. Wherever possible an idiomatic English equivalent of the Russian idiom is given. In many cases a literal translation of the Russian idiom is provided as well. Often this literal translation helps to elucidate the meaning of the Russian idiom but in some instances it serves merely to draw attention to the colourful nature of the idiom. In yet other cases, where there is no English equivalent of the Russian idiom, we provide a literal translation and if necessary an explanation of the context in which the idiom may be used.

Note that a few of the words that appear in these idioms (e.g. задо́ринка, зга, кули́чки, несо́лоно, по́лымя) have no other use in the modern language or occur only in a small number of such set expressions.

А

Нача́ть с азо́в	*to begin at the beginning* (аз is the Slavonic name of the first letter of the Cyrillic alphabet)
открыва́ть/откры́ть Аме́рику	lit *to discover America*, i.e. to *say sth well-known*

Б

бить баклу́ши	*to fritter away one's time*
Ои бро́вью не повёл.	lit *He didn't move his brow*, i.e. *He didn't turn a hair.*
броса́ться/бро́ситься в глаза́	lit *to hurl itself in one's eyes*, i.e. *to be striking*
как ни в чём не быва́ло	*as if nothing had happened*

В

(У него́) всё ва́лится и́з рук.	lit *Everything comes tumbling out of (his) hands*, i.e. *(He) is all fingers and thumbs.*

знать что́-н вдоль и поперёк	lit *to know sth along and across*, i.e. *inside out*
Ещё ви́лами по воде́ пи́сано.	lit *It's still written on the water with a pitchfork*, i.e. *It's not written in stone/It's still up in the air.*
И концы́ в во́ду.	lit *And the ends/traces into the water*, i.e. *None will be the wiser.*
как в во́ду ка́нуть	lit *like sinking into the water*, i.e. *to vanish into thin air*
выводи́ть/вы́вести на чи́стую во́ду	lit *to bring out into clear water*, i.e. *to expose, show in true colours*
Водо́й не разольёшь.	*(They're) thick as thieves.*
стре́ляный воробе́й	lit *a sparrow that's been under fire*, i.e. *an old hand*
держа́ть у́хо востро́	*to be on one's guard/keep a sharp look-out*
иска́ть вчера́шнего дня	lit *to look for yesterday*, i.e. *to waste time on sth futile, to go on a wild-goose chase*

Г

говори́ть с гла́зу на́ глаз	*to talk tête-à-tête*
гла́зом не моргну́в	lit *without blinking*, i.e. *without batting an eyelid*
закрыва́ть/закры́ть глаза́ на что́-н	*to turn a blind eye to sth*
лома́ть го́лову над че́м-н	lit *to break one's head over sth*, i.e. *to rack one's brains*
идти́/пойти́ в го́ру	*to go up in the world*
наступа́ть/наступи́ть на гра́бли	lit *to step on a rake* (so that the handle comes up and hits you), i.e. *to make a mistake which has painful consequences*; наступи́ть на те же гра́бли, *to make the same mistake again*
с грехо́м попола́м	*only just, with difficulty*

Д

ло́жка дёгтя в бо́чке мёда	lit *a spoon of tar in a barrel of honey*, i.e. *a fly in the ointment*
не ро́бкого деся́тка	*no coward*
петь дифира́мбы кому́-н	*to sing sb's praises*
У него́ душа́ нараспа́шку.	lit *He has an unbuttoned soul*, i.e. *He wears his heart upon his sleeve.*

Е

держа́ть в ежо́вых рукави́цах	*to rule with a rod of iron*
моло́ть ерунду́	*to talk nonsense*

З

заблуди́ться в трёх со́снах	lit *to get lost in three pine-trees*, i.e. *in broad daylight*
е́хать за́йцем	*to travel without paying the fare*

Ни зги не ви́дно.	lit *The path can't be seen*, i.e. *It's pitch dark.*
положи́ть зу́бы на по́лку	lit *to put one's teeth on the shelf*, i.e. *to tighten one's belt*
держа́ть язы́к за зуба́ми	*to hold one's tongue*

И

крича́ть во всю ива́новскую	*to shout at the top of one's voice* (the expression refers to Ivanovskaia Square in the Moscow Kremlin; the square is so big that it is hard to shout right across it)

К

тёртый кала́ч	*old stager, person who has been around*
держа́ть ка́мень за па́зухой на кого́-н	lit *to keep a stone in one's bosom*, i.e. *to bear a grudge against sb*
ка́мень преткнове́ния	*a stumbling block*
(Он) за сло́вом в карма́н не ле́зет.	*(He's) not at a loss for a word.*
завари́ть ка́шу	*to stir up trouble*
расхлеба́ть ка́шу	*to put things right*
входи́ть/войти́ в колею́	lit *to go into (its) rut*, i.e. *to settle down again* (of life, situation; not a negative expression, unlike Eng *to get into a rut*)
выбива́ть/вы́бить из колеи́	lit *to knock out of (its) rut*, i.e. *to unsettle*
Кома́р но́са не подто́чит.	*Not a thing can be said against it.*
своди́ть/свести́ концы́ с конца́ми	*to make ends meet*
оста́ться у разби́того коры́та	lit *to be left at a broken trough*, i.e. *to be back where one started*

Л

(У него́) лёгкая рука́.	*(He has) good luck.*
Кто в лес, кто по дрова́.	*(They're) at sixes and sevens.*
сесть в лу́жу	lit *to sit in a puddle*, i.e. *to get into a mess*
(Я/он/она́) не лы́ком шит(а).	*I/he/she wasn't born yesterday.*

М

идти́ как по ма́слу	*to go swimmingly*
медве́жья услу́га	lit *a bear's service*, said of action that is intended to be helpful but in fact has the opposite effect
ме́жду мо́лотом и накова́льней	lit *between the hammer and the anvil*, i.e. *between the devil and the deep blue sea/between a rock and a hard place*
моло́чные ре́ки, кисе́льные берега́	*a land of milk and honey*

Мура́шки по спине́ бе́гают.	lit *Little insects are running up (my) back*, i.e. *It gives (me) the creeps.*
Он му́хи не оби́дит.	*He wouldn't harm a fly.*
де́лать из му́хи слона́	lit *to make an elephant out of a fly*, i.e. *to make a mountain out of a mole-hill*

Н

уйти́ несо́лоно хлеба́вши	*to go away empty-handed*
проходи́ть кра́сной ни́тью че́рез что́-н (R3, bookish)	lit *to run like a red thread through sth*, i.e. *to stand out* (of theme, motif)
жить на ба́рскую но́гу	*to live like a lord*
жить на широ́кую но́гу	*to live in grand style*
встать с ле́вой ноги́	lit *to get up on the left foot*, i.e. *to get out of bed on the wrong side*
быть на коро́ткой ноге́ с ке́м-н	*to be on close terms with sb*
ног под собо́й не чу́вствовать	lit *not to feel one's legs under oneself*, i.e. *to be dropping (from tiredness)*
ве́шать/пове́сить нос	*to be crestfallen*
задира́ть/задра́ть нос	*to put on airs*
води́ть кого́-н за́ нос	*to lead sb a dance*
клева́ть но́сом	*to nod off*
оста́вить кого́-н с но́сом	*to dupe sb*
оста́ться с но́сом	*to be duped*

О

говори́ть без обиняко́в	*to speak plainly / without beating about the bush*
пройти́ ого́нь, во́ду и ме́дные тру́бы	*to go through fire and water* (and in the Russian *copper tubes* as well!)
из огня́ да в по́лымя	lit *from the fire into the flames*, i.e. *out of the frying-pan and into the fire*
ме́ж(ду) двух огне́й	lit *between two fires*, i.e. *between the devil and the deep blue sea*

П

па́лец о па́лец не уда́рить	*not to raise a finger*
кому́-н па́льца в рот не клади́	lit *don't put your finger in sb's mouth*, i.e. *a person is not to be trusted*
попа́сть па́льцем в не́бо	*to be wide of the mark*
смотре́ть сквозь па́льцы на что́-н	lit *to look at sth through one's fingers*, i.e. *to shut one's eyes to sth*
вставля́ть/вста́вить па́лки кому́-н в колёса	*to put a spoke in sb's wheel*
перелива́ть из пусто́го в поро́жнее	*to beat the air*

Гора́ с плеч свали́лась.	lit *A mountain's come off (my) shoulders, i.e. (It's) a weight off (my) mind.*
ждать у мо́ря пого́ды	*to wait for sth to turn up*
знать всю подного́тную	*to know the whole truth*
попада́ть/попа́сть в то́чку	*to hit the nail on the head*
стере́ть кого́-н **в порошо́к**	lit *to grind sb into powder, i.e. to make mincemeat of sb*
всё кро́ме пти́чьего молока́	lit *everything except bird's milk, said when every possible dish is served at a meal*
разби́ть в пух и прах	lit *to defeat/break up into fluff and dust, i.e. to put to rout*
стреля́ть из пу́шек по воробья́м	lit *to fire cannons at sparrows, i.e. to use a sledgehammer to crack a nut*
(У него́) семь пя́тниц на неде́ле.	*(He) keeps chopping and changing.*

Р

показа́ть кому́-н **где ра́ки зиму́ют**	lit *to show sb where the crayfish spend the winter = to give sb a dressing-down*
у кого́-н **хлопо́т по́лон рот**	lit *sb has a mouth full of troubles, i.e. sb has his/her hands full*
махну́ть руко́й на что́-н	*to give up sth as lost*
сиде́ть сложа́ ру́ки	lit *to sit with arms folded, i.e. to twiddle one's thumbs*
из рук вон пло́хо	*dreadfully, wretchedly*
рабо́тать засучи́в рукава́	lit *to work having rolled up one's sleeves, i.e. to work with zeal*
рабо́тать спустя́ рукава́	lit *to work having put one's sleeves down, i.e. to work in a slipshod manner*
ни ры́ба ни мя́со	*neither fish nor flesh, neither one thing nor the other*

С

Два сапога́ па́ра. (pej)	*They make a pair.*
подложи́ть кому́-н **свинью́**	*to play a dirty trick on sb*
ни слу́ху ни ду́ху (о ко́м-н**)**	*not a word has been heard (of sb)*
Вот где соба́ка зары́та.	lit *That's where the dog is buried = That's the crux of the matter.*
соба́ку съесть на чём-н	*to know sth inside out*
выноси́ть/вы́нести сор из избы́	lit *to take one's litter out of the peasant hut, i.e. to wash one's dirty linen in public*
роди́ться в соро́чке	lit *to be born in a shirt/blouse, i.e. with a silver spoon in one's mouth*
держа́ть что́-н **под спу́дом**	*to hide sth under a bushel*

выходи́ть/вы́йти сухи́м из воды́	lit *to emerge dry from water*, i.e. *unscathed*
без сучка́, без задо́ринки	*without a hitch*
в два счёта	*in a jiffy*

Т

быть не в свое́й таре́лке	*to be not quite oneself*
В тесноте́, да не в оби́де.	*The more the merrier.*
сбива́ть/сбить кого́-н с то́лку	*to confuse sb*
за три́девять земе́ль	lit *beyond thrice nine lands*, i.e. *far, far away* (a formula from fairy tales)
в Ту́лу со свои́м самова́ром	lit *to Tula with one's samovar*, i.e. *coals to Newcastle* (in tsarist times Tula was where samovars were made)
заходи́ть/зайти́ в тупи́к	*to go up a blind alley, to come to a dead end, reach deadlock*

У

заки́дывать/заки́нуть у́дочку	lit *to cast a (fishing-)line*, i.e. *to put out feelers*
попада́ться/попа́сться на у́дочку	*to swallow the bait*
бра́ться/взя́ться за ум	*to come to one's senses*
мота́ть/намота́ть что́-н себе́ на ус	lit *to wind sth round one's whisker*, i.e. *to take good note of sth*
из уст в уста́	lit *from mouth to mouth*, i.e. *by word of mouth*
пропуска́ть/пропусти́ть что́-н ми́мо уше́й	*to turn a deaf ear to sth*

Ф

кури́ть фимиа́м кому́-н	lit *to burn incense for sb*, i.e. *to praise sb to the skies*

Ч

замори́ть червячка́	lit *to underfeed the little worm*, i.e. *to have a snack*
у чёрта на кули́чках	*in the middle of nowhere, the back of beyond*

Ш

Де́ло в шля́пе.	lit *The matter is in the hat*, i.e. *It's in the bag.*

Щ

по щу́чьему веле́нию	lit *at the pike's behest*, i.e. *as if by magic*

Я

я́блоко раздо́ра	*apple of discord, bone of contention*
Я́блоку не́где упа́сть.	lit *There's nowhere for an apple to fall*, i.e. *There isn't room to swing a cat.*
откла́дывать/отложи́ть что́-н в до́лгий я́щик	lit *to put sth in the long-term box*, i.e. *to shelve sth, put sth off*

5.8 Proverbs and sayings (посло́вицы и погово́рки)

A proverb is a short statement expressing a supposed truth or moral lesson. Russian is rich in such colourful utterances, many of which are felt to express folk wisdom. A foreigner's knowledge of the more common among them is likely to impress a native speaker, provided that they are used correctly and sparingly.

The following list contains many of the best-known Russian proverbs. Those proverbs that are distinctively Russian and proverbs that differ in their terms from their English equivalents have been given preference in the selection. Where possible a close English equivalent is given, often with a literal translation. Where there is no close English equivalent a literal translation is offered together, if possible, with an approximate English equivalent. In a few cases (e.g. **Незва́ный гость ху́же тата́рина**) the literal meaning makes the sense of the saying obvious.

Note: occasionally stress in a word used in a proverb is on a different syllable from the syllable on which it normally falls, perhaps because of the need for an internal rhyme (see e.g. the stress on **ворота́** (instead of standard воро́та) in the first proverb in this list).

Б

Пришла́ беда́ – отворя́й ворота́.
lit *Misfortune has come, open the gate(s)*, i.e. *It never rains but it pours.*

Друзья́ познаю́тся в беде́.
A friend in need is a friend indeed.

Семь бед – оди́н отве́т.
One may as well be hanged for a sheep as a lamb.

Бе́дность не поро́к.
Poverty is no sin.

Пе́рвый блин ко́мом.
lit *The first pancake is like a lump*, i.e. *The first attempt is usually botched.*

В

Век живи́ – век учи́сь
Live and learn!

С волка́ми жить – по-во́лчьи выть.
lit *If one is to live with wolves one has to howl like a wolf*, i.e. *When in Rome do as the Romans do.*

Ста́рого воробья́ на мяки́не не проведёшь.
An old bird [sparrow in Russian] is not caught with chaff.

Пу́ганая воро́на куста́ бои́тся.
lit *A frightened crow is afraid of a bush*, i.e. *Once bitten twice shy.*

Г

Незва́ный гость ху́же тата́рина.
An uninvited guest is worse than a Tatar. (The Tatars were the sovereign power in Russia from the early thirteenth century to the late fifteenth century.)

В гостя́х хорошо́, а до́ма лу́чше.
lit *It's nice as a guest but it's better at home*, i.e. *There's no place like home.*

Д

Дурака́м зако́н не пи́сан.

Fools rush in where angels fear to tread.

Ж

Куй желе́зо пока́ горячо́.

Strike while the iron is hot.

Жизнь прожи́ть – не по́ле перейти́.

lit *Living through one's life is not like going through a field*, i.e. *Life is not a bed of roses.*

З

За двумя́ за́йцами пого́нишься, ни одного́ не пойма́ешь.

lit *If you run after two hares you will catch neither.*

К

Не плюй в коло́дец; случи́тся воды́ напи́ться.

lit *Don't spit in the well, you may need to drink out of it*, i.e. *Do not antagonise people whose help you may need later.*

Коси́ коса́ пока́ роса́.

Make hay while the sun shines.

Не всё коту́ ма́сленица, придёт и вели́кий пост.

lit *It's not all Shrove-tide for the cat, Lent will come too*, i.e. *After the dinner comes the reckoning.*

Всяк кули́к своё боло́то хва́лит.

lit *Every sandpiper praises its own bog*, i.e. people praise what is dear to them.

Л

Одна́ ла́сточка весны́ не де́лает.

One swallow does not make a summer [*spring* in Russian].

Лес ру́бят – ще́пки летя́т.

lit *You cut down the forest and the bits of wood fly*, i.e. *You cannot make an omelette without breaking eggs.*

М

Мир те́сен.

It's a small world.

В чужо́й монасты́рь со свои́м уста́вом не хо́дят.

lit *You don't go into sb else's monastery with your own set of rules*, i.e. *When in Rome do as the Romans do.*

Москва́ не сра́зу стро́илась

lit *Moscow wasn't built all at once*, i.e. *Rome was not built in a day.*

Н

У семи́ ня́нек дитя́ без гла́зу.

lit *Where there are seven nannies the child is not watched*, i.e. *Too many cooks spoil the broth.*

П

Всё перемéлется, мука́ бу́дет.

It will all come right in the end.

Поживём – уви́дим.

lit *We shall live and we shall see*, i.e. *Time will tell.*

Что посе́ешь, то и пожнёшь.

As a man sows so shall he reap.

Пра́вда глаза́ ко́лет.	lit *Truth pricks the eyes, i.e. Home truths are hard to swallow.*

Р

Своя́ руба́шка бли́же к те́лу.	lit *One's own shirt is nearer to the body, i.e. Charity begins at home.*
Ру́сский челове́к за́дним умо́м кре́пок.	*The Russian is wise after the event.*
Рыба́к рыбака́ ви́дит издалека́.	lit *The fisherman spots a fisherman from afar, i.e. Birds of a feather flock together.*

С

Сде́ланного не воро́тишь.	*What's done can't be undone.*
Сме́лость города́ берёт.	lit *Boldness takes cities, i.e. Nothing ventured nothing gained.*
Соловья́ ба́снями не ко́рмят.	lit *You can't feed a nightingale with fables, i.e. Fine words butter no parsnips.*
Сы́тый голо́дного не разуме́ет.	lit *The well-fed cannot understand the hungry.*

Т

Там хорошо́, где нас нет.	lit *It's good where we are not, i.e. The grass is always greener on the other side of the fence.*
Ти́ше е́дешь, да́льше бу́дешь.	lit *[If] you go more calmly you'll get further, i.e. More haste less speed.*

У

Ум хорошо́, а два лу́чше.	*Two heads are better than one.*

Х

Хрен ре́дьки не сла́ще.	lit *Horseradish is no sweeter than ordinary radish, i.e. There is little to choose between two unpleasant things.*
Нет худа́ без добра́	lit *There's no evil without good, i.e. Every cloud has a silver lining.*

Ц

Цыпля́т по о́сени счита́ют.	lit *People count their chickens after autumn, i.e. Don't count your chickens before they are hatched.*

Ч

Не так стра́шен чёрт, как его́ малю́ют.	*The devil is not so terrible as he is painted.*
В ти́хом о́муте че́рти во́дятся.	lit *In a quiet whirlpool devils are found, i.e. Still waters run deep.*

Я

Язы́к до Ки́ева доведёт.	lit *Your tongue will get you to Kiev, i.e. Don't hesitate to ask people.*

5.9 Similes

A simile is an explicit likening of one thing to another. Languages have a stock of such comparisons, some of which are distinctive to that language. While the foreign student should take care not to use similes excessively or ostentatiously, their occasional use in the right context adds colour and authenticity to one's language, both spoken and written. The following list gives some of the commonest Russian similes. It is arranged in alphabetical order of the key word in the comparison.

(кружи́ться) как бе́лка в колесе́	(to whirl around) like a squirrel in a wheel (said of sb frantically busy)
Дождь льёт как из ведра́.	lit It's raining as out of a bucket, i.e. It's raining cats and dogs.
как с гу́ся вода́	lit like water off a goose, i.e. like water off a duck's back
как в во́ду опу́щенный	downcast, crestfallen
как горо́х об сте́ну	like a pea against a wall (said of action that is futile)
как гром среди́ я́сного не́ба	lit like thunder in the middle of a clear sky, i.e. like a bolt from the blue
(быть, сиде́ть) как на иго́лках	(to be) on thorns/tenterhooks
как две ка́пли воды́ похо́жи	lit like two drops of water, i.e. alike as two peas
(жить) как ко́шка с соба́кой	(to live) a cat and dog life
холо́дный как лёд	cold as ice
знать что́-н как свои́ пять па́льцев	lit to know sth like one's five fingers, i.e. like the back of one's hand
как ры́ба в воде́	like a fish in water, like a duck to water, in one's element
(би́ться) как ры́ба об лёд	(to fight) like a fish against ice (said about futile struggle)
как снег на́ голову	lit like snow on one's head, i.e. like a bolt from the blue
как соба́ка на се́не	like a dog in the manger
гол как со́кол	lit naked like a falcon, i.e. poor as a church mouse
как на раскалённых у́глях	as on hot coals
как чёрт от ла́дана	like the devil from incense (said of sb shunning sth)

Note

1. The word **гла́сность** (f) is itself an example of the much smaller number of Russian words that have been borrowed by English and other Western European languages; **во́дка, интеллиге́нция, перестро́йка, спу́тник, тайга́**, are others.

6 Language and everyday life

6.1 Measurement

The metric system has been used in Russia since it was introduced on an obligatory basis by the Bolshevik government in 1918. The British imperial system will not be understood by Russians, although some of the words denoting units of measure in that system may be familiar to them. Comparisons of units of different systems in the following sections are approximate.

6.1.1 Length, distance, height

Approximate metric equivalents of imperial units of measure of length:

1 inch = 25 millimetres
1 foot = 0.3 metres
1 yard = 0.9 metres
1 mile = 1.6 kilometres

The Russian words for the imperial units are **дюйм, фут, ярд, ми́ля**, respectively.

The Russian words for the basic metric units of measure of length are:

миллиме́тр	*millimetre*
сантиме́тр	*centimetre*
метр	*metre*
киломе́тр	*kilometre*

Some rough equivalents:

10 сантиме́тров	4 inches
1 метр	just over a yard
100 ме́тров	110 yards
1 киломе́тр	five-eighths of a mile
100 киломе́тров	62 miles
мужчи́на ро́стом (в) метр во́семьдесят три (1,83)	a man 6′ tall
мужчи́на ро́стом (в) метр се́мьдесят пять (1,75)	a man 5′ 9″ tall
мужчи́на ро́стом (в) метр шестьдеся́т во́семь (1,68)	a man 5′ 6″ tall
де́вочка ро́стом (в) девяно́сто сантиме́тров (0,90)	a girl nearly 3′ tall

Note: the versions of the above phrases without the preposition **в** are more colloquial.

A plane might fly at an altitude of 30,000 feet, i.e. **на высоте́ де́сять** [R3: **десяти́**] **ты́сяч ме́тров**.

   The highest mountain in the world, Everest (**Эвере́ст** or **Джомолу́нгма**), has a height of roughly 29,000 feet, i.e. **во́семь ты́сяч восемьсо́т пятьдеся́т ме́тров**.

6.1.2   Area

Approximate metric equivalents of imperial units of measure of area:

1 square inch = 6.45 square centimetres
1 square foot = 0.09 square metres
1 square yard = 0.84 square metres
1 acre = 0.4 hectares
1 square mile = 259 hectares

The Russian adjective for *square* is **квадра́тный**. The metric unit of measure for large areas is the *hectare*, **гекта́р** (= 10,000 square metres).

   Some rough equivalents with imperial measurements:

оди́н квадра́тный метр	just over 1 square yard
10 квадра́тных ме́тров	just under 12 square yards
два гекта́ра	nearly 5 acres (about the size of 3 football pitches)
250 гекта́ров	about 615 acres (roughly the area of Hyde Park)
20,000 квадра́тных киломе́тров	nearly 8,000 square miles (roughly the area of Wales)

6.1.3   Weight

Approximate metric equivalents of avoirdupois units of measure of weight:

1 ounce = 28.35 grams
1 pound = 0.45 kilograms
1 stone = 6.36 kilograms
1 hundredweight = 50.8 kilograms
1 ton = 1,016 kilograms

The Russian words for these avoirdupois units are **у́нция, фунт, сто́ун, ха́ндредвейт, то́нна**, respectively.

   The Russian words for the basic metric units of weight are:

миллигра́м	*milligram*
грамм	*gram*
килогра́мм	*kilogram*

це́нтнер	*100 kilograms*
то́нна	*(metric) tonne* (1,000 kg)

Some rough equivalents with avoirdupois weights:

200 грамм ма́сла	about 7 oz of butter
полкило́ мя́са	just over 1 lb of meat
мужчи́на ве́сом (в) 65 кило́	a man of just over 10 stone
мужчи́на ве́сом (в) 100 кило́/	a man of about 15½ stone
оди́н це́нтнер	
маши́на ве́сом (в) 1000 кило́/	a car weighing just under a ton
одну́ то́нну	

Note: the versions of the above phrases without the preposition **в** are more colloquial.

6.1.4 Volume

Approximate metric equivalents of imperial units of measure of volume:

1 cubic inch = 16 cubic centimetres
1 cubic foot = 0.03 cubic metres
1 cubic yard = 0.8 cubic metres
1 pint = 0.57 litres
1 gallon = 4.55 litres

The Russian words for the last two imperial units are **пи́нта** and **галло́н**, respectively. The Russian adjective for *cubic* is **куби́ческий**; *litre* is **литр**. Some rough equivalents:

поллитра пи́ва	about a pint of beer
литр молока́	about 1¾ pints of milk
бензоба́к ёмкостью в 50	a petrol tank which holds about
ли́тров	11 gallons

Note: small quantities of drinks may be ordered by weight, e.g. **сто грамм во́дки**, *100 grams of vodka*; **две́сти грамм коньяка́**, *200 grams of brandy*.

6.1.5 Russian pre-revolutionary units of measure

Words relating to the earlier system of measurement will of course be found in pre-revolutionary literature and documents, and in some cases may persist in contexts in which they no longer have to do with precise measurement. The main units were:

length

вершо́к =	1¾″ or 4.4 cm
арши́н =	28″ or 71 cm
са́же́нь (f) =	7′ or 2.13 metres
верста́ =	⅔ mile or 1.07 km

Note: **ме́рить что́-н на свой арши́н**, *to measure sth by one's own standards*
ме́рить вёрсты, *to travel a long way*
хвата́ть вершки́ чего́-н, *to get a smattering of sth*

area   **десяти́на** = 2.7 acres or 1.09 hectares
weight   **пуд** = 36 lbs or 16.38 kg
liquid measure **штоф** = 2 pints or 1.23 litres
че́тверть (f) = 5 pints or 3 litres
ведро́ = 21 pints or 12.3 litres (10 × штоф, 4 × че́тверть)

6.1.6   Speed

Some rough equivalents:

60 киломе́тров в час	37 miles an hour
100 киломе́тров в час	62 miles an hour
160 киломе́тров в час	100 miles an hour
300 миллио́нов ме́тров в секу́нду	186,000 feet per second (the speed of light)

6.1.7   Temperature

The centigrade scale constructed by Celsius is used, and the Fahrenheit scale will not be generally understood. The formulae for conversion are:

$$C = (F - 32) \times \tfrac{5}{9}, \text{e.g. } 77°F = 25°C$$
$$F = \left(C \times \tfrac{9}{5}\right) + 32, \text{e.g. } 15°C = 59°F$$

Some equivalents:

По Це́льсию	по Фаренге́йту
сто гра́дусов (100°, **то́чка кипе́ния воды́**, i.e. *boiling point of water*)	212°
три́дцать гра́дусов (тепла́) (30° above zero)	86°
два́дцать гра́дусов (тепла́) (20° above zero)	68°
де́сять гра́дусов (тепла́) (10° above zero)	50°
четы́ре гра́дуса (тепла́) (4° above zero)	39°
нуль (m; 0°, **то́чка замерза́ния воды́**, i.e. *freezing point of water*)	32°
пять гра́дусов ни́же нуля́/пять гра́дусов моро́за (−5°)	23°
два́дцать гра́дусов ни́же нуля́/два́дцать гра́дусов моро́за (−20°)	−4°
со́рок гра́дусов ни́же нуля́/со́рок гра́дусов моро́за (−40°)	−40°

The normal temperature of the human body (98.4°F) is just under 37°C, i.e. **три́дцать семь гра́дусов**, more precisely **три́дцать шесть и де́вять**.

6.2   Currency

The basic unit of currency is the rouble (**рубль**; m). The smaller unit, the kopeck (**копе́йка**), of which there are a hundred to the rouble, has with post-Soviet hyperinflation become valueless. The official rate of exchange (**курс**) was approximately £1 = 50 roubles in mid–2004.

Salaries are described in monthly terms (e.g. **во́семь ты́сяч рубле́й в ме́сяц**, *8,000 roubles a month*).

Russian pre-revolutionary coins, the names of which may be encountered in classical literature and pre-revolutionary documents, included the **алты́н** (3 kopecks), **гри́вна** (10 kopecks) and **полти́нник** (50 kopecks).

The names of the main foreign currencies that are used or are familiar in Russia are: **до́ллар**, *dollar*; **фунт**, *pound*; **франк**, *Swiss franc*; and latterly **е́вро**, *euro*.

6.3   Fractions and presentation of numerals

A decimal point is indicated in writing by a comma and is read as follows:

3,1	**три це́лых и одна́ деся́тая** (**часть**, *part*, is understood)
4,2	**четы́ре це́лых и две деся́тых**
5,5	**пять це́лых и пять деся́тых**
7,6	**семь це́лых и шесть деся́тых**
8,9	**во́семь це́лых и де́вять деся́тых**

Because the comma is used to indicate a decimal point it cannot be used to separate blocks in numbers involving thousands and millions, which may instead be spaced out in the following way:

23 987	**два́дцать три ты́сячи девятьсо́т во́семьдесят семь**
2 564 000	**два миллио́на пятьсо́т шестьдеся́т четы́ре ты́сячи**

6.4   Time

The 24-hour clock is widely used for all official purposes, e.g.

Конфере́нция начина́ется в **15.00 часо́в**.

The conference begins at 3.00 pm.

По́езд отправля́ется в **21.00 час**.

The train leaves at 9.00 pm.

If the 24-hour clock is not used, and one needs to specify which part of the day one is talking about, then one of the following forms (in the **genitive** case) should follow the stated time:

утра́	*in the morning*
дня	*in the afternoon*
ве́чера	*in the evening*
но́чи	*in the night*

e.g. **в во́семь часо́в утра́**, *at eight in the morning*; **в де́сять часо́в ве́чера**, *at ten in the evening*.

Note: **ве́чер** implies any time up until bedtime, whilst **ночь** indicates the period after midnight. English-speakers should note in particular that *tonight* in the sense of *this evening* should be translated **сего́дня ве́чером**.

In R1/2 time is frequently presented in simplified forms such as **три два́дцать**, *three twenty* or **во́семь три́дцать пять**, *eight thirty-five*, rather than the more cumbersome **два́дцать мину́т четвёртого** and **без двадцати́ пяти́ де́вять**, respectively. Forms such as **полседьмо́го**, *half (past) six*, are also preferred in R1/2 to the fuller **полови́на седьмо́го**.

Russia contains eleven time zones. Speakers may therefore need to specify which time zone they have in mind, e.g. **в де́сять часо́в по моско́вскому вре́мени**, *at ten o'clock Moscow time*.

6.5   Telephone numbers

In big cities these will normally consist of seven digits, which will be divided up and read in the following way:

243-71-59 две́сти со́рок три, се́мьдесят оди́н, пятьдеся́т де́вять
391-64-27 три́ста девяно́сто оди́н, шестьдеся́т четы́ре, два́дцать семь

However, it would also be perfectly acceptable nowadays for the foreign speaker, for the sake of convenience, to treat each digit separately.

6.6   Postal addresses

These have until recently been presented in inverse order to that used in English, that is to say in the order country, postcode, town, street, building, addressee. The abbreviations **к.** (**ко́рпус**, *block*), **д.** (**дом**, *house*), **кв.** (**кварти́ра**, *flat*) may be used. The name of the addressee is put in the dative case. Examples:

Росси́я 197343,	**г. Калу́га 253223,**
Москва́,	**ул. Циолко́вского,**

ул. Ташке́нтская,   д. 3а, кв. 22,
д. 23, кв. 36,   Па́влову С.Г.
Елисе́евой В.А.

However, since 1997 Russian practice has changed, perhaps in order to bring it in line with Western European practice, so that an address should be set out in the following way:

Кому́: Ко́зыреву В.А.
Куда́: ул. Ста́рый Арба́т, д. 3, кв. 5,
Москва́,
Росси́я 119026.

6.7 Family relationships

Russian has what to an English-speaker is a bewildering multiplicity of terms to denote family relationships, including e.g. **шу́рин**, *brother-in-law* (wife's brother); **своя́к**, *brother-in-law* (husband of wife's sister); **своя́ченица**, *sister-in-law* (wife's sister); **де́верь** (m), *brother-in-law* (husband's brother); **золо́вка**, *sister-in-law* (husband's sister); **зять** (m), *brother-in-law* (sister's husband or husband's sister's husband) or *son-in-law*; and **неве́стка**, *sister-in-law* (brother's wife) or *daughter-in-law* (son's wife). Fortunately for the foreign learner, however, these terms now have largely historical significance. They were once widespread in the extended family in the rural community, and may be encountered in classical literature, but they are not used in modern urban society. One still does need, though, to know the terms for *father-in-law* and *mother-in-law*, which have to be rendered in different ways depending on whether the speaker has in mind the parents of the wife (**жена́**) or the husband (**муж**), viz:

тесть (m)	*father-in-law* (father of one's wife)
тёща	*mother-in-law* (mother of one's wife)
свёкор	*father-in-law* (father of one's husband)
свекро́вь (f)	*mother-in-law* (mother of one's husband)

To translate *brother-in-law* or *sister-in-law* an appropriate descriptive phrase such as **брат жены́**, *wife's brother*, **жена́ бра́та**, *brother's wife*, or **муж сестры́**, *sister's husband* should now be used.

6.8 Public notices

A number of grammatical structures are characteristic of public notices, the language of which may be seen as a variety of R3b.

(a) Where an order or prohibition is expressed the imperative is often rendered by an infinitive form. In an instruction the infinitive is perfective, whilst in a prohibition with the particle не it is imperfective, e.g.

Пристегну́ть ремни́. (in plane)
Fasten seatbelts.
При ава́рии разби́ть стекло́ молотко́м. (in bus and underground)
In the event of an accident break the glass with the hammer.
Рука́ми не тро́гать. (in museum)
Do not touch.
Не кури́ть.
No smoking.
Не входи́ть в пальто́. (in offices, etc.)
Do not enter in your coat.
Не бе́гать по эскала́торам. (in underground stations)
Do not run up and down the escalators.
Не прислоня́ться. (on doors of underground train)
Do not lean.
По газо́нам не ходи́ть.
Keep off the grass.

(b) Instructions and prohibitions may also be couched in the imperative, e.g.

Пройди́те да́льше в ваго́н. (in tram)
Pass down the vehicle.
Соблюда́й диста́нцию. (on back of road vehicle)
Keep your distance.
Не отвлека́йте води́теля посторо́нними разгово́рами. (in bus)
Do not distract the driver by talking to him.
Не стой под стрело́й. (on crane)
Do not stand under the arm.

(c) Prohibitions may also be expressed with a past passive participle, e.g.

Вход посторо́нним запрещён.
Unauthorised persons not admitted.
Кури́ть запрещено́.
Smoking prohibited.
Купа́ться запрещено́. Опа́сно для жи́зни.
Bathing prohibited. Danger of death. (lit *dangerous to life*)
Приноси́ть и распива́ть спиртны́е напи́тки запрещено́.
It is forbidden to bring and consume alcoholic drinks.

(d) An exhortation may be couched in a third-person-plural form, or with the words **про́сьба**, *request*, or **про́сим**, *we ask*, e.g.

У нас не ку́рят.
No smoking here.
Про́сьба закрыва́ть дверь.
Please close the door.

Про́сьба живо́тных не корми́ть. (in zoo)
Please do not feed the animals.
Про́сьба/про́сим сдава́ть су́мки. (in self-service shop)
Please hand in your bags.

(e) Statements providing information, and also prohibitions, are often rendered by a reflexive verb, e.g.

Вы́емка пи́сем произво́дится в 8 часо́в. (on letter box)
Collection of letters takes place at 8.00 (am).
Стол не обслу́живается. (in restaurant)
No service at this table.
Вход посторо́нним стро́го воспреща́ется. (e.g. on building site)
Entry to people who have no business here strictly forbidden.

(f) Some notices or instructions incorporate gerunds (see 9.7.1–9.7.2, 11.11.1), which are characteristic of R3, e.g.

Уходя́, гаси́те свет.
Turn out the light when you leave.
Опуска́я письмо́, прове́рьте нали́чие и́ндекса.
Check that you have put the postcode on when you post your letter.

(g) Miscellaneous notices:

Закры́то на́ зиму. (on train windows)	*Closed for the winter.*
Закры́то на ремо́нт. (ubiquitous)	*Closed for repairs.*
Закры́т на учёт/переучёт. (in shops)	*Closed for stock-taking.*
Иди́те. (at road crossing)	*Go.*
Жди́те. (at road crossing)	*Wait.*
Сто́йте. (at road crossing)	*Stop.*
К себе́. (on doors)	*Pull.*
От себя́. (on doors)	*Push.*
Стоп! (at road crossing, etc.)	*Stop.*
Осторо́жно! Высо́кое напряже́ние.	*Warning. High voltage.*
Осторо́жно! Окра́шено.	*Caution. Wet paint.*

6.9 Abbreviations of titles, weights, measures and common expressions

бул.	бульва́р	*boulevard, avenue*
в.	век	*century*
г	грамм	*gram*
г.	год	*year*
г.	го́род	*town, city*
г.	господи́н	*Mr*
га	гекта́р	*hectare*

г-жа	госпожа́	*Mrs*
гл.	гла́вный	*main*
гос.	госуда́рственный	*state*
д.	дом	*house*
до н.э.	до на́шей э́ры	*BC*
ж.д.	желе́зная доро́га	*railway*
жит.	жи́тели	*inhabitants*
и т.д.	и так да́лее	*etc., and so on*
и т.п.	и тому́ подо́бное	*etc., and so on*
изд-во	изда́тельство	*publishing house, press*
им.	и́мени	*named after*
ин-т	институ́т	*institute*
кв.	кварти́ра	*flat, apartment*
кг	килогра́мм	*kilogram*
к-т	комите́т	*committee*
к/ч	киломе́тры в час	*kilometres per hour*
м	метр	*metre*
м.	мину́та	*minute*
мин-во	министе́рство	*ministry*
мор.	морско́й	*naval, marine*
напр.	наприме́р	*e.g.*
нар.	наро́дный	*people's*
нац.	национа́льный	*national*
н.ст.	но́вый стиль	*New Style* (post-revolutionary calendar)
н.э.	на́шей э́ры	*AD*
о.	о́стров	*island*
об.	о́бласть	*province*
оз.	о́зеро	*lake*
пл.	пло́щадь	*square*
пр.	проспе́кт	*avenue*
р.	река́	*river*
р.	рубль	*rouble*
р-н	райо́н	*region*
с.г.	сего́ го́да	*of this year*
см.	смотри́(те)	*see, vide*
ср.	сравни́	*compare, cf.*
ст.ст.	ста́рый стиль	*Old Style* (pre-revolutionary calendar)

стр.	страни́ца	*page*
с.х.	сельскохозя́йственный	*agricultural*
т	то́нна	*tonne*
т.	том	*volume*
т.е.	то́ есть	*that is to say, i.e.*
т.к.	так как	*since*
ул.	у́лица	*street*
ун-т	университе́т	*university*
ф.ст.	фунт сте́рлингов	*pound sterling*
ч.	час	*hour, o'clock*

6.10 Acronyms and alphabetisms

Acronyms and alphabetisms function as nouns. They have a gender of their own, and many (those which can be pronounced as a single word, as opposed to a succession of individual letters) also decline, e.g. **ЗАГС**, *register office*; **ООН**, *UN(O)*, which decline like masculine nouns ending in a hard consonant.

Acronyms and alphabetisms continue to abound in the Russian press and most of those given below will therefore be widely understood.

Those acronyms and alphabetisms which denote Soviet institutions or phenomena or the names of countries or institutions in the communist world as a whole and whose significance is now mainly historical are indicated below with an asterisk.

АЗС	автозапра́вочная ста́нция	*petrol station*
АиФ	Аргуме́нты и Фа́кты	*Arguments and Facts* (weekly newspaper)
АН	Акаде́мия нау́к	*Academy of Sciences*
АН-	Анто́нов-	*Antonov* (Russian aircraft)
АСЕАН	Ассоциа́ция госуда́рств Юго-Восто́чной А́зии	*Association of Southeast Asian Nations* (*ASEAN*)
АЭС	а́томная электроста́нция	*atomic power-station*
БАМ	Байка́ло-Аму́рская магистра́ль	*Baikal-Amur Railway* (i.e. East Siberian railway)
бомж	без определённого ме́ста жи́тельства	lit *without definite abode*, i.e. *vagrant, down-and-out*
БТР	бронетранспортёр	*armoured personnel carrier*
ВВП	валово́й вну́тренний проду́кт	*gross domestic product* (*GDP*)
ВВС	Военно-Возду́шные Си́лы	*air force*
ВДНХ	Вы́ставка достиже́ний наро́дного хозя́йства	exhibition of Soviet economic achievements (in Moscow)

ВМФ	Военно-Морской Флот	*(military) navy*
ВНП	валовой национальный продукт	*gross national product (GNP)*
ВОВ	Великая отечественная война	lit *Great War of the Fatherland*, i.e. Second World War
ВОЗ	Всемирная организация здравоохранения	*World Health Organisation (WHO)*
ВПК	военно-промышленный комплекс	*military–industrial complex*
ВС	вооружённые силы	*armed forces*
ВТО	Всемирная торговая организация	*World Trade Organisation (WTO)*
ВУЗ	высшее учебное заведение	*higher educational institution*
ГАИ	Государственная автомобильная инспекция	Soviet/Russian traffic police
ГАТТ	Генеральное соглашение о тарифах и торговле	*General Agreement on Tariffs and Trade (GATT)*
ГДР*	Германская Демократическая Республика	*German Democratic Republic*, i.e. former East Germany
ГКЧП*	Государственный Комитет Чрезвычайного Положения	Committee responsible for putsch in USSR in August 1991
ГРУ*	Главное разведывательное управление	Soviet military intelligence
ГУВД	Государственное управление внутренних дел	*Ministry of Internal Affairs*
ГЭС	гидроэлектростанция	*hydroelectric power-station*
ДТП	дорожно-транспортное происшествие	*road accident*
ЕС	Европейское сообщество/ Европейский союз	*European Community (EC)/European Union (EU)*
ЖКХ	Жилищно-коммунальное хозяйство	*communal housing service*
ЗАГС	(отдел) записи актов гражданского состояния	register office
ИЛ-	Ильюшин-	*Iliushin* (Russian aircraft)
ИМЛИ	Институт мировой литературы	*Institute of World Literature* (in Moscow)
КГБ*	Комитет государственной безопасности	*Committee of State Security (KGB)*
КНДР	Корейская Народно-Демократическая республика	*North Korea*
КПРФ	Коммунистическая партия Российской Федерации	*Communist Party of the Russian Federation*
КПСС*	Коммунистическая партия Советского Союза	*Communist Party of the Soviet Union (CPSU)*

ЛГУ	Ленингра́дский госуда́рственный университе́т	*Leningrad State University*
МАГАТЭ	Междунаро́дное аге́нтство по а́томной эне́ргии	*International Atomic Energy Agency (IAEA)*
МБРР	Междунаро́дный банк реконстру́кции и разви́тия	*International Bank for Reconstruction and Development*
МГУ	Моско́вский госуда́рственный университе́т	*Moscow State University*
МНР	Монго́льская Наро́дная Респу́блика	*Mongolian People's Republic*
МО	Министе́рство оборо́ны	*Ministry of Defence*
МПС	Министе́рство путе́й сообще́ния	*Ministry of Communications*
МХАТ	Моско́вский худо́жественный академи́ческий теа́тр	*Moscow Arts Theatre*
НАТО	Се́вероатланти́ческий сою́з	*North Atlantic Treaty Organisation (NATO)*
НИИ	нау́чно-иссле́довательский институ́т	*scientific research institute*
НКВД*	Наро́дный комиссариа́т вну́тренних дел	*People's Commissariat of Internal Affairs (Soviet police agency, 1934–43)*
НЭП*	но́вая экономи́ческая поли́тика	*New Economic Policy (of 1920s)*
ОАЭ	Объединённые Ара́бские Эмира́ты	*United Arab Emirates*
ОВД*	Организа́ция Варша́вского Догово́ра	*Warsaw Treaty Organisation*
ОВИР	Отде́л виз и регистра́ции	*visa and registration department*
ООН	Организа́ция Объединённых На́ций	*United Nations Organisation (UN)*
ООП	Организа́ция Освобожде́ния Палести́ны	*Palestine Liberation Organisation (PLO)*
ОПЕК	Организа́ция стран-экспортёров не́фти	*Organisation of Petroleum Exporting Countries (OPEC)*
ОЭСР	Организа́ция экономи́ческого сотру́дничества и разви́тия	*Organisation for Economic Co-operation and Development (OECD)*
ПВО	про́тиво-возду́шная оборо́на	*anti-aircraft defence*
РАН	Росси́йская Акаде́мия нау́к	*Russian Academy of Sciences*
РФ	Росси́йская Федера́ция	*Russian Federation*
СКВ	свобо́дно-конверти́руемая валю́та	*convertible currency*
СНГ	Содру́жество незави́симых госуда́рств	*Commonwealth of Independent States (CIS)*
СП	совме́стное предприя́тие	*joint venture*
СССР*	Сою́з Сове́тских Социалисти́ческих Респу́блик	*Union of Soviet Socialist Republics (USSR)*
США	Соединённые Шта́ты Аме́рики	*United States of America (USA)*
СЭВ*	Сове́т Экономи́ческой взаимопо́мощи	*Council for Mutual Economic Aid (COMECON)*

ТАСС*	Телегра́фное аге́нтство Сове́тского Сою́за	*TASS*, i.e. the Soviet news agency
ТВ	телеви́дение	*TV*
ТНК	трѐнснациона́льные корпора́ции	*multinational corporations*
ТУ–	Ту́полев–	*Tupolev* (Russian aircraft)
ФБР	Федера́льное бюро́ рассле́дований	*Federal Bureau of Investigation (FBI)*
ФРГ*	Федерати́вная Респу́блика Герма́нии	*Federal German Republic*, i.e. former West Germany
ФСБ	Федера́льная слу́жба безопа́сности	*Federal Security Service*
ЦБР	Центра́льный банк Росси́и	*Central Bank of Russia*
ЦК*	Центра́льный Комите́т	*Central Committee* (of CPSU)
ЦРУ	Центра́льное разве́дывательное управле́ние	*Central Intelligence Agency (CIA)*
ЧП	чрезвыча́йное происше́ствие	lit *extreme event*, i.e. *emergency*, some natural or man-made disaster
ЮНЕСКО	Организа́ция ООН по вопро́сам образова́ния, нау́ки и культу́ры	*United Nations Educational, Scientific and Cultural Organisation (UNESCO)*

6.11   Names of countries and nationalities

The following lists are not exhaustive, but give the names of most countries of the world, grouped according to continent or region, together with the adjectives formed from them and the nouns denoting male and female representatives of each nationality.

The suffixes most commonly used to denote nationality are -**ец** and -**нин**, for males, and -**ка** and -**нка** for females. However, in certain instances the expected feminine form cannot be used or at least seems unnatural to native speakers (and is therefore omitted from the lists in the following sections). In other instances no noun at all is derived from the name of the country to denote nationality, or at least Russians might hesitate to use a form that does in theory exist. When in doubt as to whether a particular noun denoting nationality may be used one may have recourse to a phrase with **жи́тели**, *inhabitants*, e.g. **жи́тели Буру́нди**, *people who live in Burundi*.

In some foreign words the letter **е** is pronounced **э**; this pronunciation is indicated in brackets after the word in question. An asterisk after a place-name in this section indicates that the noun in question is indeclinable.

Note: nouns and adjectives denoting nationality do not begin with a capital letter in Russian (see also 11.16).

6.11.1   Russia and the other states of the former Soviet Union

In this table the name of the former Soviet republic is given in brackets where it differs from the name of the new state.

	country	adjective	man/woman
Russia	**Росси́я**	**ру́сский**	**ру́сский/ру́сская**
Russian Federation	**Росси́йская Федера́ция**	**росси́йский**	**россия́нин/россия́нка**

Note: **росси́йский**, as mentioned in 1.1, has come to be used to denote the nationality, which embraces people who are not ethnically Russian and things which are not culturally Russian.

	country	adjective	man/woman
Armenia	**Арме́ния**	**армя́нский**	**армяни́н/армя́нка**
Azerbaijan	**Азербайджа́н**	**азербайджа́нский**	**азербайджа́нец/ азербайджа́нка**
Belarus	**Белару́сь** (f) **(Белору́ссия)**	**белору́сский**	**белору́с/белору́ска**
Estonia	**Эсто́ния**	**эсто́нский**	**эсто́нец/эсто́нка**
Georgia	**Гру́зия**	**грузи́нский**	**грузи́н/грузи́нка**
Kazakhstan	**Казахста́н**	**каза́хский**	**каза́х/каза́шка**
Kyrgyzstan (Kirgizia)	**Кыргызста́н (Кирги́зия)**	**кирги́зский**	**кирги́з/кирги́зка**
Latvia	**Ла́твия**	**латы́шский** or **латви́йский**	**латы́ш/латы́шка**
Lithuania	**Литва́**	**лито́вский**	**лито́вец/лито́вка**
Moldova	**Молдо́ва (Молда́вия)**	**молда́вский** or **молдава́нский**	**молдава́нин/ молдава́нка**
Tadjikistan	**Таджикиста́н**	**таджи́кский**	**таджи́к/таджи́чка**
Turkmenistan	**Туркмениста́н (Туркме́ния)**	**туркме́нский**	**туркме́н/туркме́нка**
Ukraine	**Украи́на**	**украи́нский**	**украи́нец/украи́нка**
Uzbekistan	**Узбекиста́н**	**узбе́кский**	**узбе́к/узбе́чка**

6.11.2   Other regions and national minorities of Russia and the former Soviet Union

	region	adjective	ethnic group
Abkhazia	**Абха́зия**	**абха́зский**	**абха́зец/абха́зка**
Baikal region	**Забайка́лье**	**забайка́льский**	**забайка́лец**
Baltic region	**Приба́лтика** (also **Ба́лтия**)	**прибалти́йский**	**приба́лт(и́ец)/ прибалти́йка**
Bashkiria	**Башки́рия**	**башки́рский**	**башки́р/башки́рка**
black earth region	**чернозём**	**чернозёмный**	
Buriat region	**Буря́тия**	**буря́тский**	**буря́т/буря́тка**
Caucasus	**Кавка́з**	**кавка́зский**	**кавка́зец/кавка́зка**
Chechnia	**Чечня́**	**чече́нский**	**чече́нец/чече́нка**
Chuvash region	**Чува́шия**	**чува́шский**	**чува́ш/чува́шка**

Crimea	**Крым**	**крымский**	**крымча́нин/ крымча́нка**

Note: *in the Crimea*, **в Крыму́**.

Dagestan	**Дагеста́н**	**дагеста́нский**	**дагеста́нец/дагеста́нка**
Ingushetia	**Ингуше́тия**	**ингу́шский**	**ингу́ш/ингу́шка**
Kalmyk region	**Калмы́кия**	**калмы́цкий**	**калмы́к/калмы́чка**
Karelia	**Каре́лия**	**каре́льский**	**каре́л/каре́лка**
Kuban	**Куба́нь** (f)	**куба́нский**	**куба́нец/куба́нка**

Note: *in the Kuban*, **на Куба́ни**.

Mari Republic	**Мари́йская Респу́блика**	**мари́йский**	**мари́ец/мари́йка** or **ма́ри** (m and f, indecl)
Mordvin region	**Мордо́вия**	**мордо́вский**	**мордви́н/мордви́нка**; also **мордва́** (collect)
Moscow region	**Подмоско́вье**	**подмоско́вный**	
mountain region (i.e. Caucasus)	**го́ры**	**го́рный** or **го́рский**	**го́рцы** (pl; sg **го́рец**)
Ossetia	**Осе́тия**	**осети́нский**	**осети́н/осети́нка**
Siberia	**Сиби́рь** (f)	**сиби́рский**	**сибиря́к/сибиря́чка**
steppe	**степь** (f)	**степно́й**	
taiga	**тайга́**	**таёжный**	**таёжник**
Tatarstan	**Татарста́н**	**тата́рский**	**тата́рин/тата́рка**
Transcaucasia	**Закавка́зье**	**закавка́зский**	
tundra	**ту́ндра**	**ту́ндровый**	
Udmurt region	**Удму́ртия**	**удму́ртский**	**удму́рт/удму́ртка**
White Sea coast	**Се́верное помо́рье**	**помо́рский**	**помо́р/помо́рка**
Yakutia	**Яку́тия/Са́ха**	**яку́тский**	**яку́т/яку́тка**

6.11.3 Europe (Евро́па)

	country	adjective	man/woman
Albania	**Алба́ния**	**алба́нский**	**алба́нец/алба́нка**
Austria	**А́встрия**	**австри́йский**	**австри́ец/австри́йка**
Belgium	**Бе́льгия**	**бельги́йский**	**бельги́ец/бельги́йка**
Bosnia	**Бо́сния**	**босни́йский**	**босни́ец/босни́йка**
Bulgaria	**Болга́рия**	**болга́рский**	**болга́рин/болга́рка**
Croatia	**Хорва́тия**	**хорва́тский**	**хорва́т/хорва́тка**
Czech Republic	**Че́шская Респу́блика**	**че́шский**	**чех/че́шка**

Denmark	**Да́ния**	да́тский	датча́нин/датча́нка
England	**А́нглия**	англи́йский	англича́нин/ англича́нка
Finland	**Финля́ндия**	фи́нский	финн/фи́нка
France	**Фра́нция**	францу́зский	францу́з/францу́женка
Germany	**Герма́ния**	неме́цкий	не́мец/не́мка
Great Britain	**Великобрита́ния**	брита́нский/ англи́йский	брита́нец/брита́нка англича́нин/ англича́нка

Note: англи́йский, англича́нин, англича́нка tend to be used to encompass where necessary all things British or all British people unless it is intended to make specific reference to Scottish or Welsh things or people.

Greece	**Гре́ция**	гре́ческий	грек/греча́нка
Holland	**Голла́ндия/ Нидерла́нды**	голла́ндский/ нидерла́ндский	голла́ндец/голла́ндка or нидерла́ндец/ нидерла́ндка
Hungary	**Ве́нгрия**	венге́рский	венгр/венге́рка
Iceland	**Исла́ндия**	исла́ндский	исла́ндец/исла́ндка
Ireland	**Ирла́ндия**	ирла́ндский	ирла́ндец/ирла́ндка
Italy	**Ита́лия**	италья́нский	италья́нец/италья́нка
Luxembourg	**Люксембу́рг**	люксембу́ргский	люксембу́ржец/ люксембу́ржка
Norway	**Норве́гия**	норве́жский	норве́жец/норве́жка
Poland	**По́льша**	по́льский	поля́к/по́лька
Portugal	**Португа́лия**	португа́льский	португа́лец/ португа́лка
Romania	**Румы́ния**	румы́нский	румы́н/румы́нка
Scotland	**Шотла́ндия**	шотла́ндский	шотла́ндец/ шотла́ндка
Serbia	**Се́рбия**	се́рбский	серб/се́рбка or сербия́нка
Slovakia	**Слова́кия**	слова́цкий	слова́к/слова́чка
Slovenia	**Слове́ния**	слове́нский	слове́нец/слове́нка
Spain	**Испа́ния**	испа́нский	испа́нец/испа́нка
Sweden	**Шве́ция**	шве́дский	швед/шве́дка
Switzerland	**Швейца́рия**	швейца́рский	швейца́рец/ швейца́рка
Wales	**Уэ́льс**	уэ́льский/ валли́йский	уэ́льсец or валли́ец/валли́йка

6.11.4 Africa (Áфрика)

	country	adjective	man/woman
Algeria	**Алжи́р**	алжи́рский	алжи́рец/алжи́рка
Angola	**Анго́ла**	анго́льский	анго́лец/анго́лка
Benin	**Бени́н**	бени́нский	бени́ец/бени́йка
Botswana	**Ботсва́на**	ботсва́нский	жи́тели Ботсва́ны
Burundi	**Буру́нди***	бурунди́йский	жи́тели Буру́нди
Cameroon	**Камеру́н**	камеру́нский	камеру́нец/камеру́нка
Chad	**Чад**	ча́дский	жи́тели Ча́да
Egypt	**Еги́пет**	еги́петский	египтя́нин/египтя́нка
Ethiopia	**Эфио́пия**	эфио́пский	эфио́п/эфио́пка
Ghana	**Га́на**	га́нский	га́нец/га́нка
Ivory Coast	**Бе́рег Слоно́вой Ко́сти**		жи́тели Бе́рега Слоно́вой Ко́сти
Kenya	**Ке́ния**	кени́йский	кени́ец/кени́йка
Libya	**Ли́вия**	ливи́йский	ливи́ец/ливи́йка
Mauritania	**Маврита́ния**	маврита́нский	маврита́нец/ маврита́нка
Morocco	**Маро́кко***	марокка́нский	марокка́нец/ марокка́нка
Mozambique	**Мозамби́к**	мозамби́кский	жи́тели Мозамби́ка
Namibia	**Нами́бия**	намиби́йский	жи́тели Нами́бии
Nigeria	**Ниге́рия**	нигери́йский	нигери́ец/нигери́йка
Rwanda	**Руа́нда**	руанди́йский	руанди́ец/руанди́йка
Senegal	**Сенега́л**	сенега́льский	сенега́лец/сенега́лка
Somalia	**Сомали́***	сомали́йский	сомали́ец/сомали́йка
South Africa	**Ю́жно-Африка́нская Респу́блика (ЮА́Р)**	ю́жноафрика́нский	жи́тели ЮА́Р
Sudan	**Суда́н**	суда́нский	суда́нец/суда́нка
Tanzania	**Танза́ния**	танзани́йский	танзани́ец/танзани́йка
Togo	**То́го**	тоголе́зский	тоголе́зец/тоголе́зка
Tunisia	**Туни́с**	туни́сский	туни́сец/туни́ска
Uganda	**Уга́нда**	уга́ндский	уга́ндец/уга́ндка
Zaire	**Заи́р**	заи́рский	заи́рец/заи́рка
Zambia	**За́мбия**	замби́йский	замби́ец/замби́йка
Zimbabwe	**Зимба́бве***	зимбабви́йский	зимбабви́ец/ зимбабви́йка

6.11.5 America (Аме́рика)

	country	adjective	man/woman
Argentina	Аргенти́на	аргенти́нский	аргенти́нец/аргенти́нка
Bolivia	Боли́вия	боливи́йский	боливи́ец/боливи́йка
Brazil	Брази́лия	брази́льский	брази́лец/бразилья́нка
Canada	Кана́да	кана́дский	кана́дец/кана́дка
Chile	Чи́ли*	чили́йский	чили́ец/чили́йка
Colombia	Колу́мбия	колумби́йский	колумби́ец/колумби́йка
Costa Rica	Ко́ста-Ри́ка	костарика́нский	костарика́нец/ костарика́нка
Ecuador	Эквадо́р	эквадо́рский	эквадо́рец/эквадо́рка
El Salvador	Сальвадо́р	сальвадо́рский	сальвадо́рец/сальвадо́рка
Guatemala	Гватема́ла (тэ)	гватема́льский	гватема́лец/гватема́лка
Guyana	Гайа́на	гайа́нский	гайа́нец/гайа́нка
Honduras	Гондура́с	гондура́сский	гондура́сец/гондура́ска
Mexico	Ме́ксика	мексика́нский	мексика́нец/мексика́нка
Nicaragua	Никара́гуа	никарагуа́нский	никарагуа́нец/ никарагуа́нка
Panama	Пана́ма	пана́мский	жи́тели Пана́мы
Paraguay	Парагва́й	парагва́йский	парагва́ец/парагва́йка
Peru	Перу́*	перуа́нский	перуа́нец/перуа́нка
United States of America	Соединённые Шта́ты Аме́рики	америка́нский	америка́нец/америка́нка
Uruguay	Уругва́й	уругва́йский	уругва́ец/уругва́йка
Venezuela	Венесуэ́ла	венесуэ́льский	венесуэ́лец/венесуэ́лка

6.11.6 Asia (А́зия)

	country	adjective	man/woman
Afghanistan	Афганиста́н	афга́нский	афга́нец/афга́нка
Bangladesh	Бангладе́ш	бангладе́шский	бангладе́шец/бангладе́шка
Burma	Би́рма	бирма́нский	бирма́нец/бирма́нка
Cambodia	Камбо́джа/ Кампучи́я	камбоджи́йский/ кампучи́йский	камбоджи́ец/камбоджи́йка or кампучи́ец/кампучи́йка
China	Кита́й	кита́йский	кита́ец/китая́нка

Note: кита́йка cannot be used for *Chinese woman*; it used to mean *nankeen* (type of cloth).

India	**И́ндия**	инди́йский	инди́ец/индиа́нка

Note 1   The forms **инду́с/инду́ска**, originally *Hindu*, are often used instead of
инди́ец/индиа́нка.

2   The adjective **инде́йский** and the noun **инде́ец** refer to American Indians.
The feminine form **индиа́нка** may refer to an Indian woman of either
race. The noun **инде́йка** means *turkey*.

Indonesia	**Индоне́зия**	индонези́йский	индонези́ец/индонези́йка
Iran	**Ира́н**	ира́нский	ира́нец/ира́нка

Note: the forms **Пе́рсия, перси́дский**, and **перс/перси́янка** also occur, but like
their English equivalents (*Persia, Persian, Persian man/woman*) they are not
used with reference to the modern state of Iran.

Japan	**Япо́ния**	япо́нский	япо́нец/япо́нка
Korea	**Коре́я**	коре́йский	коре́ец/корея́нка

Note: **коре́йка** cannot be used for *Korean woman*; it means *brisket* (meat).

Laos	**Лаос**	лао́сский	лаотя́нин/лаотя́нка
Malaya	**Мала́йя**	мала́йский	мала́ец/мала́йка
Malaysia	**Мала́йзия**	малайзи́йский	малайзи́ец/малайзи́йка
Mongolia	**Монго́лия**	монго́льский	монго́л/монго́лка
Nepal	**Непа́л**	непа́льский	непа́лец/непа́лка
Pakistan	**Пакиста́н**	пакиста́нский	пакиста́нец/пакиста́нка
Singapore	**Сингапу́р**	сингапу́рский	сингапу́рец/сингапу́рка
Sri Lanka	**Шри-Ла́нка**	шриланки́йский	жи́тели Шри-Ла́нки or (шри)ланки́йцы
Thailand	**Таила́нд**	таила́ндский/ та́йский	таила́ндец/таила́ндка or (in pl) та́йцы
Tibet	**Тибе́т**	тибе́тский	тибе́тец/тибе́тка
Vietnam	**Вьетна́м**	вьетна́мский	вьетна́мец/вьетна́мка

6.11.7   The Middle East (Бли́жний Восто́к)

	country	adjective	man/woman
Iraq	**Ира́к**	ира́кский	жи́тели Ира́ка or ира́кцы
Israel	**Изра́иль** (m)	изра́ильский	израильтя́нин/израильтя́нка
Jordan	**Иорда́ния**	иорда́нский	иорда́нец/иорда́нка
Kuwait	**Куве́йт**	куве́йтский	жи́тели Куве́йта or кувейтя́не
Lebanon	**Лива́н**	лива́нский	лива́нец/лива́нка

Palestine	**Палести́на**	**палести́нский**	**палести́нец/палести́нка**
Saudi Arabia	**Сау́довская Ара́вия**	**сау́довский**	**жи́тели Сау́довской Ара́вии**
Syria	**Си́рия**	**сири́йский**	**сири́ец/сири́йка**
Turkey	**Ту́рция**	**туре́цкий**	**ту́рок/турча́нка**

Note: gen pl **ту́рок**, though **ту́рков** may be heard in R1.

Yemen	**Йе́мен (мэ)**	**йе́менский**	**йе́менец/йе́менка**

6.11.8   Australia and New Zealand

	country	adjective	man/woman
Australia	**Австра́лия**	**австрали́йский**	**австрали́ец/австрали́йка**
New Zealand	**Но́вая Зела́ндия**	**новозела́ндский**	**новозела́ндец/новозела́ндка**

6.12   Words denoting inhabitants of Russian and former Soviet cities

Nouns denoting natives or inhabitants of certain cities (e.g. *Bristolian, Glaswegian, Londoner, Parisian*) are rather more widely used in Russian than in English (at least in relation to natives or inhabitants of Russian cities). Moreover a wider range of suffixes (both masculine and feminine) is in common use for this purpose than in English, e.g. **-ец/-ка, -анин/-анка, -янин/-янка, -ич/-ичка, -як/-ячка**. However, it is not easy for the foreigner to predict which suffix should be applied to the name of a particular Russian city. A list is therefore given below of the nouns denoting natives or inhabitants of the major Russian cities, and of some cities of other former republics of the USSR.

Several major cities (like the names of many streets, squares and other public places) have been renamed in the post-Soviet period. (Usually the pre-revolutionary name has been resurrected.) In such cases the former Soviet name is given in brackets.

Note: in the case of some of the less important cities the nouns denoting their inhabitants may rarely be used or may have only local currency.

city	adjective	inhabitant
Арха́нгельск	**арха́нгельский**	**архангелогоро́дец/архангелогоро́дка**
А́страхань (f)	**астраха́нский**	**астраха́нец/астраха́нка**
Баку́	**баки́нский**	**баки́нец/баки́нка**
Ви́льнюс	**ви́льнюсский**	**ви́льнюсец/ви́льнюска**
Владивосто́к	**владивосто́кский**	**жи́тель(ница) Владивосто́ка**

Влади́мир	влади́мирский	жи́тель(ница) Влади́мира or влади́мирец/влади́мирка
Во́логда	волого́дский	вологжа́нин/вологжа́нка or вологоде́ц/волого́дка
Воро́неж	воро́нежский	воро́нежец/воро́нежка
Вя́тка (Ки́ров)	вя́тский	вя́тич/вя́тичка
Екатеринбу́рг (Свердло́вск)	екатеринбу́ржский	екатеринбу́ржец/екатеринбу́рженка
Екатериносла́в (Днѐпропетро́вск)	екатериносла́вский	екатериносла́вец/екатериносла́вка
Ирку́тск	ирку́тский	иркутя́нин/иркутя́нка
Каза́нь (f)	каза́нский	каза́нец/каза́нка
Ки́ев	ки́евский	киевля́нин/киевля́нка
Кострома́	костромско́й	костроми́ч/костроми́чка
Краснода́р	краснода́рский	краснода́рец/краснода́рка
Красноя́рск	красноя́рский	красноя́рец/красноя́рка
Курск	ку́рский	курча́нин/курча́нка
Львов	льво́вский	львовя́нин/львовя́нка
Минск	ми́нский	минча́нин/минча́нка
Москва́	моско́вский	москви́ч/москви́чка (also москвитя́нин/москвитя́нка; obs)
Ни́жний Но́вгород (Го́рький)	нижегоро́дский	нижегоро́дец/нижегоро́дка
Но́вгород	новгоро́дский	новгоро́дец/новгоро́дка
Новоросси́йск	новоросси́йский	новоросси́ец/новоросси́йка
Новосиби́рск	новосиби́рский	жи́тели Новосиби́рска (also новосиби́рцы)
Оде́сса	оде́сский	одесси́т/одесси́тка (pronunciation дэ also possible)
Омск	о́мский	оми́ч/омча́нка
Псков	пско́вский/псковско́й	пскови́тянин/пскови́тянка
Пятиго́рск	пятиго́рский	пятигорча́нин/пятигорча́нка
Ри́га	ри́жский	рижа́нин/рижа́нка
Росто́в	росто́вский	ростовча́нин/ростовча́нка
Ряза́нь (f)	ряза́нский	ряза́нец/ряза́нка
Сама́ра (Ку́йбышев)	сама́рский	самаровча́нин/самаровча́нка
Санкт-Петербу́рг (Ленингра́д)	петербу́ргский (ленингра́дский)	петербу́ржец/петербу́ржка (ленингра́дец/ленингра́дка)
Сара́тов	сара́товский	саратовча́нин/саратовча́нка (also сара́товец)
Севасто́поль (m)	севасто́польский	севасто́полец

Смоле́нск	смоле́нский	смоля́нин/смоля́нка
Со́чи	со́чинский	со́чинец/со́чинка
Та́ллинн	та́ллиннский	та́ллинец
Тамбо́в	тамбо́вский	тамбо́вец/тамбо́вка
Та́рту	та́ртуский	жи́тели Та́рту
Тверь (f) (Кали́нин)	тверско́й	тверя́к/тверя́чка
Томск	то́мский	томи́ч/томча́нка
Ту́ла	ту́льский	туля́к/туля́чка
Хаба́ровск	хаба́ровский	хабаровча́нин/хабаровча́нка
Ха́рьков	ха́рьковский	харьковча́нин/харьковча́нка
Я́лта	я́лтинский	я́лтинец/я́лтинка
Яросла́вль (m)	яросла́вский	яросла́вец

Note: a noun of a similar sort to those denoting inhabitants of certain cities is
derived from **земля́**, *land, earth*, i.e. **земля́к/земля́чка**, which means *person from
the same region*.

6.13 Jokes (анекдо́ты) and puns (каламбу́ры)

Анекдо́ты, by which Russians mean a joke or little story that captures
some aspect of the everyday world or a political situation in an
amusing way, have for a long time played an important role in Russian
life. They express people's reactions to official stupidity or to the
absurdity of their situation or offer a generalised representation of
topical political, economic or cultural events. They are also a useful
source of linguistic material for the foreign learner.

Анекдо́ты had a particularly important function in Soviet times,
providing people with a verbal outlet for their frustration at the
mistakes or inefficiency of party officials. The low educational level of
many party workers, for example, gave rise to the following popular
joke: Зна́ете, почему́ коммуни́сты вы́брали сре́ду парти́йным днём?
Потому́ что они́ не зна́ют как писа́ть вто́рник и четве́рг, *Do you
know why Wednesday is the day for Communist Party meetings? Because they
can't spell 'Tuesday' or 'Thursday'* (In Russian среда́ is slightly easier to
spell than вто́рник or четве́рг.)

The period of *perestróika*, especially Él′tsin's (i.e. Yéltsin's) term in
office, also gave rise to numerous jokes and puns which expressed a
jaundiced view of current affairs, e.g. **катастро́йка**, i.e. катастро́фа,
catastrophe, + перестро́йка; **дерьмокра́тия**, i.e. дерьмо́, *crap*, instead of
демо + кра́тия. People's disappointment with the results of
privatisation, when they came to feel that they were getting nothing
while a greedy few were becoming billionaires, found expression in the
coinage **прихватиза́ция**, in which the insertion of the sound *x* turns
the loanword приватиза́ция into a noun with the Russian root хват,
suggesting snatching or stealing (see also the word олига́рх in 5.1.2).

The recent inundation of the Russian language with anglicisms (англици́змы), which reflects the post-Soviet openness and receptivity to what is going on in the outside world, has prompted numerous letters to newspapers by people who have not been able to understand what they were reading in the Russian press. Misunderstanding of anglicisms also lies behind a joke in the form of a dialogue between two boys, who think that three foreign words that are unfamiliar to them all relate to the same subject (confectionery):

– Ты сни́керс про́бовал?	*Have you tried Snickers?*
– Да, класс!	*Yes, they're great!*
– А марс про́бовал?	*And Mars?*
– Су́пер!	*Fantastic!*
– А тампа́кс про́бовал?	*What about Tampax?*
– Нет!	*No, I haven't.*
– И не про́буй, одна́ ва́та!	*Well, don't, they're just cotton-wool!*

(The frequency of jokes about Tampax probably reflects unease, in the post-Soviet world in which commercial advertising has all of a sudden become pervasive, about the publicity given to a product that is so personal.)

Financial crisis, and in particular the collapse of the rouble in 1998, has been a further source of wry jokes, such as the following:

Челове́к звони́т в банк. – Как у вас дела́?	*A man phones a bank. 'How are things with you?'*
– Всё хорошо́.	*'Everything's OK.'*
– Я, наве́рно, не туда́ попа́л!	*'I must have the wrong number.'*

The similarity of the words for *bank* (банк) and *jar* (ба́нка), and the coincidence of their prepositional singular forms (в ба́нке), provide an opportunity for punning which has given rise to a further, untranslatable joke on the same theme:

– Где ру́сские храня́т де́ньги?	*'Where do Russians keep their money?'*
– В ба́нке. А ба́нку под крова́тью.	*'In the bank. And they keep it (i.e. the jar) under the bed.'*

The recent emergence in post-Soviet economic conditions of a class of very wealthy people (но́вые ру́сские) also provides fertile ground for Russian humour. English-speakers familiar with the 'Essex' jokes of the 1990s will recognise the spirit of the following:

Оди́н но́вый ру́сский говори́т друго́му: – Смотри́, како́й я га́лстук купи́л за сто до́лларов.	*One new Russian says to another: 'Look at my tie, I paid a hundred dollars for it.'*

Другóй отвечáет: – Это что, за углóм мóжно за двéсти двáдцать купи́ть.	*The other replies: 'You didn't do too well, you can get one round the corner for 220.'*

Animosity towards the *nouveaux riches* who flaunt their wealth is reflected in a spate of popular jokes based on a tale from folklore (and perpetuated in a fairy-tale by Púshkin). In the tale an old man catches a golden fish and lets it swim back into the sea without asking anything in return. To thank the old man for this act of generosity the fish tells him it will grant the old man any wish that he might have. In the current joke the roles of man and fish are reversed:

Нóвый рýсский поймáл золотýю ры́бку и говори́т ей: – Чегó тебé нáдо, золотáя ры́бка?	*A new Russian catches a golden fish and says to it: 'Well, what is it you want, golden fish?'*

It should be emphasised, finally, that many jokes flourish because of their topicality and that their appeal, like that of slang (5.1.4 above), is therefore ephemeral. At the same time it is useful for the foreign student to know that as a conversational genre the joke remains very popular and that it often depends for its success on linguistic subtlety, especially exploitation of the opportunities that Russian offers for punning, as well as on the verbal dexterity of the speaker.

7 Verbal etiquette

7.1 Introductory remarks

Every language has conventional formulae to which its speakers resort in certain situations that constantly occur in everyday life: addressing others, attracting their attention, making acquaintance, greeting and parting, conveying congratulations, wishes, gratitude and apologies, making requests and invitations, giving advice, offering condolences and paying compliments. Telephone conversations take place and letters are written within established frameworks that vary according to the relationship between those communicating and the nature of the exchange.

Ignorance of the formulae in use for these purposes among speakers of a language may make dealings with them on any level difficult and unsuccessful or may even cause offence. Or to look at it from a more positive point of view, the speaker who has mastered a limited number of these formulae will make her or his intentions and attitudes clear, set a tone appropriate to the situation and thereby greatly facilitate communication and win social or professional acceptance.

One may say that there are particular advantages for the foreign student of Russian in deploying the correct formulae in a given situation. In the first place, Russians are aware of the difficulty of their language for the foreign student and have little expectation that a foreigner will speak it well, let alone that a foreigner should be sympathetic to their customs, of which they are inured to criticism. They therefore tend to be more impressed by and favourably disposed towards the foreigner who has mastered the intricacies of their language and is prepared to observe at least their linguistic customs than are perhaps the British towards foreign English-speakers. And in the second place, it would be true to say that Russian society has remained, at least until very recently, in many respects conservative and traditional and has adhered quite rigidly to conventional procedures, including linguistic usage, at least in the public sphere.

The following sections give some of the most common conventional formulae that are of use to the foreign student of Russian. Many of the formulae may occur in very numerous combinations of their parts, only a few of which can be given here. One may introduce many formulae, for example, with any one of the following phrases meaning *I want* or *I should like to*. (The phrases are arranged with the most direct first and the least direct last.)

Я хочу́
Я хоте́л(а) бы
Мне хо́чется
Мне хоте́лось бы

Often the grammatical forms used in the formula (in particular choice of **ты** or **вы** forms) are determined by the context. A formula used exclusively in a formal situation, for example, is likely to contain only **вы** forms.

The formulae given in this chapter may be taken to be stylistically neutral and therefore of broad application unless an indication is given that they belong predominantly to R1 or R3. In general, formulae in the lower register are characterised by ellipsis (see 11.13) while those in the higher register are more periphrastic and often contain the imperative forms **позвóльте** or **разреши́те** (*allow [me]/permit [me]*).

Translations of the formulae given here are often inexact in a literal sense; an attempt has been made instead to render the spirit of the original by the most appropriate English formula.

7.2 Use of ты and вы

English-speaking students, having only one second-person form of address (*you*) at their disposal, must take particular care with the second-person pronouns in Russian. To use them incorrectly is at best to strike a false note and at worst to cause offence.

If one is addressing more than one person, then only **вы** may be used. If on the other hand one is addressing only one person, then either **вы** or **ты** may be used. As a general rule one may say that **вы** is more respectful and formal than **ты**, but a fuller list of factors that determine choice of pronoun would include the following considerations.

	вы	**ты**
degree of intimacy	to adults on first meeting to adults not well known to the speaker	to people well known or close to the speaker to one's partner, parents, children children to other children
Note:	one may switch from **вы** to **ты** as one comes to know the addressee better. This switch may take place almost immediately between people of the same age, especially young people, or it may be delayed until some closeness develops. Even when one knows a person well and feels close to them one may remain on **вы** terms; this is particularly the case among educated older people who wish to preserve the sense of mutual respect connoted by **вы**.	
relative status	to seniors in age or rank	to juniors in age or rank
Note:	one may address one's seniors as **ты** if one knows them well enough; conversely, to address a junior as **ты** appears condescending unless there is some closeness and mutual trust between the speakers.	
formality of situation	in formal or official contexts	in informal or unofficial contexts

Note: even if one normally addresses a person as **ты** one should switch to **вы** in a
            formal or official situation.

state of relations   cool, stiff, strained, excessively   disrespectful, over-familiar
                          polite

The point here is that subversion of the normal rules indicates that the
relationship is not as it should be, given the degree of intimacy, relative
status and formality or informality of the situation. The speaker
therefore chooses the pronoun which in normal circumstances would
seem **inappropriate**.

7.3   Personal names

All Russians have three names: a first or given name (**и́мя**), chosen by
one's parents; a patronymic (**о́тчество**), derived from one's father's
name; and a surname (**фами́лия**).

7.3.1   First names (имена́)

Use of a person's first name only is an informal mode of address. The
foreigner may use the first name, in its full form (**и́мя по́лное**) or in its
shortened form (**и́мя сокращённое**), if one exists, in addressing
children and students. However, it might seem impolite if one were to
use the first name on its own on first acquaintance to an adult
(particularly one's seniors in age or status) unless invited to do so
(therefore see also 7.3.2).

The majority of Russian first names have shortened forms and
diminutive forms. The foreigner must be aware of these forms, which
may be confusing in their abundance and variety, because they will be
frequently encountered in informal conversation and in imaginative
literature. However, great care must be taken both to use them only in
the right circumstances and to distinguish the nuances of the various
forms. Three principal forms must be distinguished apart from the
shortened forms that can be derived from most first names, viz:

- a truncated version of the shortened form which amounts to a form in
  the vocative case for use when a person is being called or addressed;

- a diminutive form which is a term of special endearment
  (hypocoristic). Such forms are usually derived from the shortened
  form, if one exists, by using one of the suffixes –**енька** and
  –**очка/–ечка** for men and women alike, e.g. **Са́шенька, Вале́рочка,
  Па́шенька, Ле́ночка, Ната́шенька, Та́нечка**. These forms are used
  by parents or relations in talking to their children. Among older people
  they are used only when addressing those to whom one is very close;

- a further diminutive form derived from the shortened form by using
  the suffix –**ка** (e.g. **Ви́тька, Ко́лька, Пе́тька, Ле́нка, Ната́шка,
  Та́нька**). Such forms may be used by young children addressing one

another. When used of adults about children or about other adults these forms may express disapproval or even verge on coarseness, but equally they may express affection in a jocular way towards people to whom one is very close.

The following lists give the most common men's and women's first names and some, but by no means all, of the shortened or diminutive forms that may be derived from them. Fashions vary over time and in different sections of the population, but the majority of the names given here have been widespread since pre-revolutionary times and now occur in most strata of the population.

Men's first names

full form of name	shortened form	vocative of short form	hypocoristic diminutive	pejorative diminutive
Алекса́ндр	Са́ша, Шу́ра	Саш, Шур	Са́шенька, Шу́рочка	Са́шка, Шу́рка
Алексе́й	Алёша, Лёша	Лёш, Алёш	Алёшенька, Лёшенька	Алёшка, Лёшка
Анато́лий	То́ля	Толь	То́ленька, То́лик	То́лька
Андре́й	Андрю́ша	Андрю́ш	Андрю́шенька	Андрю́шка
Арка́дий	Арка́ша	Арка́ш	Арка́шенька	Арка́шка
Бори́с	Бо́ря	Борь	Бо́ренька	Бо́рька
Вади́м	Ва́дя	Вадь	Ва́денька	Ва́дька
Валенти́н	Ва́ля	Валь	Ва́ленька	Ва́лька
Вале́рий	Вале́ра	Вале́р	Вале́рочка	Вале́рка
Васи́лий	Ва́ся	Вась	Ва́сенька	Ва́ська
Ви́ктор	Ви́тя, Витю́ша	Вить	Ви́тенька	Ви́тька
Влади́мир	Воло́дя	Воло́дь	Воло́денька	Во́вка
Вячесла́в	Сла́ва	Слав	Сла́вочка	Сла́вка
Генна́дий	Ге́на	Ген	Ге́ночка	Ге́нка
Григо́рий	Гри́ша	Гриш	Гри́шенька	Гри́шка
Дми́трий	Ди́ма, Ми́тя	Дим, Мить	Ди́мочка, Ми́тенька	Ди́мка, Ми́тька
Евге́ний	Же́ня	Жень	Же́нечка	Же́нька
Ива́н	Ва́ня	Вань	Ва́нечка	Ва́нька
И́горь	Го́ша	Гош	Игорёк	Го́шка
Константи́н	Ко́стя	Кость	Ко́стенька, Ко́стик	Ко́стька
Леони́д	Лёня	Лёнь	Лёнечка	Лёнька
Михаи́л	Ми́ша	Миш	Ми́шенька	Ми́шка

Николай	Коля	Коль	Коленька	Колька
Олег			Олёжек, Олёженька	Олёжка
Павел	Паша	Паш	Пашенька	Пашка
Пётр	Петя	Петь	Петенька	Петька
Руслан			Русик	
Сергей	Серёжа	Серёж	Серёженька	Серёжка
Станислав	Слава, Стас	Слав, Стась	Стасенька, Стасечка	Стаська
Степан	Стёпа	Стёп	Стёпочка	Стёпка
Юрий	Юра	Юр	Юрочка	Юрка
Яков	Яша	Яш	Яшенька	Яшка

Women's first names

full form of name	shortened form	vocative of short form	hypocoristic diminutive	pejorative diminutive
Александра	Саша, Шура	Саш, Шур	Сашенька, Шурочка	Сашка, Шурка
Алла		Ал	Аллочка	Алка
Анна	Аня, Нюра	Ань, Нюр	Анечка, Нюрочка	Анька, Нюрка
Вера		Вер	Верочка, Веруша	Верка
Виктория	Вика	Вик	Викочка	
Галина	Галя	Галь	Галочка	Галька
Евгения	Женя	Жень	Женечка	Женька
Екатерина	Катя	Кать	Катенька	Катька
Елена	Лена, Алёна	Лен	Леночка, Алёнушка	Ленка, Алёнка
Зоя		Зой	Зоечка, Зоенька	Зойка
Инна		Инн	Инночка, Инуся	Инка
Ирина	Ира	Ир	Ирочка	Ирка
Лариса	Лара	Лар	Ларочка	Ларка
Лилия	Лиля	Лиль	Лилечка	Лилька
Людмила	Люда, Люся, Мила	Люд, Мил	Людочка, Милочка	Людка, Люська, Милка
Маргарита	Рита	Рит	Риточка	Ритка
Марина		Марин	Мариночка	Маринка
Мария	Маша	Маш	Машенька	Машка
Надежда	Надя	Надь	Наденька	Надька

Ната́лья	Ната́ша	Ната́ш	На́точка, Ната́лочка, Ната́шенька	Ната́шка
Ни́на		Нин	Ни́ночка	Ни́нка
О́льга	О́ля	Оль	О́ленька	О́лька
Раи́са	Ра́я	Рай	Ра́ечка	Ра́йка
Светла́на	Све́та	Свет	Све́точка	Све́тка
Софи́я/Со́фья	Со́ня	Сонь	Со́нечка	Со́нька
Тама́ра	То́ма	Тама́р	Тама́рочка	Тама́рка, То́мка
Татья́на	Та́ня	Та́нь	Та́нечка, Таню́ша	Та́нька
Эльви́ра	Э́лла	Эл	Э́ллочка, Элю́ша	Э́лка
Э́мма		Эмм	Э́мочка	Э́мка
Ю́лия	Ю́ля	Юль	Ю́ленька, Ю́лечка	Ю́лька

7.3.2 Patronymics (о́тчества)

A patronymic is a name derived from the name of one's father. Russian patronymics are based on the full form of the first name and are obtained by the addition of one of the following suffixes:

	in men's names	in women's names
following hard consonants	–ович	–овна
following soft consonants or replacing **й**	–евич	–евна
replacing **а** or **я**	–ич	–ична

In colloquial speech the patronymics are shortened, and their normal pronunciation is given in the right-hand column of the table below. When the patronymic is combined with a first name, as it almost always is, then the two words in effect merge into one and only the ending of the patronymic is inflected.

first name	patronymic	colloquial pronunciation of patronymic
Алекса́ндр	Алекса́ндрович	Алекса́ндрыч
Алексе́й	Алексе́евич	Алексе́ич
Анато́лий	Анато́льевич	Анато́льич
Андре́й	Андре́евич	Андре́ич
Арка́дий	Арка́дьевич	Арка́дьич
Бори́с	Бори́сович	Бори́сыч
Вади́м	Вади́мович	Вади́мыч

Валенти́н	Валенти́нович	Валенти́ныч
Вале́рий	Вале́р(и)евич	Вале́рьич
Васи́лий	Васи́льевич	Васи́льич
Ви́ктор	Ви́кторович	Ви́кторыч
Влади́мир	Влади́мирович	Влади́мирыч
Вячесла́в	Вячесла́вович	Вячесла́вич
Генна́дий	Генна́дьевич	Генна́дич
Григо́рий	Григо́рьевич	Григо́рьич
Дми́трий	Дми́триевич	Дми́трич
Евге́ний	Евге́ньевич	Евге́ньич
Ива́н	Ива́нович	Ива́ныч
И́горь	И́горевич	И́горевич
Константи́н	Константи́нович	Константи́ныч
Леони́д	Леони́дович	Леони́дыч
Михаи́л	Миха́йлович	Миха́йлыч
Никола́й	Ннкола́евич	Никола́ич
Оле́г	Оле́гович	Оле́гович
Па́вел	Па́влович	Па́(в)лыч
Пётр	Петро́вич	Петро́(в)ич
Русла́н	Русла́нович	Русла́ныч
Серге́й	Серге́евич	Серге́ич
Станисла́в	Станисла́вович	Станисла́вич
Степа́н	Степа́нович	Степа́ныч
Ю́рий	Ю́рьевич	Ю́рич
Я́ков	Я́ковлевич	Я́ковлич

Note: the forms in the right-hand column above are not necessarily the only possible truncated forms, nor are all patronymics truncated in pronunciation.

Patronymics should as a rule be used in the following circumstances:

(a)   when a person's full name is being given (e.g. in introductions or in answer to an official question);

(b)   together with the first name, as a polite form of address to an adult with whom one is not on intimate terms. In this latter use it combines with the full form of the first name (e.g. **Ива́н Петро́вич, Еле́на Петро́вна**), not a shortened or diminutive form. This polite form of address corresponds to an English form with title and surname (e.g. *Mr Smith, Mrs Johnson, Dr Collins*).

Note: the patronymic on its own may be encountered as a form of address among older people in the countryside, e.g. **Петро́вич! Ива́новна!**

7.4 Attracting attention (привлече́ние внима́ния)

The following formulae are commonly used to attract the attention of a stranger. With the exceptions indicated all are polite if not very polite. Some include part of the request that they generally introduce, e.g. for information of some sort.

seeking directions, help, or information

Извини́те (пожа́луйста)! Как пройти́ в метро́? Прости́те (пожа́луйста)! Как пройти́ в метро́? Скажи́те, пожа́луйста, как пройти́ в метро́?	*Excuse me, how do I get to the underground?*
Вы не мо́жете сказа́ть...? Не мо́жете ли вы сказа́ть...? Вы не подска́жете...? Не могли́ бы вы сказа́ть...? Вас не затрудни́т сказа́ть...? Вам не тру́дно сказа́ть...?	*Could you tell me...*
Бу́дьте добры́, скажи́те, кото́рый час? Бу́дьте любе́зны, скажи́те, кото́рый час?	*Could you tell me the time please?*

Note: because the above formulae are all polite and suitable for use to strangers it would not be appropriate to couch any of them in the **ты** form.

Мо́жно тебя́/вас на мину́тку?	*Could I speak to you for a moment?*

Note: this expression is more familiar, may be used to acquaintances, and is commonly couched in the **ты** form.

responses to requests for information

The initial response to an approach which does not itself include a request may be as follows:

Да.	*Yes.*
Да, пожа́луйста.	*Yes, please.*
Что?	*What?*
Слу́шаю (вас).	*I'm listening (to you).*
Чем могу́ быть поле́зен/поле́зна? (R3b)	*How can I be of help?*
Я к ва́шим услу́гам. (R3b or iron)	*At your service.*
Ну? (R1)	*Well?*
Что тебе́? (R1)	*What do you want?*
(Ну) чего́ тебе́? (R1)	*(Well) what do you want?*

If the addressee is not sure that it is he or she who is being addressed, an elliptical response might be:

Вы меня?	
Вы ко мне?	*Are you talking to me?*

If the addressee has not heard or understood the request, the response may be:

Что-что? (R1)	*What was that?*
Повтори́те, пожа́луйста.	*Could you say that again?*
Прости́те, я не расслы́шал(а).	*I'm sorry, I didn't catch what you said.*
Что вы сказа́ли?	*What did you say?*

If the addressee cannot answer the question, the response may be:

Не зна́ю.	*I don't know.*
Не могу́ сказа́ть.	*I can't say.*
Не скажу́. (R1)	*I can't say.*

calling for attention

The widespread forms of address for calling people unknown to the speaker, both of them stylistically neutral, are:

Молодо́й челове́к! (to males)	*Young man!*
Де́вушка! (to females)	*Young lady!*

Note: these forms of address are used, despite the literal meanings of the terms (*young man* and *girl* respectively), to call not just young people but also people up to middle age.

At a higher stylistic level an educated person might use:

Ю́ноша!	*Youth!*

At a lower stylistic level, one might use one of the following familiar forms of address, perhaps preceded by the coarse particle **Эй!**

Па́рень! (R1)	*Lad!*
Друг! (R1)	*Friend!*
Прия́тель! (R1)	*Friend!*

The pronoun **ты** would be appropriate, indeed expected, with these forms of address (which should, however, be avoided by the foreign student), e.g.

Эй, па́рень, у тебя́ есть закури́ть? (R1)	*Hey mate, have you got a light?*

At this level, one might – provocatively – use some attribute of the addressee as the form of address, e.g.

Эй, борода́! (D)	*Hey, you with the beard!*
Эй, в очка́х! (D)	*Hey, you with the specs!*

In familiar speech, older people, especially in the country, may be addressed as:

Де́душка!	*Grandfather!*
Ба́бушка!	*Grandmother!*

Young children might address older strangers as:

Дя́дя!	lit *Uncle*! (cf. Eng *mister*!)
Дя́денька!	lit *Little uncle*!
Тётя!	*Auntie*! (cf. Eng *missis*!)
Тётенька!	lit *Little auntie*!

Children speaking to their grandparents might use the words **деду́ля**, *grandad*, and **баба́ля**, *granny, nan*.

Foreigners may be addressed as **господи́н** (*Mr*) or **госпожа́** (*Mrs*) + their surname, e.g.

Господи́н Смит!	*Mr Smith*!
Госпожа́ Бра́ун!	*Mrs Brown*!

other forms of address

До́ктор!	*Doctor*!
Сестра́!	*Nurse*!
Профе́ссор!	*Professor*!
Друзья́!	*Friends*!
Колле́ги!	*Colleagues*!
Ребя́та!	*Lads*!
Ма́льчики!	*Boys*!
Де́вушки!	*Girls*!
Де́вочки!	*(Young) girls*!
Ученики́!	*Pupils*!
Да́мы и господа́!	*Ladies and gentlemen*!

7.5 Introductions (знако́мство)

introducing oneself

Я хочу́ с ва́ми познако́миться. **Я хоте́л(а) бы с ва́ми познако́миться.** **Мне хо́чется с ва́ми познако́миться.** **Мне хоте́лось бы с ва́ми познако́миться.**	lit *I want/should like to meet you/make your acquaintance.*
Дава́й(те) знако́миться! **Дава́й(те) познако́мимся!**	lit *Let's meet/get to know one another.*
Позво́льте (с ва́ми) познако́миться. (R3) **Разреши́те (с ва́ми) познако́миться.** (R3) **Позво́льте предста́виться.** (R3) **Разреши́те предста́виться.** (R3)	*Allow me to introduce myself to you.*

All the above formulae precede naming of oneself. The form of one's name that one gives depends on the degree of formality of the situation. Young people meeting in an informal situation would give only their first name, perhaps even in a diminutive form, e.g.

(Меня́ зову́т) Влади́мир.	*My name is Vladimir.*
(Меня́ зову́т) Воло́дя.	*My name is Volodia.*
(Меня́ зову́т) Татья́на.	*My name is Tat'iana.*
(Меня́ зову́т) Та́ня.	*My name is Tania.*

In a formal situation one would give one's first name and patronymic, e.g.

Меня́ зову́т Никола́й Петро́вич.	*My name is Nikolai Petrovich.*
Меня́ зову́т О́льга Серге́евна.	*My name is Ol'ga Sergeevna.*

or even all three names (first name, patronymic and surname), often with the surname first, e.g.

Евге́ний Бори́сович Попо́в	*Evgenii Borisovich Popov*
Ири́на Па́вловна Тара́сова	*Irina Pavlovna Tarasova*
Гончаро́в, Серге́й Петро́вич	*Goncharov, Sergei Petrovich*

Note 1   The nominative case is preferred after the verb form **зову́т** when people are being named (see the examples above), although the instrumental is also grammatically possible after **звать**, e.g. **И́мя моё – И́горь, а зову́т меня́ Го́шей** (R1), *My name is Igor, but people call me Gosha.*

2   The formula **меня́ зову́т** tends to be omitted if the surname is included.

In a formal situation connected with one's work one might give one's position and surname, e.g.

Профе́ссор Моско́вского	*Moscow University Professor*
университе́та Кузнецо́в	*Kuznetsov*
Дире́ктор городско́го музе́я	*Director of the City Museum*
Гончаро́ва	*Goncharova*

Having named oneself one may proceed in the following way to ask for the same information from the other person:

А как вас зову́т?	*And what is your name?*
А как ва́ше и́мя?	*And what is your first name?*
А как ва́ше и́мя и о́тчество?	*And what is your first name and patronymic?*
А как ва́ша фами́лия?	*And what is your surname?*

responses to introductions

О́чень прия́тно!	*Very pleased to meet you.*
Мне о́чень прия́тно с ва́ми познако́миться.	*I am very pleased to meet you.*
О́чень ра́д(а)!	*Very glad (to meet you).*
Я о вас слы́шал(а).	*I've heard about you.*
Мне о вас говори́ли.	*I've been told about you.*

If the people have already met, one of the following formulae might be appropriate:

Мы уже́ знако́мы.	We're already acquainted.
Мы уже́ встреча́лись.	We've already met.
Я вас зна́ю.	I know you (already).
Я вас где́-то ви́дел(а).	I've seen you somewhere.
Познако́мьтесь, пожа́луйста.	lit Meet each other.

introducing other people

Я хочу́ познако́мить вас
с + instr
Я хоте́л(а) бы познако́мить вас
с + instr
Я хочу́ предста́вить вам + acc
} *I want to introduce you to*

Позво́льте познако́мить вас
с + instr (R3)
Разреши́те предста́вить
вам + acc (R3)
} *Allow me to introduce you to*

7.6 Greetings (приве́тствие)

general greetings

Здра́вствуй(те)!	Hello.
До́брый день!	Good day.
До́брое у́тро!	Good morning.
До́брый ве́чер!	Good evening.
Приве́т! (R1)	Hello.
Я ра́д(а) вас приве́тствовать. (formal; to audience)	I am pleased to welcome you.
Добро́ пожа́ловать! (on sb's arrival for a stay)	Welcome.
С прие́здом!	= добро́ пожа́ловать
Хлеб-со́ль!	revived archaic welcome to guests at gathering, indicating hospitality

responses to greetings

(Я) (о́чень) ра́д(а) тебя́/вас ви́деть.	(I) am (very) glad to see you.
(Я) то́же ра́д(а) тебя́/вас ви́деть.	(I) am glad to see you too.

enquiries about one's affairs and health

Как живёшь/живёте?	How are you getting on?
Как пожива́ете?	How are you getting on?
Как твоя́/ва́ша жизнь?	How's life?
Как (иду́т) дела́?	How are things going?
Что но́вого? (R1)	What's new?
Как твой/ваш муж/сын/брат/оте́ц?	How is your husband/son/brother/father?
Как твоя́/ва́ша жена́/до́чка/сестра́/мать?	How is your wife/daughter/sister/mother?
Как вы себя́ чу́вствуете?	How do you feel?
Ну, как ты? (solicitous, e.g. after illness)	How are you then?

	Замеча́тельно.	*Marvellous.*
	Великоле́пно.	*Splendid.*
	Норма́льно.	*All right.* (This is the most frequently used colloquial response of to an enquiry about how one is.)
	Хорошо́.	*Fine.*
	Непло́хо.	*OK.*
	Не жа́луюсь.	*I can't complain.*
	Ничего́.	*All right.*
	Ка́жется, ничего́ плохо́го.	*Not bad.*
	Ни ша́тко, ни ва́лко. (R1)	*Middling.*
	Так себе́. (R1)	*So-so.*
	Нева́жно.	*Not too good/well.*
	Пло́хо.	*Bad(ly).*
	Лу́чше не спра́шивай(те)! (R1)	*Better not to ask.*
	Ху́же не́куда! (R1)	*Couldn't be worse.*
	Из рук вон пло́хо! (R1)	*Dreadful(ly).*
unexpected meetings	Кака́я (прия́тная) встре́ча!	lit *What a (pleasant) meeting,* i.e. *How nice to see you.*
	Кака́я (прия́тная) неожи́данность!	*What a (pleasant) surprise.*
	Не ожида́л(а) тебя́/вас встре́тить (здесь).	*I didn't expect to meet you (here).*
	Каки́ми судьба́ми! (R1)	*Fancy meeting you here!*
	Как ты сюда́ попа́л(а)?	*How did you get here?*
meeting after long separation	Кого́ я ви́жу?	lit *Who's this?* i.e. *It's good to see you again after so long.*
	Э́то ты?	*Is it you?*
	Ты ли э́то?	*Is it you?*
	Давно́ не ви́делись.	*We haven't seen each other for a long time.*
	Сто лет не ви́делись. Це́лую ве́чность не ви́делись. Ско́лько лет, ско́лько зим!	*We haven't seen each other for ages.*
meeting by arrangement	Вот я и пришёл/пришла́.	*Here I am.*
	Ты давно́ ждёшь/Вы давно́ ждёте?	*Have you been waiting long?*
	Я не опозда́л(а)?	*Am I late?*
	Я не заста́вил(а) вас ждать?	*I haven't kept you waiting, have I?*
responses at meeting by arrangement	Я жду тебя́/вас.	*I've been waiting for you.*
	Ты пришёл/пришла́ во́-время/ Вы пришли́ во́-время.	*You're on time.*
	А, ну вот и ты. (R1)	*So here you are.*
	Лу́чше по́здно, чем никогда́.	*Better late than never.*

7.7   Farewells (проща́ние)

До свида́ния.	*Goodbye.* (lit *until [the next] meeting*; cf. Fr *au revoir*)
До ско́рой встре́чи!	*Let's meet (again) soon.*
До ве́чера!	*Till this evening.*
До за́втра!	*Till tomorrow.*
До понеде́льника!	*Till Monday.*
Проща́й(те)!	= до свида́ния or may suggest parting for ever (cf. Fr *adieu* as opposed to *au revoir*)
Всего́ хоро́шего!	
Всего́ до́брого!	*All the best.*
Всего́! (R1)	
Пока́! (R1)	*So long.*
Счастли́во! (R1)	*Good luck.*
Споко́йной но́чи!	*Good night.*
Мы ещё уви́димся.	*We'll see each other again.*

phrases associated with parting

Не забыва́й(те) нас.	*Don't forget us.*
Приходи́(те).	*Come again.*
Заходи́(те).	*Drop in again.*
Звони́(те).	*Give us a ring.*
Приезжа́й(те).	*Come again.* (to sb travelling from afar)
Пиши́(те).	*Write (to us).*
Да́й(те) о себе́ знать.	lit *Let us know about you.*
Ми́лости про́сим, к нам ещё раз.	= *You're always welcome to come again.*
Переда́й(те) приве́т + dat	*Give my regards to*
(По)целу́й(те) дете́й/дочь/сы́на.	*Give your children/daughter/son a kiss from me.*
Не помина́йте ли́хом.	*Remember me kindly.* (to sb going away for good)

formulae preceding parting

It might be appropriate as one is preparing to part to use one of the following phrases:

Уже́ по́здно.	*It's late.*
Мне пора́ уходи́ть.	*It's time I was leaving.*
Мне бы́ло прия́тно с ва́ми поговори́ть.	*It's been nice talking to you.*

At the end of a business meeting it might be appropriate to use one of the following formulae:

Мы обо всём договори́лись.	*We've agreed about everything.*
Мы нашли́ о́бщий язы́к.	*We've found a common language.*
Извини́те, что я задержа́л(а) вас.	*I'm sorry I've kept you.*
Прости́те, что я о́тнял(а́) у вас сто́лько вре́мени.	*I'm sorry I've taken up so much of your time.*

7.8   Congratulation (поздравле́ние)

Congratulations are generally couched in a construction in which the verb **поздравля́ть/поздра́вить**, *to congratulate*, which is followed by **с** + instr, is used, or more often simply understood, e.g.

Поздравля́ю вас с рожде́нием ребёнка!	*Congratulations on the birth of your child.*
С Рождество́м!	*Happy Christmas.*
С Но́вым го́дом!	*Happy New Year.*
С днём рожде́ния!	*Happy birthday.*
С годовщи́ной сва́дьбы!	*Happy wedding anniversary.*
С лёгким па́ром!	said to sb emerging from bath or shower (literally expressing a wish that a person has been refreshed by the right sort of steam in the **пари́лка** or steam room of the **ба́ня**)

The phrase might end with **тебя́** or **вас** as a direct object of the verb, but the inclusion of this pronoun is not essential. Examples:

С сере́бряной сва́дьбой тебя́!	*Congratulations on your silver wedding anniversary.*
С оконча́нием университе́та вас!	*Congratulations on graduating.*

For more formal congratulations one of the following formulae may be used:

Позво́льте поздра́вить вас с + instr (R3)	*Allow me to congratulate you on*
Прими́те мои́ и́скренние/серде́чные/горя́чие/ тёплые поздравле́ния с + instr (R3)	*(Please) accept my sincere/heartfelt/warmest/warm congratulations on*
От и́мени компа́нии/университе́та поздравля́ю вас с + instr (R3)	*On behalf of the company/ university I congratulate you on*

giving presents   Congratulations might be accompanied by the giving of presents, in which case one of the following formulae might be used:

Вот тебе́ пода́рок. (R1)	*Here's a present for you.*
Э́то тебе́. (R1)	*This is for you.*
Я хочу́ подари́ть вам кни́гу.	*I want to give you a book.*
Пожа́луйста, прими́те наш пода́рок. (R3)	*Please accept our gift.*

7.9   Wishing (пожела́ние)

Wishes are generally couched in a construction in which the imperfective verb **жела́ть**, *to wish*, is used or understood. In the full construction this verb is followed by an indirect object in the dative, indicating the recipient of the wish, and an object in the genitive indicating the thing wished for. The verb **жела́ть** may also be followed by an infinitive. Examples:

Жела́ю тебе́ сча́стья!	*I wish you happiness.*
Жела́ю вам больши́х успе́хов!	*I wish you every success.*
Всего́ наилу́чшего!	*All the best.*
Прия́тного аппети́та!	*Bon appétit.*
Счастли́вого пути́!	*Bon voyage.*
До́лгих лет жи́зни! (said to ageing person)	*Long life.*
Жела́ю поскоре́е вы́здороветь!	*Get better quickly.*

More formal wishes might be rendered thus:

Прими́те мои́ са́мые лу́чшие / и́скренние / серде́чные / тёплые пожела́ния.	*(Please) accept my best / most sincere / heartfelt / warmest wishes.*

Wishes, or an element of wishing, may also be expressed by means of the imperative or by **пусть**, *may*, e.g.

Выздора́вливай(те).	*Get better.*
Береги́(те) себя́.	*Look after yourself.*
Расти́ больши́м и у́мным. (said to child)	*Grow big and clever.*
Пусть тебе́ бу́дет хорошо́!	*May all be well for you.*
Пусть тебе́ повезёт!	*May you have good luck.*

Note: the expression **Ни пу́ха ни пера́**, *Good luck*, is said to a person about to take an examination. (Originally the purpose of this expression, which literally means *Neither down nor feather*, was to wish sb good luck as they set off to go hunting.) The response is **К чёрту!** *To the devil.*

toasts   Speeches and toasts are a very much more widespread feature of Russian life than of British life. Even at an informal gathering in the home speeches may well be delivered and toasts proposed to guests by the host and others, and the guests should themselves respond with speeches and toasts of their own. A toast might be proposed in one of the following ways:

(За) ва́ше здоро́вье!	*(To) your health.*
Я хочу́ вы́пить за + acc	*I want to drink to*
Я предлага́ю тост за + acc	*I propose a toast to*
Я поднима́ю бока́л за + acc	*I raise my glass* (lit goblet; poet) *to*
Позво́льте подня́ть бока́л за + acc (R3)	*Allow me to raise my glass to*
Разреши́те провозгласи́ть тост за + acc (R3)	*Allow me to propose a toast to*

Note: it is the preposition **за** that should be used in toasts to translate Eng *to*, not **на** (which is commonly used in error by English-speakers in this context); see also the note at the end of 7.10 below.

7.10   Gratitude (благода́рность)

Спаси́бо.	*Thank you.*
Большо́е спаси́бо.	*Thank you very much.*
Спаси́бо за внима́ние. (said to audience after talk or lecture)	*Thank you for your attention.*
Спаси́бо, что вы́слушали меня́.	*Thank you for hearing me out.*
Благодарю́ вас за гостеприи́мство.	*Thank you for your hospitality.*
Я о́чень благода́рен/благода́рна вам.	*I am very grateful to you.*
Я вам мно́гим обя́зан(а).	*I am much obliged to you.*
Я о́чень призна́телен/ призна́тельна вам за це́нные сове́ты. (R3b)	*I am very grateful to you for your valuable advice.*
Я хоте́л(а) бы вы́разить свою́ благода́рность за то, что (R3b)	*I should like to express my gratitude for the fact that*

Note: *for* is rendered by **за** + acc in such expressions.

responses to thanks   The recipient of thanks routinely dismisses gratitude as unnecessary:

Пожа́луйста.	*Don't mention it.* (cf. Fr *de rien*; but note that **ничего́** is not used in this sense)
Не сто́ит/Не́ за что.	*It's nothing.*
Ну что ты, каки́е пустяки́! (R1)	*Don't be silly, it's nothing.*

Note: the expression **на здоро́вье** is used as a response to some expression of thanks for hospitality such as **Спаси́бо за угоще́ние** (*Thanks for treating me/Thanks for the food and drink*). The expression is only used in this sense. It should not be confused with **за ва́ше здоро́вье** (see 7.9 above).

7.11   Apologising (извине́ние)

Apologies are most often framed with one of the verbs **извиня́ть/ извини́ть**, *to excuse*; **извиня́ться/извини́ться**, *to apologise*; or **проща́ть/ прости́ть**, *to forgive*.

Извини́(те), (пожа́луйста).	*I'm sorry.* (lit *Excuse me*)
Извини́(те) за беспоко́йство.	*I'm sorry to trouble you.*
Извини́(те) меня́ за то, что забы́л(а) тебе́/вам позвони́ть.	*I am sorry that I forgot to ring you.*
Прости́(те), (пожа́луйста).	= **извини́(те)**
Прости́(те) меня́.	*Forgive me.* (for more serious transgressions)

Я прошу́ проще́ния.	*Forgive me.*
Я до́лжен/должна́ извини́ться	*I must apologise to you for the fact*
пе́ред ва́ми за то, что	*that*
Я винова́т(а) пе́ред ва́ми.	*I owe you an apology.* (lit *I am*
	guilty before you)
Прими́те мои́ (глубо́кие)	*(Please) accept my (profound)*
извине́ния. (R3)	*apologies.*
Я бо́льше не бу́ду (так де́лать).	*I shan't do it again.*
(said by child)	

Note: *for* in apologies is rendered by **за** + acc.

responses to   The recipient of an apology might respond in one of the following
apologies   ways:

Ничего́!	*It's nothing.*
Не́ за что (извиня́ться).	*There's nothing to apologise for.*
Да что́ ты/вы! (R1)	*What are you (apologising for)?*
Ну, хорошо́/Ну, ла́дно уж. (R1)	*Well OK.*
Так и быть. (speaker not entirely	*All right/OK.*
happy to forgive)	

7.12   Request (про́сьба)

Requests may of course be expressed by the imperative form of an
appropriate verb (see 9.6.11 and 11.5.6). A request in the imperative
may be introduced by the following very polite formulae:

Бу́дь любе́зен/любе́зна + imp	
Бу́дьте любе́зны + imp	*Would you be so good as to*
Бу́дь добр/добра́ + imp	
Бу́дьте добры́ + imp	

Е́сли вам не тру́дно + imp	*If it's no trouble to you*
Е́сли вас не затрудни́т + imp	

However, requests may also be framed in many other ways. Inclusion
of **не** or **ли** in formulae of the sort which follow increases the
politeness of the request. Examples:

О́чень прошу́ вас + infin	*I (do) ask you to*
Я хоте́л(а) бы попроси́ть у вас +	*I should like to ask you for*
acc	
Не могу́ ли я попроси́ть вас +	*Could I ask you to*
infin	
Я попроси́л(а) бы вас не кури́ть.	*I would ask you not to smoke.*
(polite prohibition)	
Мо́жет быть, вы сни́мете сапоги́?	*Would you take your boots off?*
Вы не пога́сите сигаре́ту?	*Would you put out your cigarette?*

In R1 a request might be couched as a question in the second person singular of the perfective verb, e.g.

Завáришь мне чай?   *Will you make me a cup of tea?*

A request might also be introduced by one of the following formulae, all of which mean *Can you* or *Could you*, and all of which are followed by an infinitive:

Вы мóжете
Вы не мóжете
Вы не моглú бы
Мóжете ли вы
Не мóжете ли вы
Не моглú бы вы

Permission may be sought by means of one of the following phrases, all of which mean *May (I)*, and all of which are followed by an infinitive:

Мóжно (мне)
Нельзя́ ли (мне)
Могу́ ли я
Не могу́ ли я
Позвóльте мне
Разрешúте мне

agreement

Accession to a request may be indicated by one of the following responses:

Пожáлуйста.	*By all means.*
Хорошó.	*All right.*
Лáдно. (R1)	*OK.*
Сейчáс.	*At once.*
Сию́ мину́ту.	*Straightaway.*
Нá(те). (R1; said when sth is being handed over)	*Here you are.*
Нá, возьмú. (R1)	*Here you are, take it.*

permission

The following responses indicate permission:

Да, конéчно.	*Yes, of course.*
Да, пожáлуйста.	*Yes, by all means.*
Разумéется.	*Of course.*
Безуслóвно.	*It goes without saying.*

The following phrases might be used to indicate refusal:

refusal

Не хочу́.	*I don't want to.*
Не могу́.	*I can't.*
Жаль, но не могу́.	*I'm sorry, but I can't.*
Я не в сúлах + infin (R3b)	*I am not able to*

prohibition

Prohibition might be expressed by one of the following formulae:

Нельзя́.	*No, one/you can't.*
К сожале́нию, не могу́ разреши́ть вам + infin	*Unfortunately I can't allow you to*
Ни в ко́ем слу́чае.	*No way.*
Ни за что́.	*Not for anything.*
Ни при каки́х обстоя́тельствах.	*In no circumstances.*
Об э́том не мо́жет быть и ре́чи.	*There can be no question of it.*

7.13   Invitation (приглаше́ние)

Приглаша́ю тебя́/вас на ча́шку ко́фе.	*I invite you for a cup of coffee.*
Хочу́ пригласи́ть тебя́/вас к себе́.	*I want to invite you to my place.*
Приходи́(те) к нам.	*Come to our place.*
Придёшь/Придёте ко мне? (R1)	*Will you come and see me?*
Приезжа́й(те).	*Drive over to us.*
Заходи́(те) к нам.	*Call on us.*
Загля́дывай(те). (R1)	*Drop in.*
Входи́(те).	*Come in.*
Бу́дь(те) как до́ма.	*Make yourself at home.*

acceptance of invitation

Спаси́бо, с удово́льствием!	*Thank you, with pleasure.*
С ра́достью!	*Gladly.*
Охо́тно!	*Willingly.*
Я обяза́тельно приду́.	*I shall definitely come.*

7.14   Reassurance and condolence (утеше́ние, соболе́знование)

Успоко́йся/успоко́йтесь.	*Calm down.*
Не беспоко́йся/беспоко́йтесь.	*Don't worry.*
Не волну́йся/волну́йтесь.	*Don't get agitated.*
Не огорча́йся/огорча́йтесь.	*Cheer up.*
Не расстра́ивайся/ расстра́ивайтесь.	*Don't be upset.*
Не па́дай(те) ду́хом.	*Don't lose heart.*
Не принима́й(те) э́того бли́зко к се́рдцу.	*Don't take this to heart.*
Не обраща́й(те) на э́то внима́ния.	*Don't pay any attention to this.*
Вы́брось(те) э́то из головы́.	*Put it out of your mind.*
Всё ко́нчится хорошо́.	*It'll all end up all right.*
Всё бу́дет в поря́дке!	*Everything will be all right.*
Всё э́то пройдёт!	*It'll all pass.*
Всё э́то обойдётся! (R1)	*Things will sort themselves out.*
Я тебе́/вам сочу́вствую.	*I sympathise with you.*
Мне жаль тебя́/вас.	*I'm sorry for you.*

Ничего́ не поде́лаешь.	*It can't be helped.*
Э́то не твоя́/ва́ша вина́.	*It's not your fault.*
Я тебе́/вам и́скренне соболе́зную.	*My sincere condolences.*
Прими́те мои́ глубо́кие соболе́знования. (R3)	*Please accept my deepest condolences.*
Разреши́те вы́разить вам мои́ глубо́кие соболе́знования. (R3)	*Permit me to express my deepest condolences.*
Я разделя́ю ва́ше го́ре.	*I share your grief.*

Note: the negative imperatives in these expressions are couched in imperfective forms.

7.15 Compliments (комплиме́нты)

Ты прекра́сно вы́глядишь!	*You look splendid.*
Вы так хорошо́ вы́глядите!	*You look so well.*
Како́й вы до́брый челове́к!	*What a kind person you are.*
Вы не измени́лись.	*You haven't changed.*
Вам не дашь ва́ших лет.	*You don't look your age.*
У тебя́ краси́вые во́лосы.	*You've got beautiful hair.*
Тебе́ идёт э́та причёска.	*This hair-style suits you.*
Тебя́ молоди́т коро́ткая стри́жка.	*Short hair makes you look younger.*
Вам к лицу́ я́ркие цвета́.	*Bright colours suit you.*

Note: compliments may of course be delivered with various degrees of expressiveness by the inclusion of such words as **о́чень, так, тако́й, како́й.**

responses to compliments

Спаси́бо за комплиме́нт.	*Thank you for (your) compliment.*
Вы льсти́те мне.	*You're flattering me.*
Вы преувели́чиваете.	*You're exaggerating.*
Прия́тно э́то слы́шать.	*It's nice to hear that.*
Я рад(а), что вам понра́вилось.	*I'm glad you liked it.*
То́же мо́жно сказа́ть и о тебе́/вас.	*One could say the same about you.*

7.16 Telephone conversations (телефо́нный разгово́р)

The person picking up the telephone may use a formula of the following sort:

Ало́! (pronounced алё)	*Hello.*
Да.	*Yes.*
Слу́шаю.	lit *I'm listening.*
Петро́в слу́шает.	*Petrov speaking.*
Па́влова у телефо́на.	*Pavlova speaking.*

The person making the call might begin in one of the following ways:

Э́то Ива́н Серге́евич?	*Is that Ivan Sergeevich?*
Э́то ты, Ива́н?	*Is that you, Ivan?*

If the caller has dialled the wrong number, one of the following responses might be used:

Вы оши́блись (но́мером).	
Вы непра́вильно набра́ли но́мер. ⎫	*You've got the wrong number.*
Вы не туда́ попа́ли. ⎭	
Здесь таки́х нет.	*There's no one by that name here.*

If the caller wants to speak to someone other than the person who has answered the phone, he or she may use one of the following formulae:

Позови́(те), пожа́луйста, О́льгу Петро́вну.	*May I speak to Oĺga Petrovna please?*
Попроси́(те) к телефо́ну Влади́мира Никола́евича.	*May I speak to Vladimir Nikolaevich?*
Мо́жно Ка́тю? (R1)	*Can I speak to Katia?*
Мне ну́жно Ива́на. (R1)	*I need Ivan.*
Мне Серге́я, пожа́луйста. (R1)	*I want Sergei.*
Та́ня до́ма? (R1)	*Is Tania in?*

The person who answers the telephone may call the person whom the caller is asking for in one of the following ways:

Ири́на Алексе́евна, вас про́сят к телефо́ну.	*Irina Alekseevna, you're wanted on the telephone.*
Ла́ру к телефо́ну!	*It's for you, Lara.*
Ната́ш, тебя́! (R1)	*Natasha, it's for you.*

In a place of work a person might be more formally called to the telephone in one of the following ways:

Ви́ктор Миха́йлович, вам звоня́т из министе́рства.	*Viktor Mikhailovich, there's a call for you from the ministry.*
Семён Степа́нович, с ва́ми хотя́т говори́ть из ба́нка.	*Semion Stepanovich, someone from the bank wants to talk to you.*
Ни́на Дми́триевна, вас спра́шивают из университе́та.	*Nina Dmitrievna, someone from the university wants to talk to you.*

The person who has answered the telephone and is summoning the person whom the caller wants to speak to may say to the caller:

Сейча́с позову́.	*I'll get him/her.*
Сейча́с он(а́) подойдёт.	*He's/She's coming.*
Подожди́(те) мину́т(оч)ку.	*Just a moment.*
Одну́ мину́точку.	*Just a minute.*
Одну́ секу́нду.	*Just a second.*
Жди́те.	*Wait (please).*
Не клади́(те) тру́бку.	*Don't put the receiver down.*

If the person sought by the caller is not available, the person who answers the telephone may say:

Его́ сейча́с нет.	*He's not here at the moment.*
Позвони́(те) попо́зже.	*Ring a bit later.*
Вам не тру́дно позвони́ть ещё раз?	*Could you ring again?*

If the person sought is not available the caller may say:

Переда́й(те) ему́/ей, что звони́л Алекса́ндр.	*Tell him/her that Aleksandr rang.*
Попроси́(те) его́/её позвони́ть А́лле.	*Ask him/her to ring Alla.*
Я позвоню́/перезвоню́ че́рез час.	*I'll call again in an hour.*

In the event of problems with the telephone one might say:

Пло́хо слы́шно. Я перезвоню́.	*It's a bad line. I'll call back.*
Нас прерва́ли.	*We got cut off.*

The conversation may end thus:

Ну, всё.	lit *Well, that's all.*
Пока́. (R1)	*So long.*
Созвони́мся. (R1)	*We'll talk again.*
Целу́ю. (among people close to one another, esp women)	lit *I kiss (you).*
Я вы́нужден(а) зако́нчить разгово́р. (R3)	*I must finish.*

7.17 Letter writing (перепи́ска)

Letters may be begun with the following formulae, which range from the intimate (R1) to the formal type of address used in official correspondence (R3b).

Ми́лая Та́ня!	*Darling Tania,*
Дорого́й Па́вел!	*Dear Pavel,*
Уважа́емый Михаи́л Петро́вич!	*Dear Mikhail Petrovich,*
Многоуважа́емый Ива́н Серге́евич!	*Dear Ivan Sergeevich,*
Глубо̀коуважа́емый Андре́й Па́влович!	*Dear Andrei Pavlovich,*

Note: the form of address may be affected by the form of first name (full form or diminutive) which the writer uses to the addressee and which, like the form of address itself, indicates the degree of intimacy, distance, respect between the writer and addressee.

The following formulae, again arranged in ascending order of formality, may be used at the end of a letter immediately before the signature:

Обнима́ю тебя́,	lit *I embrace you,*
Целу́ю тебя́,	lit *I kiss you,*
Пока́, (R1)	*So long,*
Всего́ хоро́шего, (R1)	*All the best,*
До свида́ния,	*Goodbye,*
Всего́ до́брого/хоро́шего,	*All the best,*

С любо́вью,	*With love,*
С серде́чным приве́том,	lit *With heartfelt greetings,*
С наилу́чшими пожела́ниями,	*With best wishes,*
С и́скренним уваже́нием,	*With sincere respect,*

Note: Russians tend to express themselves more effusively and in more emotional terms than the English, and such formulae reflect that fact.

In the formal official/business style of R3b formulae of the following sort may be employed:

В отве́т на Ва́ше письмо́ от 1-го ма́рта . . .
In reply to your letter of 1 March . . .
Подтвержда́ем получе́ние Ва́шего письма́ от 2-го апре́ля.
We confirm receipt of your letter of 2 April.
Контра́кт незамедли́тельно бу́дет Вам вы́слан.
A contract will be forwarded to you without delay.
Мы с интере́сом ожида́ем Ва́шего отве́та.
We look forward to receiving your reply.
Прилага́ем сле́дующие докуме́нты:
We append the following documents:

Note: it is conventional in letters in this style to begin the second-person-plural forms of address with a capital letter (**Вы, Ваш**, etc.).

8 Word-formation

8.1 Principles of word-formation

The stock of words in a language is increased over time by various procedures. In Russian the main procedures have been borrowing (see 5.1.1–5.1.2), affixation (with which this chapter is mainly concerned) and composition (see 8.12).

Knowledge of the main principles of Russian affixation helps a student to extend her or his vocabulary, because it enables the student in many cases to understand the precise sense of a word and to recognise the word's relationship with other words derived from the same root.

The student needs to be able to identify the basic components of a Russian verb, noun, or adjective, i.e. its prefix (if it contains one), root and suffix (again, if it contains one), e.g.

	prefix	root	suffix
входи́ть, *to enter*	**в**	**ход**	**и́ть**
развяза́ть, *to untie*	**раз**	**вяз**	**а́ть**
стака́н, *a glass*		**стака́н**	
подстака́нник, *glass-holder*	**под**	**стака́н**	**ник**
описа́ние, *description*	**о**	**пис**	**а́ние**
чита́тель, *reader*		**чит**	**а́тель**
котёнок, *kitten*		**кот**	**ёнок**
вку́сный, *tasty*		**вкус**	**ный**
бездо́мный, *homeless*	**без**	**до́м**	**ный**

Similar principles apply in English, but they are in evidence in words of Greek or Latin origin (e.g. *psycho/logy, trans/late, in/scrip/tion*) rather than in the words of Germanic origin which constitute the bulk of the most common, everyday vocabulary of English. Some of the English prefixes and suffixes derived from Latin that are equivalent to Russian prefixes and suffixes are noted in the following sections.

It should be emphasised that while an understanding of Russian affixation and of the meanings of a word's components aids recognition of words and retention of vocabulary, the principles of word-formation cannot be applied in a wholly predictable way. The foreign student must therefore check that a word whose form may be inferred from the principles given here does actually exist.

The lists which follow are intended to illustrate the main principles of Russian affixation and in particular to give the student some knowledge of the main verbal prefixes and noun suffixes. However, the lists of affixes are not exhaustive, nor does the chapter describe all the functions that a given affix may have.

8.2 Types of consonant, spelling rules and consonant changes

It is helpful when studying Russian affixation (and grammatical inflection; see Chapter 9) to bear in mind the following factors relating to pronunciation, orthography and the transformation or insertion of certain consonants in particular circumstances.

8.2.1 Hard and soft consonants

Russian has ten letters which represent vowel sounds: **а, е, ё, и, о, у, ы, э, ю, я**. These letters may be divided into two categories, viz:

col 1	col 2
а	я
о	ё
у	ю
ы	и
э	е

The vowels represented by the letters in col 1 follow hard consonants, whereas those represented by the letters in col 2 follow soft consonants. Therefore letters in col 1, such as **а, у** and **ы**, which frequently occur in the standard endings of Russian nouns, are replaced by letters in col 2 (**я, ю** and **и** respectively) in endings which follow a soft consonant. Compare, for example, acc/gen/instr sg endings of **пила́**, *saw*, which has a hard л, with those of **земля́**, which has a soft л:

пилу́	зе́млю
пилы́	земли́
пило́й	землёй

8.2.2 Use of the hard sign

The sole function of this letter in the modern language is as a separative sign between the consonant with which a prefix ends and a root beginning with a vowel that would in other circumstances soften the preceding consonant (i.e. one of the vowels in col 2 in 8.2.1 above; in practice this vowel is usually **е**, sometimes **ё** or **я**). Thus въезжа́ть, *to drive in*; взъеро́шенный, *dishevelled*; изъе́здить, *to travel all over*; отъе́хать, *to travel away*; разъе́хаться, *to drive off in various directions*; съе́зд, *congress*.

8.2.3 Devoicing of consonants

The consonants in col 1 below are voiced, whilst those in col 2 are their unvoiced equivalents. Col 2 also contains unvoiced consonants which have no voiced equivalent.

col 1	col 2
б	п
в	ф
г	к
д	т
ж	ш
з	с
	х
	ц
	ч
	щ

If two consonants belonging to different categories fall adjacent then one of the consonants must change to its equivalent in the other category. In prefixes ending in **з** (e.g. **без-, вз-, из-, раз-**) this change is reflected in the orthography: thus бесполе́зный, *useless*, расходи́ться, *to disperse*. In other circumstances, however, devoicing of consonants is not reflected in orthography. For example, the letters in col 1, which denote voiced consonants, are used in final position even though the consonants they represent are devoiced when they occur at the end of words (e.g. the words гроб, *coffin*; Ивано́в, *Ivanov*; друг, *friend*; сад, *garden*; нож, *knife*; раз, *time*, are pronounced *grop, Ivanof, druk, sat, nosh, ras*, respectively).

8.2.4 Spelling rules

(a) After **г, к, х, ж, ч, ш** and **щ** the letter **ы** cannot occur (except in a very small number of words, especially names, of foreign origin). It must be replaced, in those endings where **ы** would be expected, by the letter **и**, e.g. ру́сский, ти́хий, as opposed to кра́сный.

(b) The letters **я** and **ю** do not occur either after **г, к, х, ж, ц, ч, ш** and **щ**, except in a few words, especially proper nouns, of foreign origin (e.g. Гю́го, *Hugo*; жюри́, *jury*; Цю́рих, *Zurich*). They must be replaced, in those endings where they would be expected, by **а** and **у** respectively, e.g. лежу́ and лежа́т, as opposed to говорю́ and говоря́т.

(c) Unstressed **о** is not found after **ж, ц, ч, ш** or **щ** and is replaced by **е** after these letters, e.g. in the neuter nominative singular adjectival ending хоро́шее (cf. the normal ending for this form, as in кра́сное, ру́сское).

(d) The vowel **ë** is always stressed, e.g. in **полёт**, *flight*. It follows that ë cannot occur if the stress in a word is on any other syllable (contrast пойдёшь and вы́йдешь).

8.2.5 Consonant changes

A number of consonants (e.g. the velars **г, к, х**) are changed in certain circumstances into consonants of a different type (e.g. the hushing consonants **ж, ч, ш**). Thus it commonly happens that the consonant with which a root ends is transformed into a different consonant when certain suffixes are added to the root or when certain adjectival or verbal flexions are added to it (see 9.3.3, 9.6.8).

The main changes, which will be encountered frequently in the examples given in the following sections, are:

г ⟶ **ж**, as in движе́ние, *movement*, from the root двиг

д ⟶ **ж**, as in броже́ние, *ferment*, from the root брод

д ⟶ **жд**, as in освобожде́ние, *liberation*, from the root свобо́д

з ⟶ **ж**, as in выраже́ние, *expression*, from the root раз

к ⟶ **ч**, as in восто́чный, *eastern*, from восто́к

с ⟶**ш**, as in отноше́ние, *attitude*, from the root нос

ст ⟶ **щ**, as in чи́ще, *cleaner*, from the root чист

т ⟶ **ч**, as in лечу́, *I fly*, from лете́ть

т ⟶ **щ**, as in освеще́ние, *illumination*, from the root свет

х ⟶ **ш**, as in тишина́, *tranquillity*, from the root тих

8.2.6 Epenthetic л

Before certain suffixes or flexions the consonant л is added to a root ending in **б, в, м, п, ф**, e.g.

у/глуб/л/е́ние, *deepening*

у/див/л/е́ние, *surprise*

из/ум/л/е́ние, *astonishment*

куп/л/ю́, *I shall buy*

раз/граф/л/ю́, *I shall rule (lines on paper)*

8.3 Verbal prefixes

There are some two dozen prefixes which may be added to a simple verb in order to modify its meaning or to create a verb with a related but different meaning. A few of these prefixes are to be found in only a small number of verbs, but the majority occur in many verbs.

Most of the common prefixes may be used in various senses. They may indicate the direction of the movement denoted by the basic verb (e.g. **входи́ть**, *to go **into***), or they may in some other way define the precise nature of the action denoted by the verb (e.g. **запла́кать**, ***to start** to cry*). In many instances the prefix, perhaps combined with some other affix, bears a subtle meaning which in English must be rendered by some adverbial modification of the verb (e.g. **застрели́ть**, *to shoot **dead**; **набе́гаться**, *to **have had enough** of running about;*

посви́стывать, to whistle **from time to time**; **при**откры́ть, to open **slightly**).

Note 1   Prefix and aspect: normally the addition of a prefix to a simple imperfective verb makes the verb perfective, e.g. писа́ть (impf), написа́ть (pf); вяза́ть (impf), связа́ть (pf). In some instances (e.g. in the verb написа́ть) the prefix has no function other than to make the verb perfective (i.e. it adds only the sense of completeness of the action to the sense already conveyed by the imperfective). However, in other instances (e.g. in the verb связа́ть) the prefix provides a further modification of the meaning (вяза́ть means *to tie*, but связа́ть means *to tie together*, i.e. *to unite, to join, to link*). (See also 8.6 on infixes.)

2   Prefixes consisting of a single consonant or ending in a consonant may have to add **o** for the sake of euphony, e.g. **во-**, **подо-**.

Most of the prefixes which verbs may bear are listed below. A few of the less common meanings which may be borne by some of the prefixes are omitted. The directional meaning of each prefix, if the prefix has such a meaning, is dealt with first in each instance.

в– (во-)   (a)   movement *into*, or sometimes *upwards*:

ввози́ть/ввезти́	to bring in (by transport), import
вовлека́ть/вовле́чь	to drag in, involve
влеза́ть/влезть	to climb into/up

(b)   + **-ся**: action carried out with care or absorption; the prefix occurs only in a few verbs in this sense:

вслу́шиваться/вслу́шаться в + acc	to listen attentively to
всма́триваться/всмотре́ться в + acc	to peer at, scrutinise

вз– (взо-)
вс– before
unvoiced
consonants

movement *up*:

взлета́ть/взлете́ть	to fly up, to take off
всходи́ть/взойти́	to go up, mount, ascend
взва́ливать/взвали́ть	to lift, load up on to

воз– (вос– before
unvoiced
consonants)

of OCS origin; borne by verbs unlikely to occur in R1:

возде́рживаться/воздержа́ться	to abstain, refrain from
возобновля́ть/возобнови́ть	to renew
воскреша́ть/воскреси́ть	to resurrect

вы–

Note: this prefix is always stressed when it occurs in perfective verbs.

(a)   movement *out of*:

вывози́ть/вы́везти	to take out (by transport), export
вынима́ть/вы́нуть	to take out

(b) action carried out to the fullest possible extent; the prefix does not occur in many verbs with this meaning:

выва́ривать/вы́варить	*to boil thoroughly*

(c) action carried out to an extent sufficient to obtain the desired result; the prefix does not occur in many verbs with this meaning:

выпра́шивать/вы́просить	*to obtain through asking*

Note: the imperfective here will carry a sense of *trying* to obtain through asking; see 11.5.3.

(d) + **-ся**: in a few perfective verbs indicating that an action has been carried out to a sufficient degree:

вы́плакаться	*to have a good cry*
вы́спаться	*to have a good sleep*

до–   (a) movement *as far as* or *up to* a certain point:

доходи́ть/дойти́ до + gen	*to reach (on foot)*
добира́ться/добра́ться до + gen	*to reach, get as far as*

(b) action supplementary to some action already carried out:

допла́чивать/доплати́ть	*to make an additional payment*

(c) + **-ся**: action carried through to its intended outcome; the prefix occurs with this meaning in only a few verbs:

дозвони́ться	*to get through (on the telephone)*

за–   (a) movement *behind*:

заходи́ть/зайти́	*to go behind, set* (of sun)

(b) in a number of verbs indicating that a call or visit is/was/will be made:

забега́ть/забежа́ть	
загля́дывать/загляну́ть	*to call in on/drop in on*
заходи́ть/зайти́	

(c) used as a prefix to render simple verbs perfective, **за–** may indicate the beginning of an action; this usage is particularly common in verbs describing some sound:

зазвене́ть	*to start to ring*
засмея́ться	*to burst out laughing*
заходи́ть	*to start pacing around/up and down*

(d) may indicate that a space is filled or that sth is covered or closed by the action:

зава́ливать/завали́ть	*to block up, obstruct, pile up with*
заполня́ть/запо́лнить	*to fill in* (form, questionnaire)

(e) used as a perfective prefix **за-** may indicate that an action, particularly a harmful one, has been carried to an extreme degree; the prefix occurs with this meaning in only a few verbs:

запоро́ть	*to flog to death*
застрели́ть	*to shoot (and kill)*

(f) **+ -ся**: may indicate that action has gone on for longer than one might expect or that the agent has been more than normally engrossed in it:

заба́лтываться/заболта́ться	*to be/get engrossed in conversation*
зачи́тываться/зачита́ться	*to be/get engrossed in reading*

из- (ис- before unvoiced consonants)

(a) in many verbs has original directional meaning *out of*, though now this meaning may not be obvious; cf. Eng *ex-* (abridged form *e-*):

избира́ть/избра́ть	*to elect*
извлека́ть/извле́чь	*to extract, derive*
исключа́ть/исключи́ть	*to exclude, rule out*

(b) action affecting the entire surface of sth; occurs with this meaning in only a few verbs:

изгрыза́ть/изгры́зть	*to gnaw to shreds*
изре́зывать/изре́зать	*to cut to pieces/cut in many places*

(c) exhaustion of a supply of sth; occurs with this meaning in only a few verbs:

испи́сывать/исписа́ть	*to use up all of* (some writing material, e.g. paper, ink)

(d) action carried out to the fullest possible extent:

иссыха́ть/иссо́хнуть (intrans)	*to dry up altogether*

(e) **+ -ся**, and in perfective forms only: to do or suffer sth unpleasant to the extent that it becomes habitual:

изолга́ться	*to become an inveterate liar*

на-

(a) movement *onto* or *into* (in the sense of collision):

налета́ть/налете́ть	*to swoop on, run into* (of vehicles)
напада́ть/напа́сть	*to attack, fall upon*

(b) in some verbs, predominantly perfectives, to denote action affecting a certain quantity of an object; the direct object is generally in the genitive case, indicating partitive meaning:

навари́ть	*to boil a certain quantity of*
накупи́ть	*to buy up a certain quantity of*

(c) **+ -ся**: in verbs (predominantly perfectives) denoting action carried out to satiety or even to excess:

	наѐсться	*to eat one's fill*
	напи́ться	*to drink as much as one wants; to get drunk*

недо–	insufficiency; attached to very few verbs:	
	недостава́ть/недоста́ть + gen	*to be insufficient*
	недооце́нивать/недооцени́ть	*to underestimate*

о– (об–, обо–)	(a)	movement *round* in various senses, viz comprehensive coverage, bypassing or overtaking, encircling or surrounding:
		обходи́ть/обойти́ — *to go all round, get round*
		обгоня́ть/обогна́ть — *to overtake*
		обрамля́ть/обра́мить — *to frame*

	(b)	thorough action covering the whole surface of sth:
		окле́ивать/окле́ить — *to paste over*
		осма́тривать/осмотре́ть — *to look over, inspect*

	(c)	in verbs derived from a different part of speech, especially an adjective; the prefix is very common in this function:
		обогаща́ть/обогати́ть — *to enrich* (from бога́тый)
		освобожда́ть/освободи́ть — *to liberate, free* (from свобо́дный)

	(d)	+ **-ся**: in verbs indicating that an action is mistaken:
		обсчи́тываться/обсчита́ться — *to make a mistake (in counting)*
		огова́риваться/оговори́ться — *to make a slip (in speaking)*

обез– (обес– **before unvoiced consonants)**	(= verbal prefix **о–** + adjectival prefix **без–/бес–**): loss or deprivation of the thing denoted by the root of the word; used with only a small number of verbs in this meaning:
	обезво́живать/обезво́дить — *to dehydrate (i.e. take away water)*
	обезвре́живать/обезвре́дить — *to render harmless, neutralise, defuse*
	обесси́ливать/обесси́лить — *to weaken (i.e. take away strength)*

от– (ото–)	(a)	movement *away from*, or *off* (cf. **у–** below); the prefix is very common in this meaning:
		отлета́ть/отлете́ть — *to fly away, fly off, rebound*
		отходи́ть/отойти́ — *to go away, go off, depart (of transport), come away from*
		отнима́ть/отня́ть — *to take away*

	(b)	in verbs with figurative meaning, may carry the sense of *back* (cf. Eng *re-*); the prefix is common in this meaning:
		отбива́ть/отби́ть — *to beat back, repel*
		отража́ть/отрази́ть — *to reflect*

	(c)	in perfective verbs, to emphasise that action is at an end or has been carried out to its required limit; the prefix is not widely used with this meaning:	

	отдежу́рить	*to come off duty*
	отрабо́тать	*to finish one's work*

пере-   (a)   movement *across* or transference from one place to another (cf. Eng *trans-*):

	переходи́ть/перейти́	*to cross (on foot)*
	передава́ть/переда́ть	*to pass (across), transfer, transmit*
	переса́живаться/пересе́сть	*to change (transport)*

(b)   to do sth again (cf. Eng *re-*); the prefix occurs in many verbs in this meaning:

	пересма́тривать/пересмотре́ть	*to look at again, review*
	перестра́ивать/перестро́ить	*to rebuild, reconstruct*

(c)   to do sth too much (cf. Eng *over-*):

	перегрева́ть/перегре́ть	*to overheat*
	переоце́нивать/переоцени́ть	*to overestimate*

(d)   + **-ся**: reciprocal action:

	перегля́дываться/перегляну́ться	*to exchange glances*
	перепи́сываться (impf only)	*to correspond (i.e. exchange letters)*

по-   (a)   in many perfective verbs, to indicate action of short duration or limited extent; it may be attached to indeterminate verbs of motion; the prefix is very common in this meaning:

	поговори́ть	*to have a talk, talk for a bit*
	погуля́ть	*to take a stroll*
	пое́сть	*to have a bite to eat*
	порабо́тать	*to do a bit of work*
	походи́ть	*to walk about for a bit*

(b)   + infix **-ыва-** or **-ива-**, to form imperfective verbs with iterative meaning (i.e. action repeated off and on for some time):

	погля́дывать	*to look at from time to time*
	погова́ривать	*to gossip, talk about every so often*
	пока́шливать	*to cough from time to time*
	посви́стывать	*to whistle off and on*

под- (подо-)   (a)   action *below* or *from below*:

	подде́рживать/поддержа́ть	*to support*
	подпи́сывать/подписа́ть	*to sign (i.e. write underneath)*
	подчёркивать/подчеркну́ть	*to stress, emphasise (i.e. underline)*

(b) movement *towards*; this is the commonest directional meaning of this prefix when it is used with verbs of motion:

подходи́ть/подойти́	*to approach, go towards/up to*
подзыва́ть/подозва́ть	*to call up, beckon*

(c) movement *upwards*:

подбра́сывать/подбро́сить	*to throw/toss up*
поднима́ть/подня́ть	*to lift, raise*

(d) action that is not far-reaching:

подкра́шивать/подкра́сить	*to tint, touch up*
подреза́ть/подре́зать	*to clip, trim*

(e) action that adds sth:

подраба́тывать/подрабо́тать	*to earn some additional money*

(f) underhand action:

поджига́ть/поджѐчь	*to set fire to (criminally), commit arson*
подкупа́ть/подкупи́ть	*to bribe, suborn*
подслу́шивать (impf only)	*to eavesdrop*

пред- (предо-) action that precedes or anticipates sth (cf. Eng *fore-*); mainly in bookish words characteristic of R3:

предви́деть (impf; no pf)	*to foresee*
предотвраща́ть/предотврати́ть	*to avert, prevent, stave off*
предска́зывать/предсказа́ть	*to foretell, prophesy*

при- (a) movement *to* a destination:

приезжа́ть/прие́хать	*to come, arrive (by transport)*
приноси́ть/принести́	*to bring (by hand)*
приходи́ть/прийти́	*to come, arrive (on foot)*

(b) attachment or fastening of an object to sth else:

привя́зывать/привяза́ть	*to tie/attach/fasten to*
прика́лывать/приколо́ть	*to pin to*

(c) action that is not fully carried out:

приостана́вливать/приостанови́ть	*to halt*
приоткрыва́ть/приоткры́ть	*to half-open*
приспуска́ть/приспусти́ть	*to lower a little*

про- (a) movement *by* or *past*:

пробега́ть/пробежа́ть	*to run past*
проходи́ть/пройти́	*to go past (on foot)*

(b) movement *through*:

проеда́ть/прое́сть	*to eat through, corrode*
пропуска́ть/пропусти́ть	*to let through, admit, omit*

(c) as a perfective prefix, in many simple verbs when the duration of the action or the distance covered by it is defined:

просиде́ть два часа́	*to sit for two hours*
пробежа́ть де́сять киломе́тров	*to run ten kilometres*

(d) thorough action:

проду́мывать/проду́мать	*to think over*
прожа́ривать/прожа́рить	*to roast thoroughly*

(e) oversight (only in a few verbs):

прогля́дывать/прогляде́ть	*to overlook*

(f) loss:

прои́грывать/проигра́ть	*to lose* (game, at cards)

(g) + -**ся**: unintentional revelation:

прогова́риваться/проговори́ться	*to let the cat out of the bag*

раз- (разо-); рас–
before unvoiced
consonants

(a) movement in various directions or distribution (cf. Eng *dis-*); verbs of motion bearing this prefix become reflexive:

разбега́ться/разбежа́ться	*to run off (in various directions)*
разлета́ться/разлете́ться	*to fly off, scatter, be shattered*
размеща́ть/размести́ть	*to accommodate, place (in various places)*

(b) action that uncovers or undoes sth (cf. Eng *un-*); the prefix is used in many verbs with this meaning:

развя́зывать/развяза́ть	*to untie*
разгружа́ть/разгрузи́ть	*to unload*

с- (со-)

(a) movement *off* or *down from*:

сбега́ть/сбежа́ть	*to run down*
слеза́ть/слезть	*to climb down/off*
снима́ть/снять	*to take off*
сходи́ть/сойти́	*to come down*

(b) convergence (cf. Eng *con-*); verbs bearing the prefix in this sense may become reflexive:

сбега́ться/сбежа́ться	*to run and come together*
сходи́ться/сойти́сь	*to come together, meet, gather, tally (of figures)*
слива́ться/сли́ться	*to flow together, blend, mingle*

(c) joining, linking:

свя́зывать/связа́ть	*to tie together, connect, link, unite*
соединя́ть/соедини́ть	*to unite, join*

(d) + indeterminate verbs of motion to form perfective verbs which indicate that the subject moved in one direction and then back again; contrast homonyms or homographs which are imperfective verbs of motion indicating movement *down* or *off* (see (a) above):

сбе́гать	*to run somewhere and back again*
сходи́ть	*to go somewhere and back again* (on foot)

у- (a) movement *away from*; this prefix differs from **от-** in that it suggests that the subject moves *right off*, whereas **от-** describes the progressive separation of the subject from the point of departure:

уезжа́ть/уе́хать	*to go away (by transport)*
уходи́ть/уйти́	*to go away*
убира́ть/убра́ть	*to remove, take away, clear away*

(b) in verbs with comparative meaning derived from an adjectival root:

улучша́ть(ся)/улу́чшить(ся)	*to improve* (from лу́чший)
уменьша́ть(ся)/уме́ньшить(ся)	*to diminish* (from ме́ньший)
ухудша́ть(ся)/уху́дшить(ся)	*to make worse* (non-refl)/*get worse* (refl) (from худо́й)

Note: the non-reflexive forms of the above verbs are transitive, the reflexive forms intransitive.

(c) removal or diminution:

уре́зывать/уре́зать	*to cut, reduce*
ушива́ть/уши́ть	*to take in (clothes)*

(d) achievement in spite of opposition; uncommon in this meaning:

устоя́ть	*to stand one's ground*

(e) abundance:

усыпа́ть/усы́пать	*to strew with*

8.4 Noun prefixes

Although the main function of the prefixes listed in 8.3 above is to modify the meaning of verbs, they do also occur, with similar meaning, in many nouns. Some idea of their function and its extent in the formation of nouns may be gained from the following list of nouns which consist of prefix + the root **ход** (indicating *going, motion, movement on foot*) + (in some cases) a noun suffix.

восхо́д (со́лнца)	sunrise
восхожде́ние	ascent
вход	entrance, entry
вы́ход	exit, departure
дохо́д	income
захо́д (со́лнца)	sunset
нахо́дка	a find
обхо́д	round (of doctor), beat (of policeman); bypass
отхо́ды	waste-products
перехо́д	crossing, transition
подхо́д	approach
прихо́д	arrival
прохо́д	passage
расхо́д(ы)	expense, outgoings
расхо́дование	expenditure
схо́дни (pl; gen схо́дней)	gangplank
схо́дство	similarity
ухо́д	departure, withdrawal

Adjectives may also be derived from some of these nouns, e.g.

выходно́й (день)	rest-day
дохо́дный	profitable, lucrative
нахо́дчивый	resourceful
обхо́дный	roundabout, circuitous
отхо́дчивый	not harbouring resentment (see 3.7)
перехо́дный	transitional
схо́дный	similar

8.5 Adjectival prefixes

A number of prefixes, some of them of foreign origin and international currency, may be attached to adjectives, e.g.

а/мора́льный	amoral
анти/фаши́стский	anti-fascist
все/си́льный	all-powerful
наи/лу́чший (bookish)	best
не/большо́й	small
не/глу́пый	not stupid
не/без/основа́тельный	not without foundation
пре/глу́пый (R1)	really stupid
про/америка́нский	pro-American
сверх/мо́щный (tech)	extra-high-powered
ультра/фиоле́товый	ultraviolet

Other prefixes, of Russian provenance, combine with the suffixes **-ный** and **-ский** to form adjectives, e.g.

без/вре́дный	*harmless*
бес/коне́чный	*infinite*
вне/бра́чный	*extramarital*
внутри/ве́нный	*intravenous*
до/вое́нный	*pre-war*
за/рубе́жный	*foreign* (lit *over the border*)
меж/плане́тный	*interplanetary*
между/наро́дный	*international*
на/сто́льный	*table* (e.g. насто́льный те́ннис, *table tennis*)
над/стро́чный	*superlinear*
по/дохо́дный	*(according to) income* (e.g. подохо́дный нало́г, *income tax*)
по/сме́ртный	*posthumous*
под/во́дный	*underwater*
под/моско́вный	*near Moscow*
после/революцио́нный	*post-revolutionary*
пред/вы́борный	*pre-election* (i.e. *just before*)
при/балти́йский	*relating to the Baltic region*
сверх/есте́ственный	*supernatural*

8.6   The verbal infixes -ыва-/-ива-

These infixes have two functions:

(a)   used in combination with the prefix **по**- they form iterative verbs (see 8.3, по- (b));

(b)   they form secondary imperfectives (e.g. **подпи́сывать**, *to sign*), i.e. forms derived from a simple verb (e.g. **писа́ть**, *to write*) to which some prefix has been added, thus creating a perfective verb (e.g. **подписа́ть**) whose meaning needs to be preserved in an imperfective form. Further examples:

secondary impf	pf with prefix	simple verb
развя́зывать, *to untie*	**развяза́ть**	**вяза́ть**
переде́лывать, *to re-do*	**переде́лать**	**де́лать**
прои́грывать, *to lose*	**проигра́ть**	**игра́ть**
оты́скивать, *to find*	**отыска́ть**	**иска́ть**
прока́лывать, *to puncture*	**проколо́ть**	**коло́ть**
подка́пывать, *to undermine*	**подкопа́ть**	**копа́ть**
разма́тывать, *to unwind*	**размота́ть**	**мота́ть**
пересма́тривать, *to review*	**пересмотре́ть**	**смотре́ть**
вса́сывать, *to suck in*	**всоса́ть**	**соса́ть**
перестра́ивать, *to rebuild*	**перестро́ить**	**стро́ить**

Note 1 Unstressed **o** in the root of the simple verb, and sometimes stressed **ó**, change to **a** in secondary imperfective forms.

2 Secondary imperfectives belong to the conjugation 1A (see 9.6.2) and are characterised by stress on the syllable immediately before the infix.

8.7 Noun suffixes

The suffixes used in the formation of Russian nouns are very numerous. They may be used to indicate:

(a) people by reference to, for example, their qualities, characteristics, occupations or places of origin;

(b) types of animal;

(c) objects;

(d) abstract concepts;

(e) female representatives of a group;

(f) an attitude, ranging from affection to loathing, on the part of the speaker towards the object in question.

Note 1 Many suffixes are used within more than one of the above categories.

2 Properly speaking some of the 'suffixes' included in this section and almost all those in 8.9 might be treated as combinations of more than one suffix, e.g. **–н-ие; –ств-о; –ист-ый; –н-ый**.

8.7.1 The principal noun suffixes

The following list of noun suffixes is arranged in alphabetical order. The suffixes **–ация, –ение, –ец, –ин, –ость, –тель** are particularly common. The suffixes relating to categories (e) and (f) above are dealt with separately in 8.7.2 and 8.8 respectively.

–ак/–як	suffixes defining people by reference to their place of origin (see also 6.12), to some characteristic, or to the object with which their occupation is associated, e.g.	
	рыба́к	*fisherman*
	бедня́к	*poor man*
	моря́к	*seaman*
	холостя́к	*bachelor*

–а́ла/–и́ла	very expressive suffixes used mainly in R1 to define people by reference to a particular action. The nouns formed with these suffixes are of common gender.	
	вороти́ла	*bigwig*
	вышиба́ла	*bouncer*

	громи́ла	*thug*
	заправи́ла	*boss*
	кути́ла	*fast liver, hard drinker*

-анин/ -янин used to form nouns that indicate a person's social status, religion, ethnicity, or place of origin (see also 6.11–6.12), e.g.

дворяни́н	*nobleman*
крестья́нин	*peasant*
марсиа́нин	*Martian*
мусульма́нин	*Moslem*
славяни́н	*Slav*
южа́нин	*southerner*

Note: in some words the suffix used is **-ин**, e.g. **болга́рин**, *Bulgarian*; **боя́рин**, *boyar*; **грузи́н**, *Georgian*; **тата́рин**, *Tatar*.

-ант/-ент suffixes of foreign origin defining people in relation to some action or object, e.g.

музыка́нт	*musician*
эмигра́нт	*émigré*
оппоне́нт	*opponent*

-ация/-яция used in very numerous verbal nouns of international currency (cf. Eng *-ation*), e.g.

администра́ция	*administration*
деклара́ция	*declaration*
консульта́ция	*consultation*
модерниза́ция	*modernisation*
организа́ция	*organisation*
приватиза́ция	*privatisation*

Note 1   In words with a stem ending in a soft consonant the suffix used is **-я́ция**, e.g. **инфля́ция**, *inflation*; **корреля́ция**, *correlation*.

   2   The suffixes **-ция** and **-иция** also occur, e.g. **инстру́кция**, *instruction*; **экспеди́ция**, *expedition*.

-ач a relatively uncommon suffix defining people by reference to their occupational activity or salient characteristic, e.g.

бога́ч	*rich man*
горба́ч	*hunchback*
скрипа́ч	*violinist*

-ёнок used to form nouns which denote the young of living creatures, e.g.

жеребёнок	*foal, colt*
котёнок	*kitten*
львёнок	*lion-cub*

	поросёнок	*piglet*
	ягнёнок	*lamb*

Note 1 After hushing consonants the suffix is **-о́нок**, e.g. **волчо́нок**, *wolf-cub*; **мышо́нок**, *baby mouse*.

    2 The plural forms of nouns with this suffix are not formed in the usual way (see 9.1.9).

-ёр   used in some words of international currency which define people by reference to their field of activity (cf. Eng *-er, -or*), e.g.

	боксёр	*boxer*
	дирижёр	*conductor* (of orchestra)
	режиссёр	*producer* (of play, film)

-ец   a very widespread suffix denoting a person by reference to (a) some action or occupation; (b) a certain quality; or (c) place of origin or residence (in which case the forms **-анец/-янец** (see also 6.11–6.12) are common), e.g.

(a)	бе́женец	*refugee*
	гребе́ц	*rower, oarsman*
	купе́ц	*merchant*
	певе́ц	*singer*
	торго́вец	*trader*
(b)	краса́вец	*handsome man*
	скупе́ц	*miser, skinflint*
(c)	африка́нец	*African*
	баки́нец	*person from Baku*
	япо́нец	*Japanese*

-ие/-ье   with adjectival roots, in neuter abstract nouns which tend to be bookish and are therefore prevalent in R3, and which denote a quality, e.g.

	вели́чие	*greatness*
	равноду́шие	*indifference*
	хладнокро́вие	*sang-froid*
	здоро́вье	*health*

-изм   of foreign origin, in nouns denoting a doctrine or system and also activities or tendencies (cf. Eng *-ism*), e.g.

	атеи́зм	*atheism*
	капитали́зм	*capitalism*
	оптими́зm	*optimism*
	романти́зм	*romanticism*
	социали́зм	*socialism*
	тури́зм	*tourism*
	фанати́зм	*fanaticism*

-ик	used in words of international currency which define a person's field of activity, e.g.

исто́рик	*historian*
те́хник	*technician*
хи́мик	*chemist* (not dispensing chemist: апте́карь (m))

-ика	a suffix of foreign origin indicating a field of knowledge, a discipline (cf. Eng *-ics*), e.g.

матема́тика	*mathematics*
фи́зика	*physics*
эконо́мика	*economics*

-ина	miscellaneous functions, including:

(a) with verbal roots, to indicate the result of actions, e.g.

впа́дина	*cavity*
цара́пина	*scratch*

(b) with noun roots, to denote an individual specimen of an object usually referred to collectively, e.g.

изю́мина (collect изю́м)	*a raisin*
карто́фелина (collect карто́фель, m)	*a potato*

(c) to denote the meat of an animal or fish, e.g.

бара́нина	*mutton*
лососи́на	*salmon*

(d) to denote dimensions, and in some other abstract nouns:

глубина́	*depth*
длина́	*length*
тишина́	*silence*
ширина́	*width*

-ионе́р	used in words of international currency to define people by reference to their activity or outlook, e.g.

коллекционе́р	*collector* (e.g. of stamps)
революционе́р	*revolutionary*

-ист	a suffix of foreign origin which defines people by reference to some doctrine they hold or art or skill they practise (cf. Eng *-ist*; see also **-изм**), e.g.

атеи́ст	*atheist*
велосипеди́ст	*cyclist*
журнали́ст	*journalist*

–ич		the suffix used to form male patronymics; it may also indicate place of origin (see also 6.12), e.g.	
		Серге́ич	*son of Sergei*
		оми́ч	*person from Omsk*

–ка	(a)	with verbal roots, in nouns denoting a process, an instrument, or the result of an action, e.g.	
		запи́ска	*note*
		запра́вка	*refuelling, seasoning*
		тёрка	*grater*
		чи́стка	*cleaning, purge*
	(b)	in R1 predominantly, with adjectival roots, to denote objects which in R2 are described by the adjective in question + a noun, e.g.	
		пятиле́тка = пятиле́тний план	*five-year plan*
		Третьяко́вка = Третьяко́вская галере́я	*Tret'iakóv Gallery*

–лка		often in R1, with verbal roots, to denote an instrument or place associated with an action, e.g.	
		ве́шалка	*clothes-hanger*
		зажига́лка	*cigarette-lighter*
		кури́лка (R1)	*smoking room*
		раздева́лка (R1)	*cloakroom*

–лог		a suffix of foreign origin denoting a specialist or person of learning in a particular field (cf. Eng *-logist*; see also **–логия**), e.g.	
		био́лог	*biologist*
		метеоро́лог	*meteorologist*

–логия		a suffix of foreign origin denoting a science (cf. Eng *-logy*; see also –лог), e.g.	
		биоло́гия	*biology*
		метеороло́гия	*meteorology*
		психоло́гия	*psychology*
		социоло́гия	*sociology*

–ние		extremely common, in verbal nouns (cf. Eng *-ing, -ment, -sion, -tion*), e.g.	
		выраже́ние	*expression*
		достиже́ние	*achievement*
		загрязне́ние	*pollution*
		объявле́ние	*announcement, declaration*
		одобре́ние	*approval*
		освобожде́ние	*liberation*

пе́ние	singing
продолже́ние	continuation
расшире́ние	widening, expansion, extension
увеличе́ние	increase
улучше́ние	improvement
ухудше́ние	worsening, deterioration

Note: consonant changes affecting the first person singular of second-conjugation verbs (9.6.8) are also in evidence in nouns of this type, e.g. **выраже́ние**.

| **-ник** | several uses, including: |
| | (a) | with noun roots, defining people by reference to their character, occupation or activity, e.g. |

зави́стник	envious person
защи́тник	defender (including sportsman)
помо́щник	helper

(b)   with verbal roots, defining people by reference to their actions, e.g.

| изме́нник | traitor |
| коче́вник | nomad |

(c)   denotation of objects which contain sth or accommodate some creature, e.g.

коро́вник	cowshed
кофе́йник	coffee-pot
рудни́к	mine

| **-ок** | with verbal roots, to indicate: |

(a)   a person who performs an action, e.g.

| едо́к | eater, mouth to feed |
| игро́к | player, gambler |

(b)   the action itself or its result (perhaps what is left over after it), e.g.

бросо́к	a throw, also spurt
зево́к	a yawn
обло́мок	fragment
объе́дки (pl; gen объе́дков)	leftovers (of food)
огры́зок	core (of fruit after eating)
оку́рок	cigarette-end
скачо́к	a jump, leap
спи́сок	list

Note: the **о** in this suffix as used in (b) is a mobile vowel, hence gen sg **броска́**, etc.

–ор	a suffix of foreign origin denoting an agent (cf. Eng *-or*; see also –**тор**), e.g.

| профе́ссор | *professor* |
| тра́ктор | *tractor* |

–ость	this suffix, and related suffixes (e.g. **–ность, –нность, –мость**), are the most widespread suffixes used in the formation of abstract nouns. They are particularly prevalent in R3. With adjectival roots, –**ость** is used to form feminine nouns denoting a quality (cf. Eng *-ness, -ery, -ity*, etc.), e.g.

весёлость	*gaiety*
возмо́жность	*possibility*
глу́пость	*stupidity*
мо́лодость	*youth*
му́дрость	*wisdom*
хра́брость	*bravery, courage*
че́стность	*honesty*
я́сность	*clarity*

Note: after hushing consonants this unstressed suffix becomes **–есть**, e.g. **све́жесть**, *freshness* (see 8.2.4(c)).

Added to the roots of present active participles, or to the roots of adjectives derived from them, the suffix –**ость** may be used to form nouns denoting a capacity or potentiality (cf. Eng *-ity*), e.g.

ви́димость	*visibility*
заболева́емость	*sickness rate*
необходи́мость	*necessity, inevitability*

Added to the roots of past passive participles, the suffix –**ость** may be used to form feminine nouns denoting a condition resulting from an action, e.g.

договорённость	*agreement, understanding*
изоли́рованность	*isolation*
срабо́танность	*wear and tear*

–ота́	with adjectival roots, to form abstract nouns denoting quality or condition (cf. Eng *-ness*), e.g.

быстрота́	*speed*
глухота́	*deafness*
красота́	*beauty*
острота́	*sharpness*
пустота́	*emptiness*
слепота́	*blindness*
чистота́	*cleanness, purity*

–ство	(a)	with roots of nouns referring to people, in nouns denoting position, quality, branch of activity (cf. Eng -*ship*), e.g.

а́вторство	*authorship*
крестья́нство	*peasantry*
чле́нство	*membership*

	(b)	With adjectival roots, in nouns denoting a quality or condition, e.g.

бога́тство	*richness, wealth*
одино́чество	*solitude, loneliness*
превосхо́дство	*superiority*

–тель (m)

a suffix added to the root of transitive verbs to form masculine nouns denoting an agent, usually a person, but also possibly a thing (cf. Eng -*er*, -*or*), e.g.

дви́гатель	*engine*
зри́тель	*spectator, viewer*
избира́тель	*elector, voter*
изобрета́тель	*inventor*
истреби́тель	*fighter* (aircraft)
люби́тель	*amateur*
огнетуши́тель	*fire-extinguisher*
писа́тель	*writer*
покупа́тель	*buyer, purchaser*
преподава́тель	*teacher* (in higher education)
учи́тель	*teacher* (in school)
чита́тель	*reader*

–тор

a suffix of foreign origin used to denote persons who do or things which carry out some activity denoted by a word with the suffix –**а́ция** or related suffixes (see –**а́ция**; cf. Eng -*(a)tor*), e.g.

авиа́тор	*aviator*
инкуба́тор	*incubator*
инстру́ктор	*instructor*
организа́тор	*organiser*

–ун

mainly in R1, a suffix applied to verbal roots to form nouns which define persons by reference to some action which they perform or to which they are prone, e.g.

болту́н	*chatterbox*
врун	*liar*
говору́н	*talker*
хвасту́н	*braggart*

–щик/–чик

suffixes defining persons by reference to some object or institution associated with their occupation; also denoting some objects by reference to their function, e.g.

	барабáнщик	drummer
	бомбардирóвщик	bomber, bomber pilot
	кáменщик	stone-mason, bricklayer
	счётчик	counter (person, i.e. teller, or instrument, i.e. meter)

-щина	a suffix added mainly, but not exclusively, to proper nouns, to indicate a syndrome or set of circumstances associated with a person or place, e.g.	
	ежóвщина	political terror associated with Ezhóv (chief of Stálin's secret police 1936–8)
	казёнщина	red tape
	облóмовщина	behaviour associated with Oblómov (eponymous hero of Goncharóv's novel)

-ье	with noun roots and a spatial prefix, to form nouns denoting region, e.g.	
	заполя́рье	polar region
	побере́жье	coast, littoral
	предгóрье	foothills
	примóрье	seaside

Note: the suffix -ие may also have this function, e.g. **подно́жие**, *foot* (e.g. of mountain).

8.7.2 Noun suffixes denoting females

Several suffixes denote females of a type. These suffixes may correspond to suffixes denoting males of the same type (e.g. африкáн/**ка**, female equivalent of африкáнец), or they may be added to a masculine noun in order to transform it into a feminine one (e.g. тигр/**и́ца**, *tigress*). Sometimes the masculine noun to which the female suffix is added already bears a suffix itself (as in учи́тель/**ница**, *female teacher*, where the suffix -**ница** is added to учи́/тель).

Some of the commonest female suffixes are listed below, together with a note on their relation to masculine nouns denoting people of the same type and with a few examples.

-анка/-янка	feminine equivalents of -**анец/-янец** and -**анин/-янин** (see 8.7.1; also 6.11–6.12), e.g.	
	америкáнка	American woman (m америкáнец)
	англичáнка	English woman (m англичáнин)
	италья́нка	Italian woman (m италья́нец)

	киевля́нка	*woman from Kiev* (m киевля́нин)

Note: the suffixes **-анка/-янка** may correspond simply to the masculine suffix -ец, e.g. **китая́нка**, *Chinese woman* (m кита́ец).

-иня/-ыня	ба́рыня	*noble lady* (m ба́рин)
	геройня	*heroine* (m геро́й)
	мона́хиня	*nun* (m мона́х)

-иса/-есса	suffixes of foreign origin, used in nouns of foreign origin, e.g.	
	актри́са	*actress* (m актёр)
	поэте́сса	*poetess* (m поэ́т)

-иха	added to masculine nouns denoting persons and also to some nouns denoting animals, e.g.	
	повари́ха	*cook* (m по́вар)
	слони́ха	*she-elephant* (m слон)
	труси́ха	*cowardess* (m трус)

Note: the root of the masculine noun may undergo some change before the suffix is added, e.g. **зайчи́ха**, *doe-hare* (m за́яц).

-ица	added to some masculine nouns without a suffix; also feminine equivalent of -ец (see 8.7.1), e.g.	
	краса́вица	*beautiful woman* (m краса́вец)
	певи́ца	*singer* (m певе́ц)
	цари́ца	*tsarina* (m царь)

-ка	also a feminine equivalent of -ец; added to nouns in -ист, -ич (see 8.7.1), e.g.	
	арти́стка	*artiste* (m арти́ст)
	москви́чка	*Muscovite woman* (m москви́ч)
	япо́нка	*Japanese woman* (m япо́нец)

-ница	feminine equivalent of -ник and also added to nouns in -тель (see 8.7.1), e.g.	
	рабо́тница	*worker* (m рабо́тник)
	учи́тельница	*teacher* (m учи́тель)

-ша	added to masculine nouns to denote female of the type; also (in R1, but nowadays rare) to denote wife of the male, e.g.	
	секрета́рша	*(woman) secretary* (m секрета́рь)
	генера́льша	*general's wife* (m генера́л)

-ья	added to nouns in -ун, e.g.	
	болту́нья	*chatterbox* (m болту́н)

8.7.3   Miscellaneous noun suffixes

Although the commonest noun suffixes have been dealt with in the preceding sections, there are also many others, as briefly exemplified in the following list. (Suffixes, or groups of related suffixes, are arranged in alphabetical order.)

вольт/а́ж	*voltage*
сабот/а́ж	*sabotage*
пис/а́ка (R1, pej)	*hack*
брод/я́га	*tramp, vagrant*
покрыв/а́ло	*bedspread*
интриг/а́н (R1, pej)	*intriguer*
груби/я́н (R1, pej)	*ruffian*
библиоте́к/арь (m)	*librarian*
слов/а́рь (m)	*dictionary*
старик/а́шка (R1, pej)	*old man*
борь/ба́	*struggle*
дру́ж/ба	*friendship*
жа́л/оба	*complaint*
уч/ёба	*tuition*
кла́д/бище	*cemetery*
убе́ж/ище	*refuge*
учи́л/ище	*college*
сердц/еви́на	*heart(land)*
пут/ёвка	*travel permit, pass* (to sanatorium)
плат/ёж	*payment*
сласт/ёна	*person with a sweet tooth*
пе́рв/енство	*first place, championship*
боле́/знь (f)	*illness*
боя́/знь (f)	*fear*
жи/знь (f)	*life*
то́пл/иво	*fuel*
дорогов/и́зна	*expensiveness*
нов/изна́	*novelty*
бронх/и́т	*bronchitis*
безрабо́т/ица	*unemployment*
больн/и́ца	*hospital*
пе́пель/ница	*ashtray*
владе́/лец	*owner*
буди́/льник	*alarm clock*
холоди́/льник	*refrigerator*
боле́/льщик	*fan, supporter*
колоко́ль/ня	*belfry*
па́ш/ня	*ploughed land*
то́п/от	*stamping*
шёп/от	*whisper*
бег/отня́	*scurrying*

прави́/тельство	*government*
закры́/тие	*closure*
бри/тьё	*shaving*
пас/ту́х	*shepherd*
лен/тя́й (R1)	*idler*
аспирант/у́ра	*postgraduate study, postgraduate student body*
литерат/у́ра	*literature*
дéд/ушка	*grandad*
весель/ча́к (R1)	*cheerful person*
мал/ы́ш (R1)	*kid*
обо́рв/ыш (R1)	*ragamuffin*
гнёзд/ышко (R1)	*little nest*
тел/я́тина	*veal*

8.8   Diminutive, augmentative and expressive suffixes

Russian is rich in suffixes which either indicate the size, especially smallness, of an object or are indicative of the speaker's attitude (which may be affectionate, tender, attentive or scornful, ironic, disparaging) towards it. Many suffixes may serve both a diminutive and an affectionate (hypocoristic) purpose. Note though that in certain nouns, or in some nouns when suffixes are used in certain meanings, the suffix has lost its original diminutive or hypocoristic function (e.g. when the noun **ру́чка** means the *handle* of a door).

As a rule diminutives and augmentatives are of the same gender as the noun to which the suffix is attached, even when the suffix ends with a vowel normally associated with another gender. For example, the noun **городи́шко**, *god-forsaken town*, is masculine like го́род even though nouns in -o are generally neuter.

Because they are highly expressive colloquial forms diminutives belong primarily to R1, although they are widely used in the literary variety of the written language and in folk poetry. They are less likely to be encountered in the neutral R2 and are generally altogether absent in the more formal varieties of R3, especially R3a and R3b.

The following lists of diminutive, augmentative and expressive suffixes are not exhaustive; they contain only some of the more productive suffixes.

8.8.1   Diminutive and hypocoristic suffixes

–енька	a diminutive of heightened expressiveness, used mainly with nouns denoting people and with proper names that are already in a diminutive form, e.g. Cáша:

ду́шенька	*darling*
Cа́шенька	*Sasha dear*

-ик	added to masculine nouns; may also convey scorn, e.g.	
	гво́здик	*little nail, tack*
	до́ждик	*shower*
	до́мик	*little house, cottage*
	но́сик	*spout* (of jug, teapot)
	сто́лик	*little table*
	студе́нтик	*so-called student*

-инка	diminutive form of suffix **-ина** when it denotes single specimens of an object, e.g.	
	песчи́нка	*grain of sand*
	снежи́нка	*snowflake*
	соло́минка	*piece of straw*
	чаи́нка	*tea leaf*

-ка	the most widespread diminutive suffix; added to feminine nouns; may also convey scorn, e.g.	
	голо́вка	*little head* (e.g. of pin)
	до́чка	*daughter*
	ёлка	*little fir-tree*
	иде́йка	*a silly idea*
	кры́шка	*lid*
	но́жка	*little leg, leg* (e.g. of chair)
	пе́сенка	*a (nice) song*
	ру́чка	*little hand, handle* (e.g. of door), *arm* (e.g. of chair)
	стре́лка	*little arrow, hand* (e.g. of clock)
	ча́шка	*cup*

-ок/-ёк	added to masculine nouns, which may have to undergo a final consonant change to accommodate the suffix (see 8.2.5); may also convey scorn, e.g.	
	ветеро́к	*breeze*
	городо́к	*small town*
	дурачо́к	*idiot, clot*
	конёк	*hobby-horse*

-це (-ице)/-цо́ (-ецо́)	added to neuter nouns, e.g.	
	зе́ркальце	*little mirror* (e.g. in car)
	пла́тьице	*little dress*
	деревцо́	*small tree*

-чик	added to masculine nouns ending in **в, й, л, м, н, р**, e.g.	
	бараба́нчик	*little drum*
	бли́нчик	*pancake*

| колоко́льчик | little bell |
| рома́нчик | novel (pej) |

8.8.2   Double diminutive suffixes

Some suffixes are really double diminutive suffixes. They may help to form nouns denoting particularly small objects or they may serve as terms of special endearment.

–о́чек	added to masculine nouns, e.g.	
	листо́чек	tiny little leaf
	цвето́чек	little flower

–е́чко	added to neuter nouns, e.g.	
	месте́чко	little place
	слове́чко	little word

–очка/-ечка/-ичка	added to feminine nouns, e.g.	
	звёздочка	tiny little star, asterisk
	стре́лочка	tiny little arrow, little hand (e.g. on watch)
	води́чка	nice little (bottle/drink of) water
	сестри́чка	dear little sister

8.8.3   The augmentative suffix -ище/-ища

-ище is added to masculine and neuter nouns, **-ища** to feminine nouns, e.g.

| городи́ще | a very large town |
| бороди́ща | a massive beard |

8.8.4   Pejorative suffixes

The basic function of pejorative suffixes is to indicate scorn or contempt on the part of the speaker or writer towards the person or object in question. At the same time these suffixes may also have a quite different function, i.e. they may express affection in an ironic tone (cf. the possible affectionate nuance of diminutive forms of first names in –ка (7.3.1)). The main pejorative suffixes are:

| **–и́шка/-и́шко** | The suffix **-и́шка** may be added to masculine animate and feminine nouns; **-и́шко** may be added to masculine inanimate and neuter nouns, e.g. |

лгуни́шка (m)	*a wretched liar*
городи́шко (m)	*an awful town*
письми́шко (n)	*letter* (pej)

Note: the form **брати́шка**, *brother*, on the other hand, is affectionate.

-ёнка/-о́нка	This suffix is applied mainly to feminine nouns. The form **-о́нка** follows hushing consonants, which may result from a consonant change in the root of the noun when the suffix is added. Examples:

бабёнка	*foul old hag* (or *dear old woman!*)
лошадёнка	*wretched nag*
книжо́нка	*dreadful book*
собачо́нка	*cur* (or *a dog one is fond of!*)

8.9 The principal adjectival suffixes

In this section some of the more common adjectival suffixes are given. Closely related suffixes are treated together.

Note: **-о́й** is used when the ending is stressed.

-анный/-янный **-аный/-ано́й** **-яный/ -яно́й**	variations on the same suffix, used in many adjectives indicating the material or thing from which sth is made, e.g.

деревя́нный	*wooden*
стекля́нный	*glass*
ко́жаный	*leather*
ржано́й	*rye*
шерстяно́й	*woollen*

Note: there are also many adjectives denoting material which do not have one of these suffixes, e.g. **желе́зный**, *iron*, **шёлковый**, *silk*.

-атый	a suffix indicating that the thing denoted by the noun from which the adjective is derived is characteristic of or conspicuous in the subject, e.g.

борода́тый	*bearded*
крыла́тый	*winged*
полоса́тый	*striped*

Note: **жена́тый**, *married* (of man to woman, i.e. *having a wife*), belongs in this category.

-енький/-онький	diminutive suffixes which carry a nuance of smallness, tenderness or sometimes disparagement; **-онький** is used after the velars **г, к, х**:

бе́ленький	*little white*
ми́ленький	*dear, sweet*

хоро́шенький	*pretty*
ти́хонький	*quiet little*

-ивый, -ливый, -чивый	suffixes which may be applied to noun or verbal roots and which indicate that the subject is inclined or prone to some conduct, e.g.

красноречи́вый	*eloquent*
лени́вый	*lazy*
молчали́вый	*taciturn*
терпели́вый	*patient, tolerant*
дове́рчивый	*trustful, credulous*
заду́мчивый	*pensive*

-ин	in R1, indicating possession; applied to roots of nouns in **-а/-я** denoting people, including diminutive forms of first names, e.g.

ма́мин	*mum's*
па́пин	*dad's*
Пе́тин	*Pete's*
Та́нин	*Tania's*

Note: these adjectives are similar in meaning to adjectives from the same roots in -**инский** and adjectives in -**овский/-евский**, e.g. **матери́нский, никола́евский** (see section (c) under the suffix -**ский** below). However, whereas adjectives in -**ин** tend to indicate possession by a particular individual, the forms in -**инский**, etc. denote general association with a person or type of person.

-ний	used in a number of common adjectives indicating place or time, sometimes with the help of a further letter or morpheme between root and ending. These adjectives are important because their flexions cannot be explained by the spelling rules which normally dictate variations from the standard type of adjectival ending (see 9.3.1), and they therefore need to be studied carefully.

по́здний	*late*
ра́нний	*early*
весе́нний	*spring*
ле́тний	*summer*
осе́нний	*autumn(al)*
зи́мний	*winter*
у́тренний	*morning*
вече́рний	*evening*
вчера́шний	*yesterday's*
сего́дняшний	*today's*
за́втрашний	*tomorrow's*
ны́нешний	*present-day*
да́вний	*of long standing*
дре́вний	*ancient*
пре́жний	*former, previous*

после́дний	*last*
бли́жний	*near, neighbouring*
да́льний	*far, distant*
ве́рхний	*upper*
ни́жний	*lower*
пере́дний	*front*
за́дний	*back*
вне́шний	*outer, external*
вну́тренний	*inner, internal*
сре́дний	*middle, medium, average*
кра́йний	*extreme*
посторо́нний	*extraneous*
дома́шний	*domestic*
ли́шний	*superfluous*

–ный/–но́й
the most common adjectival ending applied to inanimate nouns, including nouns of foreign origin, with the meanings *relating to* or *consisting of*, or denoting possession of the quality to which the noun refers, e.g.

во́дный	*(relating to) water*
вре́дный	*harmful*
перехо́дный	*transitional*
спо́рный	*debatable*
транзи́тный	*transit*
шу́мный	*noisy*
глазно́й	*eye*
головно́й	*head*
зубно́й	*tooth, dental*
лесно́й	*forest*

There are many further suffixes that are developed on the basis of this suffix, including suffixes of foreign origin which are applied to foreign roots, e.g.

суд/е́бный	*judicial*
госуда́рств/енный	*state*
неб/е́сный	*heavenly*
втор/и́чный	*secondary*
купа́/льный	*bathing*
верх/о́вный	*supreme*
душ/е́вный	*heartfelt*
убеди́/тельный	*convincing*
теа́тр/а́льный	*theatrical*
элемент/а́рный	*elementary*
прогре́сс/и́вный	*progressive*

–ова́тый/–ева́тый
used to indicate that a quality is possessed in some degree (cf. Eng *-ish*); especially common with adjectives of colour, e.g.

белова́тый	*whitish*

| | кислова́тый | *a bit sour* |
| | синева́тый | *bluish* |

–овый/–ово́й –евый/–ево́й	used with inanimate nouns. (English may make no distinction between the equivalent adjective and the noun which possesses the quality denoted by the adjective.) Examples:	
	бамбу́ковый	*bamboo*
	берёзовый	*birch*
	боково́й	*side*
	боево́й	*combat*

| –ский/–ско́й | (a) | An extremely widespread suffix that is applied to the roots of nouns, mainly masculine, to form adjectives indicating relationship to the thing denoted by the root. Many adjectives denoting nationality or describing place of origin (see 6.11–6.12) or a person's designation contain this suffix, e.g. | |

	а́вторский	*author's, authorial*
	де́тский	*child's, infantile*
	же́нский	*wife's, female*
	ма́йский	*May*
	городско́й	*town, urban*
	донско́й	*(relating to the River) Don*

(b)   There is a very large number of adjectives, formed from roots of international currency, which end in –и́ческий (cf. Eng -*ic*/-*ical*), e.g.

	географи́ческий	*geographical*
	климати́ческий	*climatic*
	реалисти́ческий	*realistic*

There are also many other adjectives in –и́ческий, formed from nouns of international currency in –ика (see 8.7.1). (Strictly speaking the suffix in these adjectives is –еский.) Examples:

| | математи́ческий | *mathematical* |
| | экономи́ческий | *economic* |

(c)   Numerous other adjectival suffixes are developed on the basis of –ский, e.g.

	африк/а́нский	*African*
	венец/иа́нский	*Venetian*
	итал/ья́нский	*Italian*
	рожд/е́ственский	*Christmas*
	альп/и́йский	*Alpine*
	матер/и́нский	*maternal*
	отц/о́вский	*paternal*
	ма́рт/овский	*March*
	никола́/евский	*(relating to Tsar) Nicholas*

8.10 Suffixes of participial origin

Many words of participial origin which bear one of the following suffixes have become established in the language as adjectives.

–аный/–еный/ –ёный	suffixes indicating that some process has been carried out. Many of the adjectives with this suffix are culinary terms. Examples:

рва́ный	*torn, lacerated*
жа́реный	*roast(ed)*
ра́неный	*wounded, injured*
сушёный	*dried*

–ачий/–ячий –учий/–ючий	adjectives derived from Old Russian participial forms which stand alongside active participles in -щий from the same verbal roots. (In cases where the use of a form of this type is restricted the adjective is given in a phrase in which it commonly occurs.) Examples:

лежа́чий	*lying, recumbent*
горя́чий	*hot* (cf. горя́щий, *burning*)
сидя́чий	*sedentary*
стоя́чая вода́	*stagnant* (i.e. *standing*) *water*
лету́чая мышь	*bat* (i.e. *flying mouse*)
колю́чий	*prickly*

–лый	adjectives derived from the roots of some intransitive verbs and describing a condition that is the result of some process, e.g.

быва́лый	*worldly-wise*
вя́лый	*limp*
зре́лый	*mature*
отста́лый	*backward*
уста́лый	*tired*

–мый/–емый	used in the formation of present passive participles (see 9.7.5; cf. Eng *-able, -ible*), many of which have become established as adjectives and which occur most commonly in R3. Participles of this type have also given rise to many adjectives with the prefix **не-** (cf. Eng *-in/un-*), e.g.

осяза́емый	*tangible*
допусти́мый	*admissible*
несгора́емый	*fireproof*
неуязви́мый	*invulnerable*

–нный/–енный/ –ённый	suffixes used to form the past passive participles of many verbs (see 9.7.6; cf. Eng *-ed*), e.g.

взволно́ванный	*agitated*
уме́ренный	*moderate*
истощённый	*exhausted* (i.e. *used up*)

-тый	used to form the past passive participle of verbs of certain types (see 9.7.6; cf. Eng -*ed*), some of which have become established as adjectives, e.g.

за́нятый	*occupied*
избитый	*beaten*; also *hackneyed*
смя́тый	*crumpled*

-ший	used to form past active participles (see 9.7.4), a few of which have become established as adjectives, e.g.

бы́вший	*former*
проше́дший	*past*
сумасше́дший	*mad*

-щий	used to form present active participles (see 9.7.3), many of which have become established as adjectives, e.g.

блестя́щий	*brilliant*
подходя́щий	*suitable*
сле́дующий	*following*

8.11   The verbal suffixes -ничать and -ануть

There are many suffixes that are used in the formation of the infinitive and stems of verbs. As a rule verbal suffixes do not bear specific meaning, but it is worth noting here two suffixes which do indicate certain types of action and which are characteristic of R1 and D respectively.

(a)   **-ничать**: used in R1 to form imperfectives, often with a jocular tone, which describe a certain pattern of behaviour, e.g.

бродя́жничать	*to be a tramp* (from бродя́га)
во́льничать	*to take liberties*
ехи́дничать	*to be malicious, go in for innuendo*
жема́нничать	*to behave in an affected way*
секре́тничать	*to be secretive*
скро́мничать	*to be over-modest*
скря́жничать	*to behave like a miser*

(b)   **-ануть**: used freely in D, to form highly expressive semelfactive perfectives indicating that an action was carried out suddenly on one occasion, e.g.

резану́ть	*to cut*
сказану́ть	*to blurt out*
тряхану́ть	*to shake*
чесану́ть	*to scratch*
шагану́ть	*to step*

8.12 Composition

8.12.1 Compound nouns

Russian has many nouns which have been formed by the various types of composition or abbreviation illustrated below.

compound hyphenated nouns	га́лстук-ба́бочка (m)	*bow tie*
	шко́ла-интерна́т (f)	*boarding-school*
	штаб-кварти́ра (f)	*headquarters*

Note: the gender of such nouns is that of the key noun of the pair, which is generally the first noun (as in the first two examples above), but may also be the second noun (as in the third example).

stump compounds

This type of word-formation was rarely used in pre-revolutionary times but became common in the 1920s, particularly in relation to political and administrative innovations in the early Soviet period. Examples:

авиа/ба́за	*air base*
авто/тра́нспорт	*road transport*
гос/безопа́сность (f)	*state security*
Гос/ду́ма (Государственная ду́ма)	*State Duma (Russian parliament)*
Евро/сою́з (Европейский сою́з)	*European Union, EU*
зав/ка́федрой (R1/2; заве́дующий ка́федрой)	*head of department*
зар/пла́та	*wages, pay, salary*
кол/хо́з (коллекти́вное хозя́йство)	*collective farm*
лин/ко́р (лине́йный кора́бль)	*battleship*
нарко/би́знес	*(illegal) drugs business*
проф/сою́з	*trade union*
са́м/бо (n, indecl; само/оборо́на без ору́жия)	*unarmed combat*
сек/со́т (секре́тный сотру́дник)	*secret agent*
стен/газе́та (стенна́я газе́та)	*wall newspaper*
тер/а́кт (террористи́ческий акт)	*terrorist act*
физ/культу́ра (физи́ческая культу́ра)	*physical training*
эс/ми́нец (эска́дренный миноно́сец)	*destroyer (naval)*

Note: nouns of this type fall within the normal declensional pattern (see 9.1.2) and their gender is determined by their ending in the usual way.

abbreviated nouns	метро́ (метрополите́н)	*underground (railway system)*
	Пи́тер (R1; Петербу́рг)	*St Petersburg*
acronyms	вуз (вы́сшее уче́бное заведе́ние)	*higher educational institution*
	СПИД (синдро́м приобретённого иммунного дефици́та)	*AIDS*

See also e.g. бомж, ЗАГС (6.10).

Note: nouns of this type fall within the normal declensional pattern (see 9.1.2) and their gender is determined as a rule in the usual way.

8.12.2   Compound adjectives

The following list gives examples of the process of adjectival formation through various types of composition.

земледе́ль/ческий	root of compound noun + adj suffix	*agricultural*
желе́зно/доро́жный	adj + adj derived from noun	*railway*
мно́го/чи́сленный	adv + adj derived from noun	*numerous*
ди́ко/расту́щий	adv + pres act part	*(growing) wild*
свѐтло-/зелёный	two adj roots	*light green*
а̀нгло-/ру́сский	two adj denoting equivalent concepts	*Anglo-Russian*
двух/ле́тний	numeral + adj derived from noun	*two-year, biennial*
все/сторо́нний	pron + adj	*thorough*
еже/го́дный	pron + adj	*annual*
огне/упо́рный	adj derived from two noun roots	*fireproof*

9 Inflection

Russian is a highly inflected language. Meaning is much more dependent on the ending of words and less dependent on word order than is the case in English. Without a thorough knowledge of the many flexions used on Russian nouns, pronouns, adjectives, numerals and verbs it is impossible not only to speak and write Russian correctly but even to arrive at an accurate understanding of what one hears or reads.

However, the difficulty of learning the numerous flexions is not so great as seems at first to be the case if the learner keeps in mind the distinction between hard and soft consonants and the spelling rules listed in 8.2.1 and 8.2.4 and takes the trouble to study the basic declensional and conjugational patterns set out in this chapter.

9.1 Declension of the noun

The Russian declensional system has six cases and distinguishes between singular and plural. The six cases are nominative, accusative, genitive, dative, instrumental and prepositional. There is a very small number of relics of the vocative case and dual number (see Glossary). Some nouns exist only in a plural form (e.g. **су́тки**), at least in certain meanings (e.g. **часы́**, *clock*; 3.6.1). Some nouns borrowed from other languages are indeclinable (9.1.12).

9.1.1 Gender

The gender of most nouns is easily determined:

masculine

(a) all nouns ending in a hard consonant, e.g. стол;

(b) all nouns ending in -**й**, e.g. музе́й;

(c) a minority of nouns ending in -**ь**, especially:

  i. all those denoting males, e.g. зять, *son-in-law* or *brother-in-law*;

  ii. nouns ending in the suffix -**тель** (see 8.7.1), e.g. покупа́тель, *shopper*;

(d) some nouns in -**a** and -**я** which denote males or people who may be of either sex, e.g. мужчи́на, *man*; дя́дя, *uncle*; слуга́, *servant*.

neuter

(a) most nouns in -**о**, e.g. окно́, *window*;

(b) most nouns in -**е**, e.g. мо́ре, *sea*; упражне́ние, *exercise*; except подмасте́рье, *apprentice* (m);

(c) all nouns in -**ё**, e.g. ружьё, *gun*.

Note: nouns derived from masculine nouns with the diminutive or pejorative suffix -**йшко** (8.8.4) are masculine.

feminine   (a)   most nouns ending in **-а**, e.g. де́вушка, *girl*; кни́га, *book*;

(b)   most nouns ending in **-я**, e.g. тётя, *aunt*; ба́шня, *tower*;

(c)   the majority of nouns ending in **-ь**, especially:

    i.   nouns denoting females, e.g. мать, *mother*;

   ii.   nouns in which the soft sign is preceded by one of the hushing consonants **ж**, **ч**, **ш**, or **щ**, e.g. рожь, *rye*; ночь, *night*; мышь, *mouse*; вещь, *thing*;

  iii.   abstract nouns ending in **-ость** or **-есть**, e.g. мо́лодость, *youth*; све́жесть, *freshness*.

Note: nouns derived from animate masculine nouns with the pejorative suffix **-ишка** (see 8.8.4) are masculine.

A few nouns, e.g. **сирота́**, *orphan*, are of common gender, i.e. they may be either masculine or feminine depending on whether they denote a male or female.

On the gender of indeclinable nouns see 9.1.12.

9.1.2   Basic declensional patterns of the noun

The main declensional types may be classified according to gender.

For the purposes of this book Russian nouns are treated as divisible into ten basic declensional patterns (three masculine, three neuter and four feminine). These patterns are illustrated below by the paradigms of the nouns **автобус**, *bus*; **трамва́й**, *tram*; **сти́ль**, *style*; **сло́во**, *word*; **по́ле**, *field*; **зда́ние**, *building*; **газе́та**, *newspaper*; **неде́ля**, *week*; **фами́лия**, *surname*; and **кость**, *bone*. Groups of nouns, individual nouns, and particular case endings which do not conform to these patterns are dealt with in sections 9.1.3 to 9.1.12 inclusive.

Note: many of the nouns which have been chosen to illustrate the various declensional types and whose paradigms are given below have fixed stress. However, the stress patterns of Russian nouns are complex, and in several of the declensional categories nouns of various stress patterns are to be found. On stress see Chapter 12.

		Hard endings		**Soft endings**	
		sg	**pl**	**sg**	**pl**
masculine[a]	nom	автобус	автобусы[c]	трамва́й	трамва́и
	acc	автобус	автобусы	трамва́й	трамва́и
	gen	автобуса	автобусов[d]	трамва́я	трамва́ев
	dat	автобусу	автобусам	трамва́ю	трамва́ям
	instr	автобусом[b]	автобусами	трамва́ем	трамва́ями
	prep	автобусе	автобусах	трамва́е	трамва́ях
				сти́ль	сти́ли
				сти́ль	сти́ли
				сти́ля	сти́лей
				сти́лю	сти́лям
				сти́лем	сти́лями
				сти́ле	сти́лях

neuter					
	nom	сло́во	слова́[e]	по́ле[f]	поля́[g]
	acc	сло́во	слова́	по́ле	поля́
	gen	сло́ва[e]	слов	по́ля[g]	полей
	dat	сло́ву	слова́м	по́лю	поля́м
	instr	сло́вом	слова́ми	по́лем	поля́ми
	prep	сло́ве	слова́х	по́ле	поля́х
				зда́ние	зда́ния
				зда́ние	зда́ния
				зда́ния	зда́ний
				зда́нию	зда́ниям
				зда́нием	зда́ниями
				зда́нии	зда́ниях

feminine					
	nom	газе́та	газе́ты[i]	неде́ля	неде́ли
	acc	газе́ту[h]	газе́ты[i]	неде́лю	неде́ли
	gen	газе́ты[i]	газе́т	неде́ли	неде́ль[l]
	dat	газе́те	газе́там	неде́ле	неде́лям
	instr	газе́той[j]	газе́тами	неде́лей[k]	неде́лями
	prep	газе́те	газе́тах	неде́ле	неде́лях
				фами́лия	фами́лии
				фами́лию	фами́лии
				фами́лии	фами́лий
				фами́лии	фами́лиям
				фами́лией	фами́лиями
				фами́лии	фами́лиях
				кость	ко́сти
				кость	ко́сти
				ко́сти	косте́й
				ко́сти	костя́м[m]
				ко́стью	костя́ми
				ко́сти	костя́х

[a] All the examples of masculine nouns given here denote inanimate objects. In nouns of the animate category the accusative form coincides in both singular and plural with the genitive (see 11.1.3).

[b] The instrumental singular form in unstressed endings after a hushing consonant is –ем, e.g. му́жем, from муж, *husband*. However, the ending –ом is retained after hushing consonants if stress is on the ending, e.g. ножо́м, from нож, *knife*.

[c] Nouns with stems in г, к, х, ж, ч, ш, щ have nominative/accusative plural in -и, e.g. враги́, *enemies*; со́ки, *juices*; ножи́, *knives*; карандаши́, *pencils*.

[d] Nouns in ж, ч, ш, щ have genitive plural in -ей, e.g. ножей, карандаше́й.

[e] Many nouns in -о distinguish genitive singular from nominative/accusative plural by means of stress, though the stress shift in the plural forms may be forward (e.g. gen sg окна́ but nom/acc pl о́кна) rather than back as is the case in сло́во. See also Chapter 12 on stress.

[f] Nouns with stem in ж, ц, ч, ш, щ have endings with **a** for **я** and **y** for **ю**; thus кла́дбище, *cemetery*, has gen sg кла́дбища, dat sg кла́дбищу, nom/acc pl кла́дбища, dat/instr/prep pl кла́дбищам, кла́дбищами, кла́дбищах, respectively.

ᵍ The same considerations of stress apply here as to сло́во (see note e above).

ʰ Feminine nouns of the animate category have accusative forms that coincide with the genitive in the plural only, e.g. acc pl же́нщин, but acc sg же́нщину.

ⁱ (a) Nouns with stems in **г, к, х, ж, ч, ш, щ** have **и** for **ы**, e.g. ногá, *leg*, has gen sg ноги́, nom/acc pl но́ги. (b) Some nouns in -**a** distinguish genitive singular from nominative/accusative plural by means of stress shift, e.g. ноги́, но́ги (see notes e and g above).

ʲ (i) The instrumental singular form in unstressed endings after a hushing consonant is -**ей**, e.g. больни́цей, from больни́ца, *hospital*. However, the ending -**ой** is retained after hushing consonants if stress is on the ending, e.g. душо́й from душá, *soul*. (ii) An instrumental singular form in -**ою** is also found (e.g. газе́тою), but in the modern language this form is used mainly in literary contexts or in poetry where the metre requires an additional syllable.

ᵏ An instrumental singular ending in -**ею** may also be found, in the same circumstances as -ою (see note j (ii) above).

ˡ The zero ending which occurs in the genitive plural forms of nouns in -**a** is in effect retained, the soft sign merely serving to indicate that the consonant remains soft in this case just as it is when followed by any of the vowels used in the other endings of this declension.

ᵐ Nouns ending in -**жь, -чь, -шь, -щь** have **a** for **я**, e.g. dat/instr/prep pl forms ночáм, ночáми, ночáх from ночь, *night*; вещáм, вещáми, вещáх, from вещь, *thing*.

9.1.3 Mobile vowels

Many masculine nouns have a mobile vowel, i.e. **o** or **e** or **ё**, which is found in the last syllable of the nominative/accusative singular form but which disappears in all other cases, e.g.

nom/acc sg	gen sg
кусо́к, *piece*	**кускá**
ого́нь, *fire*	**огня́**
ве́тер, *wind*	**ве́тра**
день, *day*	**дня**
козёл, *goat*	**козлá**
шатёр, *tent*	**шатрá**

Note 1   When a mobile **e** follows the letter **л** it must be replaced by **ь** in order to indicate that the **л** remains soft, e.g. **лев**, *lion*, has gen sg **льва.**

2   The feminine nouns **вошь**, *louse*; **ложь**, *lie*; **любо́вь**, *love*, and **рожь**, *rye*, lose their **o** in all oblique cases except the instrumental singular. Thus любо́вь has gen/dat/prep sg **любви́**, but instr sg **любо́вью.**

9.1.4 Genitive singular forms in -у/-ю

- A small number of masculine nouns, including a few abstract nouns, may have genitive singular forms in -**y** (or -**ю** if they have a soft stem). These forms may be used when the genitive has partitive meaning (i.e. when it denotes a quantity of sth), e.g.

купи́ть горо́ху, лу́ку, ри́су   *to buy some peas, onions, rice*
буты́лка коньяку́, лимона́ду   *a bottle of brandy, lemonade*

ба́нка мёду	*a jar of honey*
доста́ть кероси́ну, кле́ю, ме́лу,	*to get some paraffin, glue, chalk,*
миндалю́, пе́рцу,	*almonds, pepper,*
скипида́ру, тёсу	*turpentine, planks*
мно́го наро́ду, шу́му	*a lot of people, noise*
па́чка са́хару	*a packet of sugar*
кило́ сы́ру, чесноку́	*a kilo of cheese, garlic*
стака́н ча́ю	*a glass of tea*

Note 1   The normal genitive forms for such nouns must be used whenever a genitive is used with any meaning other than partitive meaning (e.g. цвет **мёда**, *the colour of honey*), or when the noun is qualified by an adjective, e.g. стака́н **кре́пкого ча́я**, *a glass of strong tea*.

    2   Even when the meaning is partitive the forms in –у and –ю are now infrequently used in R2/R3, except in the established phrases мно́го наро́ду and стака́н ча́ю. They are perhaps more widespread in R1 and among older speakers.

•   Genitive endings in **–у** or **–ю** also occur in some set phrases including a preposition which governs the genitive case. In this use they persist in all registers, though many of the phrases tend to be colloquial. The examples below are arranged in order according to the preposition which governs the noun in question.

Note: the stress tends to be capricious in such phrases.

бе́з году неде́ля (R1)	*only a few days*
без ро́ду, без пле́мени	*without kith or kin*
говори́ть без у́молку	*to talk incessantly*
ну́жно до заре́зу	*needed urgently*
не до сме́ху	*in no mood for laughter*
упусти́ть что́-н и́з виду	*to overlook sth*
Ей пять лет о́т роду.	*She is five years old.*
с гла́зу на́ глаз	*eyeball-to-eyeball*
умере́ть с го́лоду	*to starve to death*
кри́кнуть с испу́гу	*to cry out from fright*
спи́ться с кру́гу	*to go to seed from drink*
сбива́ть/сбить кого́-н с то́лку	*to confuse sb*

9.1.5   Locative singular forms in -у́/-ю́

Quite a large number of masculine nouns which denote inanimate objects have a special prepositional singular ending (**-у́** after hard consonants, **-ю́** when the nominative ends in **-й**) when they are used after **в** or **на** in a locative sense (i.e. when they indicate the place where sth is situated or happening). In a few cases usage wavers between this form and the normal ending for such nouns (**-e**), in which case the irregular ending may seem more colloquial.

в аэропорту́ (R1)	*at the airport*
на балу́	*at a ball* (dance)
на берегу́	*on the bank/shore*

на боку́	*on (one's) side*
на борту́	*on board* (ship, plane)
в бою́	*in battle*
в бреду́	*in a fever/delirium*
в глазу́	*in the eye*
в году́	*in a year*
на Дону́	*on the (River) Don*
в жару́	*in the heat*
на краю́	*on the edge*
в кругу́	*in a circle*
в Крыму́	*in the Crimea*
на лбу́	*on (one's) forehead*
в лесу́	*in the forest*
на лугу́	*in the meadow*
на льду́	*on ice*
в меду́	*in honey*
в мозгу́	*in the brain*
на мосту́	*on the bridge*
на носу́	*on (one's) nose*
в отпуску́ (R1; в о́тпуске in R2/3)	*on leave*
в полку́	*in a regiment*
на полу́	*on the floor*
в порту́	*in port*
весь/вся в поту́	*bathed in sweat*
в пруду́	*in the pool*
в раю́	*in paradise*
во рту́	*in (one's) mouth*
в ряду́	*in a row* (tier)
в саду́	*in a garden/orchard*
в снегу́	*in the snow*
в строю́	*in service*
в углу́	*in the corner*
в цвету́	*in bloom*
в часу́	*in an hour*
в шкафу́	*in the cupboard*

Note 1 The locative ending in -у́ is also embodied in various set expressions, e.g. име́ть в виду́, *to have in mind*; в про́шлом году́, *last year*; В кото́ром часу́? *At what time?*

2 Not all the nouns in the list above invariably have locative singular in -у́/-ю́; in certain meanings or phraseological combinations they may have the regular ending in -е, e.g. в Краснода́рском кра́е, *in the Krasnodar region*; в по́те лица́, *by the sweat of one's brow*; в це́лом ря́де слу́чаев, *in a whole series of instances*.

3 The endings -у́/-ю́ are used only after в and на, not after the other prepositions, о, по and при, which may govern the prepositional case (thus в лесу́/краю́ but о ле́се/кра́е).

4 Even after в and на the special locative endings are only used when the meaning is literally locative, and not in such phrases as знать толк в ле́се, *to be knowledgeable about timber*; в 'Вишнёвом са́де', *in 'The Cherry Orchard'* (i.e. Chékhov's play); в 'Ти́хом До́не', *in 'Quiet Flows the Don'* (i.e. Shólokhov's novel).

9.1.6 Masculine nouns with nominative plural in -á/-я

Over the last two hundred years the endings -á (after hard consonants) and -я (after soft consonants) have been steadily extended to more and more masculine nouns (both nouns of Russian origin and nouns of foreign origin). Some such nouns denote objects which, when referred to in the plural, usually occur in pairs and some are nouns of foreign origin ending in -op or -ep. Many of the indigenous nouns have stress on the first syllable in the singular.

In many instances the plural in -á/-я is now firmly established as the only possible plural for the noun in question. In other instances both the form in -á/-я and a regular form in -ы (-и after soft consonants, velars and hushing consonants) are possible, in which case the form in -á/-я may have a colloquial or popular flavour or may belong to the professional jargon of a particular group.

Note: most of the nouns in the following lists (which are not exhaustive) are inanimate and their accusative plural form is therefore the same as the nominative plural form given here; animate nouns, on the other hand, have accusative plural forms which coincide with the genitive plural form.

- Nouns with firmly established plural in -á/-я:

áдрес, *address*	адресá
бег, *race*	бегá
бéрег, *shore, bank* (of river)	берегá
бок, *side* (see 4.1)	бокá
борт, *side* (of ship)	бортá
бýфер, *buffer*	буферá
вéер, *fan*	веерá
век, *century, age*	векá

Note: the obsolete form вéки persists in certain set expressions, e.g. **в кóи-то вéки**, *once in a blue moon*; **во вéки вéкóв**, *for all time*.

вéксель, *bill of exchange*	векселя́
вéчер, *evening*	вечерá
глаз, *eye*	глазá
гóлос, *voice, vote*	голосá
гóрод, *town*	городá
дирéктор, *manager, headmaster*	директорá
дóктор, *doctor*	докторá
дом, *house*	домá
жёлоб, *gutter, trough*	желобá
жéмчуг, *pearl*	жемчугá
зáкром, *cornbin, granary* (rhet)	закромá
инспéктор, *inspector*	инспекторá
кáтер, *small boat*	катерá
кóлокол, *bell*	колоколá
край, *edge, region*	края́
кýпол, *cupola, dome*	куполá

лéмех, *ploughshare*	**лемехá**
лес, *forest*	**лесá**
луг, *meadow*	**лугá**
мáстер, *craftsman*	**мастерá**
нóмер, *number, hotel room*	**номерá**
обшлáг, *cuff*	**обшлагá**
óкруг, *district*	**округá**
óрдер, *order, warrant, writ*	**ордерá**
óстров, *island*	**островá**
óтпуск, *(period of) leave*	**отпускá**
пáрус, *sail*	**парусá**
пáспорт, *passport*	**паспортá**
пéрепел, *quail*	**перепелá**
пóвар, *cook*	**поварá**
пóгреб, *cellar*	**погребá**
пóезд, *train*	**поездá**
профéссор, *professor*	**профессорá**
рог, *horn*	**рогá**
рукáв, *sleeve*	**рукавá**
свúтер, *sweater*	**свитерá**
снег, *snow*	**снегá**
сорт, *sort*	**сортá**
стог, *stack, rick*	**стогá**
стóрож, *watchman*	**сторожá**
тéнор, *tenor* (mus)	**тенорá**
тéтерев, *black grouse*	**тетеревá**
том, *volume*	**томá**
флúгель, *wing* (of building)	**флигеля́**
флю́гер, *weather-vane*	**флюгерá**
хлев, *cattle-shed, pigsty*	**хлевá**
хóлод, *cold spell*	**холодá**
ху́тор, *farmstead*	**хуторá**
чéреп, *skull*	**черепá**
шáфер, *best man* (at wedding)	**шаферá**
шёлк, *silk*	**шелкá**
шу́лер, *card-sharp, cheat*	**шулерá**
я́корь, *anchor*	**якоря́**

- Nouns whose standard nominative plural form may be felt to be **-ы/-и** but which may have **-á/-я́** in R1, D, or professional jargon. Forms marked † may be particularly frowned upon in the standard language.

бу́нкер, *bunker*	**бункерá/бу́нкеры**
бухгáлтер, *book-keeper, accountant*	**†бухгалтерá/бухгáлтеры**
год, *year*	**годá/гóды**
дóговóр, *treaty, pact*	**договорá/договóры**
констру́ктор, *designer, constructor*	**†конструкторá/констру́кторы**
крéйсер, *cruiser* (naval)	**крейсерá/крéйсеры**
ку́зов, *body* (of carriage)	**кузовá/ку́зовы**

пе́карь, *baker*	**пекаря́/пе́кари**
прожёктор, *searchlight*	**прожектора́/прожёкторы**
реда́ктор, *editor*	**†редактора́/реда́кторы**
ре́ктор, *rector* (head of higher educational institution)	**ректора́/ре́кторы**
се́ктор, *sector*	**сектора́/се́кторы**
слёсарь, *metal-worker, locksmith*	**слесаря́/слёсари**
то́поль, *poplar tree*	**тополя́/то́поли**
тра́ктор, *tractor*	**трактора́/тра́кторы**
цех, *workshop*	**цеха́/це́хи**
шофёр, *chauffeur*	**шофера́/шофёры**
шторм, *gale* (nautical)	**шторма́/што́рмы**

9.1.7 Irregularities in the genitive plural of nouns

There are more irregularities that affect this case than any other, viz:

insertion of o or e

(a) affects many feminine and neuter nouns in which loss of final **a** or **o** of the nominative singular forms leaves a zero ending, e.g.

бе́лка, *squirrel*	**бе́лок**
ви́лка, *fork*	**ви́лок**
окно́, *window*	**о́кон**
де́вочка, *small girl*	**де́вочек**
дере́вня, *village*	**дереве́нь**
метла́, *broom*	**мётел**

(b) **e** also occurs in the genitive plural forms of most neuter nouns in **-це** and **-цо́**, e.g.

полоте́нце, *towel*	**полоте́нец**
се́рдце, *heart*	**серде́ц**
кольцо́, *ring*	**коле́ц**
крыльцо́, *porch*	**крыле́ц**

Note: яйцо́, *egg*, has **яи́ц**.

(c) **e** also occurs in feminine and neuter nouns in which the first of two consonants preceding the final **a** or **o** is soft, as indicated by a soft sign, e.g.

письмо́, *letter*	**пи́сем**
сва́дьба, *wedding*	**сва́деб**
тюрьма́, *prison*	**тю́рем**

Note: про́сьба, *request*, has **про́сьб**.

change of й to e

affects feminine nouns ending in **-йка**, e.g.

балала́йка, *balalaika*	**балала́ек**
га́йка, *nut*	**га́ек**
ко́йка, *bunk, berth*	**ко́ек**
копе́йка, *kopeck*	**копе́ек**

ча́йка, *seagull*   **ча́ек**

ша́йка, *gang*   **ша́ек**

zero ending

some masculine nouns ending in a hard consonant have a genitive plural form that is the same as the nominative singular form, e.g. **раз**, *time, occasion*. Other nouns with this so-called zero ending include:

(a) some nouns which, when used in the plural, refer to pairs of things, e.g.

боти́нок	*(ankle-high) boot*
ва́ленок	*felt boot*
глаз	*eye*
пого́н	*(military) shoulder strap*
сапо́г	*boot*
чуло́к	*stocking*

- But **носко́в** (from носо́к, *sock*).

(b) the names of certain nationalities, including those formed with the suffix –**нин** (see 6.11–6.12), e.g.

англича́н (← англича́нин)	*Englishman*
армя́н (← армяни́н)	*Armenian*
башки́р	*Bashkir*
болга́р (← болга́рин)	*Bulgarian*
буря́т	*Buriat*
грузи́н	*Georgian*
румы́н	*Romanian*
ту́рок (or ту́рков in R1)	*Turk*

- But:

бедуи́нов (← бедуи́н)	*Bedouin*
кирги́зов (← кирги́з)	*Kirgiz*
монго́лов (← монго́л)	*Mongol*
таджи́ков (← таджи́к)	*Tadjik*
узбе́ков (← узбе́к)	*Uzbek*
хорва́тов (← хорва́т)	*Croat*

(c) certain nouns denoting military personnel, e.g.

партиза́н	*guerrilla*
солда́т	*soldier*

(d) some units of measure, e.g.

ампе́р	*ampere*
арши́н	*arshin (see 6.1.5)*
ватт	*watt*
вольт	*volt*
герц	*hertz*
ом	*ohm*

Several other nouns have a variant with a zero ending in R1, but the full ending in **-ов** is considered the norm, e.g.

апельси́н	*orange*
баклажа́н	*aubergine*
гекта́р	*hectare*
грамм	*gram*
кара́т	*carat*
килогра́мм	*kilogram*
мандари́н	*mandarin*
помидо́р	*tomato*

Note 1   челове́к, *person*, also has gen pl **челове́к**, which is used after certain numerals (see 11.4.8), though in most contexts the genitive plural of лю́ди, **люде́й**, is used instead.

2   во́лос, *hair*, has gen pl **воло́с**. This noun is always used in the plural form (nom/acc во́лосы) in the sense of *hair on one's head*.

nouns in –ье, –ьё   most have genitive plural forms in **-ий**, e.g.

захолу́стье, *out-of-the-way place*	**захолу́стий**
побере́жье, *seaboard*	**побере́жий**
ущелье, *gorge*	**ущелий**
копьё, *spear*	**ко́пий**

• But:

пла́тье, *dress*	**пла́тьев**
подмасте́рье (m), *apprentice*	**подмасте́рьев**
у́стье, *mouth of river*	**у́стьев**
ружьё, *gun*	**ру́жей**

nouns in –жа, –ча, –ша, –ща   some have genitive plural forms in **-ей**, e.g.

ханжа́, *sanctimonious person*	**ханже́й**
ю́ноша, *youth*	**ю́ношей**

nouns in –я   although most nouns in –я have genitive plural in a soft consonant (see 9.1.2), some have genitive plural forms in **-ей**, e.g.

дя́дя, *uncle*	**дя́дей**
ноздря́, *nostril*	**ноздре́й**
тётя, *aunt*	**тётей**

Note: ту́фля, *shoe* (see 4.1), has gen pl **ту́фель** in R2 but the form **ту́флей** may be encountered in R1.

nouns in –ня   many nouns in –ня preceded by another consonant have a zero ending with a hard consonant rather than the soft ending that is normal for nouns in –я, e.g.

ба́шня, *tower*	**ба́шен**
ви́шня, *cherry-tree*	**ви́шен**
пе́сня, *song*	**пе́сен**
спа́льня, *bedroom*	**спа́лен**
тамо́жня, *customs* (at frontier post)	**тамо́жен**

- But:

дере́вня, *village*	дереве́нь
ку́хня, *kitchen*	ку́хонь

nouns in -ая, -ея, -уя have genitive plural forms in –ай, –ей, –уй respectively, e.g.

ста́я, *flock, shoal*	стай
иде́я, *idea*	иде́й
ста́туя, *statue*	ста́туй

nouns in -ья have genitive plural forms in –ей, e.g.

семья́, *family*	семе́й
статья́, *article*	стате́й
судья́, *judge, referee*	суде́й

о́блако (*cloud*) has gen pl **облако́в**, although in all other cases it conforms to the same pattern as standard neuter nouns in -o (see 9.1.2).

9.1.8 Irregularities in dative/instrumental/prepositional plural forms

це́рковь (*church*) in R3 generally has dat/instr/prep pl **церква́м, церква́ми, церква́х**, even though it is a noun ending in a soft sign. However, in R1 and R2 soft endings are now more usual in these cases too (**церквя́м, церквя́ми, церквя́х**).

instr pl in -ьми́ A very small number of nouns have (or may have) instrumental plural in **-ьми́**, although with some of the nouns in question such usage is restricted to certain registers or expressions:

де́ти, *children*	**детьми́** (all registers)
ло́шадь (f), *horse*	**лошадьми́** (all registers)
лю́ди, *people*	**людьми́** (all registers)
дверь (f), *door*	**дверьми́** (R1) **дверя́ми** (R2–3)
дочь (f), *daughter*	**дочерьми́** (R1) **дочеря́ми** (R2–3)
кость (f), *bone*, in the expression	**лечь костьми́** (R3, arch/rhet), *to lay down one's life (in battle)*

9.1.9 Nouns which are irregular throughout the plural

стул (*chair*)
де́рево (*tree*) A few masculine nouns which end in a hard consonant and a few neuter nouns in -o have regular endings in the singular but have plural forms of the following type:

nom/acc pl	сту́лья	дере́вья
gen pl	сту́льев	дере́вьев
dat pl	сту́льям	дере́вьям
instr pl	сту́льями	дере́вьями
prep pl	сту́льях	дере́вьях

Like стул and де́рево are:
кол, *stake*   **ко́лья, ко́льев**, etc.

ком, *lump*	**ко́мья, ко́мьев,** etc.
прут, *twig*	**пру́тья, пру́тьев,** etc.
звено́, *link (in chain)*	**зве́нья, зве́ньев,** etc.
крыло́, *wing*	**кры́лья, кры́льев,** etc.
перо́, *feather*	**пе́рья, пе́рьев,** etc.
поле́но, *log*	**поле́нья, поле́ньев,** etc.

Note 1 **брат,** *brother,* declines in exactly the same way, except that, being animate, it has acc pl **бра́тьев.**

2 **лист** declines like **стул** when it means *leaf* (i.e. *foliage*), but it declines like a regular masculine noun of the same type as **автобус** when it means *sheet of paper* (**листы́,** etc.).

3 **сук,** *branch, bough,* declines like **стул,** but undergoes a consonant change in its stem: thus **су́чья, су́чьев, су́чьям,** etc.

друг (*friend*)
сын (*son*)

These nouns are similar to **стул** and **де́рево,** but the stem for their plural forms is not the same as that for their singular forms, and they have accusative/genitive plural in –ей:

nom pl	**друзья́**	**сыновья́**
acc/gen pl	**друзе́й**	**сынове́й**
dat pl	**друзья́м**	**сыновья́м**
instr pl	**друзья́ми**	**сыновья́ми**
prep pl	**друзья́х**	**сыновья́х**

Note 1 **сын** also has regular plural forms (**сыны́, сыно́в, сына́м, сына́ми, сына́х**) when it has a figurative sense, as in **сыны́ оте́чества,** *sons of the fatherland.*

2 **князь,** *prince,* and **муж,** *husband,* have similar plural endings but no consonant change in the stem:

nom pl	**князья́**	**мужья́**
acc/gen pl	**князе́й**	**муже́й**
dat pl	**князья́м**	**мужья́м**
instr pl	**князья́ми**	**мужья́ми**
prep pl	**князья́х**	**мужья́х**

коле́но (*knee*)
у́хо (*ear*)

nom/acc pl	**коле́ни**	**у́ши**
gen pl	**коле́ней**	**уше́й**
dat pl	**коле́ням**	**уша́м**
instr pl	**коле́нями**	**уша́ми**
prep pl	**коле́нях**	**уша́х**

Note: **плечо́,** *shoulder,* has nom/acc pl **пле́чи,** but regular forms in the oblique cases (**плеч, плеча́м, плеча́ми, плеча́х**).

не́бо (*sky, heaven*)
чу́до (*miracle, wonder*)

These nouns have plural forms with a stem in **с:**

nom/acc pl	**небеса́**	**чудеса́**
gen pl	**небе́с**	**чуде́с**
dat pl	**небеса́м**	**чудеса́м**
instr pl	**небеса́ми**	**чудеса́ми**
prep pl	**небеса́х**	**чудеса́х**

сосе́д (*neighbour*)	These nouns have soft endings in the plural:	
чёрт (*devil*)		

nom pl	сосе́ди	че́рти
acc/gen pl	сосе́дей	черте́й
dat pl	сосе́дям	чертя́м
instr pl	сосе́дями	чертя́ми
prep pl	сосе́дях	чертя́х

nouns in -нин

Nouns of this type (see also 6.11–6.12) are regular in the singular but in the plural the last two letters (-ин) are removed to form the stem:

nom pl	англича́не
acc/gen pl	англича́н
dat pl	англича́нам
instr pl	англича́нами
prep pl	англича́нах

Note 1   All these nouns are animate, hence the coincidence of accusative/genitive forms.

2   **болга́рин**, *Bulgarian*, and **тата́рин**, *Tatar*, also follow this pattern, except that they have nom pl **болга́ры** and **тата́ры** respectively.

3   **цыга́н**, *gipsy*, has plural forms **цыга́не, цыга́н, цыга́нам**, etc. in the modern language, but nom pl **цыга́ны** in the nineteenth century (e.g. in the title of Púshkin's narrative poem).

4   **хозя́ин**, *landlord, host*, has plural forms **хозя́ева, хозя́ев, хозя́евам, хозя́евами, хозя́евах**.

5   **господи́н**, *master, gentleman, Mr*, has plural forms **господа́, госпо́д, господа́м, господа́ми, господа́х**.

nouns in -ёнок

Nouns of this type (see also 8.7.1) are regular in the singular (except that they have a mobile **о**), but in the plural have the following pattern:

nom pl	теля́та
acc/gen pl	теля́т
dat pl	теля́там
instr pl	теля́тами
prep pl	теля́тах

Note 1   All these nouns are animate, hence the coincidence of accusative/genitive forms.

2   **ребёнок**, *child*, does have a plural of this type (**ребя́та**, etc.), but this is a more colloquial word for *children* than **де́ти**, and it is also used in the sense of *lads*.

9.1.10   Nouns with irregular declension throughout

neuters in -мя

There is a small group of nouns ending in **-мя** which are neuter and which have a stem in **н** in all except nominative/accusative singular forms, e.g. **и́мя**, *name*:

	sg	pl
nom	и́мя	имена́
acc	и́мя	имена́

gen	**и́мени**	име́н
dat	**и́мени**	имена́м
instr	**и́менем**	имена́ми
prep	**и́мени**	имена́х

Like и́мя (but with some exceptions listed below) are:

бре́мя[a]	*burden*
вре́мя	*time*
вы́мя[a]	*udder*
зна́мя[b]	*flag*
пла́мя[c]	*flame*
пле́мя	*tribe*
се́мя[d]	*seed*
стре́мя[e]	*stirrup*
те́мя[a]	*crown of the head*

[a] No plural forms.

[b] nom/acc pl **знамёна**, gen pl **знамён**, dat pl **знамёнам**, etc.

[c] For a plural form the expression **языки́ пла́мени**, *tongues of flame*, is used; язы́к is put in the case appropriate in the context.

[d] gen pl **семя́н**.

[e] gen pl **стремя́н**.

мать (*mother*)
дочь (*daughter*)

These two nouns have a stem in **p** in all oblique cases in the singular and throughout the plural:

	sg	pl	sg	pl
nom	**мать**	ма́тери	**дочь**	до́чери
acc	**мать**	матере́й	**дочь**	дочере́й
gen	**ма́тери**	матере́й	**до́чери**	дочере́й
dat	**ма́тери**	матеря́м	**до́чери**	дочеря́м
instr	**ма́терью**	матеря́ми	**до́черью**	дочеря́ми*
prep	**ма́тери**	матеря́х	**до́чери**	дочеря́х

* in R1, instr pl **дочерьми́**.

муравей (*ant*)

	sg	pl
nom	**муравей**	муравьи́
acc/gen	**муравья́**	муравьёв
dat	**муравью́**	муравья́м
instr	**муравьём**	муравья́ми
prep	**муравье́**	муравья́х

Like муравей are **воробей**, *sparrow*; **соловей**, *nightingale*; **ручей**, *stream* (but ручей, being inanimate, has acc sg **ручей**).

путь (*way, path*)

This is a masculine noun, but its genitive/dative/prepositional singular forms are those of a feminine noun:

	sg	pl
nom/acc	**путь**	пути́
gen	**пути́**	путе́й

dat	**пути́**	**путя́м**
instr	**путём**	**путя́ми**
prep	**пути́**	**путя́х**

9.1.11 Declension of surnames

**men's names in
-ов, -ёв, -ев,
-ин, -ын**

These surnames decline like nouns ending in a hard consonant in the accusative/genitive, dative and prepositional singular forms and in the nominative plural, but in the remaining cases they have adjectival endings:

	sg	pl	sg	pl
nom	**Че́хов**	**Че́ховы**	**Пу́шкин**	**Пу́шкины**
acc/gen	**Че́хова**	**Че́ховых**	**Пу́шкина**	**Пу́шкиных**
dat	**Че́хову**	**Че́ховым**	**Пу́шкину**	**Пу́шкиным**
instr	**Че́ховым**	**Че́ховыми**	**Пу́шкиным**	**Пу́шкиными**
prep	**Че́хове**	**Че́ховых**	**Пу́шкине**	**Пу́шкиных**

Note: foreign surnames ending in -ин, however, follow the normal declension pattern for nouns of this type, e.g. instr sg **Да́рвином**.

**women's names in
-ова, -ёва, -ева,
-ина, -ына**

These surnames have accusative singular in -**у** (e.g. **Ивано́ву, Ники́тину**) and the ending -**ой** in all the oblique cases in the singular (e.g. **Ивано́вой, Ники́тиной**).

Note: surnames which end in a hard consonant (other than в or н in the above suffixes), whether they are Russian or foreign, do not decline when a woman is denoted, e.g. the forms **Ку́чер, Тэ́тчер** (*Mrs Thatcher*) are used for all cases.

**names in -ский,
-ская**

Surnames with these adjectival endings decline in exactly the same way as adjectives of this type (9.3.1).

**indeclinable
surnames**

Surnames ending in -**их, -ых, -ово, -аго** (e.g. **Долги́х, Бессме́ртных, Черны́х, Дурново́, Хитрово́, Жива́го**) are indeclinable.

Surnames in -**ко** and -**енко** (e.g. **Котько́, Решетко́, Евтуше́нко, Черне́нко**), which are of Ukrainian origin, are not normally declined, especially in R3b in which it is essential to avoid the confusion that may arise from the difficulty of inferring the nominative form of a name from an oblique case. However, some speakers may still decline these names like feminine nouns in -а.

Also indeclinable are Georgian surnames in -**адзе, -идзе, -вили** (e.g. **Чавчава́дзе, Орджоники́дзе, Джугашви́ли** (Stálin's real surname)), and foreign surnames ending in a vowel other than unstressed -а or -я, e.g. **Дюма́, Да́нте, Гюго́, Шо́у, Золя́** (*Dumas, Dante, Hugo, Shaw, Zola*).

Note 1 Most foreign surnames ending in unstressed -**а** or -**я** do decline (e.g. соне́ты **Петра́рки**, *Petrarch's sonnets*), but those in -**иа** do not, e.g. **Гарси́а**, *Garcia*.

2 Georgian names in -**ава** (e.g. **Окуджа́ва**) may decline like nouns in -а, but are sometimes also treated as indeclinable.

9.1.12 Indeclinable nouns

Russian has quite a large number of common nouns that are indeclinable, most of them fairly recent borrowings from other languages that do not easily fit into the Russian declensional pattern. The gender of an indeclinable noun may be determined by the gender of the person or creature that the noun denotes or by the gender of the generic noun that describes the class of thing to which the object in question belongs (generic nouns are given in brackets in the lists below). Indeclinable nouns may be allocated to the following types.

(a)   Nouns of foreign origin denoting inanimate objects: generally neuter, e.g.

бюро́	*office*
ви́ски	*whisk(e)y*
гётто	*ghetto*
депо́	*depot*
жюри́	*judges* (of competition)
интервью́	*interview*
кака́о	*cocoa*
кафе́	*café*
кино́	*cinema*
коммюнике́	*communiqué*
купе́	*compartment*
меню́	*menu*
метро́	*underground*
пальто́	*overcoat*
пари́	*bet*
пиани́но	*upright piano*
плато́	*plateau*
резюме́	*résumé*
такси́	*taxi*
шоссе́	*highway*

• But:

ко́фе (m)	*coffee* (influenced by the older form ко́фей)
сиро́кко (m)	*sirocco* (ве́тер, *wind*)
хи́нди (m)	*Hindi* (язы́к, *language*)
бе́ри-бе́ри (f)	*beri-beri* (боле́знь, *disease*)
кольра́би (f)	*kohlrabi* (капу́ста, *cabbage*)
саля́ми (f)	*salami* (колбаса́, *sausage*)

(b)   Nouns of foreign origin denoting people, including proper nouns: masculine or feminine depending on whether the person is male or female, e.g.

атташе́	*attaché*
Ве́рди	*Verdi*
ку́ли	*coolie*

(c) Nouns of foreign origin denoting animate beings other than people: generally masculine, e.g.

кенгуру́	*kangaroo*
ки́ви	*kiwi*
коли́бри	*humming-bird*
по́ни	*pony*
шимпанзе́	*chimpanzee*

Note: if the noun specifically denotes the female of the species then it may be treated as feminine, e.g. Кенгуру́ корми́ла кенгурёнка, *The kangaroo was feeding its cub.*

- But:

иваси́ (f)	*iwashi* (small far-eastern fish; ры́ба, *fish*)
цеце́ (f)	*tsetse* (му́ха, *fly*)

(d) Indeclinable Russian words which are not nouns but are used as such: neuter, e.g.

большо́е спаси́бо	*a big 'thank you'*
ве́жливое 'здра́вствуйте'	*a polite 'hello'*
мона́ршее 'мы'	*the royal 'we'*
све́тлое за́втра	*a bright tomorrow*

9.2 Declension of pronouns

я/ты/мы/вы					
(*I/you/we/you*)	nom	я	ты	мы	вы
	acc/gen	меня́	тебя́	нас	вас
	dat	мне	тебе́	нам	вам
	instr	мно́й	тобо́й	на́ми	ва́ми
		(мно́ю)	(тобо́ю)		
	prep	мне	тебе́	нас	вас

		m	n	f	pl
он/оно́/она́/	nom	он	оно́	она́	они́
они́	acc/gen	его́		её	их
(*he/it/she/they*)	dat	ему́		ей	им
	instr	им		ей (е́ю)	и́ми
	prep	нём		ней	них

Note 1   The letter **н-** must be added to the third-person pronouns when they occur after the great majority of prepositions, e.g. **от него́, к нему́, с ним, без неё, по ней, пе́ред ней, из них, к ним, между ни́ми**, and all prepositions governing the prepositional case. Prosthetic **н-** is not required after **вне, внутри́, благодаря́, вопреки́, подо́бно, согла́сно** (see 10.1.3–10.1.4) or after short comparative adjectives. Nor may it be used when **его́, её, их** are possessive pronouns, i.e. when they mean *his/its, (belonging to) her, their,* respectively, as opposed to *him, her, them.*

2   The instrumental forms **мно́ю, тобо́ю, е́ю** are alternatives to **мно́й, тобо́й, ей**, respectively. They may be used in the written language for stylistic or rhythmic reasons, especially with past passive participles, e.g. подпи́санный **мно́ю** докуме́нт, *the document signed by me,* and are particularly common when the pronoun is not preceded by a preposition.

сам (oneself/		m	n	f	pl
myself/	nom	сам	само́	сама́	са́ми
yourself/	acc	сам/самого́	само́	саму́	са́ми/сами́х
himself/	gen	самого́		само́й	сами́х
herself/	dat	самому́		само́й	сами́м
ourselves/	instr	сами́м		само́й (само́ю)	сами́ми
themselves)	prep	само́м		само́й	сами́х

		all genders			
себя́	acc/gen	себя́			
(oneself/myself/	dat	себе́			
yourself/himself/	instr	собо́й (собо́ю)			
herself/ourselves/	prep	себе́			
themselves)					

		all genders			
друг дру́га	acc/gen	друг дру́га			
(each other)	dat	друг дру́гу			
	instr	друг дру́гом			
	prep	друг (о) дру́ге			

мой (твой, свой)		m	n	f	pl
(my (your,	nom	мой	моё	моя́	мои́
one's own))	acc	мой/моего́	моё	мою́	мои́/мои́х
	gen	моего́		мое́й	мои́х
	dat	моему́		мое́й	мои́м
	instr	мои́м		мое́й	мои́ми
	prep	моём		мое́й	мои́х

наш (ваш)		m	n	f	pl
(our (your))	nom	наш	на́ше	на́ша	на́ши
	acc	наш/на́шего	на́ше	на́шу	на́ши/на́ших
	gen	на́шего		на́шей	на́ших
	dat	на́шему		на́шей	на́шим
	instr	на́шим		на́шей	на́шими
	prep	на́шем		на́шей	на́ших

его́, её, их
(his, her, their)

These forms are invariable when they are used as possessive pronouns. In D the adjectival form **и́хний** may be found instead of их.

э́тот		m	n	f	pl
(this)	nom	э́тот	э́то	э́та	э́ти
	acc	э́тот/э́того	э́то	э́ту	э́ти/э́тих
	gen	э́того		э́той	э́тих
	dat	э́тому		э́той	э́тим
	instr	э́тим		э́той	э́тими
	prep	э́том		э́той	э́тих

тот		m	n	f	pl
(that)	nom	тот	то	та	те
	acc	тот/того́	то	та	те/тех

gen	**того́**		**той**	**тех**
dat	**тому́**		**той**	**тем**
instr	**тем**		**той**	**те́ми**
prep	**том**		**той**	**тех**

весь
(all)

		m	n	f	pl
nom	**весь**	**всё**	**вся**	**все**
acc	**весь/всего́**	**всё**	**всю**	**все/всех**
gen	**всего́**		**всей**	**всех**
dat	**всему́**		**всей**	**всем**
instr	**всем**		**всей**	**все́ми**
prep	**всём**		**всей**	**всех**

что, ничто́, не́чего
(what, nothing,
there is
nothing to)

nom	**что**	**ничто́**	
acc/gen	**чего́**	**ничего́**	**не́чего**
dat	**чему́**	**ничему́**	**не́чему**
instr	**чем**	**ниче́м**	**не́чем**
prep	**чём**	**ни (о) чём**	**не́ (о) чем**

кто, никто́, не́кого
(who, no one,
there is no one to)

nom	**кто**	**никто́**	
acc/gen	**кого́**	**никого́**	**не́кого**
dat	**кому́**	**никому́**	**не́кому**
instr	**кем**	**нике́м**	**не́кем**
prep	**ком**	**ни (о) ко́м**	**не́ (о) ком**

Note: the elements of ничто́, не́чего, никто́, не́кого are usually split when combined with a preposition, whatever the case governed by the preposition, e.g. **ни с ке́м**, *not with anybody.*

чей
(whose)

		m	n	f	pl
nom	**чей**	**чьё**	**чья**	**чьи**
acc	**чей**	**чьё**	**чью**	**чьи**
gen	**чьего́**		**чьей**	**чьих**
dat	**чьему́**		**чьей**	**чьим**
instr	**чьим**		**чьей (чье́ю)**	**чьи́ми**
prep	**чьём**		**чьей**	**чьих**

9.3 Adjectival forms

9.3.1 Declension of adjectives

Accurate declension of adjectives should be taken for granted in the advanced student. Although there are various types of adjectival declension, the main differences are for the most part explained entirely by the spelling rules given in 8.2.4.

standard type

		m	n	f	pl
nom	**но́вый**	**но́вое**	**но́вая**	**но́вые**
acc	**но́вый/но́вого**	**но́вое**	**но́вую**	**но́вые/но́вых**
gen	**но́вого**		**но́вой**	**но́вых**
dat	**но́вому**		**но́вой**	**но́вым**

	instr	**но́вым**	**но́вой**	**но́выми**
	prep	**но́вом**	**но́вой**	**но́вых**

Note: adjectives with stressed endings have masculine nominative/accusative singular forms in -**о́й**, e.g. **молодо́й**.

stem in г, к, х

		m	n	f	pl
	nom	**ру́сский**	**ру́сское**	**ру́сская**	**ру́сские**
	acc	**ру́сский/**	**ру́сское**	**ру́сскую**	**ру́сские/ру́сских**
		ру́сского			
	gen		**ру́сского**	**ру́сской**	**ру́сских**
	dat		**ру́сскому**	**ру́сской**	**ру́сским**
	instr		**ру́сским**	**ру́сской**	**ру́сскими**
	prep		**ру́сском**	**ру́сской**	**ру́сских**

Note: adjectives with stem in **г, к, х** and stressed endings have forms in -**о́й** in the masculine nominative/accusative singular, e.g. **дорого́й**.

stem in
ж, ч, ш, щ

		m	n	f	pl
	nom	**хоро́ший**	**хоро́шее**	**хоро́шая**	**хоро́шие**
	acc	**хоро́ший/**	**хоро́шее**	**хоро́шую**	**хоро́шие/**
		хоро́шего			**хоро́ших**
	gen		**хоро́шего**	**хоро́шей**	**хоро́ших**
	dat		**хоро́шему**	**хоро́шей**	**хоро́шим**
	instr		**хоро́шим**	**хоро́шей**	**хоро́шими**
	prep		**хоро́шем**	**хоро́шей**	**хоро́ших**

Note: adjectives with stressed endings have masculine nominative/accusative singular forms in -**о́й**, and **о́** in all endings that in хоро́ший have e, e.g.

		m	n	f	pl
	nom	**большо́й**	**большо́е**	**больша́я**	**больши́е**
	acc	**большо́й/**	**большо́е**	**большу́ю**	**больши́е/**
		большо́го			**больши́х**
	gen		**большо́го**	**большо́й**	**больши́х**
	dat		**большо́му**	**большо́й**	**больши́м**
	instr		**больши́м**	**большо́й**	**больши́ми**
	prep		**большо́м**	**большо́й**	**больши́х**

adjectives in -ний

		m	n	f	pl
	nom	**си́ний**	**си́нее**	**си́няя**	**си́ние**
	acc	**си́ний/си́него**	**си́нее**	**си́нюю**	**си́ние/си́них**
	gen		**си́него**	**си́ней**	**си́них**
	dat		**си́нему**	**си́ней**	**си́ним**
	instr		**си́ним**	**си́ней**	**си́ними**
	prep		**си́нем**	**си́ней**	**си́них**

For a list of adjectives like си́ний see 8.9.

adjectives
like тре́тий

		m	n	f	pl
	nom	**тре́тий**	**тре́тье**	**тре́тья**	**тре́тьи**
	acc	**тре́тий/**	**тре́тье**	**тре́тью**	**тре́тьи/тре́тьих**
		тре́тьего			

gen	**тре́тьего**	**тре́тьей**	**тре́тьих**
dat	**тре́тьему**	**тре́тьей**	**тре́тьим**
instr	**тре́тьим**	**тре́тьей**	**тре́тьими**
prep	**тре́тьем**	**тре́тьей**	**тре́тьих**

Like тре́тий are a number of adjectives derived from the names of living creatures, e.g. **во́лчий**, *wolf's*; **коро́вий**, *cow's, bovine*; **коша́чий**, *cat's, feline*; **пти́чий**, *bird's*; **соба́чий**, *dog's, canine*.

9.3.2   Formation of short adjectives

- Short adjectives have four indeclinable forms which distinguish gender and number. The masculine form is found by removing the masculine nominative singular ending (-ый, -ий, or -ой); the feminine, neuter and plural forms are found by adding -**a**, -**o** (-**e** in unstressed endings after hushing consonants) and -**ы** (-**и** after velars and hushing consonants) respectively to the masculine form, e.g.

  но́вый, *new*: **нов, нова́, но́во, но́вы**
  све́жий, *fresh*: **свеж, свежа́, свежо́, све́жи**
  блестя́щий, *brilliant*: **блестя́щ, блестя́ща, блестя́ще, блестя́щи**
  стро́гий, *strict*: **строг, строга́, стро́го, стро́ги**
  молодо́й, *young*: **мо́лод, молода́, мо́лодо, мо́лоды**

Note 1   Some adjectives have short forms which may not be used in the whole range of meanings of which the long form is capable, e.g. **жив, жива́, жи́во, жи́вы** (← живо́й) may mean *alive* but not *lively*; **стар, стара́, ста́ро, ста́ры** (← ста́рый) may mean *old* in the sense *not young* and *not new*, but not in the sense of *long-standing*.

2   **рад, ра́да, ра́до, ра́ды**, *glad*, has short forms only.

- In many adjectives a vowel must be inserted between the last two consonants of the masculine short form, e.g.

  (a)   common adjectives with **o** inserted, e.g. **бли́зок** (← бли́зкий, *near*): **ги́бкий**, *flexible*; **гла́дкий**, *smooth*; **де́рзкий**, *bold*; **до́лгий**, *long* (of time); **кре́пкий**, *strong*; **лёгкий**, *light, easy*; **ло́вкий**, *agile*; **мя́гкий**, *soft, mild*; **ни́зкий**, *low*; **ре́дкий**, *rare*; **ре́зкий**, *sharp, harsh*; **сла́дкий**, *sweet*; **то́нкий**, *thin*; **у́зкий**, *narrow*;

  (b)   common adjectives with **e** inserted, e.g. **бе́ден** (← бе́дный, *poor*): **бле́дный**, *pale*; **вре́дный**, *harmful*; **гру́стный**, *sad*; **интере́сный**, *interesting*; **кра́сный**, *red*; **прия́тный**, *pleasant*; **све́тлый**, *bright, radiant*; **ску́чный**, *boring*; **то́чный**, *exact, precise*; **тру́дный**, *difficult*; **че́стный**, *honest*; **я́сный**, *clear*;

  (c)   common adjectives with **ё** (**o** after hushing consonants) inserted: **умён** (← у́мный, *intelligent*), **смешо́н** (← смешно́й, *funny*).

Note: **си́льный**, *strong*, has **си́лен** or **силён**.

- Many adjectives have no short form. These include all or most adjectives of the following types:

(a) adjectives denoting material, many of which end in -**áн(н)ый** or -**ян(н)ый**/-**яно́й**, e.g. **ко́жаный**, *leather*; **сере́бряный**, *silver*; **деревя́нный**, *wooden*; **шерстяно́й**, *woollen* (see 8.9);

(b) adjectives of participial origin ending in -**лый** (see 8.10), e.g. **уста́лый**, *tired*;

(c) adjectives ending in -**ний**, -**шний**, e.g. **весе́нний**, *spring*; **после́дний**, *last*; **дома́шний**, *domestic* (see 8.9);

(d) adjectives ending in -**о́вый**/-**ово́й**, e.g. **фиоле́товый**, *violet*; **полево́й**, *field*;

(e) adjectives ending in -**ский**/-**ско́й**, e.g. **англи́йский**, *English*; **мужско́й**, *male*.

Note 1   **ве́ский**, *weighty*, does have short forms (**ве́сок, ве́ска, ве́ско, ве́ски**) because its suffix is not -**ский** but -**кий**, the -**с**- being part of the stem.

2   Many adjectives in -**и́ческий** have synonyms in -**и́чный** which do have short forms, e.g. **траги́чный** (= **траги́ческий**), *tragic*: short forms **траги́чен, траги́чна, траги́чно, траги́чны**.

9.3.3   Formation of short comparatives

•   Most adjectives have a short comparative form. This form, which is indeclinable, is derived from the long form of the adjective in one of the following ways:

(a) in most adjectives, by addition of -**ee** to the stem, e.g.

но́вый, *new*	**нове́е**
интере́сный, *interesting*	**интере́снее**
поле́зный, *useful*	**поле́знее**

(b) in adjectives whose stem ends in **г, д, т, х**, or the combination **ст**, by a consonant change (to **ж, ж, ч, ш** or **щ**, respectively) and the addition of -**e** to the stem thus formed, e.g.

стро́гий, *strict*	**стро́же**
твёрдый, *firm*	**твёрже**
бога́тый, *rich*	**бога́че**
сухо́й, *dry*	**су́ше**
чи́стый, *clean*	**чи́ще**

Note: **жёлтый** has **желте́е**.

(c) in many adjectives ending in -**кий**, by the consonant change **к → ч**, and the addition of -**e** to the stem thus formed, e.g.

гро́мкий, *loud*	**гро́мче**
кре́пкий, *strong*	**кре́пче**
мя́гкий, *soft*	**мя́гче**
я́ркий, *bright*	**я́рче**

Note: **лёгкий** has **ле́гче**.

(d) in many other common adjectives, including many which end
in -**кий**, by some other means, e.g.

бли́зкий, *near*	**бли́же**
глубо́кий, *deep*	**глу́бже**
далёкий, *distant*	**да́льше**
дешёвый, *cheap*	**деше́вле**
до́лгий, *long* (of time)	**до́льше**
коро́ткий, *short*	**коро́че**
ме́лкий, *shallow*	**ме́льче**
по́здний, *late*	**по́зже** (or **поздне́е**)
ра́нний, *early*	**ра́ньше** (or **ра́нее**)
ре́дкий, *rare*	**ре́же**
сла́дкий, *sweet*	**сла́ще**
то́нкий, *thin*	**то́ньше**
у́зкий, *narrow*	**у́же**
широ́кий, *wide*	**ши́ре**

Note: го́рький, *bitter*, has **го́рче** in its literal meaning, but when used figuratively
has **го́рше**.

• The short comparative forms of the following eight adjectives, six of
which are themselves already comparatives, give particular difficulty:

бо́льший, *bigger*	**бо́льше**
ме́ньший, *smaller*	**ме́ньше**
лу́чший, *better*	**лу́чше**
ху́дший, *worse*	**ху́же**
ста́рший, *older* (of people), *senior*	**ста́рше**
мла́дший, *junior*	**мла́дше**
высо́кий, *high*	**вы́ше**
ни́зкий, *low*	**ни́же**

Note: the form **моло́же** must be used as a comparative of мла́дший when it means
younger.

• Outside R2 the suffix -**ей** may be encountered, as an alternative to -ee,
e.g. **нове́й**. This suffix may have an archaic or colloquial flavour, or it
may be used in verse for metrical reasons.

• The prefix **по-** is frequently attached to the short comparative,
especially in R1, to modify the meaning, e.g. **побо́льше**, *a little bigger*,
полу́чше, *a bit better*.

• There are many adjectives from which short comparative forms cannot
be derived, especially:

(a) those in -**ский** or -**ско́й**, e.g. **ру́сский**, *Russian*; **мужско́й**, *male*;
(b) those in -**овый/-ово́й** or -**евый/-ево́й**, e.g. **ма́ссовый**, *mass*;
передово́й, *advanced*;
(c) those of verbal origin in -**лый**, e.g. **уста́лый**, *tired*;
(d) some in -**кий**, e.g. **де́рзкий**, *bold*; **ли́пкий**, *sticky*; **ро́бкий**, *timid*;
ско́льзкий, *slippery*;

(e) miscellaneous adjectives, e.g. **больно́й**, *ill*; **ве́тхий**, *decrepit*; **го́рдый**, *proud*; **ли́шний**, *superfluous*.

9.4   Formation of adverbs

Adverbs are formed in the following ways:

(a) from adjectives with a stem in a hard consonant and from present and past passive participles (or adjectives derived from them), by addition of –**o** to the stem, e.g.

бы́стрый, *quick*	**бы́стро**
необходи́мый, *inevitable*	**необходи́мо**
взволно́ванный, *agitated*	**взволно́ванно**

(b) from adjectives with a stem in a soft consonant and from adjectives derived from present active participles, by addition of –**e** to the stem, e.g.

кра́йний, *extreme*	**кра́йне**
блестя́щий, *brilliant*	**блестя́ще**

Note: some adjectives in -ний have adverbs in -**o**, e.g. **давно́** (← да́вний); **по́здно** (← по́здний); **ра́но** (← ра́нний); и́скренний has either **и́скренно** or **и́скренне**.

(c) from adjectives in -**ский, -ско́й, -цкий**, by addition of -**и** to the stem, e.g.

дру́жеский, *amicable*	**дру́жески**
мастерско́й, *masterly*	**мастерски́**
молоде́цкий, *spirited*	**молоде́цки**

(d) by prefixing **по**- to a masculine/neuter dative form of the adjective or an adverb of the type in (c) above, to form adverbs of manner, e.g.

по-друго́му	*in a different way*
по-пре́жнему	*as before*
по-мо́ему	*in my opinion*
по-ру́сски	*(in) Russian*
по-челове́чьи	*like a human being*

(e) by a combination of preposition + short adjective or long adjective or noun, e.g.

напра́во	*to the right*
слегка́	*slightly*
вполне́	*fully*
вкруту́ю	*hard-boiled* (of egg)
наконе́ц	*finally*
подря́д	*in succession*
снача́ла	*at first*
за́мужем	*married* (of woman)
накану́не	*on the eve*

(f)   in miscellaneous other ways, such as by use of the instrumental form of a noun or on the basis of a numeral, e.g.

шёпотом	*in a whisper*
весно́й	*in spring*
пешко́м	*on foot*
вдвоём	*as a pair*

9.5   Declension of numerals

оди́н (1)

	m	n	f	pl
nom	оди́н	одно́	одна́	одни́
acc	оди́н/одного́	одно́	одну́	одни́/одни́х
gen	одного́		одно́й	одни́х
dat	одному́		одно́й	одни́м
instr	одни́м		одно́й	одни́ми
prep	одно́м		одно́й	одни́х

два/две (2),
три (3),
четы́ре (4)

	m/n	f	all genders	all genders
nom	два	две	три	четы́ре
acc	два/двух	две/двух	три/трёх	четы́ре/четырёх
gen	двух		трёх	четырёх
dat	двум		трём	четырём
instr	двумя́		тремя́	четырьмя́
prep	двух		трёх	четырёх

о́ба/о́бе
(both)

	m/n	f
nom	о́ба	о́ба
acc	о́ба/обо́их	о́бе/обе́их
gen	обо́их	обе́их
dat	обо́им	обе́им
instr	обо́ими	обе́ими
prep	обо́их	обе́их

Note: in R1 the distinctive feminine form may be lost in the oblique cases, e.g. в **обо́их** ко́мнатах, *in both rooms.*

пять (5)

nom/acc	**пять**
gen/dat/prep	**пяти́**
instr	**пятью́**

Like пять are all cardinal numerals up to **два́дцать** and **три́дцать.**

Note: the normal instrumental singular form of во́семь is **восьмью́**; the form восемью́ is obsolescent.

со́рок (40),
девяно́сто (90),
сто (100)

nom/acc	**со́рок**	**девяно́сто**	**сто**
gen/dat/instr/prep	**сорока́**	**девяно́ста**	**ста**

пятьдеся́т (50)

nom/acc	**пятьдеся́т**
gen/dat/prep	**пяти́десяти**
instr	**пятью́десятью**

Like пятьдеся́т are **шестьдеся́т**, *60*, **се́мьдесят**, *70*, and **во́семьдесят**, *80*.

Note: the genitive/dative/prepositional form of во́семьдесят is **восьми́десяти** and the instrumental form is **восьмью́десятью**.

две́сти (*200*),	nom/acc	**две́сти**	**три́ста**	**четы́реста**
три́ста (*300*),	gen	**двухсо́т**	**трёхсо́т**	**четырёхсо́т**
четы́реста (*400*)	dat	**двумста́м**	**трёмста́м**	**четырёмста́м**
	instr	**двумяста́ми**	**тремяста́ми**	**четырьмяста́ми**
	prep	**двухста́х**	**трёхста́х**	**четырёхста́х**

пятьсо́т (*500*),	nom/acc	**пятьсо́т**	**восемьсо́т**
восемьсо́т (*800*)	gen	**пятисо́т**	**восьмисо́т**
	dat	**пятиста́м**	**восьмиста́м**
	instr	**пятьюста́ми**	**восьмьюста́ми**
	prep	**пятиста́х**	**восьмиста́х**

Like пятьсо́т are **шестьсо́т** (*600*), **семьсо́т** (*700*), **девятьсо́т** (*900*).

the collective	nom	**дво́е**	**тро́е**	**че́тверо**
numerals дво́е (*2*),	acc	**дво́е/двои́х**	**тро́е/трои́х**	**че́тверо/четверы́х**
тро́е (*3*), че́тверо (*4*)	gen	**двои́х**	**трои́х**	**четверы́х**
	dat	**двои́м**	**трои́м**	**четверы́м**
	instr	**двои́ми**	**трои́ми**	**четверы́ми**
	prep	**двои́х**	**трои́х**	**четверы́х**

The collective noun **со́тня**, *hundred*, declines like a noun in -ня (gen pl со́тен).

other words denoting number

The word **ты́сяча**, *thousand*, declines like a noun in -a (instr sg **ты́сячей**), but may also be used as a numeral in which case it has instr sg **ты́сячью**.

The words **миллио́н**, *million*, and **миллиа́рд**, *billion*, are nouns and decline like other nouns ending in a hard consonant.

Ordinal numbers **пе́рвый, второ́й, тре́тий**, etc. decline like adjectives of the type in question (see 9.3.1 above).

A few other quantitative words have adjectival plural forms for use in the oblique cases, viz **мно́го**, *many*; **немно́го**, *not many, a few*; **не́сколько**, *several*; **сто́лько**, *so many*; and **ско́лько?**, *how many?*, viz:

acc/gen	**мно́гих**	**немно́гих**
dat	**мно́гим**	**немно́гим**
instr	**мно́гими**	**немно́гими**
prep	**мно́гих**	**немно́гих**

acc/gen	**не́скольких**	**сто́льких**	**ско́льких**
dat	**не́скольким**	**сто́льким**	**ско́льким**
instr	**не́сколькими**	**сто́лькими**	**ско́лькими**
prep	**не́скольких**	**сто́льких**	**ско́льких**

9.6 Verb forms

9.6.1 The system of conjugation

Russian verbs may be divided into two broad conjugations.

conjugation 1

Endings characterised by the vowel **e** (or **ё** under stress) in the second and third persons singular and the first and second persons plural (i.e. ты, он/она́/оно́, мы, вы forms). This conjugation may be subdivided into two types, one of which has four sub-types:

1A   stem of present/future tense is derived by removing final -ть of the infinitive, e.g. рабо́та/ть;

1B   stem of present/future tense is derived in some other way (in many instances because the infinitive ends in some combination other than vowel + ть, e.g. везти́, лезть, вести́, класть, жечь, идти́). 1B may be further subdivided into the following sub-types:

   i.   vowel stem + unstressed ending, e.g. мыть (**мо́-ю**);
   ii.   vowel stem + stressed ending, e.g. дава́ть (**да-ю́**);
   iii.   consonant stem + unstressed ending, e.g. ре́зать (**ре́ж-у**);
   iv.   consonant stem + stressed ending, e.g. жить (**жив-у́**).

conjugation 2

Endings characterised by the vowel **и** in the second and third persons singular and the first and second persons plural (i.e. ты, он/она́/оно́, мы, вы forms). In this conjugation the first person singular and the third person plural (i.e. я and они́ forms) are modified in certain verbs in accordance with basic spelling rules (see 8.2.4(b) above). Moreover, in the first person singular certain consonants at the end of the stem have to be changed (8.2.5) or require the insertion after them of the letter -л- (8.2.6). The endings of verbs in the two conjugations therefore are:

	conjugation 1	conjugation 2
(я)	**-ю** (**-у** after consonant*)	**-ю** (**-у** after hushing consonant)
(ты)	**-ешь** (**-ёшь** under stress)	**-ишь**
(он/она́)	**-ет** (**-ёт** under stress)	**-ит**
(мы)	**-ем** (**-ём** under stress)	**-им**
(вы)	**-ете** (**-ёте** under stress)	**-ите**
(они́)	**-ют** (**-ут** after consonant*)	**-ят** (**-ат** after hushing consonant)

* except **л** and sometimes **р**

Note: the vast majority of Russian verbs have two aspects, imperfective and perfective. The use of these aspects is dealt with below (see 11.5).

In the following tabulations of conjugation patterns there are many simple verbs from which a vast number of perfective forms (e.g. **зарабо́тать, откры́ть, наре́зать, подписа́ть, собра́ть, привести́, пойти́, заже́чь, рассмотре́ть**) are derived by the addition of prefixes (see 8.3). All such perfective derivatives conjugate in the same way as the simple verb itself.

9.6.2   1A verbs

Stem of present/future tense formed by removing final -ть of the infinitive; unstressed endings -ю, -ешь, -ет, -ем, -ете, -ют, e.g.

рабо́тать	теря́ть	красне́ть	дуть
to work	*to lose*	*to blush*	*to blow*
рабо́таю	теря́ю	красне́ю	ду́ю
рабо́таешь	теря́ешь	красне́ешь	ду́ешь
рабо́тает	теря́ет	красне́ет	ду́ет
рабо́таем	теря́ем	красне́ем	ду́ем
рабо́таете	теря́ете	красне́ете	ду́ете
рабо́тают	теря́ют	красне́ют	ду́ют

In 1A are a very large number of verbs in -ать or -ять and many in -еть (but not all such verbs); also обу́ть, *to provide with shoes*.

9.6.3   1B verbs with vowel stems and unstressed endings

мыть	организова́ть	воева́ть	ла́ять	брить
to wash	*to organise*	*to make war*	*to bark*	*to shave*
мо́ю	организу́ю	вою́ю	ла́ю	бре́ю
мо́ешь	организу́ешь	вою́ешь	ла́ешь	бре́ешь
мо́ет	организу́ет	вою́ет	ла́ет	бре́ет
мо́ем	организу́ем	вою́ем	ла́ем	бре́ем
мо́ете	организу́ете	вою́ете	ла́ете	бре́ете
мо́ют	организу́ют	вою́ют	ла́ют	бре́ют

Like мыть: выть, *to howl*; крыть, *to cover*; ныть, *to ache*; рыть, *to dig*.

Like организова́ть: the great majority of verbs in -овать, including many verbs of foreign origin, e.g. атакова́ть, *to attack*, as well as verbs from Slavonic roots, e.g. волнова́ть, *to agitate*. Similarly танцева́ть, *to dance* (танцу́ю, танцу́ешь, etc.).

Like воева́ть: most other verbs in -евать.

Like ла́ять: та́ять, *to thaw, melt*; се́ять, *to sow*; ве́ять, *to blow* (intrans); наде́яться, *to hope*.

9.6.4   1B verbs with stems in л and р and unstressed endings

коло́ть	боро́ться	колеба́ться	сы́пать
to prick	*to struggle*	*to hesitate*	*to pour*
колю́	борю́сь	коле́блюсь	сы́плю
ко́лешь	бо́решься	коле́блешься	сы́плешь
ко́лет	бо́рется	коле́блется	сы́плет

ко́лем	бо́ремся	коле́блемся	сы́плем
ко́лете	бо́ретесь	коле́блетесь	сы́плете
ко́лют	бо́рются	коле́блются	сы́плют

Like коло́ть: поло́ть, *to weed*; also моло́ть, *to grind*, but with **е** in the stem (мелю́, ме́лешь, etc.).

Like боро́ться: поро́ть, *to unstitch, thrash*.

Like сы́пать: трепа́ть, *to pull about, tousle*; щипа́ть, *to pinch, pluck*; дрема́ть, *to doze*.

9.6.5   1B verbs with vowel stems and stressed endings

дава́ть	узнава́ть	встава́ть	плева́ть
to give	*to find out*	*to get up*	*to spit*
даю́	узнаю́	встаю́	плюю́
даёшь	узнаёшь	встаёшь	плюёшь
даёт	узнаёт	встаёт	плюёт
даём	узнаём	встаём	плюём
даёте	узнаёте	встаёте	плюёте
даю́т	узнаю́т	встаю́т	плюю́т

петь	смея́ться	пить
to sing	*to laugh*	*to drink*
пою́	смею́сь	пью́
поёшь	смеёшься	пьёшь
поёт	смеётся	пьёт
поём	смеёмся	пьём
поёте	смеётесь	пьёте
пою́т	смею́тся	пью́т

Like узнава́ть: cognate verbs in **-знава́ть**, e.g. признава́ть, *to acknowledge*.

Like встава́ть: cognate verbs in **-става́ть**, e.g. остава́ться, *to remain*.

Like плева́ть: клева́ть, *to peck*; also кова́ть, *to forge* (кую́, куёшь, etc.).

Like пить (which has a stem in a soft consonant rather than a vowel, but conjugates in the same way): бить, *to beat*; вить, *to wind*; лить, *to pour*; шить, *to sew*.

Note: слать, *to send*, which has a consonant stem (шл-), conjugates in the same way (шлю, шлёшь, etc.).

9.6.6   1B verbs with consonant stems and unstressed endings

Note: the stress is often on the ending in the infinitive and the first person singular of verbs of this type, but is always on the stem throughout the remaining persons of the present/future tense.

(a)   Verbs with a stem in a hushing consonant:

ре́зать	пла́кать	писа́ть	иска́ть
to cut	*to cry*	*to write*	*to look for*

ре́жу	пла́чу	пишу́	ищу́
ре́жешь	пла́чешь	пи́шешь	и́щешь
ре́жет	пла́чет	пи́шет	и́щет
ре́жем	пла́чем	пи́шем	и́щем
ре́жете	пла́чете	пи́шете	и́щете
ре́жут	пла́чут	пи́шут	и́щут

Like ре́зать: **вяза́ть**, *to tie, knit*; **каза́ться**, *to seem*; **сказа́ть**, *to tell*; **ма́зать**, *to wipe, smear.*

Like пла́кать: **скака́ть**, *to gallop*; also **шепта́ть**, *to whisper* (**шепчу́, ше́пчешь**, etc.); **бормота́ть**, *to grumble*; **пря́тать**, *to hide*; **топта́ть**, *to stamp*; **хохота́ть**, *to guffaw*; **щекота́ть**, *to tickle.*

Like писа́ть: **теса́ть**, *to hew*; **чеса́ть**, *to scratch, comb*; also **маха́ть***, *to wave* (**машу́, ма́шешь**, etc.); **колыха́ть***, *to sway, rock*; **паха́ть**, *to plough.*

Like иска́ть: **плеска́ть***, *to splash*; **полоска́ть***, *to rinse*; also **трепета́ть**, *to quiver, tremble* (**трепещу́, трепе́щешь**, etc.), **ропта́ть**, *to murmur, grumble*; also **свиста́ть**, *to whistle* (**свищу́, сви́щешь**, etc.), **хлеста́ть**, *to lash.*

*These verbs may also be 1A in R1/D, e.g. **маха́ю**.

(b)   Verbs with a stem in **м** or **н**:

приня́ть	стать	наде́ть
to receive	*to become*	*to put on*
приму́	ста́ну	наде́ну
при́мешь	ста́нешь	наде́нешь
при́мет	ста́нет	наде́нет
при́мем	ста́нем	наде́нем
при́мете	ста́нете	наде́нете
при́мут	ста́нут	наде́нут

Like приня́ть: **отня́ть**, *to take away*; **подня́ть**, *to lift*; **снять**, *to take off.*

Note: a few other verbs from the same root, and which also have **м** stems in the present/future tense, have stressed endings throughout (see 9.6.7(b) below).

Like наде́ть: the simple verb **деть** and its perfective derivatives, e.g. **оде́ть(ся)**, **переоде́ть(ся)**, **разде́ть(ся)**.

(c)   Verbs in -**нуть**:

гло́хнуть
to go deaf
гло́хну
гло́хнешь
гло́хнет
гло́хнем
гло́хнете
гло́хнут

Like гло́хнуть:

i.   many other verbs which denote change of state, e.g. **блёкнуть**, *to fade*; **ки́снуть**, *to turn sour*; **мёрзнуть**, *to freeze* (intrans); **мо́кнуть**, *to get wet*; **слёпнуть**, *to go blind*; **со́хнуть**, *to get dry*;

ii.   many verbs derived from the following roots: **-бег-, -верг-, -вык-, -ник-, -стиг-, -тих-, -чез-**, e.g. **прибе́гнуть**, *to resort (to)*; **опрове́ргнуть**, *to refute*; **све́ргнуть**, *to overthrow*; **привы́кнуть**, *to get used (to)*; **возни́кнуть**, *to arise*; **прони́кнуть**, *to penetrate*; **дости́гнуть**, *to attain*; **зати́хнуть**, *to die down*; **исче́знуть**, *to disappear*;

iii.   many semelfactive verbs, e.g. **кри́кнуть**, *to shout*; **пры́гнуть**, *to jump*;

iv.   miscellaneous, e.g. **вспы́хнуть**, *to flash, flare up*; **дви́нуть**, *to move*; **тону́ть**, *to sink, drown* (intrans); **тро́нуть**, *to touch*; **тяну́ть**, *to pull*.

Note: there are also many verbs in -нуть that have stressed endings (see 9.6.7(c) below).

(d)   Miscellaneous verbs:

быть	е́хать	сесть
to be	*to go*	*to sit down*
бу́ду	е́ду	ся́ду
бу́дешь	е́дешь	ся́дешь
бу́дет	е́дет	ся́дет
бу́дем	е́дем	ся́дем
бу́дете	е́дете	ся́дете
бу́дут	е́дут	ся́дут

Note: **бу́ду**, etc., is the future tense of **быть**, there being no present tense of this verb in modern Russian (except the form **есть** in certain circumstances; see 4.2).

лезть	лечь	мочь
to climb	*to lie down*	*to be able*
ле́зу	ля́гу	могу́
ле́зешь	ля́жешь	мо́жешь
ле́зет	ля́жет	мо́жет
ле́зем	ля́жем	мо́жем
ле́зете	ля́жете	мо́жете
ле́зут	ля́гут	мо́гут

9.6.7   1B verbs with consonant stems and stressed endings

(a)   Various verbs with stems in **в**:

жить	плыть	звать	рвать
to live	*to swim*	*to call*	*to tear*
живу́	плыву́	зову́	рву
живёшь	плывёшь	зовёшь	рвёшь
живёт	плывёт	зовёт	рвёт
живём	плывём	зовём	рвём

живёте	плывёте	зовёте	рвёте
живу́т	плыву́т	зову́т	рвут

Like плыть: **слыть**, *to have a reputation for.*

(b) Verbs with stem in **м** or **н**:

поня́ть	взять	жать
to understand	*to take*	*to press*
пойму́	возьму́	жму
поймёшь	возьмёшь	жмёшь
поймёт	возьмёт	жмёт
поймём	возьмём	жмём
поймёте	возьмёте	жмёте
пойму́т	возьму́т	жмут

Like поня́ть: **заня́ть**, *to occupy, borrow;* **наня́ть**, *to rent, hire.* (But see 9.6.6(b) above for verbs in **-нять** which have a stem in **м** and unstressed endings.)

нача́ть	мять	жать	клясть
to begin	*to crumple*	*to reap*	*to swear*
начну́	мну	жну	кляну́
начнёшь	мнёшь	жнёшь	клянёшь
начнёт	мнёт	жнёт	клянёт
начнём	мнём	жнём	клянём
начнёте	мнёте	жнёте	клянёте
начну́т	мнут	жнут	кляну́т

(c) Verbs in **-нуть**:

гну́ть
to bend
гну
гнёшь
гнёт
гнём
гнёте
гнут

Like гнуть: **косну́ться**, *to concern;* **махну́ть**, *to wave;* **улыбну́ться**, *to smile.*

(d) Various verbs with stem in **р**:

брать	врать	умере́ть
to take	*to lie*	*to die*
беру́	вру	умру́
берёшь	врёшь	умрёшь
берёт	врёт	умрёт
берём	врём	умрём
берёте	врёте	умрёте
беру́т	врут	умру́т

Like брать: **дра́ть(ся)**, *to fight*.

Like умере́ть: **пере́ть**, *to make one's way*; **тере́ть**, *to rub* (**тру́**, **трёшь**, etc.).

(e)   Verbs in **-сти́** (with stem in **б, д, с**, or **т**) and in **-сть** (with stem in **д** or **т**):

грести́	вести́	нести́	мести́
to row	*to lead*	*to carry*	*to sweep*
гребу́	веду́	несу́	мету́
гребёшь	ведёшь	несёшь	метёшь
гребёт	ведёт	несёт	метёт
гребём	ведём	несём	метём
гребёте	ведёте	несёте	метёте
гребу́т	веду́т	несу́т	мету́т

Like грести́: **скрести́**, *to scrape*.

Like вести́: **блюсти́**, *to guard, watch over*.

Like нести́: **спасти́**, *to save*; **трясти́**, *to shake*.

Like мести́: **плести́**, *to plait, weave*; **цвести́**, *to blossom, flourish*.

класть	проче́сть
to put	*to read*
кладу́	прочту́
кладёшь	прочтёшь
кладёт	прочтёт
кладём	прочтём
кладёте	прочтёте
кладу́т	прочту́т

Like класть: **красть**, *to steal*; **пасть**, *to fall*; **прясть**, *to spin* (textiles).

Like проче́сть: **счесть**, *to count, consider* (**сочту́**, **сочтёшь**, etc.).

(f)   **идти́**
to go
иду́
идёшь
идёт
идём
идёте
иду́т

(g)   Verbs in **-зти́** and **-зть** with stem in **з**:

везти́	грызть
to take	*to gnaw*
везу́	грызу́
везёшь	грызёшь
везёт	грызёт
везём	грызём
везёте	грызёте
везу́т	грызу́т

Like везти́: **ползти́**, *to crawl*.

(h) Verbs in **-чь** with stem in **г/ж**:

бере́чь	жечь	стричь	запря́чь
to guard	*to burn*	*to cut*	*to harness*
берегу́	жгу	стригу́	запрягу́
бережёшь	жжёшь	стрижёшь	запряжёшь
бережёт	жжёт	стрижёт	запряжёт
бережём	жжём	стрижём	запряжём
бережёте	жжёте	стрижёте	запряжёте
берегу́т	жгут	стригу́т	запрягу́т

Note: **жечь** loses the **e** of the infinitive in its present-/future-tense stem, whereas other verbs of this type preserve the vowel of the infinitive in those tenses.

Like бере́чь: **пренебре́чь**, *to neglect, scorn*; **стере́чь**, *to guard, watch over*.

(i) Verbs in **-чь** with stem in **к/ч**:

печь	воло́чь (R1)
to bake	*to drag*
пеку́	волоку́
печёшь	волочёшь
печёт	волочёт
печём	волочём
печёте	волочёте
пеку́т	волоку́т

Like печь: **влечь**, *to drag, draw*; **сечь**, *to cut to pieces*; **течь**, *to flow*.

(j) Miscellaneous verbs:

ждать	лгать	ошиби́ться	расти́	соса́ть	ткать
to wait	*to lie*	*to be mistaken*	*to grow*	*to suck*	*to weave*
жду	лгу	ошибу́сь	расту́	сосу́	тку
ждёшь	лжёшь	ошибёшься	растёшь	сосёшь	ткёшь
ждёт	лжёт	ошибётся	растёт	сосёт	ткёт
ждём	лжём	ошибёмся	растём	сосём	ткём
ждёте	лжёте	ошибётесь	растёте	сосёте	ткёте
ждут	лгут	ошибу́тся	расту́т	сосу́т	ткут

Like ошиби́ться: **ушиби́ть(ся)**, *to knock/hurt/bruise oneself*.

9.6.8 Second-conjugation verbs

The stem of the present/future tense is found by removing vowel + ть (-ить/-ать/-еть/-ять) from the end of the infinitive.

(a) Verbs with infinitives in **-ить, -еть, -ять, -ать**:

говори́ть	смотре́ть	стоя́ть	гнать	спать
to speak	*to look at*	*to stand*	*to chase*	*to sleep*

говорю́	смотрю́	стою́	гоню́	сплю*
говори́шь	смо́тришь	стои́шь	го́нишь	спишь
говори́т	смо́трит	стои́т	го́нит	спит
говори́м	смо́трим	стои́м	го́ним	спим
говори́те	смо́трите	стои́те	го́ните	спи́те
говоря́т	смо́трят	стоя́т	го́нят	спят

* See (d) below for explanation of this form.

Like говори́ть: the vast majority of verbs that have an infinitive ending in –ить.

Like смотре́ть: **боле́ть**, *to hurt*; **верте́ть**, *to turn, twirl* (trans); **ви́деть**, *to see*; **висе́ть**, *to hang* (intrans); **горе́ть**, *to burn* (intrans); **зави́сеть**, *to depend*; **лете́ть**, *to fly*; **ненави́деть**, *to hate*; **оби́деть**, *to offend*; **перде́ть**, *to fart* (vulg); **свисте́ть**, *to whistle*; **сиде́ть**, *to sit*; **терпе́ть**, *to bear, endure*; also **блесте́ть**, *to shine*, though this verb may also be conjugated as a 1B verb with a stem in **щ** (**блещу́, бле́щешь**, etc.).

Note: most of these verbs undergo a consonant change in the first-person-singular form (see (c) below).

Like стоя́ть: **боя́ться**, *to be afraid*.

(b)   Verbs with a stem in a hushing consonant:

лежа́ть	молча́ть	слы́шать
to lie	to be silent	to hear
лежу́	молчу́	слы́шу
лежи́шь	молчи́шь	слы́шишь
лежи́т	молчи́т	слы́шит
лежи́м	молчи́м	слы́шим
лежи́те	молчи́те	слы́шите
лежа́т	молча́т	слы́шат

Like лежа́ть: **держа́ть**, *to hold*; **дрожа́ть**, *to shake, tremble*; **принадлежа́ть**, *to belong*.
Like молча́ть: **звуча́ть**, *to be heard, resound*; **крича́ть**, *to shout*; **стуча́ть**, *to knock*.
Like слы́шать: **дыша́ть**, *to breathe*.

Note: not all verbs ending in -жать, -чать, or -шать belong to the second conjugation. For example, **дорожа́ть**, *to rise in price*; **получа́ть**, *to get, receive*; **слу́шать**, *to listen to*, all belong to type 1A, while **жать**, in both its meanings (*to press; to reap*), belongs to type 1B (see 9.6.7(b) above).

(c)   Verbs with one of the following consonant changes in the first person singular:

д	→	ж
з	→	ж
с	→	ш
т	→	ч
т	→	щ
ст	→	щ

ходи́ть	to go	хожу́, хо́дишь
вози́ть	to transport	вожу́, во́зишь
носи́ть	to carry	ношу́, но́сишь
лете́ть	to fly	лечу́, лети́шь
посети́ть	to visit	посещу́, посети́шь
чи́стить	to clean	чи́щу, чи́стишь

Like посети́ть: all verbs in -ти́ть which have imperfectives in -ща́ть, e.g. **возмути́ть** (impf возмуща́ть), to anger; **запрети́ть**, to forbid; **защити́ть**, to defend; **обогати́ть**, to enrich; **обрати́ть**, to turn, convert; **освети́ть**, to illuminate; **ощути́ть**, to feel, sense; **укроти́ть**, to tame.

Note 1   The following 'defective' verbs have no first-person-singular form: **победи́ть**, to defeat; **убеди́ть**, to persuade, convince; **очути́ться**, to find oneself; **чуди́ть**, to behave oddly.

2   **чтить**, to honour, is a second-conjugation verb but has 3rd pers pl **чтут** as well as **чтят**.

3   **зи́ждиться** (на + prep; R3), to be founded on, has 3rd pers sg **зи́ждется**, and 3rd pers pl **зи́ждутся**.

(d)   Verbs with epenthetic **л** in the first person singular.

The consonant **л** is inserted between the present/future tense stem and the ending in verbs whose stem ends in one of the consonants **б, в, м, п, ф**.

люби́ть	to love	люблю́, лю́бишь
ста́вить	to put	ста́влю, ста́вишь
корми́ть	to feed	кормлю́, ко́рмишь
купи́ть	to buy	куплю́, ку́пишь
графи́ть	to rule (line)	графлю́, графи́шь

Like люби́ть: many verbs, e.g. **долби́ть**, to chisel, gouge; **истреби́ть**, to destroy; **осла́бить**, to weaken; **руби́ть**, to chop, hack.

Like ста́вить: many verbs, e.g. **объяви́ть**, to announce, declare; **пра́вить**, to correct, govern; **предста́вить**, to present, represent; **соста́вить**, to compile, constitute.

Like корми́ть: many verbs, e.g. **вы́прямить**, to straighten; **ошеломи́ть**, to stun; **стреми́ться**, to strive.

Like купи́ть: many verbs, e.g. **копи́ть**, to amass, store up; **ослепи́ть**, to blind; **ступи́ть**, to step; **топи́ть**, to sink, drown (trans), heat.

There are no common second-conjugation verbs in the modern language with present-/future-tense stem in **ф**.

9.6.9   Irregular verbs

бежа́ть	дать	есть	хоте́ть
to run	to give	to eat	to want
бегу́	**дам**	**ем**	**хочу́**

бежи́шь	дашь	ешь	хо́чешь
бежи́т	даст	ест	хо́чет
бежи́м	дади́м	еди́м	хоти́м
бежи́те	дади́те	еди́те	хоти́те
бегу́т	даду́т	едя́т	хотя́т

9.6.10 Formation of the past tense

The past tense has only four forms, which are differentiated according to gender and number rather than person. Masculine forms end in -л or some other hard consonant. Feminine, neuter and plural forms end in -ла, -ло, -ли, respectively; these endings are added to the masculine form in verbs in which the masculine form ends in some consonant other than л.

Note: in many 1B verbs in -езти́, -ести́ and -ечь the vowel e is replaced by ё in the masculine form of the past tense.

The following types of past tense can be distinguished:

(a) verbs with infinitive ending in vowel + ть: the final -ть is replaced by -л, -ла, -ло, -ли, e.g.

чита́ть, *to read*	чита́л, чита́ла, чита́ло, чита́ли
теря́ть, *to lose*	теря́л, теря́ла, теря́ло, теря́ли
пе́ть, *to sing*	пе́л, пе́ла, пе́ло, пе́ли
дуть, *to blow*	дул, ду́ла, ду́ло, ду́ли
откры́ть, *to open*	откры́л, откры́ла, откры́ло, откры́ли
коло́ть, *to prick*	коло́л, коло́ла, коло́ло, коло́ли
пить, *to drink*	пил, пила́, пи́ло, пи́ли
лечи́ть, *to cure*	лечи́л, лечи́ла, лечи́ло, лечи́ли

(b) verbs in -зти́, -зть: the final -ти or -ть is lost and the remaining stem serves as the masculine form, e.g.

везти́, *to take*	вёз, везла́, везло́, везли́
лезть, *to climb*	лез, ле́зла, ле́зло, ле́зли

(c) verbs in -сти́ with stems in б or с: the masculine form ends in the consonant with which the present-/future-tense stem ends, e.g.

грести́, *to row* (греб/у́)	грёб, гребла́, гребло́, гребли́
нести́, *to carry* (нес/у́)	нёс, несла́, несло́, несли́

(d) verbs in -сть or -сти́ with stems in д or т: the consonant with which the present-/future-tense stem ends is replaced with -л in the masculine form, e.g.

вести́, *to lead* (вед/у́)	вёл, вела́, вело́, вели́
мести́, *to sweep* (мет/у́)	мёл, мела́, мело́, мели́
класть, *to put* (клад/у́)	клал, кла́ла, кла́ло, кла́ли
красть, *to steal* (крад/у́)	крал, кра́ла, кра́ло, кра́ли

(e)   verbs in **-чь**: the final **-чь** of the infinitive is replaced with the velar with which the stem of the first-person-singular form of the present-/future-tense ends, e.g.

бере́чь, *to be careful* (берег/у́)	**берёг, берегла́, берегло́, берегли́**
лечь, *to lie down* (ля́г/у)	**лёг, легла́, легло́, легли́**
стричь, *to cut* (hair; стриг/у́)	**стриг, стри́гла, стри́гло, стри́гли**
мочь, *to be able* (мог/у́)	**мог, могла́, могло́, могли́**
печь, *to bake* (пек/у́)	**пёк, пекла́, пекло́, пекли́**

Note: **жечь**, *to burn* (жг/у), has **жёг, жгла, жгло, жгли.**

(f)   **идти́: шёл, шла, шло, шли**

Note: stress in **вы́шел** is on the prefix.

(g)   verbs in **-ере́ть** lose the final **-е́ть** in their masculine form, e.g.

умере́ть, *to die*	**у́мер, умерла́, у́мерло, у́мерли**
запере́ть, *to lock*	**за́пер, заперла́, за́перло, за́перли**
стере́ть, *to rub off*	**стёр, стёрла, стёрло, стёрли**

(h)   some verbs in **-нуть** with stress on stem, including verbs denoting change of state (see 9.6.6(c)), lose this suffix in the masculine form, e.g.

возни́кнуть, *to arise*	**возни́к, возни́кла, возни́кло, возни́кли**
дости́гнуть, *to attain*	**дости́г, дости́гла, дости́гло, дости́гли**
замёрзнуть, *to freeze*	**замёрз, замёрзла, замёрзло, замёрзли**
исче́знуть, *to disappear*	**исче́з, исче́зла, исче́зло, исче́зли**
поги́бнуть, *to perish*	**поги́б, поги́бла, поги́бло, поги́бли**

Note: the tendency is for verbs of this type to lose their suffix in the past tense, and forms which preserve it have an archaic flavour.

(i)

ошиби́ться, *to be mistaken*	**оши́бся, оши́блась, оши́блось, оши́блись**
ушиби́ться, *to hurt oneself*	**уши́бся, уши́блась, уши́блось, уши́блись**

9.6.11   Formation of the imperative

The second-person imperative may be formed from either aspect of the Russian verb (on usage see 11.5.6).

   The basic forms are used if the form of address used by the speaker is ты. The suffix **-те** is added to this basic form if the form of address used by the speaker is вы.

   The imperative of most Russian verbs is formed by removing the last two letters of the third person plural of the present/future tense and adding one of the following endings:

(a)   **й**, if the stem ends in a vowel, e.g.

чита́ть, *to finish* (чита́/ют)	**чита́й(те)**
объясня́ть, *to explain* (объясня́/ют)	**объясня́й(те)**
организова́ть, *to organise* (организу́/ют)	**организу́й(те)**
закры́ть, *to close* (закро́/ют)	**закро́й(те)**
петь, *to sing* (по/ю́т)	**по́й(те)**

Note: a few second-conjugation verbs with stressed endings in -ить in the infinitive have the ending **-й** in R2/3, e.g. **крои́ть**, *to cut out* (кро/я́т) → **крои́(те)**.

(b)   **и**, if the stem ends in a single consonant and the stress in the first person singular is on the ending or if the stem ends in two or more consonants and irrespective of the position of the stress, e.g.

писа́ть, *to write* (пи́ш/ут, пишу́)	**пиши́(те)**
вести́, *to lead* (вед/у́т, веду́)	**веди́(те)**
нести́, *to carry* (нес/у́т, несу́)	**неси́(те)**
говори́ть, *to speak* (говор/я́т, говорю́)	**говори́(те)**
купи́ть, *to buy* (ку́п/ят, куплю́)	**купи́(те)**
ждать, *to wait* (жд/ут, жду́)	**жди́(те)**
объясни́ть, *to explain* (объясн/я́т, объясню́)	**объясни́(те)**

Note: verbs with stems ending in the consonants **ст** or **р** + another consonant have parallel forms in **-ь** in the singular form of the imperative, e.g. **почи́сть**, *clean*; **не порть**, *don't spoil*.

(c)   **ь**, if the stem ends in a single consonant and the stress in the first person singular is on the stem, e.g.

ре́зать, *to cut* (ре́ж/ут, ре́жу)	**ре́жь(те)**
отве́тить, *to reply* (отве́т/ят, отве́чу)	**отве́ть(те)**

Note: some imperative forms derived from simple verbs which have end stress but which have the stressed prefix **вы́-** retain the ending **-и**, e.g. **вы́бежать**, *to run out* (вы́бег/ут, вы́бегу) → **вы́беги(те)**; **вы́йти**, *to go out* (вы́йд/ут, вы́йду) → **вы́йди(те)**.

● The following verbs or types of verb have imperatives that depart from the above patterns:

(a)   monosyllabic verbs in **-ить**: бить, *to beat* → **бе́й(те)**;
(b)   1B verbs in **-ава́ть**: дава́ть, *to give* → **дава́й(те)**;
(c)   **е́хать** and **пое́хать**, *to go*, both have **поезжа́й(те)**;
(d)   **дать**, *to give* → **да́й(те)**;
(e)   **есть**, *to eat* → **е́шь(те)**;
(f)   **лечь**, *to lie down* → **ля́г(те)**.

● A few common verbs may have forms in R1/D which differ from the standard forms of R2/3, e.g.

		R2/3	R1/D
взгляну́ть	*to glance*	взгляни́	**(гля́нь)**
вы́йти	*to go out*	вы́йди	**вы́дь**
е́хать	*to go (by transport)*	поезжа́й	**езжа́й**

красть	*to steal*	кради́	**крадь**
обня́ть	*to embrace*	обними́	**обойми́**
пойти́	*to go*	пойди́	**поди́**
положи́ть	*to put*	положи́	**поло́жь***

* As in the expression **вынь да поло́жь**, *here and now, on the spot.*

- The reflexive particle **-ся** is reduced to **-сь** after the vowel ending **и** and after the particle **-те**, e.g. **береги́сь, береги́тесь**, *be careful.*

9.7   Formation of gerunds and participles

9.7.1   Formation of imperfective gerunds

Imperfective gerunds are formed by replacing the last two letters of the third-person-plural form of the present tense with **-я** or (after hushing consonants) **-а**. These forms are invariable.

начина́ть (начина́/ют)	**начина́я**, *beginning*
кома́ндовать (кома́нду/ют)	**кома́ндуя**, *commanding*
жить (жив/у́т)	**живя́**, *living*
приходи́ть (прихо́д/ят)	**приходя́**, *arriving*
держа́ть (де́рж/ат)	**де́ржа**, *holding*

Note 1   1B verbs in **-ава́ть** have imperfective gerunds in **-ава́я**, e.g. дава́ть → **дава́я**, *giving.*

2   быть → **бу́дучи**, *being.*

3   In reflexive verbs **-ся** is contracted to **-сь** after the vowel ending, e.g. улыба́ться → **улыба́ясь**, *smiling.*

4   Many verbs, the vast majority of them 1B, are not capable of forming imperfective gerunds, viz. 1B verbs in **-зать** or **-сать** (e.g. **вяза́ть, писа́ть**); verbs with no vowel in their present-tense stem (e.g. monosyllables in **-ить** such as **лить, ждать, мять, рвать, слать, тере́ть**); verbs in **-чь** such as **печь**; verbs in **-нуть** (e.g. **ги́бнуть**); miscellaneous common verbs (e.g. **бежа́ть, гнить, драть, е́хать, звать, лезть, петь**). It is often possible, though, to form an imperfective gerund from a related 1A verb from the same root, e.g. **налива́ть** (← лить), **ожида́ть** (← ждать), **посыла́ть** (← слать), **вытира́ть** (← тере́ть), **погиба́ть** (← ги́бнуть) in the normal way.

9.7.2   Formation of perfective gerunds

Like imperfective gerunds, perfective gerunds are invariable. They are formed in the following ways:

(a)   in most verbs the final **-л** of the masculine form of the past tense is replaced by **-в**, e.g.

прочита́ть (прочита́л)	**прочита́в**, *having read*
откры́ть (откры́л)	**откры́в**, *having opened*
потяну́ть (потяну́л)	**потяну́в**, *having pulled*
почи́стить (почи́стил)	**почи́стив**, *having cleaned*

Note: forms in **-вши** (e.g. **прочита́вши**, etc.) have an archaic flavour but may also occur in R1 or D.

(b) most perfective verbs which do not form their past tense by adding -л to the final vowel of the infinitive are in theory capable of forming gerunds by adding **-ши** to the masculine form of the past tense, e.g. достигнуть (достиг) → **достигши**, *having attained*.

Note: in practice such gerunds are nowadays rarely used, and may be replaced, in some types of verb, by forms in -в, e.g. привыкнуть (привык) → **привыкнув**, *having become accustomed*; запереть (запер) → **заперев**, *having locked*.

(c) in perfective verbs of motion of the determinate category which have infinitive in **-ти** (see 11.7) the gerund is formed by attaching **-я** to the stem of the future tense, e.g.

войти (войд/у́)	**войдя́**, *having entered*
привести (привед/у́)	**приведя́**, *having brought*
ввезти (ввез/у́)	**ввезя́**, *having imported*
унести (унес/у́)	**унеся́**, *having carried away*

Note: alternative gerunds in **-ши** for such verbs, e.g. **вошедши**, are archaic.

(d) in reflexive verbs the perfective gerund is formed by replacing the final -лся of the masculine form of the past tense by **-вшись**, e.g. вернуться (вернулся) → **вернувшись**, *having returned*.

9.7.3 Formation of present active participles

Present active participles may be formed only from imperfective verbs. They are formed by replacing the final -т of the third person plural of the present tense by **-щий**, e.g.

покупа́ть (покупа́ю/т)	**покупа́ющий**, *who is buying*
пить (пью/т)	**пью́щий**, *who is drinking*
идти́ (иду́/т)	**иду́щий**, *who is going*
говори́ть (говоря́/т)	**говоря́щий**, *who is speaking*
лежа́ть (лежа́/т)	**лежа́щий**, *who is lying*
интересова́ться (интересу́ю/тся)	**интересу́ющийся**, *who is interested in*

Note 1   Present active participles decline like adjectives of the type хоро́ший (9.3.1).
2   The reflexive particle **-ся**, when it occurs in such participles, is not contracted to -сь after vowels (e.g. m/n gen sg интересу́ющего**ся**).

9.7.4 Formation of past active participles

Past active participles may be formed from verbs of either aspect. They are formed in the following ways:

(a) in most verbs the final -л of the masculine form of the past tense is replaced with **-вший**, e.g.

покупа́ть (покупа́/л)	**покупа́вший**, *who was buying*
петь (пе/л)	**пе́вший**, *who was singing*
купи́ть (купи́/л)	**купи́вший**, *who bought*

закры́ть (закры́/л)	**закры́вший**, *who closed*
объясня́ть (объясня́/л)	**объясня́вший**, *who was explaining*

(b) verbs whose masculine past-tense form ends in a consonant other than
л form their past active participle by adding -**ший** to that consonant,
e.g.

нести́ (нёс)	**нёсший**, *who was carrying*
мочь (мог)	**мо́гший**, *who was able*
умере́ть (у́мер)	**уме́рший**, *who died*
дости́гнуть (дости́г)	**дости́гший**, *who attained*

(c) verbs in -**сти́** which have a present-/future-tense stem in **д** or **т** retain
this consonant and add -**ший**, e.g.

вести́	**ве́дший**, *who was leading*
изобрести́	**изобре́тший**, *who invented*

Note 1 Similarly идти́ (шёл) → **ше́дший**, *who was going*.
   2 Many participles of this type, whilst theoretically possible, are rarely
      encountered in modern Russian.

• Past active participles decline like adjectives of the type хоро́ший
(9.3.1). The reflexive particle -**ся**, when it occurs in such participles, is
not contracted to -**сь** after vowels (e.g. m/n gen sg
интересова́вшего**ся**).

9.7.5 Formation of present passive participles

Present passive participles may as a rule be formed only from verbs
which are imperfective and transitive (e.g. **открыва́ть**). They therefore
may not be formed from verbs which are perfective (e.g. откры́ть) or
intransitive (e.g. стоя́ть). Nor can they be formed from reflexive verbs
(e.g. смея́ться), since these verbs are intransitive.

Present passive participles are formed by adding -**ый** to the first
person plural of imperfective verbs. They decline like adjectives of the
type но́вый (see 9.3.1), e.g.

рассма́тривать	**рассма́триваемый**, *being examined*
организова́ть	**организу́емый**, *being organised*

Note 1 1B verbs in -**ава́ть** do not form their present passive participles in the normal
      way. Instead they have forms in -**ава́емый**, e.g. дава́ть → **дава́емый**, *being
      given*.
   2 A few verbs with first person plural in -**ём** have a participle in -**о́мый**, e.g.
      вести́ → **ведо́мый**, *being led*; such forms are rarely used.
   3 Many imperfective transitive verbs have no present passive participle, e.g.
      брать, класть, петь, писа́ть, monosyllables in -**ить** (see 9.6.5).

9.7.6 Formation of past passive participles

As a rule past passive participles may be formed only from verbs which
are perfective and transitive (e.g. **откры́ть**). They therefore may not be

formed from verbs which are imperfective (e.g. открыва́ть) or intransitive (e.g. стоя́ть). Nor can they be formed from reflexive verbs (e.g. смея́ться), since these verbs are intransitive.

Past passive participles have one of the following types of ending.

–тый

The suffix **-ый** is added to the final т of the infinitive in verbs of the following types (on stress changes see 12.4.4.6 below):

(a) basically monosyllabic in **-ыть** (9.6.3): закры́ть → **закры́тый**, *shut*;

(b) basically monosyllabic in **-ить** (9.6.5): разби́ть → **разби́тый**, *broken*;

(c) basically monosyllabic in **-еть** (9.6.6(b)): оде́ть → **оде́тый**, *dressed*;

(d) in **-оть** (9.6.4): проколо́ть → **проко́лотый**, *punctured*;

(e) in **-уть**: упомяну́ть → **упомя́нутый**, *mentioned*;

(f) in **-ере́ть** (9.6.7(d)): запере́ть → **за́пертый**, *locked*; стере́ть → **стёртый**, *rubbed off*.

Note: the final **e** of the infinitive form of derivatives of тере́ть is lost, and the remaining **e** changes to **ё**.

(g) 1B in **-ать** or **-ять** which have a stem in **-м** or **-н** (9.6.6(b) and 9.6.7(b)):

нача́ть (начн-у́) → **на́чатый**, *begun*; снять (сним-у́) → **сня́тый**, *taken off*.

–нный

In verbs with infinitive ending in -ать or -ять, including 1B verbs (except those in (g) above) and second-conjugation verbs, the final -ть of the infinitive is replaced by -нный (note stress changes):

прочита́ть → **прочи́танный**, *read*
взволнова́ть → **взволно́ванный**, *agitated*
написа́ть → **напи́санный**, *written*
потеря́ть → **поте́рянный**, *lost*

–енный/-ённый

The ending -**енный** is used when stress is on the stem and -**ённый** is used when stress is on the ending. These endings are used in verbs of the following types:

(a) 1B verbs with consonant stems which do not fall into any of the above categories, e.g.

ввести́ → **введённый**, *introduced*
принести́ → **принесённый**, *brought*
смести́ → **сметённый**, *swept off*
ввезти́ → **ввезённый**, *imported*
заже́чь → **зажжённый**, *set light to*
испе́чь → **испечённый**, *baked*

Note: of the two stems which verbs in **-чь** have in their present/future tense (**г/ж** or **к/ч**) it is the stem in a hushing consonant (**ж** or **ч**) that is used in this participle.

(b) Second-conjugation verbs other than those in -ать. Any irregularities affecting the first person singular of second-conjugation verbs (consonant changes or insertion of epenthetic -л- (see 9.6.8(c) and (d))) also occur in these participles, e.g.

заморо́зить → **заморо́женный**, *frozen*
реши́ть → **решённый**, *decided*
встре́тить → **встре́ченный**, *met*
просвети́ть → **просвещённый**, *enlightened*
поста́вить → **поста́вленный**, *put*
купи́ть → **ку́пленный**, *bought*

Note 1 Verbs in **-дить** which have imperfective form in **-ждать** have the combination **-жд-** in their participle, even though this combination does not occur in their first person singular, e.g. **освобождённый** from освободи́ть (impf освобожда́ть).

2 Position of stress in past passive participles in **-енный** and **-ённый** is determined by position of stress in the second person singular of the present/future tense (замо́розишь, реши́шь, встре́тишь, просвети́шь, поста́вишь, ку́пишь, освободи́шь in the verbs given above).

(c) Some verbs which do not quite conform to the above rules:

укра́сть → **укра́денный**, *stolen*
derivatives of есть: съесть → **съе́денный**, *eaten up*
найти́ → **на́йденный**, *found*
увиде́ть → **уви́денный**, *seen*

• The long forms of past passive participles of all types decline like adjectives. Past passive participles also have short forms which, like the short forms of adjectives, distinguish gender and number, e.g.

откры́тый	откры́т	откры́та	откры́то	откры́ты
прочи́танный	прочи́тан	прочи́тана	прочи́тано	прочи́таны
поте́рянный	поте́рян	поте́ряна	поте́ряно	поте́ряны
решённый	решён	решена́	решено́	решены́
поста́вленный	поста́влен	поста́влена	поста́влено	поста́влены

Note 1 In all past passive participles ending in **-нный** only one **н** survives in the short form.

2 The short forms of participles in **-ённый** are always stressed on the last syllable, with the result that **ё** changes to **e** in the feminine, neuter and plural forms.

10 Prepositions

It is worth devoting a separate chapter to Russian prepositions, and the rendering of English prepositions into Russian. For one thing, knowledge of prepositions in a foreign language tends to be a good indicator of command of that language in general. More importantly, the meanings of Russian prepositions coincide with the meanings of their most common English equivalents only to a limited degree. Russian prepositions are also extremely precise in their meanings. The English-speaker must therefore think particularly carefully about the meaning of the English preposition in a given context before rendering it into Russian. Moreover, some of the most widespread English prepositions (e.g. *for, of, to, with*) are often not rendered in Russian by any preposition at all, since their meaning may be implicit in the use of a certain Russian case. Attention must also be paid to the fact that some common Russian prepositions are capable of governing more than one case and that they have different meanings when they are used with different cases.

This chapter examines the most important meanings of Russian and English prepositions respectively, and also lists common verbs that govern an object indirectly through a particular preposition. The last section (10.4), which deals with the rendering of each English preposition in Russian, draws attention to expressions in which usage in the two languages is quite different.

10.1 Valency of prepositions

10.1.1 Prepositions followed by apparent nominative forms

В	in a few expressions denoting change of status or promotion this preposition governs a noun which, although it is animate, has an accusative form that coincides with the nominative rather than the genitive:

пойти **в лётчики**	*to become a pilot*
выйти **в лю́ди**	*to get on in the world*
произвести́ **в полко́вники**	*to promote to the rank of colonel*

ЗА	is followed by a noun in the nominative case in the interrogative expression **Что э́то за** . . . ? *What sort of . . . is . . . ?* (cf. Ger *Was für ein Buch ist das?*) and in the interjectional expression **Что за** . . . ! *What a . . . !*

Что э́то за **маши́на**?	*What sort of a car is it?*
Что за **день**!	*What a wonderful day!*

Note:	in these expressions **за** is not actually functioning as a preposition but as part of a phrase with **что**.

10.1.2   Prepositions governing the accusative

В

(a) *into, to, in*, when movement is involved (cf. в + prep):

Она́ вошла́ **в ко́мнату.**	*She went into the room.*
Он положи́л ве́щи **в чемода́н.**	*He put his things in a case.*

(b) *at* a time on the hour or past the hour, *at* an age:

в час	*at one o'clock*
в че́тверть пя́того	*at a quarter past four*
в два́дцать мину́т шесто́го	*at twenty past five*
в де́вять лет	*at nine years of age*

Also **в по́лдень**, *at midday*, and **в по́лночь**, *at midnight*.

(c) *on* a day of the week:

в понеде́льник	*On Monday*
в сре́ду	*On Wednesday*

(d) to express dimension and measurement:

стол ширино́й **в оди́н метр**	*a table a metre wide*
дом **в два** этажа́	*a two-storey house*
моро́з **в де́сять** гра́дусов	*a ten-degree frost*

(e) to denote pattern:

ю́бка **в кле́точку**	*a check shirt*
пла́тье **в кра́пинку**	*a spotted dress* (tiny spots)
ю́бка **в горо́шек**	*a spotted skirt* (larger spots)
руба́шка **в поло́ску**	*a striped shirt*

ЗА

(a) *behind* or *beyond*, when movement into a position is involved:

Со́лнце зашло́ **за горизо́нт.**	*The sun went behind the horizon* [i.e. *set*].
Мы пое́хали **за́ город.**	*We went out of town* [i.e. *into the country*].

This is the sense in which за is used in certain phrases, e.g.

сади́ться/сесть **за стол**	*to sit down at table*
е́хать/пое́хать **за грани́цу**	*to go abroad* [i.e. *beyond the border*]

(b) *for*, when some sort of exchange or reciprocity is involved:

благодари́ть/поблагодари́ть кого́-н **за гостеприи́мство**	*to thank sb for their hospitality*
плати́ть/заплати́ть **за кни́гу**	*to pay for a book*

(c) *during, in the space of, over* a period of time:

за́ ночь	*during the night*
За три дня вы́пало две ме́сячные но́рмы оса́дков.	*In the space of three days there was twice the usual monthly rainfall.*

(d) *after a period of time*, or *over/beyond* a certain age:

далеко́ **за́ по́лночь**	*long after midnight*
Ему́ уже́ **за со́рок**.	*He is already over forty.*

(e) *at a distance* in space or time (especially in combination with **от** and **до** respectively):

Э́то произошло́ **за сто** **киломе́тров отсю́да**.	*This happened 100 kilometres from here.*
за оди́н день до его́ сме́рти	*a day before his death*

НА

(a) *on to, on*, when movement is involved:

класть/положи́ть что́-н **на́ пол**	*to put sth on the floor*
сади́ться/сесть **на стул**	*to sit down on the chair*

(b) *to, into* with those nouns listed in 10.1.6 (на (b)) which require **на** + prepositional case for the translation of *in* or *at*, e.g.

на вы́ставку	*to the exhibition*
на ры́нок	*to the market*

(c) *for* a period of time, when one is defining what period an action is intended or expected to cover (cf. use of accusative without a preposition; see 10.4 (*for*) and 11.1.2):

Он е́дет в Москву́ **на неде́лю**.	*He is going to Moscow for a week.*
Она́ прие́хала к нам **на́ год**.	*She came to us for a year.*

(d) *for* a certain purpose:

тало́ны **на мя́со**	*(rationing) coupons for meat*
обе́д **на пять** челове́к	*dinner for five people*

(e) *by* a certain margin:

Он **на два го́да** ста́рше бра́та.	*He is two years older than his brother.*
Э́ти проду́кты подорожа́ли **на ты́сячу** проце́нтов.	*These products have become a thousand per cent more expensive.*

О

against in the sense of *in contact with*:

спотыка́ться/споткну́ться **о ка́мень**	*to stumble against a stone*
бок **о́ бок**	*side by side*

ПО

up to a certain point in space or time:

стоя́ть **по ше́ю** в воде́	*to stand up to one's neck in water*
Ви́за действи́тельна **по** двадца́тое ма́я.	*The visa is valid up to 20 May inclusive.*

ПОД

(a) *under*, when movement into a position is involved:

Ко́шка зале́зла **под крова́ть**.	*The cat went under the bed.*
Я положи́л(а) кни́ги **под стол**.	*I put the books under the table.*

(b)	*towards*, in a temporal sense, or *just before*:	

под ве́чер	*towards evening*
Ему́ под со́рок лет.	*He is getting on for forty.*

(c) *to* the accompaniment of a sound:

танцева́ть под му́зыку	*to dance to music*
писа́ть под дикто́вку	*to write to dictation*

(d) *in imitation of*:

кольцо́ под зо́лото	*an imitation gold ring*
писа́ть под Го́голя	*to write in the style of Gogol*

ПРО (a) *about* or *concerning*; more or less synonymous with о + prep, but characteristic of R1; used only with the accusative:

говори́ть про Ма́шу	*to speak about Masha*
петь про любо́вь	*to sing about love*

(b) + **себя́**, *to* in certain phrases:

ду́мать про себя́	*to think to oneself*
чита́ть про себя́	*to read to oneself*

С with nouns denoting measurement, distance, time, etc., in the sense of *approximately*, *about*:

ве́сить с килогра́мм	*to weigh about a kilogram*
Мы прошли́ с ми́лю.	*We walked about a mile.*
Я про́был(а́) там с неде́лю.	*I was there about a week.*

СКВОЗЬ *through*, esp when passage through sth is difficult; used only with the accusative:

пробира́ться/пробра́ться сквозь толпу́	*to force one's way through a crowd*
смех сквозь слёзы	*laughter through tears*

ЧЕ́РЕЗ (a) *across*, *through*, or *over* when this preposition means *across*; used only with the accusative:

переходи́ть че́рез доро́гу	*to cross (over) the road*
перелеза́ть/переле́зть че́рез забо́р	*to climb over the fence*

(b) *in* (a certain amount of time from the time of speaking):

Че́рез неде́лю он верну́лся.	*In a week he returned.*

Note: there is a similar spatial use in phrases such as **че́рез две остано́вки**, *in two stops* (i.e. when one is going to get off a bus or train).

(c) *via* a place:

Он пое́хал туда́ че́рез Москву́.	*He went there via Moscow.*

(d)   *through* an intermediary:

говори́ть с ке́м-н **че́рез**   *to speak to sb through an interpreter*
перево́дчика

(e)   when an action affects alternate objects in a series:

рабо́тать **че́рез** день   *to work every other day*
печа́тать/напеча́тать **че́рез**   *to print on every other line* (i.e. *to*
строку́   *double-space*)

10.1.3   Prepositions governing the genitive

A very large number of prepositions may govern the genitive case. The most common ones are **из, от, с** and **у**. All of the prepositions listed in this section, with the exception of **ме́жду** and **с**, invariably govern the genitive case.

БЕЗ	*without:*	
(a)	**без значе́ния**	*without significance*
	без оши́бок	*without mistakes*
(b)	in expressions of time, to indicate minutes before the hour, e.g.	
	без пяти́ (мину́т) де́сять	*(at) five to ten*
	без че́тверти два (часа́)	*(at) a quarter to two*

ВВИДУ́	*in view of*, rather formal:	
	Ввиду́ вну́треннего кри́зиса президе́нт реши́л не выезжа́ть за грани́цу.	*In view of the internal crisis the president decided not to go abroad.*

ВДОЛЬ	*along* (i.e. adhering to a line; see also 10.4):	
	Нефтяно́е пятно́ растекло́сь **вдоль побере́жья**.	*The oil slick flowed out along the coast.*

ВМЕ́СТО	*instead of, in place of:*	
	Он пошёл на собра́ние **вме́сто своего́ бра́та**.	*He went to the meeting instead of his brother.*

Note: **вме́сто** should not be confused with **вме́сте**, *together.*

ВНЕ	*outside* (as opposed to *inside*):	
	вне го́рода	*outside the town*
	вне зако́на	*outside the law*

Note: **вне** is narrower in meaning than Eng *outside*, which may have to be translated into Russian with other prepositions such as **о́коло** or **пе́ред** (see 10.4).

ВНУТРИ́	*inside*, to indicate the position in which sth is located (**внутри́** is itself a form in the prepositional case):	
	Внутри́ корабля́ – торпе́ды с я́дерными боеголо́вками.	*Inside the ship are torpedoes with nuclear warheads.*
ВНУТРЬ	*inside*, to indicate movement inwards (**внутрь** is itself a form in the accusative case):	
	Войска́ бы́стро продви́нулись **внутрь страны́**.	*The troops quickly moved inland.*
ВО́ЗЛЕ	*by, near*:	
	Воздви́гли па́мятник **во́зле собо́ра**.	*They erected a monument near the cathedral.*
ВОКРУ́Г	*round*:	
	путеше́ствие **вокру́г све́та**	*a journey round the world*
ВПЕРЕДИ́	*in front of, ahead of*:	
	Впереди́ по́езда стоя́л сугро́б.	*In front of the train was a snowdrift.*
ВСЛЕ́ДСТВИЕ	*because of, owing to*:	
	Всле́дствие тума́на матч не состоя́лся.	*Owing to the fog the match did not take place.*
ДЛЯ	*for* in the sense of *for the benefit of* or *for the purpose of*:	
	пода́рок **для дру́га**	*a present for (one's) friend*
	ору́дие **для**	*a tool for*

Note:	**для** is much narrower in meaning than English *for*, which may have to be translated by other prepositions such as **за** + acc or **на** + acc (see 10.4), or indeed by no preposition at all.	

ДО	(a)	*before* and *until* in a temporal sense:	
		Э́то произошло́ **до войны́**.	*This happened before the war.*
		Он рабо́тает **до шести́ часо́в**.	*He works until six o'clock.*
	(b)	*up to* or *as far as* in a spatial sense:	
		Он дое́хал **до Владивосто́ка**.	*He went as far as Vladivostok.*
ИЗ	(a)	*out of*, when movement is involved:	
		выходи́ть/вы́йти **из ко́мнаты**	*to go out of/leave the room*
		вынима́ть/вы́нуть **из карма́на**	*to take out of one's pocket*
	(b)	to indicate that sb or sth is of a particular origin, or that an object is made of or consists of sth, or is one out of a larger number:	
		из крестья́нской семьи́	*from a peasant family*
		пла́тье **из шёлка**	*a silk dress*

| обе́д **из пяти́ блюд** | *a five-course dinner* |
| одна́ **из са́мых лу́чших книг** | *one of the best books* |

(c)   to indicate that some action results from a certain experience or feeling:

| **Из до́лгого о́пыта** зна́ю, что... | *From long experience I know that...* |
| Она́ э́то сде́лала **из любви́** к де́тям. | *She did this out of love for the children.* |

И́З-ЗА   (a)   *out from behind*:

| **и́з-за угла́** | *from round the corner* |
| встава́ть/встать **и́з-за стола́** | *to get up from the table* |

(b)   *because of* when the cause of sth is regarded unfavourably:

| Она́ не могла́ рабо́тать **и́з-за головно́й бо́ли.** | *She could not work because of a headache.* |

И́З-ПОД   (a)   *out from under*:

| **и́з-под** посте́ли | *out from under the bed* |
| торго́вля **и́з-под прила́вка** | *under-the-counter trade* |

(b)   to indicate the purpose for which an object is designed:

| ба́нка **из-под варе́нья** | *a jam-jar* |
| бо́чка **из-под пи́ва** | *a beer-barrel* |

КРО́МЕ   *except, apart from*:

| Она́ ничего́ не е́ла **кро́ме бу́лочки.** | *She didn't eat anything apart from a bun.* |

МЕ́ЖДУ   *between*; used with the genitive only in a few phrases:

| чита́ть **ме́жду строк** | *to read between the lines* |
| **ме́жду двух огне́й** | *between the devil and the deep blue sea (lit between two fires)* |

МИ́МО   *past*:

| проходи́ть/пройти́ **ми́мо до́ма** | *to go past the house* |

НАПРО́ТИВ   *opposite*:

| Мы договори́лись встре́титься **напро́тив це́ркви.** | *We agreed to meet opposite the church.* |

НАСЧЁТ   *about, as regards*:

| Как **насчёт ва́шего докла́да?** | *What about your report?* |

О́КОЛО   (a)   *near or by*:

| Он сиде́л **о́коло своего́ друга́.** | *He was sitting by his friend.* |

(b) *around, about* or *approximately*:

о́коло полу́ночи	*around midnight*
о́коло миллио́на	*about a million*

ОТ (ОТО)

(a) *away from*:

По́езд отхо́дит **от платфо́рмы**.	*The train is moving away from the platform.*

(b) to indicate distance from:

в двух киломе́трах **от це́нтра**	*two kilometres from the centre*
в пяти́ мину́тах ходьбы́ **от вокза́ла**	*five minutes' walk from the station*

(c) to indicate the source of sth:

узнава́ть/узна́ть **от кого́-н**	*to find out from sb*
Я получи́л(а) **от неё** письмо́.	*I received a letter from her.*

(d) to indicate the date of a letter:

его́ письмо́ **от пе́рвого ма́рта**	*his letter of 1 March*

(e) to indicate the purpose for which sth is intended:

ключ **от две́ри**	*the door key*
пу́говица **от руба́шки**	*a shirt button*

(f) to indicate that sth may be used to counter sth else:

страхова́ние **от огня́**	*fire insurance*
табле́тки **от головно́й бо́ли**	*headache tablets*

(g) to indicate that sth is prompted by a certain cause:

Столломи́лся **от еды́**.	*The table was groaning with food.*

(h) to describe the emotional state a person is in, when the feelings that prompted an action are being defined:

кипе́ть **от негодова́ния**	*to seethe with indignation*
дрожа́ть **от стра́ха**	*to tremble with fear*

(i) in miscellaneous common phrases:

не/далеко́ от	*not/far from*
вре́мя от вре́мени	*from time to time*
от всей души́	*with all one's heart*
от и́мени кого́-н	*on behalf of sb*

ОТНОСИ́ТЕЛЬНО

concerning; formal, used mainly in R3:

вопро́сы **относи́тельно процеду́ры**	*questions concerning procedure*

ПОМИ́МО		*besides, apart from:*	
		поми́мо всего́ про́чего	*apart from everything else*
ПО́СЛЕ		*after:*	
		по́сле у́жина	*after supper*
ПОСРЕДИ́		*in the middle of:*	
		Он стоя́л **посреди́ пло́щади.**	*He was standing in the middle of the square.*
ПОСРЕ́ДСТВОМ		*by means of, by dint of:*	
		посре́дством усе́рдной рабо́ты	*by means of hard work*
ПРО́ТИВ		*against:*	
		про́тив тече́ния	*against the current*
		выступа́ть **про́тив си́льного оппоне́нта**	*to take on* [lit *come out against*] *a strong opponent*
ПУТЁМ		*by means of, by dint of:*	
		путём хи́трости	*by means of cunning*
РА́ДИ		*for the sake of:*	
		ра́ди семьи́	*for the sake of the family*
С (СО)	(a)	*off* the surface of sth, *down from:*	
		снима́ть/снять **со стола́**	*to take off the table*
		приходи́ть/прийти́ **с рабо́ты**	*to come home from work*

Note: **с** translates *away from* or *out of* when the following noun is one of those nouns that require **на** rather than **в** to translate *in(to)* or *at/on to* (see 10.1.6, **на** (b–e)).

(b)   *since* in a temporal sense:

с нача́ла января́	*since the beginning of January*

(c)   *from* in the sense of *as a result of:*

умира́ть/умере́ть **с го́лода**	*to die of hunger/starve to death*
со стыда́	*from shame*

(d)   *with* in the sense of *on the basis of:*

с ва́шего разреше́ния	*with your permission*

(e)   *from:*

Он за́пил **с го́ря.**	*He took to drink from grief.*

Note: in this sense **с** is synonymous with (though a little more colloquial than) **от** as a preposition describing the emotional state that causes some action.

(f) in miscellaneous common expressions:

с одно́й стороны́	on the one hand
с друго́й стороны́	on the other hand
с како́й ста́ти?	to what purpose? why should I?
с пе́рвого взгля́да	at first sight
с тех пор, как	since (conj)
с то́чки зре́ния кого́-н	from the point of view of sb

СВЕРХ

on top of, over and above:

сверх зарпла́ты	on top of wages
сверх вся́кого ожида́ния	beyond expectations

СВЫ́ШЕ

over, more than; used mainly in numerical contexts:

свы́ше миллио́на люде́й	more than a million people

СРЕДИ́

among, amid:

среди́ молодёжи	among the young
Среди́ бе́женцев – старики́, же́нщины и де́ти.	Among the refugees are old men women, and children.

У

(a) *by* in the sense of *near:*

Она́ стоя́ла у окна́.	She was standing by the window.
дом у мо́ря	a house by the sea

(b) *at* in the sense of Fr *chez* and related meanings:

Мы поу́жинаем у вас.	We shall have supper at your place.
Он ещё живёт у роди́телей.	He still lives with his parents.

(c) + nouns and personal pronouns to indicate possession; in this sense corresponds to the English verb *to have* (4.1):

У нас есть но́вая маши́на.	We've got a new car.
У меня́ к вам одна́ про́сьба.	I've got a request to make of you.

(d) + personal pronouns, in R1, in lieu of possessive pronoun:

Са́ша у меня́ до́брый челове́к.	My Sasha's a good man.

(e) + nouns and personal pronouns in expressions indicating pain or discomfort:

У меня́ боли́т зуб.	I've got toothache.
У неё боли́т го́рло.	She's got a sore throat.

(f) to denote dispossession or taking away:

занима́ть/заня́ть де́ньги у кого́-н	to borrow money from sb
У нас отня́ли всё.	They've taken everything away from us.

10.1.4   Prepositions governing the dative

The commonest preposition governing the dative case is **по**, which is used much more widely with the dative than with the accusative or the prepositional, and which has many meanings. **К** is also very common, but the remaining prepositions which may govern the dative are restricted in their use.

БЛАГОДАРЯ́		*thanks to:*
	благодаря́ её хладнокро́вию	*thanks to her presence of mind*

ВОПРЕКИ́		*despite, contrary to:*
	вопреки́ мои́м распоряже́ниям	*contrary to my instructions*

К (КО)	(a)	*towards, up to* in a spatial sense:	
		Он подхо́дит **к мосту́**.	*He is going towards the bridge.*
		Она́ подошла́ **ко мне́**.	*She came up to me.*
	(b)	*by* or *towards* in a temporal sense:	
		Он придёт **к ве́черу**.	*He will arrive by evening.*
	(c)	in combination with many nouns to indicate attitude:	
		жа́лость к	*pity for*
		интере́с к	*interest in*
		любо́вь к	*love for*
		не́нависть к	*hatred of*
		отноше́ние к	*attitude towards, relation to*
		презре́ние к	*contempt for*
		равноду́шие к	*indifference towards*
		скло́нность к	*inclination towards, penchant for*
		страсть к	*passion for*
		стремле́ние к	*striving for*
		уваже́ние к	*respect for*
	(d)	in miscellaneous common phrases:	
		к сожале́нию	*unfortunately*
		к сча́стью	*fortunately*
		к тому́ же	*moreover, besides*
		к моему́ удивле́нию	*to my surprise*
		к на́шему изумле́нию	*to our astonishment*
		к ва́шим услу́гам	*at your service*
		лицо́м к лицу́	*face to face*

ПО	(a)	*along, down:*	
		Она́ идёт **по у́лице**.	*She is walking along the street.*
		Он спуска́ется вниз **по ле́стнице**.	*He is coming down the stairs.*

(b)   *round* in the sense of *in various directions*:

Он хо́дит **по ко́мнате**.	*He is pacing round the room.*
броди́ть **по го́роду**	*to wander round the town*

(c)   *according to, in accordance with*:

по расписа́нию	*according to the timetable*
по подсчётам экспе́ртов	*according to the calculations of experts*
по официа́льному ку́рсу	*according to the official rate of exchange*

(d)   *by* a means of communication:

по телефо́ну	*by telephone*
по по́чте	*by post*
по желе́зной доро́ге	*by rail*

(e)   *at, on* or *in* in the sense of *in the field of* or *on the subject of*:

чемпио́ны **по футбо́лу**	*champions at football*
специали́ст **по полити́ческим** вопро́сам	*a specialist on political matters*
мини́стр **по дела́м** Шотла́ндии	*Minister for Scottish affairs*
уро́к **по матема́тике**	*a mathematics lesson*

(f)   *on* days of the week and in other expressions of time to indicate regular occurrence:

по понеде́льникам	*on Mondays*
по пра́здникам	*on holidays*
по утра́м	*in the mornings*

(g)   + the numeral **оди́н**, *one*, and also the nouns **ты́сяча**, *thousand*, and **миллио́н**, *million*, to indicate distribution; cf. **по** + acc in this sense with other numerals (see 11.4.9):

Мы получи́ли **по одному́ фу́нту**.	*We received a pound each.*

(h)   + the negative particle **не** in phrases in which inconsistency is indicated; in this sense **по** may sometimes be translated by the English *for*:

Он **не по во́зрасту** высо́к.	*He is tall for his age.*
Э́та маши́на мне **не по** карма́ну.	*I can't afford this car.*

Note: as pointed out by Wade (see Sources), **по** has also made some progress in the language at the expense of more precise prepositions in phrases such as **програ́мма по литерату́ре** (= програ́мма литерату́ры), *programme of literature*; **приз по стрельбе́** (= приз за стрельбу́), *prize for shooting*.

ПОДО́БНО	*like, similar to:*
	крича́ть **подо́бно сумасше́дшему** *to shout like a madman*
СОГЛА́СНО	*in accordance with*; official in tone, characteristic of R3b:
	согла́сно гла́вной статье́ договора́ *in accordance with the main article of the treaty*

10.1.5   Prepositions governing the instrumental

ЗА	*behind, beyond, on the far side of*, and *at* or *over* in the sense of *behind*; when location is being defined; cf. **за** + acc when movement into a position is indicated:

за до́мом	*behind the house*
за грани́цей	*abroad (beyond the border)*
за бо́ртом	*overboard*
за столо́м	*at the table*
за роя́лем	*at the piano*
за пи́вом	*over a beer*

МЕ́ЖДУ	*between*; followed only by the instrumental case except in a few fixed expressions in which it governs the genitive (see 10.1.3):

ме́жду паралле́льными ли́ниями	*between parallel lines*
ме́жду на́ми	*between ourselves*

НАД (НА́ДО)	*over, above, on top of*, used only with the instrumental:

Над столо́м виси́т лю́стра.	*A chandelier hangs over the table.*
надо мно́й	*over me*

ПЕ́РЕД (ПЕ́РЕДО)	used only with the instrumental:
(a)	*in front of* or *before* in a spatial sense:

сиде́ть пе́ред телеви́зором	*to sit in front of the television*
пе́редо мной	*in front of me*

(b)	*before* in a temporal sense, especially *shortly before*; cf. **до** (see 10.1.3) which may indicate any time before:

пе́ред сме́ртью	*before death*

ПОД (ПО́ДО)	(a)	*under, below, beneath*, when actual or figurative location is defined; cf. **под** + acc when movement into a position is indicated:

под мосто́м	*under the bridge*
под аре́стом	*under arrest*
под влия́нием	*under the influence*

(b)   *with* a certain dressing, in culinary expressions, in which the literal meaning of *under* is retained:

| рыба **под томáтным сóусом** | *fish in tomato sauce* |
| яйцó **под майонéзом** | *egg mayonnaise* |

(c)   *in the region of*:

| **под Москвóй** | *in the region of Moscow* |

(d)   *of* in the names of battles:

| **бúтва под Полтáвой** | *the Battle of Poltava* |

C (CO)

(a)   *with*, when *with* means *together with* or *in the company of*, or when it refers to some connection or attendant characteristic; cf. omission of **c** when *with* denotes instrument (see 10.4):

Он пошёл в кинó **с сестрóй**.	*He went to the cinema with his sister.*
в связú **с э́тим**	*in connection with this*
человéк **с голубы́ми глазáми**	*a person with (light) blue eyes*
с рáдостью	*gladly (with gladness)*

(b)   together with personal pronouns in an inclusive sense, e.g.:

он с сестрóй	*he and his sister*
мы с брáтом	*my brother and I*
мы с мáтерью	*my mother and I*

(c)   in the expression **Что с вáми/с тобóй?** *What's the matter with you?*

(d)   *with* the passage of time, e.g. **с кáждым днём**, *with each (passing) day*

10.1.6   Prepositions governing the prepositional or locative

The prepositional case, as its name suggests, may only be used with certain prepositions (**в, на, о, по, при**). It is also sometimes called the locative case, since when used with the prepositions **в** and **на** it may define location.

В (ВО)

(a)   *in* or *at* to define location, the place where sth is situated or happening; cf. use of accusative when movement is involved:

| Он живёт **в Москвé**. | *He lives in Moscow.* |
| Мы сидéли **в спáльне**. | *We were sitting in the bedroom.* |

(b)   to express the distance at which sth is located:

в однóм киломéтре от цéнтра гóрода	*a kilometre from the centre of town*
в трёх минýтах ходьбы́ от шкóлы	*three minutes' walk from the school*
в пятú часáх езды́ от Парúжа	*five hours' journey/travel from Paris*

(c) *in* or *at* in certain expressions of time (to indicate the month, year, decade, century, or period of one's life, or stage in a period in which an event took place):

в январе́	*in January*
в про́шлом году́	*last year*
в двадца́тых года́х	*in the 1920s*
в двадца́том ве́ке	*in the twentieth century*
в де́тстве	*in childhood*
в нача́ле го́да	*at the beginning of the year*
в конце́ войны́	*at the end of the war*

(d) *at* half past an hour:

в полови́не пе́рвого	*at half past twelve*

(e) to describe what sb is wearing:

Она́ **в кра́сной блу́зке**.	*She's got a red blouse on.*
Он был **в чёрном костю́ме**.	*He was wearing a black suit.*

НА

(a) *on*, *in* or *at* to define location, the place where sth is situated; cf. use of accusative when movement is involved:

Кни́га лежи́т **на столе́**.	*The book is on the table.*

(b) *on*, *in* or *at* before many common nouns, where English-speakers might expect **в** to be used; many of these nouns denote some sort of occasion, or refer to both the place and the event or activity associated with it:

ве́чер, *party* (reception)	**на ве́чере**
война́, *war*	**на войне́**
вокза́л, *station*	**на вокза́ле**
вы́ставка, *exhibition*	**на вы́ставке**
заво́д, *factory*	**на заво́де**
заседа́ние, *meeting, session*	**на заседа́нии**
ка́федра, *department* (in higher educational institution)	**на ка́федре**
конфере́нция, *conference*	**на конфере́нции**
конце́рт, *concert*	**на конце́рте**
куро́рт, *resort*	**на куро́рте**
курс, *year* (of course in higher educational institution)	**на ку́рсе**
ле́кция, *lecture*	**на ле́кции**
о́пера, *opera*	**на о́пере**
пло́щадь, (f) *square*	**на пло́щади**
по́чта, *post-office*	**на по́чте**
рабо́та, *work*	**на рабо́те**
ры́нок, *market*	**на ры́нке**
сва́дьба, *wedding*	**на сва́дьбе**
собра́ние, *meeting, gathering*	**на собра́нии**

ста́нция, *station*	**на ста́нции**
съезд, *congress*	**на съе́зде**
у́лица, *street*	**на у́лице**
уро́к, *lesson*	**на уро́ке**
фа́брика, *factory*	**на фа́брике**
факульте́т, *faculty* (of higher educational institution)	**на факульте́те**
фронт, *front* (mil)	**на фро́нте**
ша́хта, *mine*	**на ша́хте**
экза́мен, *examination*	**на экза́мене**

(c) *in* with points of the compass, islands, peninsulas, mountainous regions of the former USSR, and the names of streets and squares, e.g.

на за́паде	*in the west*
на ю́ге	*in the south*
на се́веро-восто́ке	*in the north-east*
на о́строве	*on the island*
на Ки́пре	*in Cyprus*
на Ку́бе	*in Cuba*
на Сахали́не	*in Sakhalin*
на Аля́ске	*in Alaska*
на Камча́тке	*in Kamchatka*
на Кавка́зе	*in the Caucasus*
на Ура́ле	*in the Urals*
на Арба́те	*in the Arbat*
на Не́вском проспе́кте	*in Nevskii Prospect*
на Кра́сной пло́щади	*in Red Square*

Note 1   Formerly **на** was also combined with Украи́на, *(the) Ukraine*. However, now that Украи́на is used to denote an independent country rather than a space, region or mere republic the preposition **в** is generally combined with it instead. This usage puts Ukraine on a par linguistically with other former Soviet republics that have become independent countries (e.g. **в Казахста́не**, *in Kazakhstan*). Omission of the definite article in English (i.e. *in Ukraine*; cf. the older expression *in the Ukraine*) achieves a similar purpose. It should be added that use of **в** rather than **на** with Украи́на helps to dissociate the word from the etymologically related word **окра́ина**, outlying districts, borderland, which combines with **на**.

2   With names of mountain ranges outside the former Soviet Union, on the other hand, **в** + prep is more usual, e.g. **в Альпах**, *in the Alps*; **в Андах**, *in the Andes*; **в Гимала́ях**, *in the Himalayas*.

(d) *in* with certain nouns (especially nouns denoting means of transport, e.g. **авто́бус, автомоби́ль, маши́на, по́езд**) when presence in the place in question is associated with the activity for which the place is designed:

гото́вить **на ку́хне**	*to cook in the kitchen*
е́хать **на авто́бусе**	*to go by bus*
cf. чита́ть газе́ту **в авто́бусе**,	*to read a newspaper on the bus*

(e) in miscellaneous expressions of place or time, e.g.

на морóзе	*in the frost*
на сквознякé	*in a draught*
на сóлнце	*in the sun*
на рассвéте	*at dawn*
на пéнсии	*retired* (on a pension)
на откры́том вóздухе	*in the open air*
на свéжем вóздухе	*in the fresh air*
на бýдущей недéле	*next week*
на прóшлой недéле	*last week*
на слéдующей недéле	*the following week*
на э́той недéле	*this week*

О (ОБ, ОБО) when the following noun or adjective begins with one of the vowels **а, о, у, э** (i.e. a vowel without an initial *j* sound), then the letter **б** is generally added to **о** for the sake of euphony; **óбо** occurs only in the expressions given below.

(a) *about, concerning*:

Он дýмает **о брáте**.	*He is thinking about his brother.*
Поговори́м **об э́том**.	*Let's speak about this.*
обо всём/всех	*about everything/everybody*
обо мнé	*about me*

(b) *with* when the properties of sth are being described; this use is uncommon:

пáлка **о двух концáх**	lit *a two-ended stick*, i.e. *a double-edged weapon*

ПО *after, following*, or *on completion of*; most commonly found with verbal nouns; this usage is rather literary or official and confined to R3, especially R3b:

по истечéнии ви́зы	*on expiry of the visa*
по оконча́нии университéта	*on completing university* (i.e. *on graduation*)
по получéнии письмá	*on receipt of the letter*

ПРИ used only with the prepositional:

(a) *at the time of*:

Он жил **при Лéнине**.	*He lived at the time of Lenin.*
Достоéвский нáчал писáть **при Николáе пéрвом**.	*Dostoevskii started writing in the reign of Nicholas I.*

(b) *adjacent/attached to*:

я́сли **при фáбрике**	*a nursery attached to the factory*
буфéт **при вокзáле**	*a station buffet*

(c) *in the presence of:*

ссо́риться **при гостя́х**   *to quarrel in front of the guests*

(d) *given the availability of:*

Я э́то сде́лаю **при трёх**   *I'll do this on three conditions.*
усло́виях.

(e) *while sth is being done* (R3); *in this sense the phrase with* **при** *is*
synonymous with an imperfective gerund:

Мы теря́ем мно́го проду́ктов   *We lose a lot of foodstuffs while*
при транспортиро́вке.   *they are being transported.*

10.2   Prepositional phrases based on nouns

Prepositional phrases based on nouns, such as the following, are a
feature of the official register (see 1.3.4(b)):

в де́ле + gen	*in the matter of*
в отли́чие от + gen	*unlike, in contrast to*
в отноше́нии + gen	*in respect of*
в связи́ с + instr	*in connection with*
в си́лу + gen	*by virtue of*
в соотве́тствии с + instr	*in accordance with*
в тече́ние + gen	*in the course of*
в це́лях + gen	*with the object of*
за счёт + gen	*at the expense of*
на основа́нии + gen	*on the basis of*
по ли́нии + gen	*through the channel of*
по направле́нию к + dat	*in the direction of*
по отноше́нию к + dat	*with respect to*
по причи́не + gen	*by reason of*
по слу́чаю + gen	*by reason of*

10.3   Verbs followed by prepositions

Many verbs may be followed by certain prepositions. In the following
sections some of the more common combinations of verb +
preposition are given.

10.3.1   Verbs followed by prepositions governing the accusative

В + acc	ве́рить/пове́рить в	*to believe in*
	вме́шиваться/вмеша́ться в	*to interfere, intervene in*
	вторга́ться/вто́ргнуться в	*to invade*
	игра́ть в	*to play (a game, sport)*
	одева́ть(ся)/оде́ть(ся) в	*to dress (oneself) in*

		поступа́ть/поступи́ть в	*to enter* (institution)
		превраща́ть(ся)/преврати́ть(ся) в	*to turn/be turned into*
		стреля́ть в	*to shoot at* (fixed target)

ЗА + acc (a) after verbs with the sense of *taking hold of*:

	брать/взять кого́-н **за́ руку**	*to take sb by the hand*
	вести́ кого́-н **за́ руку**	*to lead sb by the hand*
	держа́ть кого́-н **за́ руку**	*to hold sb by the hand*
	держа́ться за (e.g. **пери́ла**)	*to hold on to* (e.g. the handrail)
	хвата́ть/схвати́ть кого́-н **за ши́ворот**	*to seize sb by the scruff of the neck*

(b) *for the sake of:*

	боро́ться за что́-н	*to fight/struggle for sth*
	заступа́ться/заступи́ться за кого́-н	*to stand up/plead/intercede for sb*
	пить/вы́пить за (e.g. чьё-н **здоро́вье**)	*to drink to* (e.g. sb's health)
	сража́ться/срази́ться за (e.g. **ро́дину**)	*to fight for* (e.g. one's country)

НА + acc

гляде́ть/погляде́ть на	*to look at*
дели́ть/раздели́ть на	*to divide into*
жа́ловаться/пожа́ловаться на	*to complain of*
наде́яться на	*to hope for, count on, rely on*
напада́ть/напа́сть на	*to attack, fall upon*
отвеча́ть/отве́тить на	*to reply to* (letter, question)
полага́ться/положи́ться на	*to count on, rely on*
серди́ться/рассерди́ться на	*to be angry at, cross with*
смотре́ть/посмотре́ть на	*to look at*
соглаша́ться/согласи́ться на	*to agree to* (but not *to agree with*)

10.3.2 Verbs followed by prepositions governing the genitive

ИЗ + gen

состоя́ть из	*to consist of*
стреля́ть из	*to shoot, fire* (a weapon)

ОТ + gen

отка́зываться/отказа́ться от	*to refuse, decline, turn down*
отлича́ться/отличи́ться от	*to differ from*
страда́ть от	*to suffer from*

Note: **страда́ть от** means to suffer from some temporary or slight problem as opposed to a chronic problem (in the latter meaning **страда́ть** is followed by the instrumental).

С + gen

начина́ть(ся)/нача́ть(ся) с чего́-н	*to begin with sth*
сбива́ть/сбить спесь с кого́-н	*to take sb down a peg*

10.3.3   Verbs followed by prepositions governing the dative

К + dat especially verbs indicating approach or attachment:

относи́ться/отнести́сь к	*to relate to, have an attitude to*
подходи́ть/подойти́ к	*to approach, match, suit*
приближа́ться/прибли́зиться к	*to approach, draw near to*
привлека́ть/привле́чь к	*to attract to*
привыка́ть/привы́кнуть к	*to get used/grow accustomed to*
прилипа́ть/прили́пнуть к	*to stick/adhere to*
прислоня́ться/прислони́ться к	*to lean against*
присоединя́ться/присоедини́ться к	*to join*
стреми́ться к	*to strive towards, aspire to*

Note: the verb **принадлежа́ть** is followed by **к** when it denotes membership (cf. ownership; see 11.1.8(c)), e.g. **принадлежа́ть к полити́ческой па́ртии**, *to belong to a political party.*

ПО + dat

скуча́ть по кому́-н/чему́-н	*to miss sb/sth*
стреля́ть по чему́-н	*to shoot at*

Note: used if the target is a moving or mobile one, or if random shots are fired at a target; cf. **стреля́ть в** + acc, 10.3.1:

суди́ть по чему́-н	*to judge by sth*
тоскова́ть по кому́-н/чему́-н	*to long for sb/sth*
ударя́ть/уда́рить кого́-н/что́-н по чему́-н (e.g. по щеке́)	*to hit sb/sth on sth (e.g. on the cheek)*

10.3.4   Verbs followed by prepositions governing the instrumental

ЗА + instr verbs indicating pursuit of sth, supervision or caring for sth:

идти́/пойти́ за	*to go for, fetch*
наблюда́ть за	*to supervise*
надзира́ть за	*to supervise*
присма́тривать/присмотре́ть за	*to look after, keep an eye on*
следи́ть за	*to track, shadow, follow, keep an eye on*
сле́довать/после́довать за	*to go after, follow*
уха́живать за	*to court, look after, tend to*

НАД + instr

возвыша́ться/возвы́ситься над	*to tower over*
госпо́дствовать над	*to dominate, tower above*
издева́ться над	*to mock*
рабо́тать над	*to work at/on*
смея́ться над	*to laugh at*

| ПЕ́РЕД + instr | извиня́ться/извини́ться пе́ред | to apologise to |
| | преклоня́ться/преклони́ться пе́ред | to admire, worship |

С + instr	встреча́ться/встре́титься с	to meet (by arrangement)
	здоро́ваться/поздоро́ваться с	to greet, say hello to
	знако́миться/познако́миться с	to meet, get acquainted with
	проща́ться/попроща́ться с	to say goodbye to
	расстава́ться/расста́ться с	to part with
	сове́товаться/посове́товаться с	to consult
	соглаша́ться/согласи́ться с	to agree with
	ссо́риться/поссо́риться с	to quarrel with
	ста́лкиваться/столкну́ться с	to collide with, run into

10.3.5   Verbs followed by prepositions governing the prepositional

В + prep	нужда́ться в	to need, be in need of
	обвиня́ть/обвини́ть в	to accuse of
	признава́ться/призна́ться в	to confess, own up to
	сомнева́ться в	to doubt, question
	убежда́ть(ся)/убеди́ть(ся) в	to convince/be convinced of
	уверя́ть/уве́рить в	to assure of
	уча́ствовать в	to participate in, take part in

| НА + prep | говори́ть на како́м-н языке́ | to speak in a language |

Note: used when one is specifying in which language communication takes place, e.g. на э́той се́ссии конфере́нции **говоря́т на ру́сском**, *at this session of the conference they are speaking in Russian.*

	жени́ться на	to get married to (of man marrying woman)
	игра́ть на	to play (a musical instrument)
	остана́вливаться/останови́ться на	to dwell on (e.g. of conversation, lecture)
	ска́зываться/сказа́ться на	to tell on, have an effect on

О + prep	жале́ть о	to regret, be sorry about
	забо́титься/позабо́титься о	to worry about
	знать о	to know about
	мечта́ть о	to dream about
	расска́зывать/рассказа́ть о	to recount, relate, tell
	слы́шать о	to hear about
	сообща́ть/сообщи́ть о	to inform about
	узнава́ть/узна́ть о	to find out about, discover

10.4   Rendering of English prepositions in Russian

In this section the most common Russian rendering of the principal meanings of English prepositions is given, together with some examples of equivalents of the English prepositions in certain idiomatic contexts.

ABOUT   (a)   meaning *concerning*: **о** + prep; **про** + acc (R1); **насчёт** + gen; **относи́тельно** + gen (*with regard to;* R3, esp R3b):

a book about football	кни́га **о футбо́ле**
a film about the war	фильм **про войну́** (R1)
What about your essay?	Как **насчёт** ва́шего сочине́ния?
concerning your letter of 1 June	**относи́тельно** Ва́шего письма́ от 1-го ию́ня (R3b)

(b)   meaning *around* a place: **по** + dat:

She was pacing about the room.	Она́ расха́живала **по ко́мнате**.

(c)   expressing approximation, rendered in one of the following ways: **о́коло** + gen; **с** + acc (R1); **приблизи́тельно**; **приме́рно**; by inversion of numeral and noun:

about two hours	**о́коло двух часо́в**
about a week	**с неде́лю** (R1)
about forty pounds	**приблизи́тельно** со́рок фу́нтов
	приме́рно со́рок фу́нтов
	фу́нтов со́рок

ABOVE   (a)   meaning *over, higher than*: **над** + instr; **вы́ше** + gen:

above the clouds	**над облака́ми**
above zero	**вы́ше нуля́**

(b)   in various expressions:

above all	**пре́жде всего́**
above-board	**че́стный, откры́тый**
above suspicion	**вне подозре́ния**
to get above oneself	**зазнава́ться/зазна́ться** (R1)

ACCORDING TO   **по** + dat; **согла́сно** + dat (R3):

according to Tolstoi	**по Толсто́му**
according to the timetable	**по расписа́нию**
according to the treaty	**согла́сно догово́ру** (R3)

Note: *the Gospel according to Mark,* **ева́нгелие от Ма́рка**.

ACROSS   (a)   indicating movement to the other side: **че́рез** + acc:

a bridge across the river	мост **че́рез ре́ку́**
We went across the desert.	Мы перее́хали **че́рез пусты́ню**.

Note: with transitive verbs bearing the prefix **пере-**, **че́рез** may be omitted, e.g. **переходи́ть доро́гу**, *to cross the road.*

	(b)	indicating position on the other side of: **на то́й стороне́** or **по ту́ сто́рону** + gen; **за** + instr (= *beyond*); **напро́тив** (= *opposite*):

There's a park across the road.	**По ту́ сто́рону доро́ги** располо́жен парк.
They live across the ocean.	Они́ живу́т **за океа́ном**.
They live across the road.	Они́ живу́т **напро́тив**.

	(c)	indicating movement over the surface of sth: **по** + dat:

Clouds were scudding across the sky.	Облака́ несли́сь **по не́бу**.

	(d)	crosswise, obstructing: **поперёк** + gen:

A lorry stood across the road.	Грузови́к стоя́л **поперёк доро́ги**.

AFTER	(a)	in temporal sense: **по́сле** + gen:

after work	**по́сле рабо́ты**

	(b)	indicating that a period of time has elapsed: **че́рез** + acc; **спустя́** + acc; and also **по́сле** + gen:

after a while	**че́рез не́которое вре́мя**
after a week	**спустя́ неде́лю**
after a long absence	**по́сле до́лгого отсу́тствия**

	(c)	indicating succession: **за** + instr:

day after day	**день за днём**
page after page	**страни́ца за страни́цей**

	(d)	meaning *following* or *in pursuit of*: **за** + instr; **вслед за** + instr; **вслед** + dat:

to run after a tram	бежа́ть **за трамва́ем**
He got in after the driver.	Он влез **вслед за води́телем**.
She shouted after him.	Она́ крича́ла **ему́ вслед**.

	(e)	in certain expressions:

after all	**в конце́ концо́в**
after you (when inviting sb to go first)	**прошу́ вас**
named after	**на́званный по** + dat; **на́званный в честь** + gen (= *named in honour of*)
to take after	**быть похо́жим/похо́жей на** + acc
the day after tomorrow	**послеза́втра**

AGAINST	(a)	meaning *in opposition to*: **про́тив** + gen:

I voted against the plan.	Я проголосова́л(а) **про́тив пла́на**.

Note:	with verbs indicating contest *against* may be translated by **с** + instr, e.g. **боро́ться с ке́м-н**, *to fight against sb*.

(b)   meaning *in collision with*: **о** + acc; **на** + acc:

to bang one's head against a wall	сту́кнуться голово́й **о сте́ну**
We ran up against a problem.	Мы натолкну́лись **на пробле́му.**

(c)   meaning in *contact with*: **к** + dat:

He was leaning against the door.	Он прислоня́лся **к две́ри.**

(d)   indicating protection against: **от** + gen; **на слу́чай** + gen:

to protect against disease	предохраня́ть/предохрани́ть **от заболева́ния**
precautions against infection	предосторо́жности **на слу́чай инфе́кции**

ALONG   **по** + dat; also **вдоль** + gen (= *down the side of*):

She was walking along the path.	Она́ шла **по тропи́нке.**
We were driving along the border.	Мы е́хали **вдоль грани́цы.**

AMONG   (a)   meaning *in the midst of*: **среди́** + gen:

There was a Spanish girl among the students.	**Среди́ студе́нтов** была́ испа́нка.
Among the little houses was a church.	**Среди́ до́миков** была́ це́рковь.

(b)   meaning *between*: **ме́жду** + instr:

They quarrelled among themselves.	Они́ поссо́рились **ме́жду собо́й.**

(c)   indicating one of a number, usually with superlative adjective: **из** + gen:

The Don is among the longest rivers in Russia.	Дон – одна́ **из са́мых дли́нных рек** Росси́и.

AT   (a)   indicating location: **в** + prep; **на** + prep:

at school	**в шко́ле**
at work	**на рабо́те**

Note: **на** is used to express *at* with many Russian nouns which an English-speaker might expect would combine with **в** (see 10.1.6 for lists).

(b)   indicating location in *the vicinity of* or *at sb's house*: **у** + gen:

I left my car at the station.	Я оста́вил(а) маши́ну **у вокза́ла.**
I'm having dinner at a friend's place.	Я обе́даю **у дру́га.**

(c)   indicating location *behind* certain objects: **за** + instr:

at the table	**за столо́м**
at the piano	**за роя́лем**
at the wheel (of car, boat)	**за рулём**

(d)   in certain expressions defining point in time: **в** + prep:

at half past one	**в полови́не второ́го**
at the beginning of April	**в нача́ле апре́ля**
at an early age	**в ра́ннем во́зрасте**
At what time?	**В кото́ром часу́?**

(e)   in other expressions defining point in time, including minutes past the hour: **в** + acc:

at one o'clock	**в час**
at midday	**в по́лдень**
at five past two	**в пять** мину́т тре́тьего
at that time	**в то вре́мя**
at a given moment	**в да́нный моме́нт**
at dusk	**в су́мерки**

Note: in expressions indicating time before the hour *at* is not translated, e.g. *at five to ten*, **без пяти́ де́сять**.

(f)   in yet other expressions defining point in time: **на** + prep:

at dawn	**на заре́/на рассве́те**
at sunset	**на зака́те**

(g)   in the following expressions of time: **на** + acc:

at Christmas	**на Рождество́**
at Easter	**на Па́сху**

(h)   indicating direction of an action: **в** + acc; **на** + acc:

to shoot at sth	**стреля́ть во что́-н**
to throw sth at sb	**броса́ть/бро́сить что́-н в кого́-н**
to look at sth	**смотре́ть/посмотре́ть на что́-н**
to point at sth	**ука́зывать/указа́ть на что́-н**

(i)   in miscellaneous other expressions:

at 100°	**при ста гра́дусах**
at 100 kilometres per hour	**со ско́ростью сто киломе́тров в час**
at any price	**любо́й цено́й**
at one's own expense	**за свой счёт**
at first sight	**на пе́рвый взгляд**
at home	**до́ма**
at last	**наконе́ц**
at least	**по кра́йней ме́ре**
at leisure	**на досу́ге**
at night	**но́чью**
at once	**сра́зу**
at the request of	**по про́сьбе**

BECAUSE OF		из-за + gen (esp for negative reason); благодаря + dat (= *thanks to*); вследствие + gen (= *owing to*; more formal, R2/3)	

because of an earthquake	**из-за землетрясе́ния**
thanks to your foresight	**благодаря́ ва́шей предусмотри́тельности**
Owing to the rain the fair did not take place.	**Всле́дствие дождя́** я́рмарка не состоя́лась.

BEFORE	(a)	in a temporal sense: до + gen (= *previous to, earlier than*); пе́ред + instr (= *[just] before*):

before the revolution	**до револю́ции**
long before	**задо́лго до**
We changed before dinner.	Мы переоде́лись **пе́ред обе́дом**.

(b)	when *before* is followed by an English gerund it may be translated by пе́ред + a verbal noun or by пре́жде чем + infin, e.g.

before leaving	**пе́ред отъе́здом**
before replying	**пре́жде чем отве́тить**

(c)	indicating location: пе́ред + instr:

You see before you a list.	Вы ви́дите **пе́ред собо́й** спи́сок.
before the court	**пе́ред судо́м**

(d)	in other expressions:

before long	**ско́ро**
before now	**ра́ньше**
before witnesses	**при свиде́телях**
the day before yesterday	**позавчера́**

BEHIND	(a)	indicating motion behind: за + acc:

The sun went behind a cloud.	Со́лнце зашло́ **за о́блако**.
He put his hands behind his back.	Он заложи́л ру́ки **за́ спину**.

(b)	indicating location: за + instr:

She was walking behind me.	Она́ шла **за мной**.
He was hiding behind a tree.	Он пря́тался **за де́ревом**.

(c)	in other senses and expressions:

She is behind the other girls in her class.	Она́ **отстаёт от** други́х де́вушек в кла́ссе.
The team is behind the captain.	Кома́нда **подде́рживает** капита́на.
What's behind this?	**Что за** э́тим **кро́ется?**

BELOW/ BENEATH	(a)	indicating motion below: под + acc:

The swimmer dived below the water.	Плове́ц нырну́л **под во́ду**.

(b)	indicating location: **под** + instr:	
	below ground	**под землёй**
	below the surface	**под поверхностью**

(c)	meaning *lower than, inferior to:* **ниже** + gen:	
	below average	**ниже среднего**
	below a captain in rank	**ниже капитана по рангу**
	beneath criticism	**ниже всякой критики**
	beneath my dignity	**ниже моего достоинства**

BEYOND   = *behind* in the senses described in (a) and (b) above; also in certain expressions, e.g.

	beyond belief	**невероятно**
	beyond one's means	**не по средствам**
	beyond reach	**вне досягаемости**
	beyond one's understanding	**выше понимания**

BY

(a)	indicating agent or instrument or means of transport: instrumental case with no preposition:	
	The play was written by Chekhov.	Пьеса была написана **Чеховым**.
	The building was destroyed by a fire.	Здание было уничтожено **пожаром**.
	by train	**поездом**

Note: in phrases of the following sort, which lack a verb, the genitive may be used:

	a play by Chekhov	пьеса **Чехова**
	a speech by the president	речь **президента**

(b)	meaning *in accordance with,* and also indicating means of communication: **по** + dat:	
	by nature	**по природе**
	by this clock	**по этим часам**
	by television	**по телевидению**

(c)	meaning *in the vicinity of:* **у** + gen; **около** + gen; **возле** + gen; **рядом с** + instr (= *next to*); **вдоль** + gen (= *alongside*):	
	to sit by the window	сидеть **у**/**около окна**
	She was standing by the bus-stop.	Она стояла **у**/**около автобусной остановки**.
	She was sitting by me.	Она сидела **возле меня**.
	The shop is by the theatre.	Магазин находится **рядом с театром**.
	a track by the river	дорожка **вдоль реки**

(d)	meaning *past:* **мимо** + gen:	
	She went by the bank.	Она прошла **мимо банка**.

(e)   meaning *by way of*: **че́рез** + acc:

She came in by the side entrance.	Она́ вошла́ **че́рез боково́й вход**.

(f)   meaning *not after*: **к** + dat:

by Saturday	**к суббо́те**
It always snows by Christmas.	Всегда́ идёт снег **к Рождеству́**.

(g)   indicating a margin of difference, and also expressing multiplication, division or combination of dimensions: **на** + acc:

older by one week	ста́рше **на одну́ неде́лю**
They increased my salary by a thousand pounds.	Увели́чили мою́ зарпла́ту **на ты́сячу фу́нтов**.
ten by five	де́сять **на пять**

(h)   after verbs meaning *to take hold of*: **за** + acc:

He took her by the hand.	Он взял её **за́ руку**.
I seized him by the neck.	Я схвати́л(а) его́ **за ше́ю**.

(i)   in miscellaneous other expressions:

by chance	**случа́йно**
by means of	**посре́дством** + gen; **путём** + gen
by no means	**во́все не**; **отню́дь не** (R3)
by mistake	**по оши́бке**
by the way	**ме́жду про́чим/кста́ти**
to know sb by sight	**знать** кого́-н **в лицо́**
to learn sth by heart	**вы́учить** что́-н **наизу́сть**
to pay by the month	**плати́ть/заплати́ть поме́сячно**
one by one	**оди́н за одни́м**
step by step	**шаг за ша́гом**

DOWN

(a)   meaning *along*: **по** + dat:

down the corridor	**по коридо́ру**
He is going down the road.	Он идёт **по доро́ге**.

(b)   meaning *descending along*: **вниз по** + dat; **с** + gen:

I am going downstairs.	Иду́ **вниз** (по ле́стнице).
downstream	**вниз по тече́нию**
They came down the hill.	Они́ спусти́лись **с горы́**.

DURING

(a)   meaning *at some point in*: **во вре́мя** + gen:

He died during the war.	Он у́мер **во вре́мя войны́**.
I left during the interval.	Я ушёл/ушла́ **во вре́мя антра́кта**.

(b)   meaning *throughout, in the course of*: **в тече́ние** + gen; **на протяже́нии** + gen; these expressions are used mainly with nouns which have temporal meaning:

During the 80s the USSR was collapsing.	**В тече́ние восьмидеся́тых годо́в** СССР распада́лся.

	During the last century Russian literature flourished.	**На протяже́нии про́шлого ве́ка** процвета́ла ру́сская литерату́ра.
(c)	meaning *in the reign/rule/time of:* **при** + prep:	
	censorship during the reign of Nicholas	цензу́ра **при Никола́е**
	the terror during Stalin's rule	терро́р **при Ста́лине**

EXCEPT FOR **кро́ме** + gen; **за исключе́нием** + gen (= *with the exception of*); **исключа́я** + acc (= *excepting*; R3):

Everybody left except me.	Все ушли́ **кро́ме меня́**.
All the students passed the exam except for one.	Все студе́нты, **за исключе́нием одного́**, сда́ли экза́мен.
All the conditions were agreed except for one.	Все усло́вия бы́ли согласо́ваны **исключа́я одно́**.

FOR

(a) indicating benefit, purpose, suitability or unsuitability: **для** + gen:

a present for you	пода́рок **для тебя́**
clothes for big people	оде́жда **для люде́й** больши́х разме́ров
The book is useful for foreigners.	Уче́бник поле́зен для **иностра́нцев**.
Polluted air is bad for one's health.	Загрязнённый во́здух вре́ден **для здоро́вья**.

Note: with verbs, or when a verb is understood, the person benefiting may be in the dative, e.g.

She bought a tie for me.	Она́ купи́ла **мне** га́лстук.
There's a letter for you.	**Вам** письмо́. (R1)

(b) expressing duration, time spent doing sth or distance covered: accusative case with no preposition; **в тече́ние** + gen:

He lay for a week in hospital.	Он пролежа́л **неде́лю** в больни́це.
I have been living here for a year.	Я здесь живу́ **оди́н год**.
I ran (for) a mile.	Я пробежа́л(а) **ми́лю**.
for a month	**в тече́ние ме́сяца**

(c) indicating the amount of time action is expected to last, or that sth is arranged for a certain time or intended for a certain purpose: **на** + acc:

He has gone to Moscow for a week.	Он пое́хал в Москву́ **на неде́лю**.
closed for the winter	закры́то **на́ зиму**
for a long time	**надо́лго**
forever	**навсегда́**
a meeting arranged for two o'clock	встре́ча, назна́ченная **на два** часа́
dinner for two	обе́д **на двои́х**
a house for sale	дом **на прода́жу**
for example	**наприме́р**

(d) meaning *in return for*, and also indicating support for sb or sth: **за** + acc:

I paid the cashier for the book	Я заплати́л(а) касси́рше **за кни́гу**.
We thanked them for their hospitality.	Мы поблагодари́ли их **за гостеприи́мство**.
an eye for an eye	**о́ко за о́ко**
He is voting for me.	Он голосу́ет **за меня́**.

(e) meaning *in search of*: **за** + instr:

| *I sent for a doctor.* | Я посла́л(а) **за до́ктором**. |

(f) after many nouns indicating attitude: **к** + dat:

love for one's country	**любо́вь к ро́дине**
a passion for music	**страсть к му́зыке**
respect for foreigners	**уваже́ние к иностра́нцам**

(g) in miscellaneous other expressions, e.g.

for and against	**за́ и про́тив**
for certain	**наверняка́**
for the first time	**в пе́рвый раз/впервы́е**
for hours on end	**це́лыми часа́ми**
for this reason	**по э́той причи́не**
for God's sake	**ра́ди Бо́га**
as for me	**что каса́ется меня́**
known for	**изве́стный** + instr
once for all	**раз навсегда́**
There were no houses for miles around.	**На мно́гие ми́ли вокру́г** не́ было домо́в.
to cry for joy	**пла́кать от ра́дости**
to get married for love	**жени́ться по любви́**
He is tall for his age.	Он высо́к **не по лета́м**.
to ask for	**проси́ть/попроси́ть** + acc or gen or **о** + prep
to long for	**тоскова́ть по** + dat
to look for	**иска́ть** + acc or gen
to be sorry for sb	**жале́ть кого́-н**
to wait for	**ждать/подожда́ть** + acc or gen

FROM   (a) meaning *out of* (i.e. the opposite of **в** + acc); *originating from, made of*: **из** + gen:

We went from Moscow to Minsk.	Мы пое́хали **из Москвы́** в Минск.
from afar	**издалека́**
fruit from Spain	**фру́кты из Испа́нии**
sausages made from pork	соси́ски, **сде́ланные из свини́ны**

(b)   meaning *away from* (i.e. the opposite of **до** or **к**); expressing distance *from*; indicating person *from* whom sth originates; indicating protection, freedom, concealment, separation, difference *from*; meaning *by reason of*: **от** + gen:

The train is drawing away from the platform.	По́езд отхо́дит от **платфо́рмы**.
from here/there	**отсю́да/отту́да**
two minutes from the centre	в двух мину́тах **от це́нтра**
a present from my mother	пода́рок **от мое́й ма́тери**
protection from the gale	защи́та **от урага́на**
exemption from taxation	освобожде́ние **от нало́гов**
cut off from civilisation	отре́занный **от цивилиза́ции**
Russian architecture differs from ours.	Ру́сская архитекту́ра **отлича́ется от на́шей**.
He collapsed from exhaustion.	Он свали́лся **от изнеможе́ния**.

(c)   meaning *off, down from* (i.e. the opposite of **на** + acc; therefore used to mean *from* before nouns in 10.1.6, **на** (b–e)); meaning *by reason of* in R1; and also *since*: **с** + gen:

The book fell from the shelf.	Кни́га упа́ла **с по́лки**.
from east to west	**с восто́ка на за́пад**
from the Urals	**с Ура́ла**
from above/below	**све́рху/сни́зу**
from boredom	**со ску́ки**
from 1 April	**с пе́рвого** апре́ля
from childhood	**с де́тства**

(d)   indicating removal of sth that belongs to sb else: **у** + gen:

She took the toy away from the child.	Она́ отняла́ **у ребёнка** игру́шку.
He borrowed a mower from his neighbour.	Он за́нял газоно코си́лку **у сосе́да**.

(e)   preceding a gerund: infinitive form of verb:

You are preventing me from working.	Ты меша́ешь **мне рабо́тать**.

(f)   in many other expressions:

from bad to worse	всё ху́же и ху́же
from behind	**и́з-за** + gen
from generation to generation	из поколе́ния в поколе́ние
from time to time	вре́мя от вре́мени
from under	**и́з-под** + gen
change from a pound	сда́ча с фу́нта
The town dates from the tenth century.	Го́род отно́сится к деся́тому ве́ку.
a year from now	через го́д

IN

(a) indicating location; indicating a point in a month, decade, year, century, time of life, or in the past, present or future; also describing attire: **в** + prep:

in the garden	**в саду́**
I read it in a newspaper.	Я чита́л(а) э́то **в газе́те.**
in March	**в ма́рте**
in 1994	**в** ты́сяча девятьсо́т девяно́сто **четвёртом году́**
in the last decade of the century	**в после́днем десятиле́тии** ве́ка
in the twentieth century	**в двадца́том ве́ке**
in old age	**в ста́рости**
in the future	**в бу́дущем**
in a blue shirt	**в си́ней руба́шке**

(b) indicating motion *into* or duration of an action or period: **в** + acc:

She went in the canteen.	Она́ вошла́ **в столо́вую.**
in that age	**в ту эпо́ху**

(c) expressing *in* with periods of the day and seasons of the year; expressing *in* in some adverbial phrases of manner; indicating material used in some action; also indicating method of arranging people or things: instrumental case with no preposition:

in the morning	**у́тром**
in winter	**зимо́й**
in a loud voice	**гро́мким го́лосом**
to write in ink	писа́ть **черни́лами**
in small groups	**небольши́ми гру́ппами**
in rows	**ряда́ми**

(d) meaning *in* with certain nouns listed in 10.1.6, на (b–e); defining time in relation to the beginning of a certain period; also in certain set phrases: **на** + prep:

in the street	**на у́лице**
in Cuba	**на Ку́бе**
in the north	**на се́вере**
in the war	**на войне́**
in the kitchen (in order to cook)	**на ку́хне**
in the first minute of the second half	**на пе́рвой мину́те** второ́го та́йма
in my lifetime	**на моём веку́**
in old age	**на ста́рости лет** (R1)

(e) indicating time taken to complete an action or meaning *over* a period: **за** + acc:

Five centimetres of rain fell in one day.	**За оди́н день** вы́пало пять сантиме́тров дождя́.

(f) indicating time after a certain interval: **че́рез** + acc:

I'll come back in a week.	Я верну́сь **че́рез неде́лю.**

(g) meaning *on the subject of*: **по** + dat:

an exam in geography	экза́мен по геогра́фии
research in electronics	иссле́дования по электро́нике

(h) meaning *in the reign/time of*, and in phrases indicating attendant circumstances: **при** + prep:

in Pushkin's time	при Пу́шкине
in the Brezhnev era	при Бре́жневе
in complete silence	при по́лном молча́нии

(i) in other expressions:

in advance	зара́нее
in all respects	во всех отноше́ниях
in answer to	в отве́т на + acc
in any case	во вся́ком слу́чае
in the circumstances	при э́тих усло́виях
in custody	под аре́стом
in the end	в конце́ концо́в
in the evenings	по вечера́м
in general	вообще́
in good time	заблаговре́менно (R3)
in honour of	в честь + gen
in memory of	в па́мять + gen
in a minute	сейча́с
in the name of	от и́мени + gen
in my opinion	по моему́ мне́нию/по-мо́ему (R1/2)
in respect of	по отноше́нию к + dat (R3)
in spite of	несмотря́ на + acc
in succession	подря́д
in turn	по о́череди
to believe in God	ве́рить в Бо́га
blind in one eye	слепо́й/слепа́я на оди́н глаз
deaf in one ear	глухо́й/глуха́я на одно́ у́хо
I'm in my twenties.	Мне за два́дцать.
an interest in politics	интере́с к поли́тике
just in case	на вся́кий слу́чай
to be in power	быть у вла́сти
The word ends in a soft sign.	Сло́во конча́ется на мя́гкий знак.

INSIDE (a) indicating location: **в** + prep; **внутри́** + gen:

inside the house	в до́ме
We do not know what is happening inside the country.	Мы не зна́ем, что происхо́дит внутри́ страны́.

(b) indicating motion: generally **в** + acc:

to go inside the house	входи́ть/войти́ в дом

INSTEAD OF		**вме́сто** + gen:	
		Have some juice instead of water.	Вы́пейте со́ка **вме́сто воды́**.
	Note:	this preposition should not be confused with **вме́сте**, *together*.	

INTO	(a)	generally **в** + acc:	
		They went into the hall.	Они́ вошли́ **в зал**.
		to fall into a trap	попада́ть/попа́сть **в лову́шку**
		The water turned into ice.	Вода́ преврати́лась **в лёд**.
	(b)	with some nouns denoting open spaces (see 10.1.6, **на** (b–c)); after certain verbs with the prefix **на–**; indicating division: **на** + acc:	
		She came out into the street.	Она́ вы́шла **на у́лицу**.
		I cut the loaf into pieces.	Я разре́зал(а) хлеб **на куски́**.

OF	(a)	expressing possession or quantity and in other functions: genitive case with no preposition:	
		the roof of the house	**кры́ша до́ма**
		the end of the lecture	**коне́ц ле́кции**
		a slice of bread	**ломо́ть хле́ба**
		a litre of beer	**литр пи́ва**
		a bunch of keys	**свя́зка ключе́й**
		the rector of the institute	**ре́ктор институ́та**
	(b)	expressing identity or definition: noun in apposition, or use of adjective:	
		the city of London	**го́род Ло́ндон**
		the Isle of Wight	**о́стров Уа́йт**
		the month of May	**ме́сяц май**
		the University of Oxford	**Оксфо́рдский университе́т**
		the Battle of Borodino	**Бороди́нское сраже́ние**
		the Sea of Azov	**Азо́вское мо́ре**
		Lawrence of Arabia	**Ло́уренс Арави́йский**
	(c)	meaning *out of* or *consisting of*; also indicating material of which sth is made: **из** + gen:	
		one of the students	**оди́н/одна́ из студе́нтов**
		some of them	**не́которые из них**
		a family of four	**семья́ из четырёх челове́к**
		a table made of wood	**стол из де́рева**
	(d)	indicating amount, capacity, dimension: **в** + acc:	
		an article of twenty pages	**статья́ в два́дцать страни́ц**
		an army of 100,000 men	**а́рмия в сто ты́сяч солда́т**
		a building of ten stories	**зда́ние в де́сять этаже́й**
		a field of three hectares	**по́ле пло́щадью в три гекта́ра**

(e)	in other functions and expressions:	
	of course	**коне́чно**
	your letter of 2 May	**Ва́ше письмо́ от второ́го ма́я**
	the Battle of Stalingrad	**би́тва под Сталингра́дом**
	capable of anything	**спосо́бный на всё**
	characteristic of	**характе́рный для** + gen
	typical of	**типи́чный для** + gen
	a charge of murder	**обвине́ние в уби́йстве**
	east of Moscow	**к восто́ку от Москвы́**
	envy of (one's) neighbour	**за́висть к сосе́ду**
	news of the accident	**весть об ава́рии**
	a view of the forest	**вид на лес**
	a copy of a document	**ко́пия (с) докуме́нта**
	The room smells of smoke.	**В ко́мнате па́хнет табако́м.**

OFF

(a)	meaning *off the surface of sth, down from*: **с** + gen:	
	I took the saucepan off the stove.	**Я снял(а́) кастрю́лю с плиты́.**
	He fell off the ladder.	**Он упа́л с ле́стницы.**

(b)	meaning *at a distance from*: **от** + gen:	
	two kilometres off the coast	**на расстоя́нии двух киломе́тров от бе́рега**
	not far off	**недалеко́ от** **неподалёку от**

(c)	indicating dispossession or removal: **у** + gen:	
	I borrowed a book off him.	**Я взял(а́) у него́ кни́гу почита́ть.** (R1)
	He broke the handle off the door.	**Он отби́л ру́чку у две́ри.**

(d)	in certain expressions:	
	off the beaten track	**по непроторённой доро́ге**
	off colour (unwell)	**нездоро́вый/нездоро́вая**
	(not in form)	**не в фо́рме**
	off work	**не на рабо́те**
	goods at ten per cent off	**това́ры на де́сять проце́нтов ни́же обы́чной цены́**
	Keep off the grass.	**Не ходи́ть по траве́.**
	She's off her food.	**У неё нет аппети́та.**
	He's off his rocker.	**Он спя́тил с ума́.** (R1)

ON

(a)	indicating location: **на** + prep:	
	He's sitting on a stool.	**Он сиди́т на табуре́тке.**
	on board	**на борту́**

(b)	indicating movement *on to*: **на** + acc:	
	He climbed on the roof.	**Он влез на кры́шу.**
	They got on the train.	**Они́ се́ли на по́езд.**

(c)   *on* a day of the week: **в** + acc:

on Wednesday	**в сре́ду**
on that day	**в тот день**

(d)   repeatedly *on* a certain day: **по** + dat pl:

on Saturdays	**по суббо́там**
on free days	**по свобо́дным дням**

(e)   expressing a date: genitive case with no preposition:

on 1 March	**пе́рвого** ма́рта
on 22 June	два́дцать **второ́го** ию́ня

(f)   in certain other expressions of time: **на** + acc:

on the following day	**на сле́дующий день**
on the fourth day	**на четвёртый день**
on this occasion	**на э́тот раз**

(g)   meaning *immediately after, on the expiry of*: **по́сле** + gen; **по** + prep (R3):

on arrival	**по́сле прие́зда**
on expiry of the visa	**по истече́нии ви́зы**
On graduating she went abroad.	**По оконча́нии** университе́та она́ пое́хала за грани́цу.

(h)   indicating means of transport; also in certain expressions of time: instrumental case with no preposition:

on a bus	**авто́бусом**
on horseback	**верхо́м**
on a spring evening	**весе́нним ве́чером**

(i)   meaning *on the subject of*: **по** + dat; **о** + prep:

a lecture on geology	ле́кция **по геоло́гии**
an article on Blok	статья́ **о Бло́ке**

(j)   indicating a means of communication: **по** + dat:

I heard about it on the radio.	Я слы́шал(а) об э́том **по ра́дио**.

(k)   in other meanings and expressions:

on average	**в сре́днем**
on no account	**ни в ко́ем слу́чае**
on behalf of	**от и́мени** + gen
on the contrary	**наоборо́т**
on leave	**в о́тпуске**
on the left	**сле́ва**
on the right	**спра́ва**
on the occasion of	**по слу́чаю** + gen
on the one hand	**с одно́й стороны́**

on the other hand	**с другóй стороны́**
on one condition	**при однóм услóвии**
on purpose	**нарóчно**
on the quiet	**потихóньку** (R1)
on time	**вó-время**
on time (according to	**по расписáнию**
timetable)	
on the way home	**по дорóге домóй**
cash on delivery	**с уплáтой при достáвке**
The house is on fire.	**Дом гори́т.**
I had no money on me.	**У меня́ нé было дéнег с собóй.**
The workers are on strike.	**Рабóчие бастýют.**
to work on sth	**рабóтать над чéм-н**

OPPOSITE   **прóтив** + gen; **напрóтив** + gen:

They were sitting opposite each other.	Они́ сидéли друг **прóтив** дрýга.
He is standing opposite the Kremlin.	Он стои́т **напрóтив Кремля́.**

Note: in the meaning of *opposite* **прóтив** and **напрóтив** are interchangeable, but only **прóтив** may mean *against*.

OUT OF   (a)   in most meanings: **из** + gen:

She came out of the shop.	Онá вы́шла **из магази́на.**
He took a coin out of his pocket.	Он вы́нул монéту **из кармáна.**
a chapter out of a novel	главá **из ромáна**
four out of five students	чéтверо **из пяти́ студéнтов**
It's made out of iron.	Сдéлано **из желéза.**

(b)   meaning *outside*: **вне** + gen; **за** + instr (= *beyond*):

out of control	**вне контрóля**
out of danger	**вне опáсности**
out of earshot	**вне предéлов слы́шимости**
out of reach/range	**вне предéлов досягáемости**
out of sight	**вне пóля зрéния**
out of turn	**вне óчереди**
out of town	**зá городом**
out of the country	**за грани́цей**

(c)   indicating cause or motive: **из** + gen; **от** + gen; **с** + gen (R1):

out of respect for you	**из уважéния к вам**
out of pity	**из/от жáлости**
out of spite	**от злóсти** (R2)

(d)   in certain other expressions:

out of breath	**запыхáвшийся** (act part)
	запыхáвшись (gerund)

out of doors	**на у́лице/на дворе́**
(*in the open air*)	**на откры́том во́здухе**
out of fashion	**не в мо́де**
out of order	**не в поря́дке**
(*not working*)	**неиспра́вный/не рабо́тает**
Out of my sight!	**Убира́йся!**
out of work	**без рабо́ты**
to get out of bed	**встава́ть/встать с посте́ли**
We're out of bread.	**У нас ко́нчился хлеб.**
It's out of the question.	**Об э́том не мо́жет быть и ре́чи.**

OUTSIDE

(a) meaning *in the vicinity of*: **о́коло** + gen; **у** + gen; **пе́ред** + instr (= *in front of*):

I met her outside the park.	Я встре́тился с ней **о́коло/у** па́рка.
The car's outside the house.	Маши́на стои́т **перед до́мом.**

(b) meaning *on the outside of, beyond*: **вне** + gen; **за** + instr; **за преде́лами** + gen (= *beyond the bounds of*):

It's outside my competence.	Э́то **вне мое́й компете́нции.**
There was a policeman outside the window.	**За окно́м** стоя́л полице́йский.
He is not known outside Russia.	Он неизве́стен **за преде́лами Росси́и.**

OVER

(a) meaning *across*: **че́рез** + acc; **за** + acc:

a bridge over the river	мост **че́рез ре́ку**
He crossed over the threshold.	Он перешёл **за поро́г.**
to throw overboard	выки́дывать/вы́кинуть **за́ борт**

Note: **че́рез** may be omitted when the verb bears the prefix **пере-**, which may carry the same meaning (see also 10.1.2).

(b) indicating location *beyond, on the other side of*: **за** + instr; **по ту сто́рону** + gen:

I heard a voice over the fence.	Я услы́шал(а) го́лос **за и́згородью.**
They live overseas.	Они́ живу́т **за́ морем.**
the forest over the border	лес **по ту сто́рону грани́цы**

(c) meaning *above*: **над** + instr:

A chandelier hangs over the table.	**Над столо́м** виси́т лю́стра.
A threat hangs over us.	**Над на́ми** виси́т угро́за.

(d) meaning *over the top of*: **пове́рх** + gen:

to look over one's spectacles	смотре́ть **пове́рх очко́в**

(e) meaning *on to*: **на** + acc:

She drew a blanket over the child.	Она́ натяну́ла одея́ло **на ребёнка.**

(f)   meaning *across the surface* of sth; also *by* a means of communication: **по** + dat:

A boat sped over the water.	Ка́тер помча́лся **по воде́**.
all over the world	**по всему́ све́ту**
over the radio	**по ра́дио**

(g)   meaning in the course of a certain period: **в тече́ние** + gen; **за** + acc:

The situation deteriorated over many years.	Ситуа́ция ухудша́лась **в тече́ние мно́гих лет**.
They have all fallen ill over the last week.	Они́ все заболе́ли **за после́днюю неде́лю**.

Note: **в тече́ние** emphasises duration and therefore occurs with an imperfective verb, whilst **за** emphasises the completed nature of the event and therefore tends to dictate the use of a perfective.

(h)   meaning *more than*: **бо́льше** + gen; **свы́ше** + gen (used with numerals); **сверх** + gen (= *over and above, in excess of*):

He drank over a litre of wine.	Он вы́пил **бо́льше ли́тра** вина́.
over a million voters	**свы́ше миллио́на** избира́телей
over (and above) the norm	**сверх но́рмы**

(i)   in other expressions:

over a cup of tea	**за ча́шкой ча́я**
It's over my head.	**Э́то вы́ше моего́ понима́ния.**
to go head over heels	**полете́ть кувырко́м**
to stumble over sth	**спотыка́ться/споткну́ться о** что́-н

PAST

(a)   indicating motion alongside and beyond sth: **ми́мо** + gen:

He ran past me.	Он пробежа́л **ми́мо меня́**.

(b)   indicating location *beyond*: **за** + instr:

The theatre is past the church.	Теа́тр нахо́дится **за це́рковью**.

(c)   meaning *after*: **по́сле** + gen; **за** + acc; **по́зже** + gen:

past midnight	**по́сле полу́ночи/за́ полночь**
She's past fifty.	**Ей за пятьдеся́т.**
It's past ten o'clock.	**По́зже десяти́.**

(d)   in expressions of time: no preposition:

ten past one	**де́сять мину́т второ́го**
at half past six	**в полови́не седьмо́го**

ROUND

(a)   indicating rotation and encirclement: **вокру́г** + gen; **круго́м** (+ gen; encirclement only):

All the guests were sitting round the table.	Все го́сти сиде́ли **вокру́г стола́**.

The earth revolves round the sun.	Земля́ враща́ется **вокру́г со́лнца**.

(b) expressing approximation: **о́коло** + gen:

round (about) midnight	**о́коло полу́ночи**
round a thousand dollars	**о́коло ты́сячи до́лларов**

Note: the adverbs **приблизи́тельно**, *approximately*, and **приме́рно**, *roughly*, may also be used, with no preposition, to express approximation with numbers, e.g. **приме́рно сто фу́нтов**, *round a hundred pounds*.

(c) expressing motion in various directions (often with indeterminate verbs of motion): **по** + dat:

She's walking round the garden.	Она́ хо́дит **по са́ду**.
His things are scattered round the room.	Его́ ве́щи разбро́саны **по ко́мнате**.

(d) after verbs bearing the prefix **об**- *round* may have no prepositional equivalent:

He walked round the puddle.	Он **обошёл** лу́жу.
The nurse put pillows round him.	Медсестра́ **обложи́ла** его́ поду́шками.

THROUGH (a) indicating passage through: **че́рез** + acc (also meaning *via*); **сквозь** + acc (often implying difficulty); **в** + acc:

I went through France.	Я прое́хал(а) **че́рез Фра́нцию**.
We went to Moscow through Minsk.	Мы прое́хали в Москву́ **че́рез Минск**.
He squeezed through the crowd.	Он проти́снулся **сквозь толпу́**.
through a thick fog	**сквозь густо́й тума́н**
He was looking through the window.	Он смотре́л **в окно́**.

(b) meaning *around, over, through* an element: **по** + dat:

He was walking through the streets.	Он шёл **по у́лицам**.
The ball was flying through the air.	Мяч лете́л **по во́здуху**.

(c) meaning *for the duration of, throughout*: accusative case with no preposition:

It rained all through/throughout the day.	**Весь день** шёл дождь.
Work will continue through the winter.	Рабо́та бу́дет продолжа́ться **всю зи́му**.

(d) meaning *as a result of*: **благодаря́** + dat (= *thanks to* a favourable cause); **из-за** + gen (= *because of* some unfavourable cause); **по** + dat (= *for* some abstract reason):

through far-sightedness	**благодаря́ предусмотри́тельности**

		He had to leave work through illness.	Ему́ пришло́сь уйти́ с рабо́ты **из-за боле́зни**.
		to know through experience	знать **по о́пыту**
	(e)	in other expressions:	
		to get through an exam	**сдать экза́мен**
		to go through a fortune	**прома́тывагь/промота́ть состоя́ние**
		to see through sb	**ви́деть** кого́-н **наскво́зь**

TO

(a) expressing indirect object: dative case without any preposition:

He gave his brother a book.	Он дал **бра́ту** кни́гу.
Tell us what to do.	Скажи́те **нам**, чтò де́лать.
Greetings to you.	Приве́т **тебе́/вам**!

(b) indicating direction of movement: **в** + acc; **на** + acc (with certain nouns; see 10.1.6, на (b–e)); **к** + dat (with persons and with sth approached but not entered):

We are going to Russia.	Мы е́дем **в Росси́ю**.
She is going to a concert.	Она́ идёт **на конце́рт**.
to the left/right	**нале́во/напра́во**
I am going to the rector.	Я иду́ **к ре́ктору**.
Come to the table.	Подойди́(те) **к столу́**.
to the south of Voronezh	**к ю́гу** от Воро́нежа

(c) indicating distance, limit or extent: **до** + gen; **по** + acc (= *up to and including*):

the distance from London to Moscow	расстоя́ние от Ло́ндона **до Москвы́**
to the end	**до конца́**
to a certain extent	**до не́которой сте́пени**
He got soaked to the skin.	Он промо́к **до мо́зга** косте́й.
to 1 May	**по пе́рвое** ма́я
He was standing (up) to his knees in water.	Он стоя́л **по коле́ни** в воде́.

(d) indicating attachment, membership, proximity: **к** + dat:

to add five to ten	прибавля́ть/приба́вить пять **к десяти́**
to belong [expressing membership] to a club	принадлежа́ть **к клу́бу**
a preface to a book	предисло́вие **к кни́ге**
shoulder to shoulder	плечо́м **к плечу́**

(e) expressing time *to* the hour: a construction with **без** + gen:

five to ten	**без пяти́ де́сять**

(f) meaning *to the accompaniment of* a sound: **под** + acc:

to dance to a record	танцева́ть **под пласти́нку**

(g) in miscellaneous expressions:

to my surprise	к моему́ удивле́нию
an answer to sth	отве́т на что́-н
a tendency to	скло́нность к + dat
a claim to sth	прете́нзия на что́-н
a right to sth	пра́во на что́-н
an exception to a rule	исключе́ние из пра́вила
the key to a door	ключ от две́ри
compared to	по сравне́нию с + instr
harmful to	вре́дный для + gen
near to	бли́зкий от + gen
similar to	похо́жий на + acc
a visit to (the) Ukraine	посеще́ние Украи́ны
I have been to Moscow.	Я был(а́) в Москве́.

TOWARDS

(a) in most meanings: **к** + dat:

They were travelling towards the lake.	Они́ е́хали к о́зеру.
He was standing with his back towards me.	Он стоя́л ко мне спино́й.
attitude towards	отноше́ние к

(b) in other expressions:

towards evening	под ве́чер
responsibility towards	отве́тственность пе́ред + instr

UNDER

(a) indicating location: **под** + instr:

to sit under the trees	сиде́ть под дере́вьями
to be under suspicion	быть под подозре́нием

(b) indicating motion: **под** + acc:

She shoved a note under the door.	Она́ подсу́нула запи́ску под дверь.

(c) meaning *according to*: **по** + dat:

under Roman law	по ри́мскому пра́ву

(d) in other expressions:

under five dollars	ме́ньше пяти́ до́лларов
children under five	де́ти до пяти́ лет
under those circumstances	при тех обстоя́тельствах
under Lenin	при Ле́нине
under one's arm	под мы́шкой
under repair	в ремо́нте
The matter is under consideration.	Де́ло рассма́тривается. (R3b)

UNTIL

(a) in most contexts: **до** + gen:

until Wednesday	до среды́
until three o'clock	до трёх часо́в

	(b)	meaning *up to and including*: **по** + acc:	
		The visa is valid until 1 March.	Ви́за действи́тельна **по пе́рвое** ма́рта.
	(c)	with negated verb: **то́лько**:	
		I shall not do it until tomorrow.	**Я то́лько за́втра сде́лаю** э́то.

UP	(a)	indicating location: **на** + prep:	
		The cat is up the tree.	Ко́шка сиди́т **на де́реве**.
	(b)	indicating motion: **на** + acc; **(вверх) по** + dat:	
		He went up the hill.	Он пошёл **на́ гору**.
		The smoke goes up the chimney.	Дым поднима́ется **по трубе́**.
		They sailed up the Volga.	Они́ поплы́ли **вверх по Во́лге**.

WITH	(a)	in the majority of meanings, especially *in the company of, together with*: **c** + instr:	
		I work with him.	Я рабо́таю **с ним**.
		She went there with a friend.	Она́ пошла́ туда́ **с дру́гом**.
		a man with a red face	мужчи́на **с румя́ным лицо́м**
		with pleasure	**с удово́льствием**
		I agree with you.	**Я соглаша́юсь с ва́ми**.
	(b)	indicating instrument; also indicating what sth is covered or surrounded by: instrumental case without a preposition:	
		She is eating with a spoon.	Она́ ест **ло́жкой**.
		I saw it with my own eyes.	Я ви́дел(a) э́то **свои́ми глаза́ми**.
		The lake is covered with ice.	О́зеро **покры́то льдом**.
		a house surrounded with flowers	дом **окружённый цвета́ми**
	(c)	indicating presence at sb's home, or entrustment of sth to sb: **y** + gen:	
		I lodge with them.	Я снима́ю ко́мнату **у них**.
		I left my things with the concierge.	Я оста́вил(a) свои́ ве́щи **у вахтёра**.
	(d)	indicating source or cause: **от** + gen:	
		He is trembling with cold.	Он дрожи́т **от хо́лода**.
		She is blushing with shame.	Она́ красне́ет **от стыда́**.
	(e)	in miscellaneous other functions:	
		with all one's heart	**от всей души́**
		with the exception of	**за исключе́нием** + gen
		with regard to	**в связи́ с** + instr
			по отноше́нию к + dat (R3)
			что каса́ется + gen
		with your consent	**с ва́шего согла́сия**

with your permission	**с вáшего разрешéния**
to go with/match	**подходи́ть к** + dat
satisfied with	**довóлен/довóльна** + instr
to speak with a stutter	**говори́ть заика́ясь**
Down with the government!	**Долóй прави́тельство!**
What's it to do with me?	**При чём тут я?**

11 Syntax

11.1 Use of the cases

A sound understanding of the functions of the cases in Russian is crucial to an ability to master the language, for grammatical relationships in the sentence, and therefore meaning, depend on inflection. The sections which follow examine the basic function or functions of each of the six cases of modern Russian and also the use of those cases with verbs. The use of the case after prepositions, some of which may invariably govern it and others of which govern it when they have certain meanings, is examined thoroughly in 10.1–10.3.

11.1.1 Use of the nominative

(a) The nominative is the case used to indicate the subject of a clause:

Кни́га лежа́ла на столе́.	*The book lay on the table.*
В саду́ сиде́ла **ко́шка**.	*A cat was sitting in the garden.*
Ива́н зовёт бра́та.	*Ivan is calling his brother.*

Note: in Russian the subject may follow the verb; it is inflection, not word order (on which see 11.14), that makes clear the grammatical relationships in the sentence.

(b) The complement of the verb *to be* may also stand in the nominative when the verb *to be* is not actually stated, i.e. in the present tense, e.g.

Моя́ мать – **врач**.	*My mother is a doctor.*
Он – **грузи́н**.	*He is a Georgian.*

A nominative complement is also used when the verb form **есть** is used, in the sense of *is*, and the complement is the same as the subject (see 4.2), e.g.

Пра́вда есть **пра́вда**.	*The truth is the truth.*

When the verb *to be* occurs in the past tense a nominative complement may be used (although the instrumental is now preferred; see 11.1.10(e)), e.g.

Он был **выдаю́щийся писа́тель**. *He was an outstanding writer.*

11.1.2 Use of the accusative

(a) The principal use of the accusative case is to express the direct object of a transitive verb, e.g.

Я чита́ю **кни́гу**. *I am reading a book.*

| Он пи́шет **письмо́**. | *He is writing a letter.* |
| Она́ лю́бит **отца́**. | *She loves her father.* |

Note 1 See 11.1.3 on the animate category of nouns.
    2 No reflexive verb, with the partial exception of **слу́шаться/послу́шаться** (see 11.1.5(b)), may govern the accusative.

(b) The accusative is also used, without any preposition, to express the duration of an action, the distance covered, price, and weight. In the first two meanings it often follows a verb with the prefix **про-** (see 8.3, про- (c)).

Рабо́та продолжа́лась **всю зи́му**.	*Work continued all winter.*
Они́ прое́хали **ты́сячу** киломе́тров.	*They travelled a thousand kilometres.*
Дом сто́ит **миллио́н** до́лларов.	*The house costs a million dollars.*
Маши́на ве́сит **то́нну**.	*The car weighs a tonne.*

11.1.3 Use of case to denote animate direct object

Many animate nouns must be put in the genitive case when they are used as direct objects. This usage arises from the fact that in most types of noun the nominative and accusative forms have come to coincide. Given the flexibility of Russian word order, clauses in which both subject and object are animate could be ambiguous were the grammatical forms of subject and object to remain undifferentiated. (Take, for example, the hypothetical statement Ива́н уби́л брат.) By marking the object by use of the genitive form, which in all categories of noun is distinct from the accusative, a speaker avoids confusion as to which noun is subject and which is object (cf. the similar function of the preposition **a** to mark an animate direct object in Spanish, e.g. Él mató a un toro, *He killed a bull*).

Animate nouns include those denoting people, animals, birds, reptiles, fish and insects, and embrace all three genders. The following table shows which types of Russian animate noun have to be marked in this way when they function as the direct object of a transitive verb.

accusative form preserved	genitive form required	
	masculine singular	
	бра́та	*brother*
	ти́гра	*tiger*
	орла́	*eagle*
	пито́на	*python*
	ка́рпа	*carp*
	паука́	*spider*
	masculine plural	
	сынове́й	*sons*
	слоно́в	*elephants*

		со́колов	*falcons*
		крокоди́лов	*crocodiles*
		осетро́в	*sturgeons*
		муравьёв	*ants*

feminine singular and masculine singular in -а/-я		feminine plural	
же́нщину	*woman*	де́вушек	*girls*
ло́шадь	*horse*	соба́к	*dogs*
ла́сточку	*swallow*	соро́к	*magpies*
змею́	*snake*	кобр	*cobras*
аку́лу	*shark*	щук	*pikes*
ба́бочку	*butterfly*	пчёл	*bees*
Са́шу	*Sasha*		
дя́дю	*uncle*		

neuter singular		neuter plural	
		должностны́х лиц	*officials*
млекопита́ющее	*mammal*	млекопита́ющих	*mammals*
пресмыка́ющееся	*reptile*	пресмыка́ющихся	*reptiles*
насеко́мое	*insect*	насеко́мых	*insects*

miscellaneous		miscellaneous	
толпу́	*crowd*		
наро́д	*a people*		
войска́ (n pl)	*troops*		
труп	*dead body, corpse*	мертвеца́	*dead man*
		поко́йника	*the deceased*
да́му	*queen* (cards)	ферзя́	*queen* (chess)
		короля́	*king* (cards, chess)
		туза́	*ace* (cards)
		вале́та	*jack* (cards)
		(пусти́ть)	*to fly a kite*
		бума́жного змея́	

Note 1   The words **Марс, Мерку́рий, Непту́н, Плуто́н, Ура́н, Юпи́тер** are treated as inanimate when they denote planets in the solar system but as animate when they denote the classical gods after whom the planets are named, e.g. наблюда́ть **Юпи́тер**, *to observe Jupiter*, but прогне́вать **Юпи́тера**, *to anger Jupiter*.

2   Usage is less clear-cut when the direct object denotes a low or as yet unborn form of life, e.g. **бакте́рия**, *bacterium*; **баци́лла**, *bacillus*; **заро́дыш**, *foetus*; **личи́нка**, *larva, grub*; **микро́б**, *microbe*; **эмбрио́н**, *embryo*. In everyday speech such objects tend to be treated as inanimate, e.g. изуча́ть **бакте́рии**, *to study bacteria*, but in scientific parlance they may be treated as animate (**бакте́рий**).

11.1.4 Basic uses of the genitive

(a)   To express possession, origin, relationship of part to whole, the nature, quality, measurement, or quantity *of* sth, e.g.

кни́га **моего́ бра́та**	*my brother's book*
стихи́ **Пу́шкина**	*Pushkin's poetry*
пе́рвый ваго́н **по́езда**	*the first coach of the train*
мужчи́на **большо́го ро́ста**	*a man of large stature*
за́пах **цвето́в**	*the scent of flowers*
метр **тка́ни**	*a metre of fabric*
литр **вина́**	*a litre of wine*

Note: the genitive case is not used in a number of contexts where English has *of* (see 10.4, *of* (b)).

(b)   After words indicating quantity, e.g.

ма́ло **вре́мени**	*little/not much time*
мно́го **цвето́в**	*many/a lot of flowers*
немно́го **студе́нтов**	*not many/a few students*
не́сколько **пе́сен**	*a few/some/several songs*
Ско́лько **вина́**?	*How much wine?*
Сто́лько **впечатле́ний**!	*How/So many impressions!*

(c)   To denote a certain quantity, some of a given object (cf. Fr *du pain, de l'eau*, etc.), e.g.

нали́ть **молока́**	*to pour some milk*
Она́ ничего́ не е́ла, то́лько вы́пила **ча́я**.	*She didn't eat anything, she just drank some tea.*

Note 1   The accusative case in such contexts would denote not *some* of the object but *the* object, e.g. нали́ть **молоко́**, *to pour the* (i.e. some specific) *milk*, perhaps the milk left in the bottle, the milk on the table.

2   A genitive form with partitive meaning is often found after verbs bearing the prefix **на-** in its meaning of *a certain quantity of* (see 8.3, **на-** (b)), e.g. накупи́ть **книг**, *to buy up a number of books*.

(d)   To express lack or absence of sth or sb in constructions with **нет**, *there is/are not*; **не́ было**, *there was/were not*; and **не бу́дет**, *there will not be*. These three Russian expressions, when they have the meanings given above, are invariable.

Хле́ба нет.	*There is no bread.*
Его́ здесь нет сего́дня.	*He is not here today.*
Сне́га не́ было.	*There was no snow.*
Дождя́ не бу́дет.	*There will not be any rain.*

Note: in the past or future tense absence may also be expressed by using a nominative form of the noun or personal pronoun: **Она́** не была́ до́ма, *She wasn't at home*; **Они́** там не бу́дут, *They won't be there*.

(e)   To express sufficiency or insufficiency after the impersonal verbs **хвата́ть/хвати́ть**, *to suffice* (+ **у** + gen of person who has enough/not enough of sth) and **недостава́ть/недоста́ть**, *to be insufficient/not to have enough* (+ dat of person who is short of sth):

У нас **вре́мени** не хвата́ет.	*We don't have enough time.*
Ему́ недостаёт **о́пыта**.	*He doesn't have enough experience.*

Note: the genitive has a similar meaning of sufficiency after certain reflexive verbs bearing the prefix **на-** which mean to do sth to satiety or to excess (see 8.3, **на-** (c)), e.g. Она́ нае́лась **икры́**, *She ate a great deal of caviare*; Они́ напи́лись **воды́**, *They drank a lot of water (as much as they wanted).*

(f)   After short comparative adjectives, e.g.

бо́льше го́да	*more than a year*
ни́же нуля́	*below zero*

(g)   After cardinal numerals (provided that the numeral itself is in the nominative or accusative case), except *one* and compound numbers in which *one* is the last component (see 11.4.2).

(h)   The genitive case of an ordinal numeral is used without a preposition to express *on a certain date*, e.g.

тре́тьего а́вгуста	*on 3 August*
два́дцать **шесто́го** октября́	*on 26 October*

11.1.5   Verbs governing the genitive

(a)   Many verbs which express fear, avoidance or apprehension, e.g.

боя́ться (no pf as a rule)	*to fear, be afraid of*
избега́ть/избежа́ть	*to avoid*
опаса́ться (no pf)	*to fear, shun, avoid*
пуга́ться/испуга́ться	*to be afraid of*
стесня́ться/постесня́ться	*to be shy of*
стыди́ться/постыди́ться	*to be ashamed of*

Note: in R1 these verbs may now be found with the accusative of animate nouns (i.e. of those animate nouns that have a distinct accusative form), e.g. Он бои́тся **тётю**, *He's afraid of his aunt.*

(b)   Miscellaneous other verbs, e.g.

алка́ть (impf only; R3)	*to hunger for, crave*
держа́ться (no pf in this sense)	*to keep to, hold on to*
добива́ться[a] (impf)	*to strive for*
доби́ться[a] (pf)	*to get, procure*
достига́ть/дости́гнуть	*to attain, achieve*
заслу́живать (impf)	*to deserve*
каса́ться/косну́ться	*to touch, concern*
лиша́ть/лиши́ть	*to deprive (sb of sth)*
лиша́ться/лиши́ться	*to lose, be deprived of*
слу́шаться/послу́шаться[b]	*to obey*
сто́ить[c] (no pf)	*to be worth*

ᵃ The different aspects of this verb have different meanings when the verb refers to a single instance.

ᵇ In R1 this verb may now govern the accusative of an animate object, e.g. Ребёнок слушается **Ве́ру**, *The child obeys Vera.*

ᶜ But this verb governs the accusative when it means *to cost* (see 11.1.2).

(c) A number of verbs may govern either the genitive or the accusative, e.g.

дожида́ться/дожда́ться	*to wait until*
ждать/подожда́ть	*to wait for, expect*
иска́ть (various pf)	*to look for, seek*
ожида́ть (no pf)	*to expect*
проси́ть/попроси́ть	*to ask for*
тре́бовать/потре́бовать	*to require, need*
хоте́ть/захоте́ть	*to want*

The reasons for choosing one case in preference to the other after these verbs are not very clear-cut, and educated Russians may be unable to explain them or even to agree on which case should be used in certain contexts. One may say that the genitive tends to be used if the object of the verb is general and abstract, whilst the accusative tends to prevail if the object is particular and concrete, i.e. is a specific thing or person. Thus:

- genitive object

Он ждал **отве́та**.	*He was waiting for an answer.*
Прошу́ **проще́ния**.	*I beg (your) pardon.*
Тре́буют **аре́ста** президе́нта.	*They are demanding the arrest of the president.*

- accusative object

Он ждёт **дя́дю**.	*He is waiting for his uncle.*
Он и́щет **тётю**.	*He is looking for his aunt.*
Про́сим **ви́зу** на въезд в Росси́ю.	*We are asking for a Russian entry visa.*

Note: the genitive is understood in set phrases expressing wishes (see 7.9), e.g. **Всего́ до́брого**! *All the best!*

11.1.6 Case of direct object after a negated verb

The genitive may be used instead of the accusative to express the direct object of a negated verb. The foreign student needs to know when one case or the other is obligatory or strongly preferred, but should also be aware that there are many instances where the question is finely balanced and either case might be acceptable to a native-speaker.

Note: there is no question of a genitive object being used if the negated verb is one which, when it is used affirmatively, governs the dative or instrumental case. Thus in the statement *I am not interested in music* the noun *music* would be rendered by an instrumental form (я не интересу́юсь **му́зыкой**) just as it would if the verb интересова́ться were not negated. Only verbs which, when affirmative, govern the accusative case may govern a direct object in the genitive when they are negated.

(a) The genitive is preferred in the following circumstances:

• when the negation is intensive, i.e. if the negated verb is strengthened by some form of **никако́й**, or **ни одного́/одно́й**, or **ни . . . ни**, e.g.

Никаки́х реше́ний приня́ть не смогли́.	*They could not take any decisions at all.*

• when the absence of sth or any part of sth is indicated. (The English translation in such contexts may well contain the word *any*.) A genitive object is therefore naturally to be expected after the verb **име́ть** when it is negated.

Мото́рных ло́док здесь ещё не приобрели́.	*They have not yet acquired motor boats here.*
Мы не име́ем **доста́точного запа́са** то́плива.	*We don't have a sufficient supply of fuel.*

• when the negated verb and its object combine to form a common expression, a set phraseological combination, e.g.

Э́то не игра́ет **ро́ли**.	*This plays no role.*
Я не обраща́ю **внима́ния** на э́то.	*I pay no attention to this.*
Мы не пожале́ем **сил**.	*We shall spare no efforts.*
Они́ не сложи́ли **ору́жия**.	*They did not lay down (their) arms.*
Она́ не несёт **отве́тственности** за э́то.	*She does not bear responsibility for this.*

• when the negated verb is a verb of perception, especially **ви́деть**, *to see*, or **слы́шать**, *to hear*, e.g.

Он не ви́дел **трамва́я**, кото́рый ме́дленно шёл по у́лице.	*He did not see the tram which was moving slowly down the street.*
Я не слы́шал(а) **звонка́**.	*I didn't hear the bell.*

• when the form of the verb which is negated is a gerund or active participle, e.g.

не чита́я **газе́ты**	*not reading the paper*
не написа́в **письма́**	*without having written the letter*
пробле́ма, не наше́дшая **отраже́ния** в кни́ге	*a problem which did not find reflection in the book*

• when the object of the negated verb is **э́то**, *this/that/it*, e.g.

Я **э́того** не забу́ду.	*I shan't forget this.*
Мно́гие не хоте́ли бы **э́того**.	*Many people would not want this.*

Note: it may happen that more than one of the above considerations applies and that it is therefore difficult to define the overriding criterion for using the genitive in a given context.

(b)   On the other hand the accusative is preferred in the following
      circumstances:

- when there is a double negative or when the negative occurs in a
  combination such as **чуть не**, *almost*, or **едва́ не**, *barely*, i.e. when the
  basic idea is not negative but affirmative, e.g.

Он не мог не заме́тить **пятно́**.	*He could not help noticing the stain.*
Она́ чуть не разби́ла **ва́зу**.	*She almost broke the vase.*
Как тут не вспо́мнить **э́то**?	*How can one not recall this?*

- when the object of the negated verb is qualified by an instrumental
  predicate, e.g.

Я не нахожу́ **францу́зский язы́к** тру́дным.	*I do not find French difficult.*
Он не счита́ет **э́тот отве́т** удовлетвори́тельным.	*He does not consider this answer satisfactory.*

- when it is not the verb but some part of speech other than the verb
  that is being negated, e.g.

Не он **э́то** сде́лал.	*It was not he who did this.*
Она́ купи́ла не газе́ту, а **журна́л**.	*It was a magazine, not a newspaper, that she bought.*
Они́ не то́лько сообщи́ли **ма́ссу** све́дений . . .	*They not only communicated a mass of information . . .*

- when the object of the negated verb is a place or specific concrete
  object, e.g.

Э́ти де́ньги **Нью-Йо́рк** не спасу́т.	*This money will not save New York.*
Радиослу́шатели не выключа́ли **ра́диоприёмники** в тече́ние двух неде́ль.	*Radio listeners did not turn off their sets for a fortnight.*

- when the object is a feminine noun referring to a person (or a
  masculine noun of the type Са́ша), e.g.

Я не зна́ю **Ири́ну** в лицо́.	*I don't know Irina by sight.*

(c)   The accusative is more common than the genitive (but is not
      obligatory) when the negated verb is an auxiliary verb while the verb
      which governs the direct object is an infinitive, e.g.

Он не мог поня́ть **план**.	*He could not understand the plan.*
Не ста́ну приводи́ть **конкре́тные аргуме́нты**.	*I shall not put forward any concrete arguments.*

11.1.7   Basic uses of the dative

(a)   To express the indirect object of a verb, i.e. the person or thing to
      which sth is given or done, or which is indirectly affected by an
      action, e.g.

Почтальо́н даёт ему́ письмо́.	*The postman is giving him a letter.*
Он заплати́л **официа́нту**.	*He paid the waiter.*
Портно́й сшил **мне** костю́м.	*The tailor made me a suit.*
Я пожа́л(а) **ему́** ру́ку.	*I shook his hand.*

Note: the dative form of the reflexive pronoun **себе́** is commonly used in phrases describing injury to oneself or action on part of oneself, e.g. лома́ть/слома́ть **себе́** ру́ку, *to break one's arm*; потира́ть/потере́ть **себе́ лоб**, *to wipe one's brow*.

(b)   To indicate the subject in common impersonal expressions, such as:

мо́жно	*it is possible to/one can*
на́до/ну́жно	*it is necessary to/one must*
нельзя́	*it is impossible to/one cannot/ one must not*
жаль	*to be sorry for, to be sorry to*
пора́	*to be time to*

If past meaning is intended these expressions are followed by the neuter form **бы́ло**, and if future meaning is intended they are followed by the third-person-singular form **бу́дет**, e.g.

Ему́ на́до бы́ло вы́йти.	*He had to go out.*
Нам ну́жно сде́лать пра́вильный вы́бор.	*We must make the right choice.*
Мне жаль э́тих люде́й.	*I am sorry for these people.*

Note: these impersonal expressions are also often used without any subject, e.g. Здесь **мо́жно** кури́ть, *One can smoke here*; **Нельзя́** входи́ть в пальто́, *One mustn't go in with one's coat on*.

(c)   In impersonal expressions with the neuter short form of many adjectives, e.g.

Мне пло́хо.	*I don't feel well.*
Тебе́ хо́лодно?	*Are you cold?*
Вам не ду́шно?	*It's not too stuffy for you?*
Вам бу́дет жа́рко.	*You'll be (too) hot.*

(d)   In impersonal expressions with many verbs, e.g.

каза́ться/показа́ться	*to seem to*
надоеда́ть/надое́сть	*to make tired, sicken, bore* (used in translation of *to be fed up with*)
недостава́ть/недоста́ть	*to be insufficient*
нра́виться/понра́виться	*to be pleasing to* (used in translation of *to like*)
приходи́ться/прийти́сь	*to have to*
сле́довать (no pf in this sense)	*ought, should*
удава́ться/уда́ться	*to succeed*

Examples:

мне ка́жется, что . . .	*I think (lit it seems to me) that . . .*
Нам понра́вилась э́та пье́са.	*We liked this play.*
Вам сле́довало бы сказа́ть мне э́то вчера́.	*You ought to have told me that yesterday.*

(e) With negative pronouns which mean *to have nothing to* or *there is nothing to*, etc. (see 11.2.4).

(f) To express a subject's age. The invariable forms **бы́ло** and **бу́дет** are used to convey past and future meaning, respectively.

Андре́ю пятна́дцать лет.	*Andrei is 15.*
Са́ше бы́ло пять лет.	*Sasha was 5.*
В а́вгусте **мне** бу́дет три́дцать лет.	*I'll be 30 in August.*

11.1.8 Verbs governing the dative

(a) Many verbs which indicate either advantage, assistance, permission or disadvantage, hindrance, prohibition to the object of the verb, e.g.

вреди́ть/повреди́ть[a]	*to injure, harm, hurt*
грози́ть (impf)	*to threaten*
запреща́ть/запрети́ть[b]	*to forbid, prohibit*
изменя́ть/измени́ть[c]	*to betray*
меша́ть/помеша́ть	*to prevent, hinder, bother, disturb*
позволя́ть/позво́лить	*to allow, permit*
помога́ть/помо́чь	*to help*
препя́тствовать/ воспрепя́тствовать	*to obstruct*
противоре́чить (impf only)	*to contradict*
разреша́ть/разреши́ть[b]	*to allow, permit*
служи́ть/послужи́ть	*to serve*
сове́товать/посове́товать	*to advise*
сопротивля́ться (impf only)	*to resist*
спосо́бствовать/поспосо́бствовать	*to assist, promote, contribute to*

[a] The pair **поврежда́ть/повреди́ть**, which also means *to damage, to injure*, or *to hurt*, takes the accusative case, e.g. Он повреди́л себе́ **но́гу**, *He hurt his leg*.

[b] When it is a thing that is prohibited or allowed **запреща́ть/запрети́ть** and **разреша́ть/разреши́ть** govern a direct object in the accusative, e.g. Прави́тельство запрети́ло/разреши́ло **но́вую газе́ту**, *The government prohibited/permitted the new newspaper.*

[c] When **изменя́ть/измени́ть** means *to change* or *to alter* it governs the accusative case, e.g. Дире́ктор шко́лы реши́л измени́ть **уче́бную програ́мму**, *The headmaster decided to change the curriculum.*

(b) Some verbs indicating attitude towards an object, e.g.

ве́рить/пове́рить[a]	*to believe, give credence to*
зави́довать/позави́довать[b]	*to envy*

изумля́ться/изуми́ться	*to be astonished at*
ра́доваться/обра́доваться	*to rejoice at, be gladdened by*
сочу́вствовать (impf)	*to sympathise with*
удивля́ться/удиви́ться	*to be surprised at*

[a] **Ве́рить/пове́рить** takes **в** + acc if it means *to believe in* sth, e.g. Он ве́рит **в бо́га**, *He believes in God.* Contrast the use of the two cases with this verb in the sentence Она́ не зна́ет, **во что́ и кому́** ве́рить, *She doesn't know what to believe in and whom to believe.*

[b] **Зави́довать/позави́довать** cannot govern a direct object as can the English verb *to envy* in phrases such as *I envy you your health.*

(c)   Miscellaneous other verbs, e.g.

веле́ть (impf and pf)	*to order, command*
звони́ть/позвони́ть	*to ring, telephone*
льстить/польсти́ть[a]	*to flatter*
повинова́ться (impf, and in past tense also pf)	*to obey*
подража́ть (impf only)	*to imitate*
прика́зывать/приказа́ть	*to order*
принадлежа́ть[b] (impf only)	*to belong to*
сле́довать/после́довать[c]	*to follow*
соотве́тствовать (impf only)	*to correspond to*
учи́ть/научи́ть[d]	*to teach*
учи́ться/научи́ться[d]	*to learn* (a subject)

[a] Although **льсти́ть/польсти́ть** normally governs the dative case, the accusative form of the reflexive pronoun is used in the expression **льсти́ть/польсти́ть себя́ наде́ждой**, *to flatter oneself with the hope.*

[b] When **принадлежа́ть** denotes ownership it is followed by the dative case without any preposition, e.g. Э́та кни́га принадлежи́т **моему́ бра́ту**, *This book belongs to my brother.* When on the other hand it denotes membership it must be followed by **к** and the dative, e.g. Он принадлежи́т **к лейбори́стской па́ртии**, *He belongs to the Labour Party.*

[c] **Сле́довать/после́довать** is followed by the dative case only when it means *to follow* in the sense of *to emulate.* When it means *to go after* it takes **за** + instr (see 10.3.4).

[d] After **учи́ть/научи́ть**, *to teach* and **учи́ться/научи́ться**, *to learn*, it is the subject taught or the thing learnt that is denoted by a noun in the dative case, e.g. Он у́чит сестру́ **францу́зскому языку́**, *He is teaching his sister French*; Она́ у́чится **францу́зскому языку́**, *She is learning French.* However, after the verb **изуча́ть/изучи́ть**, which means *to study*, the thing learnt is denoted by a noun in the accusative case, e.g. Он изуча́ет **матема́тику**, *He is studying mathematics.*

(d)   The adjective **рад, ра́да, ра́ды**, *glad*, which may only be used predicatively and which exists only in a short form, is also followed by a noun or pronoun in the dative, e.g. Она́ была́ ра́да **моему́ сча́стью**, *She was glad at my good fortune.*

11.1.9   Basic uses of the instrumental

(a)   To indicate the agent by whom or the instrument with which or by means of which an action is carried out, e.g.

Он был уби́т **солда́том**.	*He was killed by a soldier.*
Она́ ест **ви́лкой**.	*She is eating with a fork.*

(b)   To denote the thing with which sth is supplied or endowed, e.g.

Госуда́рство обеспе́чивает всех гра́ждан **образова́нием**.	*The state provides all citizens with an education.*
А́томная электроста́нция снабжа́ет го́род **электри́чеством**.	*The atomic power station supplies the town with electricity.*

(c)   In many adverbial phrases of manner, including indication of means of transport, e.g.

автомоби́лем	*by car*
самолётом	*by plane*
шёпотом	*in a whisper*
идти́ **бы́стрыми шага́ми**	*to walk with quick steps*

(d)   In certain expressions of time which define the point at which sth happens; cf. use of the accusative to indicate duration (see 11.1.2(b)), e.g.

ве́чером	*in the evening*
о́сенью	*in autumn*

(e)   In the literary variety of R3, to define route taken and to indicate likeness, e.g.

е́хать **бе́регом** (i.e. по бе́регу)	*to travel along the bank*
зе́ркалом (i.e. как зе́ркало)	*like a mirror*

(f)   In certain impersonal constructions indicating the agency of some force of nature, e.g.

Доро́гу занесло́ **сне́гом**.	*The road was covered in snow.*
Луга́ за́лило **водо́й**.	*The meadows were flooded with water.*
Кры́шу сду́ло **ве́тром**.	*The roof was blown off by the wind.*

11.1.10   Verbs governing the instrumental

(a)   Many verbs indicating control, command, government, direction or use. Some of these verbs are by their nature not capable of having perfective forms.

владе́ть	*to command, master, own*
дирижи́ровать	*to conduct* (orchestra)
заве́довать	*to be in charge of, manage, run*
кома́ндовать	*to command* (armed forces)

| обладáть | to possess |
| пóльзоваться/воспóльзоваться | to use, make use of, enjoy (in sense dispose of) |

Note: the verb испóльзовать (no pf), to utilise, on the other hand, governs the accusative case.

прáвить	to govern, rule, drive (vehicle)
располагáть	to have at one's disposal
распоряжáться/распорядúться	to manage, deal with
руководúть	to manage, direct
управлять	to govern, rule, drive (vehicle)

(b)   A number of verbs indicating attitude towards sth. Some of these too exist only in an imperfective form.

восхищáться/восхитúться	to admire (i.e. to be very impressed by)
гордúться (no pf)	to be proud of
дорожúть (no pf)	to value, prize
интересовáться/ заинтересовáться	to be interested in
любовáться/полюбовáться	to admire (i.e. to enjoy looking at; see 3.7)
наслаждáться/насладúться	to enjoy
пренебрегáть/пренебрéчь	to ignore, neglect
увлекáться/увлéчься	to be fond of, be carried away by, be obsessed with (see 3.7)
хвáстаться/похвáстаться	to boast of

(c)   A number of verbs which indicate movement of sth, especially of part of the subject's body, or making a sound with sth, e.g.

бряцáть (no pf) цéпью	to rattle, clank a chain
виля́ть/вильну́ть хвостóм	to wag (its) tail
двúгать/двúнуть ногóй	to move (one's) foot
звенéть (no pf) деньгáми	to jingle money
качáть/покачáть головóй	to shake (one's) head
кивáть/кивну́ть головóй	to nod (one's) head
махáть/махну́ть рукóй	to wave (one's) hand
мигáть/мигну́ть or	to wink, blink (one's) eye
моргáть/моргну́ть глáзом	
пожимáть/пожáть плечáми	to shrug (one's) shoulders
размáхивать (no pf) мечóм	to brandish a sword
тóпать/тóпнуть ногóй	to stamp (one's) foot
хлóпать/хлóпнуть двéрью	to slam a door
шáркать/шáркнуть ногóй	to shuffle (one's) foot

Note: when the part of the body belongs to someone other than the subject then the accusative is used, e.g. пожимáть/пожáть комý-н рýку, to shake sb's [i.e. sb else's] hand.

(d) Miscellaneous other verbs, e.g.

дыша́ть (no pf)	to breathe
же́ртвовать/поже́ртвовать	to sacrifice
занима́ться/заня́ться	to be engaged in, be occupied with, study
злоупотребля́ть/злоупотреби́ть	to abuse
па́хнуть (impf only)	to smell of (used impersonally)
рискова́ть (no pf)	to risk, hazard
страда́ть (no pf)	to suffer from

Note: used with the instrumental case **страда́ть** implies chronic or permanent predicament, e.g. страда́ть **диабе́том**, *to suffer from diabetes*; **страда́ть от** implies more temporary suffering, e.g. страда́ть **от зубно́й бо́ли**, *to suffer from toothache*.

(e) The instrumental is also used in nouns which function as the complement of **быть**, *to be*. Modern usage is as follows.

• The instrumental is used when the verb occurs in the infinitive (**быть**), future (**бу́ду**, etc.), conditional (**был/была́/бы́ло/бы́ли бы**), imperative (**будь** or **бу́дьте**) or as a gerund (**бу́дучи**), e.g.

Он хо́чет быть **инжене́ром**.	*He wants to be an engineer.*
Он бу́дет **дипло́матом**.	*He will be a diplomat.*
Бу́дьте **врачо́м**.	*Be a doctor.*
Бу́дучи **дурако́м**, он не по́нял.	*Being a fool, he didn't understand.*

• The instrumental is also normally used nowadays with the past tense (**был**, etc.), e.g.

В мо́лодости он был **выдаю́щимся спортсме́ном**.	*In his youth he was an outstanding sportsman.*
Толсто́й был **вели́ким писа́телем**.	*Tolstoi was a great writer.*

Note: grammarians make a distinction between temporary state (in which case the instrumental is obligatory) and permanent state (as in the second example above, in which case the nominative may be used, giving **вели́кий писа́тель**). However, the choice is not one the student needs to agonise over, and one is now on safe ground if one always uses an instrumental complement with **быть**. (On identification of subject and complement see 4.2, явля́ться, note 2.)

• When on the other hand the verb *to be* is in the present tense, and is therefore understood but not actually stated in the Russian, a nominative complement must be used, e.g.

Она́ **профе́ссор**.	*She is a professor.*
Мой брат – **инжене́р**.	*My brother is an engineer.*

Departures from this rule are rare, unless the complement is **вина́**, *fault, blame*, or **причи́на**, *cause*, e.g. Тут, коне́чно, не одно́ телеви́дение **вино́й**, *Here, of course, television alone is not to blame.*

Note: the noun which in English functions as the complement is not in the instrumental in the following type of Russian construction:

Э́то был Ива́н.	*It was Ivan.*
Э́то была́ Татья́на.	*It was Tat'iana.*
Э́то бы́ло францу́зское сло́во.	*It was a French word.*
Э́то бы́ли дере́вья.	*They were trees.*

(f)   A number of other verbs, apart from **быть**, require an instrumental complement, at least in some contexts, e.g.

вы́глядеть (impf)	*to look (like)*
де́латься/сде́латься	*to become*
каза́ться/показа́ться	*to seem*
называ́ть/назва́ть	*to call, name*
ока́зываться/оказа́ться	*to turn out to be, prove to be*
остава́ться/оста́ться	*to remain*
притворя́ться/притвори́ться	*to pretend to be*
рабо́тать (no pf)	*to work as*
служи́ть/послужи́ть	*to serve as*
слыть/прослы́ть	*to be reputed to be*
станови́ться/стать	*to become*
счита́ться (no pf)	*to be considered*
явля́ться/яви́ться	*to be*

(g)   Some verbs take a direct object in the accusative and a complement in the instrumental, e.g. **Я нахожу́** э́ту о́перу **ску́чной**, *I find this opera boring* (R2/3). Similarly:

выбира́ть/вы́брать	*to elect*
назнача́ть/назна́чить	*to appoint*
счита́ть/счесть	*to consider*

11.1.11   Use of the prepositional

This case, as its name suggests, is used only after certain prepositions (on which see 10.1.6) and can only be governed by verbs through those prepositions (see 10.3.5).

11.2   Use of pronouns

11.2.1   Use of кото́рый as a relative pronoun

The relative pronoun **кото́рый** (*who, which*) gives some difficulty, for although it declines like an adjective and must agree in gender and number with the noun or pronoun to which it refers, its case is determined by its function within the subordinate clause in which it stands. Thus in all the following examples the relative pronoun is feminine and singular, like **маши́на**, *car*, but its case varies in accordance with its grammatical role as, respectively, subject, direct object and word governed by **в**:

Маши́на, **кото́рая** стои́т пе́ред вокза́лом, слома́лась.
The car which is outside the station has broken down.
Маши́на, **кото́рую** я купи́л(а) вчера́, слома́лась.
The car which I bought yesterday has broken down.
Маши́на, **в кото́рой** е́хал президе́нт, слома́лась.
The car in which the president was travelling has broken down.

Note: **кто**, *who*, and **что**, *what, which*, may also function as relative pronouns, although they are more commonly used as interrogative pronouns. As relative pronouns they occur mainly in conjunction with some form of **тот** or **все/всё**, e.g. **Те, кто** чита́л рома́н 'Преступле́ние и наказа́ние', по́мнят о́браз Свидрига́йлова, *Those who have read 'Crime and Punishment' remember the character of Svidrigailov;* Я не согла́сен/согла́сна **с тем, что** он говори́т, *I do not agree with what he says.*

11.2.2   Use of како́й and кото́рый as interrogative pronouns

These pronouns, which may be used in questions asking *what?* or *which?*, used to be more clearly distinguished than they are now. A question introduced by **како́й** anticipated an answer describing quality, e.g. **Кака́я сего́дня пого́да?** *What is the weather like today?*, whereas one introduced by **кото́рый** anticipated an answer selecting an item out of a number of things or indicating the position of sth in a numerical series, e.g. **Кото́рую из э́тих книг вы предпочита́ете?**, *Which of these books do you prefer?*

Nowadays almost all questions requiring the use of one of these pronouns may be put by using **како́й**, e.g.

Каки́е ви́на вы лю́бите?	*What wines do you like?*
Каки́х ру́сских а́второв чита́ли?	*Which Russian authors have you read?*
– **Како́й** у вас но́мер?	*'Which room are you in?'*
– Два́дцать шесто́й.	*'Twenty-six.'*

Кото́рый, as an interrogative pronoun, can only really be considered obligatory in expressions of time such as **Кото́рый час?** *What time is it?* and **В кото́ром часу́?** *At what time?*

11.2.3   Use of negative pronouns (никто́, etc.)

It must be remembered that the negative particle **не** must precede any verb with which the negative pronouns (**никто́, ничто́, никогда́, нигде́, никуда́, никако́й, ника́к**) are combined, e.g.

Никто́ не ви́дел его́.	*Nobody saw him.*
Она́ **ничего́ не** ви́дела.	*She didn't see anything.*
Он **ни с ке́м не** говори́л.	*He didn't speak to anyone.*
Я **ни о чём не** ду́маю.	*I'm not thinking about anything.*

Мы **никогда́ не** говори́м об э́том.	*We never talk about that.*
Я никуда́ не ходи́л(а).	*I didn't go anywhere.*

Note: **никто́** and **ничто́** decline (see 9.2) and, if governed by a preposition, split into two components with the preposition between them. (See also 11.2.4.)

11.2.4 Use of не́кого, etc.

The pronouns dealt with in 11.2.3 should not be confused with similar forms which are used in contexts where English has the expressions *to have no one/nothing/no time/nowhere to* or *there is no one/nothing/no time/nowhere to*, viz:

не́чего	*to have nothing to*
не́кого	*to have no one to*
не́когда	*to have no time to*
не́где	*to have nowhere to* (position indicated)
не́куда	*to have nowhere to* (movement indicated)

Being impersonal, these expressions are invariably used with the neuter form **бы́ло**, if they are in the past tense, and the third-person-singular form **бу́дет**, if they are in the future. Examples:

Нам не́чего де́лать.	*We have nothing to do/There is nothing for us to do.*
Ему́ не́кого бы́ло люби́ть.	*He had no one to love.*
Ей не́когда бу́дет ви́деть вас.	*She will have no time to see you.*
Я́блоку не́где упа́сть.	*There isn't room to swing a cat.* (lit *There is nowhere for an apple to fall.*)

Note: **не́чего** and **не́кого**, which are accusative/genitive forms, also have dative, instrumental and prepositional forms. When these words are governed by a preposition they are generally split to enable the preposition to be inserted between the particle **не** and the appropriate form of **кто** or **что**, e.g.

Мне **не́ на кого́** полага́ться.	*I have no one to rely on.*
Ей **не́кому** дать ли́шний биле́т.	*She has got no one to give the spare ticket to.*
Мне **не́чем** есть суп.	*I've got nothing to drink my soup with.*
Ему́ **не́ с кем** говори́ть об э́том.	*He's got nobody to talk to about this.*
Им **не́ о чем** бы́ло говори́ть.	*They had nothing to talk about.*

11.2.5 Use of the particles -то, -нибу́дь, -ли́бо

Use of these particles, any of which may be added to **кто, что, когда́, где, куда́, како́й, как, отку́да, почему́**, to render *someone, something, some time, somewhere, (to) somewhere, some, somehow, from somewhere, for* *some reason*, respectively, gives the English-speaking student some difficulty. The fundamental distinction between them is that **-нибу́дь** implies that there is an element of choice from several alternatives, whereas **-то** implies that something is unknown to the speaker. The less common **-ли́бо** is a more bookish alternative to **-нибу́дь** and now sounds somewhat dated.

- **-то** will translate into English as *some* and indicates that while the speaker is sure that some event has taken place he or she does not have precise information about it, e.g. Он сказа́л что́-то, но я не расслы́шал(а), *He said something but I didn't catch it* [i.e. sth definitely was said, but the speaker does not know exactly what it was]; Кто́-то тебе́ звони́л, *Somebody phoned you* [but the speaker does not know who].

- **-нибу́дь** may be translated, depending on the context, as either *some* or *any*. It occurs with the imperative, e.g. Поговори́те с ке́м-нибудь об э́том, *Have a talk with somebody about it*. It also tends to occur:

(a) more with the future, about which there is less certainty than the present and in which therefore any one of a number of things might happen, e.g. Е́сли кто́-нибудь позвони́т, скажи́те им, что я заболе́л(а), *If anyone rings, tell them I'm ill*;

(b) in the past tense when there is a choice or range of possibilities. Compare e.g.

Ка́ждое у́тро он уходи́л **куда́-то**.	*Every morning he went somewhere* [the speaker does not know where].
Ка́ждое у́тро он уходи́л **куда́-нибудь**.	*Every morning he went somewhere* [possibly different places on different mornings].

(c) in combination with expressions such as **вероя́тно**, *probably*, **наве́рно**, *probably, I expect*, which indicate uncertainty, e.g. Наве́рно он ку́пит **что́-нибудь**, *I expect he'll buy something* [but what exactly is not yet known].

- **-ли́бо**, like **-нибу́дь**, may indicate choice or a range of possibilities, e.g. Найди́те **кого́-либо**, кто мог бы вам помо́чь с э́тим, *Find somebody who could help you with this*.

11.2.6 Use of свой

Use of this word gives much difficulty to the English-speaker, because English has only one possessive pronoun for each person. **Свой** declines like **мой** and agrees in gender, case and number with the noun it qualifies. It denotes possession by the person or thing which is the subject of the clause in which the possessive pronoun occurs irrespective of whether that subject is first, second or third person and singular or plural. It might therefore translate any of the English possessive pronouns in the following variations:

I/you/he/she/we/they have/has lost my/your/his/her/our/their money.
Я/ты/он/она́/мы/вы/они́ потеря́л(а/и) **свои́** де́ньги.

If any of the third-person possessives (*his/her/its/their*) are rendered by **его́/её/их** then those Russian pronouns indicate possession by somebody other than the subject of the clause. Compare e.g.

Он потеря́л **свои́** де́ньги.	*He has lost his (own) money.*
Он потеря́л **его́** де́ньги.	*He has lost his (sb else's) money.*

- It is not possible to use **свой**:

(a) to qualify the subject itself. In the statement *His money has been lost*, for example, in which *money* is the subject, *his* must be translated by **его́**;

(b) when the possessive pronoun indicates possession by a subject which stands in another clause. In the sentence *He knows that I have lost his money*, for example, *his* indicates possession by the person who is the subject of the sentence as a whole (*he*), but it is *I* that is the subject of the clause in which *his* occurs. The sentence must therefore be translated: Он зна́ет, что я потеря́л(а) **его́** де́ньги.

- However, in certain circumstances the point made in (a) above is overruled, viz:

(a) in set expressions in which **свой** does qualify the subject, e.g. **Своя́** руба́шка бли́же к те́лу, lit *One's own shirt is closer to the body*, i.e. *Charity begins at home*;

(b) in impersonal constructions in which the subject appears in the dative or is understood, e.g. На́до служи́ть **свое́й** ро́дине, *One must serve one's country*;

(c) in constructions with **y** + gen which equate to the English verb *to have*, e.g. У ка́ждого студе́нта **свой** компью́тер, *Each student has his own computer*.

11.3 Use of short adjectives

The short forms of the adjective may only be used when the adjective is predicative, that is to say when in the English translation of the Russian some form of the verb *to be* stands between the subject and the adjective, as in the sentences Э́тот студе́нт **умён**, *This student is clever*, Де́вушка была́ **грустна́**, *The girl was sad*.

If the adjective is not separated from the noun in this way, then only a long form of the adjective may be used, irrespective of the word order employed, e.g. Он **у́мный** студе́нт/Он студе́нт **у́мный**/**У́мный** он студе́нт, *He is an intelligent student*; Она́ была́ **гру́стной** де́вушкой, *She was a sad girl*.

Even when the adjective is predicative the short form is not invariably used. Often the long form is preferred or possible, and when some form of **быть** is used an instrumental form of the adjective is also possible. The following guidance can be given, although this is an area of grammar in which usage is relatively fluid.

- Many common adjectives are found only in the short form when used predicatively, e.g.

вино́ват, винова́та, винова́то, винова́ты	*guilty*
гото́в, гото́ва, гото́во, гото́вы	*ready*
далёк, далека́, далеко́, далеки́	*far, distant*
дово́лен, дово́льна, дово́льно, дово́льны	*satisfied with*
до́лжен, должна́, должно́, должны́	*bound to* (i.e. *must*)
досто́ин, досто́йна, досто́йно, досто́йны	*worthy of*
наме́рен, наме́рена, наме́рено, наме́рены	*intending to*
ну́жен, нужна́, ну́жно, нужны́	*necessary*
похо́ж, похо́жа, похо́же, похо́жи	*like, similar*
прав, права́, пра́во, пра́вы	*right*
свобо́ден, свобо́дна, свобо́дно, свобо́дны	*free*
скло́нен, скло́нна, скло́нно, скло́нны	*inclined to*
согла́сен, согла́сна, согла́сно, согла́сны	*agreeable to*
спосо́бен, спосо́бна, спосо́бно, спосо́бны	*capable of*

- Short forms are preferred, provided that the adjective is predicative, in the following circumstances:

(a) when the adjective is followed by some sort of complement (as many of those in the above list almost invariably are), e.g. (with nature of complement defined in brackets):

Он **равноду́шен к му́зыке**. (preposition + noun)
He is indifferent to music.
Сау́довская Ара́вия **бога́та не́фтью**. (noun in oblique case)
Saudi Arabia is rich in oil.

(b) when the subject of the statement is one of the words **то**, *that*; **э́то**, *this, it*; **что**, in the sense of *which* or *what*; **всё**, *everything*; **друго́е**, *another thing*; **одно́**, *one thing*; **пе́рвое**, *the first thing*, e.g.

Всё бы́ло **споко́йно**.   *Everything was peaceful.*
Одно́ **я́сно**.   *One thing is clear.*

(c) when the subject is qualified by some word or phrase such as **вся́кий**, *any*; **ка́ждый**, *every*; **любо́й**, *any*; **подо́бный**, *such*; **тако́й**, *such*, which serves to generalise it, e.g.

Ка́ждое сло́во в рома́не **уме́стно**.   *Every word in the novel is apt.*
Подо́бные зада́чи **просты́**.   *Such tasks are simple.*

(d)   if the adjective is derived from a present active participle (ending in -**щий**); a present passive participle (ending in -**мый**); or a past passive participle (ending in -**тый** or -**нный**), e.g.

Ваше поведение **неприемлемо**.	*Your conduct is unacceptable.*
Он **женат**.	*He is married.*

(e)   with some adjectives when they denote excessive possession of a quality, especially:

большой: **велик, велика, велико, велики**	*too big*
маленький: **мал, мала, мало, малы**	*too small*
дорогой: **дорог, дорога, дорого, дороги**	*too dear*
дешёвый: **дёшев, дешева, дёшево, дёшевы**	*too cheap*
широкий: **широк, широка, широко, широки**	*too wide*
узкий: **узок, узка, узко, узки**	*too narrow*

e.g. Эти туфли мне **малы**, *These shoes are too small for me.*

(f)   in general statements of a philosophical or scientific nature, e.g.

Душа человека **бессмертна**.	*Man's soul is immortal.*
Судьба России **загадочна**.	*Russia's fate is enigmatic.*

• The long form of an adjective is preferred, when the adjective is used predicatively, in the following circumstances:

(a)   if it is intended to particularise, i.e. to draw attention to the fact that a particular subject possesses the quality denoted by the adjective or to pick out one object from among several or many, e.g.

Темза короткая река, Волга – **длинная**.	*The Thames is a short river, the Volga is a long one.*

Note: the inclusion in English of the definite article and the pronoun *one* serves to single out the object.

(b)   in statements incorporating a phrase with **у** + gen (in which the object in question is being particularised), e.g.

Глаза у неё **красивые**.	*She has beautiful eyes [i.e. her eyes are beautiful ones].*

(c)   with some adjectives, to indicate that the quality is a permanent one, e.g.

Она – **больная**.	*She is an invalid.*

Note: cf. Она **больна**, *She is ill.*

11.4 Use of numerals

This is a particularly complex area for the foreign student of Russian. Much of the complexity arises from the fact that (a) usage of **два** and other numerals bears traces of the existence of the old dual category (see Glossary); and (b) numerals themselves are capable of declension. It is helpful to deal separately with the use of **один** (11.4.1) and then to examine separately use of the other numerals when they are themselves in nominative or accusative form (11.4.2) and use of those numerals when they are themselves in an oblique case (11.4.3).

11.4.1 Use of один

Один, which declines like the demonstrative pronoun **этот** (9.2), is generally followed, when it means *one*, by a singular noun, even in higher numbers in which it is the last component, such as *twenty-one*. It agrees in gender and case with nouns and adjectives which follow it, e.g.

оди́н дом	*one house*
два́дцать одна́ кни́га	*twenty-one books*
в одно́й изве́стной статье́	*in one famous article*

Note: **оди́н** does have plural forms which are used with nouns which themselves exist only in a plural form (see 3.6.1; e.g. **одни́ су́тки**, *one twenty-four-hour period*) or when the word means *only* (e.g. Я чита́ю **одни́ ру́сские рома́ны**, *I read only Russian novels*).

11.4.2 Use of numerals higher than *one* in nominative/accusative

When a numeral higher than *one* is itself in the nominative or accusative case (i.e. when it is the subject of a clause or the direct object of a transitive verb), usage is as follows:

- **два/две, три, четы́ре, о́ба/о́бе, полтора́/полторы́**, and any number of which one of these numerals is the last component, govern a noun in the genitive singular, e.g.

два грузовика́	*two lorries*
две кни́ги	*two books*
три по́ля	*three fields*
четы́ре ме́сяца	*four months*
о́ба телефо́на	*both telephones*
полтора́ часа́	*one and a half hours*

Note: **две, о́бе, полторы́** are feminine forms.

- adjectives after any of the above numerals are genitive plural, if the noun is masculine or neuter, or nominative/accusative plural if the noun is feminine, e.g.

два **деревя́нных** стола́	*two wooden tables*
три **гря́зных** окна́	*three dirty windows*
четы́ре **чёрные** ко́шки	*four black cats*

Note: the use of genitive plural adjectives after these numerals with feminine nouns (e.g. две **но́вых** книги), as well as masculine and neuter nouns, is old-fashioned, but is widely encountered in classical literature.

- numerals from **пять** upwards (and also **ты́сяча**, which may be treated as either a noun or a numeral, and **миллио́н** and **миллиа́рд**, both of which are nouns) govern a noun in the genitive plural; any adjectives are also genitive plural irrespective of the gender of the noun, e.g.

пять больши́х городо́в	*five large cities*
два́дцать шесть но́вых книг	*twenty-six new books*
шестьдеся́т де́вять золоты́х меда́лей	*sixty-nine gold medals*

- the above rules relating to adjectives apply also to substantivised adjectives, e.g.

три **портны́х**	*three tailors*
четы́ре **моро́женых**	*four ice-creams*
две **столо́вые**	*two dining-rooms*

11.4.3   Use of numerals in oblique cases

When the numeral itself is in an oblique case (e.g. if it is governed by a preposition or by a verb which governs the genitive, dative or instrumental), then all nouns and adjectives which follow it are, in R2/3 at least, in the same case and in the plural, e.g.

в двух вече́рних газе́тах	*in two evening newspapers*
по обе́им сторона́м доро́ги	*down both sides of the road*
Она́ позвони́ла **трём друзья́м**.	*She telephoned three friends.*
законопрое́кт, при́нятый **девяно́ста пятью́ голоса́ми** про́тив **четырёх**	*a bill accepted by ninety-five votes to four*

Note 1   All components of the numeral itself decline.

      2   In R1 a speaker might put only key components of a compound number in the appropriate oblique case, e.g. с семьсо́т шестьдеся́т **девятью́** содда́тами, *with 769 soldiers*. Not that such an example is commonly encountered in ordinary speech: a speaker would most probably use an approximation or, if a precise number had to be given, use a construction in which the numerals did not have to be put in an oblique case.

11.4.4   Use of numerals with animate direct object

Numerals have distinct accusative and genitive forms and the question therefore arises as to which case should be used when they introduce an animate direct object (see 11.1.3). However, in practice it is only with **два/две, три** and **четы́ре** that difficulty arises.

- It is felt more correct to use the genitive rather than the accusative forms of **два/две, три, четы́ре** when they are the direct object of a verb and are used with an animate noun denoting a person, particularly when the noun is masculine, e.g.

ЦРУ раскры́ло **четырёх аге́нтов**.	*The CIA discovered four agents.*
Он ви́дел **трёх де́вушек**.	*He saw three girls.*

Note: the use of a genitive form of the numeral entails the use of a plural form of the following noun.

- When the animate noun denotes an animal then a genitive form of the numeral is still considered more correct if the noun is masculine (though this usage is perhaps less clear-cut than with nouns denoting people), whilst with nouns which are feminine the use of the genitive may seem stilted, e.g.

Он ви́дел **двух слоно́в**.	*He saw two elephants.*
Он ви́дел **две коро́вы**.	*He saw two cows.*

- If the numerals **два/две, три, четы́ре** occur as the last component of a compound number, then they are likely to be used in the accusative form, esp in R1, e.g. Он ви́дел два́дцать **два** ма́льчика, *He saw twenty-two boys.*

- With the numerals **пять** and above only the accusative forms are used with animate direct objects, even in R3, e.g. Он ви́дел **пять** ма́льчиков, *He saw five boys.*

11.4.5 Use of collective numerals

The collective numerals are **дво́е, тро́е, че́тверо, пя́теро, ше́стеро, се́меро**. Higher numerals of this type (**во́сьмеро, де́вятеро, де́сятеро**) are no longer used; nor are **пя́теро, ше́стеро, се́меро** any longer commonly used in all the contexts in which **дво́е, тро́е, че́тверо** are possible.

If these numerals are used in the nominative or accusative then, like cardinal numerals from **пять** upwards, they are followed by nouns and adjectives in the genitive plural.

The collective numerals have the following uses:

(a) to indicate the number of people in a group, especially when the people are denoted by a pronoun or when the numeral stands on its own as the subject, e.g.

Нас бы́ло **дво́е**.	*There were two of us.*
Вошли́ **тро́е**.	*Three people came in.*

(b) to indicate a number of male persons or the number in a family, e.g.

че́тверо рабо́чих	*four workers*
У нас **дво́е дете́й**.	*We've got two children.*

(c)   with nouns which exist only in the plural (see 3.6.1), e.g.

двóе нóвых джи́нсов   *two new pairs of jeans*

Note: the collective numerals decline like plural adjectives (see 9.3.1). They may be used in all cases with animate nouns (e.g. мать **трои́х** детéй, *the mother of three children*), but with inanimate nouns only the nominative/accusative forms are used (e.g. **трóе** сýток, but óколо **трёх** (not трои́х) сýток, *about three days*).

11.4.6   Approximation

Approximation may be expressed in the following ways:

(a)   by reversal of the order of numeral and noun, e.g.

недéли две   *about two weeks*
часá чéрез два пóсле э́того   *about two hours after that*

(b)   by using **óколо** with a numeral in the genitive, e.g.

óколо ста километров от Москвы́   *about 100 kilometres from Moscow*

(c)   by placing an appropriate adverb before the numeral, e.g.

приблизи́тельно сто фýнтов   *approximately £100*
примéрно три́дцать студéнтов   *roughly thirty students*

Note: see also 5.4**так** (c) in .

11.4.7   Agreement of predicate with a subject containing a cardinal numeral

When a numeral is the subject of a clause, or when it combines with a noun to form the subject, then the predicate may be in the third person plural (or plural form of the past tense) or it may be in the third person singular (or neuter form of the past tense). Usage is not clear-cut, but some guidance can be given.

•   Plural verb forms tend to prevail when:

(a)   the subject is animate and the verb denotes action (as opposed to state), e.g. За негó **проголосовáли сто члéнов** парлáмента, *A hundred members of parliament voted for him*;

(b)   the numeral is qualified by a word which is itself in a plural form, e.g. **Поги́бли все дéсять** члéнов экипáжа, *All ten members of the crew were killed*.

•   Singular/neuter forms are preferred when:

(a)   the subject is a phrase defining a period of time, e.g. **Прошлó пять мéсяцев**, *Five months passed*;

(b)   attention is being drawn to the number, perhaps because of its large or small size or because the context is a statistical one, e.g. **Всегó пришлó пять** человéк, *(Only) five people in all came*.

11.4.8   Translation of *years* and *people* after numerals

(a)   After **оди́н** and numerals followed by a genitive singular noun the word **год** is used, in an appropriate form, to mean *year*, but after numerals requiring a genitive plural noun the form **лет** is used, e.g.

оди́н год	*one year*
два го́да	*two years*
сто лет	*100 years*
о́коло трёх лет	*about three years*

Note 1   The gen pl form **годо́в** does exist and is used in referring to decades, e.g. **му́зыка шестидеся́тых годо́в**, *the music of the sixties*.

  2   When the numeral is in the dative/instrumental/prepositional case then an appropriate form of **год** is used, e.g. **пяти́ года́м, пятью́ года́ми, о пяти́ года́х**.

(b)   After numerals, and also **не́сколько**, the word **челове́к** is used, in an appropriate form, in the meaning *person/people* (the form **челове́к** is genitive plural as well as nominative singular), e.g.

три́дцать четы́ре челове́ка	*thirty-four people*
де́сять челове́к	*ten people*
не́сколько челове́к	*several people*

After **ты́сяча** and **миллио́н** there is now a tendency to use **челове́к**, although **люде́й** may also be found.

  After **мно́го** and **немно́го** both **челове́к** and **люде́й** may be used; with **люде́й** it may be felt that attention is being focused on the group rather than the individuals in it.

Note: *a lot of people/not many people* may also be translated by **мно́го/немно́го наро́да** (or **наро́ду**) if it is meant that a place is crowded/not crowded.

After **ско́лько** and **сто́лько** *people* should be rendered by **челове́к** unless the meaning is exclamatory, in which case **люде́й** is preferred, e.g.

Ско́лько челове́к там бы́ло?	*How many people were there?*
Ско́лько люде́й поги́бли на войне́!	*How many people died in the war!*

11.4.9   Distributive expressions

The preposition **по** may be used with numerals to indicate distribution of a certain number of things to each of a number of objects. Modern usage in such expressions is as follows.

(a)   **Оди́н** and any nouns that follow it are put in the dative case; the nouns **ты́сяча, миллио́н, миллиа́рд** are also put in the dative case, but following nouns and adjectives are genitive plural, e.g.

Ма́ть дала́ де́тям **по одно́й сла́дкой ири́ске**.
The mother gave her children a sweet toffee each.
Он дал нам **по ты́сяче рубле́й**.
He gave us a thousand roubles each.

Note: if there is no accompanying adjective then **оди́н** is often omitted, e.g. О́бе кома́нды име́ют **по ма́тчу** в запа́се, *Each team has a game in hand.*

(b) All other numerals are nowadays put in the accusative case and the following nouns and adjectives conform to the normal rules applicable after the numeral in question (see 11.4.2), e.g.

Инопланетя́не име́ли **по три гла́за**.
The extra-terrestrials had three eyes each.
С ка́ждого гекта́ра – **по две́сти пятьдеся́т тонн овоще́й**.
From each hectare [you get] 250 tonnes of vegetables.

Note: the use of numerals from **пять** upwards in the dative followed by a noun in the genitive plural in such expressions (e.g. Он дал нам **по пяти́ до́лларов**, *He gave us five dollars each*) is now felt to be old-fashioned or bookish.

11.4.10 Time

(a) The neutral or formal way to ask the question *What time is it?* is **Кото́рый час?** Similarly **В кото́ром часу́?** *At what time?* Colloquially one may ask these questions with the phrases **Ско́лько вре́мени?** and **Во ско́лько?** respectively.

(b) *o'clock*: numeral + appropriate case (though **оди́н** is usually omitted). *At* with time on the hour: **в** + acc:

час	*one o'clock*
два часа́	*two o'clock*
пять часо́в	*five o'clock*
в четы́ре часа́	*at four o'clock*

(c) Time past the hour: numeral + **мину́та** in appropriate case + genitive singular form of ordinal number indicating the hour (first hour, second hour, etc.). *A quarter past* the hour: **че́тверть** (f) + genitive singular form of ordinal. *At* with time past the hour: **в** + acc:

(в) два́дцать пять мину́т пе́рвого	*(at) twenty-five past twelve*
(в) че́тверть седьмо́го	*(at) a quarter past six*

(d) *half past* the hour: **полови́на** + genitive singular form of ordinal number indicating the hour. *At half past* the hour: **в полови́не** (i.e. **в** + prep):

полови́на двена́дцатого	*half past eleven*
в полови́не шесто́го	*at half past five*

(e) time *to* the hour: **без** + genitive of all components of the cardinal numeral or of **че́тверть** + the hour itself. *At* time to the hour is not expressed:

без двадцати́ пяти́ пять	*(at) twenty-five to five*
без че́тверти во́семь	*(at) a quarter to eight*

Note: if a time is followed by one of the phrases *in the morning, in the afternoon, in the evening, at night*, then the **genitive** case of the word for *morning*, etc. must be used, e.g. в де́вять часо́в **утра́**, *at nine in the morning*; cf. the use of the instrumental (**у́тром**, etc.) when the phrases *in the morning*, etc. stand on their own.

11.4.11   Dates

(a)   *on a day of the week*: **в** + acc, e.g. **в сре́ду**, *on Wednesday*.

(b)   *on days of the week*: **по** + dat, e.g. **по среда́м** (in R1, **по сре́дам**), *on Wednesdays*.

(c)   *in a month*: **в** + prep, e.g. **в январе́**, *in January*.

(d)   *a date in a month*: neuter nominative singular form of ordinal number (**число́** is understood) + genitive form of the month, e.g. **пе́рвое ма́я**, *1 May*.

(e)   *on a date*: as in (d) above but with the ordinal in the genitive, e.g. **пе́рвого ма́я**, *on 1 May*.

(f)   *a year*: a compound number with an ordinal as the last component, e.g. **ты́сяча девятьсо́т девяно́сто четвёртый год**, *1994*.

(g)   *in a year*: as in (f) above but preceded by **в** and with the ordinal and год in the prepositional, e.g. **в две ты́сячи четвёртом году́**, *in 2004*.

Note: if the year is preceded by a more precise date, then the ordinal indicating the year must be in the genitive case and must be followed by **го́да**, e.g. пе́рвое ма́рта ты́сяча девятьсо́т **восьмидеся́того го́да**, *1 March 1980* (see also the note to 11.4.10(e)).

(h)   *in a century*: **в** + prep, e.g. **в два́дцать пе́рвом ве́ке**, *in the twenty-first century*.

Note: *AD* and *BC* are **на́шей э́ры** (or **н.э.**) and **до на́шей э́ры** (or **до н.э.**), respectively.

11.4.12   Distance

This may be expressed in the following ways:

(a)   with the prepositions **от** and **до** + cardinal numeral in the nominative, e.g.

От це́нтра до стадио́на два киломе́тра.
It is two kilometres from the centre to the stadium.

(b)   with **в** + cardinal numeral and following noun in the prepositional, e.g.

Стадио́н нахо́дится **в двух киломе́трах** от це́нтра.
The stadium is (situated) two kilometres from the centre.

(c)   with the phrase **на расстоя́нии** + cardinal numeral in the genitive and a following noun in the genitive plural, e.g.

на расстоя́нии двух киломе́тров от це́нтра
at a distance of two kilometres from the centre/two kilometres away from the centre

Note: the expressions **на высоте́**, *at a height of*, and **на глубине́**, *at a depth of*, are analogous to the expression **на расстоя́нии**, but in ordinary speech a large numeral following them is likely to be left in the nominative case, e.g. Самолёт лети́т на высоте́ **де́сять** ты́сяч ме́тров, *The plane is flying at a height of 10,000 metres.*

11.4.13   Nouns expressing number

These nouns (viz. **дво́йка, тро́йка, четвёрка, пятёрка, шестёрка, семёрка, восьмёрка, девя́тка, деся́тка**) decline like feminine nouns in -ка. They may denote the shape of the digit or the number of a bus or tram, or they may have some special use (e.g. **тро́йка**, *three-horse carriage*; **восьмёрка**, *an eight* (at rowing)). They may also denote playing cards (e.g. **пи́ковая семёрка**, *the seven of spades*). In the case of **дво́йка, тро́йка, четвёрка, пятёрка** they also represent, in ascending order of merit, marks in the Russian educational system.

Note: the adjective denoting the suit, *spades*, is very commonly stressed on the second syllable in R1, i.e. **пико́вый**. However, in the title of Púshkin's famous short story **Пи́ковая да́ма**, *The Queen of Spades*, it has standard stress.

11.5   Use of aspects

Aspectual usage is an area of Russian grammar which gives particular difficulty to English-speakers, not least because aspectual distinctions cut across the distinctions of tense to which English-speakers are accustomed.

11.5.1   Basic distinction between the aspects

For practical purposes one can draw a basic distinction in usage between the two aspects which is quite straightforward.

- The **imperfective**, broadly speaking, is used to denote **incomplete** actions in the past, present or future, or actions which are **frequent** or **repeated**. Imperfective verbs naturally refer to actions which take place concurrently with other actions or which are interrupted by other actions.

- The **perfective** verb has the function of presenting a single action in its **totality**. It is therefore used when the speaker is referring to an action that has been or will be successfully **completed**. The perfective will commonly be used where an action has some **result** or where the action belongs in a past or future **sequence**, because each action in a sequence is complete before the next action takes place, e.g. Она́

встáла, умы́лась, одéлась и вы́шла, *She got up, washed, got dressed and went out.* The perfective does not as a rule have present meaning, since actions in the present are by their nature incomplete.

Note: once the above distinction has been drawn, it is useful also to bear in mind the fact that whereas the perfective form has a clear or marked meaning, the imperfective is used to convey a whole range of meanings that fall outside the scope of the marked form.

11.5.2   Effect of adverbial modifiers

It is in keeping with the basic distinction made in 11.5.1 that certain adverbs or adverbial expressions should encourage, if they do not actually oblige, the use of one aspect or the other. Contrast the following sets of adverbial modifiers; those on the left tend to dictate use of the imperfective, whilst those on the right encourage use of the perfective:

imperfective		perfective	
всегдá	*always*	вдруг	*suddenly*
врéмя от врéмени	*from time to time*	неожúданно	*unexpectedly*
иногдá	*sometimes*	совсéм	*quite, completely*
кáждый год	*every year*	срáзу	*immediately*
кáждый день	*every day*	за + acc	*over, in the space of*
мнóго раз	*many times*	покá не	*until*
не раз	*more than once*	ужé	*already*
покá	*while*		
постоя́нно	*constantly*		
чáсто	*often*		

11.5.3   Use of aspect in the indicative

The function of the aspects in the indicative, and the relationship of the indicative forms of the Russian imperfective and perfective verbs to English tenses, may be summarised as follows:

imperfective	perfective

present tense

- incomplete action:

  Я читáю.
  I am reading.
  Он пúшет письмó.
  He is writing a letter.
  Онá идёт по у́лице.
  She is walking down the street.

- repeated action:

  По воскресе́ньям я **отдыха́ю**.
  I relax on Sundays.
  Почти́ ка́ждый день она́ **посеща́ет** теа́тр.
  She goes to the theatre almost every day.

future tense

- incomplete action:

  Когда́ ты придёшь, мы **бу́дем у́жинать**.
  When you arrive we shall be having supper.

- repeated action:

  По вечера́м я **бу́ду писа́ть** пи́сьма.
  I shall write letters in the evenings.

- action about to be begun:

  Сейча́с мы **бу́дем выходи́ть**.
  We're going to go out now.

- single completed action or event:

  Я **напишу́** ему́ письмо́.
  I shall write him a letter.

past tense

- incomplete or prolonged action:

  Я **у́жинал**, когда́ вошла́ жена́.
  I was having supper when my wife came in.
  Я всю неде́лю **рабо́тал(а)**.
  I worked all week.

- repeated action:

  Я не раз **объясня́л(а)** э́то.
  I have explained this more than once.

- annulled action:

  Он **открыва́л** окно́.
  He opened the window (but has now shut it again).
  Она́ **приходи́ла**.
  She came (but has gone away again).

- question or statement of fact without stress on completion of action:

  Ты **писа́л(а)** сочине́ние?
  Have you written the essay?
  Вы **чита́ли** пье́сы Че́хова?
  Have you read Chekhov's plays?
  По ра́дио **передава́ли**, что бу́дет снег.
  They said on the radio that there would be snow.
  Вы **зака́зывали**?
  Have you ordered?

- single completed action or event, sequence of actions:

  Я **вы́пил(а)** стака́н пи́ва.
  I drank a glass of beer.
  За одну́ неде́лю она́ **написа́ла** це́лую главу́.
  In the space of one week she wrote a whole chapter.

  Он **встал, поза́втракал и вы́шел**.
  He got up, had breakfast and went out.

  Он **откры́л** окно́.
  He opened the window (and it remained open).

  Она́ **пришла́**.
  She came (and is still here).

- attempt but non-achievement:

У него было напряжённое лицо: он
вспоминал, где он видел её.
He had a strained look on his face: he was trying
to recall where he had seen her (before).
Он **бил** и не забил пенальти.
He took the penalty but did not score.

сдавать or **держать** экзамен	cf. **сдать** or **выдержать** экзамен
to sit/take an exam	*to pass an exam*
доказывать	cf. **доказать**
to try to prove, i.e. *to contend*	*to prove*

Note 1   The distinctions drawn in the last section above (attempt with reference to non-achievement or achievement) apply only in relation to a single instance. In frequentative contexts the imperfective may well convey achievement, e.g. Каждый год он **сдавал** экзамены на 'отлично', *Every year he passed his exams with commendation.*

2   The imperfective forms **видеть** and **слышать** may mean *to be able to see* and *to be able to hear* respectively. The perfective forms of these verbs (**увидеть** and **услышать**), on the other hand, are not necessarily used to render English tenses that an English-speaker would normally expect to be rendered by perfective verbs (e.g. *saw, have heard,* etc.). The perfective forms tend to refer to the beginning of a perception, e.g. Сначала он ничего не **видел** вдали, но потом **увидел** маленькую лодку, *At first he could not see anything in the distance, but then he caught sight of a tiny boat.* See also 4.3, *can* (d).

11.5.4 Use of aspect in the infinitive

After certain verbs which indicate the stage that an action has reached (e.g. *to begin, to continue, to stop, to finish*) an **imperfective** infinitive is required, e.g. Он начал **собирать** марки, *He began to collect stamps*; Она перестала **петь**, *She stopped singing*; Мы продолжали **беседовать**, *We continued to chat.* The imperfective is required here because the action denoted by the infinitive cannot in this context be seen in its totality.

- An **imperfective** infinitive is required after the following verbs:

начинать/начать	*to begin, to start*
стать (pf), in the meaning:	*to begin, to start*
приниматься/приняться	*to set about*
научиться	*to learn to (do sth)*
полюбить	*to grow fond (of doing sth)*
привыкать/привыкнуть	*to get used to (doing sth)*
продолжать/продолжить	*to continue*
кончать/кончить	*to finish*
бросать/бросить, in the meaning:	*to give up, abandon*
переставать/перестать	*to stop (doing sth)*
надоедать/надоесть	*to grow tired of (used impersonally)*

| отвыка́ть/отвы́кнуть | *to get out of the habit of* (doing sth) |
| устава́ть/уста́ть | *to tire of* (doing sth) |

Note: the perfective form **продо́лжить** is rarely used except in the sense of *to prolong*, and may be followed by a verbal noun rather than an infinitive, e.g. Мы **продо́лжили** обсужде́ние, *We carried on the discussion.*

After certain other verbs, on the other hand, a **perfective** infinitive is required, e.g. Она́ забы́ла **посла́ть** письмо́ (pf), *She forgot to send the letter.*

- a **perfective infinitive** is required after:

забы́ть	*to forget* (to do sth)
оста́ться	*to remain* (to be done)
реши́ть	*to decide (to)*
уда́ться	*to succeed in, manage to* (used impersonally)
успе́ть	*to have time to*

11.5.5   Use of aspect in negative constructions

- With negated verbs in the past tense an **imperfective** verb should be used to denote complete absence of a particular action, e.g.

| Мы не **встреча́лись**. | *We have not met.* |
| Свою́ та́йну я **не открыва́л(а)** никому́. | *I have not revealed my secret to anyone.* |

Note: a perfective verb should be used, on the other hand, to indicate that an action was not performed on a specific occasion, e.g. Мы не **встре́тились**, *We did not meet.*

- The negated **perfective** may also mean that the subject was not able to carry out an action or failed to do sth which it was intended to do, e.g.

Звоно́к буди́льника не **разбуди́л** его́, так кре́пко он спал.
The alarm-clock did not wake him, so soundly was he sleeping.
Он до́лжен был прийти́, но не **пришёл**.
He was due to come but he did not come.

- Many types of negative expression and types of verb, when negated, require a following infinitive to be **imperfective**, especially those which express:

(a)   **prohibition**: modal constructions with the meaning *may not* or *should not*, e.g. Тут нельзя́ **переходи́ть** доро́гу, *One must not cross the road here* (because e.g. there is no crossing and one may be fined).

Note: constructions meaning *cannot*, on the other hand, are rendered by perfective forms, e.g. Тут нельзя́ **перейти́** доро́гу, *One cannot cross the road here* (because e.g. there is too much traffic or the road is up and it is dangerous).

(b) **dissuasion**, e.g. Он уговори́л меня́ не **остава́ться**, *He persuaded me not to stay*.

Note: the verb *to dissuade*, **отгова́ривать/отговори́ть**, also requires a following infinitive to be imperfective, e.g. Оте́ц отговори́л сы́на **меня́ть** профе́ссию, *The father dissuaded his son from/talked his son out of changing his profession*.

(c) **advice** or **request** that sth **not** be done, e.g. Врач посове́товал больно́му не **выходи́ть** на у́лицу, *The doctor advised the patient not to go out*; Председа́тель предложи́л не **откла́дывать** реше́ние, *The chairman proposed that a decision not be delayed*.

(d) a **decision**, **promise** or **intention not** to do sth, e.g. А́рмия реши́ла не **наступа́ть** на столи́цу, *The army decided not to attack the capital*.

Note: if on the other hand verbs such as **угова́ривать/уговори́ть**, **сове́товать/посове́товать**, **предлага́ть/предложи́ть**, **проси́ть/попроси́ть**, **реша́ть/реши́ть** are followed by a verb that is not negated, then the following infinitive may be of either aspect, depending on the usual considerations concerning prolongation or frequency of the action. Thus a perfective infinitive will be required if the action is performed on a single occasion, e.g. Врач посове́товал больно́му **приня́ть** [pf] снотво́рное, *The doctor advised the patient to take a sleeping tablet*.

(e) **inexpediency**, e.g. Не сто́ит **смотре́ть** э́тот фильм, *It's not worth seeing this film*; **Кури́ть** вре́дно, *Smoking is bad for you*.

11.5.6 Use of aspect in the imperative

The use of the imperfective aspect in the imperative sounds less categoric and therefore more polite than the use of the perfective. The imperfective tends to express invitations or requests whereas the perfective tends to express instructions or commands. However, imperatives of all sorts, including those expressed in the perfective, may be softened by the insertion of **пожа́луйста**, *please*, or some phrase such as **бу́дьте добры́**, *be so kind as to* (see also 7.12). In R1 the particle **-ка** (5.4 (a)) serves the same purpose, e.g. На́дя, **иди́-ка** сюда́, *Come over here, would you, Nadia*.

imperfective	perfective
• commands relating to repeated action, e.g. По воскресе́ньям **звони́** ма́ме, *Phone mother on Sundays*.	cf. **Позвони́** мне за́втра, *Phone me tomorrow*.
• invitation to do sth, e.g. **Сади́тесь**, пожа́луйста, *Sit down, please*; По доро́ге домо́й **заходи́** ко мне, *Call in to see me on the way home*.	instruction to do sth on a single occasion, e.g. **Ся́дьте** побли́же к све́ту, *Sit nearer the light*; По доро́ге домо́й **зайди́** в апте́ку, *Call in at the chemist's on the way home*.

- instruction to do sth on a single occasion expressed by transitive verb without direct object, e.g. **Читáйте** мéдленнее, *Read more slowly*; **Пишúте** аккурáтнее, *Write more neatly*.

- request to begin to do sth or to get on with sth, e.g. Кóнчили смотрéть телевúзор? Тепéрь **выключáйте** егó, *Have you finished watching television? Now switch it off*; **Вставáй**, ужé пóздно, *Get up, it's late*.

- with **не**: prohibition, e.g. Бóльше ко мне не **приходúте**, *Don't come to me any more*.

- **не** + infin: formal prohibition (see 6.8(a)), e.g. Не **прислонúться**, *Do not lean*. (on door of train)

cf. **Прочитáйте пéрвый абзáц**, *Read the first paragraph*; **Напишúте сто слов** на эту тéму, *Write a hundred words on this subject*.

with **не** (often with **смотрú(те)** or **осторóжно**): warning, e.g. Смотрú не **уронú** вáзу, *Watch out, don't drop the vase*; Осторóжно, не **упадú**, здесь скóльзко, *Be careful, don't fall over, it's slippery here*.

infin, not negated: formal instruction (see 6.8(a)), e.g. При авáрии **разбúть** стеклó молоткóм, *In the event of an accident break the glass with the hammer*.

11.6 Problems in choice of tense

Russian in some contexts requires use of a tense which is unexpected to English-speakers.

(a) **Reported speech**, in which Russian verbs are put in the tense that would have been used in the original statement or question. Reported speech may be defined for this purpose as statements introduced by verbs of thinking, knowing, hoping and even verbs of perception such as hearing as well as verbs of saying, asking and replying. This usage differs from English usage. Compare, for example, the tenses used in the reported speech in the following Russian and English sentences:

Я сказáл(а) емý, что **живý** в Лóндоне.
*I told him that I **lived** in London.*
Солдáты убедúлись, что мúна не **взорвётся**.
*The soldiers made sure that the mine **would** not **explode**.*
Он спросúл, **изучáю** ли я рýсский язы́к.
*He asked whether I **was studying** Russian.*
Онá спросúла, соглáсен ли я.
*She asked whether I **agreed**.*

Note: in reported questions *whether* is rendered by **ли** and the Russian word order, with inversion of subject and predicate, is an order possible in a question. The last two examples above illustrate the point.

(b) **Present perfect continuous**: a present tense is used in Russian to denote an action which began in the past and is still continuing, e.g.

Я пять лет **изуча́ю** ру́сский язы́к.
*I **have been studying** Russian for five years.*
Он три́дцать лет **рабо́тает** ди́ктором.
*He **has been working** as a newsreader for thirty years.*

(c) **Logical future**: the future tense, expressed by a perfective verb, is used in Russian subordinate clauses containing conditional and temporal conjunctions such as **е́сли** and **когда́** if the action clearly is yet to take place (cf. English use of present tense in these circumstances), e.g.

Е́сли вы **прочита́ете** э́ту кни́гу, вы всё поймёте.
*You will understand everything if you **read** this book.*
Когда́ он **придёт**, мы поговори́м об э́том.
*We shall talk about this when he **arrives**.*

Note: the present tense is used, as in English, with verbs of motion indicating that an action is to take place in the near future, e.g. Я **иду́** в кино́ сего́дня ве́чером, *I **am going** to the cinema tonight.*

11.7 Use of verbs of motion

There are fourteen pairs of imperfective verbs of motion which give particular difficulty to the foreign student. There is perhaps no entirely satisfactory term to define the two categories: the terms abstract, indeterminate and multidirectional are all applied to the category including **ходи́ть**, whilst the terms concrete, determinate and unidirectional are applied to the category which includes **идти́**. The fourteen pairs are as follows:

ходи́ть	идти́	*to walk, go on foot*
е́здить	е́хать	*to travel, go by transport*
бе́гать	бежа́ть	*to run*
лета́ть	лете́ть	*to fly*
пла́вать	плыть	*to swim, float, sail*
по́лзать	ползти́	*to crawl*
носи́ть	нести́	*to take (by hand), carry*
води́ть	вести́	*to take, lead*
вози́ть	везти́	*to take (by transport), convey*
ла́зить	лезть	*to climb*
гоня́ть	гнать	*to drive, pursue*
ката́ть	кати́ть	*to roll, push*
таска́ть	тащи́ть	*to pull*
броди́ть	брести́	*to wander, amble*

Note: the verb **брести́** may convey a sense of slowness or difficulty.

| **Use of verbs like идти** | The easiest way to grasp the distinction between the verbs in the two categories is perhaps to treat those like **идти** as having quite specific meaning and those like **ходить**, on the contrary, as covering a broader range of meanings outside the scope of those like **идти** (cf. the similar distinction made in 11.5.1 between the perfective aspect of the verb and the broader imperfective). |

Verbs like **идти** indicate movement in one general direction. The movement is not necessarily in a straight line, but progress is made from point A towards point B, e.g.

| Она **идёт** по улице. | *She is going down the street.* |
| Он **бежит** к автобусу. | *He is running towards the bus.* |

| **Use of verbs like ходить** | One may list a number of meanings outside the scope of verbs in the category of **идти**, and these meanings are all conveyed by verbs like **ходить**. |

(a)   **Repeated** or **habitual** action, e.g.

| По субботам мы **ходим** в кино. | *On Saturdays we go to the cinema.* |

(b)   **Round trip**, e.g.

| Я **ходил(а)** в театр. | *I went to the theatre (and came back).* |

In this sense ходить may be synonymous with быть, e.g. Она ходила в театр, *She went to the theatre* = Она была в театре.

Note: it may be difficult to separate the sense of round trip from the sense of repetition, e.g. Каждый день дети **ходят** в школу, *Each day the children go to school* (and of course come home again).

(c)   Movement **in various directions**, e.g.

| Девочки **бегали** по саду. | *The little girls were running round the garden.* |

(d)   **General movement**, i.e. movement without reference to any specific instance of it, e.g.

Ребёнок начал **ходить**.	*The child began to walk.*
Я не умею **плавать**.	*I can't swim.*
Птицы **летают**, змеи **ползают**.	*Birds fly, snakes crawl.*

11.8   Use of reflexive verbs

- Many common verbs exist only in a reflexive form but have no obvious reflexive meaning, e.g.

бояться (impf)	*to fear, be afraid of*
гордиться (impf)	*to be proud of*
пытаться/попытаться	*to attempt*
смеяться (impf)	*to laugh*

стара́ться/постара́ться	to try
улыба́ться/улыбну́ться	to smile

Note: in a few pairs the imperfective form is reflexive but the perfective form is not:

ложи́ться/лечь	to lie down
ло́паться/ло́пнуть	to burst (intrans)
сади́ться/сесть	to sit down
станови́ться/стать	to become

• In a very large number of verbs the reflexive particle renders a transitive verb intransitive, in other words it fulfils the function of a direct object, e.g.

возвраща́ть/возврати́ть or верну́ть to return (give back)	возвраща́ться/возврати́ться or верну́ться to return (go back)
конча́ть/ко́нчить to finish (complete)	конча́ться/ко́нчиться to finish (come to end)
начина́ть/нача́ть to begin (sth, to do sth)	начина́ться/нача́ться to begin (come into being)
одева́ть/оде́ть to dress (sb)	одева́ться/оде́ться to dress, get dressed
остана́вливать/останови́ть to stop (bring to halt)	остана́вливаться/останови́ться to stop (come to halt)
поднима́ть/подня́ть to lift	поднима́ться/подня́ться to go up
раздева́ть/разде́ть to undress (sb)	раздева́ться/разде́ться to undress, get undressed
увели́чивать/увели́чить to increase (make bigger)	увели́чиваться/увели́читься to increase (get bigger)
удивля́ть/удиви́ть to surprise	удивля́ться/удиви́ться to be surprised
улучша́ть/улу́чшить to improve (make better)	улучша́ться/улу́чшиться to improve (get better)
уменьша́ть/уме́ньшить to decrease (make smaller)	уменьша́ться/уме́ньшиться to decrease (get smaller)
ухудша́ть/уху́дшить to make worse	ухудша́ться/уху́дшиться to get worse

• reciprocal action, e.g.

встреча́ться/встре́титься	to meet one another
обнима́ться/обня́ться	to embrace one another
целова́ться/поцелова́ться	to kiss one another

• characteristic action: some verbs which are normally transitive and non-reflexive take the reflexive particle in contexts where they have no specific object but denote action characteristic of the subject, e.g.

Крапи́ва жжётся.	Nettles sting.
Соба́ка куса́ется.	The dog bites.
Ло́шадь ляга́ется.	The horse kicks.
Ко́шки цара́паются.	Cats scratch.

- impersonal verbs: with some common verbs a third-person reflexive form is used to indicate the physical condition or mood of a subject, e.g.

Мне хо́чется есть/пить.	*I am hungry/thirsty.*
Ему́ не **спи́тся**.	*He can't get to sleep.*
Ей не **чита́ется**.	*She doesn't feel like reading.*

- with passive sense: many imperfective verbs are used in a reflexive form with an inanimate subject to mean that sth has been/is being/will be done, e.g.

Этот вопро́с до́лго **обсужда́лся**.	*This question **was discussed** for a long time.*
Зна́ние – э́то то́же това́р, кото́рый **покупа́ется** и **продаётся**.	*Knowledge too is a commodity that **is bought** and **sold**.*
Ры́ночные отноше́ния бу́дут **стро́иться** в Росси́и ещё до́лгие го́ды.	*Market relations **will be built** in Russia over many long years to come.*

Note: this use of the reflexive belongs mainly to R2/3, as the flavour of the above examples shows.

- in combination with certain verbal prefixes (see also 8.3), e.g.

всма́триваться/всмотре́ться	*to peer at*
зачи́тываться/зачита́ться	*to get engrossed in reading*
наеда́ться/нае́сться	*to eat one's fill, stuff oneself (with food)*
расходи́ться/разойти́сь	*to get divorced, disperse*
съезжа́ться/съе́хаться	*to gather, assemble*

11.9   The conditional mood

Conditional sentences in Russian are of two types, depending on whether the speaker means that in certain circumstances (a) sth **will/will not** happen or (b) sth **might** happen. Usage in the two clauses of a conditional sentence (i.e. the subordinate clause which contains the condition, usually introduced by **éсли**, *if*, and the main clause, which states the consequence) differs in the two types of conditional sentence.

Note: in both types of conditional sentence the clause stating the consequence may be introduced by **то** or **тогда́** (Eng *then*), provided that it follows the clause containing the condition.

- Real conditional sentences, in which the speaker is saying that given certain conditions a particular consequence definitely did/does/will or did not/does not/will not follow, a verb in the past, present or future tense (depending on the context) is used in each clause, e.g.

Éсли ты ду́маешь [impf pres], что он че́стен, **то** э́то оши́бка.
If you think he's honest then you're mistaken.
Éсли вы **переста́нете** [pf fut] крича́ть, я **отве́чу** на ваш вопро́с.
If you stop shouting I'll answer your question.

Note: a future must be used in the clause containing the condition (**переста́нете** in the second example above) when the verb denotes an event that has yet to take place (see also 11.6(c); cf. English use of the present tense in such clauses).

• Hypothetical conditional sentences, in which the speaker is saying that given certain hypothetical conditions some consequence would/would not follow or would have/would not have followed, both clauses must have a verb in the conditional mood. This mood is rendered in Russian simply by the appropriate form of the past tense (masculine, feminine, neuter or plural) together with the invariable particle **бы**, e.g.

Éсли **бы** рабо́ты **начали́сь** во́время, тогда́ расхо́ды **бы́ли бы** гора́здо ни́же.
If work had begun on time [but it did not], then the cost would have been much lower.
Как **бы** вы **отнесли́сь** к тому́, **е́сли** ваш четырёхле́тний ребёнок вдруг **пропе́л бы** таку́ю пе́сенку?
How would you react if your four-year-old child suddenly sang a song like that?

Note 1   Conditional sentences of this type may relate to past, present or future time, and only from the context will it be clear which meaning is intended.

2   In the clause containing the condition the particle **бы** generally follows **е́сли** (and it may be contracted to **б**). In the clause describing the consequence **бы** generally follows the verb in the past tense. However, **бы** may also follow some other word in the clause to which it is intended to give emphasis.

3   The clause containing the condition may also be rendered with the use of a second-person singular imperative, e.g. **Живи́** она́ в други́х усло́виях, из неё вы́шел бы прекра́сный худо́жник, *Had she lived in other conditions, she would have made a fine artist.*

11.10 The subjunctive mood

As well as forming the conditional mood, the past tense of the verb + the particle **бы** renders the subjunctive in Russian. There are no sets of distinctive verbal endings or different subjunctive tenses of the sort found in, for example, French, Italian and Spanish. As in these Western European languages, though, the subjunctive in Russian is used in concessive clauses and in subordinate clauses after verbs of wishing. It may also be used, but tends in R1 and R2 to be avoided, in subordinate clauses after verbs of ordering, permitting, fearing and doubting and after various negative antecedents.

• Concessive clauses: these are clauses introduced by *whoever, whatever, whichever, however, wherever, whenever*, etc., and they may be translated into Russian by the appropriate pronoun (**кто, что, како́й, как, где,** куда́, когда́, etc.) in the form required by the context and followed by the particle **бы** + **ни** + verb in past tense, e.g.

Кем бы пото́м они́ **ни ста́ли**, а чу́вство благода́рности ва́м от них никогда́ не уйдёт.

Whoever they may become later on, the sense of gratitude to you will never leave them.

Я счита́ю, что про́шлое непреме́нно на́до бере́чь, **како́е бы** плохо́е оно́ **ни́ бы́ло**.

I think the past should definitely be preserved however bad it might have been.

Всем гра́жданам, **како́й бы** национа́льности они́ **ни́ бы́ли** и где бы они́ **ни прожива́ли**, гаранти́рованы ра́вные права́ и возмо́жности.

All citizens, of whatever nationality they may be and wherever they may reside, are guaranteed equal rights and opportunities.

Note 1   As with conditional sentences in which **бы** is used, so in such concessive clauses too a verb accompanied by this particle may refer to past, present or future actions.

2   Concessive clauses may also be translated by the use of the appropriate pronoun + **ни** + verb in the appropriate tense, e.g. **Что ни говори́те**, а прия́тно поро́й встре́тить для себя́ неожи́данное, *Whatever you say/Say what you will, it is nice sometimes to encounter the unexpected.*

3   *Whatever, whenever, wherever*, etc. do not invariably introduce concessive clauses; they may merely impart emphasis, as in the question *Wherever have you been?*, which might be translated thus: **Где же** ты был(а́)? (See also 5.4, же (d).)

• Exhortation: the particle **бы** may also be used, with a verb in the past tense, to express an exhortation or gentle command or the desirability of some action, e.g.

Вы бы **помогли́** ему́.

You should help him/should have helped him.

• Wishing: after verbs of wishing the subordinate clause should be introduced by **что́бы** (a coalescence of **что** + **бы**) and the verb in the subordinate clause should be in the past tense, e.g.

Я хочу́, **что́бы** на́ши де́ти **зна́ли** наш родно́й язы́к.

I want our children to know our native language.

• Commanding, permitting: after verbs of this type the subjunctive may also be used, e.g.

Я сказа́л(а), **что́бы** официа́нтка **принесла́** стака́н воды́.

I told the waitress to bring a glass of water.

Note: subjunctive constructions in such sentences are only alternatives to the use of an object and verb in the infinitive, and indeed the latter, simpler, construction prevails in R1/R2. Thus the above English sentence might also have been rendered thus: Я сказа́л(а) **официа́нтке принести́** стака́н воды́.

• Fearing: verbs of fearing may be followed by (a) in R2/3, a negative subjunctive (e.g. Я бою́сь, **что́бы** [or **как бы**] он **не пришёл**), or (b) in R1/2 by a verb in the future tense in a clause introduced by что (e.g. Я боюсь, **что** он **придёт**). Both sentences mean *I am afraid he may come.* When it is feared that something may not happen, then only the second construction is possible. Thus the sentence *I was afraid he would not come* may only be rendered by Я боя́лся, **что** он не **придёт**.

- Negative antecedent: **бы** and a verb in the past tense may also be used in subordinate clauses after negated verbs such as **ду́мать**, *to think*, and **знать**, *to know*, e.g.

  Я не ду́маю, **что́бы** кто́-нибудь **мог** так вести́ себя́.
  I don't think anyone could behave like that.

11.11 Use of gerunds and participles

11.11.1 Use of gerunds

- The imperfective gerund describes action which is taking place at the same time as the action described by the main verb in the sentence (though the main verb itself may be in the past, present or future tense). It may translate English expressions such as *while doing, by doing, although they do,* as well as simply *doing,* e.g.

  Войска́ на́чали осторо́жное продвиже́ние к це́нтру, ме́дленно **подавля́я** очаги́ сопротивле́ния.
  The troops began a careful advance towards the centre, slowly suppressing centres of resistance.
  Слу́шая ра́дио, мо́жно узнава́ть (or узна́ть), что̀ происхо́дит в ми́ре.
  One can find out what is going on in the world by listening to the radio.
  Обогрева́я страну́, рабо́чие на электроста́нциях не чу́вствуют, что страна́ забо́тится о них.
  Although they heat the country, the power workers do not feel the country cares about them.

- The perfective gerund describes action that has taken place, and has been completed, before the action described by the main verb (which is not necessarily in the past). It translates an English expression of the sort *having done,* or, if it is negated, *without having done,* e.g.

  Просиде́в де́сять лет в тюрьме́, он поседе́л.
  Having been in prison for ten years, he had gone grey.
  Сде́лав свой докла́д, она́ сейча́с отвеча́ет на вопро́сы.
  Having given her report she is now answering questions.
  Нельзя́ уходи́ть, не **заплати́в**.
  One mustn't go without paying [having paid].

Note 1   Gerunds **may only be used when the subject performing the action in question is the same as the subject of the main clause**, as is the case in all the above examples. A gerund cannot be used in a sentence of the type *While she reads the text I write out the words I don't know,* in which the two clauses have different subjects (*she* and *I*). This sentence must be translated thus: Пока́ она́ **чита́ет** текст, я выпи́сываю незнако́мые слова́.

2   Gerunds (mainly imperfective) have become established in certain set phrases, e.g. **пра́вду говоря́**, *to tell the truth*; **су́дя по** (+ dat), *judging by*; **сиде́ть сложа́ ру́ки**, *to sit idly* (lit *with arms folded*). With the exception of such set phrases, though, the use of gerunds is largely confined to R3.

11.11.2   Use of active participles

Active participles correspond exactly, from a semantic point of view, to phrases containing **кото́рый** + verb in the present tense (in the case of the present participles) or in the past tense, of either aspect (in the case of the past participles). The participle must agree in gender, case and number with the noun to which it relates (cf. use of **кото́рый**, 11.2.1), e.g.

Докуме́нты, **подтвержда́ющие** [= кото́рые подтвержда́ют] э́тот факт, бы́ли на́йдены в архи́вах.
Documents confirming this fact were found in archives.
Для пассажи́ров, **отправля́ющихся** [= кото́рые отправля́ются] по са́мым популя́рным авиатра́ссам, це́ны то́же вы́росли.
Fares have also risen for passengers departing on the most popular air routes.
Авто́бус, **вёзший** [= кото́рый вёз] госте́й на сва́дьбу, упа́л с моста́.
A bus [which was] carrying guests to a wedding fell off a bridge.
Компа́ния нанима́ет иностра́нцев, специа́льно **прие́хавших** [= кото́рые прие́хали] для э́того в Росси́ю.
The company is employing foreigners who have come to Russia specially for the purpose.

Note: active participles differ from semantically identical phrases with **кото́рый** in that their use is confined to R3, except insofar as some have become established in the language in set phrases (e.g. **пи́шущая маши́нка**, *typewriter*) or adjectives (e.g. **блестя́щий**, *brilliant*; **бы́вший**, *former*) or substantivised adjectives (e.g. **куря́щий**, *smoker*).

11.11.3   Use of present passive participles

These participles are rarely used predicatively, but used attributively they occur quite frequently in the modern written language, especially in R3a and R3b. They must agree in gender, case and number with the noun to which they refer, e.g.

безрабо́тица и **порожда́емые** е́ю отча́яние и гнев
unemployment and the despair and anger generated by it
среди́ зало́жников, **уде́рживаемых** экстреми́стскими гру́ппами,
among the hostages held by extremist groups . . .

11.11.4   Use of past passive participles

These participles correspond to English participles of the type *read, written, washed.*

- Long forms of these participles decline like adjectives and must agree in gender, case and number with the noun to which they refer, e.g.

  Маши́ны, **сде́ланные** в Япо́нии, сравни́тельно дёшевы.
  Cars made in Japan are relatively cheap.
  Здесь продаю́тся проду́кты, **пригото́вленные** без консерва́нтов.
  Food-stuffs made without preservatives are sold here.
  Я чита́ю кни́гу, **напи́санную** ва́шим отцо́м.
  I am reading a book written by your father.

- Short forms of these participles, like short forms of adjectives, cannot be used unless the participle is used predicatively (i.e. unless some part of the verb *to be* comes between the noun and the participle which relates to it). However, when the participle **is** used predicatively then it must be in the short form, e.g.

  Наш телефо́н давно́ был **отключён**.
  Our telephone was cut off a long time ago.
  В не́которых города́х **введена́** тало́нная систе́ма.
  A system of rationing has been introduced in some cities.
  Зда́ние **опеча́тано**.
  The building has been sealed.
  Э́ти дома́ бы́ли **постро́ены** в про́шлом году́.
  These houses were built last year.

Note 1 Past passive participles are widely used in speech but in R1/R2 there is a tendency to avoid them by using instead a verb in the active voice (in the third person plural without a pronoun; cf. the unspecified English *they*, French *on*, German *man*). Thus the above examples might be more colloquially rendered in the following way: Наш телефо́н давно́ **отключи́ли**; В не́которых города́х **вве́ли** тало́нную систе́му; Зда́ние **опеча́тали**; Э́ти дома́ **постро́или** в про́шлом году́.

2 In many passive sentences the agent is named, e.g. Он был уби́т **партиза́нами**, *He was killed by guerrillas*; Она́ была́ аресто́вана **мили́цией**, *She was arrested by the police*. Such sentences too may be rendered with an active verb, although Russian generally preserves the word order of the passive construction, with the named agent following the verb, e.g. **Его́ уби́ли партиза́ны; Её арестова́ла мили́ция**.

11.12 Conjunctions

11.12.1 Coordinating conjunctions

(a) The main coordinating conjunctions (**и, а, но, и́ли**) may be used in all registers. In R1, in which language tends to be spontaneous and less well organised, coordinating conjunctions are the principal means of linking the clauses of complex sentences and subordinating conjunctions (11.12.2) play a lesser role. The following points about the Russian coordinating conjunctions should be particularly noted by the English-speaking student.

- Both **a** and **но** may be translated as *but*. However, **a** normally suggests a stronger opposition than **но**: it excludes one factor in favour of another, whereas **но** has only a sense of limitation. Contrast:

Советую идти ме́дленно, **a** не бежа́ть.	*I suggest you go slowly, don't run.*
Советую торопи́ться, **но** не бежа́ть.	*I suggest you hurry, but don't run.*

  In the first example going slowly and running are presented as opposites and running is ruled out. In the second running is presented not as an opposite of hurrying but as an unnecessary intensification of it.

Note: **a** used in this contrastive sense may not be directly translated at all in English, e.g. 'Лебеди́ное о́зеро' бале́т, **a** не о́пера, *'Swan Lake' is a ballet, not an opera* (see also the first example above).

- **a** may also translate English *and*, when that conjunction has contrastive meaning, e.g.

Сади́тесь, **a** я постою́.	*You sit down and I shall stand.*
Они́ оста́лись, **a** мы ушли́.	*They stayed and we went home.*

- in lists, in which in English *and* is placed as a rule before the last member, **и** may be omitted in Russian, particularly in sedate narrative style, e.g.

Продава́ли о́бувь. Ту́фли, кроссо́вки, сапоги́, ва́ленки.	*They were selling footwear. Shoes, trainers, boots and felt boots.*

  Inclusion of **и** in a list might give the list an exhaustive air and is therefore more probable in the precise language of R3a/b.

(b) There are in addition a few coordinating conjunctions which are not stylistically neutral but belong to R1, especially:

- **да** (esp in N dialects), e.g.

день **да** ночь	*day and night*
ко́жа **да** ко́сти	*skin and bone*
Я охо́тно оста́лся/оста́лась бы, **да** пора́ уходи́ть.	*I'd willingly stay, but it's time to go.*
Бли́зок ло́коть, **да** не уку́сишь.	lit *One's elbow is near, but you can't bite it*, i.e. *So near and yet so far.*

- **да и**, *and besides/and what is more*, e.g.

Хо́лодно бы́ло, **да и** дождь шёл.	*It was cold, and besides, it was raining.*

- **a то**, *otherwise/or else*, e.g.

Одева́йся потепле́е, **a то** просту́дишься.	*Put some more clothes on, otherwise you'll catch cold.*
Спеши́, **a то** опозда́ем.	*Hurry or we'll be late.*

- **ли́бо**, *or*, e.g.

   Ли́бо пан, **ли́бо** пропа́л.   lit *Either a gentleman or I'm done*
                                             for, i.e. *All or nothing.*

11.12.2   Subordinating conjunctions

The conjunctions given in the following examples are standard forms. They may all be used in all registers. It should be noted though that subordinating conjunctions tend to occur more in R3 (i.e. in formal language, where a speaker or writer is perhaps concerned to establish the logical connections which conjunctions indicate) than in R1, where language is more expressive and spontaneous and ideas less clearly organised, and where coordinating conjunctions therefore prevail.

Note: some English subordinating conjunctions (e.g. *after, before, since*) may also function as prepositions (see Chapter 10 above). When they are prepositions they are followed by a noun, pronoun or verbal noun, e.g. *after dinner, before us, since graduating.* When they are conjunctions they introduce a subordinate clause, e.g. *after I had had dinner.* In Russian the two functions are distinguished. Thus **по́сле** is a preposition, but the conjunction is **по́сле того́, как**.

causal
Де́вочка пла́кала, **потому́ что** уста́ла.
*The little girl was crying **because** she was tired.*
Ле́кции не бу́дет, **так как** профе́ссор заболе́л.
*There won't be a lecture **since** the professor is ill.*

temporal
Я не зна́ю, **когда́** приду́.
*I don't know **when** I'll come.*
Он пришёл на остано́вку **по́сле того́, как** авто́бус ушёл.
*He arrived at the stop **after** the bus had gone.*
Нам на́до поговори́ть с ним об э́том, **пока́** он тут.
*We must have a word with him about that **while** he's here.*
Посмо́трим телеви́зор, **пока́ она́ не** придёт.
*Let's watch television **until** she comes.*

Note: **пока́ не** is followed by a perfective verb.

Что он де́лал **с тех пор, как** око́нчил университе́т?
*What had he been doing **since** he left university?*
Она́ осозна́ла свою́ оши́бку, **как то́лько** вы́шла из ко́мнаты.
*She realised her mistake **as soon as** she left the room.*
Едва́ самолёт взлете́л, **как** пило́т обнару́жил неполадку.
***No sooner** had the plane taken off than the pilot detected a fault.*
Ты до́лжен/должна́ дое́сть ры́бу, **пре́жде чем** взять моро́женое.
*You must eat up your fish **before** you have any ice-cream.*
Он пришёл **пе́ред те́м, как** проби́ли часы́.
*He arrived **just before** the clock struck.*
Она́ рабо́тала перево́дчиком **до того́, как** ста́ла журнали́стом.
*She worked as a translator **before** she became a journalist.*

Note: see 11.6(c) on use of tense after temporal and conditional conjunctions.

purposive	Она́ подошла́ к нему́, **что́бы** прошепта́ть ему́ что́-то на́ ухо. *She went up to him **so that** she could whisper something in his ear.* Я говорю́ э́то (**для того́**), **что́бы** вы предста́вили себе́ все опа́сности. *I am telling you this **so that/in order that** you may picture to yourself all the dangers.*
Note:	**что́бы** + past tense is used when the subjects are different, as in the last example above, but when the subject of the verb in the subordinate clause is the same as that in the main clause then **что́бы** is followed by the infinitive, e.g. Я э́то говорю́, **что́бы вы́разить** своё негодова́ние, *I am saying this in order to express my indignation.*
resultative	Маши́на слома́лась, **так что** мы опозда́ли. *The car broke down **so that** we were late.* Мы до того́ уста́ли, **что** засну́ли в авто́бусе. *We got **so** tired **that** we fell asleep on the bus.*
concessive	Я там бу́ду, **хотя́**, наве́рное, и опозда́ю. *I'll be there, **although** I expect I'll be late.*
Note:	see also modal particle **и** (5.4, и (c)). На се́вере страны́ хо́лодно зимо́й, **тогда́ как** на ю́ге тепло́. *It's cold in the north of the country in winter, **whereas** in the south it's warm.*
conditional	**Е́сли** вы не понима́ете, я объясню́. ***If** you don't understand I'll explain.* Я уе́ду в командиро́вку, **е́сли то́лько** вы одо́брите мой план. *I'll go on a business trip **provided** you approve my plan.*
Note:	see 11.9 on conditional sentences and also 11.6(c) on use of tense in them.

11.12.3 Subordinating conjunctions used in R1 or R3

Some subordinating conjunctions that are not standard in R2 may also be encountered. These may be divided into (a) those which are still used but which belong mainly in R1 or R3 (including, in R3, many compound conjunctions), and (b) those which are considered obsolete in the modern literary language (although they will be found in classical literature and in some cases may persist in R1, especially in dialect).

restricted use	**раз** (R1)	*if*, e.g. **Раз** ты реши́л э́то сде́лать, де́лай, *If you've decided to do it, get on with it.*
	благодаря́ тому́, что (R3)	*thanks to the fact that*
	в связи́ с тем, что (R3)	*in connection with the fact that*
	в си́лу того́, что (R3)	*by virtue of the fact that*
	ввиду́ того́, что (R3)	*in view of the fact that*
	всле́дствие того́, что (R3)	*owing to the fact that*

	и́бо (R3)	*for*, e.g. Вся́кий труд ва́жен, **и́бо** облагора́живает челове́ка, *All labour is important, for it ennobles a man.* (Tolstoi)
	невзира́я на то, что (R3)	*in spite of the fact that*
	по ме́ре того́, как (R3)	*in proportion as*
	посто́льку, поско́льку (R3)	*insofar as, to the extent that*
	при усло́вии, что (R3)	*on condition that*
	с тем что́бы + infin (R3)	*with a view to (doing)*
obsolete or colloquial	**бу́де** (N dialects)/**да́бы**	*if, provided that* = что́бы
	доко́ле (**доко́ль**)	*as long as, until*
	е́жели	= е́сли (possible in R1)
	ко́ли	*if* (possible in R1, esp dialect)
	коль ско́ро	*so long as* (possible in R1)
	пока́мест	= пока́ (possible in R1)

11.13 Syntactic features of colloquial speech

The language of R1 is characterised by a number of other syntactic features, as well as predominance of coordinating conjunctions over subordinating conjunctions and the use of some coordinating conjunctions not widely used in R2, e.g.

(a) ellipsis, which may be produced by omission of the verb (especially – but not exclusively – of a verb of motion) or of some other part of speech, e.g.

Вы ко мне?	*Are you coming to see me?*
Вдруг мне навстре́чу па́па.	*Suddenly dad was coming towards me.*
Мам, за до́ктором!	*Mum, get the doctor!*
Вы́стрел. Я че́рез забо́р.	*There was a shot and I leapt over the fence.*
Два на во́семь часо́в.	*Two [tickets] for eight o'clock.*
Мне пора́.	*It's time for me to go.*
Вы меня́?	*Is it me you're asking?*
Как дела́?	*How are things going?*
Всего́ хоро́шего!	*All the best.*

(b) combination of a verb denoting condition or motion with another verb in the same form to indicate that the action is carried out in a certain state, e.g.

Она́ сиде́ла ши́ла.	*She was sitting sewing.*
Е́дем, дре́млем.	*We were travelling along in a doze.*

(c) repetition of the verb to emphasise the protracted nature of an action, e.g.

Е́хали, е́хали и наконе́ц прие́хали.	*We travelled and travelled, and eventually we arrived.*

(d)   combination of two verbs from the same root, separated by **не**, to indicate the fullness of an action, e.g.

Она́ ра́дуется не нара́дуется на сы́на.	*She just dotes on her son.*

(e)   a construction containing a form of **взять** (often the imperative) and another verb in the same form, the two verbs being linked by **да** or **и** or **да и**; the construction expresses sudden volition on the part of the subject, e.g.

Он **взял да убежа́л**.	*He was up and off.*
Она́ **вдруг возьми́ да и разозли́сь** на меня́.	*She suddenly went and got angry with me.*

(f)   the very colloquial construction **то́лько и де́лает, что/то́лько и зна́ет, что**, together with another verb in the same form, indicating a single, exclusive action, e.g.

Мы с бра́том **то́лько и де́лали, что игра́ли** в ша́хматы.	*My brother and I just played chess all the time.*
День-деньско́й **то́лько и зна́ет, что смо́трит** телеви́зор.	*He does nothing but/All he does is watch TV all day long.*

(g)   use of **знай (себе́)** with a verb to indicate that the subject perseveres with the action in question in spite of unfavourable circumstances or obstacles, e.g.

Де́ти крича́ли. Ма́ма **знай себе́ смотре́ла** переда́чу.	*The children were shouting. Mum just went on watching the programme quite unconcerned.*

(h)   use of **смотри́(те)** and a negative imperative in the sense of *mind you don't*, e.g.

Ты **смотри́ не говори́** про меня́!	*Mind you don't talk about me.*

11.14   Word order

Word order is much more flexible in Russian than in English, since it is primarily inflection that establishes the relationship between the words in a Russian utterance. Whereas the order of words in the English statement *John loves Mary* cannot be altered without a consequential change of meaning, in Russian one may say, depending on the context or emphasis, either **Ива́н лю́бит Мари́ю** (*Ivan loves Mariia*) or **Мари́ю лю́бит Ива́н** (*It's Ivan who loves Mariia*).

However, Russian word order, while being flexible, is not random. On the contrary, it conforms to certain principles and rules. Moreover, it may be affected, like other aspects of language, by register. The following guidance can be given.

(a) Neutral word order: as a general rule the same sequence of subject + verb + object/complement which characterises English statements is observed in matter-of-fact statements in Russian too, e.g.

Ма́ма пи́шет письмо́.	*Mum's writing a letter.*
Охо́тники пойма́ли льва.	*The hunters caught a lion.*
Са́ша ста́нет инжене́ром.	*Sasha will become an engineer.*

(b) New and known or given information (**но́вое и да́нное**): the point in an utterance on which the speaker or writer wishes to focus attention, i.e. the novel element in it, is placed at or towards the end of the Russian utterance, since it carries more weight there. The earlier part of the utterance, on the other hand, contains the information which leads up to the novel point, i.e. information that is already familiar or taken for granted or less important. Contrast e.g.

По́езд пришёл.	*The train arrived.*
Пришёл по́езд.	*A train arrived.*
Ко́шка сиде́ла на печи́.	*The cat was sitting on the stove.*
На печи́ сиде́ла ко́шка.	*A cat was sitting on the stove.*

Note 1   What is new in a statement varies of course according to the point in a conversation or narrative that has been reached.

2   If it is the subject of the statement that represents the new information then the order of subject and verb will be inverted.

3   The distinctions achieved in Russian by variations of word order may be achieved in English by choice between the **definite** article (*the* introduces known information) and the **indefinite** article (*a* introduces a new element).

(c) Other rules that obtain in specific circumstances: the following guidance can be given (note differences from English usage).

• Subject and verb are inverted in statements in which the verb denotes natural event, existence, process, state, becoming or occurrence, e.g.

Идёт снег.	*It's snowing.*
Существу́ет риск пожа́ра.	*There's a risk of fire.*
Прошли́ го́ды.	*The years went by.*
У меня́ боли́т голова́.	*I've got a headache.*
Наступи́ла зима́.	*Winter came.*
Произошёл взрыв.	*There was an explosion.*

Note: it will be seen that in all these sentences the word order is consistent with the point made in (b) above about known and new information: in each instance the weight of the utterance is contained in the subject, while the verb is a weak word with relatively inconsequential meaning.

• Inversion is also common when the place where an action occurred is indicated at the beginning of the statement, e.g.

С за́пада шли облака́.	*Clouds were coming from the west.*

• The order of subject and verb is also inverted in questions introduced by an interrogative word and after reported speech, e.g.

Где нахо́дится вокза́л?	*Where's the station?*
Когда́ начина́ется фильм?	*When does the film begin?*
Я уста́л, – сказа́л он.	*'I'm tired', he said.*

- Object pronouns are frequently placed before the verb, e.g.

Я **вас** слу́шаю.	*I'm listening to you.*
Мы **вам** сказа́ли, что . . .	*We told you that . . .*
Тру́дности бы́ли, но мы с **ни́ми** спра́вились.	*There were difficulties, but we coped with them.*
Он **ничего́** не зна́ет.	*He doesn't know anything.*

- Objects indicating the person in impersonal expressions also tend to be placed before the predicate, e.g.

Мне на́до идти́.	*I must go.*
У **нас** не хвата́ет де́нег.	*We haven't got enough money.*

- Infinitives as a rule follow the verb or expression on which they are dependent, e.g.

Мы прие́хали **отдыха́ть**.	*We have come to rest.*
Собира́юсь **уе́хать**.	*I'm about to go away.*
Ну́жно **рабо́тать**.	*It's necessary to work.*

- In the modern language attributive adjectives, as in English, normally precede the noun they qualify, but they may follow the noun in menus or catalogues, e.g.

хоро́шая пого́да	*fine weather*
ско́рый по́езд	*a fast train*
напи́тки **прохлади́тельные**	*soft drinks*
сала́т **столи́чный**	*'capital-city salad'*

Note: predicative adjectives, on the other hand, generally follow the noun irrespective of whether they are long or short, e.g. Кни́га **интере́сна**, *The book is interesting*; Зада́ча была́ **тру́дная**, *The task was a difficult one.*

- Adverbs tend immediately to precede the verb they modify, e.g.

Всегда́ сия́ет со́лнце.	*The sun always shines.*
Он **ещё** спит.	*He's still asleep.*
Она́ **хорошо́** вы́глядит.	*She looks good.*
И́скренно благодарю́ вас.	*I sincerely thank you.*

Note 1   Adverbs indicating language used, on the other hand, follow the verb, e.g. Она́ говори́т **по-ру́сски**, *She speaks Russian.*

2   Certain adverbs which are used with a limited number of verbs and most of which are derived from nouns also generally follow the verb, e.g. идти́ **пешко́м**, *to go on foot*; ходи́ть **босико́м**, *to go about barefoot.*

(d)   In expressive registers, e.g. R1, R3c and the language of belles-lettres, emphasis or emotive effect is achieved by infringement of the rules given above. Consider the following examples which all embody some departure from neutral word order as it has been described in the preceding paragraphs:

Был **он** добрый малый.	*He was a nice fellow.*
Романы читаете?	*Do you read novels? (as opposed to e.g. plays)*
Простояли **мы** час в очереди.	*We stood in the queue for an hour.*
Все **смеяться** стали.	*Everybody started laughing.*
Она **плавать** очень любит.	*She likes swimming very much.*
Работать нужно.	*One must work.*
Я вам расскажу анекдот **смешной**.	*I'll tell you a funny story.*
Поэт земли **русской**.	*A poet of the Russian land. (rhet; e.g. in newspaper headline)*
В степи **глухой**.	*Deep in the steppe. (poet; e.g. in folk song)*
Печально это место в дождливый день.	*This place is miserable on a rainy day.*

11.15 Punctuation

Russian usage with regard to punctuation differs significantly from English usage, and since Russian usage is also more rigid the student aiming for a high degree of accuracy in the language needs to pay some attention to the Russian rules in this area.

- The full stop (**точка**), the question mark (**вопросительный знак**) and the semi-colon (**точка с запятой**), broadly speaking, are used as in English, to mark, respectively: the end of a sentence, the end of a question, and a division within a sentence that is more marked than that indicated by a comma.

- The colon (**двоеточие**) too is used in a similar way in both English and Russian, i.e. it may introduce:

(a) a clause that explains or expands on the preceding clause, e.g.

Она опоздала на лекцию: поезд, на котором она ехала, был задержан.
She was late for the lecture: the train she was travelling on was delayed.

(b) direct or reported speech, e.g.

Он провёл рукой по лбу:
– Нет, я не буду.
He passed his hand over his brow. 'No, I'm not going to.'
Все сказали одно и то же: чтобы я работал(а) побольше.
Everybody said the same thing: that I should work a bit harder.

(c) a list, e.g.

Выращиваем всякого рода овощи на огороде: картофель, морковь, лук, капусту . . .
We grow all sorts of vegetables on the allotment: potatoes, carrots, onions, cabbages . . .

(d)　a quotation, e.g.

Мо́жет быть, по́мнишь слова́ Пу́шкина: 'Весна́, весна́, пора́ любви́!'
Perhaps you remember Pushkin's words: 'Spring, spring, the time of love!'

However, the remaining punctuation marks used in English (the comma, the dash, the exclamation mark, quotation marks, brackets, omission dots) require more attention.

• Comma (**запята́я**): this is used in Russian to serve many of the purposes of the comma in English, for example to indicate minor pauses as in lists, to separate adjectives qualifying the same noun or adverbs modifying the same verb, after **да** and **нет**, and so forth, e.g.

Она́ говори́т по-ру́сски, по-по́льски, по-неме́цки и по-да́тски.
She speaks Russian, Polish, German and Danish.
Э́то до́брый, весёлый, у́мный челове́к.
He's a kind, cheerful, intelligent man.
– Вы уме́ете пла́вать?
– Да, уме́ю.
'Can you swim?' 'Yes, I can.'

However, use of the comma is also obligatory in Russian in the following circumstances in which its use may be optional in English or in which English usage tends to be lax:

(a)　to separate clauses linked by coordinating conjunctions, e.g.

Са́ша гимна́ст, а Пе́тя штанги́ст.
Sasha's a gymnast and Petia's a weight-lifter.

Note:　when the conjunction is **и**, a comma is not used if the subject of the verb in the two clauses is the same, e.g. Она́ легла́ на дива́н **и** засну́ла, *She lay down on the sofa and went to sleep.*

(b)　to mark the division (or divisions) between a main clause and any subordinate or relative clauses, e.g.

Он сказа́л, что э́того не забу́дет.
He said he would not forget this.
Э́то бы́ло два го́да тому́ наза́д, когда́ я рабо́тал(а) в Москве́.
It was two years ago, when I was working in Moscow.
Гости́ница, в кото́рой мы остана́вливались, была́ постро́ена в про́шлом году́.
The hotel in which we were staying was built last year.

(c)　to mark off any phrases containing gerunds or participles, e.g.

Нача́в чита́ть, я сра́зу по́нял(а) значе́ние э́того докуме́нта.
Having begun to read, I at once realised the importance of this document.
Лю́ди, нося́щие одно́ и то же и́мя, называ́ются «тёзками».
People who have the same name are called namesakes.

(d)   to mark off any parenthetical words, e.g.

Мой брат, наве́рное, ста́нет врачо́м.
My brother'll probably be a doctor.
Я всё могу́ прости́ть лю́дям, да́же преда́тельство, так как счита́ю
э́то сла́бостью.
I can forgive people anything, even treachery, because I consider it a weakness.

(e)   to mark off any comparative phrases, e.g.

Он говори́т быстре́е, чем я.
He speaks more quickly than I do.

- Dash (**тире́** [э́]; indecl): this punctuation mark, which may be longer than an English dash, has several important uses, e.g.

(a)   to indicate some sort of omission, either of a copula (as is the case when it is necessary to render in Russian the English verb *to be* in the present tense) or of some part of an utterance expressed elliptically, e.g.

Мой брат – студе́нт.
My brother is a student.
Серёжа – к воро́там, но вдруг из до́ма послы́шался крик.
Seriozha was off towards the gate, but suddenly from the house there came a shout.

Note: the dash is not normally used to indicate a missing copula when the subject is a pronoun, e.g. **Он студе́нт**, *He is a student.*

(b)   to introduce direct speech, and (if the verb that indicates that direct speech is being reproduced follows the speech itself) to close that speech, e.g.

Он спроси́л:
– Ско́лько про́сишь?
Ди́ма назва́л це́ну.– Ого́! – вы́пучил он глаза́. – Тебе́ повезёт, е́сли
найдёшь дурака́ на таку́ю це́ну.
He asked:
'How much are you asking?'
Dima named his price.
'Oho!' he opened his eyes wide. 'You'll be lucky if you find a fool prepared to pay that.'

Note: the direct speech introduced by the dash must begin on a fresh line.

(c)   to draw attention to something unexpected, to mark a syntactic change of direction, or to give a sense of energy to an utterance, e.g.

Я ожида́л(а), что они́ пригла́сят меня́ – а они́ не приглаша́ли.
I expected them to invite me – but they haven't.
Ире не приноси́ли посы́лок – то́лько пи́сьма шли в её а́дрес.
They didn't bring any parcels to Ira; she was just sent letters.
Безрабо́тица – э́то са́мая о́страя пробле́ма, стоя́щая пе́ред
прави́тельством.
Unemployment is the most serious problem facing the government.

(d)   a pair of dashes may mark off a parenthetical remark in a more
emphatic way than a pair of commas, e.g.

Следы́ э́того пери́ода её жи́зни – боле́знь, преждевре́менная
ста́рость – оста́лись у неё навсегда́.
*The traces of this period of her life – illness and premature old age – remained
with her for ever.*

- Exclamation mark (**восклица́тельный знак**): this tends to be used
more widely than in English. It is placed, for example, after
instructions expressed by some part of speech other than an imperative
and after greetings (7.6), congratulations and wishes (7.8–7.9) and
forms of address at the beginning of letters (7.17), as well as after
interjections (see 5.5) and other phrases that would be followed by an
exclamation mark in English too, e.g.

Здра́вствуйте!	*Hello.*
Споко́йной но́чи!	*Good night.*
С днём рожде́ния!	*Happy birthday.*
Дорога́я Ири́на!	*Dear Irina,*
Многоуважа́емый Никола́й Петро́вич!	*Dear Nikolai Petrovich,*
тсс!	*Hush!*

- Quotation marks (**кавы́чки**) of the sort used in English (' ' or " ") are
now appearing in Russian as a result of the widespread introduction of
personal computers. Guillemets (« ») are also used to enclose titles,
quotations, unusual words, e.g.

Я чита́ю «Преступле́ние и наказа́ние».	*I am reading 'Crime and Punishment'.*
Что тако́е 'тайга́'?	*What is 'taiga'?*

Note: quotation marks may also be used as an alternative to a dash as an introduction
to direct speech if the verb which indicates that direct speech is being
reproduced precedes the speech itself, e.g. Го́рка пи́сем нараста́ет, кто́-то
се́рдится – 'вы мне не отве́тили!', *The pile of letters grows and somebody gets
angry: 'You haven't replied to me!'*

- Brackets (**ско́бки**): these indicate a parenthesis that is more strongly
marked off from the surrounding material than a parenthesis that is
marked off by commas or dashes.

- Omission dots (**многото́чие**): these are quite widely used in Russian to
indicate that a thought is incomplete or that speech is hasty or
awkward, e.g.

Он . . . вы не ду́маете . . . он не вор . . .	*He . . . you don't think . . . He's not a thief . . .*

Note: since this is an expressive device it is unlikely to be encountered in R3a or
R3b. In the written form of the colloquial language and in the language of
the internet, on the other hand, it will occur frequently.

11.16 Use of capital letters

Capital letters are used much more sparingly in Russian than in English. In particular the foreign student should note that:

- capital letters are not used in Russian at the beginning of words naming days of the week or months of the year, or indicating nationality or religion, place of origin or language, e.g.

понеде́льник	*Monday*
янва́рь (m)	*January*
англича́нин	*Englishman*
мусульма́нин	*Moslem*
москви́ч	*Muscovite*
ру́сский язы́к	*Russian (language)*

- in titles of organisations, institutions, posts, journals, newspapers, books and so forth, it is usual for only the first word in the title to begin with a capital letter (cf. the English practice of beginning each noun and adjective with a capital), e.g.

Европе́йский сою́з	*the European Union*
Ло́ндонский университе́т	*the University of London*
Мини́стр оборо́ны	*the Minister of Defence*
Аргуме́нты и фа́кты	*Arguments and Facts* (a contemporary newspaper)
Ра́ковый ко́рпус	*Cancer Ward* (Solzhenítsyn's novel)

- in place-names the generic name (e.g. **океа́н, мо́ре, о́стров, река́, о́зеро, пло́щадь, у́лица**) is usually written with a small letter and the proper noun and accompanying adjectives with capitals, e.g.

Ти́хий океа́н	*the Pacific Ocean*
Се́верный Ледови́тый океа́н	*the Arctic Ocean*
Каспи́йское мо́ре	*the Caspian Sea*
о́стров Сахали́н	*the Island of Sakhalin*
Гибралта́рский проли́в	*the Strait of Gibraltar*
Суэ́цкий кана́л	*the Suez Canal*
тро́пик Козеро́га	*the Tropic of Capricorn*
Се́верный по́люс	*the North Pole*
Кра́сная пло́щадь	*Red Square*
Зи́мний дворе́ц	*the Winter Palace*
Петропа́вловская кре́пость	*the Peter and Paul Fortress*

However, in some names the above conventions are not observed, e.g.

Да́льний Восто́к	*the Far East*
Организа́ция Объединённых На́ций	*the United Nations Organisation*
Соединённые Шта́ты Аме́рики	*the United States of America*
Росси́йская Федера́ция	*the Russian Federation*

12 Stress

12.1 Introductory remarks

Most Russian words have fixed stress, but many do not and it is these that give difficulty to the foreign learner. Stress patterns are numerous and complicated, but the student may take some comfort from the fact that there *are* patterns.

In this chapter we first set out the main patterns of stress in Russian nouns, adjectives and verbs and then indicate some of the deviations from standard stress that may be encountered.

Stress in Russian is very important for two reasons. Firstly, it is strong. Therefore a word pronounced with incorrect stress may not be understood. Secondly, there are many homographs which are distinguished from one another only by means of stress and consequential pronunciation of unstressed vowels, e.g. ве́сти, *news*, and вести́, *to lead*; мо́ю, *I wash*, and мою́, *my*; пла́чу, *I cry*, and плачу́, *I pay*; сло́ва, *of the word*, and слова́, *words*.

It should be remembered that in some words **e** will change into **ё** when the syllable in which it occurs attracts the stress.

Conversely **ё** will change into **e** when the syllable in which it occurs loses the stress (as it does in some perfective verbs bearing the prefix вы́-, e.g. вы́шел, *I/he went out*, in which the element шёл has lost the stress that it normally bears (as in пошёл, *I/he went*)).

12.2 Stress in nouns

In considering stress on Russian nouns one needs to bear in mind:
(i) the position of the stress in the nominative form of the word, and
(ii) the number of syllables that a noun has (i.e. whether it is monosyllabic (e.g. ночь, *night*; слон, *elephant*), disyllabic (e.g. топо́р, *axe*; ка́рта, *card, map*; окно́, *window*), trisyllabic (e.g. телефо́н, *telephone*; доро́га, *road*; о́зеро, *lake*) or polysyllabic (e.g. жа́воронок, *skylark*; оборо́на, *defence*; сочине́ние, *essay*)).

Most nouns have fixed stress. Shifting stress occurs mainly in monosyllabic or disyllabic nouns.

Nouns of different genders are associated with somewhat different stress patterns. The three genders are therefore treated separately in the following sections.

Note: the following lists of words to which a particular pattern of stress is applicable are not exhaustive.

12.2.1 Masculine nouns

Many masculine nouns have fixed stress. In the remaining masculine nouns, in which stress shift does take place, there are three possible patterns: (i) shift to end stress in all forms after the initial form; (ii) shift to end stress in all plural forms; and (iii) shift to end stress in the genitive, dative, instrumental and prepositional plural forms.

12.2.1.1 Masculine nouns with fixed stress

- polysyllabic nouns, e.g. **жа́воронок**, *skylark*;

- most nouns of more than one syllable that end in **-ай, -ей, -ой, -уй, -яй**, e.g. **попуга́й**, *parrot*; **музе́й**, *museum*; **геро́й**, *hero*; **поцелу́й**, *kiss*; **лентя́й**, *lazy person*;

- nouns formed with the suffix **-тель**, e.g. **покупа́тель**, *buyer*; **чита́тель**, *reader*. Usually stress is on the syllable before this suffix, but NB **морепла́ватель**, *navigator*;

- most nouns in **-н**, e.g. **бараба́н**, *drum*; **зако́н**, *law*; **карма́н**, *pocket*; **магази́н**, *shop*; **стака́н**, *glass* (for drink); **туркме́н**, *Turkmen*. Stress is usually on the last syllable in such nouns, but NB nouns with the suffix **-а́нин**, e.g. **англича́нин**, *Englishman*, etc.;

- many nouns of more than one syllable that end in **-т**, e.g. **аппети́т**, *appetite*; **арти́ст**, *artiste*; **биле́т**, *ticket*; **дикта́нт**, *dictation*; **институ́т**, *institute*; **пило́т**, *pilot*; **результа́т**, *result*; **салю́т**, *salute*;

- nouns in **-ал**, e.g. **журна́л**, *journal*; **кана́л**, *canal*; **материа́л**, *material*;

- nouns in **-и́зм**, e.g. **коммуни́зм**, *communism*; **реали́зм**, *realism*;

- disyllabic and polysyllabic nouns in **-б, -в, -д, -з, -м, -р, -с** with stress on the second syllable: **ара́б**, *Arab*; **зали́в**, *gulf*; **верблю́д**, *camel*; **парохо́д**, *steamer*; **сою́з**, *union*; **паро́м**, *ferry*; **мото́р**, *engine*; **вопро́с**, *question*; **интере́с**, *interest*.

Note: exceptions: **рука́в**, *sleeve*; **кома́р**, *mosquito*; **столя́р**, *carpenter*; **топо́р**, *axe*, all of which have end stress after the initial form.

12.2.1.2 Masculine nouns with stress on the ending after the initial form

- many common monosyllabic nouns, e.g. **стол**, *table*:

	sg	pl
nom	**стол**	**столы́**
acc	**стол**	**столы́**
gen	**стола́**	**столо́в**
dat	**столу́**	**стола́м**
instr	**столо́м**	**стола́ми**
prep	**столе́**	**стола́х**

Similarly: **бинт**, *bandage*; **блин**, *pancake*; **боб**, *bean*; **бобр**, *beaver*; **болт**, *bolt*; **бык**, *bull*; **винт**, *screw, propeller*; **вол**, *ox*; **враг**, *enemy*; **герб**, *coat-of-arms*; **гриб**, *mushroom*; **двор**, *yard, court*; **дрозд**, *thrush*; **жук**, *beetle*; **зонт**, *awning*; **кит**, *whale*; **клык**, *fang, tusk*; **кнут**, *knout*; **кот**, *tomcat*; **крест**, *cross*; **крот**, *mole*; **куст**, *bush*; **мост**, *bridge*; **пласт**, *layer, stratum*; **плод**, *fruit*; **плот**, *raft*; **полк**, *regiment*; **пост**, *post*; **пруд**, *pond*; **раб**, *slave*; **рубль**, *rouble*; **серп**, *sickle*; **слон**, *elephant*; **сноп**, *sheaf*; **ствол**, *trunk* (of tree), *barrel* (of gun); **столб**, *pillar*; **суд**, *court*; **труд**, *labour*; **ум**, *mind, intellect*; **хвост**, *tail*; **хлыст**, *whip*; **холм**, *hill*; **холст**, *canvas*; **шест**, *pole*; **штык**, *bayonet*; **шут**, *clown*; **щит**, *shield, dashboard, control panel*.

- many nouns of two or more syllables which end in one of the velars **г, к,** or **х** and have stress on the final syllable in the initial form, e.g. **язык**, *language, tongue*; **жених**, *fiancé, bride-groom*:

	sg	pl	sg	pl
nom	язы́к	языки́	жени́х	женихи́
acc	язы́к	языки́	жениха́	женихо́в
gen	языка́	языко́в	жениха́	женихо́в
dat	языку́	языка́м	жениху́	жениха́м
instr	языко́м	языка́ми	женихо́м	жениха́ми
prep	языке́	языка́х	женихе́	жениха́х

Similarly: **пиро́г**, *pie*; **сапо́г**, *boot*; **утю́г**, *iron*; **бедня́к**, *pauper*; **бело́к**, *egg-white*; **выпускни́к**, *graduate*; **игро́к**, *player, gambler*; **крючо́к**, *hook*; **кула́к**, *fist*; **мая́к**, *lighthouse, beacon*; **моря́к**, *sailor*; **потоло́к**, *ceiling*; **рыба́к**, *fisherman*; **стари́к**, *old man*; **сунду́к**, *trunk*; **учени́к**, *pupil, student*; **пасту́х**, *shepherd*; **пету́х**, *cockerel*.

Note: exceptions: **бара́к**, *hut*; **поро́к**, *vice*; **пото́к**, *current*; **уро́к**, *lesson*, all of which have fixed stress.

- many nouns of two or more syllables which end in **-ц** or one of the hushing consonants **-ж, -ч** or **-ш** and have stress on the final syllable in the initial form, e.g. **отец**, *father*; **падеж**, *case* (gram):

	sg	pl	sg	pl
nom	оте́ц	отцы́	паде́ж	падежи́
acc	отца́	отцо́в	паде́ж	падежи́
gen	отца́	отцо́в	падежа́	падеже́й
dat	отцу́	отца́м	падежу́	падежа́м
instr	отцо́м	отца́ми	падежо́м	падежа́ми
prep	отце́	отца́х	падеже́	падежа́х

Similarly: **боéц**, *fighter*; **венéц**, *crown, wreath* (poet); **гордéц**, *arrogant man*; **конéц**, *end*; **кузнéц**, *blacksmith*; **мудрéц**, *wise man, sage* (rhet); **огурéц**, *cucumber*; **певéц**, *singer*; **хитрéц**, *cunning man*; **гарáж**, *garage*; **грабёж**, *robbery*; **монтáж**, *assembly, installation*; **мятéж**, *mutiny, revolt*; **платёж**, *payment*; **рубéж**, *boundary, border*; **чертёж**, *draught, sketch*; **шантáж**, *blackmail*; **этáж**, *storey*, and some monosyllables, e.g. **ёж**, *hedgehog*; **нож**, *knife*; **стриж**, *swift* (bird); **уж**, *grass-snake*; **калáч**, kind of white loaf; **кирпи́ч**, *brick*; **москви́ч**, *Muscovite*; **силáч**, *strong man*; **скрипáч**, *violinist*; **сургýч**, *sealing wax*; **тягáч**, small tractor for pulling trolleys, and some monosyllables, e.g. **врач**, *doctor*; **грач**, *rook*; **ключ**, *key*; **луч**, *ray*; **меч**, *sword*; **мяч**, *ball*, and patronymics, e.g. **Ильи́ч**; **голы́ш**, *naked child*; **малы́ш**, *kid*; **шалáш**, *hut* (of branches and straw) and some monosyllables, e.g. **грош**, *half-kopeck piece* (i.e. fig *farthing*); **ёрш**, *ruff* (fish), *brush*; **ковш**, *ladle*.

Note: in some words of foreign origin that end in -ж stress is fixed, e.g. **витрáж**, *stained-glass window*; **пейзáж**, *landscape*; **пляж**, *beach*; **репортáж**, *reporting*; **трикотáж**, *knitting*; **шпионáж**, *espionage*; **экипáж**, *crew*.

- most nouns which end in –ун, –ль, or –рь and have stress on the final syllable in the initial form, e.g. **бегýн**, *runner*; **корáбль**, *ship*:

	sg	pl	sg	pl
nom	бегýн	бегуны́	корáбль	корабли́
acc	бегунá	бегунóв	корáбль	корабли́
gen	бегунá	бегунóв	корабля́	кораблéй
dat	бегунý	бегунáм	кораблю́	корабля́м
instr	бегунóм	бегунáми	кораблём	корабля́ми
prep	бегунé	бегунáх	кораблé	корабля́х

Similarly: **болтýн**, *chatterbox*; **валýн**, *boulder*; **ворчýн**, *grumbler*; **драчýн**, *quarrelsome person*; **колдýн**, *sorcerer*; **крикýн**, *shouter*; **лгун**, *liar*; **летýн**, *flier, drifter*; **опекýн**, *guardian*; **табýн**, *herd* (esp of horses or reindeer); **чугýн**, *cast iron*; **шалýн**, *naughty child* (but not **трибýн**, *tribune*, which has fixed stress); **журáвль**, *crane* (bird); **ковы́ль**, *feather-grass*; **корóль**, *king*; **косты́ль**, *crutch*; **феврáль**, *February*; **фити́ль**, *wick*; **хрустáль**, *cut glass*; **богаты́рь**, hero of Russian folklore; **буквáрь**, *primer, ABC*; **глухáрь**, *woodgrouse*; **декáбрь**, *December*; **календáрь**, *calendar, fixture list*; **монасты́рь**, *monastery*; **ноя́брь**, *November*; **октя́брь**, *October*; **пузы́рь**, *bubble*; **секретáрь**, *secretary*; **сентя́брь**, *September*; **словáрь**, *dictionary*; **сухáрь**, *rusk, dried-up person*; **фонáрь**, *lamppost*; **царь**, *tsar*; **янвáрь**, *January*; **янтáрь**, *amber*.

12.2.1.3 Masculine nouns with stem stress in the singular and stress on the ending in the plural

- some monosyllables, e.g. **сад**, *garden*:

	sg	pl
nom	сад	сады́
acc	сад	сады́
gen	са́да	садо́в
dat	са́ду	сада́м
instr	са́дом	сада́ми
prep	са́де	сада́х
	(в саду́)	

Similarly: **бал**, *ball (dance)*; **бой**, *battle, fight*; **вал**, *billow, earthen wall, shaft*; **воз**, *cart, wagon*; **дар**, *gift*; **долг**, *duty, debt*; **дуб**, *oak tree*; **жир**, *fat, grease*; **круг**, *circle*; **мир**, *world*; **пар**, *steam*; **плуг**, *plough*; **след**, *trace*; **слой**, *layer, stratum*; **суп**, *soup*; **сыр**, *cheese*; **таз**, *basin, wash-basin*; **тыл**, *back, rear*; **ус**, *whisker*; **хор**, *choir*; **чай**, *tea*; **час**, *hour*; **шаг**, *step, pace*; **шар**, *sphere*; **шкаф**, *cupboard*.

- the quite numerous masculine nouns which end in a hard consonant or a soft consonant and which have nominative plural (and if they are inanimate, accusative plural too) in stressed –**а́** and –**я́** respectively (see 9.1.6), e.g. **го́род**, *town, city*, **учи́тель**, *teacher*:

	sg	pl	sg	pl
nom	го́род	города́	учи́тель	учителя́
acc	го́род	города́	учи́теля	учителе́й
gen	го́рода	городо́в	учи́теля	учителе́й
dat	го́роду	города́м	учи́телю	учителя́м
instr	го́родом	города́ми	учи́телем	учителя́ми
prep	го́роде	города́х	учи́теле	учителя́х

Similarly: **а́дрес**, *address*; **бе́рег**, *bank, shore*; **ве́чер**, *evening*; **глаз**, *eye*; **го́лос**, *voice*; **до́ктор**, *doctor*; **дом**, *house*; **ко́локол**, *church bell*; **лес**, *forest*; **луг**, *meadow*; **ма́стер**, *foreman, skilled workman*; **о́стров**, *island*; **по́вар**, *cook*; **по́езд**, *train*; **профе́ссор**, *professor*; **снег**, *snow*; **сто́рож**, *watchman*; **то́поль**, *poplar*; **хо́лод**, *cold, cold spell*; **я́корь**, *anchor*, and many others.

12.2.1.4 Masculine nouns with stress on the ending in gen/dat/instr/prep plural only

- some monosyllabic or disyllabic masculine (and some feminine) nouns which end in a soft sign and are stressed on the first syllable in the initial form, e.g. **го́лубь** (m), *pigeon, dove*, and **пло́щадь** (f), *square*:

	sg	pl	sg	pl
nom	го́лубь	го́луби	пло́щадь	пло́щади
acc	го́лубя	голубе́й	пло́щадь	пло́щади
gen	го́лубя	голубе́й	пло́щади	площаде́й
dat	го́лубю	голубя́м	пло́щади	площадя́м
instr	го́лубем	голубя́ми	пло́щадью	площадя́ми
prep	го́лубе	го́лубя́х	пло́щади	площадя́х

Similarly the following masculine nouns: **гость**, *guest*; **гусь**, *goose*; **зверь**, *beast, wild animal*; **ка́мень**, *stone*; **ко́готь**, *claw, talon*; **ле́бедь**, *swan*; **ло́коть**, *elbow*; **но́готь**, *fingernail*; **па́рень**, *lad*; and the following feminine nouns: **бровь**, *brow*; **весть**, *piece of news*; **вещь**, *thing*; **дочь**, *daughter*; **кре́пость**, *fortress*; **ло́шадь**, *horse*; **мать**, *mother*; **ночь**, *night*; **печь**, *stove*; **по́весть**, *short story, novella*; **речь**, *speech*; **роль**, *role*; **сеть**, *net*; **ска́терть**, *tablecloth*; **ско́рость**, *speed, gear*; **сте́пень**, *degree, extent*; **цепь**, *chain*; **часть**, *part*.

Note: exceptions include the following monosyllables, which have fixed stress on the stem throughout: **боль**, *ache, pain*; **грань**, *border, verge*; **ель**, *fir-tree*; **казнь**, *execution*; **мазь**, *ointment*; **мысль**, *thought, idea*; **связь**, *link, connection*; **ткань**, *fabric*; **цель**, *aim, goal*; **щель**, *crack* (all feminine), and **стиль**, *style* (masculine).

- some other monosyllabic nouns, e.g. **волк**, *wolf*:

	sg	pl
nom	волк	во́лки
acc	во́лка	волко́в
gen	во́лка	волко́в
dat	во́лку	волка́м
instr	во́лком	волка́ми
prep	во́лке	волка́х

Similarly: **вор**, *thief*; **слог**, *syllable*.

12.2.2 Feminine nouns

12.2.2.1 *Feminine nouns with fixed stress*

- nouns in -**ница** derived from nouns with the masculine suffix -**тель**, e.g. **учи́тельница**, *teacher*;

- nouns in -**ия**, e.g. **фами́лия**, *surname*. Stress in these nouns is usually, but not necessarily, on the syllable preceding this suffix;

- nouns in -**ость**, e.g. **неприя́тность**, *unpleasantness*; **сла́бость**, *weakness*;

- disyllabic nouns in -**а** or -**я** with stress on the first syllable, e.g. **ка́рта**, *map*; **ла́мпа**, *lamp*; **шко́ла**, *school*; **дя́дя**, *uncle*; **пе́сня**, *song*.

12.2.2.2 *Feminine nouns with end stress in the singular and stress on preceding syllable in the plural*

- disyllabic nouns in -**a** or -**я** with stress on the ending in the initial form, e.g. **страна́**, *country*:

	sg	pl
nom	страна́	стра́ны
acc	страну́	стра́ны
gen	страны́	стран
dat	стране́	стра́нам
instr	страно́й	стра́нами
prep	стране́	стра́нах

Similarly: **война́**, *war*; **волна́**, *wave*; **гроза́**, *thunderstorm*; **доска́**, *blackboard*; **змея́**, *snake*; **коза́**, *goat, she-goat*; **мечта́**, *daydream*; **овца́**, *sheep*; **река́**, *river*; **свеча́**, *candle, sparking-plug*; **свинья́**, *pig*; **семья́**, *family*; **скала́**, *cliff, crag*; **сосна́**, *pine-tree*; **стена́**, *wall*; **стрела́**, *arrow*; **струя́**, *jet, spurt*; **судьба́**, *fate, destiny*; **судья́**, *judge*; **труба́**, *pipe, tube, trumpet*.

Note 1 It is only by means of stress that genitive singular forms are differentiated from nominative and accusative plural forms in nouns of this type.

2 Some nouns in this category have stress on the first syllable in the accusative singular as well as in plural forms: **вода́** (*water*; **во́ду**); **душа́** (*soul, spirit*; **ду́шу**); **зима́** (*winter*; **зи́му**); **нога́** (*leg, foot*; **но́гу**); **рука́** (*arm, hand*; **ру́ку**).

3 In some nouns of this type **e** in the first syllable changes to **ё** under stress: **слеза́** (*tear*; **слёзы, слёз**); **щека́** (*cheek*; **щёки, щёк**).

4 Some nouns of this type have stress on the second syllable in the dative, instrumental and prepositional plural forms: **гора́** (*mountain*; **гора́м, гора́ми, гора́х**); **губа́** (*lip*; **губа́м, губа́ми, губа́х**); **нога́** (**нога́м, нога́ми, нога́х**); **рука́** (**рука́м, рука́ми, рука́х**); **слеза́** (**слеза́м, слеза́ми, слеза́х**); **щека́** (**щека́м, щека́ми, щека́х**).

5 In some of the above nouns stress is on the second syllable in the genitive plural form (**ове́ц, свине́й, семе́й, суде́й**).

6 The noun **мечта́** has no plural form; the noun **мечта́ние** (genitive plural **мечта́ний**) should be used instead.

- nouns ending in the suffix -**ота́** which have end stress in the singular but are stressed on the penultimate syllable in the nominative plural and on the same syllable thereafter, e.g. **высота́**, *height*:

	sg	pl
nom	высота́	высо́ты
acc	высоту́	высо́ты
gen	высоты́	высо́т
dat	высоте́	высо́там
instr	высото́й	высо́тами
prep	высоте́	высо́тах

Similarly: **долгота́**, *longitude*; **красота́**, *beauty*; **острота́**, *witticism*; **сирота́**, *orphan*.

Note 1   Some nouns with this suffix do not have plural forms, or at least they do not have commonly used plural forms, e.g. **темнота́**, *darkness*; **чистота́**, *cleanness*.

2   In nouns in **-ота** which have initial stress not on the ending but on the first or penultimate syllable (e.g. **гра́мота**, *deed* (official document); **забо́та**, *worry, concern*; **пехо́та**, *infantry*; **рабо́та**, *work*) stress is fixed.

12.2.2.3   Stress in feminine nouns with pleophonic forms (-о́ло- or -о́ро-)

Pleophonic forms (i.e. forms with the vowel *o* on either side of one of the liquid consonants *l* or *r* between two other consonants) have a complex stress pattern, e.g. **голова́**, *head*, and **сторона́**, *side*:

	sg	pl	sg	pl
nom	голова́	го́ловы	сторона́	сто́роны
acc	го́лову	го́ловы	сто́рону	сто́роны
gen	головы́	голо́в	стороны́	сторо́н
dat	голове́	голова́м	стороне́	сторона́м
instr	головой́	голова́ми	стороной́	сторона́ми
prep	голове́	голова́х	стороне́	сторона́х

Similarly: **борода́**, *beard*; **борозда́**, *furrow*; **борона́**, *harrow*; **полоса́**, *stripe, zone*; **сковорода́**, *frying-pan*.

12.2.3   Neuter nouns

12.2.3.1   Neuter nouns with fixed stress

- nouns in **-ие**: **зда́ние**, *building*; **упражне́ние**, *exercise*. In these nouns stress is usually on the syllable before this suffix (but NB **иссле́дование**, *investigation, research*; **обеспе́чение**, *securing, guaranteeing, provision*; **странове́дение**, *regional studies*; **телеви́дение**, *television*);

- nouns derived from masculine nouns with the suffix **-тель**, e.g. **прави́тельство**, *government*.

12.2.3.2   Disyllabic neuter nouns with end stress in the singular and stem stress in the plural

The stress pattern of disyllabic neuter nouns in **-o** (and **-ё**) with stress on the ending in the initial form is similar to that of end-stressed disyllabic feminine nouns in **-a** or **-я**, i.e. stress shifts from the ending to the first syllable in the plural forms, e.g. **письмо́**, *letter*:

	sg	pl
nom	письмо́	пи́сьма
acc	письмо́	пи́сьма
gen	письма́	пи́сем
dat	письму́	пи́сьмам
instr	письмо́м	пи́сьмами
prep	письме́	пи́сьмах

Similarly: **вино́**, *wine*; **кольцо́**, *ring*; **крыло́**, *wing*; **лицо́**, *face*; **окно́**, *window*; **перо́**, *pen, feather*; **пятно́**, *spot, stain*; **ружьё**, *hand-gun, rifle*; **село́**, *village*; **стекло́**, *glass, pane, windscreen*; **число́**, *number, date*; **яйцо́**, *egg*.

Note 1   It is only by means of stress that genitive singular forms are differentiated from nominative and accusative plural forms.

     2   When the vowel in the first syllable is **e** it will change to **ё** under stress in the plural forms. Thus **село́, стекло́** have **сёла**, etc., **стёкла**, etc., respectively.

     3   Some nouns of this type, e.g. **крыло́, перо́**, have irregular plural forms in **-ья**, etc. (**кры́лья**, etc.; **пе́рья**, etc.; see 9.1.9).

     4   In some nouns of this type a mobile vowel appears in the genitive plural form, e.g. **о́кон, пи́сем, стёкол**.

     5   **кольцо́** and **яйцо́** have genitive plural forms **коле́ц** and **яи́ц**, respectively.

     6   **плечо́**, *shoulder*, has plural forms **пле́чи, пле́чи, плеч, плеча́м, плеча́ми, плеча́х**.

12.2.3.3   *Disyllabic neuter nouns with stem stress in the singular and end stress in the plural*

The opposite process takes place in some disyllabic neuter nouns in **-o** and **-e** in which stress in the initial form is on the first syllable, i.e. stress shifts to the ending in the plural forms, e.g. **сло́во**, *word*; **мо́ре**, *sea*:

	sg	pl	sg	pl
nom	сло́во	слова́	мо́ре	моря́
acc	сло́во	слова́	мо́ре	моря́
gen	сло́ва	слов	мо́ря	море́й
dat	сло́ву	слова́м	мо́рю	моря́м
instr	сло́вом	слова́ми	мо́рем	моря́ми
prep	сло́ве	слова́х	мо́ре	моря́х

Similarly: **де́ло**, *deed, business, affair*; **ме́сто**, *place*; **по́ле**, *field*; **пра́во**, *right*; **се́рдце**, *heart*; **ста́до**, *herd, flock*; **те́ло**, *body*.

Note 1   It is again only by means of stress that genitive singular forms are differentiated from nominative and accusative plural forms.

     2   In some nouns of this type **e** in the first syllable changes to **ё** under stress. Thus **ведро́**, *bucket*, and **весло́**, *oar*, have plural forms **вёдра, вёдра, вёдер, вёдрам, вёдрами, вёдрах** and **вёсла, вёсла, вёсел, вёслам, вёслами, вёслах**, respectively.

3   **нéбо**, *sky, heaven*, has plural forms **небесá, небесá, небéс, небесáм, небесáми, небесáх**. Similarly **чýдо**, *wonder, miracle*, has **чудесá**, etc.

4   **ýхо**, *ear*, has plural forms **ýши, ýши, ушéй, ушáм, ушáми, ушáх**.

5   **сýдно**, *vessel*, has **судá, судá, судóв, судáм, судáми, судáх**.

6   In a few disyllabic neuter nouns stress is fixed on the first syllable in all forms, plural as well as singular, e.g. **блáго**, *blessing*; **блю́до**, *dish*; **блю́дце**, *saucer*; **крéсло**, *armchair*; **плáтье**, *dress*; **срéдство**, *means*; **ýстье**, *mouth* (of river).

12.2.3.4   Trisyllabic neuter nouns with stress shift

In some trisyllabic neuter nouns stress shift also takes place, in one direction or the other, e.g.

-   moving one syllable towards the end of the word. Thus **óзеро**, *lake*, has plural **озёра, озёр**, etc.;

-   moving one syllable towards the beginning of the word. Thus **ремеслó** has plural **ремёсла, ремёсел**, etc.;

-   moving from the first syllable to the ending. Thus **зéркало**, *mirror*, **крýжево**, *lace*, and **óблако**, *cloud*, have **зеркалá, кружевá** and **облакá**, etc., respectively (except that **крýжево** has genitive plural **крýжев**; NB also that the genitive plural of **облакá** is **облакóв**).

12.2.3.5   Disyllabic neuter nouns in -мя

The few nouns of this type also have stress on the first syllable in the singular and on the second syllable in the plural, e.g. **и́мя**, *name*:

	sg	**pl**
nom	**и́мя**	**именá**
acc	**и́мя**	**именá**
gen	**и́мени**	**имён**
dat	**и́мени**	**именáм**
instr	**и́менем**	**именáми**
prep	**и́мени**	**именáх**

Similarly: **врéмя**, *time*; **вы́мя**, *udder*; **плéмя**, *tribe*; **сéмя**, *seed*; **стрéмя**, *stirrup*; **тéмя**, *crown of the head*.

Note 1   **знáмя**, *flag, banner*, has plural forms **знамёна, знамёна, знамён, знамёнам, знамёнами, знамёнах**.

2   **вы́мя, тéмя** have no plural form.

12.2.4   Irregular stress in certain prepositional singular forms

-   The ending **-у** which some (mostly monosyllabic) masculine nouns have after the prepositions **в** and **на** used in a locative sense is always stressed, e.g. **в шкафý**, *in the cupboard*; **на полý**, *on the floor*.

- In a few feminine nouns ending in a soft consonant the ending -и is also stressed after the prepositions **в** and **на** used in a locative sense, e.g. **в двери́**, *in the door*; **в грязи́**, *in the mud*; **в крови́**, *in blood*; **в степи́**, *in the steppe*; **в тени́**, *in the shade*.

12.2.5   Prepositions that attract stress in certain phrases

For the purposes of stress (and pronunciation) most prepositions should usually be treated as part of the following word, e.g. **на столе́**, *on the table*, **передо мно́й**, *in front of me*, **с бра́том**, *with (my) brother*. However, in certain combinations of monosyllabic preposition + noun with stress on the first syllable in the case governed by the preposition, the preposition bears the stress, e.g. **за́ год**, *over the space of a year*; **за́ город**, *out of town*; **за́ день**, *over the space of a day*; **за́ зиму**, *over the winter*; **за́ ногу**, *by the leg*; **за́ ночь**, *during the night*; **за́ руку**, *by the hand*; **на́ год**, *for a year*; **на́ голову**, *on to one's head*; **на́ гору**, *up the mountain*; **на́ день**, *for a day*; **на́ зиму**, *for the winter*; **на́ ногу**, *on to one's foot/leg*; **на́ ночь**, *for the night*; **на́ руку**, *on to one's arm/hand*; **на́ спину**, *on to one's back*; **по́ уши**, *up to one's ears*; **по́д вечер**, *towards evening*; **по́д гору**, *downhill*; **по́д ноги**, *under one's feet/legs*; **по́д руку**, *under one's arm/hand*. Stress also falls on the preposition in the phrases **пропа́сть бе́з вести**, *to go missing (in action)*; **бе́з толку**, *senselessly*; **до́ дому**, *as far as one's home*; **до́ ночи**, *until nightfall*; **и́з дому**, *out of one's home*; **и́з лесу**, *out of the forest*; **по́ два**, **по́ двое**, *two each*; **по́ три**, *three each*.

12.3   Stress in adjectives

- Long forms of adjectives (e.g. **большо́й**, *big*; **прекра́сный**, *fine*; **си́ний**, *dark blue*; **тре́тий**, *third*; **хоро́ший**, *good*) have fixed stress throughout their declension.

- In adjectives with the suffixes -**ичный**, -**альный**, -**онный**, and also in adjectives with one of the four suffixes of participial origin -**учий**, -**ючий**, -**ачий**, -**ячий**, stress is always on the penultimate syllable, e.g. **типи́чный**, *typical*; **печа́льный**, *sad*; **традицио́нный**, *traditional*; **могу́чий**, *powerful*; **колю́чий**, *prickly*; **коша́чий**, *feline*; **горя́чий**, *hot* (to the touch).

- In adjectives with the suffix -**ический**, stress is always on the antepenultimate syllable, e.g. **автомати́ческий**, *automatic*.

- In disyllabic adjectives the stress usually shifts to the ending in the feminine short form, e.g. **важна́, сильна́, страшна́, темна́, храбра́, ясна́** from **ва́жный**, *important*, **си́льный**, *strong*, **стра́шный**, *terrible*, **тёмный**, *dark*, **хра́брый**, *brave*, **я́сный**, *clear*, respectively. The same process takes place in some trisyllabic adjectives, mainly adjectives with a stem in к, e.g. **велика́, горяча́, далека́, хороша́** from **вели́кий**, *great*, **горя́чий**, *hot* (to the touch), **далёкий**, *distant*, **хоро́ший**, *good*, respectively.

- In the short comparative form of disyllabic adjectives stress is on the first syllable of the ending, e.g. **нове́е**, *newer*, **сильне́е**, *stronger*.

- In the superlative form of disyllabic adjectives and trisyllabic adjectives with a stem in **к** stress is usually on the penultimate syllable, e.g. **нове́йший**, *newest*, **сильне́йший**, *strongest*, **глубоча́йший**, *deepest*.

Note: in adverbs in -**и́чески** that are derived from adjectives in -**и́ческий** stress is also always on the antepenultimate syllable, e.g. **автомати́чески**, *automatically*.

12.4 Stress in verbs

Stress patterns in Russian verbs are considerably simpler than stress patterns in Russian nouns. It is only in the indicative forms of the second conjugation and the past-tense forms of some verbs that they give much difficulty.

12.4.1 Stress in first-conjugation verbs

- In verbs classified in 9.6.2 above as 1A (e.g. **рабо́тать**, *to work*; **теря́ть**, *to lose*; **красне́ть**, *to go red, blush*) stress remains on the same vowel in the infinitive and throughout the indicative (i.e. in imperfective verbs the present tense and in perfective verbs the simple future tense), e.g.

1st pers sg	рабо́таю	теря́ю	красне́ю
2nd pers sg	рабо́таешь	теря́ешь	красне́ешь
3rd pers sg	рабо́тает	теря́ет	красне́ет
1st pers pl	рабо́таем	теря́ем	красне́ем
2nd pers pl	рабо́таете	теря́ете	красне́ете
3rd pers pl	рабо́тают	теря́ют	красне́ют

- In 1B verbs with vowel stems (9.6.3 and 9.6.5 above) stress remains on the same vowel throughout the indicative (i.e. in imperfective verbs the present tense and in perfective verbs the simple future tense), e.g. **мыть**, *to wash*, **дава́ть**, *to give*:

1st pers sg	мо́ю	даю́
2nd pers sg	мо́ешь	даёшь
3rd pers sg	мо́ет	даёт
1st pers pl	мо́ем	даём
2nd pers pl	мо́ете	даёте
3rd pers pl	мо́ют	даю́т

Note: in many 1B verbs in -**ова́ть** or -**ева́ть** (9.6.3) stress may be on the ending in the infinitive form even though it is on the stem in the indicative form, e.g. **организова́ть**, *to organise*, but **организу́ю**, etc.

- In 1B verbs with consonant stems (9.6.4 and 9.6.6–7) some verbs (e.g. **ре́зать**, *to cut*) have unstressed endings throughout the indicative, others (e.g. **жить**, *to live*) have stressed endings throughout the indicative, and others (e.g. **писа́ть**, *to write*) have stress on the ending in the first person singular but on the stem in all the remaining persons, e.g.

1st pers sg	**ре́жу**	**живу́**	**пишу́**
2nd pers sg	**ре́жешь**	**живёшь**	**пи́шешь**
3rd pers sg	**ре́жет**	**живёт**	**пи́шет**
1st pers pl	**ре́жем**	**живём**	**пи́шем**
2nd pers pl	**ре́жете**	**живёте**	**пи́шете**
3rd pers pl	**ре́жут**	**живу́т**	**пи́шут**

In verbs of more than one syllable (not counting any prefix) that conform to the first of these patterns (e.g. **пла́кать**, *to cry*, **гло́хнуть**, *to go deaf*, **е́хать**, *to go (by transport)*, as well as **ре́зать**) stress is on the stem in the infinitive. In verbs of more than one syllable (not counting any prefix) that conform to the second pattern (e.g. **вести́**, *to lead*, **идти́**, *to go (on foot)*, **везти́**, *to take (by transport)*, **бере́чь**, *to guard*) or the third pattern (e.g. **коло́ть**, *to prick*, **иска́ть**, *to look for*, **маха́ть**, *to wave*, as well as **писа́ть**) stress is on the ending in the infinitive.

12.4.2 Stress in second-conjugation verbs

In the indicative and infinitive forms of verbs of the second conjugation (as in 1B verbs with consonant stems) three different stress patterns are found, as outlined below.

12.4.2.1 *Stress on ending in infinitive and all indicative forms*

infin	**говори́ть**
1st pers sg	**говорю́**
2nd pers sg	**говори́шь**
3rd pers sg	**говори́т**
1st pers pl	**говори́м**
2nd pers pl	**говори́те**
3rd pers pl	**говоря́т**

Similarly: **блесте́ть**, *to shine*; **боле́ть**, *to hurt*; **боя́ться**, *to fear*; **висе́ть**, *to hang*; **включи́ть**, *to include, switch on*; **возмути́ть**, *to anger*; **гляде́ть**, *to look at*; **горе́ть**, *to burn* (intrans); **дрожа́ть**, *to tremble*; **запрети́ть**, *to forbid*; **защити́ть**, *to defend*; **звони́ть**, *to ring*; **звуча́ть**, *to (re)sound*; **истреби́ть**, *to destroy*; **крича́ть**, *to shout*; **лежа́ть**, *to lie*; **лете́ть**, *to fly*; **молча́ть**, *to be silent*; **обогати́ть**, *to enrich*; **обрати́ть**, *to turn, convert*; **объясни́ть**, *to explain*; **освети́ть**, *to illuminate*; **ослепи́ть**, *to blind*; **ошеломи́ть**, *to stun*; **ощути́ть**, *to feel*; **повтори́ть**, *to repeat*; **помести́ть**, *to place*; **порази́ть**, *to strike*; **посели́ть**, *to settle*; **посети́ть**, *to visit*;

прекрати́ть, *to stop, discontinue*; **принадлежа́ть**, *to belong*; **прости́ть**, *to forgive*; **реши́ть**, *to decide, solve*; **свисте́ть**, *to whistle*; **сиде́ть**, *to sit*; **стоя́ть**, *to stand*; **стреми́ться**, *to strive*; **стуча́ть**, *to knock*; **укроти́ть**, *to tame*. Also many related verbs, e.g. **заключи́ть**, *to conclude, confine*; **прогляде́ть**, *to look through, overlook*; **загоре́ть**, *to get a (sun)tan*; **улете́ть**, *to fly away*; **просвети́ть**, *to enlighten*; **перемести́ть**, *to move*; **зарази́ть**, *to infect*; **пересели́ть**, *to resettle*; **разреши́ть**, *to permit, resolve*; **устоя́ть**, *to keep one's balance, stand one's ground*.

12.4.2.2 Stress on stem in infinitive and all indicative forms

infin	встре́тить
1st pers sg	встре́чу
2nd pers sg	встре́тишь
3rd pers sg	встре́тит
1st pers pl	встре́тим
2nd pers pl	встре́тите
3rd pers pl	встре́тят

Similarly: **ве́рить**, *to believe*; **ви́деть**, *to see*; **гла́дить**, *to stroke, iron*; **е́здить**, *to go (by transport)*; **жа́рить**, *to roast*; **зави́сеть**, *to depend*; **знако́мить**, *to acquaint*; **ненави́деть**, *to hate*; **оби́деть**, *to offend*; **осла́бить**, *to weaken*; **оста́вить**, *to leave*; **отве́тить**, *to reply*; **пра́вить**, *to rule*; **предста́вить**, *to (re)present*; **расши́рить**, *to widen, extend*; **слы́шать**, *to hear*; **соста́вить**, *to compose*; **ста́вить**, *to put*; **сто́ить**, *to be worth*; **чи́стить**, *to clean*. Also many related verbs, e.g. **прове́рить**, *to check*; **заста́вить**, *to make, compel*; **попра́вить**, *to correct*; **очи́стить**, *to cleanse*.

12.4.2.3 Stress shift from ending to stem after the first person singular

infin	люби́ть
1st pers sg	люблю́
2nd pers sg	лю́бишь
3rd pers sg	лю́бит
1st pers pl	лю́бим
2nd pers pl	лю́бите
3rd pers pl	лю́бят

Similarly: **вари́ть**, *to cook, boil*; **верте́ть**, *to turn, spin*; **гнать**, *to chase* (**гоню́, го́нишь**); **губи́ть**, *to ruin*; **держа́ть**, *to hold*; **дыша́ть**, *to breathe*; **копи́ть**, *to amass, store*; **корми́ть**, *to feed*; **коси́ть**, *to mow*; **купи́ть**, *to buy*; **кури́ть**, *to smoke*; **лови́ть**, *to catch*; **объяви́ть**, *to announce, declare*; **останови́ть**, *to stop*; **очути́ться**, *to find oneself*; **плати́ть**, *to pay*; **поглоти́ть**, *to swallow*; **положи́ть**, *to put*; **предложи́ть**, *to offer, propose*;

проси́ть, *to ask (for)*; **руби́ть**, *to chop, hack, mince*; **служи́ть**, *to serve*; **смотре́ть**, *to look at, watch*; **ступи́ть**, *to step*; **терпе́ть**, *to bear, endure, tolerate*; **топи́ть**, *to heat, melt, sink* (trans), *drown* (trans). Also many related verbs, e.g. **завари́ть**, *to make, to brew* (drink); **содержа́ть**, *to contain*; **раскупи́ть**, *to buy up*; **прояви́ть**, *to manifest*; **оплати́ть**, *to pay for*; **заложи́ть**, *to lay*; **допроси́ть**, *to interrogate*; **просмотре́ть**, *to survey, look through, overlook*; **уступи́ть**, *to cede, yield*. Also the following verbs of motion and all their derivatives: **води́ть**, *to lead*; **вози́ть**, *to take (by transport)*; **носи́ть**, *to carry*; **ходи́ть**, *to go (on foot)*.

12.4.3 Stress in past-tense forms

- In most verbs the stress in all four past-tense forms is on the same syllable as in the infinitive, e.g. **рабо́тать**, *to work*; **теря́ть**, *to lose*; **красне́ть**, *to go red, blush*; **дава́ть**, *to give*; **ре́зать**, *to cut*; **писа́ть**, *to write*; **коло́ть**, *to prick*; **говори́ть**, *to speak*; **встре́тить**, *to meet*; **люби́ть**, *to love*:

m	f	n	pl
рабо́тал	рабо́тала	рабо́тало	рабо́тали
теря́л	теря́ла	теря́ло	теря́ли
красне́л	красне́ла	красне́ло	красне́ли
дава́л	дава́ла	дава́ло	дава́ли
ре́зал	ре́зала	ре́зало	ре́зали
писа́л	писа́ла	писа́ло	писа́ли
коло́л	коло́ла	коло́ло	коло́ли
говори́л	говори́ла	говори́ло	говори́ли
встре́тил	встре́тила	встре́тило	встре́тили
люби́л	люби́ла	люби́ло	люби́ли

- In 1B verbs in **-ти́** and **-е́чь** the stress will shift on to the **-а**, **-о** and **-и** in the feminine, neuter and plural forms respectively, in order to remain on the final syllable, e.g. **везти́**, *to take (by transport)*; **вести́**, *to lead*; **грести́**, *to row*; **нести́**, *to carry*; **мести́**, *to sweep*; **бере́чь**, *to guard*; **течь**, *to flow*:

m	f	n	pl
вёз	везла́	везло́	везли́
вёл	вела́	вело́	вели́
грёб	гребла́	гребло́	гребли́
нёс	несла́	несло́	несли́
мёл	мела́	мело́	мели́
берёг	берегла́	берегло́	берегли́
тёк	текла́	текло́	текли́

Similarly: **влечь**, *to drag*; **волочь** (R1), *to drag*; **запрячь**, *to harness*; **мочь**, *to be able*; **печь**, *to bake*; **пренебречь**, *to neglect*; **сечь**, *to cut, flog*, and compounds of these verbs.

Note 1　In **жечь**, *to burn*, and **идти**, *to go (on foot)*, and their compounds the ending in the feminine, neuter and plural forms is the sole vowel in the word (**жёг, жгла, жгло, жгли; шёл, шла, шло, шли**.

　　　2　Exception: **стричь**, *to cut* (hair or nails), which has stress on the stem throughout (**стриг, стригла**, etc.).

- In some monosyllabic verbs of the conjugation 1B and a few monosyllabic verbs of the second conjugation the stress shifts to the ending in the feminine form only of the past tense, e.g. **быть**, *to be*; **пить**, *to drink*; **дать**, *to give*; **спать**, *to sleep*:

m	f	n	pl
был	была́	бы́ло	бы́ли
пил	пила́	пи́ло	пи́ли
дал	дала́	да́ло	да́ли
спал	спала́	спа́ло	спа́ли

Similarly: **брать**, *to take*; **вить**, *to wind*; **гнать**, *to chase*; **жить**, *to live*; **звать**, *to call*; **красть**, *to steal*; **лить**, *to pour*; **снять**, *to take off*.

Note:　other common monosyllabic verbs have stress on the stem in all past-tense forms, e.g. **бить**, *to beat*; **выть**, *to howl*; **деть**, *to put*; **дуть**, *to blow*; **есть**, *to eat*; **жать**, *to press/reap*; **класть**, *to put*; **крыть**, *to cover*; **мыть**, *to wash*; **петь**, *to sing*; **сесть**, *to sit down*; **стать**, *to become*; **шить**, *to sew*.

- In some 1B verbs with a consonant stem (e.g. derivatives of -**мере́ть** and of -**нять**) stress falls on the ending in the feminine form and shifts to the first syllable (i.e. the prefix) in the masculine, neuter and plural forms, e.g. **поня́ть**, *to understand*; **приня́ть**, *to accept, receive*; **нача́ть**, *to begin*; **умере́ть**, *to die*:

m	f	n	pl
по́нял	поняла́	по́няло	по́няли
при́нял	приняла́	при́няло	при́няли
на́чал	начала́	на́чало	на́чали
у́мер	умерла́	у́мерло	у́мерли

Similarly: **заня́ть**, *to occupy, borrow*; **отня́ть**, *to take away*; **подня́ть**, *to lift, raise*.

Note:　derivatives of **быть**, *to be*, **дать**, *to give*, **жить**, *to live*, **лить**, *to pour*, and some other verbs may follow this pattern or they may follow the same pattern as **быть** (see preceding section; see also 12.5 below).

12.4.4 Stress in gerunds and participles

12.4.4.1 Imperfective gerunds

- Although it is the third-person-plural form of the present tense that provides the stem for imperfective gerunds, stress in these gerunds is on the same syllable as in the **first-person-singular** form, e.g.

начина́ю	начина́я
кома́ндую	кома́ндуя
прихожу́	приходя́
держу́	держа́

Note: exceptions: **лёжа**, *lying*; **мо́лча**, *(being) silent*; **си́дя**, *sitting*; **сто́я**, *standing*. These forms function as adverbs rather than gerunds.

12.4.4.2 Perfective gerunds

- Although it is the masculine form of the past tense that provides the stem for the perfective gerund, stress in these gerunds is generally on the same syllable as in the **infinitive** (which in some verbs (see 12.4.3 above) has different stress from the masculine form of the past tense), e.g.

прочита́ть	прочита́в, *having read*
откры́ть	откры́в, *having opened*
почи́стить	почи́стив, *having cleaned*
нача́ть	нача́в, *having begun*
приня́ть	приня́в, *having received*
прода́ть	прода́в, *having sold*

Note 1 The above rule holds good for reflexive verbs, which form their gerund with the suffix -**ши**, e.g. **заинтересова́вшись**, *having got interested*.

2 In perfective verbs which have infinitive in -**ти́** and a gerund in -**я** (see 9.7.2) this ending is stressed, e.g. **войдя́**, *having entered*.

12.4.4.3 Present active participles

- In first-conjugation verbs stress falls on the same syllable as in the third-person-plural form of the indicative from which the participle is derived (see 9.7.3), e.g.

начина́ют	начина́ющий, *who is beginning*
кома́ндуют	кома́ндующий, *who is commanding*
иду́т	иду́щий, *who is going*

- In second-conjugation verbs stress normally falls on the same syllable as in the infinitive, e.g.

говори́ть	говоря́щий, *who is speaking*
приходи́ть	приходя́щий, *who is coming*
держа́ть	держа́щий, *who is holding*

Note: in some second-conjugation verbs in which stress shifts after the first-person-singular form of the indicative (see 12.4.2.3 above), stress in the present active participle also moves to the syllable preceding the syllable that is stressed in the infinitive, e.g. **ле́чащий**, **лю́бящий**, **слу́жащий** (from **лечи́ть**, *to cure*, **люби́ть**, *to love*, **служи́ть**, *to serve*, respectively).

12.4.4.4   Past active participles

- Stress is on the same syllable as in the infinitive, except in the case of verbs in -**сти́**, in which stress is on the same syllable as in the masculine form of the past tense from which the participle is derived (see 9.7.4), e.g.

покупа́ть	**покупа́вший**, *who was buying*
закры́ть	**закры́вший**, *who closed*
нача́ть	**нача́вший**, *who began*
приня́ть	**приня́вший**, *who received*
купи́ть	**купи́вший**, *who bought*
вёз (from **везти́**)	**вёзший**, *who was taking (by transport)*
нёс (from **нести́**)	**нёсший**, *who was carrying*
смёл (from **смести́**)	**смётший**, *who swept off*
дости́г (from **дости́гнуть**)	**дости́гший**, *who achieved*

Note 1   **Уме́рший**, *who died*, from **умере́ть** (past tense, m form **у́мер**).
2   In verbs in -**сти́** which have a present-/future-tense stem in **д** or **т**, the **ё** in the masculine past-tense form may change to **е** in the past active participle (e.g. **ве́дший**, *who was leading*, from **вести́**; **изобре́тший**, *who invented*, from **изобрести́**), although stress remains on the same syllable as in the masculine past-tense form (see 9.7.4).

12.4.4.5   Present passive participles

- In first-conjugation verbs stress is on the same syllable as in the first-person-plural form of the indicative from which they are derived (see 9.7.5), e.g.

рассма́триваем	**рассма́триваемый**, *being examined*
испо́льзуем	**испо́льзуемый**, *being used*

Note: the same rule applies to those present active participles in which **ё** is replaced by **о**, e.g. **ведо́мый**, *being led*, from **вести́** (1st pers pl **ведём**).

In present passive participles derived from second-conjugation verbs stress is normally on the same syllable as in the infinitive. The rule applies also to the many adjectives (some of them negative) that are modelled on present passive participles (although they may be derived from perfective verbs). Examples:

ви́деть	ви́димый, *visible*
люби́ть	люби́мый, *beloved, favourite*
уязви́ть	уязви́мый, *vulnerable*
повтори́ть	неповтори́мый, *unrepeatable*
проходи́ть	непроходи́мый, *impenetrable*
улови́ть	неулови́мый, *uncatchable*

12.4.4.6   Past passive participles

- In past passive participles ending in -**анный** or -**янный** that are derived from verbs with the stressed endings -**а́ть** or -**я́ть**, respectively (see 9.7.6 above), stress moves on to the preceding syllable, irrespective of the conjugation to which the verb belongs, e.g.

прочита́ть	прочи́танный, *read*
взволнова́ть	взволно́ванный, *agitated*
написа́ть	напи́санный, *written*
прода́ть	про́данный, *sold*
прогна́ть	про́гнанный, *driven (away)*
потеря́ть	поте́рянный, *lost*

Note: in verbs stressed on the stem in the infinitive (e.g. обду́мать, *to think over,* услы́шать, *to hear*) stress remains on the same syllable in the past passive participle, e.g. обду́манный, услы́шанный.

- Stress also moves one syllable nearer to the beginning of the word in past passive participles ending in -**тый** that are derived from verbs with the stressed endings -**о́ть**, -**у́ть** (9.7.6), e.g.

проколо́ть	проко́лотый, *punctured*
упомяну́ть	упомя́нутый, *mentioned*

Note: this stress shift does not apply, however, to verbs derived from monosyllabic verbs in -**ыть**, -**ить**, -**еть**, e.g. закры́тый, *closed,* разби́тый, *broken,* оде́тый, *dressed,* from закры́ть, разби́ть, оде́ть, respectively.

- In the short feminine, neuter and plural forms of past passive participles in -**ённый** (e.g. введённый, *brought in, introduced;* принесённый, *brought;* сметённый, *swept off;* зажжённый, *lit;* пересечённый, *intersected;* решённый, *decided;* see 9.7.6) stress shifts to the last syllable, with consequential change of **ё** to **e** in the preceding syllable, e.g.

m	f	n	pl
введён	введена́	введено́	введены́
принесён	принесена́	принесено́	принесены́
сметён	сметена́	сметено́	сметены́
зажжён	зажжена́	зажжено́	зажжены́
пересечён	пересечена́	пересечено́	пересечены́
решён	решена́	решено́	решены́

Note: in participles ending in unstressed -енный (e.g. поста́вленный, *put*) stress remains on the same syllable in all forms.

12.4.5 Miscellaneous points

- The negative particle **не** attracts the stress before the past tense of the masculine, neuter and plural forms of the verb **быть**, *to be*: **не́ был, не́ было, не́ были**.

- The prefix **вы-** is stressed on all **perfective** verbs, irrespective of whether they are disyllabic: **вы́дать**, *to issue*; **вы́йти**, *to go out*; **вы́лечить**, *to cure*; **вы́тащить**, *to drag out*.

- This prefix is also stressed on most other disyllabic words, e.g. **вы́дра**, *otter*; **вы́ход**, *exit*; **вы́ше**, *higher*.

12.5 Variation in stress

The stress in a word, like its pronunciation, inflection or even gender, may change over time or may vary from user to user and in different situations. A few miscellaneous points may finally be made in this connection.

- One group of words in which stress is particularly unstable, and for which reference works often suggest alternative stress, is the set of past-tense forms of certain verbs that consist of a monosyllabic basic verb + prefix, e.g.

	m	f	n	pl
прибы́ть, *to arrive*	при́был	прибыла́	при́было	при́были
пробы́ть, *to stay*	про́был	пробыла́	про́было	про́были
зада́ть, *to set*	за́дал	задала́	за́дало	за́дали
изда́ть, *to edit, publish*	изда́л	издала́	и́здало	и́здали
отда́ть, *to give back, hand in*	о́тдал	отдала́	о́тдало	о́тдали
прида́ть, *to attach*	прида́л	придала́	прида́ло	прида́ли
прода́ть, *to sell*	про́дал	продала́	про́дало	про́дали
пережи́ть, *to survive*	пе́режил	пе́режила́	пе́режило	пе́режили
прожи́ть, *to live, stay*	про́жил	прожила́	про́жило	про́жили
зали́ть, *to flood*	за́лил	за́лила́	за́лило	за́лили
обли́ть, *to pour over*	о́блил	облила́	о́блило	о́блили
проли́ть, *to shed*	про́лил	про́лила́	про́лило	про́лили

Note: in the verb **разда́ть**, *to give out, distribute*, the vowel in the prefix changes when the prefix bears the stress: **ро́здал/разда́л, раздала́, ро́здало/разда́ло, ро́здали/разда́ли**.

The variants of these past-tense forms with stress on the prefix are now less common than those with stress on the stem of the verb in the masculine, neuter and plural forms (or the ending in the feminine forms). However, no firm guidance can confidently be given on usage in these verbs.

- In R1 stress on the stem is now encountered in the feminine past-tense form of some monosyllabic verbs, or verbs derived from monosyllabic verbs, which in the standard language have stress on the ending (see 12.4.3 above), e.g. **бра́ла, жда́ла, нача́ла, приня́ла, собра́ла, сня́ла, спа́ла** (instead of standard **брала́**, *took*; **ждала́**, *waited*; **начала́**, *began*; **приняла́**, *accepted, received*; **собрала́**, *gathered*; **сняла́**, *took off*; **спала́**, *slept*, respectively).

  At the same time in the neuter past-tense forms of certain verbs stress may be found on the ending instead of the stem, e.g. **ждало́, приняло́, собрало́, сняло́** (instead of standard **жда́ло**, *waited*; **при́няло**, *accepted, received*; **собра́ло**, *gathered*; **сня́ло**, *took off*).

- Stress in the indicative forms of some second-conjugation verbs is also unstable in R1. In some such verbs which in the standard language have stress on the ending throughout the indicative (12.4.2.1 above) stress now shifts to the stem in the second-person-singular form and subsequent forms (as in verbs listed in 12.4.2.3 above), e.g. **вклю́чим**, *we shall include/switch on*; **обле́гчит**, *(s)he will facilitate*. This change is unsurprising, given that stress may now fall on the stem in the infinitive form (**обле́гчить** instead of standard **облегчи́ть**).

  Past passive participles may be similarly affected, e.g. **заклю́чен**, *concluded, confined*, and **вне́сен**, *brought in, inserted*, instead of standard **заключён** and **внесён**.

- Stress has been particularly affected over the last fifteen or twenty years by the broadcasting of the speech of politicians and presenters with regional speech habits. For example, the non-standard stress of the infinitive form of certain common verbs (e.g. **за́нять**, *to engage, occupy*; **на́чать**, *to begin*; **при́нять**, *to accept, receive*; **углу́бить**, *to deepen*) came to be disseminated as a result of the prominence of Gorbachóv, who comes from the Stávropol' region of southern Russia.

- One may hear alternative stress in adjectives and nouns, as well as in various parts of the verb, e.g. **укра́инский** (*Ukrainian*; adj), **укра́инец** (*Ukrainian*; noun), **цену́** (acc sg of **цена́**, *price*) and **долла́р**, *dollar* (instead of standard **украи́нский, украи́нец, це́ну, до́ллар**, respectively). In some nouns ending in the suffix -ение, in which stress has hitherto been on the stem in the standard language, the suffix is now attracting the stress (no doubt by analogy with the vast majority of nouns ending in this suffix, in which the stress does fall on the antepenultimate vowel), e.g. **намере́ние**, *intention*, and **обеспече́ние**, *securing, guaranteeing, provision*, instead of standard **наме́рение, обеспе́чение**. The important thing for the student is to know which variant is still considered standard.

- Finally, it should be noted that deviation from standard usage in stress may be associated with the speech of certain social groups. Thus the word **ко́мпас**, *compass*, may be stressed on the second syllable (**компа́с**) in the speech of seamen. Similarly drivers might prefer the form **шо́фер** (*driver, chauffeur*) to the standard form **шофёр**. The eminent linguist Academician Vinográdov seems to have been acknowledging the possible social basis of variation in stress when, in reply to a question about the position of the stress on the word for *kilometre*, he is said to have observed that he would use **киломе́тр** if he was speaking in an academic institution but **кило́метр** if he was talking to his chauffeur.

Index of Russian words, phrases and affixes

This index contains words (including interjections and particles), phrases and affixes (i.e. prefixes, infixes, suffixes) on which specific information is given in Chapters 1-6 and 8-12 inclusive. Only sparing reference is made here to the phraseological formulae given in Chapter 7 on verbal etiquette.

The following are *not* included in this index:

- words given as examples of various types of word-formation in Chapters 1 and 8;
- words used as examples of standard or non-standard pronunciation and stress in 1.5;
- individual words that exemplify use of a certain suffix or type of word to which reference is made in commentaries on the texts given in Chapter 2;
- the alphabetically arranged lists of loanwords and neologisms of various sorts in 5.1.2, 5.1.3 and 5.1.4;
- the lists of computing terms in 5.1.5;
- the list of obscenities in 5.6;
- the key words in the lists of idioms in 5.7, proverbs and sayings in 5.8, and similes in 5.9;
- the list of abbreviations in 6.9 and acronyms and alphabetisms (6.10);
- the geographical names and words derived from them in 6.11 and 6.12;
- the forenames and patronymics given in 7.3.1 and 7.3.2, respectively;
- words given as illustrations of spelling rules in Chapter 8;
- words given as examples of standard types of noun and adjectival inflection in Chapter 9;
- verbs listed as examples of the conjugation patterns illustrated by the paradigms in 9.6.2–9.6.8;
- examples of verbs that may be reflexive or non-reflexive in 11.8;
- lists of words given as examples of or exceptions to one of the stress patterns illustrated by the paradigms set out in Chapter 12.

In the case of nouns, adjectives and pronouns that occur in the book in more than one form it is generally the nominative singular form that is given here.

Both aspects of a verb are usually given together, with the imperfective form invariably first, although in many cases the point dealt with in the text relates to use of only one aspect. It should be noted that the perfective forms given here are not all invariably used as the perfective of the imperfective in question. Where one aspectual form differs markedly from the other (e.g. брать/взять) the two forms may also be given separately.

For the purpose of arranging forms in alphabetical order, phrases and hyphenated words are treated as indivisible in this index.

General index